DARK MOON

Apollo and the Whistle-Blowers

Mary Bennett

David S. Percy

λ

Aulis Publishers
London

Aulis Publishers
25 Belsize Park
London NW3 4DU
England

First Published in Great Britain 1999

Hardback   ISBN 1 898541 051
Paperback   ISBN 1 898541 108

Ordnance Survey maps reproduced with permission from
The Controller of her Majesty's Stationery Office MC 88720M0001

A CIP catalogue record for this book is available from the British Library

Printed and bound by SRP Ltd Exeter England

For the children of the Universe

Acknowledgements: To those who have gone before.

Special thanks to:

Cate Alfano, Darryl Anka, Richard Allenby Jr, HJP Arnold, John Brooks, Vivien Burrough, Mark Carlotto, Stephen Clementson, Jim Collier, Caroline Davies, Frank Domingo, Colette Dowell, Frederick Doyle, Farouk El-Baz, Mike O'Farrell, Goldstone's Bill Wood, Stan Gooch, David Groves, Clive Dyer, Soren Gunnarsson, Bill Kaysing, Michael Knupffer, Stan Lebar, Hamish Lindsay, Sir Bernard Lovell, Jan Lundberg, Charles Martinelli, John Michell, Carl Munck, Larkin Niemyer Jr, Martin Noakes, Peter Oakley, Linda Parker, Victor Pelevin, Marcus Price, Bob Pritchard, Ralph René, Ed von Renouard, Una Ronald, Wolfgang Schindler, David Sarkission, Percy Seymour, Peter Sharp, Erol Torun, Kalina Villeroy, Harold Watson, Jerry Wiant, Bill Wood.

Contents

Prologue   1

Part One   FOREGROUND ACTION

Chapter One   Photo Call   7
Chapter Two   Northern Exposures   50
Chapter Three   Radiant Daze   77
Chapter Four   Rocket Rackets   115
Chapter Five   'masters of infinity'   164

Part Two   MIDDLE DISTANCE

Chapter Six   Truth or Consequences   205
Chapter Seven   Distant Horizons   245
Chapter Eight   Servants of Circumstance   290
Chapter Nine   Slaves of Limitation   332

Part Three   BACKGROUND EXPLORATION

Chapter Ten   Essentials   382
Chapter Eleven   THE Triangle   426
Chapter Twelve   Prints of Mars   462
Chapter Thirteen Hurmaze   504

Chapter Notes   514

Appendix   532

Index   557

Prologue

The main thrust of this book is to question the entire validity of the official record of mankind's exploration of the Moon especially the Apollo lunar landings themselves.

We are *not* however claiming that astronauts from Earth have never walked on the Moon. Our personal interpretation of the evidence is that *surrogate* astronauts were employed.

It is our further view that the famous *named* astronauts for example Neil Armstrong, Buzz Aldrin and Ed Mitchell in all probability never left Earth orbit, remaining in the safe zones below the radiation belts and so avoiding the exposure to hazardous radiation which (in our present state of technology) awaits all those who venture into deep space.

The psychological behaviours of the named astronauts in the intervening years since Apollo—which in our opinion are those of men guilty of silence concerning the full truth—plus their rude physical health would be evidence enough for our claims. But the numerous inconsistencies clearly visible in the Apollo photographic record is quite irrefutable. Some of the many errors we evidence were due to haste and poor thinking. Others were deliberately planted by individuals we have dubbed 'Whistle-Blowers', who were determined to leave evidence of the faking in which they were unwillingly involved. Probably the most emphatic of these whistles was a bottle that rolled across the 'moon' landscape on the TV screens in Western Australia during a 'live' transmission from the 'moon'.

Yes, our claims in this book do border on the incredible. One can imagine the first reaction of even reasonable people to our evidence:

"Why would NASA do such a thing? It's too unbelievable."

"Surely, too many people would have been involved."

"What a ridiculous idea, they couldn't possibly expect to pull it off."

Such reactions will be even more likely as we unfold our scenario further.

1

The 'science fact' that we have discovered hidden within the Apollo mythos is as fantastic as any of the science fiction from the pens of Jules Verne or Edgar Rice Burroughs.

If it is of any consolation to the reader, we too at first could not believe what we were uncovering as our investigation proceeded. Yet as each new stone was turned over it revealed a conspiracy of labyrinthine proportions.

Naturally, as in a court of law, we examined, re-examined and cross-examined all our evidence carefully before reaching our verdict. And in the book we present our evidence in this step-by-step way so that the reader can reach her or his own decision upon it. These matters are contained in "Foreground Action" and "Middle Distance". These sections and their evidence stand alone in their own right.

Then in the third section "Background Exploration" we come to other related subjects which some will find, yes, even harder to accept!

These concern evidence of extra-terrestrial involvement in human affairs—evidence, moreover, of which certain individuals, governments and military authorities—including what was to become NASA—were fully aware and were in part reacting to. The element of urgency in the space exploration program was certainly a key response to the perceived 'threat' of ET intervention.

What then is our evidence for ET involvement? One crucial item is the so-called Roswell Incident which occurred in 1947, when (carefully placed) wreckage of a non-terrestrial craft was found at a particular site in America. Now, let us say at once that this incident has been quite deliberately surrounded, on the part of the authorities, with a mass of misinformation and disinformation—so much so (and this, as we will show, was the precise point of the exercise) that any reasonable person examining the data and the circumstances will simply throw up their hands and say:

"Oh come on, this is all nonsense".

So what then are our own reasons for accepting the Roswell Incident as genuine and meaningful? Well, one of them is the fact that the incident/placement occurred in 1947—and indeed at the mid point of 1947.

At this juncture the reasonable reader might again throw up their hands and mutter: "Oh dear. These poor people really are mad".

Yet we are quite sure that when we demonstrate the significant role played by the mathematical value 19.47° in astrophysics, alongside all our other evidence, any doubting readers will retract and reconsider.

Perhaps we should also emphasise at this point that we not alone in making some of the claims we have outlined so far. Other researchers have also produced hard evidence concerning massive fraud in the space program and especially in the cover-up by the authorities of information concerning extra-terrestrials, not just on this planet, but on the Moon and Mars.

We have, further, made several direct approaches with our findings and questions to NASA and other institutions involved in these various matters, and have received widely differing responses from officials.

The first was outrage at our suggestion that the record of these missions had been hoaxed. Yet when it came to answering our direct and often scientifically-based questions relating to Apollo, these same people responded with some very illogical and circuitous answers. The second reaction from the sharp end—those who actually worked on various aspects of information processing—was rather different. Confident in their ability to handle anything that was thrown at them, some of these individuals nevertheless ran for cover when they could not (or would not) answer our questions. Others were clearly ill at ease, and provided answers that were logical enough when received as the sole, stand alone answer—but were in direct contradiction to the 'official script' and when cross-referenced with other responses from colleagues in the same industry.

It could be argued that capitalising on a position of total power is virtually inevitable unless a mechanism is in place to regulate accountability. Any group with the ability to yield real power can potentially take advantage of such power whenever the opportunity presents itself. Indeed any organisation or government agency could be formed with the express intention of exploring an arena (e.g.

space) located far from the gaze of the ordinary citizen, in order to be able to experiment and perhaps even stumble periodically without practising any meaningful accountability. Such a course of action is only acceptable if it does not affect the neighbours—NASA's policies *affect us all,* as you will see.

NASA itself has elected not to answer *any* of our questions *unless* we can answer one of its questions first! During an interview with Sky TV (who were making a news special featuring our findings) Brian Welch, the Acting Director of Media Services at NASA's Washington Headquarters, first protested that he did not have time to look into matters that were nearly thirty years old, and followed that up by throwing down the gauntlet! Here is the challenge he issued to us—in his own words:

I would throw an optical question back at these folks [the authors]. It's one piece of tangible evidence that we actually did go to the Moon and it is very simple. [On] several of the Apollo expeditions, the astronauts planted [equipment] as part of the Apollo Lunar Surface Experiment Package (ALSEP). They planted retro-reflectors on the Moon for laser beams to be bounced off from Earth. And indeed, at least one observatory in the United States (the McDonald Observatory down in Texas) has been routinely bouncing laser beams off of those retro-reflectors to be able to get a very accurate distance measurement of the Earth to the Moon.

How is that possible if we never went to the Moon?

Once they have got the answer to that, I will be happy to talk to them.

By the time we had the answer to Brian Welch's question we were to discover much more than he had bargained for, and Brian Welch might regret having issued such a challenge, given that the organisation he represents has shown every sign of wishing to be neither accountable nor responsible for its actions of thirty years ago.

The US space agency are by no means the first institution to foster the suppression of information and the denial of knowledge. There

is absolutely nothing new in the organised withholding of newly-found discoveries. More than two thousand years before space travel was a reality, in the 6th Century BC, Pythagoras and his group of mathematical philosophers who lived in Greece found themselves in just such a situation.

The late Dr. Carl Sagan reminded us in his work *Cosmos* that the Pythagoreans considered the four regular basic solids made up terrestrial matter: earth, air, fire and water but they associated their discovery of the fifth solid with the heavens—it was named the dodecahedron, pentagons making up its twelve faces. (see illustration in Appendix)

A crisis of doctrine also occurred when the Pythagoreans discovered that the square root of two could not be represented accurately as the ratio of two whole numbers, for the square root of two was irrational. It was not a whole number and these people regarded whole numbers as fundamental, as all other things could be calculated from them.

For the Pythagoreans, this knowledge was difficult to assimilate into their previous 'database', as we would describe it today. This knowledge presented a serious threat. So instead of sharing in their recently-acquired and perhaps not completely understood discoveries, the Pythagoreans suppressed knowledge of both the dodecahedron and the square root of two on the grounds that it was too dangerous for the public and 'ordinary people'.

The outside world was not to know!

Did history repeat itself (as it has done so many times before) when, instead of using the experiences acquired during the preparations for manned space travel to advance our understanding of the Universe beyond this planet, it was determined to deny access to the findings concerning space and physics that have been made? Discoveries that were made both prior to and during our emergence as a civilisation learning to struggle into space?

Poor decisions and ill-considered actions by the space agencies and their masters have accumulated over the last fifty years or so and the consequences of this behaviour *still* block the threshold of the doorway marked "Progress of

3

the Human Civilisation". For even in the late 1990s there are scientists who are opposed to sharing with 'ordinary people' certain scientific knowledge.

The Apollo record, as it currently stands, is not the sum of the whole but only the part that has been revealed to the public—until now. Irrespective of any individual opinions as to the validity of the exploration of space, to dismiss the Apollo Space Project because it was too long ago, or unimportant, is to permit a history based on a false premise to stand un-challenged. In so doing we become the slaves of an elite who it seems will stop at nothing to achieve their aims—and the one firm objective they hold is the domination of this planet via the medium of space. This is no exaggeration, for as you will read, they have said as much themselves, the only trouble was that nobody paid much attention at the time.

In the greater scheme of things, thirty years is no more than the blinking of an eye, so we should not castigate ourselves for not realising before now that all is not what it seems regard-ing Apollo.

We can wake up and wipe the sleep from our eyes whenever we like.

We would do well not to wait much longer.

Part One

FOREGROUND ACTION

Chapter One

Photo Call

Did astronauts really visit the Moon from 1969 to 1972 under the banner of the Apollo space program? Perusing the answer to this question, we examine in detail a number of images from the Apollo record released by NASA. To determine some fundamentals we meet Eastman Kodak's appointed representative and discuss certain aspects of the Apollo photographic challenge.

Oh, what a tangled web they wove ...

Neil Armstrong may *not* have walked on the Moon. The Apollo missions broadcast to the world on TV may *not* have been transmitted live from the lunar surface.

Strong words indeed.

How can we justify these statements? Moreover, if our claims are correct, why would NASA & Co. go to such lengths to convince us all that twelve Apollo astronauts landed on the Moon and returned to Earth? Are we, the authors, completely deluded by yet another 'conspiracy theory' run amok? Naturally, we think not! In 1969 there was no absolutely guaranteed way to transport men to the Moon —and return them to Earth *alive* and *well*. This is equally true in the late 1990s.

We also maintain that if Apollo did go to the Moon and back, none of us have yet seen a true photographic record of the event.

In this chapter we shall begin our demonstration that the Apollo images released by NASA have been 'tampered with' in various ways. Using scientific methodology our findings show that NASA's photographic material is full of anomalies and inconsistencies. This research suggests that the images were both faked, and at the same time skilfully encoded with deliberate mistakes. In our view these mistakes were introduced by some of those working on the project in order that the true scenario might one day be reconstructed. The various individuals responsible are some of our Whistle-Blowers.

The diverse aspects of these apparently outrageous statements will be discussed in the chapters that follow. We will throw some fresh light into the dark recesses of the records and examine what really happened before, during, and after the so-called 'space race'.

Throughout aviation history and space exploration, the prime and lasting record of our achievements has been preserved as photographic images, movie film and in recent times, television coverage. We naturally assume that these records reflect the actual events as they occurred, disasters and triumphs included. Perhaps in the case of Apollo all of us have been far too trusting.

1. 'Apollo 11' crew.   NASA

In space exploration (and going to the Moon is one example) where there are no independent witnesses to the actual events, we have the right to expect the record to be genuine, honestly portrayed, and responsibly reported. Taking into consideration the weight of evidence in this book it is apparent that our expectations have not always been fulfilled and it would be disastrous if future space projects were carried out under similar conditions. The reaction in some quarters to our research findings regarding the Apollo data has been astonishing and, from NASA HQ in Washington, disheartening.

It brings us no joy to write these words. It was a painful process of realisation as we gradually discovered the background to the flaws in the data and information emanating from NASA, and we are greatly saddened that such a situation could have ever occurred.

Who are the Whistle-Blowers?

Nearly thirty years after the event, we are waking up to the probability that NASA's photographic record, plus all the original film/TV transmissions of the Apollo program has been modified, or may not even be genuine. Those whom we call Whistle-Blowers appear to have carefully *encoded* the information that would be needed for us to come to this conclusion. This evidence of encoding is found in the photography, in the processing and in the final compositing of the images—moreover, this activity occurred under the very nose of NASA.

It is our claim that the encoding of these pictures took place at each faking stage in total secrecy—the Whistle-Blowers involved had

representation in all the production departments ranging from those scripting the action, conceptual design, photography and lighting, to set dressing, continuity, photo image retouching and optical compositing. Unhappy with what they were expected to do, and unable to speak out, some of these people opted to 'booby-trap' the images by encoding clues into the respective areas of their work. This courageous encoding was not in vain.

Even if it has taken over 20 years for us to finally realise the actual dimensions of Apollo, the fact is, we all believe what we want to believe, see what we want to see—or at least what we expect to see. This aspect of human behaviour is one of the reasons why NASA has succeeded in 'pulling the wool over our eyes' for so long—eyes which were blind to this often subtle but significant encoding process.

The evidence clearly shows that there are continuity errors and serious discrepancies between the photographs and the recorded TV coverage of any given event in the Apollo record. At first the vast majority of us were so overawed with mankind's achievement as portrayed, that no one noticed these 'mistakes'. But over the decades these 'mistakes' have increasingly nudged certain professionals—familiar of

2. Apollo Saturn V launch.   NASA

course with the way light behaves. Professional photographers were best equipped to notice any tell-tale signs indicating the use of light sources other than natural sunlight.

Obviously you cannot just turn up on the Moon with an Instamatic-type camera and expect that your photographs will turn out satisfactorily. There would have been special requirements for the cameras and film stock to ensure a satisfactory photographic record of mankind's first-ever visit to another world.

So we needed to confirm at least two essentials:

- What were the conditions like for still and movie photography on the Moon?
- What was special (if anything) about the cameras and film taken to the Moon?

In seeking precise answers to such questions we set out to tackle the experts, people who had been closely associated with the photographic technology in the 1960s. Initially we contacted NASA's film stock suppliers, the Eastman Kodak Company based in Rochester, New York, USA. Through their main office in Hemel Hempstead, England, the company put us in touch with the assistant to the Managing Director of Kodak Ltd during the period we were investigating. We also travelled to Sweden to meet the executive responsible for the creation of the Lunar camera at Victor Hasselblad AB in Göteborg.

It is important to bear in mind that at the time of these discussions both gentlemen had no reason to doubt that the Apollo missions really happened 'as billed'. Indeed, at the outset we were simply seeking explanations for the photographic anomalies that were evident on close examination. Moreover, if the answers to our enquiries had allayed our suspicions we would have been somewhat relieved.

Reflex gestures

HJP ("Douglas") Arnold was with Kodak in the UK (1966-74) during Apollo. He kindly invited us to his home in July 1996, and spent some time talking to us about the photographic challenges of the space program.

The still camera selected for use on Apollo was a Hasselblad—considerably modified for the task. This converted Hasselblad was a medium format reflex, using 70mm sprocketed film stock—we should remember that this photographic kit was going to be taken to an environment totally different from Earth. The Apollo Command & Service Module (CSM) operated with pure oxygen for breathing and therefore any electrical spark would be disastrous, the electrical contacts within the camera had to be secured. In addition, the leatherette camera finish would 'outgas' in the reduced pressure environment, giving off really offensive and potentially poisonous odours.

Apparently there was to be no glass within the CSM or the Lunar Module (LM). So the reflex mirror, *one of the essential parts of the*

3. The Hasselblad 500 C.   HASSELBLAD

4. Long focal length lens used on the Lunar camera.   AULIS

Hasselblad, had to be removed but for some reason there was no objection to the lenses that *were* made of glass. A number of interchangeable lenses were available for the special camera, ranging from super-wide angle to various rather bulky long focal length lenses.

Douglas Arnold pointed out that "the Lunar Surface Camera had a Biogon 60mm wide-angle lens which provided a safe field of view. The longer lenses were usually used for imaging from the CSM by the third member of the crew".

The Hasselblad was lowered to the lunar surface by means of the lunar equipment conveyor (LEC), which was a line or pulley arrangement between the LM door and the surface. This necessitated film magazines being fitted with a tether ring. The moonwalk (EVA) magazine was designated pre-flight by the code 'S' and after processing the film was given the magazine number 40. When the EVA was over, the magazine was detached from the camera.[1]

Interestingly, "the camera body was discarded

and left on the Moon, only the film magazine was brought back," Douglas Arnold pointed out. Was there a reason other than marginal weight saving, for leaving the camera behind?

Douglas agreed that for an astronaut standing on the lunar surface the difficulty of changing the camera's magazine whilst clothed in a pressure suit was considerable. And Douglas confirmed that it had always been a problem, chiefly on account of the very awkward pressurised gauntlets they wore.

"That was why they had wings put onto the camera dials for altering the aperture and timing, so that they just pushed them with a finger instead of fiddling with them, which was an impossibility in those gauntlets." Douglas explained.

Even with the said wings on the controls the action would have been virtually impossible when pressurised. Later we were to discover, by putting our hands inside even an unpressur-

---

Photography by numbers

The Apollo images published by NASA were catalogued by two letters and a series of numbers: for example AS 11 40-5872. Apollo Spacecraft, followed by mission (11), magazine (40) and frame number.

Example of an 'Apollo 11' 70mm frame.   NASA

ised gauntlet, exactly how impossible that task would have been. We remembered that in 1993 researcher Ralph René constructed a special vacuum chamber for a demonstration of a neoprene coated, cotton-lined glove. Once his demo glove ballooned, it required great effort to move either fingers or hand.[2]

It was intended that during the EVAs—meaning extra-vehicular activity—the astronauts would NOT hold the camera at eye level, but would take all their pictures with the camera mounted on a chest bracket.

"Neil Armstrong told me that it was his idea that the spacesuits had a bracket for the cameras, instead of holding them in their gloved hands," said Douglas.

"Since Apollo 11's flight, whenever I have corresponded with him, he has always been very helpful but he always struck me as being extremely businesslike. There is no 'time of day' if you like. He responded to the point raised, and that was it. Quite typical, the thing about Armstrong which impressed me, is that he was (and is) a very private individual. He has always kept himself to himself. During the various celebrations he has tended to appear you might say, as limited as decency would allow. I think he is on record as saying that he doesn't want to become an historical event or an institution. Which one can understand, the publicity exposure in those earlier years must have been enormous."

"That sequence of photos taken by him with that one camera has never been bettered, in my opinion. Almost every one of those *Armstrong images appeared to be splendidly composed.* You remember the classic, face-on picture of Aldrin with his visor reflecting the entire lunar landscape including Armstrong taking the photograph. It's a marvellous picture." (emphasis added)

"When the camera was eventually used on the lunar surface, the astronauts were obliged to guess where the lens was pointing," Douglas confirmed. "During Apollo 15, they landed near Hadley Rille, a canyon that threaded through the edge of the Apennine Mountains. They wanted to photograph the structure and strata of the area and for that they flew a

5. The 'classic'.   NASA
Aldrin on the Apollo '11' EVA.

500mm lens. This camera was hand held with the astronaut Dave Scott sighting along the edge of the barrel," said Douglas.

We then asked Douglas about taking these irreplaceable images that would go down in history—they had to be right—some might consider it quite a challenge to take pictures with a camera that has no viewfinder?

"Well," retorted Douglas, "I think that they had a reasonable amount of training. For example: they had been instructed that for geological photos: set the lens at seven feet, and then according to the Sun angle, set the aperture to f/8, f/5.6 or f/4 or whatever it was—and then 'shoot'. Then go to another particular angle, alter the aperture because of the Sun difference and then 'shoot'."

6. Close up Lunar camera on its chest bracket.   NASA

Vulnerabilities

- A planet with no atmosphere or radiation protection is totally exposed to X-rays or any other form of galactic cosmic radiation, which is constant throughout space. These conditions would fog the film, seriously affecting the results.
- Excessively high temperatures alter any film's characteristics, and therefore its performance, making it difficult to calculate the correct exposures.
- Lunar temperatures in the 'daytime'(which lasts for approx. 14 'Earth days') can be in excess of +200°F/93°C.
- In the shade and during the lunar night (which also lasts for approx. 14 'Earth days') the temperature can drop to below -200°F/129°C. (see Appendix)
- This situation is also applicable to all areas wherever and whenever in shadow—i.e. out of direct sunlight.
- There is a considerable variation of temperature from the lunar equator to the poles.

"Being large magazine loads, the film was sprocket driven, and I do remember that they found stress marks or tears on some of the sprockets, which presumably could be put down to the pressure differences; and there were, in fact, film jams (as you would get in any mechanical system) but none of these resulted from the 'alien' atmosphere in which they found themselves," stated Douglas.

Any conclusion that the alien atmosphere was a non-contributory factor is based on data from NASA and/or belief that these images are the authentic photographic record. And even if the pictures released by NASA were perfect, such a fact would not automatically mean that images actually taken on the true lunar surface were originally problem-free, technically.

Heat and dust

Conditions on the surface during a moonwalk could certainly be described as hostile. A key aspect of the lunar photographic challenge would have been coping with the temperature extremes. What was Douglas' view on how the astro-photographers managed?

"In the sunlight, temperatures can go up as far as plus 200°F/93°C, which is very hot. And then again, to minus 200°F/129°C in the shadow areas, because there is no atmosphere to equalise the temperatures. Although the emulsion on the film in the camera could be severely affected by prolonged subjection to high temperatures, the fact that the astronauts were alternating between sunlight and shadow mitigated this problem—to the best of my knowledge," Douglas responded.

However, the metal casing of these cameras had no special insulation from the excessive heat in the radiated sunlight nor from the cold of the shadow areas that would have been experienced on the Moon.

The Apollo mission EVAs were scheduled to take place on the near side of the Moon and during the lunar day. The temperature variations from minus 180°F to plus 200°F/93°C during each mission would surely have been hot enough to soften any normal film emulsion after a number of minutes of exposure and then chill it sufficiently to make the emulsion rather brittle. As the camera was sometimes in the sunlight and sometimes in the shade, this sequence was being repeated continually as the

TechnoSpeak

- The films used are all made on thin Estar polyester film base. The strength of this enables a thinner base to be used (0.00025in as opposed to the 0.0052in thickness of normal triacetate film base) thus doubling the available space in the film magazine for a given film length. The polyester base also has great dimensional stability.
- Under the low atmospheric pressure obtaining in the spacecraft cabin (one-third normal sea-level pressure and pure oxygen) a triacetate film base would give off solvents, extremely unpleasant for the astronauts.
- Kodak Instamatic cameras were among many types considered for space photography, but it was found on test that under the low atmospheric pressure the plastic film cartridges gave off solvents.

British Journal of Photography 7 Nov 1969

astronaut moved backwards and forwards be-tween the shadow of the LM and his sunlit work sites.

It was intended that all the missions should land during the lunar morning because this gave them a relatively low Sun angle which then threw long shadows. But this low Sun angle situation was not the case all the time, as we will see!

So what was this super film that could with-stand the extremes of heat and cold, to say nothing of the hazards of space radiation and the resultant fogging of the filmstock?

"The interesting thing is," said Douglas "that with the exception of the Estar thin base (which enabled them to pack a lot more frames per magazine) for the most part the film that was flown on these missions was basically the standard Ektachrome 64 ASA that we used on Earth (nowadays we would say ISO and not ASA). This film stock had about 100 frames or so of colour or 200 frames black and white to the magazine. The lunar surface film was faster, 160 ASA (ISO) because the film was less 'contrasty' and with a faster film it was possible to use smaller stops. You could also 'stop down' a bit more, which gave a lessening of the 'hard' shadows in the space environ-ment."

One could argue that it would be difficult to obtain any lessening of 'hard' shadows on the lunar surface, because there is just as much a vacuum on and around the Moon as exists in deep space—there was a real paradox here: in all the Apollo pictures, the hard black shadows of the Moon's natural landscape were set against the extra-lunar objects (the LM, the equipment and the astronauts) which always had detail in the shadows. They were 'filled-in' on the shadow side with extra light from a reflector or an artificial light source (as we will see later in this chapter). Of course, those man-made items should have been as 'hard' a black as the shaded side of the lunar rocks, and we could not really understand how the film stock on its own was able to perform such differenti-ating 'tricks of the light'.

For some reason NASA chose to use reversal film stock, rather than colour negative film which would have provided a far greater expo-sure latitude.

"There were two reasons for this," Douglas explained, "and the matter was given a great deal of thought at the time. Firstly, when you present the lab with a negative film for them to produce the positives, they would normally expect to have some gauge by which to print it. On Earth we would use skin tones, but dressed from head to toe in a spacesuit, you do not have that availability and so the labs don't

---

Milestone mystery

It is absolutely remarkable that a film stock which can withstand extreme temperatures and damaging X-rays—coupled with an extensive exposure latitude never reached the open market.

Surely if Kodak had released such a product it would have been a commercial success!

Perhaps there is another reason for this reticence to publicise the use of Kodak film on the Moon.

Is there a clue in this extract from Kodak's company history, that covers the Apollo period?

- 1969—Construction began on Kodak Colorado Division—a manufacturing unit for films and papers located in Wind-sor, Colorado.
- A very special stereo camera made by Kodak accompanied astronauts Aldrin and Armstrong when they set foot on the Moon.
- Kodak received an "Emmy" award for its development of fast colour film processing for television use.
- The number of share owners passed the 200,000 mark. KODAK *Milestones* 1933-1979

What about Kodak film being used for the first time on another world?

No mention of this whatsoever.

Did Kodak wish to distance themselves from such a project, for reasons that we are only just beginning to discover?

have a norm from which to print. With a transparency the colours are locked in the film; secondly you had higher resolution with transparency film compared with negative/positive film."

Nevertheless, in our view, negative/positive film *could have been used* if, at the start of each roll and especially at each new location, the astronauts were to have exposed a colour chart (lit by the same light that was falling on the surrounding terrain) then there would be a very accurate colour reference for the processing laboratory. This procedure is common practice in the motion picture industry, which uses colour negative stock and had such film been used it would have provided greater flexibility.

No spin rate

All these points notwithstanding, it would appear that the Kodak film performed very well under the difficult conditions on the Moon. Therefore it is interesting, as Douglas pointed out, "in photographic terms I think I am correct in saying that there was very little, if anything, that came from the space program which was subsequently introduced into either earthbound cameras or indeed, earth-bound film". And "from the point of view of film stock development—nothing that I am aware of".

Potentially, there was a tremendous amount to be gained out of all this—going to the Moon is one of mankind's greatest achievements. And for companies like Eastman Kodak not to 'tell the world about it' to any great extent does seem rather surprising.

"Now I think that the very prosaic reason for this discreet approach," Douglas commented

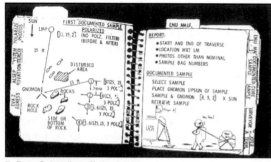

7. Pete Conrad's cuff check. AULIS NASA

8. Exposure guide on camera magazine. AULIS

9. Exposure card, the basic guide for achieving accurate exposures. AULIS

"was that although various other brands of film were tried out by NASA, to all intents and purposes it was only Kodak film that was used during Project Apollo. One can therefore understand that the corporate management in Rochester might be concerned about a monopoly situation in the American market, and decide to play down the reliance of NASA on Kodak film for Apollo. Personally, although I understand that decision, it is saddening to think of the opportunities that have been lost."

So having made it all the way to the Moon with a specially-developed camera and reliable film stock how did they manage to obtain correct exposures? Keeping in mind that these were not modern automatic cameras, apparently they had built up an awareness of typical exposures which would yield the best results under certain conditions. Their photographic training

documents, and items like the decals affixed to their Lunar Surface Cameras plus their cuff check lists indicate that they had generated what were called 'nominal settings'.

"Typically," Douglas explained, "they either had a written table of settings for certain subjects, or more usually it was presented as a clockface, and for a given shutter speed, a series of aperture settings was indicated around the sides of this clockface—f/11 taking the place of, say three o'clock etc.; the astronaut assumed the position of the clock hands at the centre of this dial, and could then select the appropriate aperture in relation to the Sun's position."

Close examination of the recorded TV footage failed to show anyone using an exposure meter on the lunar surface but there were instances where instructions came down the line from Houston regarding what exposures to use! We wondered about shots taken in shadow areas immediately followed by pictures taken in bright sunlight—or even part shadow, part bright terrain—which were always correctly exposed. Then of course there was the big question of radiation affecting the film.

Many of us remember how the early generation of X-ray machines used to cause havoc to our film stock. So with space photography, either on the Moon or orbiting around the Moon, what sort of challenges would there have been from solar and other space radiation?

"That's an interesting question," commented Douglas. "There is an enormous amount of radiation in space, potentially it affects film, and its prime effect is on contrast. The tests that were done indicated that the storing of the film magazines in special containers within the CSM (which was itself shielded to some degree from radiation) was obviously enough."

This response is based on the information supplied by NASA; however, if these pictures were not actually taken on the Moon they would obviously be OK, would they not? And in any event, how could NASA carry out radiation protection tests that were the equivalent of the lunar surface, before actually landing anyone on the Moon? To use a probe for that purpose would mean returning the film to Earth

and they were unable to do that prior to 1969—allegedly. Even if the CSM and the LM *did* have special film storage containers the Hasselblad camera itself was wholly vulnerable as it was unprotected from solar radiation and X-rays once carried onto the lunar surface. As we investigated further there were always more things that could go wrong than could go right, it seemed.

"Most mortals don't get to see the original films, kept in pressurised and temperature-controlled vaults in Houston." But Douglas assured us: "I have seen the top quality duplicates of the original film taken on the Moon, and there is no indication of any radiation effects whatsoever."

Douglas owns a duplicate roll of 70mm film. It was a contact copy of magazine number 40 from the 'Apollo 11' mission.

10. HJP ("Douglas") Arnold with a duplicate roll of 70mm film from a Hasselblad Lunar Surface Camera.   AULIS

"This was given to me by the people at the photographic technology division at Houston, there were a few dozen of these duplicates made at the time and this is quite an historical record which I am delighted to possess."

And what about the magazines themselves, were they like a regular film magazines?

"Basically yes," responded Douglas. "They had to be somewhat modified to take the longer length of the thinner-based film and also to maximise freedom from jamming. Though when you have got some ham-fisted individual trying to load the film, it would jam. Not all the astronauts were good at this manoeuvre and it did jam quite often."

Anybody wearing those pressurised gauntlets most certainly would be ham-fisted to a serious degree—in any location. The astronauts were also required to remove a thin backing plate and keep it safe somewhere, then re-fit it later before changing magazines again (11). Which pocket of the spacesuit was reserved for this exercise one wonders? It is also virtually impossible to carry out such a manipulation wearing pressurised gauntlets. The stub-ended fingers on these gauntlets could scarcely be bent at all, much less to the degree required for such a delicate operation as this.[3]

What was the situation regarding the bracketing of exposures? "Usually the astronauts were hurrying and they didn't have time to bracket," replied Douglas.

In addition to the Hasselblad, there was another piece of photographic equipment called the Data Acquisition Camera (DAC). It was a

Maurer, a specially-designed motion picture 16mm film camera. Not really a movie camera in the conventional sense, it could fire at a variety of rates (or frames per second) and still images could be made from any one of these frames. "This camera was fixed in one of the

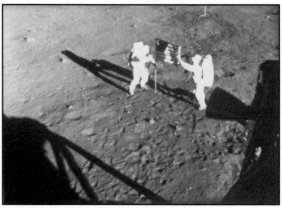

12. Armstrong and Aldrin   NASA
photographed from the Data Acquisition Camera.

triangular windows of the LM. That's the window through which the DAC shot the landing sequences that we always see," explained Douglas. "It was all pre-programmed of course, that camera was simply configured to point at where they were working on the lunar surface and it was firing all the time, at a very slow rate: one or two frames per second."

One of the missions that preceded Apollo was the Lunar Orbiter project in which Douglas Arnold had been very much involved. "The Lunar Orbiters were considered as the most successful, comprehensive space program there had been. This project's film system was kept very much under wraps, called the Kodak Bi-Mat Transfer System, it had evolved from primitive spy satellite technology. NASA flew it from 1966 to 1967."

AULIS

11. Hasselblad magazine with thin backing plate /darkslide and wire handle for removal/replacement while on the lunar surface.   AULIS

This was interesting, because we already knew that the spies 'on the other side' had been using a similar method since Luna 3 was launched from Baikonour in October 1959!

Douglas went on to explain how this system worked. "The film was processed automatically on board the orbiter. It passed through a series of rollers, was developed and fixed and then it passed in front of a flying light scanner, which moved across the film and read it out in strips of modulated light back to receivers on Earth, where the film was reconstructed. There was enormous resolution, marvellous detail, in spite of the scan lines on the film. The other probes, the crash lander Rangers and the soft lander Surveyors had TV-type systems."

We then wanted to define the height from which these images were taken, and asked Douglas to confirm his information that the Lunar Orbiters were reasonably near the surface of the Moon.

"Well," Douglas said, "they could dip to as low as 28 miles off the lunar surface but one of the cameras had a telephoto lens so that you could see detail of around 33 feet/10 metres, and they could, via shadow information, pick

13. Lunar Orbiter 2 image. NASA

out the Surveyors that had already landed on the surface. At the time, the scientists complained that the Orbiters were used too much for the Apollo landing project and not enough for lunar geological information."

14. Surveyor TV camera and mirror. NASA/NGS
The Surveyor craft were equipped with a single TV camera having a photo-sensitive vidicon tube and a lens which was permanently aimed at a motor driven mirror. This radio-commanded mirror was able to scan an almost complete 360° circle of the ground or the horizon from a position at approximately 'man height' (5.5 feet).

It is quite certain that the vast majority of people associated with the Apollo project were contracted to work on a 'need to know' basis only. Although an acknowledged expert in his own field, Douglas, like everyone else, would not have had access to the whole picture. Bearing that in mind, we asked Douglas if he had anything to add concerning the challenges of space photography. Douglas made the following points:

"On the whole I think that we have a marvel-

15. The Soviet's Luna craft with TV camera that scanned from about 'knee height'.   NOVOSTI

lous record of the space program. Despite that famous joke: 'NASA—Never **A** Straight **A**nswer'—which I think is quite unfair!" (By the end of this book many readers might think it entirely appropriate after all!)

"As distinct from the Soviet space program where everything was shrouded in secrecy the NASA-run American space program was done in the full glare of publicity. And this marvellous imagery was made available to the public. We have seen hardly anything from the Soviet missions."

"My one major regret," Douglas next declared, "is the absence of a top quality still frame of Neil Armstrong, the first man to touch the lunar surface. Now I researched this matter in depth and there's a story to this."[4]

"Granted it was the first lunar landing. There was a flight program for them which called for almost all of the photography to be done by Neil Armstrong and he did it magnificently."

"Subsequently, when those films came back to Houston and after the quarantine period when the films were in the labs, Dr. Bob Gilruth, head of Houston Manned Space Center, the photographic specialist and NASA's top PR man at that time were all examining the films as they were cranked over a light box."

(see box below)

"I have it on first hand account that the quest was: 'Let's look for the best set of pictures of Neil'. Then their faces tended to drop somewhat and by the end they were saying 'Well, let's find *any* picture of Neil'. In fact there was only one: of Neil standing near the LM, but it was a distant shot, part of a geological panorama sequence photographed by Aldrin."

"I'm somewhat surprised that nobody appeared to have realised that there was not going

---

Looking for needle in a HayShack

Houston's Astronaut Shack, better known as the Lunar Receiving Lab (LRL) took up 83,000 square feet at the Houston Manned Space Center.

One-third of this vast building (27,666 square ft) housed the astronauts' quarantine area through which they entered via a sterile plastic tunnel (remember the movie *E T?*). Among other facilities, the LRL contained biomedical labs, computer rooms, data transfer rooms and storage for the CSM. In all, two-thirds of this $15.8m building was dedicated to the R&D of the equipment and materials for 'Apollo 11'.

16. Armstrong photographed by Aldrin.
 Notice the astronaut is filled-in with light although he is standing in the full shadow of the LM.

NASA

to be a 'portrait' of the first man on the Moon. Because by 1969, NASA as an organisation was so aware of the importance of these images to communicate the endeavours of the space program to the public. It's rather like Columbus stepping onto the shores of the New World while his shipboard artist sketches the palm trees at the other end of the beach. *History has no record!* There are fuzzy TV frames from the 'step down' in black and white; grotty colour frames from the movie camera in the Lunar Module, but knowing the quality of the Hasselblad, it is a great regret that there isn't as good a shot of Armstrong as that superb picture he took of Aldrin."

As we concluded our time with Douglas, we remembered how Andrew Chaikin, in his book *A Man on the Moon,* relates that Aldrin only occasionally got to use the camera and that when he did use it, he photographed the LM and the terrain around the module—and alleg-

edly—the famous picture of his foot! Chaikin justifies this situation by telling the story of Sir Edmund Hillary on Everest, who said that there were no photos of that event as Tenzing did not know how to use a camera, and that Everest was not the place to teach him.

However, this all rather begs the question. NASA possessed high quality Hasselblad cameras and apparently the astronauts had been especially trained in the art of recording their adventures. The entire photographic assignment had been carefully planned, for this was indeed an historic first in the evolution of mankind. Our first steps beyond the bounds of this planet, our first steps on another celestial sphere. The ramifications of such an adventure were to be of world-wide proportions and yet the proof that we had achieved our aims lay in the hands of two men—one of whom, Chaikin implies, was not a good photographer, yet the evidence suggests that NASA probably relied

---

Mountain mystery

Before Tenzing died he said that Hillary had reached the summit first, but there are still unanswered questions as to exactly how that came about.

The fact that neither party would speak of the matter, the attitude of Hillary towards a mountain held sacred by the Nepalese and the fact that what should have been the highlight of his life was an episode that weighed upon Tenzing up until his death, has strange parallels with the Apollo program and the behaviour of the astronauts following their missions.

on Aldrin's landscape and technical photographs. It would be astonishing if the NASA machine 'forgot' to program in this very important photograph.

- Is it not inconceivable that Armstrong declined to be included in the 'official' visual historical record?
- The absence of Armstrong's image might not be an oversight after all.

The lunar photographic 'brief':

As our studies of NASA's photographic demands became more detailed, the absurdity of any individual actually fulfilling their criteria became increasingly obvious. Therefore at this point we are inserting what is best described as a 'spoof' photographic brief to the Apollo astronauts. Whilst this brief may at first appear to be rather frivolous, our brief is no spoof at all. It details what would be required of them as astro-photographers during their moonwalks. The real spoof may have been asking us to accept that the astronauts could actually deliver usable pictures.

"We are giving you an unusual photographic assignment. Not only do we expect the vast majority of the pictures you take to be usable, but in particular:

- Photos must be correctly and accurately exposed, in focus, well composed, and suitable for promotional purposes.
- The rolls of film from your camera magazines will be duplicated and handed out to various VIPs as souvenirs of the mission, so the pictures should look convincing when they are all seen 'together' on the roll.
- Every three or four pictures are to be of a different 'set-up' to the preceding photographs but each new scene is to be technically acceptable. We expect you to take between 100 and 150 photos per roll of Ektachrome colour film, 180 or so when using black & white film stock.
- Although you might find this assignment easier in a studio, we are sending you to an exterior location where film lighting is needed—especially in the dark areas—but you will be given no lighting whatsoever.

- In fact, you will be working under unique lighting conditions in a place never visited before by human beings!
- To make it more challenging, even if it would help you to get the exposures correct, NO LIGHT METERS are allowed!
- A processing 'clip test' is only possible once per roll of 150 pictures or so, therefore your exposures must be spot on.
- But we will give you an exposure card rather like the guides on the side of film boxes—Bright Sun = f/11 etc.
- You will be expected to photograph 'into the Sun' and get the exposure exactly right—and after changing to the next, different, set-up get that exposure right too.
- There is to be little or no 'bracketing of exposures'. In other words, we do not want you to open up the lens stop; or close it down in adjacent exposures—actions which would ensure that you return with a usable set of pictures.
- We have decided to give you the film type (reversal or transparency or slide) with the worst tolerance in exposure, as it will reproduce best in publicity material and magazines such as the prestigious *National Geographic,* the organ of one of our sponsors.
- It's not a joke, but there is NO VIEWFINDER on the camera that we are supplying! We know that this is a minor handicap and the inability to see what you are taking must make it extremely difficult—but that's our decision.
- When photographing *PANORAMA* shots without a viewfinder remember that we must, of course, be able to join them all up nicely without bits missing or excessive overlaps. You will be expected to compose and focus pictures correctly, even after using cameras with different focal length lenses.
- You will be expected to change magazines and mount a polarising filter onto the front of the camera's super-wide and/or the 60mm camera lens. However, with the absence of a viewfinder, there is no way you can see the effect of this to get the filter into the best orientation, but the rotation of the filters must be correct nevertheless! Don't forget

17. Armstrong's pressurised gauntlets. NASA

18. Could you change filters wearing these? AULIS

that you will have to calculate your exposures correctly when using the polariser.

- You will be wearing pressurised gauntlets—which take away any sensitivity when handling filters, and will make it almost impossible for you to bend your fingers. We have made some controls on the special camera easy to manipulate (but difficult to read) however, we must admit that we overlooked the problem of making filter adjustments when wearing these 'clumsy' gloves.
- The temperature in which you'll be working will average a baking +180°F/82°C. This should not soften the film *too* much! We do realise that the temperature is well out of the designed range of the film stock and we hope it will not seriously affect your chances of getting the right exposures.
- In the shade it will dip to a freezing minus 180°F/118°C, and so we hope that the emulsion will not become too brittle! We could have insulated the camera against this hostile environment, but we elected not to do that.
- Your worst problem will be this: the area you will be visiting is full of hazardous radiation. You must not get any of this onto the camera or magazine, otherwise, as you

know, a dose as low as 25 rem will seriously fog (lighten) the film, rendering it useless.

- Do you want the job? We are offering it to you simply because as a non-professional photographer you qualify.
- The bad news is that the location is on the Moon—but the good news is that you will be using the new Hasselblad 500 EL/70 Lunar Surface Camera.
- Despite the fact that your photos and TV coverage will be the only record that man has stepped onto the lunar surface, this photography business is only *INCIDENTAL* to your trip and you will be under considerable pressure to undertake many other tasks during your time on location—broadcasting live TV for instance."

Imagine having to fulfil such a photographic brief (which we consider virtually impossible); setting up and organising live TV transmissions and combining these two tasks with the already heavy physiological and psychological demands placed upon the first humans to set foot on the little-known territory of a planet beyond their own.

Be sure your sins will find you out

Through detailed photographic analysis of certain NASA images we have gathered compelling evidence that there was indeed a falsification of the record and no matter how NASA chooses to justify its actions during the 'space race' in our opinion there can be no defence for such a policy.

As we consider a number of basic photographic rules, we will see how the Apollo photographs stand up to scrutiny.

Photo rule No 1. *Light travels in straight, parallel lines at any given moment. Shadow directions are constant because the light comes from the Sun—a single light source—some 93 million miles away.*

Take a look at (19) and (19a), pictures of typical tree shadows. Notice the parallel lines of shadow—and also that the shadow side of the trees is very dark (19a). There is no visible detail there on the dark side, this is logical and therefore not surprising. Now compare the

19. Parallel shadows, sunlit side.

19a. Parallel shadows   AULIS

pictures of these trees with the panoramic shot over the page, allegedly taken on the Moon (20). This is a flat plain, the designated landing site of 'Apollo 14'.

One can calculate from the diverging shadows that the source of light is overhead, within the area of the scene! It is possible to work out exactly where the lighting was positioned, because the shadows converge to a point when in fact they ought to be parallel. The shadows cast by the rocks in the foreground should have been east-west, like the LM's shadow on the right. When natural sunlight is illuminating objects on a flat terrain such a result is impossible, with or without an atmosphere.

Compare NASA's image (20) with our computer-modified image (21). The light source in our composite is located far to the west, and in our demonstration all the shadows are falling naturally due east.

We must therefore irrefutably conclude that an artificial light source was used in close proximity (indicated with a spotlight) in order for NASA to obtain the result in photo (20).

Another image for which the same comments apply is (22) which not only exhibits diverging shadows, but contains more surprises: the shadow side of the astronaut (on the upper right) is not black, and the shaded side of his gold visor actually reflects a bright source of light!—(not from the LM). Both circumstances

are indeed rather astonishing for they *cannot* occur naturally. The rock shadow in the right lower corner is what one would expect.

Given that natural sunlight cannot generate shadows like those in (20) and (22), these images suggest that such pictures were not taken on the Moon. We therefore offer these as examples of artificial lighting in a fully controlled 'studio environment'. Now any top lighting cameraman or experienced effects photographer could have lit these scenes so that these diverging and converging shadows were not apparent: and clearly it is simply *not possible* to have variations in shadow direction *on flat terrain* (22 lower) within any one picture, if that photograph is genuine. So is it unreasonable for us to conclude that this handiwork was deliberate?

Daytime on the lunar surface lasts for a period of approximately 14 'Earth' days (noon occurring on the seventh day and night-time starting at the end of the 14th day) but in the Apollo images, shadow lengths vary *within* the time frame of any alleged mission and particularly compared to the Sun angle at the time of the supposed trip. For example, the arrival of 'Apollo 11' on the lunar surface was timed for a Sun angle of *10°* above the horizon.

Shadows due East

South East

20. Diverging shadows on the Moon, typical of the Apollo pictures lit by 'unnatural' lighting. NASA

Some 6 hours 38 minutes after Armstrong had announced: "The Eagle has landed", the astronauts had exited the Lunar Module (LM) for an EVA of just over two hours, commencing the moment Armstrong stood on the first rung of the ladder.

But the examples on page 25, that is, photographs (23) and (24) exhibit nothing like the approximate 13.55° to 15° angle we should have seen on that occasion. What we do find are many pictures with angles of 26.0° (or more) in

21. Computer-generated demonstration of correct parallel shadows as they would be if naturally formed by the Sun.

the published photographic and TV recorded footage of this time period for this mission.[5]

Any Sun angles displaying virtually double what should have been recorded at a specific location on a specific date are totally impossible, so we are left with no other alternative than to conclude that here are more examples of a Whistle-Blower's subtle manipulation of shadow length in order to encode the data that reveals the hoax. Should you protest that NASA would have spotted such a flagrant ploy, ask yourself why *you* have not noticed these differences before now.

23

The Sun?

Filled-in
with light

22. More converging/diverging shadows on the Moon.

NASA

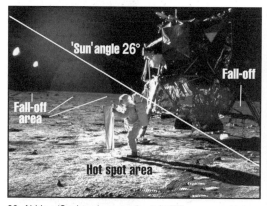

23. Aldrin—'Sun' angle approximately 26° it should have been nearer to 14°.   NASA

24. TV Frame—Armstrong standing by the LM—the light source more than double the natural Sun angle.

Varying shadow lengths within any given picture or TV scene imply either more than one light source placed in close proximity, or tampering with the shadows at a later stage of the image processing.

In (25), initially the viewer is distracted by the bright light above the full image. One has to look closer. In (26) the close-up, one can see that the shadows are all over the place. There are long shadows, short shadows, grey shadows, a few very dark shadows, some rocks filled-in and some not filled-in. This variety of 'booby-traps' undeniably

and effectively emphasises the deliberate manipulation of the image.

The two 'Apollo 11' astronauts in (27) captured by the Data Acquisition Camera mounted high on the *LM each have very different shadow lengths.* How can it also be that they are not consistent with the approx. 13.55° to 15.0° Sun elevation for the time they allegedly spent walking on the lunar surface? Furthermore, they not even consistent with the

25. 'Apollo 12'   NASA
—the complete image.

26. Close-up rock detail in foreground of picture (25).   NASA

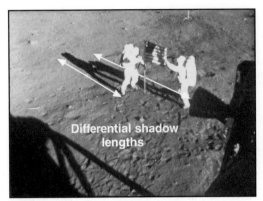

27. 'Apollo 11' shadow length differences   NASA
on flat terrain.

28. TV frame from 'Apollo 12'.   NASA
This is a *higher* Sun angle—but a *longer* shadow.
Compare with 'Apollo 11' (27).

shadow lengths created by the 26.0° or so Sun angle apparent in other pictures and TV images (see photographs 23 & 24).

Our only explanation is that these two men are standing in such close proximity to a large artificial light source, that as either one moves nearer to, or further away from this light, the shadow of each astronaut changes accordingly.

It is interesting to compare a similar view (28) from the 'Apollo 12' mission, where the astronaut has an *even longer* shadow length, despite the fact that the Sun was at a *higher angle* than the preceding mission! More importantly, in the 'Apollo 12' Hasselblad stills, the same astronauts' shadow lengths do not tally with those recorded by the Data Acquisition Camera.

Sloppiness—or deliberate manipulation?

Additionally, there is visual evidence of a large, very close, ARTIFICIAL source of light. The three TV images (29) show reflections of a light source occupying at least 25% of the astronauts' *convex* visors.

This result is indicative of a light that is incredibly large and extremely close. In our opinion these images could only manifest this result if photographed by the light of something other than the Sun. Compare for instance the small size of the reflected Sun in the visor of Bruce McCandless during the first untethered spacewalk from Challenger on February 7 1984 (29a). An average of 237,800 miles difference between low Earth orbit and the *lunar surface* cannot increase the amount of sunlight reflected in a visor to such an extent.

'Apollo 15'.   'Apollo 17'.   NASA
29. TV frames depicting an exceedingly large, close light source reflected in the astronauts' visors. Compare (29a & 29b).

29a. Pin-point of reflected Sun in visor during an   NASA
untethered space walk February 1984 (in LEO).

29b. Ed White during a Gemini EVA (pre-Apollo).   NASA

Photo rule No 2. *Light in a vacuum is high
contrast—i.e. very bright on the Sun side,
very dark on the shadow side—and on the
Moon there is no atmosphere to help fill-in
or soften/lighten the shadows.*

Telling tales?

'Apollo 12' voice recording,
the TV camera was allegedly faulty:
Pete Conrad: "That Sun's bright, it's like somebody is
shining a spotlight on your hands!"

Pete Conrad: "I tell you...it really is. It's like somebody's got a super-bright spotlight!"

Photograph (30) is one of many examples in
which the shaded part of the astronaut is artificially 'filled-in' with supplementary lighting.
Without this additional lighting, the entire
front of the astronaut would be totally black.

30. 'Apollo 16'.   NASA

31. Mongolian herdsman,   HO KAN-KEUNG
naturally backlit by the Sun—the scene is a silhouette.

We have filled-in (30) the original NASA
picture and created image (32) in order to demonstrate that the only way this scene could
look (without additional lighting) is the way
unlit surfaces *actually reproduce* in a natural
photograph. Now compare NASA's astronaut
in (30) with the Mongolian herdsman in (31).
Despite the fact that this descendant of Genghis
Khan has the benefit of atmospheric haze and
airborne dust to help diffuse the shadows he is
still totally blacked out.

32. Apollo astronaut, naturally backlit on the Moon —should be a silhouette! *(Our adjusted version of 30).*

33. Typical result of reflected lighting in automobile photography.

The fact that (30) does not look like either (31) or (32) indicates beyond doubt that reflectors or other fill-in and/or secondary light sources were deployed—yet no such equipment was seen to be used in the recorded TV coverage, which included the setting up of the equipment for these scenes. Such additional lighting would need to be suspended from some high position, out of camera shot. A studio rig or gantry would do the trick. And before you ask, the only tall structure available on this mission, the LM, has no specifications for providing such a light source. We shall come back to this very important point later.

Let us look at a terrestrial example that requires the use of reflected light in photography. When photographing automobiles in a studio an extensive amount of reflected light 'bounced' from various sources (studio walls and ceiling panels) is necessary in order to avoid unpleasant hot-spots on the paintwork (33).

The automobile in (34) is illuminated to show it at its best, using established studio techniques deploying reflected light—but then the astronaut too, as we have pointed out, was illuminated by artificial reflected lighting at the time of the Apollo photography, so of course the lighting styles match! (30 & 34). That is why the Toyota advertisement works as a convincing composite image.

Every amateur snapper knows that unless you use the flashgun on your camera (these days usually automatic) results shot 'into the Sun' are often disappointing. So, by frequently presenting us with exactly this type of 'contrajour' set-up, the Whistle-Blowers are clearly and metaphorically highlighting the 'situation'!

'Apollo 17' at the Taurus Littrow location (35) is an example of selective filling-in of shadow detail: The astronaut is filled-in, but the rocks are untouched—their shadows are

THE LITTLE CAR IN FRONT WITH THE BIG IDEAS IS THE ⊕ TOYOTA STARLET.

34. Astronaut and car in a 1997 campaign for Toyota.

Sun angle incorrect

Rocks NOT filled-in

Filled-in with light

35. 'Apollo 17'—a composite of two images.　NASA

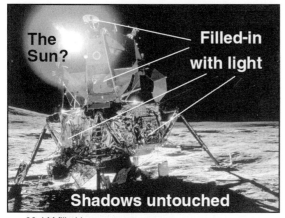

The Sun?

Filled-in with light

Shadows untouched

36. LM filled-in.　NASA

Hot spot

37. Clearly-lit equipment on the shadow side of the LM.

opinion, this was once again intentional Whistle-Blowing. A demonstration that the astronaut was filled-in by an artificial light source or reflector at the time of photography. Because if the picture had been taken in the high contrast conditions prevalent on the Moon there would be no detail available in these totally black shadows to 'bring up' during any subsequent retouching processes.

NASA, together with the suppliers of the backpacks (PLSS) and the spacesuits were no doubt pleased to see their product clearly, perhaps not primarily interested in the rocks—no immediate promotional benefits there! The black rocks also look menacing and thus enhance the bravery of 'our boys' and these could be reasons that the Whistle-Blowers were able to get this category of image passed for publication without question.

The use of fill-in light is not limited to astronauts. What about the amount of light required to be re-directed towards the LM? In photo (36), the hatch is illuminated, the 'United States' is visible and in (37) we can even see very clearly the piece of equipment which is *standing in the shadow*. All this, despite the fact that the photographer is shooting directly into the full glare of what we are to supposed to believe is the Sun.

If this picture were genuine, the side of the LM nearest the camera would be totally black. Some very fed up Whistle-Blowers in action here, utilising a great deal of light to counter the intensity of the prime light source, so that detail in the shadow side of the LM is visible. This photograph is therefore the result of an entirely artificial set-up.

At this point it is already clear:

- That the Apollo stills do not correspond to images taken with the appropriate film stock.
- That colour reversal film for transparencies or slides was used when colour negative film would have been be best, the latter having a good exposure latitude.
- The film they used would have to be accurate in its exposure to within ½ an *f* stop or so!

totally black. What an absolute give-away that this image was not taken on the Moon! In our

---

TechnoSpeak

1. Negative film for colour prints: Good exposure latitude. Nearly every amateur photographer uses this film stock. It cannot be used in a slide projector being in 'negative' but it's cheap to make prints by machine from colour negatives.
2. Transparency, or reversal film for colour slides. Minimal exposure latitude compared to 1. Reversal processing is also more expensive. This film type is used by serious photographers, prints cost more but can be of superior quality to 1. Reversal stock is ideal for commercial and professional output. Transparencies are used by picture libraries who supply professional photographs for journals and magazines etc.
3. Eastman Kodak's Kodachrome was always the best for amateurs, now rivalled by Fuji, according to some experts.
4. Kodak's Ektachrome produces softer colours than 3, and is good for reproduction in colour magazines, journals and newspapers.
Note: The bigger the 'negative' size, the better the print or slide, because the film area is greater, the lens assembly is physically larger, thereby producing higher quality results.
Some cameras, such as Hasselblads, have removable film magazines (cassettes) so that the film can be changed according to requirements.
Removable magazines are a good alternative to carrying several cameras.

But reversal film was precisely the right stock for glossy colour photographs that would reproduce well in *National Geographic* magazine. It would appear that without a viewfinder and the benefit of an exposure meter they obtained accurate exposures—there were some lovely results!

To give an idea of the problems associated with slide or reversal film stock that would have been encountered by the Apollo astronauts, here is an extract from a 1966 publication entitled *Colour Films.*[6]

Regarding exposure latitude:
The exposure of reversal colour films calls for considerably more accuracy than is required for black-and-white ...and...colour negative films. Indeed, theoretically, if all transparencies are to be evenly matched for projection, *there is no exposure latitude at all,* since the density of the colour image is the direct product of exposure, assuming standard laboratory processing conditions (emphasis added).

And again:

Reversal film exposure latitude is very limited...correct exposure not only has to reproduce tone values in proportional densities, but also it has to start the tone scale with the right minimum density. If this minimum density is too low, the image is overexposed. If it is too high, the picture looks too dark and is unacceptable, even though all steps of the subject brightness range are on the straight-line portion of the curve.

Reversal film therefore has considerably less exposure latitude than a negative film. In practice the exposure for best results with transparencies should be correct *within half a stop*, and the subject lighting contrast should not be too great.

If a subject's brightness range exceeds the recording limits of the film, the darker shadows will lose detail and in many cases show distorted colours. *There is nothing that can be done about this (other than lighting up the shadows with fill-in light)* since the exposure must be correct to get good highlight reproduction.

Exposure latitude in the reversal process is restricted by the fact that after the negative image has been developed to metallic silver, there must be left exactly the right amount of unaltered silver halide to produce the positive image.

Appreciable overexposure is therefore fatal, since no intensifier known can restore an image that has been dissolved away in the course of processing. Moderate overexposure, for the same reason destroys delicate detail in the highlights of the picture.

Underexposure in the camera leaves an excess of neutral dye over the whole picture. With gross underexposure *nothing will restore missing detail in black, empty shadows*.

The correct exposure for optimum viewing, as distinct from optimum originals for graphic reproduction, is normally that which will leave the highest specular highlight just transparent after reversal processing.

So an exposure meter is virtually indispensable for determining exposures with a reversal colour film.

In a colour transparency intended for reproduction in print, the highest attainable standard of technique is essential to reduce inevitable quality losses in the reproduction process to a minimum. A commercial photographer just cannot afford many of the compromises that are acceptable in a colour picture for one's private pleasure.

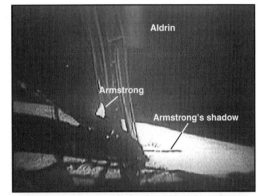

39. TV frame showing Armstrong in relation to Aldrin when taking (38). *Aldrin: "I'm on the top step and I can look down over the RCU and the landing gear pad."*

Exposure measurements for reversal colour film should be based on incident light or artificial highlight readings.[7]

Photo rule No 3. *Dark, unlit areas cannot naturally be illuminated with directional lighting emanating from the side and creating strong shadows or 'hot spots'.*

In our view it would have taken many hours to light this shot, one of several, allegedly of Aldrin descending the ladder during 'Apollo 11'. Clearly, from the TV coverage we could see that no flash, no additional lights and no auxiliary power were available *on the Moon*. Furthermore, the astronauts did not have any time to spend on setting up elaborate lighting during any of the 'Apollo' missions. Yet in order to take photograph (38) a light *had* to have been placed near the camera axis.

Snakes and ladders laboratory tested

In an attempt to disprove our own additional lighting hypothesis, Quantec Image Processing in the UK carried out a series of laboratory tests on a

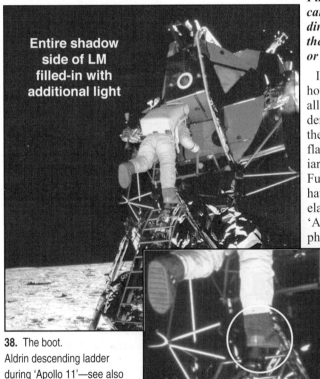

Entire shadow side of LM filled-in with additional light

38. The boot.
Aldrin descending ladder during 'Apollo 11'—see also (38b) on page 34.

38a. Blow-up of the hot spot on right over-boot.

number of NASA photographs from 'Apollo 11'. David Groves PhD who founded Quantec is more than adequately qualified to undertake such a project. He has a BSc (Hons) Class 1 in Applied Physics and his PhD was in Holographic Computer Measurement. He is also a Chartered Physicist and a Member of the Institute of Physics. Initially David Groves was determined to disprove our theories.

"When they first approached us," he said, "I thought 'here we go, a bunch of people who have misunderstood the nature of the images'. But as a professional in image processing, I was surprised to find that these pictures are full of contradictions and inconsistencies."

This particular photograph (38) was selected by us for a full test. Firstly, we asked David Groves to investigate the 'hot spot' of light on the heel protector of Aldrin's right over-boot, using the technique of 'ray tracing'—a technique for tracing paths of light. David labelled this photograph D(38) and here is the summary of his report:[8]

The source of illumination in the Astronaut Descending Ladder image photo D(38) is located between 23.6cm and 34.0cm to the right of the camera position, assuming the source of illumination is at the same distance from the Lunar Module as the camera.

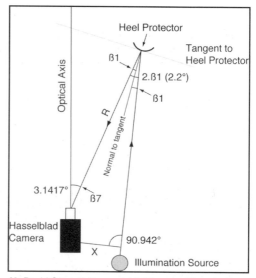

40. David Groves' diagram of lighting conditions for the boot hot-spot photo (38). The source of illumination was between 23.6cms and 34.0cms to the right of the camera. *(Distances compressed in this illustration.)*

The best estimate of the horizontal direction of illumination (using the photograph) can be determined from the position of the highlight on the heel of the right hand boot.

Illustration (40) shows the position of the (indisputable) illumination source located to the right of the subject.

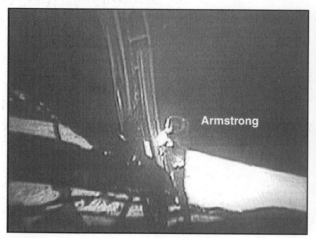

41. TV frame.
Armstrong: "...Looks like your PLSS is clearing OK."

42. Aldrin emerges.   NASA

The proof is in the detail

So an additional source of light was indeed responsible for the illumination in this set-up and evidence for this is to be found in the tell-tale 'hot spot' (the bright highlight) on the heel of the astronaut's right over-boot.

One might have argued that the photogra-pher's spacesuit was possibly acting as a reflec-tor for Aldrin descending the ladder. But this could not have been the case, as the light source is located to the right of the camera.

In TV frame (41), Armstrong is standing at the foot of the ladder, *virtually in the full shadow of the LM*. The lighting in the resultant

43. TV Frame.

44. Aldrin 'closes the hatch'. NASA

Aldrin: *"I want to er...back up and partially close the hatch, making sure not to lock it on the way out (Armstrong laughs), it's our home for the next couple of hours, we wanna take good care of it."*

45. TV frame.

46. Aldrin 'fourth rung up...'. NASA

Aldrin: *"OK, I'm gonna leave that one foot up there and...er...both hands [garbled] at about the fourth rung up."*

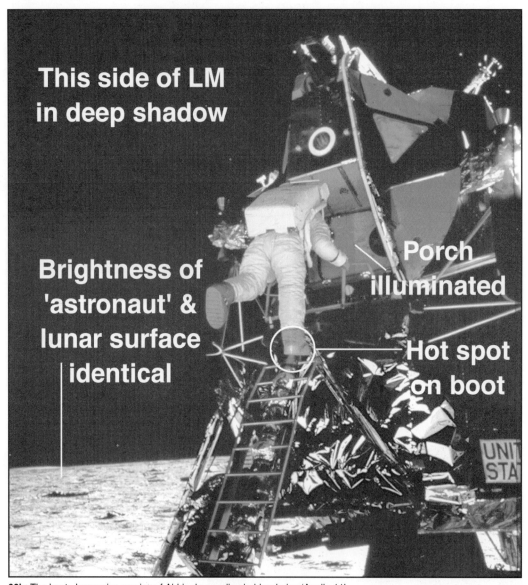

38b. The boot. Large-size version of Aldrin descending ladder during 'Apollo 11'. NASA

photograph (42) has the same characteristics as photo (38). We can see Aldrin very clearly. So as Armstrong is standing in the shade, his spacesuit is *unable to act as a hypothetical reflector*. Our conclusion therefore regarding the use of additional lighting holds firm. Moreover, the *introduced* artificial lighting is sufficiently effective to illuminate the entire area, not only into the porch, but also *into the LM itself.*

It only required one single element in this sequence of stills (the 'hot spot' on his right boot) that could be analysed at some future date to demonstrate that this series of pictures could not possibly have been taken on the Moon.

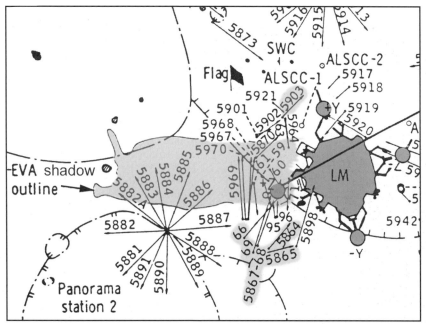

47. Part of the map of the EVA photographs taken at the 'Apollo 11' landing site.   NASA

As NASA has indicated (47), the theoretical EVA shadow outline of the LM at the end of the moonwalk (extending to the left of the LM and corresponding to about 15°) demonstrates a shadow length that confirms our Sun angle calculations.

QUESTION: How can so many of the photographs and TV sequences of Armstrong and Aldrin, as discussed in this chapter, have shadow lengths that are almost double this figure of 15°?

QUESTION: Why has NASA omitted to include the positions for the pictures of Aldrin exiting the hatch prior to descending the ladder? Their frame numbers in this sequence 5862 and 5863 are not even on this plan (47).

Photo rule No 4. *Flat surfaces are always evenly lit by the Sun.*

Aldrin, standing alone in the famous 'Apollo 11' shot we have dubbed the 'classic', cannot be standing in natural sunlight, otherwise there would be no fall-off into shadow in the background. If you were standing in an open field on Earth in sunlight, all parts of the surrounding area would be equally lit by the Sun. There would be no reduction in light as you moved across the field or away from a particular point. Hence it is clear that Aldrin has to be standing in a pool of local, artificially-generated light that does not adequately cover the entire area.

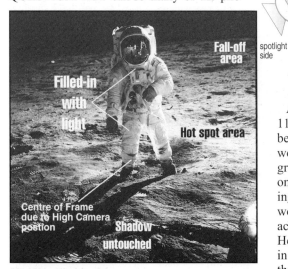

48. Aldrin, the 'classic'.   NASA

35

TechnoSpeak

Fall-off is the term used for areas within the frame of a photograph where the light source fails to illuminate the scene to the same degree as the main arena. It can only occur when the spread of the lighting is insufficient to cover the entire field of view at the same intensity.

After further careful examination of photograph (48), it is also becoming clear that the Whistle-Blowers involved in this set-up have ensured that Aldrin was photographed from *eye level.* So probably not by Armstrong then!

The main cross-hair (reticle) is centred over the subject's right ankle, indicating a camera position much higher than the Hasselblad chest-bracket level. However, the reflection in Aldrin's visor is of a photographer (supposedly Armstrong)—not on a rig, not on a platform and not on a rock—but standing firmly on the ground with his camera fixed on his chest bracket.

This was the second picture selected for testing by David Groves.[9] It was labelled photograph A(48), and David Groves' report concluded that:

The centre of the imaging plane of the camera was between 1.446 metres and 1.527 metres above the surface when photograph A(48) was recorded. In other words, it was imaged from eye level as can be seen in the illustration below (49).

It has been shown conclusively that the position of the camera above the surface of the Moon was at the same level as the line of the horizon extrapolated across the visor of the astronaut imaged in photo A(48). It has also been demonstrated that photograph A(48) was taken from eye level.

However, the image of the photographer astronaut in the visor, clearly visible in photograph A(48), shows the camera to be positioned well below this level, beyond the 'error' range stated in the report.

It can only be concluded that the reflection in the visor is not that of the actual photographer of the image.

So not only was the astronaut standing alone clearly faked. The reflected image in the visor was faked as well! (see Appendix)

The exaggerated contrast version of this picture (50) shows that Aldrin is definitely standing in the beam of what can only be described as a 'super spotlight', positioned high and behind him to the right of the image, with another secondary light source or reflector deployed to lighten-up the detail at the front and to the left, so that we can see him clearly on the shadow side—which, as we have already firmly established, would otherwise be dark.

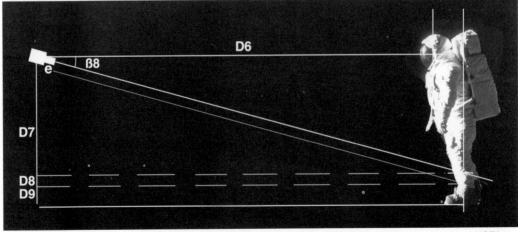

49. David Groves' analysis of camera height of (48) indicating that the photograph was taken from eye level and *NOT* from the chest bracket—the position claimed for the recording of this image (full report in Appendix).

Normal to horizon passing through centre of image

y

Horizon

Line across Visor

outside edge of left leg

x

X

48a. The 'classic' photograph of Aldrin by Armstrong was *taken from eye level* and not from chest height. NASA Therefore, the reflection in the visor [which does not have a camera positioned at eye level] cannot be that of the actual photographer of the image (full report in Appendix).

THE CENTRE OF THE IMAGING PLANE OF THE CAMERA WAS BETWEEN 1446mm & 1527mm
ABOVE THE SURFACE OF THE MOON WHEN PHOTOGRAPH A(48) WAS RECORDED.

The calculations provide an accurate estimate of the camera's height above the surface, provided all the assumptions stated in the report are valid. The only assumption which could make a significant difference if not valid is the assumption that the terrain beneath and between the photographer and astronaut is flat. This assumption can be tested and a 'typical' value for the variation in height of the surface between the astronaut and photographer can be estimated using the shadow on the surface of the outside edge of the astronaut's left leg.

The maximum height of the rise and fall between the astronaut and photographer is in the order of only 10cm, indicating that the surface's height beneath both the astronaut and photographer is not significantly different.

David Groves PhD

48b. Close up of visor from the Aldrin 'classic' picture.   NASA

"The reflection in the visor [which does not have a camera positioned at eye level]
cannot be that of the actual photographer of the image".

David Groves PhD

Full report in Appendix.

50. Exaggerated contrast version of (48).

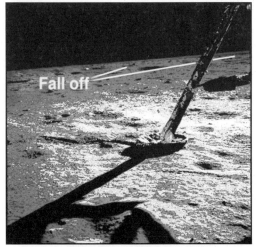

51. Close view of a LM leg, exaggerated contrast. NASA

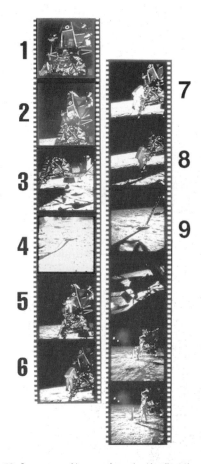

NASA

52. Sequence of images from the 'Apollo 11' Hasselblad camera—a section from magazine number 40.

This lighting technique or 'signature' was not restricted to astronauts. In image (51) the leg of the LM was also bathed in a *pool* of light and there is fall off, both to the side and further back into the picture. According to the way the sequence was presented by the Whistle-Blowing compilers of this set of images, a similar picture of the LM's leg appears (frames numbers 3 & 4) *sandwiched between* the sequence of photographs of Aldrin descending the ladder (52).

Although Armstrong had orders to record the status of the LM after landing on the lunar surface, it is amazing he chose that precise moment—*just as Aldrin was exiting the LM*—to begin that task. Had Aldrin slipped during his descent we might have missed it! Ostensibly it is a rather mean gesture, implying somehow that Aldrin's actions were less important to posterity than the parts of the machine that Armstrong photographed while he waited. In reality it is more likely that the real photographer(s) and/or compositor(s) of this sequence, due to the very unlikely sequencing, could well have been blowing a whistle.

Before we leave this 'Apollo 11' scenario, here is an exchange between Armstrong and

---

Miles of mystery

Armstrong allegedly declared that he had trouble defining the distances on the lunar surface, that everything looked nearer than it was. Other astronauts have underlined this statement.

Andrew Chaikin *A Man on the Moon*

However during a TV panorama sequence Armstrong said: "The little hill beyond the shadow of the LM is a pair of [garbled] craters. Probably, the pair together is 40 feet long and 20 feet across and probably six feet deep".

QUESTION: How could Armstrong make such positive statements of measurement when, by his own admission, it was difficult to judge distances on the Moon?

Houston concerning the TV camera. It confirms the fact that without a viewfinder or a television monitor it is very difficult (if not impossible) to know what is actually within the frame of an image.

Armstrong: "Houston, how's that field of view...er...gonna be..."

Houston: "Neil this is Houston. The field of view is OK—[actually it is not OK, the LM is only partly in the TV picture]—we'd like you to aim it a little bit more to the right, over."

Armstrong moves the camera, this time too far to the right.

Armstrong: "OK...OK that's all the cable we have...I'll start working on the solar..."

Houston (Interrupts): "Er...a little bit too much to the right—can you bring it back left—about four or five degrees?"

Armstrong makes another correction.

Houston: "OK, that looks good Neil."

Even after all that, the LM is still not central in the picture!

A short time later, Armstrong attempted to line up on the LM after a panorama (with about an hour and six minutes or so of mission time elapsed).

Armstrong: "How's that for a final orientation?"

Houston: "For a final orientation we'd like it to come left about five degrees—over."

Armstrong adjusts the TV camera yet again, but as before, too far.

Houston: "Back to the right, about half as much."

Armstrong adjusts the camera, and only then does he finally get it right.

QUESTION: So if this is all so difficult when Houston can 'guide' them, how on Earth—or rather on the Moon—did Armstrong ever manage to compose all those *still* photographs so well? How did he manage *that*?

Spot the difference

Picture (53) is a NASA photo of a space-suited individual photographed from chest height in a studio and lit primarily from the right of the image. In this picture the rectangular fill light *is clearly visible,* being *reflected in the visor.* Lighting from the fill side

spotlight side

Fill side

53. Astronaut in a photographic studio.   NASA

spotlight side

Fill side

54. Astronaut 'on the Moon'—snap!   NASA

is the only way to bring detail into the left of the image. Thus does NASA (probably inadvertently) conclusively illustrate the very same fill-in technique that was used in the Apollo lunar surface photographs.

However, if the ruse is to work, any unwanted reflected image of the lighting unit has to be 'lost', 'painted over' or 'replaced' with a false reflection so as not to give the game away. Compare (53) with (54), a filled-in 'astronaut' allegedly on the Moon, and equipped with an 'appropriate' reflection in his visor. Then remember David Groves' conclusion that: "the reflection in the visor is not that of the actual photographer of the image".

Photo rule No 5. *In perspective views, images produce lines of convergence (the leaning back effect, as with photographs of tall buildings taken from ground level).*

Standing on the lunar surface and photographing from chest height, it is only possible to 'look up' at the LM as it is virtually 23 feet high. We should therefore see a form of convergence. This image of the LM (55) was certainly not taken from chest height. It was taken either from a high camera position about 12ft/3.7m or by an exceedingly tall astronaut—a giant among men!

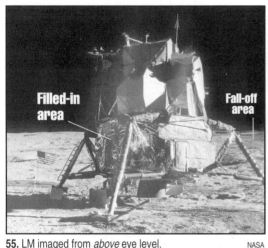

55. LM imaged from *above* eye level. NASA

Similarly, as we have established with our analysis of (48) the 'classic' picture, the astronauts have to be photographed from chest height. How then is picture (56) possible? As with the 'classic', the reflected horizon in the visor passes through at the same level as the

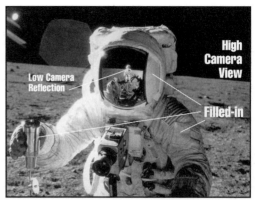

56. A high-level imagery during 'Apollo 12'. NASA

background horizon, denoting a higher-than-chest-level viewpoint. And if that were not enough, rather than a camera held higher, the low or absent camera depicted in the 'incorrect' visor reflection indicates that the reflected astronaut could not possibly have taken this photograph—yet another 'booby-trapped' image!

57. Example taken from chest height. NASA

For comparison, (57) above shows an astronaut photographed from a 'correct' astronaut camera position where is the camera is definitely at chest level. Look at the visor and notice the relationship between the horizon and the astronaut, the horizon intersects well below shoulder height.

Those who have eyes, let them see

In the NASA shots 'X' never, ever marks the spot! In (58) notice the 'C' embossed on this big rock (so that the set dresser could locate it in the right position). Note the matching 'C'

58. 'C' Rock close up.

60. The 'wrong' angles? Shady doings in the lunar Cs.

59. 'C' Rock full image.   NASA

61. The 'C'- less rock—air brushed out as published in the 1974 *Concise Encyclopaedia of Science* compiled by Robin Kerrod.

The 'C' rock is actually in the lower part of photograph (59). We can observe its relationship to the full image which also has other anomalies:

The shadow directions are all over the place (60). They do not fall in the same direction. Additionally, the lines of the Rover's track are inconsistent with a machine that has been driven but totally consistent with a vehicle that has been dragged or placed into position.

Finally, in another version that appeared in the *Concise Encyclopaedia of Science,* (61) the 'C' has been made to disappear![10]

on the ground just in front of this rock (we have enhanced it very slightly just for clarity) This 'rock', originally spotted by researcher Ralph René, gives by the appearance of papier-mâché or material stretched over a frame.

62a. Close-up, emphasising fabric arrangement.

62. The 'jump salute'. TV frame, 'Flag B'.   NASA

Photo Rule No 6. *Events taking place SIMULTANEOUSLY happen in parallel, even when viewed from different positions in close proximity.*

Therefore, if they are supposed to have been filmed and actually photographed at the same time, the recorded TV coverage and the still photographs *have to correspond* as to the final result. Rather obvious, is it not?

In the TV frame of 'Apollo 15' we 'see' the snap being taken of the 'jump salute' as we have called it. (62) The top of the flag in the TV frame is at approx. 70° from the vertical. Yet in the still photo of the same event (63) the flag is at a spanking 90° right angle. How can that be? There is no way around the fact that it has to be at the same angle in both pictures. It is not possible to reproduce this effect relying on perspective convergence (an oblique viewpoint) for a similar result. In order to explain away this anomaly one might argue that the flag in the TV image is not square on, it is simply 'pointing away'. However if that were the

case, the total surface area of visible flag would be considerably reduced. Whereas in these two pictures these areas are approximately the same, to within 10%. So in both images the flag is virtually square on. For such an equivalence, the flag either has to have been moved—or it is not even the same flag (compare 62a with 63).

It must be remembered that these two images were recorded *opposite* one another. The TV camera was on the Rover which can be seen on the far side of the flag in the still picture (63).

Was the still shot taken on another day? Or perhaps after a lunch break? For there is another problem—or clue—to be addressed within this scene. When the flag is taken out of

63. The 'jump salute', Hasselblad photograph.   NASA

64. TV frame 'Flag A'. NASA

• Reached the location.
• Selected the exact spot.
• Hammered the lower part of the flag mast into an unknown surface.
• Inserted the upper part of the mast with flag attached.
• Adjusted the folds to best effect.
• Removed himself from the scene.
• All this—in just sixty nine seconds!

Through this use of two flags, our set dressing Whistle-Blower would appear to have encoded the fact that the American flag flyers on the Apollo program were surrounded by double standards (pun intended!).

65. **66.** NASA
The 'Apollo 17' flag photographic session; and the TV frame of the moment when 67) below was allegedly taken . . .

the LM and unfurled (let us call this flag 'flag A'), the lack of folds indicate that it is different from a second flag, 'flag B'.

'Flag A' is the flag taken out of the LM (64). But in the recorded TV footage, the erected flag is 'Flag B', a different flag.

The fabric itself hangs differently in each image, and furthermore, as this flag is taken out of view by the astronaut who exits the frame to his left (64), the TV camera (on the Rover) pans round to *the right*, to reveal the flag, already fully erected!

That nifty bit of flag handling is a very tall order! Our astronaut is truly taking giant steps, for although he is wearing very cumbersome gear, he has:

• Left the LM, passing behind the TV camera.

67. The claimed resultant photograph, with the folds on the NASA
edge of the flag adjusted in a totally different manner to (65/66).

44

In an 'Apollo 17' scenario we find another situation in which the American flag has been used by Whistle-Blowers to encode clues that all is not well. On the left is the flag on its own (65). It is important to appreciate that the fold on the right hand edge of the flag is positive on the TV camera side. This fact is confirmed by the brightness of that part of the flag and the shadow to the left of it.

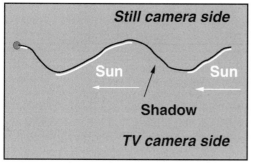

68. Guide plan view of lower folds of flag in (65/66).

The second TV image (66) is supposed to be the moment of photographing the still picture on the right. Not only is the Hasselblad clearly pointing straight ahead, *but without doubt* at such an angle it would be unable to include the Earth, which we can see framed carefully at the top of the resultant picture (67). Most impor-

tantly, the flag in this allegedly resultant still photograph is now billowing *positive* on the still camera side, where it should be *negative* (68), demonstrating that both images cannot be right—they should complement each another—and sadly, they do not.

Barely any single moment of any recorded TV coverage matches *exactly* any still image of any 'Apollo' mission! It is as if the TV coverage was treated as one shoot and the stills as a separate exercise—intentionally. Continuity is sacrosanct in studio work, so in the fact that the flag was altered at all, lies the clue. Moreover, the inflexibility of the astronaut's pressure suit and PLSS would have prevented him from assuming the *low viewpoint* required to produce the final picture (67). So how *did* the photographer guarantee that Earth was actually in the top of the frame without a viewfinder to compose it properly? (67). Clearly another creative set-up designed to alert us to the 'reality' of the situation.

Say "cheese!"

Photographs do not just happen. Much has to be set up. It requires a period of time to prepare product pack-shots, group shots, even traditional wedding pictures. NASA wanted and needed high quality posters, postcards, and

69. Well-composed shot requiring considerable direction before the shutter can 'click'. NASA

essential publicity material including well-illustrated magazine articles as part of an on-going process to assure further funding.

After a lifetime in the business it is our professional opinion that the time it would take an advertising agency to get the scene in (69) right would be a 'long day'—at least. The ingredients of astronaut, flag, LM, (together with an illuminated 'United States' on the *shadow* side of LM) the umbrella antenna, and the good dog Rover are all far too perfectly arranged for a mere snapshot. This is a category of photograph that *just does not compose itself.* It is not simply a case of having a 'photographer's eye', the grouping itself has to be *directed.* Everything here is just overlapping, to create a very well-composed shot.

This scenario is exactly the same as the official wedding photographer's nightmare, yet it was allegedly done in seconds flat! "Turn around, click that's it. Next? Walkies, Rover!"

At this point you might say: "Surely NASA was allowed a few publicity pictures?" Then we would ask you to tell us the difference between the publicity shots and the real McCoy. The substitution of even one publicity picture in the place of a real Moon image—without such a picture being clearly labelled as a promotional image—implies not only the purposeful

use of an artificial moon set, and the installation of light sources and authentic equipment for reasons other than astronaut training (which we know occurred in just those circumstances). It implies at the very least the wish to dissimulate certain facts and at the very most, wilful intent to deceive.

You might say: "Perhaps they *retouched* the pictures to bring up the detail of the astronauts?" Any retouching of images cannot apply to 'Apollo 11' pictures. We have examined a duplicate or copy of the roll of film from *magazine #40* that purports to come from Armstrong's camera—it is a roll with well over 100 colour images. Retouched or publicity images cannot get onto a *continuous* roll of film. So none of these images can have been retouched unless they have been collectively photographed under entirely different technical conditions than we have been led to believe. Or are the duplicate rolls *duplicity rolls?* Made up of carefully selected studio images which could have been retouched as required and then *re-photographed* together on a roll?

In taking such actions NASA would have deceived even their closest collaborators.

QUESTION: Why did astronauts only occasionally need to discuss the correct settings for

---

Astro-bloopers

Here, taken from the recorded transmissions, are a few typical astronauts' bloopers, indicating unfamiliarity with photographic terminology.

'Apollo 14'
Astronaut on Moon: "OK Houston, I've got a 40 foot zoom now—how does that look?"
Houston: At first no reply—then "Looks good."
(Should have been ..."I've got a FOCAL LENGTH of 40 on the zoom...")

'Apollo 15'
Astronaut on Moon: "How's a 250th and an 8th look to you?"
Houston: "Sounds good."
(Should have been....."....and f/8 look to you?" In any event, 'look' is an inappropriate term.)
And again:
Houston: "I forgot the 16mm. We want you to change out that mag, run the camera at one foot per second for 10 seconds and then go back to normal."
(The term is 'change the mag'. And Houston should have said "One FRAME per second". One FOOT per second is absolutely incorrect and totally meaningless.)

'Apollo 16'
Charlie: "I'm putting magazine Bravo...OK mag Bravo...is going onto the Commander's camera.
I've just tried to blow off the dust Tony." *(Very funny, how do you blow off dust through a visor? Or at all?)*

their camera equipment with Houston? How did they manage when they did *not* consult, and how is Houston in a better position to advise than those out there 'on location'? Unless cosmetic chit-chat incidents are just to fill up the hours of programming that they had to generate? In our view, the dialogue in these recordings is often an affront to the viewer's intelligence. It is so blatantly obvious that either the cast is Whistle-Blowing or they are thumbing their noses at the uninitiated—us.

70. Mock-up model of Surveyor 1 in a 'moon set'.　　HUGHES

When first they practised to deceive

There is at least one serious error or anomaly in all these Apollo images and it only takes *one* to be proven a fake. We have demonstrated that there are *many* faked or mocked-up images.

This revealing photograph above (70) was really taken in a studio complete with simulated lunar surface and black background. The studio in this particular instance is illuminated with 'flat' overall (non directional) lighting to facilitate inspection and adjustments by technicians of the Hughes Aircraft Company—a corporation founded and headed up by Howard Hughes and a major contractor to the American Government, including NASA.

From the evidence in these photographs we are led to conclude that the images attributed by NASA to the Apollo missions were created in similar, albeit larger photographic studios.

The problem with faking or simulation is that you require a 'moon set', in fact several sets in several studios. The photographers would have needed to *emulate* sunlight on the interior sets, and on the larger exterior sets as well, because in order to get a *black sky* the exteriors could only been used at night. These studio sets under their *total control* would enable them to create all the lunar landing sites and the EVA locations.

These sets would then be illuminated by an enormous, incredibly bright, focused, single source of *directional* light to simulate the Sun.

Once the set has been constructed, the script written, the actors familiar with their lines and their stage directions, the tape machines could roll. As any writer or movie director will appreciate, whether amateur or professional, the scenario then begins to take on a life of its own. The actors go through each scene over and over again until perfect, as indeed the astronauts' training program demonstrated.

Thereafter, with one 'giant leap' we go to the Moon, everything in the Apollo simulation project becomes the event that takes place 'on the moon'. The astronauts write about it. The very act of recording and interpreting this event by the world's recognised historians and science writers immediately (though only seemingly) endorses and validates the hoax. Numerous documentaries are produced covering the event. All these media angels either wittingly or unwittingly become a part of the very process that they are recording—until the 'record' is so well woven into the tapestry of our lives that the facsimile becomes the reality, culminating in the near impossibility of ever 're-opening' the scenario for serious re-examination.

One might challenge this statement by asking questions such as:

• "How can you tell the difference between the 'real' thing on the Moon—since you have never been to the Moon—and an artificially created event?"

• "There is no way that you can tell, so how can you comment?"

We consider that there *is* another way to find out and that is to analyse the information that has been made available by NASA and see if it stands up to close scrutiny.

It would appear that the Whistle-Blowers have ensured that their message would be read, as and when the technology to do so became available. Nearly thirty years on, countless desktop computers have more power at their disposal than *all* the computational power available to NASA throughout the entire United States in the 1960s.

We have cracked the Whistle-Blowers' encodings, and the computer technology with which we have analysed some of these images is itself a development of the space program!

The wheel has turned full circle!

Off the cuff

What else has prevented us from suspecting that anything to do with the Apollo program might be wrong? Most people are inherently honourable and would not even consider that such a momentous event in humankind's development would be transgressed.

It is important that those who care appreciate the situation that we all find ourselves in now, thanks to the decisions and actions of a relatively small but influential group of individuals.

It comes as a distressing shock to realise that the core values of truth, consideration and integrity have been so completely ignored. Does the fact that it was so easy to deceive the majority so blatantly mean that we are more naive than we imagine ourselves to be?

Not necessarily. It was and is the *emotion* of the event that forms the glue that keeps it all together—yet another element that enabled NASA & Co. to pull this off. Powerful emotions can prevent us from ever doubting an event's validity.

We have in our possession a copy of a letter written in June 1996 by the 'Apollo 8' astronaut Jim Lovell to Bill Kaysing, who used to work for Rocketdyne (contractors to NASA). Mr Kaysing was head of technical publications in the Propulsion Field Laboratory in the Simi Hills, California from 1956 until 1963. He has been blowing a loud whistle for many years (we hear from him again in later chapters) and has written a book concerning the Apollo simulation program, a copy of which he sent to Jim Lovell. In his response Mr Lovell first advises Mr Kaysing that:

> I have read your manuscript *We Never Went To The Moon* and if there is any fabrication concerning the Apollo program it is in your book!

In the next paragraph he then declares:

> I personally made two trips to the Moon—Apollo 8 in December 1969 and Apollo 13 in April 1970 . . .

Now that is rather clever, because 'Apollo 8' actually went moonwards in December *1968* (not 1969). He certainly should remember the occasion, because the day before they left Earth (December 20), while in pre-flight routine, Jim Lovell met the man who had so inspired him as a teenager—the enigmatic aviator Charles Lindbergh.

To forget one life-changing event and its date may be regarded as a misfortune, to forget two such occasions, looks like carelessness, as Oscar Wilde nearly wrote! Unless, of course, Jim Lovell does not read his letters before signing them.[11]

The American public, though maybe not speaking directly to Lovell, have also expressed doubts on the authenticity of the lunar missions. In July 1969 European newspapers questioned the validity of Apollo, but this

---

Moon marks

In a 1994 TV interview, Aldrin related that each time he placed his foot on the surface of the Moon the dust flew upwards and outwards *in perfect arcs*, all equidistant from his feet, unhindered by any atmosphere. *Yet we have no clear signs of this movement of dust on any photograph, nor in the recorded TV material when the astronauts are moving about.*

Maybe *the set* was called 'the moon'. . .

query was not taken up by the American national press. In 1970 a newspaper group polled 1,721 US residents in six different cities and discovered that 30% were not inclined to believe that Apollo really happened on the Moon. Today certain top NASA officials admit that worldwide 'many millions' do not subscribe to the Apollo lunar landings and *recent* polls show that now, less than 50% of the American population believe that their government, via NASA, sent astronauts to walk on the Moon.[12] These results are based on individuals' feelings about Apollo. At last in this book we are able to demonstrate to anyone concerned that these feelings are well founded.

The Whistle-Blowing photographic studio crew within NASA *need not* have taken any pictures at eye level! Nor used lights to create such obvious results but they *chose* to do so!

They *need not* have recommended the removal of the viewfinder from the Hasselblad camera, there was already glass in the lens and in the reticle so what difference would a little more glass make? Alternatively, they could have recommended a wire frame finder. No finder *at all* is the real give-away, it was a 'set up' which the chiefs at NASA obviously did not recognise.

In summary, the still images do not correspond to:

- Any given TV/ film location on the Moon;
- The way sunlight really behaves;
- The appropriate shadow lengths (on flat terrain) for any given mission,
- Images taken without studio lighting and without a viewfinder in the camera.

The fact that the pr-recorded TV coverage was videotaped in the *same* lunar settings and sets indicates that the 'live' TV transmissions were also targeted by the Whistle-Blowers. There are certainly grave continuity errors between the two mediums, as we have demonstrated.

With the accumulated evidence we have presented thus far we sadly have to conclude that:

- Either mankind did go to the Moon—but what we have been shown was not the true record of that visit.
- Or Apollo did not go to the Moon at all.

An Oscar for Neil?

HJP ("Douglas") Arnold has expressed the regret that there was only one distant shot of Neil Armstrong near the LM. By 1997 Neil Armstrong apparently was not so sure that this *was* a photograph of himself. Is this another case of the Wildian 'Earnests', or is it a faint puff at a tiny whistle? How could Armstrong forget, what about the list of assignments, the mission timeline? *Or was he not there?* And if he was not there, then was there an actornaut or A N Other astronaut in that pressurised suit?

If the alleged man on the spot did not know what was going on, then why should NASA be surprised that *we* are not at all convinced by their official Apollo photography?

Chapter Two

Northern Exposures

We continue our investigation into the disturbing situation concerning the Apollo photographic and TV images. We visit Sweden and consult the senior Hasselblad engineer who was responsible for building the special Lunar Surface Camera for NASA. Constellations and consternations begin to emerge.

Starlight suppressed . . .

The surface of the Moon would be an ideal location for astronomical observation of deep space. With none of the light pollution we have created for ourselves on Earth, and no atmospheric conditions to inhibit imaging, optical telescopes could function far better, as has been dramatically the case with the Hubble Space Telescope. Radio telescopes would also deliver far superior results without any interference from Earth-based noise if they were installed on the far side of the lunar mass.

From our earthbound point of view it is difficult to imagine the significant differences in environment between these two celestial bodies. It is possible to walk on the lunar surface beneath thousands and thousands of stars, and to be *simultaneously* lit by sunlight. A few degrees away from the Sun's direct glare the stars and planets would be brightly visible. Observed directly, without the barrier of a diffusing atmosphere such as the Earth's, the stars shine down, *unblinking* and perfect.

The correct definition of daylight is: sun-illuminated atmosphere. Our atmosphere creates a 'threshold' around the planet. It acts like a distorting lens and creates the effect of a prism. This effect can for instance bend the starlight so that it is perceived as having the colours of the light spectrum within it. This atmospheric aberration also creates the effect of rotating and twinkling stars. On the Moon there is no such sun-illumined atmosphere and thus the 'sky' is eternally dark with both Sun and stars simultaneously visible.

Some photographic experts say that on the lunar surface it is necessary to expose for *either* the stars *or* the sunlit terrain and thus they explain the absence of stars in the lunar photographs.

We asked Douglas Arnold about this starlight problem. "Of course you can't see stars in the bulk of these pictures, for an obvious reason (which photographers will understand). If you are exposing for an astronaut or an object in the foreground or taking a shot of the LM from the CSM, you will be using a fast exposure. As an astro-photographer I know that an exposure on stars will take many seconds, if not minutes. So the stars are not there because they are under exposed."

50

QUESTION: How could the astronauts see the reflected light from the Earth (on average 238,900 miles distant—centre-to-centre) but allegedly not be able to see any of the stars?

Photographically Douglas' explanation or claim may be only partially correct. David Groves informed us that the stars *would* nevertheless show in the images, because they are *extremely bright* pin-sources of light, undimmed by any atmosphere. Lack of stars in the photographs will not suffice as an explanation for being unable to *see* the stars from the lunar surface. Surely another Whistle-Blowing exercise instigated by advisors who knew that NASA did not have the answers, but allowed the agency to pursue the scenario of "no visible stars" in deep space in order that eventually someone might understand this rather complex matter and realise this explanation is false.

Through a glass darkly . . .

To our knowledge, NASA has never satisfactorily responded to any question posed as to why the stars are absent from their space pictures—certainly they have never admitted the possibility of technical deficiencies with their imaging. It would be perfectly acceptable to experience technical limitations, especially when functioning in an *unknown* environment with relatively untried technology.

- The lunar probes orbiting the Moon in the 1960s sent back *star data* to NASA in order that the *exact* locations of their lunar imaging could be determined by NASA analysts.
- In 1994 the Clementine lunar probe had two additional cameras which were actually called *Star-Trackers,* precisely because they used the stars to determine the craft's position.

QUESTION: How can there be any reliance upon star-tracking cameras for orientation purposes, when NASA spends all its time telling us—and certainly showing us—that no stars are visible around the Moon?

We suggest that there are other reasons why NASA was obliged to invent and then maintain its star-fiction scenario. If there were numerous technical difficulties stemming from other problems, among which is radiation (including galactic cosmic rays—GCRs—and solar radiation/particle events—SPEs) it is easy to see why NASA chose to remain silent over this issue of stars. It is also our contention that there were problems with the real Moon surface images—if indeed there were any—totally unrelated to NASA's technological challenges, which those concerned had (and still have) little chance of successfully overcoming, given

---

Kodak Kare

An Eastman Kodak brochure from the 1950s

Protection from X-rays

In hospitals, industrial plants, and laboratories, all films, regardless of the type of packing, must be protected from X-rays, radium, and other radioactive materials. For example, films stored 25 feet away from 100 milligrams of radium require the protection of 3 ½ inches of lead around the radium.

An Eastman Kodak brochure from the 1990s

Protect Film From X-rays

X-rays can fog unprocessed film when the level of radiation is high or when the film receives several low-level doses, because the effects of X-ray exposures are cumulative.

---

the accepted, current understanding of physics.

NASA could have thrown open such problems to the scientific community, but no doubt that would have meant delaying the space program, perhaps by many years. Such a course of action would have been unacceptable. NASA, not entirely for political reasons, was determined to 'get there' fast at whatever the cost and no delays were to be tolerated. We shall be exploring the ramifications of our remarks further on. We suggest that President John Kennedy's message to the American people was the public face of this most secret and urgent matter.

For the public, NASA would need means by which they could present a totally convincing, 'photographic record' of these Moon landings, to which they were totally committed—failure was simply not an option. With little idea of what awaited them in terms of human explora-

tion on the Moon, we suggest that (if only for contingency purposes) the agency decided to create or fake the Apollo photographs and prepare the pre-recorded TV coverage, as we have discussed in the previous chapter.

The stars as seen from Earth would not be usable at all, because they would be incorrect from the viewpoint of an astronaut on or near the Moon. There are plenty of expert astronomers who would have been ready to calculate the correct starfield for any given mission and instantly notice if there were any inaccurate configurations. These starfields would have been impossible to reproduce in studio sets. Although according to some sources they may have tried, and could not get the effect to work, so they left the stars out altogether!

As, for purely technical reasons, NASA had no *need* to hide the fact that they could not photograph the stars, the agency's biggest mis-

The public face

"America should commit itself to achieving the goal, before the decade is out, of landing a man on the Moon and returning him safely to Earth."

President John F Kennedy 1961

take was to have the astronauts declare, many times, that the stars were invisible. This strategy compounded the mistake, because the individual stories were not always the same. Some astronauts forgot their lines and this 'non-existent starfield' myth still pertains today. Some Shuttle astronauts are having to repeat the same inconsistent stories, for to acknowledge the presence of stars in space would be to jeopardise the very fabric of the Apollo mythos.

Moonshine

Back in the former USSR this same problem was treated with an extra creative zing. In 1973, thanks to data from their probes and especially Lunikhod 2 (the Luna 2's rover) the Soviets ascertained that the Moon would be excellent for observational use—during the lunar night. Telescopic observations during the lunar day would be hampered by a swarm of dust particles that allegedly surround the lunar surface, "a kind of atmosphere" as they put it. "To have observational use for only fourteen days every month," the Soviets said, "was not considered worthwhile." To our knowledge these alleged dust particles had not been publicly mentioned either previously or since!

QUESTION: If there is no atmosphere, and the Moon has little or no magnetic field, how are such particles being generated and maintained?

QUESTION: Are they due to some electrostatic

field, or is all this just moonshine?[1]

Star quality

Here are a number of extracts from various publications, the first four from the *National Geographic* magazine, which further illustrate these contradictions concerning the visibility or otherwise of stars in space.

- Among the many impressive features [of the Apollo training equipment] is an out-the-window display which gives the crew a panoramic, make-believe journey through half a million miles of space. Nine tons of optical equipment produce this celestial extravaganza *so accurately* that astronauts can practice their critical star navigation and simulate their Moon landings (emphasis added).[2]

QUESTION: Why bother? Since allegedly astronauts cannot see the stars when in space or on the Moon!

- Regarding the Gemini missions: In a space not much larger than a phone booth, the two astronauts would share their space with equipment that included a complex optical and colour TV system which reproduced the view of the Earth.

- From 100 miles up, you can see pin-point stars in a black sky and a sunlit blue-green Earth, stretching almost 900 miles to the horizon.[3]

- Commander David Scott 1971: "I steal a

Shooting themselves in the Moon boots

Who took these pictures? These photographs are generally credited as Buzz taking his own Boots. Other sources including *National Geographic* magazine December 1969 credit Neil Armstrong.

moment and glance straight up into the *black sky*. Earth gleams in the abyss of space . . ." [4]

- ". . . in attempting to line yourself up with a large satellite, starkly illuminated by direct sunlight against the *velvet black background* of deep space . . ." Joe Allen, physicist and Shuttle astronaut 1996.[5]

QUESTION: If Joe Allen calls the area below the Van Allen belts 'deep space' what did the astronauts call the area of space around the Moon tens of thousands of miles further out?

QUESTION: The implication of these statements is that the sunlight is so bright that it drowns out the starlight. If this is the case, then how can the following also be possible?

- "I will always remember Endeavour [CSM] hurtling through that strange night of space. Before us and above us stars spangled the sky with their distant icy fire." ('Apollo 15')
- In a 1996 UK TV documentary, a female Shuttle astronaut said how much she enjoyed looking at the stars out in space.
- The *Star Trek* film crew at Paramount have an ex-NASA astrophysicist working with them as a consultant—and all the space backgrounds to *Star Trek* episodes are full of pin-point stars.

However,

- During the 'Apollo 16' scenario, astronaut Ken Mattingley made a point of saying that he had to lift up his gold visor during his supposed EVA (extra vehicular activity) *in order to see the stars*.

QUESTION: Is this requirement of raising his space helmet visor disinformation or Whistle-Blowing?

QUESTION: Are they planting the notion that these visors *screened-out* the starlight?

QUESTION: If Ken Mattingley could not see the stars through his gold visor, then how could the lunar surface walkers describe the subtle colours of the rocks they were apparently collecting?

We could conclude that if NASA wishes to imply that gold visors screened-out the stars, then possibly the imaging equipment also had specially produced gold-coated lenses or filters! Apparently the cameras had neither, but we did go to meet with Hasselblad, the NASA contractor that supplied the cameras for the named Apollo Moon walkers, just to make sure.

The Hasselblad account

Hasselblad, a Swedish company with formidable experience and a proud history of photographic 'firsts', have been at the forefront of photographic development from the Second World War through to the Space Age. With the manufacture of an aerial camera for the Swedish Air force in 1941, Hasselblad has always worked closely with its own Swedish

1. HK7—hand-held aerial camera for the Swedish Air Force, 1941-45. HASSELBLAD

National Defence Industry, and was therefore uniquely equipped to work on secret developmental projects with the American Government's civilian agency, NASA. Hasselblad launched its first civilian camera on the market

---

The learning curve

The Second World War came. The Swedish Air Force needed cameras.
But Sweden was cut off from the world and the need for cameras was urgent. Victor Hasselblad was asked if he could produce them. He had no workshop but there was a great hurry and he said, "Yes".
That work gave valuable lessons on how to construct fast shutters which functioned even in cold temperatures, the value of motor operation systems with interchangeable cassettes and also with roll film, and the value of fast interchangeable optics with high resolution.

Extract from the *History of Hasselblad*

in 1948 and went on to such commercial success that its annual accounts have not been in the red since the late 1950s.

Prior to our visit we received the press handouts from Hasselblad's PR department. From these we learned that the Hasselblad Company had started life in 1820 shipping a wide variety of miscellaneous items into Sweden including the first importation of thermos bottles. Manifest curiosity combined with good business acumen were the hallmarks of a company at the leading edge of commercial exploitation and development of the latest innovations. Yet nearly 150 years later, this same company does not even mention a world-wide 'first': the production of a camera that was specially selected

---

1996-01-23

The story of Hasselblad

1841 The trading company FW Hasselblad is established.

1885 FW Hasselblad is one of Sweden's most prosperous trading companies. Starting import of photographic products i.e. cameras and film.

1888 Importer of Eastman Kodak Co. products.

1906 Fritz Victor Hasselblad is born.

1908 Hasselblad's Fotografiska AB is formed and becomes the exclusive distributor on the Eastman Kodak AB. Laboratories and a nationwide net of retail dealers.

1937 Victor Hasselblad opens his own photo shop "Victor Foto" as well as a photo lab.

1940 A German military aeroplane was shot down over Swedish territory, a camera was found inside it. The Royal Swedish Air Force sent an inquiry to Victor Hasselblad: "Can you make a camera like this?" "No, I can make a better one", was the answer.

1941 Victor Hasselblad AB is formed in order to produce aerial cameras for the Swedish Air Force.

1942 Victor Hasselblad's father dies. Victor and his wife Erna buy the majority of the shares in the family company FW Hasselblad.

1948 The first civil Hasselblad Camera was introduced at a press conference in New York. It was regarded as a sensation.

1953 Expansion and increased profitability for the camera business.

1962 The images from the NASA space mission, shot with a Hasselblad camera, arise a tremendous interest.

1968 Victor Hasselblad was awarded the degree of honorary doctor of technology at the Chalmers University of Technology.

1968 Victor Hasselblad sells the distribution company and retailer net "Hasselblad Fotografiska AB" to Kodak.

1976 The investment company Säfveån AB buys Victor Hasselblad AB.

1978 Victor Hasselblad dies. His will includes a donation of 78 MSEK to the "Erna and Victor Hasselblad Foundation". The purpose of the foundation is to support scientific education and research. A photographic prize and a medal is awarded yearly. In 1995 the Prof. Robert Häusser was awarded.

1984 VHAB is introduced at the Stockholm Stock Exchange, Säfveån keeps 57,5% of the shares.

1985 VHAB establishes the subsidiary Electronic Imaging AB for the development, production and marketing of digital imaging systems and systems for digital transmission of images.

1985 the Swedish company Incentive AB acquires 58,1% of the shares in VHAB.

1991 Incentive takes over 100% of the shares. VHAB is not any more at the Stoch Exchange.

For further information please contact Information Dpt., VICTOR HASSELBLAD AB, PO Box 220, s-401 23 Göteborg, SWEDEN. Phone +46 (0)31 10 24 00. Fax +46 (0)31 13 50 74.

HASSELBLAD

2. Reproduction of the Hasselblad 1996 press handout.

Hollow plotting

Even the relatively coarse pictures taken by the astronauts using hand-held cameras, showed how out of date or inaccurate most maps [of the Earth] are.

National Geographic magazine January 1969

---

to be taken to the Moon by the Apollo astronauts.

Surely a Public Relations department would have adored the tag line "The Camera that was used on the Moon" or "The first camera chosen to be taken to another world". Yet, the first-ever Hasselblad camera in space is summarised in one sentence, "1962—the images from the NASA Space mission arouse a tremendous interest". *And the Apollo Moon landings are not even mentioned.*

After reading these handouts, we contacted the PR department of Hasselblad who recommended that we meet with Gustav Lagergren, an executive who was in office at the time of the American Space Program. Now retired, he had been alerted by Hasselblad that our phone call was imminent. The very first thing that he said was, "I was dreading your call".

We attempted to set up a meeting but Mr Lagergren prevaricated, saying that he would be out of town, that it would be difficult to get together and so forth. He then requested a list of questions which we duly sent. After a long silence an answer was eventually forthcoming. He could not meet us after all. Without mentioning our questions he arranged that we meet Jan Lundberg, the designer and co-ordinator of the Apollo Lunar Camera Project—who at the time still worked at Hasselblad.

Our meeting took place on August 30 1996 at Hasselblad's head office in Göteborg, Sweden. Soren Gunnarsson, Hasselblad' historian explained the link between Kodak and Hasselblad. We asked Soren how long there had been an association between the Eastman-Kodak Company and Hasselblad.

"For a long time, for a very long time," he replied. "In 1888 the grandfather of Victor Hasselblad met George Eastman at a wedding party and they came to an agreement, which they sealed with a handshake, to import Kodak products into Sweden. That is how it all started."

That would probably explain why they used only Kodak film in the Hasselblads we commented.

"Yes, it would," said Soren. "In 1948 when the first Hasselblad camera was launched—Victor Hasselblad preferred New York City for the launch—at that time there was no Zeiss lens on it, it was a Kodak lens. So during the first years they supplied the camera with this Kodak lens."

We then went on to talk with Jan Lundberg, the project engineer responsible for building the Lunar camera. Jan received us in the corpo-

3. Jan Lundberg, Group Manager Space Projects 1966-'75.
AULIS

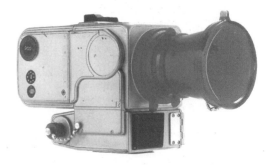

4. 500 EL/70 (the Lunar Surface Camera) electric drive with Biogon 60mm lens, plus polarising filter on the front of the lens—the camera's 'Polaroid sunglasses'. HASSELBLAD

rate presentation area, complete with its impressive glass-fronted display cases of Hasselblad products. It would be true to say that the peak of Jan's career coincided with the most historic time for space photography.

"Yes, I was responsible for building the Lunar camera," said Jan. "And during that period I almost had a season ticket for the Sweden-USA round trip! I went to Houston and Cape Kennedy very, very often. I was a designer for Hasselblad and from 1966 onwards I was mainly occupied with the design and modification of the NASA camera. We started with the electric model in 1967, and then I had a group building the cameras, seven people in the design department and two in the workshop."

"We built all of them, there were hundreds, and we had very good communications with NASA. There was a lot of paperwork which I supervised along with the design development, while others were at their drawing boards or testing models. And that continued until the end of the lunar missions."

"Then I think they ran out of money," Jan continued. "They had the Space Shuttle project and I think they spent, over the years, many millions of dollars. However, when they started to fly the Shuttle, the Hasselblad was there all the time. So from 1963, possibly up

until now, we have been on every space flight, with one or more cameras. We have established a Space Log which goes up until fairly recently, but now it is all becoming quite banal so we have stopped doing it."

So in what way, apart from the lack of a viewfinder and items like that, was the Hasselblad Lunar camera actually different from a production camera?

"Well," replied Jan, "it was stripped of everything that was considered unnecessary, which was all the 'cosmetics'. NASA wanted to avoid too much plastic and needed it to be metal wherever possible. The main thing was to make it lighter than the original model."

The modifications to the selected camera, the manual, non-electric 500C (picture 5), were carried out at their factory in Sweden. NASA made its initial adaptations in a sub-basement workshop outside the Houston Space Center.

Jan went on the explain that "originally, NASA made all the alterations themselves. Then they presented to us their prototype and asked us, 'can you do this?' We said 'Yes, we can and we can do it better'."

"So after that," Jan continued, "we would

5. 500 C 1957-70 (Earth camera) manual operation.

6. 500 EL 1965-72 (Earth camera) electric drive.

Myth Sweden
During World War Two, a German Bomber was shot down over Swedish territory. It contained an interesting camera.
Swedish Air Force experts sent for Victor Hasselblad and asked if he could make one like it.
"No" he said. "But I can make a better one."

Extract from the *History of Hasselblad*

Early history	
1962	Wally Schirra assigned the adapted 500C.
1963	Gordon Cooper assigned the 500C.
1965-1966	Gemini Missions 1 to 8 assigned the 500 C and the Hasselblad Super-Wide Camera appeared during the Gemini program assigned together with the 500 C to Gemini 9.
	The Super-Wide Camera was the only Hasselblad assigned to Gemini missions 10, 11 and 12.

7. Hasselblad Super-Wide Camera with Zeiss Biogon 38mm lens, manual operation (Space version). HASSELBLAD

present a technical specification which was approved by NASA and then all the alterations were made in our factory."

Jan continued, "while NASA was working on all this, the 500 EL was presented to the market, and so NASA changed its mind, they said that it would be an advantage to have this electric drive on the cameras, as the astronauts complained about winding the film on by hand—cranking all the time. So when planning for the lunar mission, they decided to use the electric camera."

"The 500 EL/70 Lunar Surface Camera had a modified standard 70mm back, it used a special drop-in film and they got, I think as a maximum, 200 exposures per roll. But then the magazine had to be loaded in a darkroom."

"Would they have had a plate to protect the film in the magazine from the light until it had been fitted onto the camera, and then would they have removed the plate afterwards?" we asked.

"Yes," was Jan's reply, "there were protective plates both on the camera and on the film magazine."

"How easy was it for them to remove the plate, or dark slide and put it back again?"

"That was quite easy," Jan confirmed. "On the other hand the attachment to the camera was more sophisticated than on the commercial model. They had a special lock that pulled the magazine towards the body and locked it there."

We noted that this account was slightly at variance with Douglas Arnold's opinion of the problems associated with the manipulation of the magazine while wearing the pressurised gauntlets.

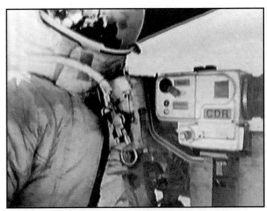

9. CDR (= Commander) on the Hasselblad Lunar camera. NASA

"Now, on the silver-bodied Lunar camera, we remember seeing some pictures depicting 'CDR' on the side. But looking at your model

1963	Hasselblad completed the prototype 500 EL.
1965	Hasselblad introduced the 500 EL to the market.
1966-1967	Space model, a redesigned and modified version of 500 EL/70.
1968	First assignment of the 500 EL/70 was to the 'Apollo 8' mission.

Arctic antics

When actor Michael Palin's crew filmed at the Earth's South pole the exterior temperature was about -22°F/-30°C.
He stated that the cameras were seizing up due to the cold.
What chance then for an uninsulated Hasselblad in the shadow of the LM at temperatures as low as -180°F?

---

of this camera in the showcase, there aren't any markings on the side at all."

"It was probably some designation that they made themselves," Jan suggested. "We delivered the camera and they painted them silver with aluminium paint. And made all kinds of strange notes on them, for the astronauts to recognise."

"How would they have actually protected the camera from the heat and cold?" we then asked.

"Well, the original ones were not protected at all," explained Jan. "The ones they brought to the lunar surface needed to deflect the Sun's heat. Because they had found that the camera's insides heated up when it was exposed to the very strong Sun. The cold was not too difficult—so the challenge was, to keep them cold."

"Exactly," we affirmed, "the outside temperature could get as high as +180°F/+82°C. So how would you keep the film inside cool?"

"Well, in space, in an absolute vacuum, the heat you get is purely from the sunlight." Jan then elaborated: "the actual environment itself is quite cold and if you can reflect most of the Sun's radiation you will get only very limited heating inside [the camera]. So what NASA did was to paint the cameras with this aluminium paint and [the astronauts] didn't keep them out too long. They rushed them in or kept them in the shadow. Because as soon as you go from the direct sunlight into the shadow, its very cold again . . . *nothing* gets heated."

"Yes, we understand that, but if you look at the live TV transmissions, they're wandering around outside with the camera fixed to their chest bracket for *hours on end*."

"Well, as far as I *know*," said Jan, "they had

no trouble with overheating of the film.

"The film can take quite a reasonable heat, because they used a polyester base and very thin coating and I think it worked for them. I didn't hear any complaints about the film getting too warm. On the other hand they might have had some trouble if the film got too cold, because then it would have cracked."

"Well that's exactly the same problem in reverse, because then it must go down to minus 180°F/118°C in the shade?" we asked.

"Yes," Jan replied, "so the instructions were, 'don't keep them [the films] in the shadow'. We didn't hear of any problem."

On our behalf, SKY TV News had asked NASA's Brian Welch much the same question, "What about the film stock, given the temperature range on the lunar surface, isn't it extraordinary that all of the photographs should come out the same, with pretty perfect quality?"

To which Brian had replied, "Well, actually the film was specially produced for NASA by Kodak. It involved the use of thin gels and special emulsions for this film. The idea was that it would have to stand up to a vacuum, extremes of heat and cold on the surface of the Moon. Some of this film was tested in the actual cameras that went to the Moon in vacuum chambers in Houston, before the astronauts would leave for the lunar expeditions—and we did our job well."

Brian Welch did not answer our question regarding the claimed performance of the stock under such extremes of temperature. Bearing in mind the information from Kodak, the actual *film emulsion* was *NOT* specially produced, so it would appear that the agency was misleading SKY TV in giving this response.

Radiation realities

"On the Moon particle radiation would fog the pictures. Radiation would enter through the camera lens."
Dr. Percy Seymour, University of Plymouth, England.

November 1995

Jan Lundberg now continued: "Cold was more of a problem in the vacuum, because you got exposed to static discharges on the film's surface when you wound the film on. And since there was no atmosphere, the charges ran across the film's surface making tracks, like some dendritic pattern on the film."

We thought that this point was certainly noteworthy—no mention of this problem from Kodak's expert Douglas Arnold. Nor had there been any clear evidence of dendritic patterning in the published Apollo photographs.

"The other thing," we continued, "that is associated with heat and cold on the Moon is cosmic radiation. How did the camera actually cope with radiation from space, and particularly X-rays, which one certainly doesn't want to get onto the film?"

"Well X-rays," replied Jan, "do not expose the common emulsion. We could see no signs of [exposure] to X-rays. So pure cosmic radiation and X-ray radiation, for that short period, obviously didn't disturb the film. Nor did it disturb the function of the camera at all."

"That's very interesting," we commented. "Because when we used to travel around the world as a film crew, going from country to country, passing our equipment through those early generation X-ray machines, we only had to go through six times or so with our film rushes (we were using Ektachrome at about the same speed as the lunar film stock) and they would get fogged pretty badly. We had to put the film into lead-lined bags, or make sure that the stock was hand searched."

"I think, that compared with the X-rays they used for your luggage," Jan responded, "the concentration in space is, I would say, hundreds of times lower than that because it's actually what's reaching you from the Sun and the concentration is very low.

"Otherwise the people would have suffered too!"

"And so far," Jan continued, "NASA hasn't recognised or reported anything of the kind. I mean you have had these cosmonauts being out for half a year, and although they are in the capsule, their shielding is not very strong—no

lead used there! But so far, I haven't heard of any damage caused like that."

So, *because the pictures were OK* there were no X-ray problems! That's a point to ponder. And similarly for the remark, "otherwise the people would have suffered too." We were aware that when he referred to "staying out half a year" Jan was not talking about the lunar mission but about the cosmonauts in the Russian Space Station MIR. But this station operates in relative safety *below* the Van Allen radiation belts (which we will discuss in the next chapter), and while not an ideal location, is certainly much safer than anything with which the alleged Apollo missions had to contend. Jan is right about one thing though: NASA have not recognised or reported any serious problems, publicly at least.

"As I said," Jan continued, "the vacuum is a challenge because any kind of lubrication [in the camera] will boil away, due to the very low pressure. So that was one of the problems we had to solve, which we did fairly easily. Partly by using as little lubrication as possible and secondly by making sure the amount we did use was designed not to leave any residues in the mechanism, nor leave any residues on the lens surfaces."

Most people do not get a chance to see a Lunar camera, but looking at the copy of a 500 EL/70 that went to the Moon, we noticed that there are only normally-etched scales for adjusting aperture and so forth. As the *f*-stop numbers on the lenses and other settings were not any easier to read than on a conventional camera, surely it would have been virtually impossible to check the settings whilst fully clad in space suit and helmet on the Moon?

Not actually commenting on this point Jan replied: "We put tabs on the setting rings, for different functions, the [shutter] speed and the aperture. Normally they used only one or two aperture settings and as far as I know, just one or two shutter speeds. They had these large tabs and they had a lot of practice so that they could feel what the setting was, because once on the lunar surface, in the pressure suit, *you couldn't see the camera. They couldn't bend*

> **TechnoSpeak**
> A polarising filter is used to photograph a subject clearly
> through a reflective surface, such as the windshield of a car (or spacecraft).

their head that far down to see the scales." (emphasis added)

"They also had no viewfinder," Jan continued. "They had to aim by moving their body. But of course they spent months and months in the Arizona desert practising this. So the habit was built into their spines!" said Jan laughing at the thought.

So what about changing lenses, filters and magazines?

"They didn't change lenses *on* the surface," Jan affirmed, "they did that inside the capsule. So once they went out they had one set for a particular [EVA] mission, then they went back in, changed whatever they needed to change—for instance film magazines or lenses and then they went back out again."

But that was not actually what we had seen in the TV recordings of the Apollo EVAs. There was at least one occasion when an astronaut made a magazine change *outside* the LM.

"The camera was bolted to a small bracket on their chest," Jan continued. "In some of the pictures taken on the Moon you can see it there."

"We noticed in your showcase a filter on the front of the lens. What kind of filter is that?" we asked.

"That's a polarising filter which the astronauts were instructed to set in three different settings: left, straight up and right. Which meant that they changed the polarising pattern through two steps, to be able to analyse the surface through changes in reflection."

Then we enquired if they ever removed this filter for normal use, or was it always fitted to the camera lens.

"It was sitting on the camera." Jan confirmed.

"So every shot they took was in fact through a polarising filter?"

"Well," responded Jan thoughtfully. "Yes, if they used that particular lens; because the filter was not on all the lenses. It was also not permanently fixed. They could change the lens and take the polarising filter off that lens and

10. Close-up of an 500 EL/70 camera on location without a polarising filter. NASA

choose to use it [either] on that or another lens. But they never made any such changes outside *because of course the gloves were made so that they couldn't grip anything smaller than about an inch.* And they had little feeling at their fingertips, due to the pressurisation. They needed to do as little fine mechanics as possible on the outside." (emphasis added)

We were interested to hear more about the challenges of working with these pressurised gauntlets. Firstly, we knew that during lunar EVAs the LM was not pressurised, so the astronauts could not have removed their gloves without first re-pressurising the cabin.

Secondly (to our knowledge) once outside, none of the astronauts were scheduled to return to the LM's interior during an EVA.

Thirdly, the polarising filter uses up light and in its maximum position would mean the loss of one to two stops of light, perhaps even more.

And fourthly, many of the photographs do not show this supposedly permanent polarising filter on the Zeiss Biogon 60mm lens as for example in pictures (10 and 11).

This alleged fitting of a polariser is a real Whistle-Blowing situation, as use of such a filter is thwart with difficulties! Due to a polariser 'using up' several stops of light, it requires compensation when arriving at the correct exposure. This difficult and fiddly manoeuvre of fitting and removal was supposed to have been done on location, calculating the correct exposure with nothing but a simple exposure guide. There are even sound and TV recordings of Houston requesting astronauts to *fit* a polarising filter during an EVA—whilst working on the lunar surface.

Moving on to another subject, we then asked Jan: "Did they have any other accessories such as flash on their cameras?"

"No. Only lenses and magazines," Jan responded. "The only accessory they had was a small—what we call a 'ring sight'—with a circular finder. This finder gave very good directional information. But that was not used on the lunar surface, that was used on the camera they hand-held for photography through the LM capsule window."

"And how do you think they managed with exposure?" we asked. "Because the first time they went with Apollo 11, they wouldn't have known what the brightness values really were on the surface?"

"Oh yes they did!" Jan interrupted. "Because the scientists had analysed the reflective properties of the lunar surface very carefully. And they had a very narrow register of exposures. I would say, about four different settings. What setting they would use was dependant upon which way they directed the camera, with reference to the Sun. And it was successful. I mean, the films that they used would normally have a latitude of 2, 2½, maybe 3 stops and that was quite enough, almost anything was possible."

"Oh!," we replied, rather astonished, "the latitude was 2 to 3 stops?"

"Yes," asserted Jan.

Such an exposure latitude would mean that it would most certainly have been possible to *register* the bright starlight, even while exposing for a lunar-based subject. Which would eliminate the technical reason for not seeing

11. Astronaut Schirra with his 500 EL/70 & 60mm lens without a polarising filter. NASA

even the vaguest *hint* of stars in the lunar photographs.

"That's very interesting," we commented. "Because normally when you're using Kodak's Ektachrome film for transparencies, you need to get the exposure accurate to about half a stop."

"Well, what they did was to take small parcels [clips] of film for analysing," responded Jan. "They developed everything themselves and they tried to find methods to modify the development to give them a [greater] latitude. Also if the astronauts were in doubt about which setting they should use, they changed the setting between pictures but generally, the light on the lunar surface *is very even* and easy to determine. It mainly depends in which direction you take the photograph, with reference to the Sun."

This notion of taking a 'clip test' is a rather intriguing one as it is only possible to do one test per roll, unless you wish to risk cutting a unique photograph in half! But as each roll has 100 exposures or more, and as it was required of them to take a constantly changing variety of subjects under a variety of lighting conditions, surely it would be *virtually impossible* to get all these combinations correctly covered with the correct exposures.

We continued: "There was something else that Douglas Arnold pointed out to us. He said that when Armstrong was taking the pictures of Aldrin coming down the LM ladder,

12. Aldrin emerges without flash or other lighting. NASA

continuing through his helmet, and on this picture, are two people, the one that is photographed and the photographer reflected in the visor? Considering that the photographer had to aim by moving his body, I think that is remarkable."

Yes, it was indeed remarkable, we thought. In fact, Douglas Arnold had said that he thought the astronauts varied in their ability. We explained to Jan that we had been studying a particular sequence of Aldrin descending the ladder. We showed Jan one of the first of the series of still pictures—Aldrin exiting through the hatch (12).

"This is one of the reasons why we asked you if there was a flash or any other lighting, because to our eyes as photographers, it looks as though the scene has been lit. There is light inside the hatch and it's also catching the bottom of his Life Support Pack."

"Yes. That is quite normal," replied Jan.

"Quite normal?"

"Yes," Jan continued. "Because the one big reflector that you have is the lunar surface. Actually light is coming from below [when it's not directly in the Sun] and I've looked at the shadows and it seems to me that they are working very close to the terminator, which means that the Sun is very low over the horizon. The idea was to keep the radiation as low as possible so they always worked as close to the terminator as they could."

In fact it is the height of the Sun over the Moon's horizon that dictates the Sun angle and this is the result of the lunar cycle and *not* the terminator.

"We understand that," we commented. "But do not see how the light—*if it is* bouncing off

Armstrong being a good photographer, had remembered to open up the lens aperture as Aldrin was descending in the dark shadow." (see 12 above)

"Well, yes, it might be so," Jan replied. "We think that they were fairly good cameramen, all of them. They did train a lot. They spent days and days photographing out in the desert. So they had very much built-in responses. Many of them were very good, they were not only able to handle the camera technically but also were good at choosing nice motifs. You remember the famous picture of an astronaut standing against the horizon which is almost

Sun angles on the lunar surface at touchdown				
Mission	Landing date	Location	Sun Angle	Time on lunar surface
'Apollo 11'	July 20 '69	Sea of Tranquility	+10°	21 hrs 36 mins
'Apollo 12'	Nov 19 '69	Ocean of Storms	+15°	31 hrs 31 mins
'Apollo 13'	April 11-17 '70 aborted, after 'accident' occurred on April 13 1970			
'Apollo 14'	Feb 05 '71	Frau Mauro	+20°	33 hrs 30 mins
'Apollo 15'	July 30 '71	Hadley Appenine	+10°	66 hrs 54 mins
'Apollo 16'	Apr 20 '72	Descartes	+10°	71 hrs 02 mins
'Apollo 17'	Dec 11 '72	Taurus Littrow	+05°	74 hrs 59 mins

These morning sunrise angles are calculated for the day of arrival on the lunar surface (not the day of departure from Earth). We have used 'earth day' references because the astronauts were keeping their watches on Houston time.

13. 'Apollo 12'—artificially illuminated in a similar manner to 'Apollo 11'.   NASA

"Well, as I said, they possibly used specially designed film. I don't know which film they used on this sequence but I know that they had Kodak make special colour film for them in the beginning. Later on they used more normal Ektachrome but in the beginning they had both black and white and colour film made especially for them." (Same apparently incorrect story here as from Brian Welch of NASA.)

"Well, let's say, for the sake of argument," we said, sticking with the point, "that it was regular film stock. Relating it to the way people use film on Earth—and using Ektachrome EF, which is what Kodak say the astronauts were using . . ."

"Yes," interrupted Jan, "but they also had some special formulas made up for themselves I think they considered it too expensive later on and not necessary, so they abandoned that policy." Jan was laughing again as he added:

"These special [processing] formulas never got into commercial production." (emphasis added)

To abandon the continued use of specially produced film stock "because of the expense", on critical Moon missions already costing an absolute fortune and then fail to commercially exploit

14. 'Apollo 15' mostly in shadow except for astronaut.   NASA

the surface—actually gets inside the porch and can create highlights or hot-spots. And then how the exposure in the shade is actually *matching* the bright sunlight in the distance on the lunar surface. Because we shouldn't forget that he was coming down in *total shadow* and if you open up the stop to expose for him, under normal circumstances you'd expect the lunar surface to be very burned out (over exposed), wouldn't you?"

15. Black rock. Rock *not filled-in* with any reflected light.   NASA

16. Illuminated gold foil and equipment standing in full shadow on the claimed *unlit side of the LM.* NASA

this already perfected special film stock—made no sense at all to us.

"But even that wouldn't explain that it looks as though he's specially lit, when in fact he is in full shadow," we persisted.

"Still I know that they had no extra lighting no flash or equipment like that. It has to be the reflection from the surface. I mean the LM looked like a real 'contraption' They didn't have to take any aerodynamics into consideration when they built it—they built it the way it was necessary and that's why it looks like a flying iron bed, or something like that!"

"Just coming back for a moment to the possibility of the lunar surface lightening the shadows," we insisted. "Looking at wide lunarscapes the shaded part is totally black (15), which is what you would expect in a vacuum. But then why do we have shadows at all [as Jan maintained earlier] if the lunar surface is lightening those very deep shadows?"

"Well of course, the lunar *surface cannot lighten the shadows* on the lunar surface because the angles don't match and also the radiated light from the Sun is much stronger than the reflection from the surface."

(Jan appears now to have recanted somewhat on his previous remark.)

"The Sun is clearly behind the LM in this picture," To make our point we showed Jan pictures of the LM (13) and a photograph of the rocks that we looked at in "Photo Call" (15). "You'd expect the part nearest the camera, in total black shadow, to exhibit no detail of the LM's shadow side at all. After all, if it were to behave in the same way as the lunar rocks, which are *always* black in the shadow side, it should to be totally black shouldn't it?"

We then showed Jan another picture we saw in Chapter One (16), the illuminated piece of equipment placed on the surface in the shadow side of the LM. "...But instead, that piece of equipment is conspicuously visible."

"Well," responded Jan, "I think because it is standing in the shadow, indirectly illuminated by the Sun [and] it has a reflective surface. Maybe as it is rounded it reflects the light from the lunar surface. Yes, that's the explanation, that's *my* reaction to this picture. It *has* to be that way."

"There is no other explanation?" we questioned.

"No. They had *no* extra light sources with them. Still, the lunar surface has a very high albedo."

"What would you say that was?" we asked.

TechnoSpeak
Albedo is the ability of a celestial body to reflect light.
It is the ratio of the total amount of light (reflected in all directions) to the amount of incident light (the light hitting it).
Earth's albedo is 37%. The Moon's average albedo is 7% of sunlight reflected,
which is about the reflectivity of asphalt—not a lot!
(Black totally absorbs the light spectrum, while white reflects virtually all of it.)
The lunar albedo is calculated as an average because the lunar albedo is *darker* on the maria
(subject of the photograph being discussed here) and lighter in the highlands.
Bearing in mind that 1.0 indicates a perfectly reflecting surface and 0.0 indicates a totally black surface
that absorbs all incident light, 0.07 (i.e. 7%) is actually very different from most people's estimates.

"Albedo. That is the reflectivity."

"OK in general terms," we asked Jan, "would you say the Moon reflected 50% of the sunlight striking its surface?"

"It's even more, I think," Jan responded. "It's between 60% and 70% of the cooler radiation. The heat radiation is lower, but considering that the surface is mainly made up of fine dust it absorbs a lot of the long-wave radiation and reflects the visual light a lot."

"So in the visual spectrum, it's reflecting more than half of light?"

"Yes, I believe it does, yes," confirmed Jan.

Interestingly, most people are generally under the impression that the Moon's reflectivity is as high as 60% to 70%, when it is actually nearer to *10%* of 70%, namely an average of only 7% or so—the reflectivity of asphalt.

"Just one final question, here's another photograph, probably Armstrong's most famous picture. Now, what it seems to show is differential lighting around him. There's a bright hot-spot of light, then the horizon 'falls off' in brightness. In other words, there's a difference in brightness in the area around the subject, compared with the background. It falls off very, very considerably—more than two stops."

"Yes," agreed Jan. "Considering the direction of the Sun and the curvature of the surface, what you see is more and more of the shadow part of whatever item is there, the rocks, or whatever. So that's the reason the illumination falls off."

"But in the foreground to the left of this picture," we pointed out, "it's darker, and in the central area there is also what looks like a pool of light."

"Yes, it seems like he is standing in a spotlight," said Jan, "and I can't explain that. Umm, that escapes me why. So maybe you have to find Armstrong and ask him! Maybe he is standing on a slope or something—would that be possible?"

We knew that could not be so, as the 'Apollo 11' LM, Eagle, was recorded as landing on a relatively flat plain of the Sea of Tranquility. Also when Brian Welsh was asked about some of the factors involved in this 'classic' photo of

17. The 'classic' photograph of Aldrin, once again.   NASA

"Yes, it seems like he is standing in a spotlight," said Jan, "and I can't explain that. Umm, that escapes me why. So maybe you have to find Armstrong and ask him!

Aldrin his response was not nearly so measured as his previous replies. In fact for a representative of NASA, his vocabulary defies belief:

SKY TV NEWS "What about the finding (the fact that the camera is positioned too high for it to have been taken by a standing astronaut) considering the horizon level in the visor of the Aldrin 'classic' picture?"

Brian Welch: "I think that is pseudoscientific nitpicky claptrap! I don't know why we should spend even a moment trying to judge that."

It is possible however, to judge NASA by that outpouring and come to the conclusion that something is probably very wrong indeed.

Furthermore, we should remember that David Groves has shown conclusively that the plain near the LM undulated very little indeed, no more than about 10cm (see previous chapter).

We then changed the subject with Jan Lundberg.

"When we first contacted Hasselblad they sent us the story of the company from 1841 to

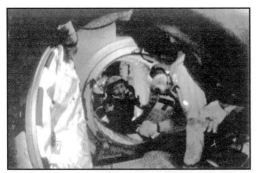

18. Handshake in orbit during Apollo-Soyuz.   NASA

1991 and we were rather surprised that it doesn't mention the Lunar camera at all!"

"That's because it is the *company* history, not the product history," replied Jan. "There are no products featured on that list, just the company's story."

"But surely one of the highlights of the company's story must be having a camera that was used on another world?" we queried.

"Well, sure. I don't know who made this up. Can you remember who gave it to you?"

"It came with all the background material," we replied. "Unless we are mistaken, this was a pivotal moment for the Hasselblad Company? Yet this document mentions neither Apollo nor the Moon . . ."

"It doesn't mention anything at all as far as I can see," Jan interrupted. "There is that single line about the 'images from the NASA space mission shot with a Hasselblad camera arise (sic) a tremendous interest'."

"And that's 1962," we commented.

"I wouldn't call this history complete at all. So we shall try and give you another one."

"Thank you,, it was rather disappointing."

"Yes, for me too—because I have been working with all those products. We were also on the Apollo-Soyuz project (in 1975). We built a special camera, with a viewfinder," Jan explained, "and this viewfinder had to be reversible so that they could shoot over their shoulders. I don't know why."

We remembered Douglas Arnold's view of the 1975 Apollo-Soyuz link up, which he saw as an exercise in politics: "There was still a Cold War around at that time and the picture of two adversaries' first handshake (Stafford and Leonov) was an historic picture. It was taken with one of the Apollo DAC cameras (picture 18). It's a small frame [16mm], blown up, as grainy as hell, and while a reasonable record it certainly isn't of the quality that one would expect now.

"However, the Apollo-Soyuz Test Project was very much a political breakthrough. Even a political gimmick according to many people. It was a bridge-building exercise, I think. You had the usual sorts of photos being taken by the two crews, demonstrating bonhomie in space between the Americans and the Russians. I remember that the removal of the last door between the two vehicles was due to take place just over the South of England but I checked the flight record and thanks to a few problems in actually opening this door, by the time it happened they were flying over central Europe!"

19. Examples of objects in front of camera reticles.   NASA

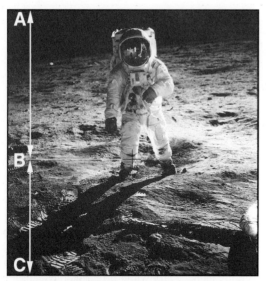

20. Full area of the 'classic' (image # AS11-40-5903).   NASA
The vertical line A-B-C demonstrates the off-centre position
of the large reticle that *should* be in the centre of the image.

Crossed wires?

Back at Hasselblad we went on to investigate another problem, the case of the disappearing cross hairs. All Apollo pictures have these reticles or cross hairs (19). A reticle is set in the focal plane of the camera, virtually in contact with the film and is recorded on the photographed image. So how in heaven, or on Earth, does an object *get in front of the reticle?* Putting it another way, how could any reticles get behind objects? This is a technical impossibility—unless the photograph has been adjusted or 'diddled with' which is very loud Whistle-Blowing.

"What is the correct technical description of these cross-hairs?" we asked.

"We call them reticles," responded Jan. "They are crosses accurately placed, mapped up to half a micron on the location. They used them to correct for distortion of the lens and they can measure the distance between the crosses and determine if the film has 'curved' because if so, these crosses will be slightly dislocated. *They did not help [NASA] in judging lunar distances.*

This statement was in direct contrast to NASA representative Brian Welch's reply. When asked by SKY TV News (August 1997 interview) to explain the reticles he had replied:

> Those are there in the photos in order to provide the engineers with the ability to measure distances. Knowing the way the photo was put together they would be able to use that to measure things off in the distance.

"Were these reticles engraved on the film plane?" we then enquired of Jan Lundberg.

"No," he replied, "firstly, these reticles were established on the plate by metal evaporation, at Zeiss. It is a common technique for mapping cameras. It was almost on the film plane, but not completely, because they didn't want to scratch the film. The plate had small ridges on the film transportation edges which raised it about 800th of a millimetre above the surface of the film."

When SKY TV asked Brian Welch: "Why is the centre reticle not actually in the centre of the image?" (20) The reply they received was absolutely astonishing:

> The exact answer to the question is I don't really know and haven't even bothered to go and find out. The reason is, this is thirty year old stuff.

But the fact of the matter is that the large centre reticle always has to appear in the centre of the image—because it is an integral part of the camera. For the reticle to be off-centre in any photograph is another technical impossibility and a very loud blow on the whistle (20). It implies that such a photograph was taken without reticles and that the reticles on this particular image were intentionally added later.

"And lastly," said Jan, "they had a pole that you have seen in the photos, called a gnomon, which enabled them to determine the angle of the camera and the scale in the vicinity of that pole. And this gnomon was held in a universal joint so that it always hung at the vertical."

So with that, we had reached the end of our most instructive time with Hasselblad in Sweden.

Garden gnomes

NASA

"Gnomon is an island" *(astronaut Schmitt).*
The gnomon facilitated the calibration of pictures by providing a shadow and a definition of length, plus a colour
chart—which surely could have been deployed for a guide had negative colour film been used.

Surprisingly, not one single camera used during the Apollo space program is on display in the exhibition cases at Hasselblad in Göteborg.

What did we learn from building the moon camera?

The System

HASSELBLAD

22. Hasselblad advertisement December 1969.

This is apparently because all the 500 EL/70 camera bodies taken by the astronauts were supposedly left on the lunar surface. The space cameras in Hasselblad's showcase are product samples that have never left home. NASA has only given them one 'souvenir' magazine from an Apollo trip! However, as we all know, 'Apollo 13' allegedly did a round trip, with no stops and was equipped with three HEDC cameras. Is it not extraordinary that not one of those cameras has been returned to Hasselblad as a memento? 'Apollos 8' and '10' were also billed as journeying around the Moon with several Lunar Surface Cameras on board and no claimed stops for garbage dumps on the lunar surface.

The next remarkable commercial incident in the life of the Hasselblad company (mentioned in their press release) was the sale of the distribution company and retailer network Hasselblad Fotografiska A3—to Kodak! And this happened in 1968, the year of 'Apollo 8'.

In the 1990s more and more Nikon cameras are being flown by NASA. It was in 1991 that Hasselblad stopped keeping a record of their cameras on board NASA's spacecraft. Too banal, as Jan had said—or not enough of them being flown?

During our visit we were presented with a glossy booklet, a history of the company which spans the years between 1941-1991 in photographs. There is no mention of the 1968 sale to Kodak, just a line on the fact that the deal with Kodak lasted—until 1966! (Compare the History of Hasselblad on page 55.) Is it not extraordinary that the company history is full of these inconsistencies?

More importantly still, this book makes no reference to the arrival of the first Hasselblad on the lunar surface, nor indeed to any other lunar mission. A careful search reveals this:

> Hasselblad cameras have accompanied all American space flights since 1962. NASA has chosen Hasselblad because of the high technical quality and the camera's ability to handle all types of assignments in extreme conditions.

The company has published a second glossy booklet specifically dedicated to thirty years in space. Out of 41 space photographs, 29 were taken in Earth orbit; only 6 depict the Apollo astronauts on the Moon and 6 picture frankly bizarre lunarscapes. And the famous 'classic' of Aldrin standing alone *is printed the wrong way round!* The text is notable for its meagre reference to the Apollo missions. In this booklet of 63 pages 'Apollo 11' is linked with Hasselblad only *twice*.

> The Eagle moon lander came to rest on the Moon, carrying Neil A Armstrong and Edwin E Aldrin. The parent vessel was called Apollo 11. The camera was called Hasselblad.

- Why not mention the model and type of Hasselblad camera?
- The CSM (the parent vessel) is named incorrectly. The *mission* was named Apollo 11, the parent vessel was called Columbia.

Then further on it states that 'Apollo 11' arrived on the Moon on *June 1* 1969 (instead of July 20).

How can Hasselblad, of all people, possibly forget the date of 'Apollo 11'? Here is another extract from this space booklet—after our conversations at Göteborg and an analysis of their company history it sounds rather like an extraordinarily loud blast on that whistle:

> The ancient rock carvings near Victor Hasselblad's home carried a message.

Just like the space photographs of our own age. *It is up to us to interpret them correctly* and let our feelings and knowledge work in harmony, as we enter a new millennium (emphasis added).

We cannot help feeling, that somewhere, something has gone a little awry. Both Kodak and Hasselblad have acted as though they may be uncomfortable about their products being used on the Moon. Has their close proximity to NASA led them to suspect that all is not well with the historical record? Do they perhaps feel 'guilty by association'?

More hassles with cameras

The Apollo **colour TV camera** *was designed to military specifications* and built under the direction of Larkin Niemyer, the Engineering Manager of the Apollo TV Camera Program at the aerospace division of Westinghouse in Baltimore, USA. (see Appendix) Mr Niemyer, together with Stan Lebar kindly sent us a copy of the operations manual for this camera.

On 'Apollo 12' the mission only returned *sound* to Earth during its alleged EVA on the Moon. This lack of television coverage was blamed on a TV camera failure, just after its installation on the lunar surface. As a clever ploy to turn the American public away from their screens, we can think of no better way to generate indifference! Afterwards NASA could

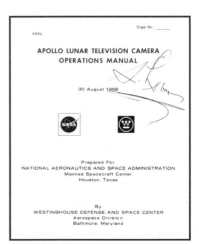

22. The Apollo Lunar TV Camera Operations Manual.

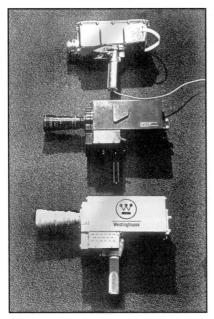

23. The Apollo TV cameras.   WESTINGHOUSE

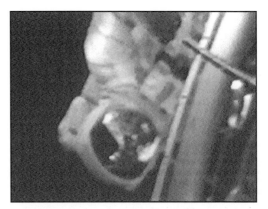

24. 'Pre-TV failure' astronaut descending ladder as actually seen on TV, December 1969.   NASA

say, with some justification, that the public had lost interest in the Apollo space program.

Here is the Westinghouse press release:

> Immediately after the Apollo 12 color camera was lifted from the modular equipment stowage assembly (MESA) compartment, it was inadvertently pointed at the Sun. The imaging tube burned and television coverage of the moon was blacked out.

The only problem with this scenario is that wherever they actually were, the camera had not in fact failed to function.

QUESTION: If this camera was totally inoperable, how could picture (25) be possible and how could each of the three images in sequence (26) be different from each other?

It would appear that the Westinghouse press release is rather misleading or even incorrect.

QUESTION: Why did Houston fail to instruct the astronauts to 'pick up the TV camera and place it on the stand?' In fact the TV camera was totally ignored—clearly part of the script.

On page nine of the Apollo Lunar TV Camera Operations Manual for the B&W camera the following is underlined:

> The camera . . . should not be pointed directly at the Sun or directly at bright lamps.

Firstly, the astronauts (including the 'Apollo 12' crew) were clearly alerted to the dangers of pointing at the Sun and secondly, this warning equally covers any studio light sources!

Also in bold print on the same page of the manual, there was this warning:

25. An image from the recorded TV material, frame grabbed during the relocation of the camera at least 45 minutes after the alleged TV camera failure. One can make out images whilst it was being moved around. This 'post-failure' TV frame shows a crater on the left and has lens flare diagonally across the picture from bottom left to top right.

THE CAMERA CASE SHOULD NEVER BE ALLOWED TO REACH A TEMPERATURE COLDER THAN MINUS 30°F OR HOTTER THAN PLUS 120°F.

Apparently a thermal control system prevented the temperature of the camera from exceeding 120°F. But that is still an interesting challenge to astronauts photographing in the Sun for long periods at a lunar surface temperature of anything between 180°F and 250°F! The 1969 Westinghouse press release further stated:

> To ward off direct rays of the Sun and the glare from the lunar surface, Mr Lebar (Manager of the Apollo TV Camera Program) said, the housing of the camera has a highly polished bottom and top cover treated with special heat-resistant paint. Other than these simple features, the camera requires no heating or cooling elements for operation.
>
> *Apollo 11 Color TV*
> Westinghouse also provided the 13-pound camera which will be carried in the command module during Apollo 11 to televise astronaut activity en route to and returning from moon orbit.
>
> The variable focus zoom lens on the Westinghouse color camera has a focal length ranging from 12.5mm to 75mm.

One minute of your time ...

We have listened to these experts, and compared their statements with our own findings. We have also examined various statements made by the astronauts, at the time of Apollo

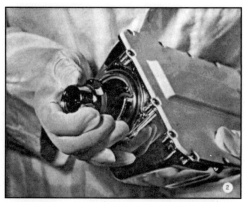

27. Technician fitting a lens to the Apollo TV camera.
WESTINGHOUSE

and over the years that followed, especially concerning the photographic aspect of their respective missions. In the next chapters we will bring still more evidence to support our conclusion that:

- The photographic evidence for the Apollo missions is fabricated.
- We probably did not go to the Moon with any of the named American Apollo astronauts belonging to 'Apollo 8', '10' and '11 through to 'Apollo 17'.
- Any *anomalies* that might have occurred in any *real* lunar surface pictures, which no doubt would have rendered many of the *real* lunar surface images useless, appear to have been exchanged for major *inconsistencies* in the faked Apollo photographic record.

We could ask why one of the twelve American astronauts who are supposed to have walked upon the lunar surface was not scheduled to take one minute of his time, place one

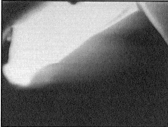

26. Three images from the TV camera—just 'left on the ground'.
NASA

camera upon one rock, and take *one* colour picture of the magnificent canopy of stars under which he was privileged to work? Thus recording that wondrous view of those ever-present and unblinking luminosities for all on Planet Earth to see—especially for those who had paid to send astronauts to the Moon, either with their income, their integrity, or with their lives.

It might not have been a perfect exposure and perhaps such a picture has been taken. If such an image does exist, the vast majority of us have not seen it.

As we have already amply demonstrated, the photographic record with which we are all familiar has been shown to be fake. It is our contention that only a *select few* know what the lunar surface *really* looks like at close quarters, and how a star, viewed from the Moon, unhindered by an atmosphere, *really* shines.

28. US flag at the South Pole.

The standard flag

Here is a rare occasion when those involved have admitted to great lighting on the Moon!

'Apollo 11': Mike Collins (in CSM Columbia): "...How is the quality of the TV?"
Houston: "Oh, it's beautiful Mike, it really is."
Collins: "Oh, gee, that's great. Is the lighting half way decent?"
Houston: "Yes, indeed. They've got the flag up now and you can see the Stars and the Stripes on the lunar surface."

QUESTION: Where else other than allegedly on the Moon is there a sole American flag marking an important point on a planet in our solar system?
ANSWER: Planet Earth, the South Pole.
Ironically the markers at the South Pole mirror the flag A & B system applied in the production of the Apollo lunar surface photographs.

In the Antarctic there is an official flagpole with the flags of at least ten nations in a hemisphere surrounding a red and white striped marker decorated with a dark blue top. This then is the site at which visiting dignitaries have their photograph taken, endorsing the impression that Antarctica is a truly international place of scientific research. However, 'X' never, ever, marks the spot! Those who wish to experience the exact 0°S longitude must hike some way from this multi-flagged arena to find *the actual geographic centre of the South Pole*. On arrival there, they will discover an explanatory noticeboard, a simple wooden marker and a single flagpole. From this pole, a lone but very large flag is flying—is it a symbol of unity, representing the allegedly international territory of the Antarctic? Well... not exactly. Longitude 0°S has been quietly claimed by one nation alone and the flag that flies there is the Stars and Stripes!

Dr. Donald's SFX trickery

SFX is the film industries' term for special effects and throughout this book, there will be sections entitled Dr. Donald's SFX trickery, which will deal with film, TV or media events relevant to the matter in hand and for the most part involving 'special effects'.

29. US flag on the Moon. NASA

The three-card trick

Early on in the history of the moving picture business, documentary film images were doctored for political, sociological and commercial propaganda purposes.[6] The American media were right there from the very start.

For example, a significant battle during the American Civil War was later recreated in film studios with model ships filmed against a painted backdrop and with the film cameraman's wife making simulated cannon fire—puffing cigarette smoke on cue. This faked footage was then palmed off on the unsuspecting public as the authentic record. On a tabletop, Edison faked film sequences of the 1906 San Francisco Earthquake that outsold the authentic footage of the disaster. The British media were not far behind the Americans.

On Wimbledon Common, (a London suburb) actors in costume were filmed thrashing about in the pond and then struggling into a lifeboat, the director exhorting them to dramatic ges-

tures of desperation throughout the several takes that it took to get this footage 'right'. This film was then presented to the public as being *authentic* newsreel of *real* survivors of the sinking of the Lusitania.

Nobody questioned this item originally because the general public did not know what technology was involved in capturing those images and where the bounds of possibility lay. It did not occur to the audience that there had to be a cameraman in a boat to film this scene and that producing these images was beyond the bounds of circumstantial possibility.

We suggest that exactly the same situation existed with regard to the Apollo images. Until recently we were all ignorant of the cinematic challenges inherent in space photography. With the advance of our analytical technology we can now understand how something we had previously considered a possibility is in reality an impossibility—that is, within the

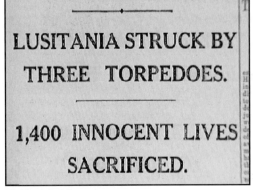

30. The fall of the gods.

In the can

- In 1834 Roget (of Thesaurus fame) explained the relationship between the brain and the eye and demonstrated how the *Zoetrope* toy worked.
- Invented by WG Horner, the *Zoetrope* consisted of a series of pictures on a rotating drum which appeared to move.
- Niepce, Daguerre & Fox-Talbot pioneered photography.
- In 1877 Eadwearde Muybridge set up a series of 24 cameras that photographed in sequence and so was able to record the motion of a moving horse.
- Ottomar Anschutz then devised an apparatus to view such images.
- Etienne-Jules Marey designed a single camera for the same job and in 1884 George Eastman invented celluloid film.
- In 1891 Thomas Edison (together with his assistant WL Dickson) introduced 35mm film with four sprocket holes per frame to advance it.
- This film was used inside a peepshow, viewable by one person at a time. Indeed this type of film stock is still standard in the Motion Picture Industry.
- On December 28 1895 moving film was projected for the first time to an audience in Paris by the brothers Louise and Auguste Lumière, a surname of destiny surely? Lumière is the French word for 'light'.[7]

---

stated circumstances of the lunar exploration allegedly carried out by NASA.

Reverting to past history, where the audience had some *experience* of the event, they were quick to spot anything that was a fake. There is the classic example of a boxing match that was rigged up by the newsreel makers, who were not able to film the event itself. The audience, familiar with the sport, spotted the inadequacies of the actors hired to represent the boxing champions, and immediately denounced the whole film as a hoax. In the early days of commercial aviation, George Bernard Shaw, roped in to authenticate its usefulness, cheerfully announced to the audience: "You think that this is a real event. It isn't—it's all a fake—a set-up for the camera!" Today, we would recognise and acknowledge that he was in fact participating in an advertisement.

Yet in the early days of factual movie making, when the Newsreel was an integral part of the cinema programme, the audiences were given to understand, and indeed believed, that *everything they saw* on the screen was actually happening—the real thing. That is precisely what *we* were given to understand by those who created the *pre-recorded* Apollo TV material and still images.

In a sense, in the 1960s we were as innocent in our response to media manipulation as were those very early movie audiences.

NASA

31. 'Apollo 16' image featuring a camera intended to take pictures by ultra violet light, seen here on a stand in the centre of the photograph. This piece of equipment was placed in total shadow—so it should be absolutely black. However, a secondary source of illumination was deployed, on this occasion emanating from the *left of the camera position* so that it would be visible. Yet another example of an image laden with inconsistencies.

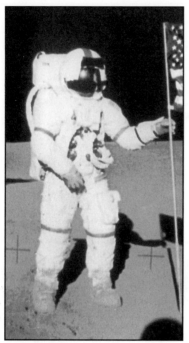

32. Astronaut 'on the moon'.   NASA

33. Astronaut on a 'moon' set.   NASA

Is it not also true that rather than a truly objective view, our daily dose of TV news stories, our radio and our newspapers essentially reflect the views of the journalists and the policies of media networks and in some cases, governments? For example, did any newsreels produced by the Allies during WWII ever show footage depicting the *heroism* of individual German or Italian soldiers?

With the ever-expanding art of cinematography, developments in still cameras, movie cameras, and latterly video cameras and their attendant technology, the ordinary person has gradually became far more familiar with the use of effects and trick photography in the making of motion pictures.

We all understand that certain scenes have to be 'cheated'. But even now, as then, we expect the SFX trickery to occur *only* in dramatic films—*never* in national and international news items and *absolutely not* in documentary material. ■

Heat and Radiation

David Groves PhD conducted tests on Ektachrome ISO (ASA) 160 Professional colour reversal film
to see how it would stand up to radiation exposure and temperatures of +180°F/+82°C on the lunar surface.

Groves found that even a modest radiation dose to the film—5 rem of ionising radiation—(8MeV X-rays)
would produce **significant reduction of contrast and image density in the resulting transparencies**.

Extended exposure to the higher end of NASA's anticipated temperature range
on the lunar surface may be expected to **significantly decrease the image density**
thus **adversely affecting the quality of the resulting Ektachrome transparencies**.

Report in Appendix

Chapter Three

Radiant Daze

"Radiation is a key issue—one of the biggest show stoppers in mankind's exploration of the Universe!"—according to an expert at the Defence and Research Agency, Farnborough, England. We explore the natural barrier that would challenge the United States when attempting to achieve its declared aim: to send NASA's named Apollo astronauts to the Moon and bring them home again—safely.

R is for Radiation

Why did NASA feel obliged to fake the lunar photographic record? Was there more than one reason, or even a galaxy of reasons, for the unfortunate actions of this government agency?

The three Rs are generally considered to refer to reading, 'riting and 'rithmetic but we have taken this old adage, applied it to other equally essential principles (which we shall explore further on) and added a fourth 'R': an invisible but potent component with which space travellers must contend—radiation.

It is unsurprising to us, the authors, that one of the most taboo subjects associated with the Apollo missions—galactic cosmic rays and solar radiation—is one of the 'biggest show stoppers' ever. After all, in 1871, a full 98 years before 'Apollo 11' supposedly set forth for the Moon, Ralph Waldo Emerson had already got the right idea when he wrote: "A man should not go where he cannot carry his whole sphere or circle with him—not bodily but atmospherically".

Just as a human baby is protected by the maternal environment of the womb so are we, on Earth, protected to an appreciable extent from the effects of radiation by the physics of our planet. We benefit from an environment which is the ideal requirement for the evolution and maintenance of life as we know it. We are all protected and clothed in our atmosphere and shielded from harmful radiation by the Earth's magnetic field. A baby generally does not leave the womb until around 272 days after conception, at a point when it is mature enough to survive outside that safe environment. Premature babies have a very tough time, needing incubators and careful human nurturing, and even so, many do not survive.

However, we are all expected to believe that the Apollo astronauts have boldly travelled into deep space full of known and unknown hazards, beyond the safety of our naturally created environment, without suffering any harmful consequences. Yet radiation will alter anything that it strikes.

As early as 1958 it was acknowledged that cosmic rays would penetrate metal hulls effortlessly. Depending upon their composition, metals were affected by radiation to different degrees. Glass was found to deteriorate when subjected to cosmic radiation and it was recommended that any windows in spacecraft would need to be tinted and equipped with filters.[1] (Of course recording images through tinted windows would surely add to the challenges of taking acceptable colour photographs.)

The Good, the Bad, and the Rems & Rads

Firstly, we need to have some 'basics' simply established. This is not an academic textbook, so we are attempting to deal with a complex and very technical subject in the simplest way possible. Our intention is to look at the very real dangers of space travel and see how they were (and are) addressed by the space 'experts'. At this stage we ought to grasp the jargon used by scientists when dealing with radiation evaluation. Currently, there are several terms—rems, rads, ergs, rens, sieverts, millisieverts and bequerels are all employed—to the great confusion of the uninitiated who generally stop asking questions at this point.

Maybe that is the general idea, as author John Davidson who is an expert on radiation with a degree in biological sciences from Cambridge University has written: "Nobody fully understands how radioactivity harms us, what levels—if any—are safe and why its effect varies from person to person".[2]

As a guide to radiation terminology:

- One rad is the measure of the actual amount of radiation absorbed by living tissue. It is used to measure all types of radiation and is a unit of energy equal to 100 ergs delivered to 1 gram of tissue.
- One erg is a basic unit of energy in which all other energy units such as watts, mass, etc. can be expressed.
- Radiation doses expressed in units of rem are called dose equivalent.
- The rem is an acronym from Roentgen Equivalent Man and is a unit of biological response to the radiation dose, derived from adjusting the rad by the quality (Q) factor.
- In the late 1980s the rem was generally replaced in Europe by the term: sieverts, cSv (centi-Sieverts) or mSv = milli-Sieverts. All these units (rems and sieverts) take account of the Relative Biological Effectiveness (RBE) of the particular kind of radiation.

The amount of radiation that is naturally present on the surface of the Earth and absorbed by a human being is about 1 rem per year. For reasons not yet fully understood by scientists, we all tolerate radiation to varying degrees but generally for a short exposure (which would include solar flares) 118 rem is considered lethal to 10% of human recipients and a dose of 345 rem lethal to 50% of humans.[3]

Arthur C Clarke's quote (below) notwithstanding, there are consequential effects of radiation during space travel on the purely physical body which can be categorised as 'stochastic' and 'deterministic'. Stochastic effects are the longer term consequences that occur following exposure to radiation—cancers and similar issues. The study of deterministic effects is based on any disablement or impairment that occurs immediately after exposure to radiation.

Leaving aside the hazards to crew and environment from man-made nuclear reactors on board spacecraft, there are three primary sources of natural space radiation:

Up above the Clarke belt

"Space itself, to the considerable surprise of most people, has turned out to be a benign environment; It is only the planets that are hostile."

Arthur C Clarke Sri Lanka 1980[4]

Rads, Rems and Q

A radiation absorbed dose (rad) is an absolute measure of energy absorbed by tissue exposed to radiation. Different types of radiation are found to produce varying degrees of tissue damage for the same absorbed energy dose. It is the irradiation of the nucleic acid in the DNA that kills cells.

The absorbed dose of each type of radiation is multiplied by the Q factor (Q) to obtain the dose equivalent. The Q factor has nothing to do with James Bond. It means the Quality Factor.

1. X-rays, gamma rays and beta particles: Q factor 1.
2. Slow neutrons: Q factor 2.5.
3. Fast neutrons and alpha particles: Q factor 10.
4. Heavy nuclei (GCR): Q factor 10-15.

The rem (dose equivalent) is an expression of 'harm done' by the radiation.

$$1 \text{ Sv} = 100 \text{ rem}$$
$$1 \text{ cSv} = 1 \text{ rem}$$
$$1 \text{ mSv} = 0.1 \text{ rem (or 100 mrem)}$$

J R Murphy *Medical Considerations for Manned Interstellar Flight* JBIS 1981 Vol 34

---

1. *Van Allen belts*—a specific doughnut-shaped region of space encircling our planet which traps high energy particles.
2. *Solar particle events* (SPEs) as the name suggests emanate from the Sun (these were previously called solar flares). SPEs consist of protons, alpha particles and small fluxes of heavy nuclei.
3. *Galactic cosmic radiation* (GCR) is the radiation ever-present in deep space, the background radiation in the galaxy containing extremely high energy protons, alpha particles and heavy nuclei.[5]

In June 1997 we were privileged to talk with Professor Clive Dyer, DERA Senior Fellow at the UK's Defence and Research Agency, Farnborough, England about the effects of radiation. The numerous framed certificates lining a wall of his office testifying to the long-standing and close relationship Professor Dyer has with NASA.

We first asked Clive Dyer if he could describe the typical immediate effects of radiation.

"The immediate, or deterministic effects," said Clive Dyer, "mean being disabled. You have experienced so much radiation, for example, that you vomit, you have diarrhoea, the lining of the stomach is destroyed, and cells are destroyed. These are the obvious immediate disabling effects from nuclear radiation."

"Do these symptoms start occurring after a dose of—say 75 rem?" we asked.

"Oh yes," replied Clive. "Cataracts come in at that sort of level. But you do realise I am not a medical expert as such."

"Yes, of course," we responded. "So if you get 'zapped' at the agreed minimum level (as an astronaut in your craft on your way to Mars, for example) you are going to get quite poorly—albeit not permanently—would that be correct?"

"Yes, for sure," said Clive. "With so many critical functions to perform, somewhere around the 100 rem mark could be potentially disabling."

After such information we might be forgiven for suggesting that the principal reason why none of our space craft travelling beyond the safety boundary of our planet's atmosphere and magnetic field are currently manned, is due to a very simple fact: We do not know how to cope in a practical sense with the effects of solar or galactic cosmic radiation, neither during the voyage nor upon arrival on another celestial body.

The deterministic chart over the page pinpoints the very real dangers to which the authorities were prepared to expose space travellers—allegedly. We cannot emphasise enough how fortunate the named Apollo astronauts were to have apparently escaped the dangerous game of 'Russian Solar Flare Roulette'. It is our conclusion that NASA's named astronauts—introduced to us as the Apollo program's lunar visitors—did not venture beyond

Expected Immediate (Deterministic) Effects of acute radiation doses			
Single Doses		(NVD = Nausea, Vomiting & Diarrhoea)	
rem	sieverts	Effects	Mortality
000 - 030	0.0 - 0.3	Possible blood changes	—
035 - 070	0.3 - 0.7	NVD 5%-10% + poss. blood changes	—
075 - 160	0.7 - 1.6	NVD 25% exposed personnel	
		Eye lens—detectable opacity	10% 30-60 days
170 - 220	1.7 - 2.2	NVD 50% exposed personnel	
		Eye lens—vision impairing opacity	20% 30-60 days
230 - 300	2.3 - 3.0	NVD up to 100% personnel	
		Bone marrow damage	
		Eye lens—vision impairing opacity	40% 30-60 days
310 - 490	3.1 - 4.9	NVD 100% first day	
		Inflammation of lung tissue	
		Bone marrow damage—mod/severe	
		Permanent sterility at app 350 rem	
		Eye lens—vision impairing opacity	50% 30-60 days
500 - 620	5.0 - 6.2	NVD 100% within 4 hours	
		Lung problems—serious	
		Damage to gastrointestinal tract	
		Cataracts + loss of vision	
		Bone marrow damage—severe	
		Permanent sterility	100% 30-60 days
630 - 950	6.3 - 9.5	NVD 100% within 1 to 2 hours	
		Lung damage—severe	
		Damage to gastrointestinal tract	
		Cataracts + loss of vision	
		Bone marrow damage—severe	
		Permanent sterility	100% 10-20 days
960 +	9.6 +	Incapacitation almost immediately	100% 01- 7 days

1. Compiled from data obtained from the Royal Marsden NHS Trust UK; The National Radiological Protection Board UK; The Naval Research Laboratory USA; Severn Communications Corp USA, and the National Council on Radiation Protection and Measurements (NCRP) USA.

our safety boundary—for otherwise they would have run the risk of becoming very ill or even of dying.

Next to this little-discussed basic radiation problem, the much-discussed subject of the lengthy duration of future interplanetary voyages pales into insignificance. The plight of manned space travel in the late '90s is still the equivalent of that premature baby trying to survive, equipped only with a primitive incubator, an unreliable life support system and tended by an incompetent nurse!

The what's what of 'out there'

In terms of aviation, avionics and the development of its associated technologies, humanity has progressed so fast that it is difficult for many of us to realise that from the late 1940s through to the '60s, we knew very little indeed about the safety of the environment beyond a distance of 25 miles above the surface of the Earth.

Even today our real knowledge of the effects of space radiation is still relatively scant and certainly inadequate in terms of navigating

2. An early view of the Earth from the edge of space.   NASA

safely and freely through the oceans and currents of space. In the 1950s matters were even more conjectural. Primitive rockets and high altitude unmanned research balloons had revealed initial data suggesting that a major problem facing space exploration was the presence of cosmic rays.   These are now called galactic cosmic rays or GCRs.

During the early days of space exploration both the Soviets and the Americans experimented with animals such as tortoises, mice, rats, dogs, and monkeys. These animals were put into orbit relatively near to Earth. Yet,

3. Space mice.   NASA

whatever the physical metabolic equivalence between animals and human beings, there are still considerable differences between the *psychological* requirements of an animal and a human being travelling through space.

The unfortunate animals subjected to these tests were examined for the effects of radiation. In one experiment two colours of mice were subjected to cosmic rays, a test that was apparently painless (though how did the experimenters know that for sure?). The black mice returned with their hair streaked through with grey so obviously it was not a stress-free experiment for the mice. The white mice did not register a colour change; presumably their hair already being a whiter shade of pale had something to do with that. Mice not being known for speaking up about their finer feelings, these colour changes were remarked upon but not taken into consideration and these tests were considered successful.[6]

Near the surface of the Earth, there is, as we know, the Earth's atmosphere. This name from the Greek for 'vapour' and 'ball', designates the gaseous envelope surrounding a celestial body. Our atmosphere consists of twelve layers, ranging from the troposphere (about 18 miles thick at the equator, thinning to about 4 miles above the poles) up to the exosphere (about 311 miles above the surface and 62 miles thick). Each of these layers has different characteristics, which many physics books will go into in great detail, here we are concerned with the overall protective capacities of these twelve layers.

- The Earth's atmosphere provides a radiation shield equivalent to about 32ft/10m of water.
- The atmosphere, together with the Earth's magnetic field, reduces the space radiation dose rate for a human being standing on the Earth's surface to about one-third of the typical total dose rate.
- The typical total dose rate incorporates an evaluation of dosage from radioactive material both on the Earth's surface and within its crust.

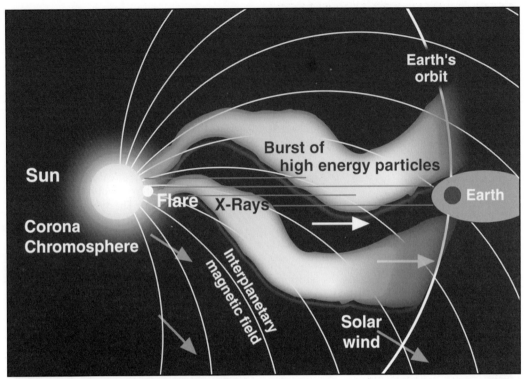

4. Solar radiation field lines and solar wind.

After SMART 1988

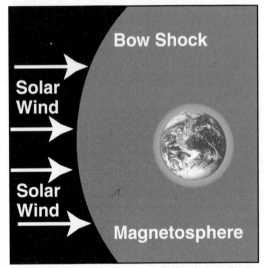

5. Earth's protection by its magnetic field and atmosphere.

So now we know how protected we are, let us see what exactly might be 'out there' that can hurt us. The early space scientists of this century discovered that space is a hard vacuum, which means it is relatively pure with no oxygen (or any other gases) available for breathing and no protection against solar illumination, high radiation levels and the hazards of micrometeorites. In fact these scientists found that, from the point of view of 'getting up there' and moving through it at speed, space started much nearer to the Earth than we had previously imagined, affecting the human metabolism in a variety of ways.

If our atmosphere is thought of as an ocean, then we can liken ourselves to fish living on the floor of such an ocean. The pressure on this 'ocean' from the weight of air is at its greatest at the bottom, as is the case on the true ocean floor. On our planet we can only breathe comfortably because our bodies are specifically designed for this environment. As a matter of fact we would die if we did not breathe air at this pressure. As we inhale, the chest wall expands and the diaphragm pulls away from the lungs and exhalation, the inverse of this action

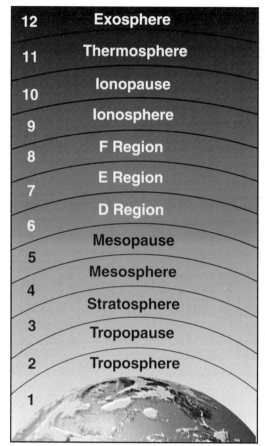

12	Exosphere
11	Thermosphere
10	Ionopause
9	Ionosphere
8	F Region
7	E Region
6	D Region
5	Mesopause
4	Mesosphere
3	Stratosphere
2	Tropopause
1	Troposphere

6. The Earth's atmosphere.

produces the deflation of the lungs. Atmospheric pressure then forces air into the lungs which inflate. A pressurised spacesuit in the vacuum of space replaces the action of our atmosphere and obliges an astronaut's lungs to 'drink their fill' of his or her 'in-house' oxygen system.

Back here on Earth, when climbing to high altitudes, the quantity of oxygen present in the air remains roughly constant, but the air pressure and its density decrease so that insufficient air is forced into the lungs. As we go even higher we find we cannot survive without arti-

ficial help. From 49,000ft/14,934m lack of oxygen to the brain would kill a human being within seconds, and from 63,000ft/19,200m the lack of pressure means that the blood would boil, tissue would expand and then burst. Those exploding bodies from sci-fi horror films would become reality. Working in the United States, Dr. Hubertus Strughold considered that these two altitudes were significant, representing what he described as "the physiological conditions of the total space equivalence". Hubertus Strughold also stated that: "The conquest of the outskirts of the atmosphere and eventually space, is a revolutionary event, comparable only to the transition of the aquatic animals to the land in geologic times" (sic).[7]

Minute traces of our atmosphere can be found up to approximately 600 miles above the surface of the Earth—but from 15 miles up the air contains ozone which is a form of oxygen that rots rubber, corrodes metal and poisons human beings. (The molecules in ozone contain three atoms instead of the two found in the common form of oxygen.) Thus a further need for designing pressurised spacecraft equipped with air-locks is emphasised.

The remarkably elastic Van Allen belts

After all these hurdles we next encounter the wall at the boundary of the park—The Van Allen radiation belts.

These two radiation zones within the magnetosphere were named after Dr. James Van Allen who, together with his colleagues, was the first to register his findings and is therefore credited with the discovery of these bands of magnetic radiation. He received these data from the US satellites: Explorer 1, launched February 1 1958 and Explorer 3, launched March 25 1958. (Explorer 2 March 5 1958 failed to reach orbit and fell to Earth 2,000 miles downrange of its launch site.)

Up and down in space
The presence of an atmosphere makes returning to Earth a hazardous procedure due to air-friction heating. On the other hand, the absence of an atmosphere makes landing on a planet *even more hazardous* due to the lack of aero-dynamic support.

William J Walter, author of *Space Age*[8] states that Van Allen and his team *together* with Wernher von Braun (and allegedly behind the backs of most of the authorities involved in space policy) had been preparing a scientific payload to be deployed, should such an expedition ever be sanctioned. It was—and the rest is history—but that may not be the entirety of the matter. Walter maintains that the discovery of the Van Allen belts was a first ever for a space probe. However according to one report, as early as November 1957, the Soviet scientist Vernov had already discovered much the same data from Sputnik II. The Soviets were unable to formally register this information due to a transmission failure between Sputnik II and ground control[9]—yet other sources state that this matching data *was received* by the USSR.

Sputnik II was equipped to evaluate cosmic radiation and solar radiation, so no doubt the effects of radiation were being evaluated on Laika (the dog passenger) as well. Officially, the effects of zero gravity on her circulation and digestive system were monitored as were data on breathing, blood pressure, pulse and psychological reactions. Also officially, Laika died painlessly when the oxygen supply ran out, but since 1957 another version of events has emerged.

New information available in 1988 states that the insulation ripped away from the satellite at the moment of its insertion into orbit around Earth and that the rapid rise

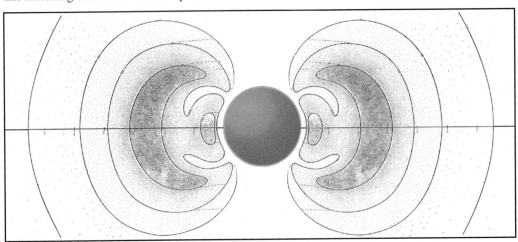

7. Based on Dr. James Van Allen's original illustration for the belts of trapped radiation around the Earth.

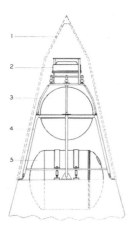

1)   Protective cone
2)   Solar radiation detection equipment
3+4) Instrumentation
5)   Animal chamber.

8. Sputnik II: Full scale replica, Moscow.   AULIS

8a. Solar radiation detection equipment fitted in section number two in Sputnik II.

in temperature within the satellite would have caused Laika to suffer a painful death. However even this statement is not entirely correct. Made of ceramic materials the nosecone of the Sputnik—designed to protect the satellite from atmospheric heating during the ascent from Earth—was *programmed* to be discarded when orbital height was attained.

My mind is made up— don't confuse me with the facts

Prior to 1957 *NOBODY* on Earth had any idea that such a high level of radiation existed around our planet. The only way that these belts were detected was by their negative effect on data-collecting instruments within the space probe—they failed to register the radiation, not because there was none present but because there was too much. The instruments went 'off the scale', and it took a little while for ground-based scientists to work out what had occurred.

Given that between scientists at least, there were relatively few, if any, secrets withheld from either side, it is more likely that the Soviets had indeed discovered these belts, shared the information with their American counterparts and that the 'unofficial' preparations by Van Allen and his team were, in fact, the very official beefing up of scientific instruments better able to register the mighty force of the planet's radiation zones—a level with which the Sputnik II's instruments were incapable of dealing comprehensively.

Science prides itself on stating facts. Which makes our following discovery all the more problematic: since the initial release of the data concerning this zone of intense radiation, right through to the present day, the evaluation of the depth of the Van Allen belts varies dramatically according to the source of information. There are significant differences of opinion, not just relating to understandable discrepancies of a few miles but to thousands of miles.

Let us have a look at why that should be so.

85

Early probes				
Probe	Orbit/miles	Inclination	Launch Date	End Date
Sputnik I	141 x 581	65.1°	Oct 14 1957	Jan 4/Feb 25* 1958
Sputnik II	131 x 1031	65.3°	Nov 3 1957	April 14 1958
Explorer 1	225 x 1594	33.24°	Jan 31/Feb 1* 1958	Mar 31 1970
Explorer 3	117 x 1740	33.5°	Mar 25 1958	June 28 1958
Sputnik III	135 x 1158	65.18°	May 15 1958	April 6 1960

*Depending on source

No single source of information will provide all these details and no source necessarily corresponds with another—as can be seen from the discrepancies in dating for Explorer 1. Surely the first American satellite to leave the launch pad should be an incontrovertible fact?

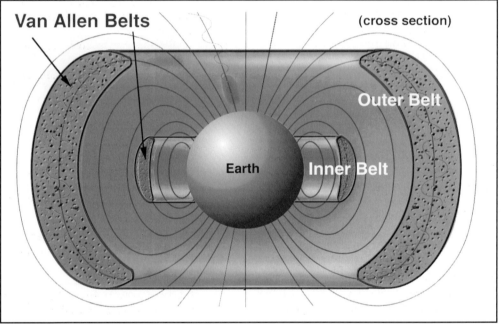

9. The two Van Allen radiation belts. While there is no clear interface between the two Van Allen belts, they do constitute two distinct regions which are often referred to as the lower (inner) and the upper (outer) belt. These names stem from the order in which one reaches them from the surface of the Earth. It is more accurate to use the term 'inner and outer belts' as the lower belt is actually surrounded by the upper belt.

- In *Spaceflight and Rocketry: A Chronology* David Baker has an entry dated March 20 1959 for an announcement of further radiation belt data from Professor James Van Allen, stating that that the inner belt extended from 1,500 to 3,000 miles, the upper belt from 8,000 to 55,000 miles. This information was based on data received from Pioneer 4 (launched on March 3 1959 and destined for a lunar flyby—incidentally, it failed) but

was tracked for nearly three and a half days to a distance of 407,000 miles from Earth.

Yet in that same year, in the highly respected *Scientific American* James Van Allen stated that the radiation zone actually extends to a distance of 64,000 miles out. This is an increase of 9,000 miles over the Pioneer 4 data and a difference of 41,000 miles compared with the received wisdom still bandied about by the scientific community today.

Trapped radiation is harmful

"Our planet is encircled by two zones of high-energy particles, *against which space travellers will have to be shielded.*"

Dr. James A Van Allen 1959.

Scientific American Vol 200 No 3

- An American sci-fi movie in the late 1950s featuring the Van Allen Belts as part of its plot gave 300 miles from the surface of the Earth as the lower limit of the radiation belts.
- In 1997 NASA web sites quoted the starting point of the Van Allen Belts at between 250-750 miles from Earth. Hardly a start point, more of a vague zone!
- Also in 1997 British university students were informed that the Van Allen Belts extend from 621 to 3,107 miles for the lower belt and that the upper belt only continues to a mere 12,430 miles![10]
- The above distance is even more astonishing, with the upper belt apparently ending 51,570 miles short of Van Allen's own data.
- According to one source there is a discrepancy of 32,000 miles in the claimed limit of the upper belts!

May the Force be with you

A few more very significant points:

- Below 6,200 miles within the lower radiation belt, the trapped particles consist mostly of rather low energy electrons (a few MeVs) and protons.
- In LEO (low Earth orbit) the flux of electrons and ions heavier than a proton is "appreciable only at low energies, and is easily shielded against" so states the United States' Naval Research Laboratory. This laboratory claims that "trapped protons and their secondary nuclear interaction are the only significant hazard at this orbital level" [LEO].
- Matter, which mostly consists of minute particles called atoms, interacts by packets of energy (quanta) being thrown back and forth which transmit their force.
- Energy and matter can be converted into each other.
- It is generally recognised that there are four fundamental forces in nature:

   1. The Weak force
      —which causes radioactive decay.
   2. The Strong force
      —which binds the atom together.
   3. The Electro-magnetic force (electromagnetism underlies all chemistry).
   4. Gravity (which is considered to be the weakest force of all).

These forces can be arranged diagramatically to illustrate the four levels (see illustration 10).

The great barrier grief

As the information concerning the dangerous areas within the Van Allen belts differs depend-

---

Radiation belts—the facts

(All measurements taken at the equator.)

- The radiation trapped within the Van Allen belts is most intense from *620 miles* above the Earth's surface through to a height of 18,634 miles.[11]
- There are peaks at 1,863 miles and again at 13,665 miles.[12] (Other sources state 5,945 miles for the first peak.[13])
- At these specific altitudes, the intensity of radiation *exceeds* the peak intensity of the largest solar energetic particle event *ever recorded by human beings.*

   To summarise: Starting at a height lower than 300 miles from the Earth's surface there is a continuous zone of at least 54,000 miles of hazardous radiation. (The geosynchronous orbit at around 22,300 miles is within the upper belt.)

   While a *solar* event is sporadic and impermanent, the radiation in the Van Allen Belts is constantly present and is the gauntlet to be run on our way to deep space.

   Upon the discovery of the belts Van Allen's colleague Ernie Ray proclaimed: "All space must be radioactive".[14]

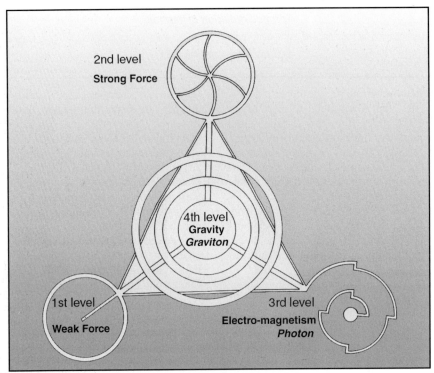

10. Our hierarchical representation the four forces of nature.

ing upon the source, we asked Professor Clive Dyer for his opinion.

"What about the challenge of the Van Allen belts?" we asked.

"That's a very intense zone," replied Clive. "No one lingers in the middle of that region for long. The Shuttle and the MIR space station are located at about 250–310 miles/400–500 kms up, which only gets the inner lower fringes several times a day. The belts are nearest to Earth over Brazil. Craft flying inclined orbits in LEO intersect this dominant-dose region—called the South Atlantic Anomaly.

"The Apollo manned missions went through the radiation belts very quickly," Clive continued. "What they did was park in low Earth orbit (the equivalent of where the Shuttle orbits now) and when they had rearranged their spacecraft, they travelled through the Van Allen belts at a great rate so they didn't pick up too much of a dose."

"But they would still have spent about an hour or so in the belts?" we queried.

"Something like that...that's acceptable," responded Clive. "I have a lot of Apollo dosimetry data, I worked on some of the later Apollo missions myself and its not too bad at all, quite acceptable."

"So what would be an average background level in the belts?"

"It varies by many orders of magnitude," replied Clive. "The worst place to be is the heart of the lower (inner) radiation belt, measured from the Earth's surface, that is about 1.5 earth radii out [2,000 miles from the surface].

"The upper (outer) belt peaks at about 3.5 to 4 radii out [between 10,000-12,000 miles from the Earth's surface] and if you were to stay *there* too long, you'd get rates which are lethal to electronics, let alone humans."

"Compared with say 50 rem per year (the average cosmic radiation level) what would it be in the belts?" we asked.

"It would be worse that that, a lot worse than that," responded Clive. "There is no question of men sitting there ... it could be ten times as bad."

"So that would be 500 rem?"

"Typically with electronics," said Clive (not directly answering the question), "if you were to sit in those worse situations and don't shield enough, you are getting tens of kilorads —tens of thousands of rads per year." (see table 1 on page 80 earlier in this chapter)

"So you want to get through them pretty quickly?" we continued.

"You do, yes!" Clive confirmed. "But there is no *real* problem though."

We wondered at this point why it is that so many experts and consultants to NASA freely *admit* and acknowledge the severe dangers of this radiation, but at the same time advise us that there is *no real problem* with these levels?

"And what about X-rays and their affects?" we asked Clive.

"The X-rays themselves don't go very far, they are stopped by less than a centimetre of aluminium, so they are not really a hazard."

QUESTION: If less than a centimetre of aluminium can stop X-rays then why do radiologists take the precaution of leaving the room and use lead-sheeted aprons when taking X-ray pictures?

QUESTION: If less than a centimetre of this material is so effective, then why are radiographers' aprons not manufactured from aluminium, lighter to wear and far cheaper to produce?

QUESTION: Astronauts have varying degrees of difficulty in walking after even fourteen days in space, a problem currently attributed solely to the problems of zero gravity. Could the effects of radiation be playing a part in this incapacitation?[15]

It is rather obvious from all the data we have studied that when passing through the intense trapped radiation of the Van Allen belts, astronauts would experience problems if not provided with adequate protection. Despite the publication of many scientific papers on this subject, we question whether there is currently sufficient public debate regarding the factors involved.

David Baker writes: "It was feared that the intensity of radiation would prohibit astronauts from spending long periods within the lower zone".[16] And that is our bone of contention: NASA has always emphasised that the astronauts travelled through the belts very quickly, staying less than an hour within these intense zones of radiation.

These radiation belts, extending to at least 54,000 miles out, are in fact *over twice the depth* compared with the data generally available from NASA. Therefore, any Apollo astronaut travelling through these belts would have spent *over two hours* in each direction within the belts, *absorbing high levels of radiation for a total of approximately four hours.*

At this juncture we could ask if NASA's statements concerning these dangers are based on 'doctored' information as to the true extent of these belts? If these zones of radiation were *not* a real threat to living organisms and if adequate protection from the hazards of radiation was *not* beyond the capacity of NASA's technology, then perhaps there would be no need to 'adjust' the data and there would therefore be only one official version of these figures. (See NCRP Report on page 376 in "Slaves of Limitation".)

In fact by the time a human being has travelled 24,000 miles beyond the surface of this planet he or she will have encountered all the medical problems that space travel embraces,

---

In sickness

NASA infers that 'Apollo 8' astronaut Frank Bormann suffered from nausea and diarrhoea after his passage through the Van Allen belts.

A Man on the Moon Andrew Chaikin

As NASA wishes to maintain the scenario that all these astronauts really made it to the Moon and back, it is still hard to believe that out of the 27 named US astronauts who are supposed to have travelled through the Van Allen belts only one suffered any noted radiation effects, and he is still alive and well, living in Las Cruces, New Mexico.

GCRs, SPEs, micro meteor-
ites and of course, weightlessness. Needless to say, all
the above factors have to be
taken into account and coun-
teracted by any who wish to
stand on the airless surface of
the Moon.

Magnetic charms

Now we need to understand
how the Van Allen Belts interact with the solar wind.
The Sun is the generator of
the solar wind which was first
detected in 1962, *after*
Kennedy's announcement that
the Americans were going to
the Moon. The Sun's activity
carries a continuous outward

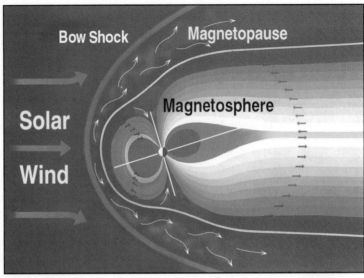

12. The solar wind and the magnetopause around Earth.

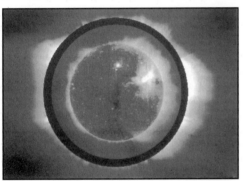

11. The Sun and the solar wind—the area beyond the
ring (ultraviolet light photograph).   ESA/SOHO

flow of a tenuous ionised gas (called plasma)
from the corona of the Sun, so the word 'wind'
is somewhat a misnomer. The solar wind extends throughout the solar system.

This relentless solar windflow is first inter-
cepted by the Earth at the magnetosheath: a
turbulent magnetic field beyond the magnetopause enclosed by a shockwave—the bow
shock. The magnetic field lines of the Sun and
the Earth reconnect across the sunward surface
at the magnetopause.

This magnetic reconnection allows energy
and particles to transfer from the solar wind to

the magnetosphere, and these charged particles
are henceforth under the control of our planet's
magnetic field. Our magnetosphere (see illustration 5) extends to 37,267 miles on the sunward side of the planet, but on the side of the
planet away from the Sun, as the solar wind
continues on its way through the solar system
it pulls the magnetosphere into a magnetotail
stretching many times this distance (12).

Within our magnetosphere, these charged particles, consisting mainly of protons and electrons, are trapped by the Van Allen belts. The
outer Van Allen belt contains charged particles
of both atmospheric and solar origin. The protons of the outer belt have much lower energies
than those of the inner belt, and their fluxes are
much higher. The protons of the inner Van
Allen belt originate from the decay of neutrons
produced when these high-energy cosmic rays
from outside the solar system collide with atoms and molecules form the planet's surface
and the Earth's atmosphere.[17] As the particles
approach either of the magnetic poles, the increase in the strength of the field causes them
to be reflected. On account of this so-called
magnetic mirror effect, the particles bounce
back and forth between the magnetic north and
south poles of our planet spiralling around
Earth's magnetic field lines. Superimposed

upon this spiralling motion are the slow drift of the positively-charged protons westwards; whilst the negatively-charged electrons drift eastwards.

The Earth's magnetic field protects astronauts from potentially lethal GCRs and SPEs for distances up to 500 miles above the Earth's surface. The year 1958 was one of extreme solar activity, one reason it was declared an International Geophysical Year. During the Apollo era, 1969 and 1970 were also years of high solar radiation—perhaps not the best time to venture out—given the lack of knowledge at that juncture.

The fact is that if the named astronauts really had been sent to the Moon during those years, they would all have suffered from exposure to solar radiation at one of the highest levels in the eleven-year solar cycle. According to one of our Whistle-Blowers, all of the test bio-organisms sent beyond our 500 miles safety zone have died from radiation exposure.[18] However in reality, we were not that ignorant, as we have seen from the amount of information collated by both the NASA and Soviet satellites. Does the remarkably elastic nature of these Van Allen radiation belts, on paper at least, merely reflect basic ignorance or a loss of innocence?

Micrometeorites and other macroproblems

In 1958 Carsbie Adams stated that small meteorites striking a spacecraft would explode upon impact and might penetrate the hull. Large meteorites would pass through the craft "as if it were made of cheese". Adams also concluded that if the craft were to enter a meteorite swarm, then the hull would be punctured faster than the crew could repair it—if indeed they had that capacity.

Constant etching by micrometeorites would destroy any exterior protective surface and reduce reflectivity which would of course increase the heat of the craft. A puncture by even one meteorite would ensure explosive decompression of the ship with the loss of all life aboard. Aluminium was found to be particularly susceptible to penetration while stainless steel fared rather better.

At the time of these assessments, it was understood that to build a craft strong enough to resist all impacts would be impossible. It came down to a decision based on how much of the rocket needed special protection, given that every square foot of hull added 2lbs of weight to the craft. Adequate coverage could then run into tons, mass which the Americans certainly were not capable of putting into orbit. So in the late 1950s it was thoroughly understood that any good size meteor, to quote Adams "would be fatal or near fatal", and he drew the parallel with the Wright brothers. "They might have been able to make their aeroplane a good deal safer," he wrote, "but then it would not have flown, being too heavy for their engine's capacity". The same could be said for the American's space craft.

13. The Russian Space Station MIR.   NASA

14. LEO and GEO Satellite orbits.

The vacuum conditions encountered in space demand that we encapsulate both our apparatus and our passengers in a vehicle and/or create equipment that can operate without an 'air' environment. For example, it was found in the early days that the cooling and electronics systems became problematic in space and that any moving mechanical parts required special lubricating systems. These tended to 'stick together' when operating in the vacuum of space.

The sunlight that arrives on the surface of Earth has been filtered through all the protective layers that we have been discussing. In space unfiltered sunlight—solar radiation—can cause illuminated portions of a spacecraft to rise to very high temperatures, while simultaneously the shaded portions often fall well below the freezing point of liquids such as water and storable rocket fuels. On spacecraft all fluid containers and fuel lines are commonly equipped with electrical heaters, while the overall temperature of the craft is moderated by rotating the craft along an axis perpendicular to the spacecraft/Sun line—officially called passive thermal control. The popular astronaut's term is 'Barbecue Mode'. Unmanned space probes to the inner planets have to be equipped with parasols to deflect unwanted solar heat. Those sent to the outer solar system, or to the lunar surface (where one night lasts for two of our Earth weeks) usually use radio-isotope heaters. (In other words they contain nuclear products.) The Apollo scientific packages allegedly set out on the lunar surface by the named Apollo crews were nearly all powered in such a manner. These items supposedly travelled to the Moon fixed to the outside of the craft and were set in place on the packages by our intrepid friends who had been specially trained in the manipulation of these hazardous items.

Astonishingly, it was conveniently estimated by NASA that the chances of meteor impact were relatively small, despite the fact that with the exception of the known meteor showers, (such as the Perseids) *these objects arrive totally unexpectedly.* Another category of space projectiles is accumulating at a rate of knots. Lost clothing (yes!) and tools, old pieces of satellite and booster rockets eventually collide with each other and create even more pieces. It is estimated that there are many thousands of such items of space junk, from the substantial through to the microscopic.

Trash in the geostationary Earth orbit (GEO—22,300 miles/35,888 kms up) can stay there for centuries. Objects in LEO (around 300 miles/480 kms up) eventually decay (fall out of orbit) but can nevertheless survive for months or years. A particle the size of a speck of paint has actually caused a small pit 0.02 inches wide on a Shuttle window (7th mission). A slightly larger speck of paint, about an inch in diameter, travelling at high speed, could in fact endanger the lives of the crew.

Radiation hazard

Astronaut Michael Collins stated in 1988 that: (on the way to Mars):

". . . Radiation from solar flares could kill the crew, if unprotected, within a couple of days".

National Geographic magazine Nov 1988

'Die Meister Tinkers'

Satellites in LEO are protected by the magnetosphere from the solar charged particles and a large percentage of the cosmic rays arriving from space. Vehicles operating on interplanetary missions or at GEO receive the full force of this radiation. NASA's Skylab orbited in LEO, 270 miles above the Earth from May 1973 to February 1974. Yet when a solar panel failed to deploy, Skylab was unable to operate its protection against the already intense solar heat. The astro-mechanics who went to rescue the overheated ship (with 'string and tape' in true NASA style) found *that all the stored film stock was ruined*. In practical terms this means that either it was fogged or that the high temperature conditions had rendered the emulsion useless.[19]

It has been recorded that during solar storms (periods of intensive activity on the solar surface affecting the solar wind) a space version of 'static electricity' builds up, resulting in electrical sparking that causes severe problems with the a spacecraft's on-board electronics. Better design, the fruits of experience, has reduced but not eliminated the effects of these influences.

'X' does not mark the spot

We have already heard from Douglas Arnold about the effects of radiation on equipment. Here is what Professor Clive Dyer had to say on the subject:

"And things like cameras," we asked, "would they not be subject to X-ray problems? For example, after the accident in Chernobyl the on-site photographer found that his film was fogged."

"There are problems with those things [cameras and imaging equipment] from all types of radiation," replied Clive Dyer. "X-rays are quite readily shielded, but if they did get in through thin optics, yes, they would fog any film. But all these particles we are talking about, the cosmic rays and the solar particles produce effects in CCD (digital) cameras and on regular photographic film. There is a background level of bright spots you get all the time."

TechnoSpeak

Information from Kodak's 1950s Color Data publication

Protection from Heat

- Neither regular nor tropical packing is heat proof. Regardless of the type of packing, do not leave films near steam pipes or other sources of heat. In warm weather, do not leave them on the top floors of uninsulated buildings or in closed automobile compartments.
- During summer heat (over 75°F/24°C) in temperate or tropical zones, store films in moisture-tight packing in iceboxes or mechanical refrigerators, preferably the latter.
- *When intended for professional work, films in moisture-tight packing should always be stored in a refrigerator.*

  (emphasis added)
- Where possible, the maximum storage temperature should be 60°F if the films are to be used within three months, and 50°F/10°C if it is necessary to store the films for a longer period of time.
- Keeping effects can be arrested almost completely for long periods of time by actually freezing the film in one of the freezing units commercially available. Storage in a unit of this type at zero°F is an ideal way to keep films, provided they are in moisture-tight packing.
- When special storage precautions are not practical, it should be borne in mind that a moderate temperature and relative humidity, such as 60°F/15.5°C with 40% relative humidity, are better than a low temperature with high relative humidity, such as 40°F/4.4°C with 80% relative humidity.

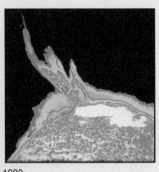

Solar prominence

1969   1973-Skylab   1980

Centre: 1973 Skylab image of a sunspot leaping approximately 376,00 miles/588,000 kms out into space.   NASA

Interesting! We were not aware of any such background level of spots on any Apollo duplicate transparencies that we have examined.

"Again," Clive continued, "the cosmic rays [GCRs] are pretty acceptable but when you get those huge flare enhancements, Star Trackers and other systems such as the Hubble Space Telescope and probes like Galileo get confused, go wrong, and are unusable for a period of time. During the peak of a flare, even the Hubble Telescope is pretty near unusable. There are times when you have to forget about the data, and just throw it away."

We were well aware that the Hubble Telescope orbits *below* the Van Allen belts.

"So the X-ray situation actually varies?" we then asked.

"Compared with these [solar] particles," Clive responded, "solar X-rays are not very penetrating and are readily stopped. However, they are often signatures of solar particle events, during which you might not have a usable system. These SPEs are most definitely a problem, their penetrating radiation goes through many centimetres of material. In fact sometimes it gets worse as it goes through material."

We knew that the Apollo missions were all scheduled at around a time of solar maximum and that at such a time, fifteen of the daily quota of solar flares emitted detectable X-ray energies.

"So radiation really is a problem for electronic equipment and cameras?"

"Right, it is, yes," Said Clive. "For example in the MIR Space Station (13), on average three times a day the laptop computers crash."

"So how would you categorise the type of problem that would be encountered?" we enquired.

"The background noise problem really," replied Clive. "The background level of events. Average flares last a couple of days and come along approximately every month. But the real big ones are only two or three per solar cycle."

In recent years, minimum shield thickness recommendations for manned spacecraft have been published, particularly in reference to long

---

Just passing through

Cosmic rays have been known to penetrate integrated circuits in spacecraft autopilots and to alter data and commands! These rays can also deliver a radiation dose to the human crew.

When galactic cosmic rays pass through matter (inanimate or animate) the atoms in their path become agitated in relation to the radiation frequency—leaving the atom either positively or negatively charged. The electrons can become so agitated that they can either eject from their normally stable orbit further from the nucleus or even eject from the atom altogether, leaving behind an ionised atom. This creates a free radical. Ionised atoms are chemically reactive, and within a living cell exposed to such radiation, the molecules are subject to these chemical changes. The DNA is then capable of genetic mutation.

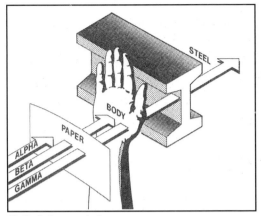

15. Radiation penetration.

journeys to Mars.[20]

Nature ignores statistical averages and disabling SPEs can occur during any voyage *at any time*. Provision for a storm shelter *within* the spacecraft is required, with shielding more than four times the minimum recommended amount. This is the density considered to be adequate enough to protect the human body in a worst-case scenario, i.e. a maximum dosage of radiation. According to leading American radiation experts: "Not even 30 cm of aluminium prevents astronauts from receiving a disabling dose (above 1,000 mSv/100 rem) from the conceivable, but highly unlikely, worst-case event". Remembering that the British John Davidson considers 100 rem quite enough to kill rapidly, any scenario worse than that is hard to imagine.

These American scientists also report:

From the viewpoint of radiation protection, the most hazardous space environment we have discussed is free space, unprotected by magnetic fields, atmospheres, or planetary bodies. Long-term exposure to such a space radiation environment can be expected on the long-duration mission to Mars and its moons, and on space stations in Geosynchronous orbit. In this environment astronauts will receive a dose of 200 to 500 mSv [20-50 rem] per year (depending on solar activity) from galactic cosmic radiation. In addition, radiation doses up to, or exceeding, 400 mSv

[40 rem] can be anticipated from solar energetic particle events.

About 7.5 cm of aluminium shielding is required in all habitable areas of spacecraft on long-duration missions if we wish to ensure that astronauts receive a dose less than 500 mSv [50 rem] per year.

During the August 1972 solar flare the radiation dose would have been about 960 rem with no spacecraft shielding. This falls to 40 rem with 9 cm of aluminium shielding. The higher dose is lethal, while the shielded dose would have resulted in no short-term health problems for astronauts in general.[21]

For short exposures, a dose of about *118 rem is lethal to 10% of human recipients, and about 345 rem to 50%*.[22]

Other American scientists have this to say:

The worst-case solar flare dose suggests that there is a potential for all human activity in free space to be interrupted, at infrequent intervals, unless extreme measures are taken to protect astronauts and space workers.[23]

The art of prophesy

As we can see, these complex reports dissect various frameworks with much talk of the size of a storm shelter in relation to total inner volume of the craft. These reports also calculate to what extent radiation dosages can be affected by the astronaut spending specific portions of time within the storm shelter, irrespective of the solar flare activity.

As one cannot predict solar flares, would it not be preferable to calculate all spacecraft protection requirements in terms of the worst-case scenario, independent of the length of the trip? After all the chances of an SPE for lunar travellers is no less due to its relative nearness to Earth, compared with Mars' distance from Earth. And lunar travellers of the 1960s were *in no way* protected from any such event, despite this vain attempt to justify the good health of the named Apollo astronauts from Brian Welch of NASA:

Regarding the supposition that the film should be fogged from cosmic rays, well indeed there were cosmic rays in space

---

Radiation reality

The intensity of space debris and radiation has been considered to be so low that no special protection has been built into manned spacecraft so far.   *Your Spaceflight Manual* David Ashcroft & Patrick Collins 1990

Alternative radiation reality

" Cosmic particles are dangerous, come from all sides, and require at least two meters (6 ft 6 inches) of solid shielding around all living organisms."   *Prospects For Interstellar Travel* John A Maudling 1992

[during Apollo] and you have the radiation flux that you have to deal with out there. We understood that, we monitored the Sun very, very carefully, we did not send expeditions to the Moon at times when there was the possibility of a particle event on the Sun. We didn't want to subject the astronauts to any radiation from a solar flare or a prominence or an event like that, we thought it through very carefully. We planned our way through that.

Yes, it does appear that NASA planned its way through that part of the script!

In 1958 Carsbie Adams concluded that the rule of thumb should be: to protect things that cannot be repaired in space together with the people who ride in the craft, so that they could fix the problems. This fundamental principle seems to have been overlooked. Was NASA therefore playing 'Russian Solar Flare Roulette'—with their first space travellers to another world—'pulling the trigger' once per day? Or could it be that these particular astronauts were not really going into dangerous territory, so there was no need for any such precautions?

Another Galactic Ghoul for NASA

Some of the scientists who work on NASA's unmanned spacecraft projects such as the Mars probes have blamed equipment failures on the 'Great Galactic Ghoul'. A large cartoon mural of this ghoul featured in at least one TV documentary on the Jet Propulsion Laboratories, NASA/JPL, California, where the design work for many space probes is undertaken. With an uncanny resemblance to NASA's attitude towards radiation, when we mentioned this 'ghoul' to Bill Wood, our Goldstone/JPL contact, he pleaded ignorance regarding the existence of this mural.[24]

Concerning this particular galactic cosmic radiation ghoul, in the late '90s scientists currently assume that these GCRs are generated from sources within the galaxy and confined within it for tens of millions of years by its complex and weak galactic magnetic field. These GCRs, the most energetic of the three principal types of radiation, are of the lowest intensity but have the largest fraction of highly ionising heavy nuclei—such as oxygen, neon, magnesium, silicon and iron. Irregularities in

---

Lunar reality

Solar Wind

Solar Wind

The Moon *totally unprotected* from the solar wind and SPEs.

The American Lunar Orbiter *Explorer 35*
July 19 1967 mission confirmed:
• The near total absence of a lunar magnetic field;
• The absence of radiation zones or belts;
• The absence of an ionosphere.
These findings indicate that there is no protection from the full force of the solar wind for anyone whilst standing on the lunar surface—and that means anywhere on that surface.
The solar wind is carried throughout the solar system and is present even when sunlight is not actually striking the lunar surface.

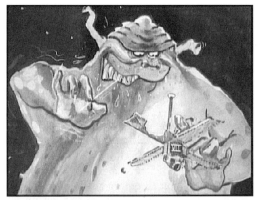

16. NASA/JPL's Great Galactic Ghoul.   NASA/JPL

the flow of these GCRs accelerate these particles, which travel at nearly the speed of light (as currently expressed).

Travel—a nasty dose of medicine

Returning to Professor Clive Dyer again:

"When we spoke about eleven months previously Clive, you said that radiation is 'the biggest show-stopper affecting mankind's exploration of the Universe'."

"It's a severe hazard that needs to be taken into account," confirmed Clive. "The galactic cosmic rays are pretty well known, they [NASA] know the solar cycle effects on them. Unshielded they are something like 50 rem a year, which is pretty severe."

"What about solar flares?" we asked.

"Solar flares are the real nasties," replied Clive, "GCRs are bad enough, but what is worse, if intense solar flares come along, they are potentially very harmful in the short time scale."

"The ability to predict solar fares seems to be very..."

We had hardly finished our question when Clive interrupted: "...it's very poor! Yes it is! What you can say is that you are likely to get, say two or three very severe flares each solar maximum, somewhere spread around that maximum."

"But apart from the big solar flares," we continued, "there are small solar flares daily or weekly aren't there? Surely, solar flares occur all the time?"

"Not all the time, no," said Clive. "There are small radio and optical emissions, but they are very much grouped around the solar maximum period. However, there are solar flares and then there are solar particle-producing flares. Solar particle flares are a subset of general solar flares. These solar particle flares don't occur all the time, they are also very much grouped in the years around solar maximum. You do tend to get four quiet years out of eleven when you don't get any worth speaking of. So those would be the years to go for if you were travelling in space."

On the chart (on the next page) we have highlighted the month of each claimed Apollo mission. The italicised numbers highlight the ideal times for venturing into space: from December 1974 to May 1977 and from September 1984 to March 1987. Notice the very high count of 839 flares for 'Apollo 10', an average of 27.96 flares per day! We know that quantity does not equate with quality, for although that May 1969 count is around 300 events higher than the 515 flares registered for August 1972 we also know that it was during the August '72 minimal period of solar activity that the greatest flare ever registered by human beings erupted, rating 960 rems. Instant death!

Individual flares are basically random occurrences, superimposed on the 11.6 year cycle. Nonetheless:

- There can be a high flare count for short periods, even during the low of the cycle.
- There can be a low count for short periods during the peak of the cycle.
- Immense proton and X-ray emitting flares can randomly occur at any portion of the cycle.
- It is virtually impossible to predict solar flares!

Despite these four facts, the named Apollo astronauts (allegedly) sauntered out into space at a time of high solar activity and all of them escaped without a hair on their heads being harmed. They must have been issued with a special password because the solar energetic particles associated with larger events generally last one or two days.

Grouped solar flares													
Year	Jan	Feb	Mar	Apr	May	June	July	Aug	Sept	Oct	Nov	Dec	Total
1967	796	589	1009	694	771	629	907	911	573	946	775	1109	9709
1968	1037	773	519	460	768	697	573	611	616	772	556	**640**	8022
1969	581	504	669	655	**839**	694	**489**	551	540	643	**566**	422	7153
1970	466	646	578	**688**	722	836	954	780	811	797	687	667	8632
1971	**589**	**505**	387	546	461	430	**713**	**673**	518	375	431	394	6031
1972	384	599	621	**361**	614	541	404	515	371	408	175	**210**	5203
1973	221	171	410	453	388	270	232	182	353	201	136	163	3180
1974	127	148	.079	364	255	204	360	187	270	366	153	*081*	*2594*
1975	*068*	*082*	*069*	*019*	*042*	*085*	*196*	*346*	*068*	*038*	*127*	*025*	*1165*
1976	*069*	*018*	*180*	*060*	*038*	*048*	*006*	*047*	*057*	*023*	*013*	*055*	*0614*
1977	*054*	*077*	*018*	*076*	*064*	210	140	140	250	252	107	336	1724
1978	274	588	338	526	330	460	533	346	554	499	418	648	5514
1979	926	781	731	731	907	772	750	821	901	1018	888	786	10012
1980	703	689	621	1092	811	956	763	720	924	988	1027	838	10132
1981	578	782	914	915	658	592	893	982	680	836	773	615	9218
1982	631	766	803	490	553	769	696	753	615	544	564	748	7932
1983	332	220	337	346	609	561	427	389	289	298	088	152	4048
1984	353	461	366	440	492	185	151	161	*095*	*036*	*092*	*069*	*2901*
1985	*104*	*029*	*038*	*119*	*129*	*116*	*185*	*053*	*025*	*108*	*019*	*050*	*975*
1986	*051*	*158*	*054*	*056*	*068*	*003*	*071*	*012*	*014*	*174*	*056*	*013*	*730*
1987	*036*	*007*	*052*	192	205	061	132	185	172	198	273	114	1627
1988	217	109	413	328	274	551	502	375	513	429	508	584	4803
1989	689	539	658	485	686	971	473	684	699	535	640	507	566

'Apollo 8' December '68 'Apollo 10' May '69 'Apollo 11' July '69 'Apollo 12' November '69 'Apollo 13' April '70   Data from
'Apollo 14' January-February '71 'Apollo 15' July-August '71 'Apollo 16' April '72 'Apollo 17' December '72   NOAA/René

But some of these flares can deliver more energetic particles in a few hours than GCRs could deliver in 10 years. That is potent and quite enough for a lethal dose, under flimsy shielding conditions!

Official opinions appear to differ as to the damage potential. Here is a paragraph by the US Naval Research Lab published in 1987:[25]

Most solar energetic particles are of low energy, below 100 MeVs protons, but heavier nuclei are present.

A statement which is in direct contradiction to the following from John H Mauldin PhD. With a Masters in Physics, Mauldin is a member of the American Astronautical Society and a consultant to NASA on the Voyager space missions:

Solar flares can deliver GeV protons in the same energy range as most cosmic particles, but at much higher intensities. Increase of energy accounts for most of the increased radiation danger because GeV protons or their products will penetrate several meters of material.[26]

In the grouped solar flare chart we can see that the accepted theoretical apex of the 20th solar cycle was from December 1968 through to December 1969. Around this period Apollos '8', '10', '11' and '12' allegedly left the protection provided by the atmosphere and the Earth's magnetic fields and entered deep space.

The record states that the Apollo missions spent approximately one hour travelling through the increased radiation trapped within the belts. (This time period is calculated on the narrowest width of the belts). Yet this exposure is minuscule compared to one big solar flare. Here is John Mauldin again on this:

Solar flares (or star) flares of protons, an occasional and severe hazard on the way out of and into, planetary systems, can give a dose of *hundreds* to *thousands* of rem over a few hours at a distance of miles from Earth. Such doses are fatal and *millions of times* greater than the permitted dose. Death is likely after 500 rem in any short time, whereas 500 rem spread over a lifetime is not likely to cause problems although clearly not safe (emphasis added).[27]

And here is an extract from a paper by Dr. Percival D McCormack, the Manager for Operational Medicine, in the Life Sciences Division of NASA:

In the case of...deep space, the greatest acute threat to humans is the solar particle event (SPE)—that solar flare actively associated with the emission of high-energy ionising particles. SPEs are transient in nature, occur randomly (and almost exclusively during the solar maximum period) and consist of protons and alpha particles with energies in the range from a few KeV to several hundred MeV. The anomalously large event (AL) can deliver over 600 rem to the blood-forming organs (BFO) which would be acutely lethal. Such events occur at a frequency of 1 to 2 every 4 years. The AL event of August 1972 would have delivered 960 rem with no shielding.

The other important source of energetic particles outside the Earth's magnetosphere is solar flares. Flares deliver very high doses over short periods (a few hours or days). Without shielding, exposure to anomalously large events would be deadly to astronauts.
Exposure to an anomalously large event particle flux during EVA in a 'soft' space suit would result in a lethal dose.

And regarding the "difficulties of prediction of SPEs" McCormack says:

The capability of predicting individual solar fluence rates and of anticipating which flare will produce energetic protons escaping the vicinity of the Sun and reaching the orbit of the Earth [or Moon] has not advanced to the point of being able to predict the precise day an event will occur at the Earth [or Moon]. The ability to predict the occurrence of a SPE and its subsequent peak fluence, is still in a primitive stage of development, particularly for events originating from flares in the eastern solar hemisphere.[28]

QUESTION: How did NASA predict that there were not going to be any solar flares specifically during these missions, when by their own admission, they were unable to predict solar flares at all? How could a vomiting, vision-impaired visitor to deep space have performed his duties?

After looking at the radiation effects above, it is clear that it would only require one flare delivering a dose as low as one or two hundred rem (2 Sv), to pose a potentially serious risk to an Apollo astronaut on the way to the Moon.[29] Surely, even with the best rockets in the world, if their astronauts were getting zapped by radiation, it was not going to be worth the effort!

Here is Michael Collins again, of 'Apollo 11' writing in the *National Geographic* magazine November 1988:

Radiation poses a major concern. Human response to harmful radiation can range from nausea and vomiting to fever and death. Long term effects, which may not arise until years after exposure, include cataracts, tumours and leukaemia.

The named Apollo astronauts are, however, a remarkably healthy bunch considering that during the nine alleged trips to the Moon 1,506 solar flares were recorded—an average of 16.92 per day per mission. J A McKinnon NOAA expert on solar flares states that 10 to 20% of solar flares could be considered a Medium X-ray emitter event and 1%, the deadliest of all, a Class X event.[30] So these astronauts should have encountered from 16 to 33 Class M events and at least one Class X event *on each mission*.

The Oscar for the category 'meeting misfortune during Apollo' goes to the mission combining the highest number of recorded solar flares during the greatest amount of time spent in space. And the winner is—'Apollo 15'.

Their mission occupied 14.6% of the overall Apollo profile of 89 days and the average of 268 solar flares recorded during that time was 17.7% of the total number of flares that actually occurred during the Apollo period. Considering the inability of the agency to clad its craft against lethal radiation—and with figures like these—how long each astronaut actually spent on the surface of the Moon, exposed to

taken from astronaut dosimeters functioning in LEO well below the Van Allen Belts, as we will show shortly.

When astronaut Jim Irwin died on August 8 1991 aged 61, the cause was said to be cardiac arrest. Interestingly, Irwin had agreed to talk to Whistle-Blower Kaysing about his Apollo experiences but the meeting never took place, as he died in the meantime. Jim Irwin had previously told Andrew Chaikin that on the Moon he felt the presence of God. He also felt strongly that the special crystalline rock that he had discovered sitting on a pedestal of rock, had been prepared for him.

When he made that statement was Irwin blowing a whistle?

We shall never know.

Year	Mission	Days in space	% total days	Avge flares /mission	% total flares/mission
1968	'Apollo 8'	21 - 27 Dec = 7	7.9%	145	9.6%
1969	'Apollo 10'	18 - 26 May = 8	8.9%	224	14.8%
	'Apollo 11'	16 - 24 July = 9	10.1%	142	9.4%
	'Apollo 12'	14- 24 Nov = 10	11.2%	189	12.5%
1970	'Apollo 13'	11 - 17 Apr = 7	7.9%	161	10.6%
1971	'Apollo 14'	31 Jan-9 Feb = 10	11.2 %	145	9.6%
	'Apollo 15'	26 July-7 Aug = 13	14.6%	268	17.7%
1972	'Apollo 16'	16 - 27 April = 12	13.5%	144	9.5%
	'Apollo 17'	07 - 19 Dec = 13	14.6%	88	5.8%

During the total of 89 days spent in space 1,506 solar flares were officially recorded.
Of these 1,506 at least 15.6 events were classified as deadly by the NOAA.
At an average of 1.73 of these Class X events per mission, surely at least one of the Apollo crews should have encountered such a killer?
How did the named Apollo astronauts who walked on the Moon survive without any radiation protection?

lethal radiation, is fairly academic. Nevertheless, anyone with an inclination for statistics will find a chart for the lunar EVAs in the Appendix.

Of the twelve men who allegedly spent time on the lunar surface, to date (June 1998) only one has since died. What are the odds on this outcome, after the evidence presented in this chapter concerning the dangers of radiation? Officially, we are informed that the alleged maximum dose experienced by any astronaut (to 1987) was only about 18 rem![31] Which may well be true, but may *actually* be readings

If all goes well . . .

This section title is one of NASA's stock phrases. The likelihood of all actually going well with the rocket riders when it comes to radiation is getting slimmer by the page. As it only requires a dose of 35 rem to induce vomiting, nausea and diarrhoea, and 75 rem to result in 10% fatalities, surely any Apollo astronaut, without protective shielding is playing 'Russian Solar Flare Roulette' (or should we say American Solar Flare Roulette?) Will he or won't he become incapacitated during his journey to and from the Moon? Clearly, any of these named Apollo astronauts could have become very ill at any time with the resultant incapacity to perform his duties.

QUESTION: Can you imagine Aldrin or Armstrong so sick that they are throwing up into their spacesuits and suffocating on their own vomit?

QUESTION: Can you imagine watching them dying?

QUESTION: Would you take the chance on live TV broadcast to the world that everything would go well?

QUESTION: Is not this circumstance alone sufficient for NASA to have taken the decision to fake the entire Apollo record and adopt the Surrogate program?

QUESTION: What would your decision have been?

Ironically, that 'Barbecue Mode' we mentioned earlier—rotating the unprotected craft—actually would have ensured that the Apollo astronauts were like chickens on a spit: cooked, fried, baked, radiated (call it what you will) on all sides! The crew would have been better protected from solar radiation by not rotating the CSM and using an appropriate shield on the sunward side of the craft. However such protection provision would have been incompatible with the payload capability of the Saturn V, as we shall see in the next chapter.

Here is another extract from the *Aerospace America* paper published in October 1987:

Aluminium shielding thickness is most effective at stopping primary heavy nuclei, the type of cosmic radiation that causes the most damage to living tissue. Components of the annual cosmic-ray dose equivalent vs. shielding thickness are shown below at a time of minimum solar activity. High energy protons interact with shielding material to generate additional secondary particles.

With about 7.5 cm of aluminium, the normal dose equivalent is reduced from 50 rem to 35 rem. Calculations for a very large solar flare series, like events of August 1972, show that the lethal unshielded dose of about 1,000 rem is reduced to 40 rem with 9 cm of aluminium shielding.[32]

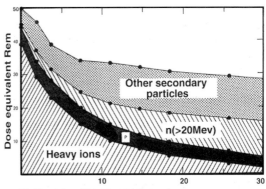

18. Aluminium Shielding thickness (cm) required at solar minimum.

Rein Silberberg, Chen H Tsao, James H Adams Jr—US Naval Research Lab, and John R Letaw—Severn Communications Corp.

However, the named Apollo astronauts did not enjoy the benefits of any aluminium shielding to help protect them from SPEs during their Apollo sorties.

Anyone for another game of American Solar Flare Roulette?

Sir Bernard Lovell

For another expert opinion on this serious matter of radiation dangers we contacted Sir Bernard Lovell of The Nuffield Radio Astronomy Laboratories at Jodrell Bank, England.

He told us:

In the 1960s I was a frequent visitor both to the United States and to the Soviet Union and I was surprised by the attitude to this danger [of solar radiation] by the authorities in the two countries. In America one of the principal medical advisors to NASA was unconcerned and dismissed the idea that there should be a concern for the relative [sic] short astronaut flights to the moon then in prospect. The Soviet attitude about radiation danger and, indeed, to the whole problem of the safety of cosmonauts was in marked contrast. If one asked about their manned lunar plans the response was always that they would attempt a manned lunar landing when they were confident of securing the safe return to earth of their cosmonauts.[33]

101

If advisors to NASA 'dismissed the idea that there should be a concern for the relative short astronaut flights to the moon', could it have been because they already had fully evolved their 'Plan B'—namely the Apollo Simulation/ Surrogate program?

"It was easier to tell everyone that the radiation levels were OK!" said one of our Whistle-Blowers.

18. Professor Bernard Lovell with Professor Alla Masevich— Vice President of the Soviet Academy of Sciences (who was responsible for Sputnik tracking arrangements) during a visit to Jodrell Bank Radio Telescope, February 1960.   PRESS ASSN

The midas touch

When we were talking to HJP ("Douglas") Arnold, previously employed by Kodak, about radiation and film stock, he made some comments concerning crew safety.

"Radiation is more of a problem than anything else," said Douglas. "NASA took this into account when planning the Apollo missions and they had physicists around the world carefully monitoring the Sun's activity during the missions. Fortunately, because nature can do unpredictable things, a solar flare never happened. They were protected against normal

levels of radiation by the CSM of course. Though on the Moon they would have been totally unprotected outside the LM. However, a form of cosmic ray did sometimes enter the module. There are famous stories of the astronauts 'seeing' a trail go across their eyes, as it were. It was the impact of a cosmic ray. Actually I remember Buzz Aldrin talking about this in particular."

The Biomedical Results of Apollo lists these flashes as "High energy cosmic rays entering the spacecraft and passing through the astronaut's eyes". Buzz Aldrin asserted several times that he had seen these flashes in the darkness of the capsule, much to the annoyance of Armstrong.[34]

QUESTION: Was this event actually experienced by Aldrin, or was he voicing information on this phenomenon that had been gathered by other means?

QUESTION: Was Aldrin making sure this information got onto the official Apollo record as validation for their mission?

QUESTION: Why would mention of this event during a post-Apollo debriefing annoy Armstrong to the extent that the historian Chaikin would feel it worth recording?

Farouk El-Baz, a NASA geologist of great influence at the time of Apollo, during an interview with Saga Magazine, stated that tests made on the astronauts (no specific names mentioned) ascertained that these cosmic rays penetrated the skull, the brain and the optic nerve. Later in the same interview he contradicted himself and stated that these rays only penetrated the optic nerve. Many astronauts had seen flashes when they closed their eyes, he said. He then added insult to injury by inferring that Ken Mattingley ('Apollo 16') had a physical constitution different to that of his colleagues! "...His optic nerve, whatever—was such that he was not able to record the light flashes that the other guys had been recording."[35] Forgive us, but this vagueness concerning a tested medical phenomenon does rather smack of make-believe. The use of the word 'whatever' is an Americanism whereby one word usefully fills out for the rest of an unspoken phrase.

102

> **Space balls**
>
> Remembering that these astronauts are always orbiting *below* the Van Allen radiation belts, *1996* space scientists have analysed Shuttle astronauts' helmets under an electron microscope.
>
> They found that laser-like paths had ploughed through the perspex visors, and through the back of the helmet.
>
> If this is the trail of atomic destruction in a relatively safe zone, rays ploughing through the eyeball and then the skull, surely would have wreaked far more serious damage to the brain tissue of the named *Apollo* astronauts.
>
> Just as age restraints are being relaxed for astronauts, doubts are emerging about the effects of cosmic radiation on the older astronaut.
>
> In July 1996, Dr. Bernard Rabin of Maryland University, maintained the 1955 Dr. Herman Schaefer scenario, namely that one's life expectancy is shortened if one travels in space. Cosmic radiation damages nerve cells and Dr. Rabin postulated that the older the astronaut, the greater the danger.

Following Douglas Arnold's spontaneous comment concerning cosmic rays, we asked him for his opinion on the dangers of radiation and its effect on the astronauts.

"Who knows how exposure to above normal—if not lethal—radiation levels have affected the Apollo mission astronauts over the years? But, to the best of my knowledge, in a potentially very, very bad scenario, no major radiation incident affected the Apollo astronauts. However, you are absolutely right," continued Douglas, "if there had been a major solar flare during an Apollo mission to the Moon it would have been extremely serious to say the least—and not just for the film stock. In fact it would have been lethal [for the astronauts]. So far, I am not aware that we have a technology which can protect the astronauts, even during minimal solar flares."

QUESTION: If such technology was not available in 1996, when this remark was made, then how could it possibly have been available in the 1960s?

Now consider this quote from Andrew Chaikin, who is either Whistle-Blowing or being too poetic about the 'Apollo 16' mission—Mattingley had left the CSM 'Casper':

The Sun was so staggeringly bright that Mattingley immediately pulled down his gold-plated visor...in [Casper] he had seen stars: where were all the stars?
Charlie Duke [standing in Casper's hatch looking after the 50 foot umbilical line attached to Mattingley] kept saying, "My God, it's dark out here."

Mattingley was sure that the 'disappearance' of the stars was due to his gold visor. The doctors had advised him to leave the reflector down, *lest he be exposed to harmful solar radiation,* but he couldn't stand it any more. He blinked the visor open just long enough for the Universe to show a familiar face. (emphasis added)[36]

Just long enough to risk damage to himself too. And just long enough to imply that this is a fairytale. Perhaps the Universe was showing the familiar face of Mother Earth not 200 miles beneath him? Or could it be that this is an attempt at a whistle-blow by an otherwise muzzled astronaut? And how did image (19) —(from a TV recording) get passed for release—is this yet another Whistle-Blowing set up? For here is Schmitt allegedly walking on the surface of the Moon with his visor up and staring full into the 'sun' (or more likely some other light source). There is an interesting piece of dialogue that accompanies the NASA TV recordings of this particular mission:

Houston: "Hey, er Jack—we see your gold visor up—you may want to put it down, out here in the Sun."
Jack: "Well, I think I might...I can't see with it down—it's scratched!"

QUESTION: Why does Houston say, "Out *here*" and not "Out *there?*" Could it possibly be that Schmitt is not some two hundred and forty seven thousand miles away from the lights, camera and action but on the same planet as once trod that legendary director with the same name? We are of course referring to Mission Control *in* Houston!

QUESTION: In any event, how could a scratched visor prevent Schmitt from being able to see?

In true NASA contradictory style, the Apollo transcripts revised and edited by one Eric Jones (of whom more later) have Schmitt commenting on his scratched helmet within the LM cabin, three hours before rendezvous with the CSM.

19. TV frame depicting Schmitt with NO gold visor during an 'Apollo 17' EVA. NASA

185:55:11 Schmitt: "Let's do it. (Pause) I got a scratch on my helmet!"[37]

QUESTION: Has this line of dialogue been inserted in order to 'retrieve' the situation?

QUESTION: Since when has clear perspex been an adequate protection (especially for the eyes) against solar or galactic cosmic radiation?

QUESTION: In any event, surely it is absolute folly to walk on the surface of an atmosphereless planet with nothing more to protect the body from radiation and the further the risk of an unexpected solar flare than a linen-based space suit, a helmet that has an additional gold-coated perspex visor (but not used), gloves and plastic over-boots? And nowhere to hide should even a moderate solar flare occur.

If Schmitt really *had* been standing on the Moon, and there was a solar flare that had delivered a dose even as low as 35 rem, he could have been very unwell indeed whilst on the lunar surface, live on TV for all to witness. If there had been a more energetic flare he (or any astronaut in that position) would have been fatally affected.

QUESTION: Would that situation have been good for NASA's image and its assurance of continued funding?

QUESTION: Do you think NASA was really prepared to take the risk of such a disaster striking at any time?

All dressed up and nowhere to go

In December 1969 an article in the *National Geographic* magazine stated that:

> Part of the space suit assembly, the Thermal Meteroid Garment, also shielded the astronauts against those very high energy nuclear and electromagnetic particles that speed throughout the universe and would have a deadly effect when they strike human tissue—if there were no atmosphere to slow them down and stop them.

There is further description of 'Apollo 11's suits as: "many layered marvels of engineering that work like thermos bottles (remember Hasselblad?) and can stop micro-meteoroids travelling at 64,000 miles per hour, 30 times the speed of a military rifle bullet".[38]

Remembering that there is no atmosphere on the Moon and that micro-meteoroids are massless particles and can pass through anything, including a space craft, an astronaut's skull and

---

Hop along Conrad

There is a story of Conrad during 'Apollo 12' allegedly walking around on the surface they called the 'moon' in a pressure suit that was a fraction short in one leg.

Why? Well, apparently during a last minute suit fitting, he was not allowed to wear *used* tubed-underwear inside the space-ready suit. He therefore wore 'space-ready' long johns without tubes and had to *guess* how much shoulder room his water cooling tubes would take up, and he failed by $^1/_4$ inch on the right leg.

Yes, we too think it sounds rather ridiculous!

---

out through the other side of the space craft again. As another doubter has put it, NASA tell us that their layers of cloth, doped with silicon rubber, aluminium and a coating of Teflon, could stop particles that may be up to 2 gigavolts (2 billion eVs) of power.[39]

These suits were part of an inventory that included: "Heavily corrugated plastic over-boots that can resist temperatures from +180°F down to -180°F. Gloves that were covered with a fine mesh of chromium and nickel alloy to protect the glass-fibre and Teflon material of these gloves from abrasion."

"When pressurised to 3.5 lbs per square inch the suits were as hard as a football and added 190 lbs to the weight of a man standing on Earth—due to the gravity differential, this meant a burden of 31.66 lbs on the lunar surface. It also meant that their centre of gravity was altered and their activity hampered. Bending down would have been almost impossible."[40]

But in the 1989 publication detailing the 'true' story of the 'Apollo 11' Moon landing we are informed that ease of movement was a factor in the design of these suits and that when Armstrong was suited up and still in the Houston facilities, he dropped a film cassette on the floor and "...fairly easily bent down and picked it up".[41]

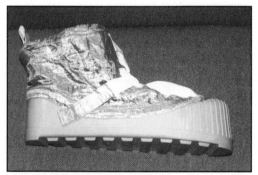

20. Cernan's right over-boot—original. AULIS

There are no signs of any movement problems on any recorded TV coverage that we have viewed. So who is telling the truth? Why do the accounts differ so dramatically and widely?

QUESTION: Had Armstrong not already discovered and learnt that during simulation practice on Earth?

QUESTION: If these suits were so effective, then what could they do in an atomic reactor? There are no signs of our nuclear workers being equipped with such a useful, life-enhancing spin-off from the 'space race'. Obviously when the Russians sent inspectors into the Chernobyl disaster area they were inadequately clad.[42]

21. Apollo space suit—replica. AULIS

'Lunarnaut': "...We quickly discover locomotion on the Moon has its own peculiar restrictions...I learn to get under way by thrusting my body forward, as though I were stepping into a wind. To stop, I dig in my heels and lean backward".[43]

22. Clearing up at Chernobyl—due to the radiation the photographer's film was badly fogged. NOVOSTI

In 1968, the 'Apollo 7' space suits weighing 15.21 lbs were 6.21 lbs heavier than the original Apollo design but apparently far more flameproof. These suits, more flexible than their predecessors were manufactured from layers of:

A. Aluminised Kapton.
B. Neoprene-coatedNylon.
C. Beta cloth (flameproof).
D. Sections of Chromel-R at the knees, elbows and shoulders. (Chromium & Nickel alloy heavy duty protection as in the gauntlets.)

David Shayler gives us another recipe for the 'Apollo 11' suit.[44] He is working from the outside in, so we have inserted the relevant layer letter in order for you to compare with the above list.

1. Five oz inner layer of Nomex.
2. Two-layer fire resistant, filament-coated Beta cloth, with extra protection at knees, elbows and shoulders (C&D).

This weighed 35 lbs and is the version for intravehicular activity which Collins wore within the CSM. While Armstrong and Aldrin donned theirs with another 20 lbs of material comprising:

3. Two layers of neoprene-coated Nylon. (B)
4. Seven layers of Beta/Kapton spacer laminate. (A)
5. One layer of Teflon-coated Beta fabric.

They also wore overshoes to protect the soles of their spacesuits from damage while transferring from Houston to the spacecraft. So Shayler in his account has an inside layer and an exterior layer unaccounted for in the first version.

The pressure helmet at that time consisted of a transparent polycarbonate shell attached to an aluminium neck ring designed to connect and lock onto the matching ring on the neck of the body suit. The helmet contained a feed port at the front and a vent port at the back through which the oxygen would flow to the face area.

The close-fitting hats that the astronauts wore underneath these pressure helmets were nicknamed 'Snoopy Hats' and look much the same today as then. In 1968 they enclosed communications equipment consisting of two microphones, two earphones, a dosimeter pocket and

23. Apollo space helmet. NASA

106

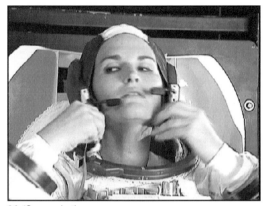

24. 'Snoopy hat'.   NASA

a 21-pin electrical connector.

While this suit was more bulky than the earlier models, the elbows and knees were fitted with 'bellows' so that movement was easier for the astronaut. Two versions of this suit were developed by ILC (the International Latex Corporation in Dover, Delaware, USA) the intravehicular and the extravehicular. The extravehicular suit being strengthened with 'additional protection from micrometeroids' by having an Integrated Thermal Meteroid overlayer. However, for 'Apollo 7', with no EVA scheduled, only the intravehicular suit was used.

By 1969 the spacesuit had acquired seventeen layers of material but the Shuttle spacesuit of 1996 had dwindled to only nine layers. This

suggests that whoever may have gone to the Moon was apparently given the best chance, in theory at least.

So what happened to the intervening layers? Apparently all the materials currently in use were existent at the time of the Apollo missions. Space has not changed its physical attributes and decreased the amount of danger it presents to the ill-equipped. The reason why the Shuttle astronauts need fewer layers is that they are not travelling outside their protective planetary environment.

Breathing space

In the closed circuit system of a spacesuit, carbon dioxide (the waste product of used air) expelled by the astronaut has nowhere to go, and excessive build up of this CO_2 would be toxic. Therefore a chemical 'scrubber' is inserted into the Personal Life Support System (PLSS). Lithium Hydroxide molecules were introduced which reacted with the CO_2 molecules. This system, we are informed, had the advantage of being light in weight and only required a little water to work at its maximum and provide several hours of PLSS time. The astronaut provides this amount of water through his natural body evaporation (sweat) within the confines of the spacesuit. The disadvantage of this system is that there is no possibility of recycling the end product, lithium carbonate. It therefore has to be expelled from the suit.

25. Getting into a space suit in the 1990s.   NASA

26. Long John underwear with tubes attached   NASA
across the back, as worn in the 1990s.

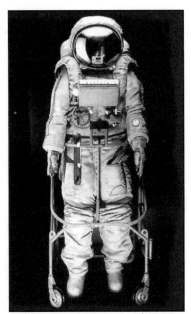

27. Soviet Krechet lunar space suit.   SMITHSONIAN INSTITUTE

28. Recent Soviet space suit.

QUESTION: Where are the signs of this discharge around the Apollo astronauts during EVAs? Surely sometimes we should see the 'vapour' of these expelled lithium carbonates making contact with the exterior environment? NASA does not address this point. But why do they feel the need to be coy about the elimination of these and other waste products? Surely every astronaut should be accompanied from time-to-time by a small personal 'exhaust cloud' which, of course, would not make for

exciting photography. We might not be able to see the flags on their spacesuits!

In addition, the result of the astronauts personal cooling process, steam (according to rocket expert Bill Wood) or expelled ice particles (according to writer/researcher Ralph René), would also have been visible periodically as it was forced outside the spacesuits and vaporised. If these were genuine images from the Moon we should see evidence in the photos of cooling discharges and other elimination

---

Stop press!

". . . in that cold and boundless emptiness . . . [space]"

". . . shield me from the blistering +150°F surface heat of the lunar morning."

David Scott, 'Apollo 15' *National Geographic* 1973

There is no atmosphere to retain the heat that hits the Moon although the regolith (lunar surface) will retain some heat. NASA is continually attempting to inform us that space is COLD, but this is not true. It is as hot in the sunlight of deep space as it is on the sunlit surface of the Moon.

Astronauts blow hot and cold

Jim Irwin is quoted as saying that he became dehydrated due to not selecting sufficient cooling in his liquid-cooled underwear, and that he had no replacement electrolytes available.

However, on another occasion he informed the author that they had to dry out their suits after nine hours continuous wear.[45]

Conversely, Russian cosmonauts supposedly wrapped themselves in layers and layers of wool to keep *warm*, they did not need any cooling equipment . . .

---

from the astronaut's spacesuits.[46]

It would appear that we have been given a false representation of what it is really like for astronauts to be on the Moon. Perhaps the depiction of expelled waste, steam or ice particles in an Earth-bound studio was impossible to fake so, like the stars, they ignored them altogether.

In 1996 NASA spokesman, Glenn Lutz, the sub-systems manager at Johnson Space Center assured us that NASA are still using the lithium hydroxide system, as the advantages of recycling do not match the disadvantages of carrying extra weight which any other method would require.[47] We suggest that, given the limitations of the Saturn V launch vehicle, any increased payload was not an option in the 1960s either.

In any event, one fastidious researcher has stated that there was something seriously wrong with NASA's description of the Apollo PLSS. It was, it would seem, too small for the job.[48]

The internal capacity of the PLSS was a mere 2.7 cu ft. and designed to last four hours on the lunar surface in terms of its oxygen supply, CO_2 scrubber, dehumidifier, two water bladders, heat exchanger, body temperature condi-

tioning, communication systems to Mission control, four litres of water and electrical power for everything. Close call for 'Apollo 12' then, with a lunar EVA of 3 hours and 56 minutes!

These units had to warm up the astronauts when in the cold of the shadow regions, perhaps averaging minus 180°F, and instantly alternate with cooling capabilities when in 180-200°F sunlight. For these ridiculously small PLSS back packs to have really operated as claimed, they must, as Ralph René has so beautifully put it, "have been fabricated by the Wizard of Oz".[49]

We know that the lunar surface is an utterly hostile environment for human beings. Astronauts would need to wear their pressurised space suits at all times, without which it would take no more than thirty seconds for their blood to boil. If the suit were to lose pressure no astronaut would be 'usefully conscious' for longer than twelve seconds. Safety measures could never be broken, without incurring extreme danger.

Current evaluations of the amount of protection required from the dangers of radiation, for colonies of people living on the Moon require that they live underground at a depth of at least 32ft/10m. Even then, our scientists would not guarantee against genetic mutations of the DNA which could result in physical deformities in future generations of 'Moon Humans'.[50] We cannot say whether this calculation is based on realistic and honest information or if it is a continuation of that old chestnut, left over from the 1945 A-bomb tests: "Two foot of the good earth will protect you, soldier boy".

"They say Manhattan"

The American National Council on Radiation Protection (NCRP) has established a scale of dose equivalent limits:

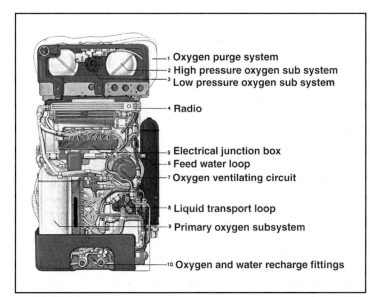

1 Oxygen purge system
2 High pressure oxygen sub system
3 Low pressure oxygen sub system

4 Radio

5 Electrical junction box
6 Feed water loop
7 Oxygen ventilating circuit

8 Liquid transport loop

9 Primary oxygen subsystem

10 Oxygen and water recharge fittings

29. Main PLSS systems.

General population: 0.5 rem per year
Radiation workers: 5.0 rem per year
Volunteer astronauts   50.0 rem per year
Idem, with a limit of 200.0 rem/10 years

You might ask: If the Apollo astronauts were 'volunteers' does that also imply that there were also conscripted astronauts? If so, would they 'benefit' from these limits or were they expendable? It is certainly a good question, because history shows that when new technologies are being developed the interests of the individual are often sacrificed for the 'project', as was the case during the development of the WWII A-bomb Operation Echo.

In 1955 the stated expert opinion on galactic rays was that our atmosphere shielded us to the equivalent of a three-foot thick lead plate. We now know the correct model is more like 32ft/10m of water. Hence the 32 feet of soil for a lunar base. Upwards of 23 miles from the Earth's surface there is total penetration by all these cosmic rays. Additionally, some primary rays could penetrate the atmosphere down to about 13 miles. However, we are assured that most of this primary atomic radiation is believed to be "within accepted dosage limits". But the truth of that statement depends upon who establishes the limits and for what reason those limits are defined. Are these stated limits to protect the astronaut, or are they there to sanction space travel at any cost? Does the end justify the means to these limit definers? The general scientific viewpoint on the radiation problem suggests that it is probably not critical—at least during 'limited flight periods'. It has also been admitted by the US Military that shielding of craft would be impossible, on account of the unacceptable launch weight problems that would be engendered.

The German scientist Hermann J Schaefer, an expert on radiation assigned to the American Navy, upon his arrival in the States after WWII reminded his new masters that there was both immediately discernible damage to the human body as well as genetic damage, which would emerge much later.

In the mid 1950s, nobody knew if these GCRs would affect the brain, the reproductive glands or the retina of the eye—allegedly. In the late '90s we now know these statements to be incorrect. This information *was* known. The research scientists had made it their business to take the data and derive information from extensive tests that they had conducted on their own (often unwitting) people.

Old McDonald had a farm

The fact that the Americans were well aware that no other nation was developing an atomic weapon is often glossed over in the historical record of the development of the A-bomb. In 1943, the vast amount of funding for this development was initially granted as a result of 'rumours' that Germany was already working on such a bomb. Well before the end of the war, the Americans knew this statement to be untrue but by then their desire was to be first with THE deterrent—and never mind the consequences. That at least is the consensus version of events.

Codenamed 'Manhattan Project', the development of the A-bomb was one of at least two super-secret projects of the last World War. The research and development for this A-bomb was established at a location inhabited mainly by scorpions and centipedes, and decorated with Yucca plants. Omnisciently, the local name for this site had always been 'Jornado del Muerto'—the 'Journey of Death' or dead man's trail. A pavilion-like homestead in the middle of the site area belonged to one David McDonald. This the US Army leased for use as a Field Laboratory and Military Police Station. Rather sadly they called their new headquarters Trinity. Preliminary tests were carried out in New Mexico and Nevada—and the final result, the A-bomb was first exploded at the Trinity site.[51]

In their pursuit of knowledge concerning the results of nuclear weapons upon human beings, the Americans ran Operation Echo. From 1945 through to 1963, the American Military subjected over 235,000 of their personnel—both male and female—to the effects of radiation from A-bomb testing in the Nevada Nuclear Test Site, north of Las Vegas (the Ranch or the location known as Area 51 is part of that Nevada base).

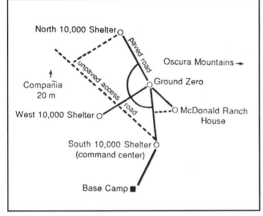

30. The Trinity Test Site.

Around 25,000 experiments were carried out and the tolerance dose to which the army personnel were subjected was steadily increased from 5 rem to 8 and then up to 14 rem. This test data was achieved by placing the troops nearer and nearer to Ground Zero (the site of the blast) and/or by providing them with ever-decreasing levels of protection. Few of these personnel were fully cognisant of the dangers they were facing, having been told that two feet of earth or soil would keep them safe from the effects of an A-bomb explosion—if they were lucky enough to have trenches.

It was only in 1955 that it was publicly acknowledged that the lens of the human eye actually concentrated the glare from an A-bomb explosion and the retina was then burned. These nuclear tests were euphemistically called 'medical school research' and we are cosily assured that 'safe' viewing distances and the other protective measures had been established by the medics of the Randolph Air Force Base in Texas. Because this fact has been demonstrated as being manifestly untrue, it is clear that the decision makers behind the Echo project treated these people as cold-bloodedly as the inmates of the concentration camps had been treated, and were as indifferent to their induced stress as they were to the fate of the animals they also used in these nuclear tests. This is an attitude, or policy if you will, which we consider has continued throughout the space

program, which could also be called 'space medical school research'.

Interviewed in the 1990s about the tests, one soldier, who was aged 22 at the time, recounted how he and his friends were utterly shocked by the experience of being in such close proximity to the detonation of an A-bomb. They had been told to keep their right sides towards Ground Zero and to raise their right arms in the 'ward off' position. Although he was in a trench, when the flash went off this young soldier could see the two bones inside his forearm, and he felt utter fear. When the loudspeakers ordered them out of the trenches and instructed them to walk towards the mushroom cloud, none of the soldiers said a word—*they were all in such a state of shock.*

31. Observers entering trenches at the test site.

111

After this harrowing experience, they were brushed down by a man with a yard broom—supposedly if you removed the dust, you removed the radiation. The American Army personnel had been informed by some of their medical advisors that they were putting their troops too close to the detonation site, but the Army went ahead and did it anyway. The American Atomic Energy Commission's information issued to towns neighbouring the test sites was initially believed to be in the population's interests. However, these same trusting citizens found

32. Military Personnel ordered to advance towards a test A-bomb explosion.

themselves with abnormal numbers of mentally and genetically defective children, only nine months after the fallout from testing had swept over their town and have since expressed the feeling that "they now dare not trust their government any more".[52]

Searing truths

The American civilian public apparently perceived the A-bomb as 'the bringer of peace' and assumed that the Japanese would capitulate under such a threat. The American public did not perhaps appreciate that for the potency of that threat to be understood a demonstration would be needed. However the use of the A-bomb, even the making of such a bomb, did not have its roots in the conflict with Japan. "It was not a military decision," stated General George C Marshall. Although President H S Truman always maintained the use of the bomb against Japan was dictated by military necessity, the evidence uncovered since those days reveals that this was not the case.

Nearly all the top brass in both the US Army and Navy were against the use of the bomb as a means of forcing the Japanese to surrender. General MacArthur, Supreme Commander in the Pacific, did not believe in using a military weapon against civilian populations. General Dwight Eisenhower told the Secretary of War, Henry Stimson, and President Truman not to use this weapon. General Carl Spaatz of the US Army Strategic Air Force did not know why the second bomb had been used and Averril Harriman, wartime Ambassador to the Soviet Union, was able to concur with this opinion as he had heard it in 1945 expressed by others within the Air Force in Washington.

So who was *actually* making the policy decisions in the United States at that time? With hindsight, the decision to design and build the A-bomb, and then use it, had far more to do with the conquest of space. It must be obvious to any thinking person that dropping the A-bombs on Hiroshima and Nagasaki provided the Americans with the opportunity to gather

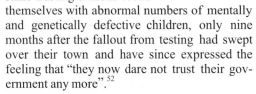

Robert Oppenheimer

Head of the A-bomb Project, watched the initial test at the Trinity Test Site and quoted from the ancient Indian text, the Bhagavad Gita.

"It flashed through my mind that I had become the Prince of Darkness, the destroyer of universes."

---

first-hand knowledge of the deterministic effects of radiation upon human beings. And it enabled them to evaluate the stochastic development (the after-effects) over the decades that followed. The Americans started monitoring the Japanese victims of their A-bomb attacks at least as soon as the Emperor surrendered on behalf of the Japanese nation. Through both the photography and medical examination of these individuals American scientists were able to add their conclusions to the results already obtained from the previous experiments on their own people.

After Hiroshima in 1945, the American nuclear physicists estimated that it would probably take from three to five years for another power to create their own bomb. This deduction was made in the full knowledge of the state of the nuclear fission art in the Soviet Union.[53] However in May 1947 the British Joint Chiefs of Staff sent this top secret report to the British Cabinet:

All our intelligence sources indicate that Russia is striving, with German help (referring to the scientists that were shared out between the Allies at the end of WWII) to improve her mili-

> **Indie 4**
>
> "... When we didn't need to do it,
> and we knew we didn't need to do it,
> we used them [the Japanese] as
> an experiment for two atomic bombs."
> *Brigadier-General Carter W Clarke* [54]
>
> It was on Independence Day 4th July 1945,
> that under the Quebec Agreement the British gave
> their approval to the Combined Policy Committee
> for the bombing of Japan with the A-bomb.

tary potential and to catch up technically and scientifically. We must expect that from 1956-57 Russia will be in a position to use some atomic bombs that she may have developed.

We find the discrepancy of timing interesting. If the Americans thought that another power—and the Soviet Union specifically—could make a bomb from scratch twice as fast as the British estimate, did the Americans know something that the British did not? Was there perhaps some kind of done deal? In other words, were the Russians given an 'unofficial' helping hand? We have reason to think so.[55] As it turned out, despite the overtly covert spying that went on around the Manhattan Project and whatever other help the Soviets might have been given, the Soviet Union only started assembling their scientists, building special research centres and infrastructures to support their effort for developing atomic power during 1947 and were not ready to explode their first A-bomb until the early Autumn of 1949. The American estimates were accurate to within a year, either way!

One could say that without WWII the Americans would not be attempting to head out

33. Aftermath of the Hiroshima A-bomb, August 6 1945. ARCHIVE

into deep space today. It would appear that several elements of WWII were specifically designed, an overall plan into which were written key components that would form part of the scripted scenario.

It is important to remember that today the academe of science flatters itself that it has everything under control. But the unbridled forces of nature which include space radiation are not at the command of man. Our scientists are totally unable to second-guess nature.

We have endeavoured to paint a realistic, truthful picture of the immense challenges to be faced with regard to the chronic problems of space radiation. As Clive Dyer stated, radiation surely must be the showstopper preventing mankind's exploration of the Universe. And surely that includes NASA's ability to venture forth safely with its named Apollo astronauts on short term flights. Until a totally different method of space travel is developed, the agency is destined to traverse the most hazardous parts of the Van Allen radiation belts.

Our firm conclusion on this subject has to be that with the prevailing capabilities at the time of 'Apollo 11' we were (and still are) unable to shield ourselves sufficiently against the potentially lethal radiation of space. Could it be that NASA was in fact unprepared to take these very considerable risks? It would be reasonable to decide against taking such a chance, with the entire world looking on. However, this would not excuse opting for the total fabrication/simulation of Apollo, employing surrogate astronauts, and/or any number of other permutations, instead of owning up to the problems.

We also suggest that the majority of the difficulties encountered by NASA in attempting to land a man on the Moon and return him home in one piece would not have been overcome without many more disasters and possible deaths than has been officially recorded.

But to acknowledge such matters would jeopardise the very future of space exploration.

What a quandary!

Chapter Four

Rocket Rackets

From Snoopy to Droopy—thanks to a Prussian Baron. How space development progressed from the V-I to the N-I and earned the 'award of the lemon' within a period of thirty years. We delve into the turbulent adventures in the development of rockets and rocketry and discuss why there is much more to the business of lifting a payload off the ground than a roaring engine with clouds of smoke. We meet experts in this field who help to explain the technological difficulties involved in manned deep space travel.

This chapter is for any of us who have never given a thought to the mechanical miracles required to get tons of metal aloft, out of its orbit around the Earth, on its way to the Moon and at the same time ensuring that the occupants stay alive and well. We have demonstrated that without adequate shielding, human beings would not survive for very long in the hazardous environment that lies beyond the protection of the Earth's atmosphere and its magnetic field. But manoeuvring in space is also hazardous to any machines we might send forth—be they satellites to orbit the planet or probes to explore the solar system.

In the first instance, these vehicles have to be launched into space. In the USA, the principal launch sites are located at Cape Kennedy in Florida, Wallops Flight Center in Virginia and Vandenberg Air Force Base in California (2).

Spacecraft often suffer severe jolts at lift-off and the launch itself sometimes aborts. Even if they survive that initial process, craft can fail

to reach the required orbit or bypass the orbital path and continue on into space, to be seen no more!

When the probe or satellite achieves its destined path, it will still be on the receiving end of numerous hazards lying in wait to challenge any space mission. For example solar flares can alter its trajectory and affect its primary func-

1. The Chinese were the human inventors of the very first solid fuel rockets used for aggressive purposes, way back in 1232 AD.

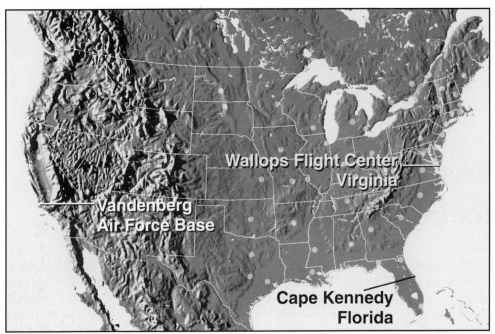

2. United States Space centres.

tions, wisps of our outer atmosphere can affect its speed, gravity fields of the Earth, Moon and Sun influence its path and sunlight itself can also have an effect on a satellite.

However, these matters are not the real problem. Rockets themselves are the problem.

In order to provide adequate protection for the Apollo astronauts the appropriate materials necessary for optimum radiation shielding would have created very significant weight increases. This protection would have been needed for the CSM as well as the LM. In turn, these specially-protected modules would have required an exceedingly powerful launch capability—a far more powerful rocket than anything that the US have so far developed. The truth of the matter is they could not have launched an adequately protected spacecraft out of the Earth's gravity 'well' and on course for the Moon.

To put it bluntly—they couldn't get it up!

Having to 'make do' with this somewhat 'impotent' rocketry concerns our past as well as our future. So we shall begin by digging around at the development stages of the space program. In a practical sense this first took off towards the end of WWII, by which time scientists had devised some fairly diabolical ways for killing people. The climax of mankind's barbarity to mankind, occurred on the 6th and 9th of August 1945, when the two A-bombs were unleashed over Japan.

As this chapter focuses on the 'hardware'—the technology that led to the Apollo period, of necessity we will only mention the events of WWII in order to follow the timeline. In the next chapter we will go back into this period in some detail and examine the 'software'—the personalities and their intricate backgrounds which would influence many of the policies behind the space programs of both the United States and the Soviet Union.

Dropping A-bombs was not the only activity involving explosives of a hitherto unparalleled brutality. Desperate to rebuild their army after the First World War, the Germans had spotted a loophole in the restrictive conditions concerning rearmament laid down by the Treaty of Versailles at the end of WWI. Having realised that the manufacturing of rockets had not been

Although spurred on by the news that the Nazis were also developing a V-3 for launching against the eastern coast of the United States, it was not until the end of March 1945 that the Allies finally eradicated this threat to their respective countries. In truth, rocket scientist Hermann Obcrth was the intellectual impetus behind the practical beginnings of German rocket science and, by extension, the instigator of practical space

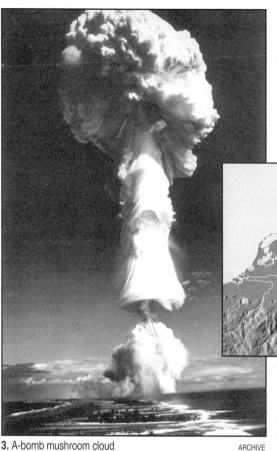

3. A-bomb mushroom cloud.   ARCHIVE

4. The Peenemünde site, Germany.

flight including the V-2. However, it is Wernher von Braun, the Technical Director at Peenemünde, who is generally regarded as the driving force behind both Peenemünde and the subsequent American missile and rocket program.

The series of weapons created at Peenemünde, of which the V-2 was the fourth weapon developed, was initially codenamed Aggregate. This explains its other code name: A-4, adopted by the Soviets as the 'base' name of this rocket.

The V-2 would become the starting point for development of the American sounding rockets used for research into upper atmospheric conditions. The later Viking and Aerobee rockets were also based on this V-2 technology.[1] In attempting to thwart the German V-2 rocket development and manufacture, Peenemünde had been the target of attack by Allied air raids between 1943-45. So consequently the Nazis spread their technicians and manufacturing bases further afield and worked underground.

envisaged by the architects of this treaty, the Germans went into action and developed a rocket fuelled by liquid propellants. The V-2 model which they used against England and mainland Europe during WWII was the most advanced in the world.

In April 1937, two years before the official declaration of war by Great Britain, the Germans transferred all their rocket testing sites from Kummersdorf and Berlin to a newly established secret rocket base on the island of Usedom, situated at the mouth of the Peene River off the Baltic coast. This site was selected by one Wernher von Braun who then used it to create and test the Vengeance Weapons—the Nazi's official name for the V-I aeroplane and V-2 rocket.

5. V-2 production hangar at Peenemünde.   ARCHIVE

6. V-2 test stand at Peenemünde in 1942.   ARCHIVE

The spoils of war—Air Matériel

The result of the final phase of the war—the capturing of these German rocket bases and their equipment—was quite simply the transfer of the Nazis' most precious assets to the Allies. Although the French and the British benefited from this Operation Overcast, as designated by the American Army, the lion's share of the technicians, blueprints and remaining weaponry were assigned to the United States and the Soviet Union. Most of the Nazi weapons bases were within Soviet occupied territory. On taking over these bases the Soviets worked on-site or removed the assets—lock, stock and barrel—back to the Soviet Union. Sometimes there was a mixture of both methods, with materials initially being worked on in situ and only later being moved to the Motherland. A number of technicians were also taken to the Soviet Union at this time where they comprehensively transferred their skills to Soviet technicians.[2]

The Americans were also busy—in contravention of the terms of the Yalta Agreement—parts and blueprints for about one hundred V-2s were shipped to the United States

---

WvB—The Busy Bee, Part I

Wernher von Braun, born March 23 1912

1930-32	Demonstrated his proficiency with rocketry to the German Army at Kummersdorf.
1932	Received a Bachelor's degree from Berlin Institute of Technology, aged 20.
1933	Adolf Hitler came to power. The German Army Weapons Department, GAWD(!) formed under General Walter Dornberger provided a research grant to WvB & his colleagues.
1934	Gained his Doctorate of Physics from the University of Berlin, aged 22. *(Very short degree course!)* Used the Island of Borkum, near Emden, for his secret experiments.

under the aegis of Operation Overcast. The Yalta Agreement expressly stipulated that it was illegal to remove any captured technical equipment from its location in occupied territory. Nevertheless a special team of four American Army personnel, together with some ex-Peenemünde engineers organised the shipping of this material to the United States via Antwerp, Belgium. The first shipment left from the underground rocket works at Nordhausen in Bavaria on May 22 1945 and nine days later a total of 341 freight cars had made the journey to the coast. The cargo was then shipped over to New Orleans in 16 Liberty ships.

Belgium and New Orleans have the French language as a common bond. Is this how the army designation 'Air Matériel' came about?[3]

7. V-2 rocket on a rail launcher.   ARCHIVE

Was the naming of this particular cargo an 'in-joke' that stuck?

Either the Yalta Agreement was not worth the paper on which it was written or there were wheels within wheels operating, for this cargo had been removed from Nordhausen Mittelwerks with the full knowledge, but not the active participation of the US Transportation Corps. The American Army's 'official' smugglers removed the 'Air Matériels' from Nordhausen only days ahead of the Soviet occupation. Moreover, they had removed the Peenemünde blueprints and documentation from their hiding place near Dornten in the Hartz Mountains only hours before the Soviets and the British were to occupy the area.

It is hard to believe that such barefaced lack of attention to a vitally important international agreement could have been carried out without the approbation of all parties involved. If there had been serious competition for these spoils of war, why then did the Soviets not press forward to reach Peenemünde—as the Germans had anticipated? Even though it was within their grasp the Soviets took their time; and when they commenced reconstruction the Mittelwerks at Nordhausen in the south, they did not complain that all the toys were gone. They found plenty left for themselves.

It is our contention that they already knew what their share would be. The US Transportation Corps may have feared remonstrations by the other parties to the Yalta Agreement, but further up the chain of command the overall plan was falling into place very nicely. For the men in black knew very well that in the battle for political and military supremacy, those who controlled space would control the political future of this planet.

They knew that rockets were the first step towards that ultimate control.

The 'Rockettes'

In an extension of Operation Overcast, the selection of the captured technicians was carried out under the codename Operation Paperclip. How precisely that came about would seem to depend upon the source of information consulted and how much any given source wants to convey. Generally the military (Nazi) aspect of this affair is played down, the emphasis is on 'scientists caught in the maelstrom of war'—which is somewhat inaccurate as we shall see.

Having read numerous histories of this period we have come to the conclusion that either the United States selected the top engineers from the Peenemünde base, or that the US was allocated the top planners. One thing however *is* certain. Every member of the chorus line sang his heart out to their interrogators, and just *weeks* after their best efforts had been focused on attempts to annihilate the forces of their captors, the 'Rockettes' of Germany were removed to a new country of residence.

8. V-2 test flight at White Sands in the late 1940s.   ARCHIVE

WvB—the Busy Bee, Part II

Wernher von Braun

1945   WvB and over 100 engineers were interrogated, then offered contracts with the US Army. Research was initiated at Fort Bliss, Texas (near White Sands Missile Range, New Mexico) then at Redstone Arsenal, Huntsville, Alabama. Army ballistic missiles were developed between 1945 and 1958.

1958   The Redstone rocket (modified) placed the first US satellite into orbit.

1960   July 1—WvB and his team were drafted to NASA, WvB became Head of the NASA Marshall Space Center, Huntsville, Alabama.

1970   WvB *resigned* from the Space Program aged 57 and became Deputy Associate Administrator for Planning at NASA, Washington DC, working on 'advanced programs'.

1972   Six months before 'Apollo 17' WvB resigned completely from NASA to become Vice President of Engineering and Development at Fairchild Industries, Germantown, Maryland, USA. An old friend, astronaut Ed Mitchell, arranged a meeting with WvB in order to introduce Uri Geller.[4] Meeting held at Fairchild Industries August 29 1972. WvB was most impressed by Uri Geller's talents.

1977   WvB whose lifelong dream had been to send men to the Moon, died aged 65.

QUESTION: Why did WvB resign from a program in 1972 that *apparently* was achieving his lifelong aim?
Had he only fulfilled the technical requirements of his role, i.e. built a Saturn V?
Were these requirements at odds with his real ambition?

Wall games

As the Nazi Rocketteers settled into their new regimes, the resultant products of the clandestine Manhattan Project were flown out of New Mexico and dropped onto the Japanese towns of Hiroshima and then Nagasaki. The nuclear age had truly arrived and, thanks to that most influential of film directors Stanley Kubrick, to many of us it is inextricably linked with his Dr. Strangelove's view of the world. Or should we really say Strange-Glove? Gunter Anders, addressing the International Students Conference on Nuclear Disarmament in 1957 described the event as "The End of Times". The possibility of planetary annihilation now became a reality and overshadowed every single person's life. This shadow only marginally began to recede at the 'official' end of the Cold War in the mid 1980s.

From the end of the 1940s those who were of an age to understand would never forget the tension created by the fact that one single misunderstanding between the protagonists of the Cold War could have meant the end of human life on this planet. This state of affairs was in fact fostered by the authorities, and actually reinforced by such events as the construction of the Berlin Wall in 1961 and the Cuban Crisis in 1962. In retrospect perhaps now we should ask ourselves if the Cold War was ever real? It would appear that there was a different scenario for each segment of the population, with only a very few ever having had sight of the original 'script': in much the same way that a large multinational corporation with many subsidiaries has employees who do not necessarily know the senior executives and the CEO at Head Office, only being familiar with their

9. Ernst Stuhlinger, Hermnann Oberth, Wernher von Braun and Eberhard Rees (with Commanding Officer Major General H Toftoy, Operation Paperclip) working at the Army Ballistic Missile Agency, Huntsville, Alabama in 1956.   NASA

particular department within the structure of their own company subsidiary.

Once the basic principals of 'need to know' are understood, together with the resulting manipulation of information, it is easy to observe this process in action—indeed every day, via our media, we are led by the nose along the 'required' path and we generally go quietly, because we have been well trained.

It is entirely possible that many of our historic events reflect this general pattern, including the establishment of the doctrine of communism in specific arenas around the globe.

However, there are two sides to every quid coin! It was the resulting tension from the post-war Dr. Strangelove era, for example, that brought forth the eruption of the 'peace and love' movement in the 1960s, as a public counter-reaction to the political circumstances established by our 'leaders'. That decade became the benchmark for change and in 1968 when the shockwaves hit France via the students' revolution, that country (symbolic of maintenance of the status quo, despite its declaration: 'Liberté Fraternité, Egalité') was forced to its knees by its own youth, and subsequently underwent some profound changes on many levels. So clearly tensions engendered by dreadful circumstances can also bring about change for the better—which gives us all some grounds for hope.

The Strangelove era, we suggest, came about as a direct consequence of the redistribution of the Peenemünde 'Rockettes'. That single event back in May 1945 engendered a situation that is still an issue today. The odds that this division of labour was simply an accident of fate are unlikely in the extreme. Documents surfacing in the 1990s belie the notion of a Cold War between the top brass in the USA and the USSR as it was then. Indeed, by the end of this chapter we shall see that there is every reason to believe that the Soviet Union's retreat behind the Iron Curtain was merely a dramatic marionette show run by puppeteers who manipulated the emotions of their childlike audience (us all) with every jerk of the strings. For it is quite clear from a close analysis of the documents pertaining to the race to space that very early on in the development of rocketry, the space agencies in the two countries shared information between themselves. This is not surprising, for scientists are not generally given to putting politics first—and research second. Furthermore, the majority of the rocket technicians both in the USA and the USSR had come from the same place—Nazi Germany. However, when the Peenemünde 'Rockettes' were reorganised, the 'planners and public relations' people resurfaced in America and the 'movers and shakers' of the world of rocketry went to ground in the Soviet Union.

What state of affairs would these whiz kids find in their new places of residence?

Mexican jumping beans

In America, Robert Goddard was considered to be the father of rocketry. Inventor of a bazooka during WWI, Goddard published a paper on rocketry in 1919 and began experimenting with

10. Robert Goddard. ARCHIVE

liquid propellants in 1921. On March 16 1926 his first liquid-propelled rocket achieved a height of 41 ft and landed 184 ft from its launch stand, having travelled at 60 mph on liquid oxygen and gasoline. In May 1935, Goddard launched a rocket to a height of 7,500 ft from his research site near a town that would become forever linked with the military, nuclear warfare, rockets, astronauts, NASA, space and ET–Roswell.

Monkey business

With the arrival of the boys and their toys in 1945 the American military literally set to work with a vengeance and by June 1948 Wernher von Braun and his newly-formed team of German and American rocket scientists were ready to use the V-2 rocket to launch small monkeys and later chimpanzees (in the 1950s) into space. These early launches were to experiment with the then unknown effects of space flight dynamics on living organisms—this first series of tests was called Project Blossom.

These poor animals were often wedged into a space actually smaller than their physical body length, For example, Albert 1 was anaesthetised and sent aloft with his head nearly doubled upon his chest. It is hardly surprising that he suffocated. Anthropomorphised with names such as Albert, Patricia or Michael these experimental animals were officially described as 'Simulated Pilots'. In the early stages, the researchers were seemingly able to emotionally insulate themselves from the effects of their treatment on the animals. Since those first experiments with rockets many different sentient life forms have been used for scientific research into the biological effects of space flight.

It is claimed that these flights have contributed to the definition of an astronaut's basic requirements: the necessity for an oxygen system of a sufficient size to last throughout the entire mission; a chemical-based system designed to cleanse the waste products of exhalation; medical monitoring systems for each individual. The astronaut's backpack, which became known as the PLSS (Portable Life Support System) was designed to fulfil all these established requirements.

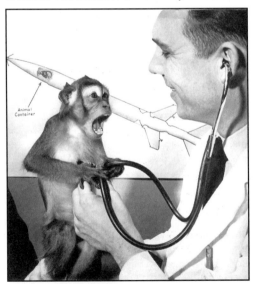

11. Space monkey that rode an Aerobee rocket to a height of 36 miles. NASA

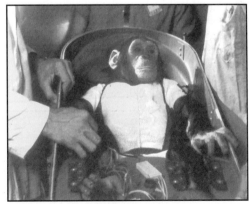

12. Ham, the first Chimpanzee in space. NASA

While these animals returning from trips into space provided dramatic publicity photographs, it was not an especially scientific methodology and a machine could have been constructed to provide the required data faster and more economically.[5] But it did make it *look* as if NASA was doing something towards getting 'out there'. Sometimes just getting up was a nightmare for the animal. In January 1961 Ham the chimpanzee was sent aloft atop a Redstone rocket—which unfortunately consumed all its fuel five seconds too early. This accident resulted in the spacecraft being shot higher and faster than its designed trajectory. Ham experienced more than twice the expected amount of gravity (Gs) and apparently inside the craft itself nothing worked properly. Each task Ham performed was rewarded with an electrical shock instead of a banana pellet. He ended up crash-landing in the ocean over a hundred miles from the planned landing site. When he was finally rescued he was a half-drowned, very angry chimpanzee. It was also made clear by this event that NASA had a long way to go before sending a human astronaut safely into space. As a postscript to this incident, *Space-flight*, published in 1995 by the Smithsonian Institute, had the temerity to state that the flight *passed off without incident*. History had been rewritten—yet again.

At sixes and sevens

Having analysed the photographs together with all the recorded TV coverage published by NASA and then having investigated the problems caused by radiation hazards, another factor puzzled us. There were some tell-tale signs that the rocketry involved in the Apollo project might not be quite as wonderfuel(!) as we had been led to believe. As with any new technology the space program would have its devel-

opmental problems but for a greater insight we needed to consult some experts.

Our enquiries led us to the doorstep of Bill Kaysing, an established Whistle-Blower concerning Apollo. Kaysing is an authority on rockets and their propellants, with engineering qualifications and a degree in English literature from the University of Southern California. He worked for Rocketdyne, a division of North American Aviation, for seven years (from 1956 to 1963). Employed as a technical writer

13. The Mercury-Redstone (1961).

and later head of technical publications for the Rocketdyne Research Department, Kaysing held both *Secret* and *Atomic Energy Commission* clearances at the time Rocketdyne was developing Apollo program technology. Whistle-Blower Kaysing confirmed that the building blocks of such missiles as the American *Redstone* and *Thor* rockets were really the tried and tested engines of the old German V-2 rocket. (The Mercury-Redstone derived from the Redstone MRBM was 83ft long and generated 78,000 lbs thrust in its first stage.) Subsequent designs evolved into the American Atlas and Titan.

The hardware for these military rockets therefore became the platform for all subsequent rocket systems and the designs selected were always based on engines that operated with liquid propellants. At that time these propellants were considered to be the way of the future but they had a very serious drawback— combustion instability. A problem that exists

---

TechnoSpeak
Rocket propulsion system:
The engine or powerplant that produces thrust by ejecting propellant, stored within a vehicle.
These rocket propulsion systems are classified according to these criteria:
1. Energy source—chemical, combustion, nuclear, solar etc.;
2. The amount of thrust produced;
3. The type of vehicle supplied—missile, sounding rocket, space craft.

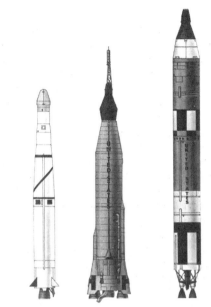

to this day.

Combustion instability results from hundreds of pounds of propellant being burned in a
very short space of time (called a high flow
rate). The result is a 'continuous explosion'
which has a side effect; it engenders acoustic
resonances, called 'acoustic transients'.

The type of propellants used, combined with
the fact that they are burning up within a very
short time period means that noise levels as
high as 150 decibels can cause anomalies in the
burn. Standing waves flash back and forth
within the rocket chamber and these waves can
concentrate high temperatures at certain points
within the chamber, burning the thin walls and

14. Left to right:

Thor-Able Star (1960) 79.3ft long, 72,000 lbs thrust 1st stage.

Mercury-Atlas (1962) 95.3ft long, 367,000 lbs thrust 1st stage.

Gemini-Titan II (1964) 109ft long, 430,000 lbs thrust 1st stage.

TechnoSpeak

The efficiency of rocket engines is measured by a quantity known as 'Specific Impulse' (SPI). This item is an
evaluation of the duration of time for which 1 lb of propellant can produce 1 lb of thrust. (a pound for a pound).
The higher the exhaust velocity and of the rocket engine, the more efficient it is.

Liquid propellants in order of their increasing SPI

Fuel	Oxidiser	Fuel	Oxidiser
1. Hydrogen peroxide	with self		
2. Ethylene oxide	with self	7. Hydrazine	Liquid Oxygen
3. Furfuryl alcohol	white fuming Nitric Acid	8. Hydrazine	Liquid Ozone
4. Hydrazine hydrate	white fuming Nitric Acid	9. Hydrazine	Liquid Fluorine
5. Hydrazine	Hydrogen Peroxide	10 Hydrogen	Liquid Fluorine
6. Kerosene	Liquid Oxygen	11. Hydrogen	Liquid Ozone

- *Solid fuel systems* tend to have values to approximately 200 SPI.
- Liquid propellants (e.g. kerosene & oxygen) to 250 SPI.
- *Hypergolic systems* (e.g. hydrazine & nitrogen tetroxide) where components ignite upon contact can have values
  that exceed 300 SPI.
- *Electric systems* (e.g. cryogenic oxygen & hydrogen NI) can deliver values to 450 SPI.
- *Cryogenic:* the management of temperatures from -238°F/-150°C to absolute zero. (Usually defined by the
  Kelvin scale.)
- *Nuclear engines* can deliver up to 800 SPI but the potential for disaster and launch failure leading to long term con-
  tamination of the area is the chief problem with the development of nuclear fission reactor rocket propulsion.

causing total failure of the engine.

Bill Kaysing saw many, many such failures, blow-ups and premature engine cut-offs at Rocketdyne's Santa Susana Laboratories in California. It was announced by the US Department of Defense on April 20 1964 that the Atlas D, E and F rockets endured thirteen consecutive failures during the summer and autumn of 1963.

If the Atlas rocket was still unreliable after almost ten years in development, one may well ask how was a further development, the *Saturn* series going to be any better? All these rockets had emerged from the von Braun academy, but the Saturn rocket was *it*—*the* state of the art for Wernher von Braun. It had taken him from

---

The ranch

North of Las Vegas, in the Nevada desert, there is vast area known as the Nellis Air Force Range and Nuclear Test Site. Within the test site a location called 'Frenchman's Flats' was used for a series of night-time A-bomb tests which were seen by the Las Vegas casino gamblers, some 75 miles away.

North of the test site a remote USAF facility on the ancient bed of the dried out Groom Lake boasts the longest runway in the world. This facility is commonly referred to by UFO spotters either as Area 51, The Ranch, Watertown Strip, or Dreamland. The USAF do not refer to it at all, except to post signs around its perimeter stating that the area is off limits to the public.

If NASA *did have* UFO-type technology the agency would have no need to experiment with nuclear engines. Notwithstanding the testing of NERVA, this site has seen much testing of materials designed to be radar proof and radiation proof. In its attempts to conquer the Van Allen radiation zones, NASA and Co. are still endangering lives and this research alone is a very good reason for keeping the general public well away from this area.

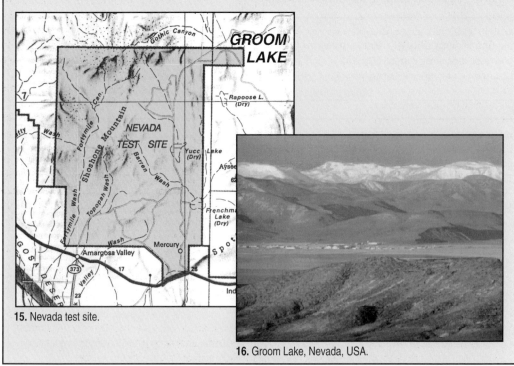

15. Nevada test site.

16. Groom Lake, Nevada, USA.

1958 through to January 1964 to achieve the Saturn 1's first launch with all stages working.[6]

(The Saturn 1B was 224ft in length and powered by B-1 engines producing 1,640,000 lbs thrust in its 1st stage.)

After several modifications, the Saturn V emerged some three years later. With its five F-1 boosters, it was larger and more powerful than any launcher previously built for NASA. Test-launched in 1967 and 1968, the record states that it performed flawlessly throughout the entire Apollo program.

But the early Saturn V F-1 engine tests were absolutely disastrous, with catastrophic explosions on the test stand. This was a rocket designed to carry astronauts into space and to the Moon, not to blow up on the launch pad—and time was ticking away. Yet according to Whistle-Blower Bill Kaysing, as late as Spring 1963 (although it was widely believed to be due to combustion instability), Rocketdyne were still trying to establish the specific causes of these engine failures.

Naturally—and as we had come to expect—the NASA public relations machine kept a very low profile on these serious problems. When we asked for copies of the F-1 test data, we were advised that the data is unclassified but unfortunately 'not available'. Obviously freedom of information is a selective process.

We needed the opinion of a rocket engineer on these matters and so we paid a visit to the

17. The Saturn 1B.

United States to meet Bill Wood during 1996.

Whistle-Blower Wood has a BSc in Aerospace Engineering, an MSc in Mechanical Engineering and Degrees in maths, physics and chemistry. He knows a great deal about rocket technologies, having worked on US Air Force rockets, including the Minuteman ICBM (Inter-Continental Ballistic Missile) from 1964-1968 as a munitions specialist. Wood was then employed on classified projects for the US Navy under secret security clearances. From 1977-1993 he worked on numerous secret and top secret US Government rocket programs. He also worked with MacDonnell Douglas on the Delta Satellite launch vehicle and with many of the engineers who had worked on the Saturn V. Bill Wood has published classified and unclassified papers on rockets and ramjet propulsion and served as Chairman of the ASME Propulsion Technical Committee. Since 1993 he has also acted as consultant on a number of non-governmental rocket programs. We cannot doubt his credentials. Therefore it is very significant that he has strong doubts concerning the authenticity of Apollo, basing his opinion on thirty years of his own investigations. He also agrees with many aspects of Bill Kaysing's independent findings, and considers that, at launch, the Saturn V highlighted some very 'interesting' anomalies.

The Saturn V

Five F-1 motors (as displayed at the Kennedy Space Centre) were the first-stage engines for the Apollo missions to the Moon, allegedly producing 1.5 million pounds of thrust, each.
That is a sum of 7.5 million pounds thrust at take-off.

Information from one of NASA's sponsors, The *National Geographical Society*, stated that the Saturn V launcher had the most powerful engines in the world and used 15 tons of kerosene and liquid oxygen per second.
Please wait for the section on Soviet rockets before accepting everything as gospel!

"Film footage of the Saturn V launch records the five F-1 motors producing an 800 foot long highly fuel-rich exhaust plume together with extensive atmospheric after-burn," Bill Wood says. "These exhaust plumes are dark for the first eight feet from the end of the nozzle, then ignition of a very fuel-rich exhaust occurs in the atmosphere. The recorded effect is not typical of other known rocket engines utilising the same propellants. So could it be that the rocket motors in this Saturn V were in fact the *smaller B-1 engines, inserted into the centre of an F-1 motor shell?*" Bill asks.

"These B-1 engines were proven rocket motors with lower thrust, originally used in the Saturn 1B rocket." He continued: "These substitutes would then have had extra kerosene injected into the annular space between the rocket motors. This fuel would then be vaporised and burned in the atmosphere. While it would not provide much increase in thrust, it would have been reliable, and would also account for the 'flame-thrower' effect visible at launch."

Bill paused at this juncture for his own 'effect' to sink in.

"Why would this be done," we asked?

"The reason would have been to make the rocket appear to be more powerful that it really was—and we all know that flamethrowers produce very little thrust!" Bill responded.

His reply certainly sank in.

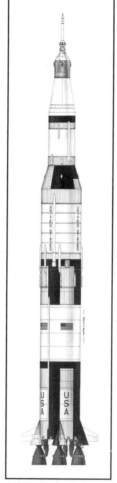

18. The Saturn V.

A game of pogo

The problem of combustion instability which caused what was is known as the 'pogo effect' (the industry term for those internal oscillations we mentioned earlier) was in evidence from early testing of the Saturn rocket right through to the 'Apollo 10' launch—after which everything worked perfectly!

Apparently this very real problem was solved by "cutting off the centre of the five first-stage rocket engines, before the pogo oscillations were likely to begin".[8] But is this not utter rubbish? If you cut off the central engine to restore stability, you diminish the thrust capability; surely the Saturn V then becomes a 'Saturn IV' and even less effective.

Other chroniclers of the 'space race' infer that the problem was solved by cutting out this central rocket engine during the second stage and letting the other four rockets burn a little longer to compensate for the consequent overall lack of thrust. How would this help? The pogo effect occurred during the first stage. Within these variations perhaps we find back-up for Bill Wood's observation of the odd fuel mix emanating from Saturn V's rocket exhaust.

On the opposite page chart (19) is a list of failures from a NASA index to the year 1970, but these many and various catastrophes did not stop with the advent of the Apollo phase of the space program. So how did the Saturn V suddenly come right, delivering the Apollo astronauts safely into space without another single incident? After all the people and the technology were still the same, and Bill Wood tells us that the Saturn V was supposed to contain over 2 million separate parts, surely a virtually impossible challenge to fulfil, mission after mission?

Project Apollo

The Apollo program, the section of the American space program designed to actually deliver the astronauts to the lunar surface, started not with a bang, nor with a whimper, but with a

tragedy. On January 27 1967 Gus Grissom, Ed White and Roger Chaffee all died high up on launch Pad 34 at the Cape from asphyxiation—caused by fire in the cockpit of their test capsule, probably triggered by an unshielded electrical switch in an oxygen environment. There are several in-depth accounts of this saddening event.[9] We mention this accident here to emphasise the accumulating problems that were developing within the Apollo program. The urgency to get out into space seemed to be dominating a timetable which should have been dictated by the technical requirements.

NAME	LAUNCH	VEHICLE	MISSION/REMARKS

Selection of NASA failures:

NAME	LAUNCH	VEHICLE	MISSION/REMARKS
1 PIONEER	August 1958	Atlas ICBM	Exploded at launch.
PIONEER 1	Oct 11 1958	Atlas ICBM	Third Stage failure.
PIONEER 2	Nov 8 1958	Atlas ICBM	Failed to reach Moon, travelled only 1000 miles.
PIONEER 3	Dec 6 1958	Atlas ICBM	Failed to reach Moon, travelled 66,000 miles.
RANGER 1	Aug 23 1961	Atlas-Agena	Agena engine failed to restart.
ATLAS E	Nov 10 1961	Atlas E	Monkey 'Goliath' died when craft destroyed by range safety officer.
RANGER 2	Nov 18 1961	Atlas-Agena	Agena engine failed to restart.
RANGER 3	Jan 26 1962	Atlas Agena	Missed the Moon.
RANGER 4	April 23 1962	Atlas-Agena	Crashed on lunar far side.
RANGER 5	Oct 18 1962	Atlas-Agena	Missed the Moon.
RANGER 6	Jan 30 1964	Atlas-Agena	Failed and crashed on Moon
GEMINI Rendezvous	Oct 25 1965	Atlas-Agena	Failed, Agena blew up.
GEMINI IXA	Jun 3 1966	Titan II ICBM	Manned: Unable to dock with
	Jun 1 1966	Atlas	ATDA when shroud failed to clear docking adapter.
APOLLO SATURN	July 5 1966	Uprated Saturn	Flight terminated during liquid hydrogen pressure and structural test.
SURVEYOR III	Sept 20 1966	Atlas Centaur	One of three vernier engines failed to ignite causing incorrectable tumbling. Contact lost. Crashed?
GEMINI XII	Nov 11 1966	Delta	Manned: The target vehicles' primary propulsion not usable for elliptical orbit manoeuvre.
APOLLO I	Jan 27 1967	Saturn	Spacecraft fire at Complex 34—three astronauts died.
SURVEYOR III	April 17 1967	Atlas Centaur	Closed loop radar failed during landing.
SURVEYOR IV	July 14 1967	Atlas Centaur	All communication lost with spacecraft. Crashed?
APOLLO 6	April 4 1968	Saturn V	2nd stage failed to ignite, propulsion difficulties with 3rd stage, 20 major failures.
ATS IV	Aug 10 1968	Atlas Centaur	Spacecraft failed to separate from Centaur.
'APOLLO 13'	April 11 1970	Saturn V	Manned: lunar landing attempt aborted.

19. (Various sources)

Deeds not words

As late as 1967, the Apollo spacecraft was still considered dangerous by the astronauts.
The spacecraft had clocked up 20,000 systems failures—of which 200 belonged to the environmental control system.[10]
In early tests a thruster nozzle had shattered on being fired.
This vital nozzle would place the craft in lunar orbit and then be required to set the craft's return course to Earth.
On another occasion the heatshield split open and
the $35 million dollar craft SANK to the bottom of the pool over which they were carrying out a splashdown test.
Such had been the state of affairs when Gus Grissom walked away from the test craft
leaving a lemon perched upon it, representing his very low esteem for the vehicle.

Baron vs. Barons

The North American Aviation quality controller Thomas Baron, working on the Apollo Program since 1965, was convinced that "the Apollo CSM was a lethal machine and unsafe for men to fly in space"[11] and Baron put it on record in 1966, producing an itemised written report to the CSM contractors (North American Aviation) on December 23 1966.

Quality controllers were used to inspect and evaluate all aspects of workmanship during the installation procedures involved in the assembly of space craft. This process included the adhesion of the work force to the on-site safety standards and procedures, during both installation and astronauts' tests. Their checklists were the result of carefully established criteria, and the comments made by these men were respected by the authorities. Among this group of observant men, Thomas Baron was considered a fastidious inspector, a perfectionist; and he had earned the nickname D R (Discrepancy Report) Baron.

North American Aviation should have been happy to have such a good inspector on their side. This was obviously not the case, because on January 5 1967—twenty two days before the fatal flight test, *Baron was suspended from duty.*

Later, at the official hearing regarding the Pad 34 accident held in April 1967, Baron testified detailing the evidence that he had accumulated, presented in two reports of 55 pages and 500 pages respectively. Incidentally, two years previously, in December 1965, a highly critical report of manufacturing standards, workmanship and timekeeping had been sent to North American Aviation by the Director of the entire Apollo program, Major General Samuel Phillips of the USAF. The *Baron Report* and the *Phillips Report* were very similar in their criticisms. The following letter had been sent to NAA from Major General Samuel C Phillips one year before the fatal fire that took the lives of Grissom, Chaffee and White.

A Miracle!

"No fire fighting methods have been developed that can cope with a fire in pure oxygen."
So wrote F J Hendel of North American Aviation in *Journal of Spacecraft & Rockets,* 1964.
Yet three years later the same company created a miracle: a pure oxygen environment that stifles air!

"Flammability tests within a model of the redesigned CSM proved, that once begun, a fire would *actually extinguish itself* in pure oxygen," reported North American Aviation after a test on an Apollo 7 module, May 1967.

A publication on 'Apollo 11' states that after the fire on Pad 34:
"All aspects of flammable equipment and hardware were addressed and corrected.[12]
Instead of the nitrogen/oxygen mixture on Earth, the crew breathed pure oxygen with a pressure of 5 lbs/sq. inch compared with an Earth surface pressure of 14.7 lbs/sq. inch."

Why does this author attempt to gloss over the fact that the Apollo 1 cabin *was* filled with pure oxygen?
This fact is exceedingly well known and his description is disinformative.
Therefore, the breathing mixture had NOT been corrected, it was exactly the same mix.

NATIONAL AERONAUTICS AND SPACE ADMINISTRATION

Washington 25, D C

December 19, 1965

IN REPLY REFER TO: MA

Mr J L Atwood
President
North American Aviation, Inc.
1700 E Imperial Highway
El Segundo, California

Dear Lee:

I believe that I and the team that worked with me were able to examine the Apollo Spacecraft and 5-II stage programs at your Space Information Systems Division in sufficient detail during our recent visits to formulate a reasonably accurate assessment of the current situation concerning these two programs.

I am definitely not satisfied with the progress and outlook of either program and am convinced that the right actions now can result in substantial improvement of position in both programs in the relatively near future.

Enclosed are ten copies of the notes which were compiled on the basis of our visits. They include details not discussed in our briefing and are provided for your consideration and use.

The conclusions expressed in our briefing and notes are critical. Even with due consideration of hopeful signs, I could not find a substantive basis for confidence in future performance. I believe that a task group drawn from NAA at large could rather quickly verify the substance of our conclusions, and might be useful to you in setting the course for improvements.

The gravity of the situation compels me to ask that you let me know, by the end of January if possible, the actions you propose to take. If I can assist in any way, please let me know.

Sincerely,

(Signed)
SAMUEL C PHILLIPS
Major General, USAF
Apollo Program Director

20. Copy of original.

There was one notable difference between these two plain-speaking individuals.

As a consequence of his courageous speaking out, Thomas Baron did not survive the process, he was eliminated from the Apollo program. The hearing officially concluded that an electrical failure caused the fire in the cap-sule—using language that left little to the imagination when referring specifically to the appalling state of the wiring.[13]

Following this enquiry, NASA renamed the Apollo tests so that the ill-fated flight was memorialised as Apollo 1 in honour of the three deceased astronauts. From the similar findings presented by General Philips and

Thomas Baron it was clear that the Apollo program had not improved its technical abilities to put a manned mission into space in the intervening months between their assessments, nor had that situation improved by January 27 1967 when the three Apollo astronauts were killed. It is less widely known that on January 31 1967—four days after the tragedy that killed the Apollo 1 crew—two airmen, William F Bartley Jr and Richard G Harmon were killed in a flash fire within the pure oxygen environment of a high altitude chamber at Brooks Air Force Base, Texas. Details concerning this fire were sent to the Apollo 1 investigation team and on February 1 1967 NASA finally called a temporary halt to manned tests in pure oxygen environments.

Cobweb of deceit

In 1997 Journalist Piers Bizony published an article in which he asserted that, during the Washington enquiry into the Pad 34 fire, NASA Administrator James Webb basically protested that he had never seen the Major General Samuel Phillips December 1965 report.[14] On October 7 1968, Webb quietly resigned from NASA and Tom Paine took over. Webb's resignation (accepted with alacrity by President Johnson on the very September day that it was offered) became a reality only four days before the departure of 'Apollo 8', the first manned mission scheduled to travel beyond the Van Allen radiation belts.

Bizony also catalogued another sorry tale: in this rather complicated saga the Senator for Oklahoma was a figure of some significance. Owner of both Kerr McGee (an oil and nuclear fuel corporation of consequence) and the Fidelity Bank of Oklahoma, Senator Kerr had helped Webb get his job at NASA. He was officially appointed by President Kennedy as NASA administrator in 1961. And guess what, previously Webb had been a senior president in Kerr McGee. James Webb was a political animal and used his energies to keep Congress in line, deploying any means at his disposal.

Enter a certain Fred Black, an influential lobbyist (especially concerning the space program) and owner of Serv-U Vending Machines. North American Aviation—those guys again—did a deal with Kerr to build factories in Oklahoma, thus boosting Kerr's chances of re-election. According to Bizony, Senator Kerr then apparently authorised not only an enormous security-free loan of $500,000 but also a valuable contract to install vending machines into North American Aviation's premises—to one Fred Black!

A further demonstration of this particular 'web's' efficiency is apparent here: Initially NASA had given the Command Module contract to Martin Marietta, but apparently Black heard about this, phoned Kerr and informed him of the situation. Consequently, Webb overturned his NASA manager's decision and awarded the contract to North American—despite the fact that they were already up to their necks trying to build a Saturn rocket that would work. Apparently subsequent investigations by the FBI revealed Black to be the linkman between Kerr, Webb and North American Aviation. Chaikin tells us that James Webb had "an uncanny knack for knowing where congressional skeletons were hidden". We would suggest that he also had Fred Black at his beck and call. Like us, Bizony feels that the 'space race' had nothing to do with the Cold War contest. He considers that it had more to do with corrupt big business. We agree that big business was right up there but we suggest that monetary gain was the inevitable fall out from the larger scam we are describing.

However, partially as a result of all these shenanigans, *one-third* of the Apollo spending program, Bizony tells us, was in the hands of North American Aviation. He asserts that its

---

New name, same game

Just to help us all to forget what had happened, several names were changed following the accident on Pad 34. North American Aviation was merged with Rockwell-Standard Corporation and became North American Rockwell. Token scapegoats, one each from NAA and NASA, were removed from their managerial posts.

> ### *Consider this:*
>
> "Think of all the thousands of parts and instruments—
> *many of them furnished by the lowest bidder!*—that had to work properly."
>
> Stuhlinger & Ordway III *Wernher von Braun Crusader for Space*

management team was incompetent and its engineers good at the talk but evidently not so good at the walk.

No wonder poor Grissom hung that lemon on a command module one sad day at NAA.

Following the Apollo 1 disaster and inquiry, major overhauls were also instigated 'on the ground'. The Apollo capsule had 5,000 changes made to its design within a period of just 21 months. That was at rate of 8 changes per day for the entire 21 months period! But still Apollo tests 2 through 5 had hundreds of technical failures. Whistle-Blower Bill Kaysing tells us that Apollo 6 was an unmitigated disaster, even by NASA's standards!

• The second stage did not light;
• the vehicle did not achieve Earth orbit;
• there were over 20 major failures in the flight.

Apollo 6 testing was intended to 'man rate' the Saturn V rocket ('man rate' in this case means testing for its capacity to carry humans safely) and this it clearly failed to do.

• No significant changes or improvements were made between Apollos 6 and 7. Yet, within *six* months, the very next testing—Apollo 7 was pure perfection!
• Nothing in the *basic* structure of the American space program was *redesigned* between Apollo 7 and 'Apollo 17'. Yet a mere 23 months after the fire on Pad 34 we are expected to believe that 'Apollo 8' went on a jaunt around the Moon and back.

'Apollo 8' was scheduled to re-enter our atmosphere at a rate that gave it a specific kinetic energy twice as high as Apollo 7's Earth orbit re-entry. But even more dramatic, this flight was billed as performing an exercise that had never been tried before: the re-entry manoeuvre through our atmosphere of a spacecraft *containing human beings. For some reason, NASA*

was in such a hurry that the agency did not even send a trial unmanned craft of an equivalent weight to test this re-entry procedure first.[15]

• Yet in defiance of the laws of probability, statistics and just simple mechanics, everything had changed.

QUESTION: Is it possible for a program to become 'perfect' virtually overnight without the addition and implementation of *real* technological advancements?

More monkey business

As late as June 28 1969 and after the 'Apollo 8' mission, NASA launched a biosatellite containing a 14 lb monkey, scheduled to spend 30 days in orbit. Officially, the mission was 'not considered a success'. In order to verify what had really happened during this test, we were obliged to cross-reference a number of space histories. Only by digging deeply were we able to establish that the monkey had died very early on during this low Earth orbit (221 x 241 miles) flight. The satellite was brought down into the Pacific on July 6 after just 8½ days. An autopsy report dated July 8 1969 concluded that the animal had died of a heart attack, brought about by the problems associated with weightlessness *and a lower than normal body temperature.*

QUESTION: Why did NASA provide different researchers with variations of the truth, and very economical variations at that? What is wrong with stating clearly "the monkey died"?
QUESTION: If, when testing monkeys on long space flights such animals could not survive eight days or so, why should any of us give credence to the claim that the astronauts of Apollos '8' and '10' survived the full duration of their flights? Moreover, how are we to believe that less than a month after this biosatel-

lite failure, 'Apollo 11' left for its much publi-cised successful voyage to the Moon?

After these 'made in USA' trials and tribula-tions, how were the 'Rockettes' getting on over in the Soviet Union?

Back in the USSR

As early as 1833, Konstantin Tsiolkovsky had calculated that a rocket would work in the vac-uum of space. The man was a visionary, detail-ing many of the requirements of a space age which would only begin to take shape decades later. In 1895 he published an article postulat-ing space travel as a possibility and in 1898 published findings that were to be of the great-est importance: namely that liquid propellants would be more efficient than solid propellants and that of these, a mixture of either of oxygen and hydrogen or of oxygen and kerosene, would be the most suitable for rocket engines.

21. Konstantin Tsiolkovsky.

In 1903 Tsiolkovsky published a treatise on space travel, which included the basic premise that still applies today: the need for the cos-monauts to recline at take off—in order to withstand the forces of acceleration, the neces-sity for a pressurised double-skinned hull to prevent meteoroid damage and that staging rockets (rockets that fire in sequence dropping away as soon as their fuel is spent, the next then firing and so on) should be used. In this way deadweight would be reduced and greater acceleration achieved within a shorter time pe-

22. Konstantin Tsiolkovsky's statue in Moscow.   AULIS

riod. Thereby rocket-fired craft would be able to leave the gravitational pull of the Earth.

Tsiolkovsky also recognised that gyroscopes and thrusters (small stabilising rockets) would be necessary and he proposed that people even-tually living in space stations needed to do so in spinning habitats which would create artifi-cial gravity.

The first of the 'firsts'

Tsiolkovsky's work was somewhat eclipsed by the German Zeppelin's work on dirigibles, and subsequently WWI as well as the Russian Revolution slowed any practical research into rocket technology. Such would remain the situation until the emergence of the Soviet Union from the ashes of the Tsarist regime.

The Soviets have always been pioneers in space flight. When the Transylvanian Hermann Oberth (later to join the Americans) published a book on rocketry in 1923—hailed as the

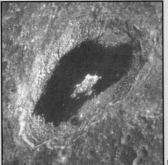

Tsiolkovsky Crater

NASA

To honour of Konstantin Tsiolkovsky, the most significant volcanic crater on the lunar surface was named after him. About 120 miles wide, it is situated on the far side of the Moon at between 19° and 22°S.

"first of its kind"—the Soviets protested that this was not so, for Tsiolkovsky had already been published in the preceding century!

Baikonur, 'city' of the double image

Until the mid 1990s it was difficult to evaluate the Soviet capacity at the time of the Apollo phase of the space program because all information in the public domain was coloured by the Western attitude, which of course favoured NASA über alles. Fortunately, that situation is now beginning to change. Nevertheless, the cosmonaut launch sites of Baikonur Cosmodrome, the Volgograd Station and the Northern Cosmodrome were the scenes of a series of successes in the domain of space exploration never equalled by the Americans.

The name of the Soviet Union's space base in southern central Kazakstan was a code name designed to confuse Westerners as to its exact location, taking the name of a town some 200 miles distant. This doubling of names initially caused much confusion for *Soviet* observers not 'in the know'. Used for the manned missions throughout the 1960s, this base was built on the north bank of the River Syr near the old town of Tyuratam in 1955. The Soviets always referred to their launch complex at that location as Tyuratam, not Baikonur. For ease of use we shall use the name Baikonur. A new town named Leninsk (now known as Korolëv) was constructed to provide the housing and facilities for the Baikonur Cosmodrome and the railway system extended to service the base.

It is said that for the Soviets, a prime advantage of the Baikonur site was the fact that it was allegedly beyond the reach of American intelligence listening posts based in Turkey. However, Whistle-Blower Bill Kaysing recalls

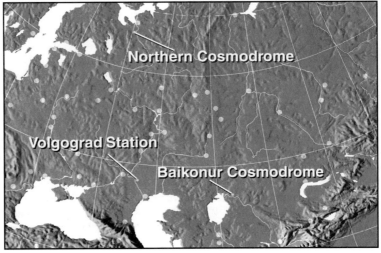

23. Soviet launch sites.

Baikonur briefing

In 1995 it was announced that Lockheed Khrunichev Energia International, a *Russian-American commercial venture,* was spending $23 million on updating the Baikonur Cosmodrome.

working on Soviet rocket data that emanated from these very listening posts, or at least that was the information passed to him. The task was so secret that not even his own superior was aware of what he was doing. Kaysing knew of other American scientists who were working on secret data supplied by the American intelligence network, albeit utterly frustrated as they were not given sufficient data to fulfil their job specification.

The bias of the Western reporting of history painted the Soviet Union as the big bad bear in the eyes of the American public, while reassuring the West that their technology was better than that of the Soviets.

However, the facts speak otherwise. Contrary to the desires and the information released by Western propaganda, the Soviets have *always* had the most powerful rockets on the planet, rockets capable of launching exceedingly heavy payloads. Even after the premature death of Korolëv in 1966, the Soviets continued to achieve feats in space technology well beyond the capabilities of their American counterparts.

Korolëv, the Chief among the Indians

The individual primarily responsible for the development of Soviet rocketry during the main thrust of the Soviet space program, was their chief engineer Sergei Korolëv, the rocket wizard. The large number of prestigious technological achievements that he realised for his country is nothing short of stunning. He was kept pretty much hidden as were most of the activities at the Baikonur Cosmodrome. This secrecy applied as much to the common Soviet people as to the uninitiated Western observers. We are told as many misleading stories about Korolëv, as we are about the base of Baikonur. Sergei P Korolëv was born on December 30 1906. He became a rocket engineer in the 1930s but as he would

24. Sergei P Korolëv with Yuri Gagarin. Smithsonian

not become a communist, Korolëv was sent to a gulag in Siberia during the Stalin purges. This valuable, unknown genius was kept in a special prison where prisoner scientists could work on special military projects—laboratories surrounded by bars. By 1945, with the recruitment in Eastern Germany of the Peenemünde 'Rockettes' he was released to oversee the organisation of these men and to lead, as the chief designer, what was to become the Soviet space program.

Following the death of Stalin, Korolëv was personally in contact with Nikita Kruschev, his successor. Then at the peak of his career, Korolëv died on the operating table on January 14 1966. According to Western sources of this information: "Korolëv's plans for sending probes to the Moon were frustrated by engineering failures" and "the first successful automated landing did not happen until two weeks after his death".

No mention of the successful crash landing of Luna 1, no mention of the successful imaging of the far side of the Moon, no mention of the fact that Korolëv's probes *reached the Moon.*

The Americans at that time had failed to get two Rangers even into Earth orbit. Their first fly-by was three years later and three times fur-

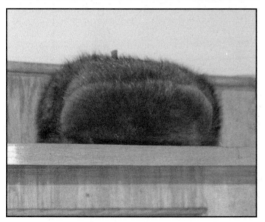

25. Korolëv's house in Moscow, his desk and hat just as he left them before going into hospital in January 1966.

In 1966 Sergei Korolëv asked his Doctor how long his heart would last. The reply was "about twenty years"—to which Korolëv replied: "Ten years will be enough".

ther out from the Moon than the Soviets; and the Americans only began obtaining near-side photographs of the lunar surface the year before the Soviets *finished* imaging the entire far side!

It is little known outside the aerospace industry that back in 1957 at the time of launching both Sputnik satellites the Soviet rockets were already lifting loads far in excess of anything that the Americans could manage. The satellites designed by Yevgeni Frolov of the Korolëv Bureau and launched from Baikonur were launched by an R-7 (AKA A-1).[16] These Sputnik launches were announced months in advance, but nobody in the West took them seriously. Some of the photographs that we reproduce in this book were first issued by the Soviet Embassy—in 1957. So much for the 'secrecy and competition' storyline. Sputnik I weighed 223 lbs and was *eleven times heavier* than anything that the United States was capable of launching at that time (their maximum being about 20 lbs—(for the Vanguard and Explorer satellites).

Sputnik II launched a month later on November 3 1957 weighed in at 1,117 lbs, five times the weight of Sputnik I and fifty-five times the weight of American launch capacity. This second Sputnik contained Laika the dog.

Gravity wells

The escape velocity for leaving Earth is 6.83 miles per second or 24,588 mph.

In order to leave a planetary body it is necessary to travel at a speed fast enough to release the rocket from the planet's gravitational field.

The required speed is called the escape velocity and accurate calculations related to this speed are naturally crucial to the amount of fuel carried by the craft.

The LM used hypergolic fuels and these take up weight and space. During the design stage all the components of the Apollo spacecraft to be launched by the Saturn V had undergone Operation Scrape—the elimination of all superfluous weight.

This exercise included the LM.

The escape velocity for leaving the Moon is just over 1.138 miles per second or 4,097 mph.

26. Soviet space rockets to 1966. The SL13 (far right) with 2,355,000 lbs thrust was *50% more powerful* than the USA's Saturn 1B (with only 1,640,000 lbs thrust).

27. USA space rockets to 1966 (Saturn 1B on the far right.).

First Prize—21/19

If one consults the list of Soviet firsts in the 'space race' it is clear that they had very talented engineers backed up by vast undisclosed facilities. Soviet engineers achieved the remarkable feat of scoring *twenty one* space *firsts* within nineteen years. After studying the progressive development of Soviet rocketry, it is logical to conclude that the Soviets always had every intention of sending men to the Moon.

1st satellite: Sputnik	October 4	1957
1st ICBM firing 4,000 miles/6,400 kms	August 21	1957
1st gamma ray data	October	1957
1st near miss of Moon (by only 4,600 miles)	January	1959
1st man-made object to land on Moon: Luna 2	September 13	1959
1st lunar far-side photos: Luna 3	October 4	1959
1st living creatures to orbit & return to Earth	August 19	1960
1st man into space: *Yuri Gagarin* *	April 12	1961
1st woman in space: V Tereshkova Vostok 6	June 16	1963
1st three-man crew orbit: Voskhod 1	October 12	1964
1st spacecraft to use an ion propulsion system	Vostok I	1964
1st space walk (two crew): Voskhod 2	March 18	1965
1st lunar soft landing: Luna 9	January 31	1966
1st photographs of the surface of the Moon	February	1996
1st lunar orbit: Luna 10 (April 3 Bernard Lovell)	August 24	1966
Largest & most complex spacecraft to date: Soyuz 1	April	1967
1st EVAs: two Cosmonauts leave Soyuz 5, transfer to		
Soyuz 4, undock, re-enter Earth's atmosphere & land		1969
1st lunar soil sample (100 gms): Luna 16	September 12	1970
1st lunar rover deployed: Luna 17 + Lunikhod	November 20	1970
1st human artefact to land on another planet: Mars 3		1971
1st deep soil sample (7ft depth): Luna 24	August 9	1976

* See later chapters

records that the Soyuz 1 crashed to the ground, killing Cosmonaut Komarov when the drogue lines became entangled—this matter allegedly leading to the delay of the Soyuz and Lunar programs. However a comparison of both countries' lunar timetables demonstrates how very neatly the American flights slot into the Soviet gaps. Even the above Soviet 'gap' is not as large as we are led to believe because despite delays, throughout 1968 one Luna mission and two Zonds were flown.[17]

In 1964—two years *before* the Americans developed the Saturn 1B—the Soviets were using a launch vehicle equal in lifting capacity. The Soviets called their rocket the D booster and this craft was capable of lifting 20 tons. Both the size and the power of the Soviet launch vehicles was increased with the advent of this Proton D rocket, which was used for the launch of the Proton satellite as well as the Cosmos, Zond, Luna and Salyut programs.

It is now known that in 1965, the Soviets started building a launcher equivalent to the Saturn V that America would eventually build. It was planned to test fly the N-1 craft in the latter part of 1967. Referred to by some as the 'Super Booster' this rocket generated 10 million lbs of thrust—from *30 engines in the first stage* alone—somewhat in excess of the American's 7.6 million lbs of thrust from their Saturn V.

The heavier the craft, the more powerful the launcher needs to be. Contrasting with the American desire to make lighter and lighter spacecraft, the Soviets were launching aloft much heavier payloads. Either they had less access to certain lighter materials then available in the USA, and/or their superior launch capacity was due to something else—*better engineering.*

Around the rugged rock . . .

The first Soviet in space was also sent aloft on top of an A-1. The A-2 launched the *Voskhod I* and an uprated version of this rocket launched the Soyuz spacecraft. Western information

28. Soviet A-2.

139

29. Twenty engine nozzles visible on an A-2 launcher at Bikonur.

ALLGEMEINER DEUTSCHER NACHDIENST

The N-1 rocket engines, were codenamed NK-33 and the prospective Soviet lunar craft was codenamed OK-L-1. It was claimed that the vehicle had a unique and safe structure. In all, five hundred organisations and twenty six ministries and government departments were involved in the development of the N-1 vehicle.[18]

The first flight was officially re-scheduled for February 21 1969. Many writers are at pains to state that the Soviet 'Super Booster' did not work and that the Soviets had to abandon their chances of getting to the Moon for the want of a capable launcher in addition to internal politics within their space program. We feel that these stories of the launch problems of the N-1 throughout the years of 1967-1970 could well be the product of organised disinformation.

Key points in the program were:

• On February 21 1969 the Soviets first test-flew their N-1. It used liquid kerosene and oxygen, had a weight of 9.1 million lbs, produced 10 million lbs of thrust, had 30 first stage engines and stood 307.5 feet high with a base diameter of 52.5 feet. We are informed that a fire in the tail compartment

30. The Soviet N-1.

shut down the engine 70 seconds after launch. The second firing in July 69 also apparently failed. The N-1 was tested again in June 1971 and November 1972.

• Suvorov's diaries disagree with these dates.[19]

• In 1994 we learnt that the Russian N-1 engines were currently being tested for use in American rockets! Now that *was* an apparent turn around!

• The Japanese had N-1 main engine(s) and a number of strap-on boosters.

• Data published in 1995 indicated that since 1965 more than 200 Proton craft have been launched.

• In the late 1990s a Proton could take aloft a payload of 9 tonnes.

QUESTION: If the Soviets had been so unsuccessful in their quest to build powerful rockets, how can it be that the Russians are currently charging various countries, including the Americans, commercial rates for space launches?

... the ragged rascals ran

The Soviets built their machines for functionality and not for show business. These machines were tougher, more efficient and had greater durability than their American counterparts. Soyuz, flown in 1967 (at the same time as the Gemini phase of the American program), was still functioning 15 years later. If Soyuz allegedly did not perform and killed their cosmonauts, why did the Soviets continue with its use? Of their manned craft, Voskhod 1 was capable of taking a crew of three. It was a major advance over the first series, being 1,500 lbs heavier and containing many technical improvements. It was considered so safe that cosmonauts did not need to wear their pressure suits during flight. The Soviets considered that an accident serious enough to split the crew module would kill the cosmonauts anyway, so that it was irrelevant to provide spacesuit environmental feeds, except for EVAs or whenever the cabin was to be depressurised.[20] Our information is that the Voskhod cosmonauts used drogue parachutes and retro-rockets to land on the hard surface of Earth, compared with the Vostok pilots who had to parachute from their spacecraft.

The Soviet crew command module design of 1967 was that of a bell with flattened sides and a hemispherical heat shield across the base. It was designed to carry three cosmonauts in a shirt-sleeve environment of nitrogen and oxygen at sea-level pressure.

The Soviets used this nitrogen/oxygen mix in their manned craft instead of the pure oxygen environment that the Americans favoured. In the early days of Apollo, Charlie Felz of North American Aviation wanted to use this two-gas mixture as it was safer than the very hazardous pure oxygen. NASA overruled this request because considerable technical problems would have arisen, including the need for instrumentation developments before such a mixture could be used.

One wonders how the Soviets managed so well!

It is our contention that the Soviets have always been at the forefront of rocket development and that they never did abandon their intention of going to the Moon. We suggest that much of the propaganda released by the US regarding the Soviet space program was just that—propaganda. Costly failures, management insisting that missions be tried without enough testing, technical problems with solar panels during flight, tragic accidents which affected the schedule with the entire program were virtually dependent on just one major item.

For the Soviets, their rocket launcher.

For the Americans, their lunar lander.

Both countries' space scenarios appear to have been written by the same script writers.

Drama doctoring

During the 'Apollo 16' mission the record states that the astronauts experienced technical problems, even during the first stages of separation of the LM Orion from the CM Casper. The drama of this landing was heightened by their tardiness, they were *six hours late* when they finally touched down at their designated lunar site. According to space historian Andrew Chaikin, had the flight been much further behind schedule, the landing would have been reprogrammed for the following morning (Earth time). This action was considered an impossibility due to the lighting conditions.

The foregoing statement is totally absurd.

At the time this *actual arrival* was scheduled the Sun was at 10 degrees of arc, a delay of between 12 to 24 hours would only increase the Sun angle by 6 to 12 degrees or so. If an entire lunar mission costing billions of dollars is jeopardised by a brief delay of six hours, then it does not say much for the planning department at Houston, who would appear to have selected either the wrong site or the wrong time of the lunar month—or both! But from a purely creative point of view, the script writing was excellent, the whole episode made for a great adventure with plenty of dramatic tension. A great ending for a storyline featuring a craft designed as a lunar lander and which was an equally dramatic prop!

L is for LEM

The Lunar Excursion Module later known as the LM, (pronounced *lem*) was an excellent piece of set dressing, a vitally important component in the unfolding NASA space drama. The LM was basically an arrangement of two engines and their attendant fuel tanks. Even hypergolic fuels take up space, and during the design stage, the LM (which used such fuels)—like all the other components of the Apollo spacecraft to be launched by the Saturn V—had undergone Operation Scrape, the elimination of all superfluous weight. Created uniquely for the astronaut's descent to the surface of the Moon from the Command Module, the LM was specifically designed to function with either a one-man or a two-man crew,[21] although two astronauts were very hard pressed to be comfortable in such conditions, as we shall discover. This machine would sit on the surface during the EVA and "if all went well" as NASA were fond of saying, it would leave the Moon and rejoin the CSM. The Lunar Module design in some ways is equivalent to a wigwam. Both have two apertures (one in the side, one at the top), flimsy supports, thin

31. North American Indian wigwam.

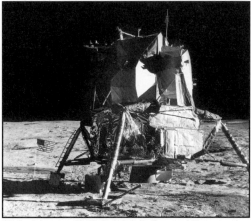

32. A wigwam no North American Indian would be seen dead in.　　NASA

walls and a central fire!

This 'flying wigwam', specifically designed for functioning uniquely in a vacuum, was totally incapable of supporting its own weight on Earth, and certainly incapable of surviving the heat of re-entry into the Earth's atmosphere. Given its inability to travel anywhere once down on the lunar surface, NASA at an early stage decided to drop the word 'excursion' from its title.

So how would the LM perform in the environment of space and on the lunar surface? Before 'Apollo 11' allegedly landed on our satellite, the Moon, *no LM* had ever been tested to its *full* functionality in space.

This means that:

- No LM had ever been in manned lunar orbit lower than a distance of nine miles above the lunar surface. This height was allegedly reached during the 'Apollo 10' test flight of May 1969;
- No LM had ever touched the lunar surface;
- No trials had ever been made for the *ascent* from the lunar surface, either by a remote-controlled or by a manned LM. That at least is what we have all been told.

Given the number of unknowns inherent in these manoeuvres, would it not have been advisable—or rather absolutely mandatory—to test these procedures with a remote-controlled LM before risking the lives of human beings in one? Even more so since NASA and the Soviet Union had both experienced disturbing gravitational anomalies during lunar orbits involving their respective unmanned craft.

The LM was the culmination of many years of design and research. It was constructed for NASA by the Grumman Aircraft Engineering Corporation and its affiliated contractors.

Founded in 1930, Grumman's expertise (much like that of Hasselblad) was acquired through the necessities of United States' national defence industries. Builders of naval aircraft such as amphibious aeroplanes, hydrofoil boats, seaplanes etc., Grumman also produced 17,000 combat aircraft during WWII, including the Hellcat, Wildcat and Avenger series.

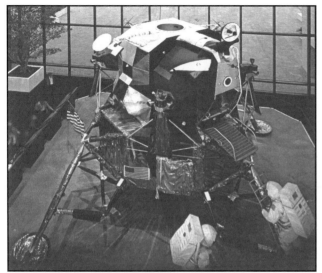

33. Lunar Module in the US National Air and Space Museum. (see also Appendix)

The company only began making commercial (i.e. civilian) aircraft after the war. Space was a domain into which they first ventured publicly in 1960 with the contract for a series of astronomical satellites designed for Earth orbit.

Although they were not to sign the contract with NASA for the LM development until 1962, Grumman had been investing time and money in LM design principles and requirements since 1958. From that date until 1965, Grumman worked through three variations on a basic theme, before finalising the design into the 'flying wigwam' (or spider as some have called it) that we are familiar with today. Their final design was *remarkably* similar to RA Smith's original 1947 proposal (see next page). That first concept incorporated the principals of liquid propellant technology, a base supported by legs and vertical ascent from the lunar surface.

QUESTION: Why is it that most space chroniclers consider that Grumman only worked on the LM from 1962 onwards?

QUESTION: Have they been deliberately mislead?

QUESTION: Were Grumman philanthropists or speculators, that they used their own time

and money to develop a product for which they might never receive a contract?

ANSWER: No.

QUESTION: Then whose money was used to finance the Grumman LM in-house studies from 1958-1962?

ANSWER: They received development funding.

It is usual for potential contractors to produce a written proposal of a size and detail commensurate with the allocated program budget. For example the LM program was evaluated at $6.9 *billion*. That is a very large sum indeed and was worth a great deal more back in the 1960s. A budget of that size would normally require a program proposal of anything between 5,000 to 86,000 pages. Whistle-Blower Bill Wood informs us that ten other proposals he had examined for programs of that $ value averaged over 38,000 pages.

Yet Grumman produced a Lunar Excursion Module program proposal totalling only 110 pages! This size of document would have been appropriate for a mere $1.4 million project.

QUESTION: Why was Grumman's LEM program proposal so skimpy ?

QUESTION: Could it rather be that they already knew in advance that they would secure the contract and therefore did not have to 'bother' with the very detailed proposal normally required to secure such projects?

QUESTION: Or could it be that certain key individuals were advised that this craft would *actually not be required to perform to its full official specification?*

Reservations

The LM was basically a pair of flying engines, designed to carry the astronauts from the Command Module orbiting around the Moon down to the lunar surface. The LM would be their 'home' for the duration of their visit, and would then ascend from the lunar surface and rendezvous with the Command Module. An

---

The British Interplanetary Society

was founded in 1933 specifically to evaluate *how three men could be landed on the Moon and returned safely to Earth* (does that remind us of anyone else's words?).
Many of this Society's original concepts, including the LM, have been incorporated into aspects of the space program.
R A Smith, the designer of the first lunar lander had already designed a spaceship by 1939—many aspects of this craft appear to be rather more sensible than those ultimately put into practise by NASA.

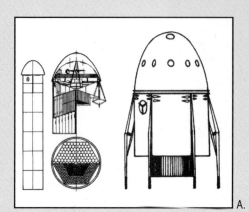 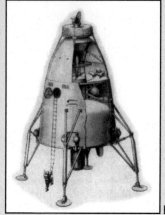

A) British Interplanetary Society Lunar Spaceship 1939.
B) Lunar Exploration craft BIS member R A Smith's 1947 design.
The BIS had already considered that chemical scrubbers would be necessary for the removal of carbon dioxide and water vapour from the astronauts' breath.
Founder members of the BIS include Arthur C Clarke.

---

ambitious program certainly, but theoretically feasible. In order to achieve these aims, the flying wigwam consisted of two sections: The *descent stage*, which provided the power for the first part of the mission; and then th*e ascent stage* which housed the crew of two astronauts, became their base camp while on the Moon and then provided the propulsion and control systems for their return to the orbiting CSM.

With the redundant descent stage remaining on the Moon, the departure from the lunar surface required the provision of separate fuel tanks and ascent engine. This was a good design feature. During the descent period, the LM had the potential to abort a landing and fire the ascent stage from mid-descent, should there be a malfunction or an impediment to landing. This capability of course was only available down to a certain height—after which it would

be too late to obtain the required impetus from the ascent engine—the LM would then crashland onto the Moon. Another advantage to the dual stage concept meant that the LM could be much lighter overall, and less fuel was required on board than if the whole apparatus had to be returned to the Command Module.

The lander was entirely constructed around the engine housing and fuel tanks. Two astronauts stood in front of the engine housing (located on top of the ascent engine) and were surrounded on all four sides—front, back, left, and right—by fuel tanks. At the angles between these tanks were the triangular storage bays for the scientific equipment, geological specimen returns, and other necessities. These, together with eight radio systems, life support systems, cameras and other instrumentation gave the LM of 'Apollo 11' a launch weight of 14.82 tons. This was increased to 16.18 tons on later LM models. The LM was stowed, fully loaded with its hypergolic fuels, on top of the third stage of the Saturn V rocket.

Being uniquely designed to fly in the vacuum of space, the Lunar Module's structure was so delicate (according to many sources) *that it could not support its own weight in an Earth environment.*

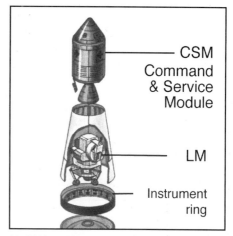

35. CSM and LM in their launch configuration on top the Saturn V.

34. Artists impression of LM landing and clearly producing a very obvious exhaust. NASA

Yet that same LM would have had to endure the maximum thrust of the Saturn V's first and second stage at full acceleration, an imposition of at least 7 Gs—that is an equivalent *weight* of 103.74 tons. If the module could not even support its *own* weight, then it would certainly have required some *very* special support or suspension during lift-off from Earth!

Just before he died, Gus Grissom had noted that NASA's inability to ade-

quately communicate between their spacecraft and ground control—while still on the launch pad—did not bode well for the missions themselves.

When Armstrong was nearly killed during a training exercise on the LM simulator and had to eject before it crashed to the ground, he was unable to hear anything from the control tower through his headphones, due to the excessive noise of the jet engine.

How can it be that the pressurised interior of the LM was virtually silent? The thunderous noise inside this pressurised flying wigwam should have been tremen-

36. LM Trainer/simulator. NASA

37. Interior view of a LM.   NASA

38. Cernan and Schmitt during training in a LM.   NASA

dous, with the rocket engine roaring just under the occupant's feet, yet the sound recordings on all the alleged direct communications with Houston are *unhindered by any vibration or significant sound in the background whatsoever*. They are also miraculously unhindered by any breakup in communications, not many of the "...Say again Houston?" lines in these carefully written scripts!

Armstrong was standing immediately above a rocket engine producing *10,000 lbs of thrust!* And we hear *nothing?*—silent whistles!? And then what about the total lack of shake, or stress in his voice?—the heat and vibration transmitted to the entire frame of the craft would surely have been an utterly bone-rattling nerve-shattering experience.

NASA described the LM descent engine as being covered with a Titanium shield, made to contain the radiating heat estimated at nearly 2,000°F/1,093°C) according to some sources, or even as high as 3,000°F/1,649°C.[22]

With the best will in the world, it is difficult to conceive of the silent, shirt-sleeved environment that we were presented with on the Apollo missions—except of course, as seen in movies such as *2001; A Space Odyssey.*

Pushing the envelope—*of our gullibility*

NASA shows us Aldrin aboard the LM Eagle in his coveralls. Some technical sourcebooks assert that the LM was designed for the astronauts to fly in light coveralls, in a pure oxygen

---

Cranky Yankees

Jet engines make a great deal of noise.

For sake of a comparison, the noise of a single jet taking off from an aircraft carrier can reach 140 decibels, roughly the amount of noise generated by an orchestra of 75,000 musicians.

Above 145 decibels, the *human body vibrates* from the intensity of these sound waves.

Long exposure to such an intensity of sound, creates physiological and psychological stress.

During the early days of aircraft flight decks, catapult crews wore special earmuffs, which filtered out the high frequency noise but these crews still suffered from stress and depression.

---

environment of 248 mm Hg.[23] Others state that the astronauts were required to be clad in their pressure suits as the oxygen feeds *transited* through the suits and *then* through the cabin environment.

Chaikin relates that Armstrong and Aldrin took six hours to put on their suits, while the astronauts of 'Apollo 15' were supposedly the *first* astronauts *not* to have to wear their pressure suits within the LM.[24] They said that it was a pleasure to wear coveralls while they slept.

QUESTION: If *you* really were travelling in an untested craft, when the slightest problem might cause your immediate demise, would you be doing it in your shirt sleeves? Would you travel thusly, when apparently, you could maximise your chances of survival by wearing the protective clothing that went with your ticket?

In Europe, we insist that motor cycle riders wear crash helmets at all times and on construction sites hard hats are compulsory.

However, astronauts, travelling at speed in a virgin and reputedly tricky craft, through an unfamiliar environment, on an untried trajectory to an unknown landing surface are supposedly doing all of this just in their pilot's coveralls!

Back on Earth, before launch, each astronaut was suited up by several attendants, working in a spacious arena. Yet we are expected to believe that the astronauts were able to dress and undress *themselves* in the *severely restricted* interior of the LM. We are also advised that they slept in their space suits and some of them allegedly felt the cold whilst the LM stood on the lunar surface. So much for the claimed complete environmental system that

39. 'Apollo 11' the shirt-sleeve environment of the LM Eagle.

NASA

these suits afforded the wearer.

QUESTION: How could they possibly become *cold* in a cabin standing in the Sun of the lunar day. In a cabin that supposedly had been thermally insulated, pressurised and specifically designed for their requirements?[25] If anything they should be too *hot*, with outside temperatures of around +180° to 200°F, and at least one half of the cabin exposed to the full blast of the Sun.

Whichever account you read of these astronaut's LM adventures, there is only one certainty—they never, ever tally. Not ever.

Grumman's wigwam

At the heart of the LM—the habitable area was of aluminium alloy fabrication using conventional aircraft construction techniques. This cabin was surrounded by cylindrical propellant

---

LM precautions

The complete descent stage was protected by a thermal and micrometeoroid shield, the top and side panels having an extra tough nickel mesh protection.

The engine temperatures radiated by the descent engine would heat the engine compartment, and so titanium was used as a protection.

Mylar and H film blankets were fitted to distribute heat from the Sun and absorb the energy of tiny micrometeorites.

There was also a Teflon-coated titanium blast shield to deflect engine exhaust from the ascent stage when it took off after separating from the descent stage, which was to remain behind.

---

tanks, altitude control thrusters and all their associated 'plumbing'. The drum shape of the ascent engine protruded into this 'living' space. The peculiar shape of the LM was due mostly to the aluminium 'stand-offs', which contoured these propellant tanks and plumbing and also supported the thermal blankets. These blankets were made of at least 25 layers of aluminised Mylar (or H film).

There was another layer external to this Mylar, supported by an extension of the standoffs. This second layer was an anti-micrometeoroid shield, a flexible skin of sheet aluminium. It was this flexible outer skin that gave rise to the legend of the LM's fragility, where an astronaut could "put his foot through the wall" at any moment.

The front section was equipped with the two triangular windows, and there was a larger rectangular window in the roof of the LM. During the testing of the first LM, aluminium shades were lowered over these windows. Why did they not test the windows as they would have been used by the astronauts—i.e. without covers? Or conversely, should not these windows have been covered by aluminium *at all times,* bearing in mind the GCRs and particularly the solar radiation problems with which NASA were continually grappling?

It has been acknowledged that micrometeorites can traverse the perspex and polycarbonate helmets worn by the astronauts, and it is known that cosmic rays have also penetrated craft. One of the LM's triangular windows had a camera fitted behind it. Yet we have no evidence, actual or admitted from NASA, that any film stock, exposed or otherwise was ever damaged or exhibited any effects from any of these ultra high speed particles.

More drama doctoring

Having created this machine the real question was: could the LM even land on the Moon? The record states that during the alleged 'Apollo 10' testing of the LM both in orbit around the Moon and continuing down to nine miles above the surface, the LM suffered from wild gyrations, which were later put down to: "an abort switch that had been snapped on, unnoticed"! Another official comment on this incident was: "the Lunar Module had performed far beyond what (sic) engineers believed would ever have been demanded of the skittish machine". A machine does what it is supposedly designed for—in this case, goes to the Moon and descends near enough to simulate *some* of the conditions required for landing, then departs and rejoins its Command Module—and its engineers are astonished! However, given that it is highly unlikely that this trip was a manned mission these descriptions could be script writing, Whistle-Blowing or even a bit of both.

We note that the machine was still considered to be 'skittish' two months before 'the big one'—nevertheless, when this flying wigwam apparently went to the Moon it behaved *perfectly*—as it did thereafter on *five* subsequent manned lunar landings!

Those engineers were right to be astonished! Because leading up to this manned 'Apollo 10' flight (wherever it actually flew) Grumman had been in serious trouble with the development of the LM. The LM1 test did not fulfil expectations, with the Ascent Propulsion System (APS) bursting into flames and breaking up as the two stages separated. The computer also became confused and malfunctioned, depleting the propellants from the thruster system and,

---

Horses for courses

Skittish is generally used as a description of lively but unreliable behaviour.
It is often applied to horses difficult to ride, being inclined to starting
or shying for no reason.
This is an interesting definition of a craft that needs to be utterly reliable
and extremely responsive to the astronaut's every whim.
Or perhaps the officials intended the word in its other context:
to ridicule or caricature, by means of a skit?

The boggle factor

During manufacture, stress corrosion cracks began to appear in the aluminium structures of some LMs.

Grumman's inspectors checked the LMs in the areas accessible to inspection, but did not disassemble any module—apparently for fear of dropping behind with their delivery dates.

They *gambled* that, as they had not found any cracks in the *accessible* parts,

the chances of corrosion happening in the hidden parts of the structure were:

"Sufficiently low to assume there were none!"

They hedged their bets by switching to a different alloy for subsequent LM fabrication.

We have been unable to find any trace of this alloy swap in the history records available.

Is this 'drama doctoring' or plain commercial greed?

of LM3. But among other difficulties, all the LMs experienced *wiring* problems to varying degrees and naughty Grumman were told to be more careful.

So history repeats itself once more: in mid 1968, some 14 months after the fatal electrical faults that killed Grissom, White and Chaffee we are again hearing of electrical wiring installation and malfunction problems in a major component of the Apollo program. Two near disasters were announced in that year, one of them in the very month that 'Apollo 8' was scheduled to leave for its mission. Theoretical flight simulations were held between the Cape and Houston. Physical flight simulations took place at Ellington Air Force Base.

The physical LM simulator had a centrally-placed jet engine which shot it 1,000 feet into the air. The astronaut then threw a switch which throttled back the engine to compensate for $5/6$ths of the LM's weight. The remaining $1/6$th weight made the vehicle fall at just the correct speed towards the ground and the pilot used his thrusters to manoeuvre and balance the LM's descent.

There is film footage of Armstrong's ejection from the LM simulator in May 1968 when it ran out of attitude control fuel for the thrusters. The machine became totally unstable to the point of almost killing Armstrong. This prob-

on a second firing of the APS, closed down systems which then forced the LM into an uncontrollable tumble. Yet, astonishingly, this result was considered by NASA as satisfying minimum test operations. The LM1 'officially' passed this test with flying colours—so much so that NASA thought another unmanned test unnecessary! They then skipped to the testing

The box of tricks.

It was on July 20 1962 that James Webb said NASA needed a real time computer complex (RTCC) at the Manned Spacecraft Center in Houston, thus unifying existing computers with the Space Task Group at Langley, Goddard and the Cape.

IBM were given the job and the transfer of Mission Control from the Cape to Houston was completed three years later by the time of the Gemini IV flight on June 6-7 1965. Although primitive by today's standards, at the time of Apollo the US computing technology was the most advanced in existence—and this was the vital adjunct to their rocket technology. Yet all the computing ability in the world would be of no consequence if their *spacecraft's* computers were unable to handle the radiation of the Van Allen belts and thereafter in deep space.

In the *Scientific American* of March 1959, Dr. James Van Allen wrote that any craft containing astronauts would require shielding against radiation.

If their computers were unable to deal with this hazard, then what chance would a bio-organism have?

The sixties bug?

An interesting explanation as to why the 'Apollo 11' astronauts had alarm bells ringing 5 mins 38 secs into the *descent to the landing site:* Mission Control was unaware, as were the astronauts, that the LM's computer was *incorrectly programmed for the descent trajectory* down to the lunar surface![26]

TechnoSpeak update	
Cryogenics:	The management of temperatures from -238°F/-150°C down to absolute zero. Molecular motion at absolute zero is as close as possible to ceasing completely.
Hypergolics:	Fuels which ignite *upon contact with each other,* thus requiring no external aid.

lem was declared a *design* flaw and not an operational blip. For a design flaw to result in a lack of fuel is pushing Operation Scrape a bit far, is it not?

In December 1968 test pilot Joe Algranti also had to eject from the LM simulator due to an (unspecified) aerodynamic problem. When the 'Apollo 8' flight around the Moon was scheduled for December that year, no LM was considered flight ready.

Wonderfuel

Whistle-Blower Bill Kaysing has evaluated, as have others, that the LM was under capacity in fuel provision for the claimed descent to the lunar surface. He infers that the LM neither landed on the Moon nor took off again according to the scenario published by NASA. The LM consumed more than half its own weight during the descent stage, which should have brought the amount of propellants to around 8 tons for the LM *Eagle's* descent. Eagle's descent fuel tanks held 8 tons of propellant while the ascent tanks stored 2.3 tons.[27] Neil Armstrong apparently landed with about 2% of available fuel remaining.[28] (Each published account gives different figures and even different actual weights for the LM. One cannot blame the various authors for these discrepancies, but it does help to fudge the record, contributing to the continuance of the notorious Never A Straight Answer policy.)[29] Armstrong overshot the lunar landing site by 1,000 feet, which apparently cost an extra 40 seconds, leaving 400 lbs of fuel in the descent tanks. If 400 lbs is 2% then 100% is 20,000 lbs which is around 9 tons. *That makes one ton more fuel than they started out with at launch.* (Those

rumours must be true then: 'They' are out there, running a Cislunar filling station!)

Grumman's engineer

In June 1996, we talked to George Pinter previously of Grumman Aerospace who was actively involved at top level in the development of the cryogenics for the Lunar Module.[30]

The company had formal discussions with Rocketdyne in California concerning the development of a helium-injected engine. Rocketdyne had been awarded the contract to develop the LM's descent propulsion system (Bell Aerosystems were awarded the Ascent Propulsion System) on January 30 1963, but they had run into difficulties. Pinter was so valuable that for a period he was seconded to Rocketdyne to help them out. For this project was considered as a 'pacing item' around which the whole Apollo program would revolve.

The Manned Spacecraft Center had drawn up the specifications for this descent engine and stipulated that it should have a throttleable range of 10:1. However, Grumman put out to tender the Descent Propulsion System again on March 14 1963, this time requesting an alternative design, using mechanical throttle linkage rather than chemical thrust reduction as in the helium system.

By May 1 that year, Grumman had authorised Rocketdyne to proceed with the Helium concept and selected Space Technology Labora-

Rockets dying
In 1963, Rocketdyne was a division of North American Aviation, the company that manufactured the Apollo 1 Command Module which was destroyed by fire killing three astronauts.

40. George Pinter at Grumman Aerospace, September 1970.

G PINTER

tories (STL) to proceed with the mechanical engine. Money was certainly not in short supply! STL carried out its first (we are advised successful) test firing of this engine in January 1964, a year after the Rocketdyne contract had been agreed. By April 1964, STL had established a new facility for the Lunar Module DPS at San Juan Capistrano, California and in July they were testing out at Reno, Nevada—using simulators to run tests up to a theoretical 24 miles altitude.

Back at Rocketdyne, in January 1965, two years after their contract had been awarded, Rocketdyne were ordered to cancel what was now interestingly termed "their competitive concept". Was this role reversal or parallel development of two systems for two different purposes? And were these parallel contracts designed to discretely slow the pace of the space program?

Whatever the real reason for this shift of approach, one thing is certain: a great deal of money had gone to North American Aviation as a result of that successful tender.

On June 15 1996 we were very fortunate to be able to put several questions to George Pinter. He was now retired and in delicate health but there was nothing wrong with either his mind or his memory.

An Associate Fellow of the American Institute of Aeronautics and Astronautics, his work involved the technical supervision of the specialists as well as the management of the project. With numerous qualifications and four

patents to his name, George Pinter was recipient of a Grumman 'Certificate of Excellence', plus a NASA 'Apollo achievement award'.

"Why do you think that the makers of the film *Apollo 13* produced a red exhaust from the LM engine when there was no such exhaust in the 'real thing'?" we asked.

"It was theatrical license," George replied.
"But the LM used *hypergolic propellants,*" was our response, "therefore there should have been thick, dense, opaque, dark red smoke in 'the real thing'."

"It was *white* smoke," George insisted.
"But there were always red exhaust gases produced during the tests in California," we pointed out.

"Oh! The red gases were the tests for the chemicals used for the attitude control thrusters," responded George.

41. Close up detail of a LM thruster.

J COLLIER

We knew that George Pinter was highly qualified to answer such questions and he was certainly in full possession of the facts. Being intimately involved with the cryogenics for the LM he had to be fully aware that his answer was glaringly incorrect and that we would easily be able to establish that it was 'wrong'. It would appear that George Pinter was blowing a clear, albeit discreet whistle.

"Well, let's move on to another point. How could anybody see anything out of the window of the LM during landing on the lunar surface, with this totally obscuring hypergolic exhaust smoke belching out of the engine?"

42. Hypergolic tests in the Simi Hills, California—which produced thick, dense, opaque, dark red smoke.   W KAYSING

"There absolutely could not be *any* smoke," replied George, "because they *had to see to land.* They just picked up a little dust."

This crucial question of the lack of exhaust from the descent engine (and from the ascent engine as well) is absolutely fundamental to the veracity of the LM lunar landings.

We wondered if George Pinter was saying that the lack of the thick, dense, opaque, dark red (or even white) smoke is a clue that hypergolic fuels were *not* used?

Or rather that there is something altogether in error with the record of the landings? Was he, in effect, agreeing that hypergolic fuels do produce the effects mentioned, but that *Armstrong* did not see smoke through his window, because *Neil Armstrong had to be able to see* and therefore *Armstrong* did not land on the Moon?

The single common factor in all these alleged events would have been the emissions from the LM's actual exhaust, no matter where the landing location.

43. Artists impression of LM's ascent stage   NASA
taking off, producing a very obvious exhaust.

"These hypergolic fuels burn with thick, dense, opaque, dark red smoke, through which, at close distances it is impossible to see."[31]

Therefore we must conclude:

NO EXHAUST = NO HYPERGOLIC FUELS = NOT A TRUE RECORD OF AN ACTUAL LUNAR LANDING.

44. Actual TV frame of 'Apollo 17' LM ascent stage apparently taking off, generating NO SMOKE OR ROCKET EXHAUST WHATSOEVER.   NASA

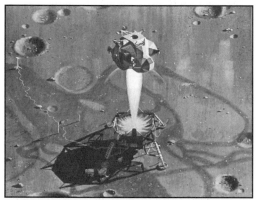

45. Artists impression of LM's ascent stage taking off, producing an obvious exhaust.   NGS

We returned to this key question with George Pinter. "There is another point concerning the landing of the LM on the lunar surface," we said. "When the space agency [and Grumman] were preparing their early 'artist's impressions'

of future landings on the Moon they had the artist include the red exhaust gas *and* a crater underneath the LM.   So why was there no *crater* in the real thing?"

"That's a good question. You should write to the American Consulate and ask them," George   suggested.   We thought that this cratering aspect was crucial so we asked George about it once again.

"Just to press the point—by what circumstance is it possible to hover and then land on rock with an engine burning at 3,250°F/1,788°C (when throttled back to 65%) and neither affect the rock nor *MELT* the dust directly under the engine, let alone 'not dig a hole'. And wouldn't that also have damaged the gold Mylar on the legs and deposited dirt on the LM's footpads?" we asked.

"Two more good points. You should write to the American Consulate in London for the answer to those questions," was the firm reply.

"During the take-off from the lunar surface why were no exhaust gases and smoke from the

46. Grumman LM and generated crater.   GRUMMAN

153

ascent engine visible?" we queried.

"In a vacuum the gases must disperse very widely and these gases must have become so thin that they were invisible"(!) George responded.

In this last answer, George Pinter was of course admitting (wittingly or unwittingly) that *there are* indeed visible exhausts from a hypergolic engine when operating—even in a vacuum.

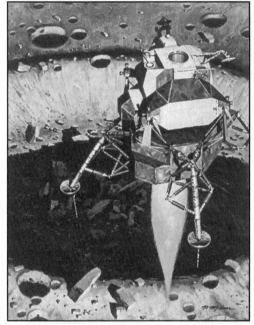

47. Artists impression landing on the Moon with a large crater beneath the LM.   NGS

However, he had not thought of this answer earlier on when he had said: "There could not be any smoke". In a vacuum, these thick, dense, opaque, exhaust gasses would certainly be visible, no matter how widely they had dispersed.[32] But to comply with his own earlier answer and the recorded TV material of the alleged ascents of the LM modules, these gases would have to *disperse instantly*—a very tall order. On take off, we should have seen the exhaust generated by the engine. In fact we saw nothing, just a special effect rather like a champagne cork popping.

We maintain that there were no exhaust gases visible during take off, because *the TV footage*

48. No lunar dust whatsoever on the surface of LM footpad.   NASA

is not a true record of an actual take off from the Moon. A take off which might never have occurred—even if there were any surviving astronauts.

QUESTION: What is the difference between a wigwam and the LM—apart from the fact that a wigwam cannot fly?

ANSWER: A wigwam has ventilation for the *white smoke* from the central fire. The LM apparently did not create *any* 'smoke' at all.

QUESTION: Why does George Pinter tell us to ask the American Consulate in *England* for the answers—an act of absolute Whistle-Blowing in his case. Firstly "go and ask another American official" is a very good response from someone 'unable' to speak out. Or

49. LM 'on Moon', with no melted dust, no crater, no disturbance whatsoever—only a footprint or two!   NASA

Manoeuvring difficulties

In its Orbital Manoeuvring Subsystem & Reaction Control System, the Space Shuttle uses the same fuel and oxidiser as the LM—*clearly visible when firing.*

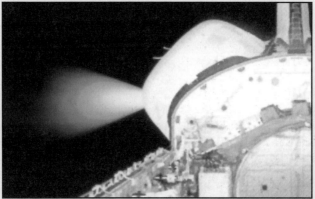

NASA

"The forward primary thrusters sound like exploding cannons at thrust onset; and during their firing, jets of flame shoot out from the orbiter's nose. The orbiter reacts to the primaries' shove by shaking slightly and moving very noticeably. For the crew on board, a series of attitude changes using primaries resembles a World War I sea battle, with cannons and mortars firing, flashes of flame shooting in all directions, and the ship's shuddering and shaking in reaction to the salvos."

The above account posted on the Internet by David Wozney in 1998 is an extract by one Joseph P Allen, better known as Apollo astronaut Joe Allen.

The LM ascent and descent engines used *hypergolic* propellants. Nitrogen tetroxide the oxidiser and Aerozene-50 the fuel, both stored in separate tanks: Aerozene-50 is a blend of hydrazine and unsymmetrical dimethylhydrazine.
This mix was identical to that used for the LM thrusters. Hypergolic fuels ignite upon contact without external aid.

---

could it be that the American Consulate in the UK would equally be unable to enlighten us as to why there was no sign of hypergolic fuels being used in the Apollo LMs?

Very sadly, George Pinter died a few months after our conversation but we followed his recommendation and wrote to the American Consulate, who acknowledged our letter. The Consulate stated that they were not in a position to help us; they therefore had forwarded our questions to the appropriate departments in NASA.[33] That was in 1996. Not surprisingly, to date we have had no response whatsoever on this serious matter from NASA. We concluded that George had foreseen such an outcome and that in waiting for a reply which would never appear, we would then query *why* George had indicated this particular Embassy. Was George really telling us that the Apollo lunar missions

50. Rock melted at 1,800°F/1,000°C during the Mount Etna volcanic eruption in 1986.   AULIS

No smoke—only dust!

Apollo 11: "At 115 feet the thrust from the engine begins to disturb the loose dust on the surface. The intensity of lunar dust cloud increases sharply making the out-of-the-window observations difficult." *Apollo 11* D Shayler

(Yet from the same source, at 65 feet Armstrong is apparently hovering and *looking* for a place to land!)

Apollo 11: "During the last forty feet or so, the rocket engine exhaust sent the dust of the Moon flying. Not billows of dust; instead the disturbed particles flew out at low angles and high velocity, like rays of light, with no atmosphere to buoy them or impede them." *National Geographic* magazine

Apollo 11: "Much like landing through light ground fog. The moment the engine shut off, however, the view out of the window was completely clear again." Neil Armstrong

Apollo 15: "As Jim Irwin and I wait for the dust to settle . . ." *National Geographic* magazine

Apollo 15: "Sixty feet above the Moon the blast of our single rocket churns up a gray tumult of lunar dust that seems to engulf us. Blinded, I feel the rest of the way down on the gauges. With an abrupt jar the Lunar Module strikes the surface and shudders to rest." *National Geographic* magazine

Apollo 15: "When they landed they had the now usual experience of *dust blowing up from the surface* and visibility was totally obscured 60 feet from the ground (emphasis added). *A Man on the Moon* A Chaikin

had international political connotations to which he was bound by his oaths of secrecy (for the defence of the United States) not to reveal? For we discovered that the American Embassy in London is the *only* American Embassy in Europe with an extensive legal library. A library that specifically contains the *treaties* entered into by the United States during the last two hundred years.

There is no fire without smoke

Rock melts at approximately 1,800°F/ 1,000°C. Whistle-Blower Bill Wood confirmed that the heat of the descent engine would have a combustion of around 5,000°F when it left the chamber, (and even if the engine was throttled back to 65% power, burning at 3,250°F) it would still be intense enough to actually melt the rock.

We must point out that not only would there have been a localised area with a changed appearance beneath the engine, we should have seen the markings of a *trail* of melted dust and softened rock as the hovering craft neared its touch-down point.[34] Another important detail left out by the creators of the visual record.

Sumerian summer

In the Summer of 1996, at White Sands Proving grounds, New Mexico, tests on the Delta rocket (DC-X) were carried out, with the rocket

51. DC-X exploding after falling over on landing.

landing in a vertical descent onto a specifically prepared site of highly compacted gypsum. The idea of this project was to design a reusable vertical take off and landing craft. This engine produced a two foot-deep crater underneath the rocket and lumps of gypsum flew up and impacted the sides of the Delta rocket, causing significant damage. The crater was so wide there was concern that the rocket would fall over into it. And hey presto! During a subsequent test, this DC-X rocket *did in fact* keel over, and then exploded.

In contrast to the alleged successful deployment of four long legs on the LM in 1969, the DC-X failed to deploy one of its relatively

52. DC-X Vertical take off rocket 1996.

short legs. We understand that the developmental DC-X project was subsequently abandoned. This DC-X experiment is one example of the state of our capabilities in respect of landing a vertical craft *(unmanned)* in the mid-to-late 1990s!

NASA is still trying to find a team of engineers who can get a rocket to land safely in a vertical descent—27 years *after* Apollo is supposed to have done exactly that, not only six times in succession, but without leaving a physical trace of such a landing! And while there is not the slightest hint of softened rock or melted dust in the lunar surface still and recorded TV pictures, nor even a speck of material covering any of their LMs, let alone any signs of damage to same, by contrast, images of the 1975 Viking lander on the surface of Mars clearly show a quantity of debris collected in its footpads.

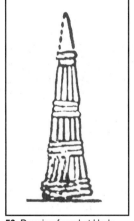

53. Drawing found at Uruk, Sumeria.

Speedy spider

It has been said that it took just 18 months for Grumman to reach the definitive external form of the LM. The implication being that American industry is the ultimate, that even an extraordinary concept such as a lunar landing vehicle can be built quickly, employing the genius that is behind NASA & Co. The numerous technical problems were quietly ignored and the public reassured that its money was being well spent and that the United States *would* beat the Soviets to the Moon.

We are beginning to see that as far as the space program is concerned, the reported facts are not necessarily the complete story. In this instance building an external shape amounts to the wrapping paper around an empty box, and a package without the contents is generally a disappointment. The reality of the situation is that it took Grumman and its associates at least 11 years (from 1958 through to 1969) to construct a machine—founded on a previous British design dating from 1947. The three year period from the Grumman/NASA contract signature in 1962 through to initial approval of the first basic design in October 1965 was only a small part of the whole LM enterprise.

In January 1965 Dr Robert R Gilruth, at that time Head of NASA's Manned Space Center near Houston, in an article in the *National Geographic,* described the LM flying simulator based at Edwards AFB as a "jet powered daddy longlegs" that "performs here on Earth as it will on the Moon".

QUESTION: How could Gilruth know *that fact for sure,* when the article was published *nine months before the approval of the first basic design?*

When we examine the developmental problems experienced by the American rocket engineers and especially when we take note of details from the interview with Grumman's George Pinter, we come to the sad conclusion that it did not matter if the LM worked or not, it was not going to bring anyone back from the Moon—but it had to *behave* as if it was.

54. LM 10. Note the clear rocket engine exhaust.

Notwithstanding that, the LM was always go-ing to be a showcase craft for NASA. Its much vaunted temperament would enhance the 'courage' of the astroboys. Whether inten-tional or not, giving it the same *characteris-tics* as a wigwam, albeit remoulded by the technological requirements of the day, could be seen as a statement. Twentieth century pro-gress was allied to the fact that these incomers (who now considered themselves as the right-ful owners of their own land) were once again appropriating a territory and all that went with it. This time it was our Moon, not a country and as we shall see, it was for their own pur-poses—not for all mankind.

As a post scriptum to the possibilities of landing safely on the lunar surface and the fact that the images of the LM are apparently fake pictures, let us just remember the historical record relating to the Surveyor 'soft landers'.

In 1966, following the June 2 landing of Surveyor 1 on the lunar surface, the space his-torian David Baker wrote that these craft used a solid propellant main retro-rocket to slow its speed from 5,000 mph to 290 mph in 40 sec-onds. Then small liquid propellant variable-thrust vernier rocket engines brought it to a quasi-standstill 13 feet above the Moon, from where it went into a free fall at a rate of 10 feet per second to the surface. This high free fall was made 'to minimise surface contamination and disturbance from exhaust gases', Baker wrote. The 649 lb Surveyor (Earth weight,

108 lbs lunar weight) bounced and oscillated slightly but came to rest undamaged. Its footpads dug about an inch into the lunar surface. QUESTION: If a Surveyor, weigh-ing a mere 108 lbs went into free fall from 13 ft *to avoid damaging the surface with its exhaust gases,* then why did not the LM contami-

55. Surveyor tests, Earth 1966.
HUGHES AIRCRAFT

nate or disturb the surface with its exhaust gases, not to mention severely altering its configuration by producing a crater? Espe-cially when the LM had a lunar weight of *over two tons* and no engine cut off until—only *5ft 8ins, less than 2m,* from the lunar surface.

When Surveyor 3 had landed on the Moon it had bounced into the air twice, once to a height of 33 ft and then to a height of 9.8 ft, its radar apparently confused by *highly reflect-ing surface rock.* Rebounded probably would be a better choice of words for leaps of such heights! Yet this probe had landed on a *dusty* surface out of which it was allegedly scooping soil samples—to a depth of 7 inches. So

56. Imprints of Surveyor's footpad 'bounce' on landing.
NASA

'Apollo 12'

From Astronaut Pete Conrad on landing the LM:
"Just like Neil, I didn't dig any crater at all!"
And from Al Bean:
"Look at that descent engine it *did not even dig a hole!*"
Infamous first words.

'Apollo 12' astronauts say that the Surveyor was no longer white when they found it but a light tan colour. They wondered if they had covered it with lunar dust when they landed. (But then how could they have done that when, in their own words, they "hardly disturbed the dust"!) Of this landing, Andrew Chaikin wrote: "Six hundred feet away, on the crater rim, the Lunar Module *Intrepid* looks like a *tiny scale model...*" Spot on, Mr Chaikin, so it does. The more one studies his book, the more one hears the whistles *he* appears to be blowing—intentionally or otherwise.

Whether there are Surveyors actually on the Moon or whether they too were simulated landings, we cannot say. However, the discrepancies outlined here are more evidence of inconsistencies within the NASA record of its Moon missions. And as for the

57. Note the lack of dust on the Surveyor and the careful placing of the 'Apollo 12' LM *exactly* on the horizon so that it stands out clearly against that black sky! It would be interesting to know who actually took this picture—taken from a considerable height, as the astronauts were allegedly *standing* on the surface! Compare *sequence of aerial images* on page 160.   NASA

where were the mirror-like surface rocks?

Then, just to confuse the issue even more, 'Apollo 12' astronauts inform us that the geologists had warned them to expect a soft, thick dust blanket at Surveyor 3's landing site—yet they apparently found firm ground and a good footing. Photograph (56) shows two of the Surveyor's imprints and the footpad resting on the surface beside the second imprint.

sharing of scientific information during a period of Cold War, here is a further example that backs up our claim that there were no secrets within the space programs of America and the Soviet Union:

What Surveyor saw after it landed, was of course, not totally new. Three Ranger spacecraft had sent back pictures.

159

Russia's Luna 9 landed on the Moon last February and took a handful of close up photographs.[35]

The above statement implies that NASA could well have seen these photographs. And why should the American author refer to the Soviet Union as Russia, unless the *political differences between their two regimes were considered irrelevant to the matter in hand—The exploration of space?*

What is certain is that at least one surveyor craft—Surveyor 3—associated closely with

---

10 out of 12

As 'Apollo **12**' LM was coming in to land on the Moon, the astronauts had the capability, the miraculous capability, despite being restricted to very limited vision through the small triangular window, of panning the camera to maintain a shot—which lasted for at least **10** seconds—of the Surveyor, allegedly on the lunar surface.

NASA

TV frames from the 'Apollo 12' LM which allegedly filmed Surveyor 3 during the LM's descent to the surface.

This sequence was filmed as one continuous shot (requiring a large panning capability). But this was apparently taken from the small triangular forward-facing window of the 'Apollo 12' LM! To obtain such a shot on Earth would require a special camera and mount—to give plenty of *sideways camera movement* while the craft maintained level flight.

Either a camera and mount fitted to a helicopter with its door removed, or a control rig in a studio would do the trick.

In our opinion, this material is absolute Whistle-Blowing and this particular scene totally faked.

But then if the astronauts had not been near the Moon but were credited with having filmed the Surveyor during their mission—it would have to have been specially created, would it not?

'Apollo 12'—is seemingly featured in a studio version of events.

A new stage

Fifteen years after the development of the Saturn V, and two years later than scheduled, the Space Shuttle was launched, using a rocket three quarters the size of the Saturn V.

The Shuttle then spent nearly three years in *redevelopment* following the Challenger disaster. In 1990s terms each Shuttle launch costs over three times as much as a Saturn V launch. Yet the Shuttle can only carry ⅙th as much payload as the Saturn V.

QUESTION: Why, nearly 30 years after Apollo, are the Americans unable to build a rocket equalling the *claimed* performance of the Saturn V?

QUESTION: In other words, if the Saturn V was so good why was it abandoned?

QUESTION: Why not use the Saturn V as the launch vehicle for the Shuttle? The initial development costs had already been covered—the Saturn V was 'bought and paid for'.

QUESTION: Equally, why was the Shuttle not designed to be used with the Saturn V launching system?. It would have been economically viable and technically feasible.[36]

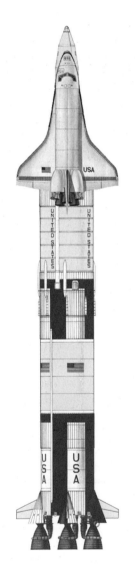

58. Mock up of the Space Shuttle with its Saturn V launcher—never to be.

QUESTION: Why are the Americans currently using a system so lacking in performance compared with the apparent capabilities of the Apollo program?

QUESTION: Can the answer to all these questions support our claim that there were serious technological problems with Apollo?

If there were shortcomings with the Saturn V as Bill Wood has suggested, launching the heavier mass of the Shuttle even into a lower orbit would have been a problem. Was the Saturn V impotent, had it *never* been able to get it up?

"One more reason for not producing any more Saturn Vs would be if they did not work in the first place," said Wood. "If their claimed performance was a hoax, then there is no point in making any more of them. That's why they might have started all over from scratch, with something that was going to work!"

It has become clear to us that the roots of this story went back further than the 1960s. It is our understanding that the Soviets had far more success with their rocket technology than the Americans, quite simply because they had the better engineers. Furthermore, the Soviet's machines did not have to 'look good', they were built to *function* in space. The Soviets did not have to justify either their expenses or their failures to their citizens and they could work and experiment in relative privacy. It is of course quite normal to have failures when developing wholly new technologies but the American way does not really tolerate a succession of visible failures to be an inherent part of the struggle towards evolution. The Soviet Union's list of successful breakthroughs allowed the Americans to 'use' that success rate as the carrot to dangle in front of the American Congress, largely responsible for approving/allocating funds to the space program.

Publicly, NASA sneered at the Soviets' failures, and masked its own. It is our belief that NASA privately partnered the Soviet space effort. The American/Soviet space timetable demonstrates how carefully progress in space had been shared out between them, with alternating monthly flights in some cases. This can only have been the result of close planning and continuous liaison at the very highest levels. (see Appendix)

Bearing this situation in mind, together with the problems posed by two basic factors, solar radiation challenges and rocket engineering difficulties, we come face to face with another problem.

QUESTION: Why did a relatively small cabal esteem it necessary to adhere to the announced agenda of landing on the Moon by December 1969, despite the many and obvious technical problems encountered along the way?

QUESTION: What had stimulated such indecent haste? The American journalist Walter Lippman writing in *Newsweek*, on February 13 1967 after the fire on Pad 34 made some particularly pertinent comments:

> This competitive timetable [the December 1969 deadline of putting a man on the Moon] has not been set by the scientists themselves....
> The risk of explosive fires is only one risk in this artificially accelerated program....
> At the risk of their lives, these men are being sent on a mission for which the scientific preparation is far from adequate.

Whistle-Blower Bill Kaysing estimated that there were 85 completely separate manoeuvres involved in a lunar landing. Statisticians have calculated that the chances of completing this set of manoeuvres six times, without a single failure, were totally beyond the realms of probability.

In 1967, Sir Bernard Lovell (the Director of Jodrell Bank Radio Astronomy Laboratories in England) was quoted as saying that:

> The risks of being placed in Earth orbit are so enormous that an entirely new degree of human courage has been demanded.

For the technology involved, given the difficulty of launching the required weight into space from the Earth's surface, launching from LEO would be more practical, cheaper and enable greater weights to be sent into deep space. It would also grant more freedom of action to our space heroes to behave as they wished. Hence the requirement for a space station.

Attaining LEO creates *enormous* risks, so what would be the risk evaluation for landing on the Moon and returning home safely—gargantuan or plain impossible for our technological resources at that time? If orbital procedures concerning the Moon are not finely tuned, then the craft will miss the Moon and continue onwards, forever. Sir Bernard Lovell:

> Apollo will be hurtling towards the Moon at a speed of over 6,000 miles per hour. At a time which must be correct *to a fraction of a second* the firing of retrorockets will slow down the spaceship so that it enters a lunar orbit at a height of about 60 to 100 miles above the lunar surface.

Then there is the question of the re-entry of the craft into our atmosphere. Excessive drag and deceleration produced by approaching Earth's atmosphere at too steep an angle creates G forces that could injure or kill the crew. Sir Bernard again:

> On the return trip to Earth if the craft enters at too steep an angle it will burn up. If the angle is too shallow the craft *will skip out of the atmosphere and be lost forever in space.*[37] (emphasis added)

Sir Bernard Lovell concurred with Walter Lippman when he too, stated that:

> The project has never had the unanimous backing of scientists—indeed astronomers, whose science might be

expected to be the chief beneficiary, have been almost wholly opposed.[38]

It is the contention of Bill Kaysing, Ralph René, ourselves and others, that well before 1967 it had been decided that *simulation* was going to be the modus vivendi of the Apollo program. Secret intentions, even if verbalised between *very* few people, have a way of spreading their energy or 'atmosphere' around the project to which they are related. At some intangible level, this decision would necessarily have taken the 'edge' off the attention to detail. Technicians such as Thomas Baron, unaware of such an audacious plan, would understandably be astonished at the amount of laxity in the work place. Whistle-Blower Bill Kaysing cites several technicians who have told him that they 'knew' as soon as they arrived at their work sites, that the entire Apollo program was a fake. This situation was never verbalised, they could just 'sense' that it was the case.

Walter Lippman expressed the thought that the Space program should: "Rid itself of the destructive intrusion of propaganda and public relations". There would be no chance of that happening, for those two elements were the 'soot and whitewash' of the Space program, as integral to it as the dark and light surfaces of the Moon itself.

But then these dark and light surfaces were also integral to the Whistle-Blower's subtle denunciation of Apollo, and the discovery of the encoded messages within these pictures led us to further questions that would not go away:

• Why go to all the trouble and expense of simulating or faking an event that was *really happening*—unless such an action was absolutely necessary?

• Why construct a number of extraordinarily equipped studios, requiring virtually unlimited budgets to simulate lunar conditions?

• Why accept the consequential obligations: Namely that those who participated would become inextricably obliged to contain and defend (albeit tacitly) this action indefinitely—unless *that action* was absolutely necessary?

• What (and/or who) was it that drove this program?

• What was the *real* agenda behind all this?

We had come to the point in our research where we realised that the roots of the real Apollo story went back much further than the 1960s and that as fantastic as it might seem, we had to consider that the game of 'space racing' was in fact a script acted out by the principals and supported by a cast of many thousands. Of this great show, it would be true to say that most of the people involved were totally unaware of the actual intentions and objectives of the program. Only a very select few at the heart of this dark structure, knew (and still know) not only the full extent of the hoax but also the real reasons for which it was being carried out. In other words—the answers to our questions.

As they were obviously not about to tell any of us their secrets, we decided to go back into history in order to go forwards in our understanding of the real scenario behind Project Apollo.

Chapter Five

'masters of infinity'

In *Rocket Rackets* we dealt with the technology created by the rocket scientists and engineers Wernher von Braun, Sergei Korolëv, Hermann Oberth & others. Now we are going to look more closely at the 'software'—the people involved—with a view to adding more background detail and colour to this portrait of Apollo.

The canvas

The results of our own research have shown us that it is unsurprising that NASA, while protesting greatly, is not particularly concerned by the accusations of 'hoax' when it comes to the Moon landings.

Such a reaction is similar to that of any sophisticated and highly intelligent group—the accused—under interrogation. The interrogators, convinced that they have pieced together many facts of the case, are attempting to extract confessions from the accused. However, the ammunition for the questioning is, in part, based on disinformation and so the accused sits there, quietly amused at the interrogator's ineptitude. The accused feels secure in the knowledge that ultimately their group cannot be convicted because, as both parties know, there are missing parts to the picture.

The levels of disinformation and inconsistencies concerning Apollo and indeed this planet's entire space project are complex and layered. When thinking people voice their concerns that something is wrong with the Apollo record, NASA merely side-steps such observations.

As researchers are generally armed with facts initially provided by NASA, they tend to fall into the traps placed in their path by the very people they are accusing. In order to manoeuvre around the edge of such hazards it is necessary to examine the surrounding terrain, to see exactly where the ground has been disturbed.

We put our trust in those we elect, who all too often usurp that trust and exercise their power to become the manipulators of our ultimate fate. NASA is an organisation ostensibly run by those in power—the American Government—and with regard to Project Apollo NASA simply *refuses to be accountable for its actions.* Nor is NASA acting with *responsibility* in its reluctance to answer our claims that the Apollo record is full of inconsistencies. This utter disregard for these two most fundamental requirements for any institution appears to be 'company policy'. NASA's attitude is all the more worrying, considering it is supported by US taxpayers and also by avowals to 'represent all mankind'.

Yet similar behaviour played a role in a regime of recent times—one that spawned some of the individuals responsible for the very foundations of the Apollo technology. That was of course, *the Third Reich* when Adolf Hitler adopted the title of Führer or supreme leader of the National Socialist German Workers party—remembered by the entire world as the Nazis. This matter is entirely relevant, for without the remnants of Hitler's war machine, our first steps into space would probably have occurred decades later.

The fact that the rocket scientists, their documentation and rocket hardware were transferred to the Allies is a matter of record. The ways and means by which this transfer was achieved, and the roles played by these chief protagonists of the future Apollo program is not as clearly recorded as it might have been.

It would appear that the basecoat for the canvas of this commissioned work was mixed from pigment pots labelled 'Peenemünde Purple' and 'Prussian Puce'. And to stay with the chosen medium of astronaut-turned-artist Al Bean, their much vaunted 'masterpiece' is now in need of complete restoration. An examination of this painting's detail—the events and the people involved—is essential. Apollo is only the foreground of this space painting, for the sorry catalogue of serious discrepancies, numerous inconsistencies and downright distortions of the truth began well before the establishment of an agency outwardly and allegedly dedicated to the exploration of space for peaceful purposes—NASA.

The sheer quantity and intensity of these inaccuracies have produced a muddied image. It is only by removing the layers of dirt and remixing the palette (from recently available sources) that we have we been able to restore this painting—and its subjects—to their true colours. We have assembled the salient moments of the events surrounding these subjects, which of necessity incorporate the pre-and post-war period in Germany. As a result of this exercise, it has become abundantly clear to us that there has been a consistent attempt to retouch and alter the original many times over.

The end justifies the means

War, or the strategy of creating a threat of conflict, has generally been the prime driving force

behind the advancement of technology. War, or the threat of war, has oftentimes been used to focus the minds of the people on fear and distrust. The urgency not to be attacked and defeated is a 'tension generator' that pushes naturally peaceful peoples into overdrive and thus forces the creation of technologies that in normal peacetime would be considered too expensive to develop, and even totally unnecessary. It would seem vital that we now reach a stage of awareness whereby this principle is inherently understood and thus rendered obsolete and that we achieve this result without losing our societal courage along the way. The collective consciousness of the majority on this planet can prevail over the persistent aggressive tendencies of the governing few. But in order for that to happen we need to be aware of our options. Withholding events, and knowledge derived from such events, deprives us of those options. As a species we are now mature enough to harness our creative energies towards the development of technologies for the *truly* peaceful exploration of space—without the need to focus our competitive energies on any other nation or species as an enemy target. But our military leaders and politicians seem to find change a threat and not a challenge. For the most part, they are cocooned within a mind set that has produced thoughts such as these:

> Control of space means control of the world . . . From space the masters of infinity would have the power to control the Earth's weather, to cause drought and flood, to change the tides and raise the levels of the sea, to divert the gulf stream and change the climates to frigid.
> There is something more important than the ultimate weapon. That is the ultimate position—the position of total control over Earth that lies somewhere in outer space . . . And if there is an ultimate position then our national goal and the goal of all free men must be to win and hold that position.[1]

However if this is truly to be a national goal, then it cannot be the goal of all free men, for the USA is not the nation of "all free men". We might then consider that Lyndon B

Johnson really meant: "Our goal (that of the masters of infinity) must be to win and hold that position". These masters by LBJ's definition therefore run (amongst other things) the space program and we have taken his lead and used this title to signify the very small group of international powerbrokers who were completely in the know regarding the reasons why, where, who, what and when of Apollo. At the time this was considered by some to be a blustery statement designed to galvanise the American people into standing behind the exploration of space. With the benefit of hindsight we can see that in fact this statement was a true reflection of the intent of the self-proclaimed 'masters of infinity'. These words of Senator Lyndon Baines Johnson (at the Senate Democratic Caucus of January 7 1958) were a prime example of how the truth can be said but not necessarily heard. The press generally portrayed this speech as politician's rhetoric, designed to stimulate but not to be taken literally. Indeed, for any critic to have thought otherwise, would probably have earned him the label of paranoid schizophrenic. Today we would use the term conspiracy theorist.

Now it is time to remove the layers of dirt and reveal the detail concerning the subjects of that painting. To do this we will turn the clock back to the decade preceding the rise of the Third Reich.

1927 Berlin

In the twelve years preceding the outbreak of WWII a group of like-minded individuals obsessed by their desire to get into space—at any cost—were working together in Germany. Many internationally renowned rocket researchers belonged to their club, the Verein für Raumschiffahrt (the VfR or Association for Space Travel). The VfR was founded in Berlin on June 5 1927, with Johannes Winkler as president. Founder members Hermann Oberth and Dr. Walter Hohmann were followed by Dr. Franz von Hoefft, the Austrian Professor Guido von Pirquet, the Frenchman Robert Esnault-Pelterie and the Russian Nikolai Rynin. Despite much muddling by the chroniclers of history it was only *after* the war that the group calling themselves the German Rocket Society was founded.

However, the men who were to become the driving force behind the American space program lived and worked in Germany during the thirties and early forties. Some of these would stop at nothing, even resorting to duping their colleagues and superiors in order to ensure the continuance of their research. In practical terms the survival of their dreams was the same then as it is today: finding the means of achieving the sustained attention—and consequent funding—that their burgeoning rocket technology demanded.

The *official* records emphasise the fact that these German researchers were only desirous of exploring "the frontiers of space" and that they were not interested in making war machines. From the information now available from various and diverse biographies, memoirs and histories associated with this period, it is evident that the official record was written with a view to 'whitewashing' the wartime occupations of most of these Nazi rocket engineers—men, we must emphasise, who were transformed into post-war *American* rocket engineers. The wartime *actions* of Wernher von Braun and Hermann Oberth demonstrate more clearly than all the *words* uttered then or since, that their overriding belief was that the end justifies the means. The combination of their ruthless scien-

---

An opinion

There isn't any other end but power.

What delight is there but to be part of great events?

The sheer sense of control—power is the only end—and if you don't like the code of the game, what is it then?

Love of country? Let me see it in people who *really* command.

How did the Tudors, Cecils, Brahmins rise?

The source of power is money.

Joe Kennedy Snr

Opposites

"Science itself has no moral dimension; it is neither good nor evil. We must apply our own moral yardstick to judge its ethical value."

Wernher von Braun

"Science and theology should be harmonised to provide a self-consistent view of reality. Science lacks an ethical basis and fails to speak to much we humans experience."

Sir Bernard Lovell, astronomer [2]

tific ambitions, in association with the Nazi regime to whom they gave their allegiance (whether in mind or just in body), became the driving force behind the practical beginnings of the space program.[3]

1928 Prussia

Wernher von Braun joined the VfR in 1930, when it had grown to 900 members. But it was during his school years that WvB began to hone the skills that were to serve him throughout his life: the art of persuading people to do what he wanted, combined with the ability to organise people into working teams dedicated to fulfilling his ambitions. For example, when he needed a much larger and more expensive telescope, he persuaded his teachers at Spiekeroog Island School that 'they' needed a telescope. He then organised his schoolfellows into a team of carpenters and electricians and they built the observatory to house the telescope. What Wernher wanted, Wernher got—generally at very little outlay to himself. Thus WvB established the system to which he was faithful all his life: someone else should provide Wernher with all the materials and/or funds that Wernher needed, in exchange for which he would offer his energy and knowledge to the benefactor.

1929 Moscow

Korolёv qualified as an aero-mechanical engineer and started work full time for an aircraft design bureau—OPO4. Principally established to design seaplanes of several different types, it actually concentrated on one single torpedo bomber, TOM-1.

1930 Berlin

Willie Ley, science writer and rocket specialist, member of the VfR and publicist for these rocketmen *par excellence*, introduced Wernher to his boyhood hero, Hermann Oberth. This simple introduction would result in a formidable team of shaman showmen. WvB worked on rockets with Oberth at Plotzensee. Willie Ley would leave for the States just before the accession of Hitler in 1933 and become very much involved in the American space program.[4]

1931 Berlin

Von Braun met with Walter Dornberger for the first time. The nineteen year old von Braun and the thirty-six year old Dornberger immediately formed a mutual admiration society which would last for the rest of their lives, the differences in age becoming less marked as the years went by.

Captain Walter Dornberger of the German Army was the prime active link between the future Nazi regime and these rocketeers of the VfR. Dornberger, a qualified engineer, was promoted to General at the head of the German Army and Air Force Rocket Development programs, then to Major-General and Director of Peenemünde (1943-1945). In 1945 Dornberger was transported for interrogation to England

Dornberger & von Braun—close encounters of some kind

"The degree of mutual dependence, but also of mutual trust and personal attachment between the two exceeded the bounds of normal friendship."

"Their encounter may be the most decisive single factor that led to the development of spaceflight in our time."[5]

Or maybe not. We think that a close encounter of the third kind wins that prize.

before being sent to America, via Operation Paperclip that same year. He worked firstly as a consultant for the USAAF and then became the Vice President of Bell Aircraft Company before the Apollo phase of the space program was set in motion. Then in 1960 Dornberger retired to Mexico, where he died some twenty years later.

2. Hermann Oberth.   ARCHIVE

1. Walter Dornberger.   ARCHIVE

1932

WvB received his Bachelor's degree in aeronautical engineering from Charlottenburg Institute of Technology. Some sources say he received an MA not a BA.[6] With the rise of Hitler, his father Baron von Braun, unwilling to participate in the Nazi regime, resigned from Ministry of Agriculture and returned to his Prussian estate. Baron von Braun repeatedly talked to Wernher about the negativity of the "Nazi madness" but Wernher ignored his opinions on the subject and chose to remain in Berlin and pursue his contacts with the German Army.

GAWD (The German Army Weapons Department) was formed and provided research grants to the VfR. Von Braun wittingly opted for the German Army as the solution to his financial problems, considering himself fortunate to have been taken up by the "powerful and wealthy organisation of the German Army" under the supreme command of Adolf Hitler.[7] It was then decreed that rockets would only serve as items of 'national defence'. Any private research groups working outside state supervision were declared illegal and closed down. Rolf Engel, an acquaintance of Wernher von Braun, attempted to pursue individual rocket research and ended up in prison. It was WvB's Nazi connections that secured Engel's release.

WvB was on the ground floor of the select band of technicians forming the core of the Nazi rocket program, having been selected by Dornberger and then 'advised' by Professor Becker to study for a degree in physics at the Military Science Faculty of Berlin University, choosing the subject of liquid propellants for his thesis. In exchange for his co-operation he would be granted access to the Army's Kummersdorf testing facilities for his practical work. Despite already having testing grounds with his associates at the VfR, von Braun accepted this offer and immediately joined Dornberger's staff, working in the Ordnance Ballistics Section. The German War Ministry included Lt-Col Becker, Major von Horstig, engineer Captain Walter Dornberger and engineer Wernher von Braun, who soon had a staff of fifty to eighty people with whom to operate. Yet WvB also managed to earn his pilot's license whilst a Luftwaffe cadet.[8]

QUESTION: How did it happen that Wernher von Braun was simultaneously a member of the German Army *and* the German Air Force?

168

1933 Germany
Adolf Hitler became Chancellor of the Third Reich.

3. Wernher von Braun and J F Kennedy at Redstone Arsenal in 1962.   ARMY ORDNANCE, REDSTONE

1933 Moscow
Korolëv published *Towards the Rocketplane* in the *Vechernaya Moskva* newspaper.

1934 Berlin
WvB received his Doctorate of Physics from University of Berlin, aged 22. The papers that gained him this qualification were curiously classified as 'secret' by the German Army and never published. Yet throughout his life von Braun would feel distanced from other scientists. Why? Did he feel inadequate in their presence for any particular reason?[9]

At this time von Braun was participating in practical, secret rocket research which was now being carried out on the Island of Borkum, near Emden.

1935 Germany
Wernher von Braun spent much of his time travelling, often in his own aircraft (perhaps, in reality, the Luftwaffe's?) looking for new testing sites for his ever more powerful rockets. It is said that his mother had suggested the area of Peenemünde, where his grandfather went duck shooting—and von Braun had agreed that the location was ideal for his purposes.

1936 Berlin
Dornberger and von Braun persuaded Adolf Hitler to visit the Kummersdorf rocket test site near Berlin, in order to demonstrate the fact this location had become too small for their needs. Very shortly thereafter, the town of Wolgast sold the Peenemünde island site to the Nazis for 750,000 Reich marks. In August, work began on the Rocket site at Peenemünde. WvB had already started working on the rocket destined for attacking America—the A-3.

4. The Baltic coast, Island of Borkum near Emden and Usedom Island with the peninsula of Peenemünde.

1937 Moscow
The NKVD of the Soviet Union started spying on Wernher von Braun's rocket tests.[10] Reports were sent to Molotov, together with Timoshenko, Beria and Stalin.

1938 Moscow
Korolëv, aged 31 and holding a position of authority at the Soviet Reaction Scientific Research Institute (RNII) was arrested by Stalin's henchmen the NKVD, later replaced by the KGB, on June 27. As he related to Gagarin and Leonov a few days before

169

his death, Korolëv was blamed for spending too much money on his work budget at the RNII. Denounced by three of his colleagues (one of whom was his rival Valentin Glushko, himself arrested three months earlier), Korolëv was taken away to Lefortovo prison for interrogation. Beaten and told to confess, he denied having committed any crime. His interrogator shouted back at him: "None of you swine have committed a crime". He was sentenced to ten years in prison and taken to work the gold mines at Kolmya Gulag in the province of Magadan (Eastern Siberia).

Kolmya came under the jurisdiction of Glavzoloto, the Eastern division of the Ministry of Non-Ferrous Metallurgy and conditions were so hard that several thousand prisoners died every month. After only five months, Korolëv was called back to Moscow for a reappraisal of his case.

Tales from the fire side

Amazingly Korolëv recounted to Gagarin and Leonov that he hitchhiked to Magadan, 150 miles away, only to miss the last boat for the next leg of his trip. Fate had obviously intervened, for days later this boat was lost at sea with all hands. Korolëv envisaged staying in Magadan for the winter but first he had to find somewhere to spend that night. Without enough warm clothing, with no money and starving, he tried to find shelter from the temperatures of 50°F below zero but was thrown out of an army barracks in which he had sought refuge. Then a miracle occurred. He came across a loaf of warm bread lying in the snow. Ravenous he fell upon it and then returned to the army barracks, managed to hide beneath a bed and was subsequently discovered the next day with his clothes frozen to the ground. He alleged that he never knew from where the loaf of bread came, and wondered about it all his life. In the Spring, having supported himself with miscellaneous jobs he headed in the direc-

tion of Moscow by rail. Suffering from scurvy, with bleeding gums, his teeth falling out and nearly dead, he was taken off the train in Khaborovsk. Korolëv then recounted that an old man massaged his gums with kolba, a herb something akin to garlic, which healed them. Within a week he was well enough to catch another train to Moscow.

Most of the other versions of the imprisonment of Korolëv state that he was in Kolmya for a year, his case having been reviewed in 1939 and the sentence reduced to eight years. Many historians doubt the veracity of Korolëv's tale but it is clear that whether information or disinformation this was the version of events that Korolëv wittingly purveyed. To us it is astonishing that nobody escorted Korolëv back to Moscow from Kolyma, and whether he was a 'special requisition' or a 'convoy prisoner' is not made clear.[11] It is also astonishing that Korolëv was left to work throughout the winter and early spring and that he then returned *voluntarily* to Moscow. There are also large gaps in the timing of events. If Korolëv was sent to Kolmya straight after interrogation and is only in Kolmya for five months, this brings the timing to the end of November/beginning of December 1938. Travel to Magadan and stopover took until the spring of 1939. Korolëv arrived in Moscow in May 1939 and was not sent back to the gulag, but only to the Tupolev Sharaga on Radio Street in September 1940.

These Sharaga prisons, where Korolëv ended up, were reserved specifically for scientists and engineers. The living and working conditions were good and he maintained reasonable health during this time. Korolëv was in fact to continue his research into rocketry during the six years that he spent in various Sharaga—for these men were certainly kept away from the dangers of war and moved around the country, according to the shifting of the front lines. In *The Gulag Archipelago* Solzhenitsyn tells us

---

The pirates of Peenemünde

"Man must establish the principle of freedom of space as he has done with freedom of the seas. And like everything else, we can establish this only from a position of strength."[12]

Wernher von Braun

that the convicts' slang for them was 'Sharash-kas'. In these 'Paradise Islands', as he also called them, the only labour was super-secret mental work and the inmates were kept warm and fed. In Russian slang 'sharaga' means 'a sinister enterprise based on bluff or deceit'.[13] Perhaps we should refer to the space program as the Apollo Sharaga Project.

Nights at the round table— 1938 Peenemünde

WvB was appointed Technical Director of Peenemünde German Rocket Research Centre by the Nazis. This wild island site of heather, pine and oak trees, home to deer and duck, was scarred forever by various buildings, paved streets and railway tracks. The boundaries were protected by a series of fences arranged in concentric circles. Very, very few people had permits entitling them to approach the very heart of the rocket centre.

Dispel any images of a band of lofty scientists struggling with the isolated rigors of life on the rough Baltic coast. The nearby coastal town of Wolgast was a resort town for the German residents. This Peenemünde research site had lawns, flowers, gardeners, servants, together with plentiful supplies of food and materials, including air raid shelters. After working extensively on their rocketry, von Braun and his colleagues would relax in comfortable chairs around a circular table in the 'Hearth Room' illuminated by the light from crystal and gold chandeliers. Albert Speer, the Reichminister for Armaments and Munitions was an intensely enthusiastic supporter of the Peenemünde project and used his authority to ensure that it flourished even through the latter days of 1939 when Hitler designated rocket research a low priority.[14]

1939 Peenemünde September

A secret conference on the future and development of long range rocketry was held at the resort town of Peenemünde. The Conference President was none other than Wernher von Braun. And it was the secret agent Paul Rosbaud who informed the Allies of this meeting.[15]

The necessary supplies for the Peenemünde rocket development project came partially from munitions factories in another country, seemingly working with the Nazis in absolute immunity. It is now considered a truism that if

---

The art of sweet talk

Austria 1940. The official record states that during the development of the V-2 (then in the planning stage at Peenemünde) Hermann Oberth, genius of rocket research, was at Felixdorf near Vienna working on top secret rocket research.

Oberth was supposedly kept in the dark about the ultimate results of his work, only to find out later that he had been working on the designs and data for the V-2. This remark is on a par with a chef devising a recipe and then professing ignorance about the taste of the resulting creation!

Hermann Oberth was born in Nagyszeben in Austria-Hungary which is now Sibiu, Romania. Like Fritz Lang, Oberth served as an officer in the *Austrian* Army during the First World War. By 1940 he was considered to be too valuable an asset to be allowed to roam free beyond the borders of Germany and the Gestapo had *offered* him the choice of becoming a German citizen or going to a concentration camp. He rather obviously chose the former and subsequently found that he was no longer *offered* jobs. Instead he was *ordered* to the Army Experimental station at Peenemünde, where he found himself under the command of the Technical Director, Wernher von Braun.

This story has to be another piece of moonshine. The Nazi regime only conferred German nationality on people of 'proven German stock'. Either Oberth fulfilled this criterion or he was given 'associate citizenship'. This was granted to those loyal to the regime and the SS were quite happy to incorporate 'loyalists' into their ranks. Any other category of non-German person living within the Third Reich was considered as 'stateless'. Compare the foregoing account with the glamorised version: "Wernher von Braun *invited* Oberth to participate as a consultant [at Peenemünde] thus providing professional security during the wartime period".[16]

---

these particular supply facilities had not existed, the war would have been shortened by months, if not years.[17] These were protected from attack either by land or air. How could that be? Were they situated in a country beyond the reach of the allied air forces or land armies? Geographically, the country in question may have been over the hills, but it was not far away. We all know it as Switzerland and their defence systems were gilt edged. The Swiss Minister for Foreign Affairs during that time, M Pilet-Golaz, was very pro-Nazi and allowed the export of arms, munitions and other supplies to Germany. Conversely, coal supplies were despatched to Switzerland by the Nazis in order to keep the factories going and the country's railway network was also utilised. It was not until October 1944 that the Allies were able to pressurise Switzerland into ceasing the export of all war materials, by which time even the Swiss could see that Hitler was losing the war. To be on the wrong side of the curtain when the show was over was not an option, for, as author Adam LeBor wrote in *Nazi Bankers:* "A Europe from which Switzerland could not profit financially was unthinkable".[18] Regarding Swiss accountability and responsibility, in the 1990s questions are being asked that require answers now—both concerning the Swiss authorities' knowledge and degree of participation in the deportation via the Swiss railway network of wanted Nazi prisoners (including Jews) and also concerning the unrestored monies that were legitimately placed in Swiss bank accounts both before and during WWII. The Zurich gnomes are finally going to have to give an account of themselves and *The Sound of Music* is perhaps something more than just a popular musical.

1940 Moscow

Korolëv was moved into Tupolev Sharaga on Radio Street, Moscow. Despite rivalry from other design bureaux (and in particular Valentin Glushko) it was Korolëv who was chiefly responsible for enabling the Soviets to realise the development of ICBMs and thereafter the space program. He was to work under three Soviet leaders, Stalin, Krushchev and Brezhnev.

1940 Peenemünde May 1

Wernher von Braun had by now joined the Nazi party and earned the rank of Untersturmführer (2nd Lieutenant) in the infamous SS, under Himmler. Stuhlinger and Ordway described this as only an honorary position, one resented by WvB, who apparently left 'the uniform' in his closet. This account is slightly inaccurate. Each rank of the SS was equipped with many uniforms of varying degrees of splendour for different occasions. If WvB permanently left his uniforms in his closet then Himmler, not renowned for kindness, would seem not to have taken umbrage, for three years later he would endow von Braun with an even higher rank in the SS.[19]

1941 Siberia

Korolëv was moved 1,400 miles from Moscow to the Sharaga in Omsk, Siberia. He made many claims of innocence throughout these years. His wife however, is not on record as having protested against his arrest.

1942 Kazan

At the end of the year Korolëv was moved to the Sharaga in Kazan, about 400 miles from Moscow, and found himself working with none other than his arch rival, Glushko.

1943 Berlin April

Following a dream, Hitler was on the point of cancelling the rocket project at Peenemünde. Dornberger's memoirs note that Hitler considered this dream's message reinforced by an 'intuitive trance' that was also experienced by Adolf. These two related events led Hitler to believe that "the disturbance of the etheric fields" around the planet by the V-2 would enact a "dreadful vengeance upon humanity",[20] and were sufficiently impressive for Hitler to stop production on the rocket for two months.

1943 Peenemünde June 28

Himmler upgraded von Braun to SS Sturmbannführer (Major). Regarding our earlier point as to whether WvB actually wore the many uniforms that went with these grades we should note that his close friend Carsbie

Adams, stated that Wernher "always acted in conformity with the people around him".[21]

1943 July 7

Albert Speer arranged for Peenemünde's Director (Dornberger) and Technical Director (WvB) to meet Hitler at his headquarters *The Wolf's Lair* near Rastenburg in Prussian East Germany. *"The organising genius and extraordinary powers of persuasion of WvB were exercised to the full."*[22] In fact Dornberger and WvB pleaded their cause for hours and *finally succeeded in convincing Hitler* of the true value of the rocket as a *WEAPON.*

Given Hitler's known fascination with the occult and his strong belief in dreams and portents, we can imagine how very persuasive these two men had to be, and that point brings us to some appreciation of the extraordinary powers of Wernher von Braun in this regard. On this same occasion, von Braun also pushed for the establishment of an underground launch facility, showing Hitler a model of just such a complex that he had designed.[23] Astonishingly and sadly, this is the very same von Braun who is quoted as having said: "We created the rocket to conquer other planets, not to destroy our own".

1943 Rastenburg July 8

Hitler, won over by his visitors' arguments of the preceding day, increased the budget for rocket research and nominated Speer as overall head of the V-2 program. Wernher von Braun received the honorary title of 'Professor' from Hitler in recognition of his achievements.

1943 Peenemünde August 17-18

Thanks to information from Germany supplied by Paul Rosbaud, codenamed 'Griffin', the British put Operation Hydra into action, designed to eliminate 1) the engineers' residential quarters 2) the missile pre-production facility and 3) the R&D laboratories/offices. From nine minutes past midnight on August 18 and over forty seven minutes, 600, yes *six hundred,* Royal Air Force aircraft marked targets and then dropped 1,593 tons of high explosives and 281 tons of incendiary bombs onto Peenemünde. However, from the beginning the start point of the bombing run was altogether mis-identified—the northern peninsular of Peenemünde being lit by the target indicators rather than the designated Ruden Island situated two miles further north. As a result of this initial 'blunder', the air raid failed in two-thirds of its avowed objectives. During Operation Hydra, the RAF lost at least thirty nine aircraft, and of the eight hundred personnel on the ground who did die about half were from the prisoner labour force (mostly Soviets) and the other half were technicians and their families. After this raid, the irreplaceable Hermann Oberth was transferred to the safety of the Reinsdorf works near Wittenberg, to continue working.

Instructions from the highest level, it seems, had been to target personnel and certainly *not the V-2 rocket production facilities.* It was clearly *CRUCIAL* that these rockets, plans and parts were spared. Is it not conceivable that the original bombing directives from the British War Office were contravened in order to bring about the 'sparing of Peenemünde'? The alteration of the co-ordinates relating to the bombing run start point certainly would have ensured that the advance pathfinders placed the marker flares 'too short' and/or 'too long', thus ensuring the safety of the individuals and rocket technology desperately needed by those that knew—the 'masters of infinity'.

1943 Poland August 21

The V-2 test firing complex was now moved from Peenemünde into an SS camp in Poland. The Nazis moved as much of their rocket technology as was practicable away from the allied air raids and as far as was possible into underground facilities some 250 miles south from Peenemünde, near Nordhausen. Renamed the 'Mittelwerk' by the Nazis in '43 this infamous rocket factory was constructed inside the base of Mt Konstein of the Harz mountain range. Originally an old gypsum mine, the tunnels had been expanded and used as an oil depot in 1934. Two parallel tunnels ½ mile long and 40 feet in diameter, connected by cross tunnels at intervals, made it resemble a ladder. It was

173

capable of turning out up to thirty-five V-2s every day. For the thousands of concentration camp prisoners who were used as slave labour during the conversion and then as workers on the rocket assembly lines, the subterranean and subhuman conditions were unendurable and murderous.[24]

1944 Stettin March

WvB was *allegedly* imprisoned by his own army. 'Accused' of thinking too much about space in general and not enough about the V-2 in particular(!) WvB was 'released' 14 days later, after intervention by his friend Major General Walter Dornberger.

This 'reason for arrest' is hardly credible when we also learn that von Braun was awarded the special Knight's Cross of the Iron Cross for his work on the V-2 and beggars belief when we remember the details of the meeting with Hitler on July 7 1943.[25] David Baker gives the date of arrest as being February 21 with Dornberger turning up "a few days later". Baker reports that Riedel and Grottupp were also with WvB adding "planning to escape to England with the V-2 documentation" as a motive for the arrest. Shades of Hess![27]

1944 Caucasus

Korolëv was moved to a rocket Sharaga housed in a former hunting lodge of Tsar Nicholas II situated in Krasnapolyana in the Caucasus. This Sharaga would eventually be moved to Moscow where on June 27 Korolëv was officially discharged, with previous convictions expunged. Glushko was made chief designer of the bureau, with Korolëv his deputy. While not denying that this procedure was a terrible way to treat individuals, the 1938-1945 timing of Korolëv's unjust prison sentence leads us to ask if an ulterior motive for some of these arrests was not both far-sighted and well planned by the Soviet leadership. By detaining many of their best scientists and engineers in these Sharaga for the duration of the war, the state's intellectual and scientific heritage was honourably and safely preserved from the dangers of armed combat without turning such a policy into a public issue.

It is notable that despite being imprisoned, Korolëv worked with great devotion to his country, as did others in the same circumstances. Although many of his colleagues on the Soviet space program thought that his years of incarceration had affected his character, we have noted how *similar in drive and methods* Korolëv was to his German counterpart Wernher von Braun. Korolëv was considered by some to have been outright Machiavellian while others described him as opportunistic, cunning, ruthless and cynical. Like von Braun, Korolëv adapted to whatever particular regime was in force at the time and used people to get what he wanted. If he was required to produce a missile shield for the Soviet Union, as well as design a lunar rocket, then so be it.

Korolëv's daughter recalls that the date of her father's discharge was August 10 1944. He remained working at his Sharaga as a free man until the spring of 1945. But astonishingly, Harford states in his biography that Korolëv arrived in Germany on September 8 1945 "fresh from Kazan, *still not officially rehabilitated*" (our emphasis). How can these two accounts be reconciled?

5. Korolëv's statue, Moscow.   AULIS

1944 Peenemünde, July 18 , August 4 & August 25

Three American raids on Peenemünde resulted in only limited technical and hardware damage. Our opinion is identical to that stated for August 17-18 1943, that the nature of *all* the allied bombing raids on this base indicate a

---

Neutrality—Swedish style

When Wernher von Braun accidentally fired a rocket into Swedish neutral territory on June 13 1944,
the jackboot was on the other foot!

Hitler predicted that the Swedes would copy his secret weapon.

The Nazi high command reasoned that if Sweden tried to copy the rocket or send the pieces to England for back
engineering, they would be violating their neutrality. At which point Hitler could and would attack them.

This story glosses over the reality of the Swedish/German situation during WWII. Hitler was no doubt far more worried
about the threat to his imports from Sweden. Throughout the war, as well as allowing the Germans access to Norway via
their railways, the Swedes in a "consistent and determined effort" shipped iron ore and steel ball bearings across the
Baltic sea to Germany, and despite allied protests continued this trade until the end of December 1944.

As for von Braun's stray rocket, American aviators sent the remains of this rocket to England, thus obviating any
further incident, but thoroughly alarming the British who now fully realised the magnitude of
the Nazi Rocket Project aimed at their shores.

---

clear demonstration of forward planning: *the intention not to damage the V-2 material, while rendering the base itself inoperable, in order to subsequently reap the full benefit of German rocket research.*

1944 Poland August 5

At Winston Churchill's request of July 13, a group of British spies and missile experts visited Poland and met with Soviet specialists, in order to locate fragments of a V-2 left by the fleeing Germans. These were shipped to the Soviet Union where the Soviets who examined the material were surprised and shocked by the advanced state of the technology they found—as the English had been in June 1944 upon receiving stray missiles sent from Poland (May 20 1944) and Sweden (June 13 1944). Up until this time the Soviets had been working on the dangerous nitric acid and kerosene mix as rocket propellants, whereas the Germans were using alcohol and liquid oxygen.

1944 Belgium September 8

Wernher von Braun's creation the A-4, renamed the V-2, launched from mobile launchpads in Belgium, fell from the skies onto Paris and London.

1945 Peenemünde January 31

SS General Hans Kammler appointed WvB to oversee the evacuation of Peenemünde. WvB prepared their departure from a base increasingly protected by SS, allegedly both to keep the rocket scientists in and also to defend the base against the approaching Allies. All of which makes nonsense of the statements that WvB and his friends felt increasingly threatened by the SS—*they were the SS!* WvB and his cronies apparently decided that they would surrender to the West rather than the Soviets. However, it turned out that Peenemünde was not considered a prime target for the *Soviets,* who would not reach there until May 5.[26] February 14, St Valentine's day, saw the last missile fired and February 17 through to mid-March saw the removal of all essentials including personnel 250 miles south to the Mittelwerks at Nordhausen. Test stands were set up at nearby Bleicherode.[27]

- One source states that by the time the 1944 Peenemünde air raids took place, the SS had already moved most of the rocket team to Nordhausen together with as much equipment as was practicable.[28]
- WvB allegedly organised 10,000 men and 2,000 tons of materials out of Peenemünde to the Harz mountains of Central Germany.[29]
- Dr. Helen Walters' 1964 biography, 'authorised' by a foreword from WvB himself, recounts that WvB moved only 5,000 men, and even found time during these preparations to negotiate the German Army roadblocks encircling Peenemünde in order to visit his parents on their farm and then his cousin (and future wife) Maria von Quistorp. Stuhlinger and Ordway also state that 5,000 men were removed from Peenemünde.

- Walters states that WvB broke his arm in a car accident during the removal from Peenemünde and that by Easter that year (April 1) he had settled his five thousand men in Bleicherode in the Harz mountains. These same mountains would serve as a hiding place for their films and records, material they were unable to take to the West.

1945 Bavaria April 3

Kammler then ordered Walter Dornberger (not Wernher von Braun as generally stated) to select the top five hundred of his technicians and move them from Bleicherode to Oberammergau in the Austrian Alps. There they were distributed among the various villages, WvB and Dornberger ended up in Oberjoch.

Austria 1945

Variations on a theme—various biographers offer diverse accounts of the same event.

Gartzmann: Following the establishment of his people in Bleicherode, WvB and his close friends travelled to Oberjoch in the Bavarian Alps "to spend weeks of idleness..." [just under four to be precise] "...sitting in the sun discussing rocket projects of the future— totally isolated from reality they waited for the Allies to catch up with them". Apparently von Braun and Dornberger were wearing uniforms when they travelled from Peenemünde to Oberjoch, for

they had to find civilian clothes before meeting the Americans.

The question is, which uniforms were they sporting, those of the German Army or the SS elite? If anyone had been ordered to Oberjoch by Kammler, surely they would be wearing their elitist uniforms!

Whereas *Stuhlinger and Ordway* recall that von Braun *flew* south to Bleicherode ahead of his evacuating men, organised their accommodation and the hiding of technical papers in the Harz mountains. The SS then requested WvB to prepare to leave for Oberammergau, further south in the Austrian Alps. WvB travelled there by car (special dispensation because of his broken arm, allegedly). The team of five hundred men that *he* had selected to go with him travelled by train. From there, Dornberger and WvB persuaded the SS that it was too dangerous for all these irreplaceable scientists to be in the same location and that they should go to different villages. Dornberger, WvB, his brother Magnus and several others then moved out to the small village of Oberjoch, where they took up residence in Haus Ingeburg—which is where this version of events joins with the others.

This 'persuasion' version does not ring true. It is much more likely that the initial plan established by the SS in conjunction with Dornberger and von Braun, already included the distribution of these scientists amongst the civilian population of these Austrian villages as a protective measure against allied bombing raids.

WvB's version as told to the Americans is fairly accurate, but the timing may have been a little different: WvB apparently injured his arm and shoulder during the evacuation from Peenemünde to Bleicherode (although this does not square with the Stuhlinger & Ordway version of this event!). This provides a date of mid-March 1945. He had a new cast fitted to his arm while in Oberjoch, prior to the suicide of Hitler on April 30, some forty days later. In July, WvB wearing a sling, was photo-

6. The hills are alive—the Oberjoch Guest House in Bavaria.　ARCHIVE

graphed boarding an American C-47 aircraft in Munich. Why then was it still in a sling upon his arrival in the United States on September 20—*At least 24 weeks* after the initial injury? QUESTION: Was the acquisition/retention of a sling and the numerous photos of WvB with his arm in plaster, a publicity ploy, designed to soften the public attitude towards him when these were subsequently released? Or was it all a ruse, perhaps to facilitate the transportation of ultra secret documents?

7. Hand Uber Alles! Magnus and Wernher von Braun (with broken arm) with PFC Fred Scheikart after surrendering to the US Army.

QUESTION: How many British people were advised that one of the perpetrators of their wartime miseries, Wernher von Braun visited England (and Paris) between May and September 1945? Allegedly for interrogation—we would rather describe these meetings as *discussions*.

1945 Nordhausen April 11

The Americans arrived at the Mittelwerks to find that the Germans had vanished, leaving their 4,500 former workers either fending for themselves in the surrounding countryside—or dead. The Americans then 'quickly' organised Operation Overcast in order to evacuate the Mittelwerks' V-2 components—and insensitively used the remaining prisoners, or at least those who could still function, to do so. David Baker records that the Soviets, under the

terms "of a high level agreement" were due to arrive on June 1. This reference is a delicate allusion to the Yalta agreement! And is an interesting massage of history because the Soviets arrived in Bleicherode only 12 days later.

1945 Bleicherode April 23

Upon their arrival in Bleicherode, Soviets Boris Chertok and Isaev, both rocket designers, coincidentally (for those who like coincidences) took over the very house in which von Braun had stayed. Their mission was to collect the documents, technology and the rocket specialists for removal to the Soviet Union. Korolëv arrived in Bleicherode some months later, looking exceedingly healthy and very smart in his Red Army uniform.

1945 Nordhausen May 1

Baker reports that the Russians took over the Mittelwerks and found that the Americans had *already* ransacked the place. This is actually contradictory to his entry for May 22, which has Major James Hamill (later to accompany von Braun from Washington to Fort Bliss) supervising the shipping out of about 100 V-2s from the Mittelwerks facility.[30] Baker says that the last train left the Mittelwerks on May 31, the day *before* the Russians "were expected to occupy the place".

From our perusal of the various biographies and chronologies of this time we would say that:

- Either the Soviets and the Americans were at Mittelwerk together;
- Or these dates are wrong. Which is highly unlikely given the extreme accuracy and attention to detail employed by David Baker.

These discrepancies most certainly uphold our theory that this entire period was being organised as a cohesive whole and was not just a 'race' against time to see who could bag the bigger haul of documents, materials and men. This plan was surely a precursor to the 'space race' story, which was also designed to look like one thing but actually to function in a completely different way.

James Harford relates that "by agreement with the Allies" the Soviets took over the underground V-2 factory at Nordhausen but found that they could not bear the atmosphere of the place. They worked on assembling the remaining V-2 parts (of which they found plenty) at nearby Klein Bodungen. It is said that a total of 250 V-2s were found in the Mittelwerks facility, which left around 150, plus parts with which the Soviets could work. [31] According to Harford, the Soviets had about 1,000 people working "at Mittelwerk", of which around 500 were German, including sixty technicians from Peenemünde. While according to Baker, the Soviets had rounded up about 3,500 people whose job was to re-establish the documentation taken by von Braun.

Postscript

In an interesting postscript to this abuse of the Yalta Agreement, some 13 years later, in August 1958, Robert Maxwell and his wife attended two symposia in Moscow: the International Astronomical Union and the final meeting of the International Geophysical Year (for which Maxwell's Pergamon Press had been the official publisher).

One morning Maxwell, returning to the hotel in something of a hurry, produced sixty-three pages of "important book titles" and asked his wife to photograph this enormous bundle before lunch, when these papers had to be returned "without fail". Dr. Elizabeth Maxwell recounts how she, together with Professor Fred Whipple's wife Babbie, proceeded to use the Whipples' 16mm movie camera to do the job "using the best film available and tripling the normal exposure time".

Most interestingly, she recounts how, by page thirty-two she noticed that they were not book titles at all, but were: "Die deutschen Firma, deren Einrichtung demontiert und zur Ausfuhr nach der Sowjetunion bestimmt sind". Which translates as: "German firms whose

equipment is to be dismantled and transported to the Soviet Union". She did not tell her friend Babbie Whipple what she had discovered but carried on. Just before lunch Maxwell turned up to collect the papers, and departed as quickly as he had come. The matter was never mentioned between them again! Dr. Maxwell recounts that years later Robert Maxwell had "told *The Sunday Times* that he had been opposed to the dismantling of the German plants by the Soviets, which was contrary to 'Ally policies'". At the time, *Maxwell had been instructed to drop the matter by his superiors.*

In Moscow, his wife thought that he had found the proof that he was right all those years previously. We have seen how the Americans were behaving towards the Yalta Agreement, now we see that the British were equally au fait with the Soviet activity. [32] It is significant that this Soviet shopping list was written in *German*.

Why was it not in Russian?

1945 Oberjoch May 2

Wernher von Braun, in typical fashion of assuming that he knew best, arbitrarily sent brother Magnus off on his bicycle, dressed in civvies, to find the Americans in nearby Reutte. It was only when Magnus had pedalled safely away that Wernher announced the fact to his colleagues. He had chosen Magnus for the job, as he "spoke the best English" but when Richard Porter of General Electric interviewed WvB at the Allies' holding camp, he noticed that Wernher himself actually spoke very good English! Given the atrocious conditions at Mittelwerk and the deprivation of the civilian populations at the end of this war, it is noteworthy that an American GI guarding von Braun was heard to observe that von Braun was well fed and fat. This fact is also visible in the photographs of that time.

1945 Peenemünde May 5

The Soviet Army capturing the Peenemünde base found most of it destroyed by the departing Nazis but retained the few remaining engineers.

1945 Washington and Paris, May 5—London calling

Despite the fact that Baker recalls that General Toftoy put together the plan to remove the V-2s from the Mittelwerks "in a hurry", other sources report that Operation Overcast had been organised in the USA by the American Army, *"while the war was still raging"*.[33] Toftoy and his assistant Major James Hamill based themselves in Paris for the application of their plans. Their operation went by the ALSOS book and culminated not only in the shipment of 'matériels' but also in the interrogation and relocation of the cream of the Nazi scientists, technicians and scholars.

In fact the Peenemünde operation was a twin of the ALSOS operation run by Boris Pash for General Groves in August 1944. So the basic preparation time for Overcast dates from at least then, if not earlier. It is interesting to compare and contrast the two operations in their basic format:

1) ALSOS: (Greek for Grove, as in General!) Application: From August 25 1944 to April 30 1945.

- The verification of the status of Nazi technology regarding nuclear fission and especially the A-bomb. They discovered that the Nazi atomic scientists had never been far enough advanced in their experiments to become a threat.

- The recuperation of 1,200 tons of high quality uranium ore which the Germans had stolen from the Belgian Union Minière in 1940. Note that when they finally recovered 1,100 tons of this ore, the Americans did not return it to the Belgians but packed the ore into 10,000 strong paper bags and by April 17 1945 it was ready for shipping, via Toulouse, to Oak Ridge USA (as 'Air Matériel'?) to be prepared for the A-bomb 'Little Boy'.

- Using a British and American search team of soldiers and scientists, the crucial atomic scientists were located. They had retreated to Heigerloch in Southern Germany. Most of them were recuperated from this "small picturesque town" on St George's Day April 23 1945. Selected scientists were interviewed and removed to the States where they were soon hard at work for the Americans. However, two key players, Hahn and Hiesenberg were waiting in outlying villages. Hahn was picked up on April 25. Hiesenberg was collected from his Bavarian lakeside house shortly thereafter.

2) OVERCAST: (As in the weather code—US version—rare thunderheads gathering in the East.) The V-2 rocket scientists and their wares. Application: from May 1945 to spring 1946.

- The verification of the status of Nazi technology with reference to rocket missiles, especially the V-3. They discovered that the Nazi scientists were on a par with Goddard but more experienced in practical experimentation.

- The recovery of as many working parts of V-2 rocketry as was possible. In contravention to the 'official' Yalta Agreement, this 'Air Matériel' was shipped out via France to New Orleans, USA.

- Using the same search and interview methods adopted by Pash and Groves the rocket scientists were selected, interviewed and removed to the States. These men had retreated to the small picturesque town of Oberjoch

---

Rare birds

'Griffin' owned the rights to a vast body of scientific work which he had collected throughout the 1930s when the Third Reich suppressed the circulation or publishing of scientific data outside its borders. Griffin met with Robert Maxwell (apparently engineered by the British secret services) and this eventually resulted in Maxwell's Pergamon Press, which was 75% financed by Charles Hambro's Bank. As an open pipeline for scientific information from firstly Germany and then Russia to the West, Pergamon Press was unrivalled. Without the knowledge and contacts that Paul Rosbaud had, Pergamon Press would not have existed. Rosbaud was an active partner and 25% shareholder in the firm until October 1955 when his services were seemingly of little further use to Maxwell.

Incidentally Robert Maxwell was also out in Germany 'interviewing' prominent Nazis at the end of the war.[34]

> ### Garbage in—garbage out
> "If we haven't caught the biggest scientist in the Third Reich, we've sure bagged the biggest liar."
> *Anonymous American Soldier at the 'Dustbin' internment camp in Austria referring to Wernher von Braun.*[35]
> The name of this camp smacks of British involvement.
> Americans use the term garbage, trash or trash can, not Dustbin. They had also captured the man in charge of the
> Mittelwerks—Magnus von Braun, and he went to America too.

where they waited to be picked up. As with the A-bomb scientists, the key rocket men, von Braun and Dornberger were waiting in an outlying village.

One would almost think they heard a pre-arranged code to tell them what to do and when. Now how could that have been accomplished? Well, there was a certain Paul Rosbaud ('Griffin') who, from his background as a scientist and then publisher of scientific papers, had a wealth of knowledge and had already provided the Allies with invaluable help throughout the war prior to 1945. 'Griffin' also determined the list of scientists that he considered valuable assets for the West.[36] Given such information, and despite von Braun taking the credit for having selected his team, it must be said that the Allies would have already have written out their basic shopping list before leaving home.

1945 Austria

Most of these willing or unwilling illuminati of the Nazi regime, including WvB, Hermann Oberth and his cronies, were eventually held at an internment camp in Garmisch-Partenkirchen —the so-called 'Dustbin'. Those Germans that were chosen to go to the States had a card pa-

perclipped to their file, hence the code name Operation Paperclip.

Every version of Operation Overcast (except that of Baker) has the interrogation of von Braun happening at the 'Dustbin'. Baker informs us of another interrogation in Kochel, Bavaria by the US Naval Technical Mission, represented by Dr. Hsue-Shen Tsien from GALCIT and that it was Hsue-Shien Tsien who asked WvB to prepare his summary of future rocketry technology.

1945 Bavaria May 27

The Americans removed 14 tons of documents from a mine in Dornten, allegedly 'hours' before the Soviets arrived. Baker reports that the idea of sending one hundred (whittled down from the WvB original demand of six hundred) top scientists to the USA was receiving high priority in Washington and Paris. The inference that this was a 'new idea' is humbug, as we have seen. Baker states that a total of 350 men were eventually sent to the United States of which 100 were rocket scientists. This total number does not, however, tally with other versions of this event.

Then again Baker has Operation Overcast beginning on July 19 and the selection process starting in July 24. His version of events has

> ### Chinese chequers
> In 1936, Dr. Hsue-Shen Tsien founded the Guggenheim Aeronautical Laboratory of the Californian Institute of Technology, together with Theodore von Karman and Frank J Malina. The GALCIT was the ancestor of JPL, the Jet Propulsion Laboratory.[37]
> First Goddard Professor at Caltech, Dr. Tsien was one of the great contributors to American rocket research in the 1930s and '40s.
> During the MacCarthy witchhunt era Dr. Tsien was arrested and forbidden the right to return to China. He did leave the States in the end however, and for the last 20 years or so Dr. Tsien has been at the top of the Chinese rocket program.
> This is ultimately very good for world peace but if ever the Chinese are designated as our next 'threat' remember history and that the old boys network is already firmly established—
> everybody went to the same school!

Close call for the ball bearer

During the trip to Fort Bliss von Braun was in conversation with an American who asked him where he came from. Von Braun chose to be a Swiss ball-bearing businessman(!)

The innocent American thanked von Braun, saying that if it hadn't been for the Swiss, he doubted that the Allies could have beaten the Germans.

If only he had known to whom he was speaking and also the secret history of the Swiss.

In fact it was another 'neutral' country, Sweden, that supplied steel ball-bearings to Germany throughout the war.[38]

---

the name change from Overcast to Paperclip only occurring in March 1946, *after* the arrival of the Germans in the USA, which is pretty much at variance with every other source. Baker states that Toftoy finally met von Braun and his team in August 1945 (where, Paris?) *at which time* they were offered contracts with the US Army.

Baker then records 113 German scientists arriving in the States. Thirteen too many for the one hundred limit, and exactly fourteen too few for every other source of information. All other sources confirm that Wernher von Braun was involved in the process of choosing the rocket technicians and other men that he would take with him to the USA. One hundred and twenty seven (including WvB) men were finally offered contracts with the US Army. Then we have a parting of ways, again. According to one version these men arrived in the US within a few months. Whilst according to another, it was not until 1946 that they set foot on American soil. Both versions have some measure of accuracy—in fact six of these Peenemünde 'Rockettes', including von Braun, were transported to Paris in September 1945, whereupon they were flown from Orly (via the Azores and then Newfoundland) to Delaware, USA. From there they were flown to Boston, Massachusetts and then taken by boat to Fort Strong, in Boston Harbour, for further 'interrogation'. A fortnight later five of these men were transferred to Aberdeen Proving Ground, Maryland. The sixth, Wernher von Braun was taken to Washington for debriefing at the Pentagon. Von Braun then travelled with an escort by train to Fort Bliss, Texas, where he would remain for the next four years.

Now follows some interesting arithmetic. We are told by Baker that the German scientists began arriving at Fort Bliss in October 1945 (that is the advance guard of von Braun and his small team of five) and by March 1946 their numbers had peaked—at the grand total of thirty nine.

Stuhlinger and Ordway inform us that there were three shipments and *a total of 118 men* arriving in America between November 1945 and February 1946. So by 1946 the American Army have already lost 85 scientists. Were they declared AWOL or were they housed elsewhere, and not at Fort Bliss? Were some of them at Almogordo perhaps? From 127 total German rocket scientists allowed into

---

The goose that laid the golden egg-heads

In an alleged response to the proliferation of German U boats in the Atlantic, the flying boat HK-1 Hercules 'Spruce Goose' was commissioned by the American government in 1942 at an initial cost of *$18 million* to provide "a safer troop carrier".

Four years later (16 months after the war had ended) the 200 ton giant was ready by June 1946, but it did not have an initial test until November when the aircraft flew one short experimental hop at a height of 100 feet for 60 seconds! Hughes Aircraft abandoned the Goose after this effort.

That must be some kind of brevity record.

Perhaps it had already laid its golden egg?

This is the official version (according to the Smithsonian Institute and the National Air & Space Museum in Washington) but not quite the same version of events that emerged from a 1998 British TV documentary, *The Secret History of Howard Hughes.* We shall come to this variation on a theme later.

Quackers

Was the Howard Hughes aircraft 'Spruce Goose' another example of using one project to hide and finance another?
It is said that Hughes put $7 million of his own money into this dead duck
(the exact amount invested varying according to the biographer).
To spend the entire war perfecting a wooden plane that was not ready in time to fulfil its brief and did not work properly
after four years of development sounds rather like goosefeathers; though this is a very good way of 'absorbing'
US Government cash and could well be the origin of the rumour that Hughes had something to do with the
importation of vast numbers of German scientists.
Did the cost of building this DOD-sponsored flying boat provide part of the funding for Operation Overcast?
The Spruce Goose was actually built of birch, so are we back to army code names?
Spruce Goose = Smart Goosestepper = Clever Nazi.

America under Operation Paperclip we have a total of 6 + 118 = 4. These men were initially set to work as instructors to technicians from both the American Army and the General Electric Corporation.

There were "two further shipments later in 1946". Apart from the professional details of the 223 other German technocrats and scholars that were selected and shipped over, it would be of great interest to know why three scientists were missing from the first shipment. Who were they? Were they held at the 'Dustbin' for all that time, or was it the case that the Americans had trouble locating them in the chaos of post-war Germany? Was one of these late arrivals, Dr. Hubertus Strughold, the close collaborator of von Braun in the realm of space medicine research?

Yet another version of these events credits Howard Hughes, the aviation and electronics genius, for bringing the German scientists into the country. Psychiatrist Anthony Dietrich asserted that Hughes was a collector and then cited the time that "right after WWII, Hughes imported a whole group of German scientists, but then left them sitting idly by for years; it was enough that they were there".[39] Hughes himself once said: "I play chess with people. In a chess game, you see how long you can keep a person in a certain move". The United States was wholly dependent upon Hughes for its vital defence systems during WWII and Hughes' companies enjoyed many government contracts. It is far more likely that if Hughes was involved in the importation of the Peenemünde 'Rockettes', he was working on behalf of people *within* the US Government while *displaying* the whims of a collector.

1945 Bleicherode September 8

Having been promoted to Colonel in the Red Army during the summer, Korolëv flew out to Germany to join the Soviet V-2 research team. He returned to Moscow in 1946. Most importantly, while acknowledging the work of von Braun and his team, Korolëv had assessed the state of German rocket technology. He realised that the V-2 was not capable of fulfilling the rocketry requirements of the Soviet Union and said as much to Stalin at the earliest opportunity.

The Soviets eventually procured around 5,000 German technicians including the Peenemünde *guidance and control expert* Helmut Grottrup. Unlike the Americans who put von Braun et al. into Fort Bliss in Texas for several months and did not allow families to travel with them, the Soviets billeted Grottrup and his family in comfortable quarters in Bleicherode. The Soviets mainly concentrated on back engineering on site and it was nearly a year later before they moved their German technicians into Soviet territory.

1945 London September 8

Meanwhile back in England, David Baker tells us that on this day the British Interplanetary Society (BIS) was created out of several smaller British astronautical societies. But that the official inauguration of the BIS was not held until December 31 1945, whereupon Wernher von Braun was appointed an honorary fellow(!)[40] Arthur C Clarke, an early member of the BIS, confirms the 1945 WvB honorary fellowship but states that the BIS was founded *before* the war. Kenneth Gatland, another BIS member, offers the date of 1933. As Clarke puts it: "The BIS had been in suspended animation" from 1939 through to 1945. And as for this honorary fellowship, Stuhlinger and Ordway have set the date of this honour as the very vague *"late 1940s"* while WvB's 'authorised' biographer Helen Walters, categorically states 1949. The executive secretary of the BIS conceded the delicacy of the situation and insisted that the appointment was honouring the pre-war work of WvB in the VfR! That is pretty feeble. WvB was 18 years old in 1930 when he *joined* the VfR. Three years later the VfR was on its last legs and he had joined forces with Dornberger and the German Army.

QUESTION: Why was it necessary to reform a society already in existence?
QUESTION: Why did the British hasten to grant such an award to the man who only nine months before, was responsible for the annihilation of so many people in London and the Home Counties?
QUESTION: Why did both the British (and von Braun) wish to play down the real timing, if everybody felt comfortable with the reasons for honouring WvB?

To us the nomination of this award smacks of political expediency. As indeed does the very establishment of this society. Could it be that its focal point as a publisher of technical papers on rocketry and its efficacy at disseminating news gave the BIS precisely the proper credentials for becoming the discreet middle-man between the Soviet and American space program scientists? The Soviet Embassy in London had a subscription for twenty copies of the BIS bi-monthly (then) journal and Arthur C Clarke received a list from the Embassy of the final destinations of these magazines—which he passed on to the 'appropriate' (allegedly disinterested) authorities.[41] With WvB "honoured and obligated" the British would maintain a high grade 'official' source of information concerning the development of rocket technology.

1945 Baltic coast October 15

Operation Backfire. The British held three test firings of captured V-2s that they had reassembled. These rockets were launched from Cuxhaven, west of the River Elbe on the North German sea coast. The Soviets attended the third test firing. Meanwhile in Germany the Soviets had two special trains built for them by a German railway company. These trains were entirely equipped as mobile laboratories-cum technician's living quarters and were used to prove out missile equipment. The great advantage of these convenient trains was that they could perform anywhere they were required.

1946 Hollywood

Fritz Lang premièred *Cloak and Dagger,* badly received by the critics, who were not at all convinced by it. The last of his films to deal with the Nazi issue and—shades of Mittelwerk—it featured an A-bomb factory in the Bavarian Alps. Switch A-bombs for V-2s and there you have it. Willie Ley and "a scientist from Los Alamos" were the technical advisers on this film. The discretion with which this announcement was made leads one to guess the name of the other colleague of Ley—could it be Wernher von Braun, at the time maintaining a very low profile in the States? Lang was known to attend anti-A-bomb meetings with Ley, and he was said to have been "most concerned about the issue of former Nazis who were brought over to America in order to work on future weapons technology".

The whole issue of his relationships with these men is revelatory and we now take a break from post war rocketry for a large dose of Dr. Donald's mede-ciné-ma.

Dr. Donald's SFX trickery— Part Two

The examples of photographic fakery discussed in *Northern Exposures* fell mainly into the category of manipulation for commercial purposes. In the domain of political manipulation there is also a precedent—one that would set the pattern for the later Apollo film faking.

Die Artful Dodgers-Germany 1927-1933

This fakery principally involved six people. Four were to become the backbone of the American space program—Willie Ley, Wernher von Braun, Walter Dornberger and Hermann Oberth. The other two were one of the great teams of German cinema—Fritz Lang and Thea von Harbou.

According to the Fritz Lang biographer, Patrick McGilligan, it was in the autumn of 1929, at the invitation of Fritz Lang, that the rocket scientist Hermann Oberth (then living in Medias, Romania) arrived in Berlin to be the principal technical consultant on the little-known silent movie *Frau im Mond, Woman in the Moon.*

This film owed much of its genesis to the friendship that Lang and his then wife, Thea von Harbou, had with Wille Ley, the scientist and specialist writer on

rocketry, whom they had first met in 1927.

Frau im Mond, the last silent movie to have a plot based on spaceflight, dealt with a trip to the Moon and required many special effects (SFX) and technically challenging sets. Enormous quantities of bleached sand were trucked into the sound stage in Berlin and Lang's designers created the lunar mountains and dunes from this material.

The results were in fact *very* similar to those portrayed in the first artistic impressions of the Moon released by NASA and its contractor Grumman see picture (8) below.

Critics noted that the actual rocket launch only took a few pages in Thea von Harbou's book for the film but accounted for nearly half the movie's total running time on screen. The

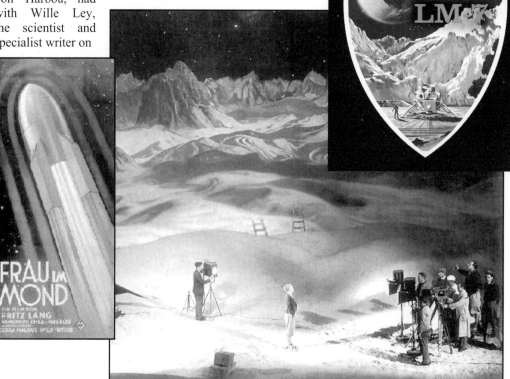

8. The film set for *Frau im Mond* and the 'Apollo 13' LM 7 badge.

Wolf whistle

Lang was a fervent nationalist but professed to be anti-Nazi.

Yet this film abounds in *pro* Nazi gestures (such as half disguised stiff arm salutes)

and even his characters' names are revelatory.

Could it be another reason why this film is so little-known?

For an anti-Nazi, Wolf Helius, the name of the 'hero' in *Frau im Mond* is interesting: Hitler's Alsatian dog was called

Wolf; his mountain fortress was dubbed 'The Wolf's Lair' and Helios was the son of Hyperion, father of

Uranus & Gaia and one of the Titans.

In fact Titan in the singular is interchangeable with Hyperion.

Helios succeeded Hyperion as the Greek god of the Sun and

himself was succeeded by—Apollo.

Life imitating art.

---

rocket design for the Lang film was based on 'Model B', one of Oberth's theoretical rockets.

There are as many variations on this collaboration between scientist and cinéaste as there are historians. One version of the 'official' history tells us that the rocket model was subsequently incorporated by Oberth into practical experimentation at the VfR's proving ground in the suburbs of Berlin.[42]

Another version (Heinz Gartzmann) has Willy Ley, proposing (on behalf of the VfR) that Oberth, in his capacity of technical adviser to Lang, used his time with the production team to carry out real-life tests using genuine rocket models, thus incorporating the costs for such tests into the film budget. Naturally enough, that idea did not meet with the approval of the film's financial backers. Ley nearly managed to persuade Ufa (the company in charge of publicity) of the value to be gained from launching a real rocket on the same day that the film would première, but since he could not guarantee the efficiency and readiness of such a rocket, this plan was initially vetoed—until Fritz Lang, who was enthusiastic about the idea, apparently offered to pay half of the costs towards this publicity coup.

This situation now left Oberth with problem areas. His technical consultation work partly consisted of advising the film's designers who were far more concerned with the visual and dramatic aspects of their sets rather than scientific realism. Oberth finally arrived at a set that conformed to his scruples as a scientist. He then had to oversee the design of the model rocket used in the film, as well as build and experiment on the real rocket, all within three months, in readiness for the opening night.

This première was to be held on October 15 1929. Taking autumn as commencing on McGilligan's date of September 21, for Oberth's arrival on set, it only gives him four weeks to achieve his aims. As nearly half the film is concerned with the rocket launch and the interiors of the space craft cabin, it is highly unlikely that Oberth was brought into

---

Frau im Mond credits

Director	Fritz Lang
Writers	Thea von Harbou, Fritz Lang
Photography	Curt Courant, Oskar Fischinger
Special Effects	Konstsantin Tschetwerikoff
Background Photographs	Horst von Harbou
Art Directors	Otto Hunte, Emil Hasler, Karl Vollbrecht
Music	Willy Schmidt-Gentner
Characters	Prof. George, Manfeldt, Wolf Helius, Hans Windegger, Frieda Venten, Gustav, Walt Turner, Mrs Hippolt, Grotjan, Financiers, Flower vendor, Foreman, Josephine, 'the Mouse'.

the production schedule at such a late date. However, one of the Oberth biographers, Heinz Gartzmann, has Oberth arriving in Berlin in the Autumn of 1928, a whole year earlier, as "upon completion of the scenario, a scientific adviser was needed". Given the dedication of these biographers to accuracy, such discrepancies in the stories of Lang and Oberth are worthy of note. As a German acquainted with the rocket scientists of the Third Reich, Gartzmann might well have had access to facts perhaps unavailable to others.

Despite the proximity of his VfR rocket association, it seems that Oberth did not have the technicians on hand that he needed to produce a real liquid propellant rocket, and he placed an advertisement in the press for help. This assistance came, in the form of Rudolf Nebel, engineer and ex-wartime pilot (in the opinion of many not nearly such a war hero as he made himself out to be) and Alexander Shershevsky. Sent by his government to study aircraft engineering in Berlin, Shershevsky had outstayed his 'official' visit and was now said to be afraid to return to Moscow. Oberth called him "the second laziest man I had ever met—he was bone idle". For the *real* rocket, Nedel proposed that they build a much smaller rocket with only a half-gallon propellant capacity but the film production company insisted that the rocket be at least a 45ft/13.72m long. Eventually a compromise was reached at 7ft/2.13m, with a two gallon capacity. So with the very odd choices of a lazy-bones and a 'fly-boy' to help him, Oberth now set out to create this real rocket publicity event for the film, actively aided by Willy Ley.

Gartzmann states that Oberth's calculations indicated his rocket would climb to about 25 miles. The film's PR department, with scant regard for the truth, immediately increased this distance to 40 miles. Oberth then nearly killed himself trying out a propellant mixture of petrol and liquid oxygen. As one of the foremost experts on rocketry at that time, he would certainly have been aware that here was a lethal mixture, exploding on contact, but he allegedly considered that the availability and cheapness

of these fuels outweighed the major disadvantage—probable death.

Does any of this sound familiar? Remember Apollo 1? Remember Challenger? In this example of greed and expediency endangering the safety of a 'mission' we learn from Gartzmann that Oberth perforated one eardrum and severely damaged his eyes. The resulting costly delay lasted for *six weeks* and the expenses for the equipment and time lost had to be met by the resources of the production company. Yet none of these details are mentioned by Lang's biographer, who is otherwise meticulous in his detail concerning the progress of each film. McGilligan merely says that: "Problems arose when the costs mounted and the final experiment fizzled," prior to the Berlin première.

During the six weeks that Oberth was somewhat incapacitated, the real rocket's body was being constructed and Gartzmann relates that (Shershevsky having finally been dismissed) Oberth and Nebel gained some time when Fritz Lang himself over-ran his shooting schedule. (No mention of this overrun in the *Lang* biography.)

But even the genius of Oberth could not (would not?) solve the problem of the appropriate combustion mix for the 'demonstration' model. But despite working over twelve hours at a stretch, Oberth was not going to be ready and he finally abandoned any pretence at a 'real' rocket. Instead he built a simplified 'demonstration' model that would suffice for the film's publicity needs. Nebel photographed a wooden test model of the rocket falling down a long chimney. The picture was then turned upside down and issued by the publicity department as a 'trial launch' of the real rocket. Does *this* scenario sound at all familiar? When the film opened in Berlin on October 15 1929, no actual rocket launch accompanied the event. We are told that the film was a success and that the public quickly forgot about the real rocket launch they were meant to have seen.

This piece of history is an interesting demonstration in promising one event, producing a similar but fictitious event in its place and leaving the audience totally happy, having forgotten the initial promise.

If the film was finally premièred in October 1929 and Oberth was indeed first approached in the Autumn of 1928, Oberth actually had nearly twelve months for the development of his rocket rather than the three months that the above story relates. Which would make "time ran out and Oberth had to abandon his careful construction of a proper high altitude rocket" a dramatic storyline but an inaccurate statement.

Gartzmann's version of events then goes on to describe how much valuable data was accrued from the *Frau im Mond* period and that "the VfR took over Oberth's 'real' rocket parts from the film company and continued with the research". But the VfR *is* Oberth, one of its founder members! This action was allegedly harder than it sounds, as most of the parts were with the manufacturers, awaiting payment. He records that nevertheless, "somehow the bills were met". Of the same event McGilligan tells us that the VfR then had in its possession the parts, the tools for assembly and a large launching cradle—all kindly *given* to them by the film's production company—Fritz Lang GmbH.

If Lang was underwriting 50% of the cost of this rocket, would he not have made sure that the parts were ready for the publicity event, and recuperated his excess costs via Oberth's fee? Indeed McGilligan recounts that Lang had initially personally invested his 5,000 Deutschmarks out of Oberth's own pocket and that Oberth finally left Berlin, "stranding investors and in financial and moral ruin". This account does not accord with Gartzmann's, but then McGilligan is only getting Fritz Lang's side of the story, and there may have been vested interests here, as we shall see.

Gartzmann relates that by 1929 Oberth's club, the VfR had not a pfennig with which to pursue its research. Whether it really had exhausted its funds is cause for debate. What is certain is that the VfR was reputed to have been flirting with the military. Gartzmann states that: "Oberth's sporadic attempts to interest the War Ministry and the Luftwaffe (German Air Force) in his plans had repeatedly failed to meet with any response, for reasons which have never been satisfactorily explained". Yet early in 1930, Dr. Ritter, Director of the Reich Institute of Chemistry and Technology at Plotsenzee near Berlin allowed Oberth to use his facilities for the development of a liquid propellant rocket, which would then be launched and authenticated under the aegis of the institute. Oberth and Nebel were able to set to work again, and took on three new assistants: Klaus Riedel a young engineer, and two other eighteen year old boys, Rolf Engel and a certain Wernher Freiherr von Braun. By July 23 1930 the rocket was ready and was fired successfully (no doubt not using petrol and liquid oxygen then!).[43] Nebel and the young men continued working *in Berlin* while Oberth supposedly returned to Medias. However, some fifteen pages later in Gartzmann's account, we learn that at the conclusion of the July 23 test, Nebel and Riedel went to a farmhouse *in Saxony* (owned by Nebel's grandparents). Here they began experiments on their 'Mirak' rocket which took from the end of July through to *September 27 1930* when they returned to Berlin to test the Mirak at Reinickendorf, a disused firing range near Berlin granted to *Oberth* by the Reich authorities for a peppercorn rent. Thus did the VfR get its own testing site and others including Wernher von Braun together with Rolf Engel who joined them at that time.

Heinz 59

After the war the spirit of the VfR was rekindled. On January 29 1948 student Hermann Kolle and Juppe Gerhards (ex-wartime colleague of Oberth's, turned publisher) founded the German Society for Space Research. Heinz Gartzmann, scientist and author, was one of the first fifty nine members.

These various scientists are popularly depicted as being impoverished throughout this period, living on welfare and spending any money they did have on their experiments. They begged various German suppliers for parts and affluent visitors were actively encouraged to visit the testing site. A careful list of donors was kept. Years later Rolf Engel estimated that the VfR had raised over 300,000 Deutschmarks by 1933, when the VfR's bookkeeping system lapsed. Gartzmann infers that Rudolf Nebel did not bother to keep the books thereafter, whereas the truth of the matter is that after the VfR was incorporated into the Nazi regime there were no books to keep.

In the next paragraph of this muddlesome tale, we are told that on leaving the July 23 test site at Plotsenzee, Oberth was to stay in Translyvania for the next *ten* years. So how can it be that by 1938, only eight years later, Hermann Oberth was to be found at Felixdorf, near Vienna (then part of Greater Germany) working on top secret rocket preparations with the Nazis? These events appear to be a mixture of truth and disinformation. Which comment leads us to another cinematic adventure, a fakery which resolves the problems of the preceding story and which contains the seeds of the future Apollo hoax.

Die racketeers

Somewhere between October 1929 and 1933, the VfR, Oberth and von Braun were involved in the production of a 'promotional' movie designed to convince the German authorities of the viability and possibilities of their rocket research. This production was achieved by intercutting images of successful rocket tests with scenes from the Fritz Lang film *Frau im Mond* (a classic 'cheat' therefore) and presenting the finished whole product as 'fact' to Adolf Hitler. Greatly impressed, the Nazi leader gave engineer Captain Walter Dornberger (head of the German Army Weapons Department) and the VfR virtual carte blanche to proceed with their experimental developments. Dornberger allegedly then warned von Braun that the 'fiction' would now actually have to become 'fact' or they would all be in trouble!

On March 14 1933 the National Ministry of Public Enlightenment and Propaganda was set up under the direction of Goebbels and took control of the film industry in Germany during the Third Reich.

In 1995, two years prior to the details published in the McGilligan biography of Fritz Lang, we received independent information from a Whistle-Blower who *must* remain incognito under the circumstances. He told us that not only did the Nazis take over the records and the men of the VfR in 1933 but also that the Nazis went all over Europe tracking down and destroying all the film prints of the Lang movie that they could find, to minimise any risk of the initial hoax being uncovered.

The pieces of the puzzle began to fall into place when we later ascertained that it was actually *Fritz Lang* who asserted that Oberth had set in motion a "series of actions" by which the Gestapo confiscated all Lang's plans and mod-

---

'masterly' mergers

The deal between Oberth and Lang was interesting—to say the least.

- If Oberth's rocket was a commercial success, then Lang would benefit by receiving 50% of the film's profits—*until the year 2020.*
- If the rocket did not work—during the lifetime of the film contract—then Oberth would not have to honour this agreement (which could have come to millions of marks).
- The film contract's 'lifetime' was defined as lasting until the film production company Fritz Lang GmbH had ceased operating.
- This get-out clause of rocket failure also provided a reason for Oberth to pursue his research on this rocket after the film's release, which of course gave him an excuse for removing all the plans, drawings and models, thus eliminating them from the cinematographic record, forever. Moreover, if Oberth already had the intention of selling his rocket to the German Army, and did not feel confident that the company would be wound up speedily, there was every reason for Oberth to take out personal 'insurance' by producing a 'failure' of a rocket, even at the risk of life and limb, for he would not want to bring a crippling monetary deal onto the bargaining table along with his rockets.

Rather unsurprising then that Fritz Lang GmbH was wound up—shortly after the release of *Frau im Mond*.

els for the film and then "called in from world release every print of our films when he went to work on rocket research for the Third Reich". The date was pin-pointed as 1933 and in Lang's opinion, Oberth was an "ardent Nazi".

Lang himself thought that the reason for this confiscation was because the film might contain technological information. However McGilligan quite rightly points out that Oberth's rocket was hardly the only, or even the best prototype then in research. Furthermore, the film had already been released in the States in 1931. Logically the Americans had already had two years to scrutinise the film for any relevant technical details. And Fritz Lang would have known that fact, therefore his statement is misleading to say the least. Lang went on record in 1944 as saying that: "Nowhere in the *world* today (our emphasis) can be located a copy of *Frau im Mond"*, without indicating how he knew this to be so. This statement was not true either, as at least two film prints have escaped confiscation.

It is of course quite possible that he himself was involved in the whole scenario from start to finish.

Reels within reels

Both Lang and his wife, the pro-Nazi Thea von Harbou, were interested in spaceflight and they had known Willie Ley since 1927. Lang set up his own company *Fritz Lang GmbH* in June 1928 which gave him complete control over production, while Ufa with whom he had worked since 1922, retained the management of advertising, publicity and distribution. An ideal world for a creative film director and yet Lang only made two films with this production company: *Spione* which had begun production in December 1927 and appeared in March 1928 and *Frau im Mond* (from script to première, April 1928 through to October 1929). Gartzmann recounts that the film was a great success with cinema audiences yet Lang's biographer asserts that the film's lack of success contributed to the demise of Fritz Lang GmbH. And that the final blow to the company was the request by Ufa that Lang add sound to the movie, which he absolutely refused to do. If this film was secretly being prepared for further cutting and insertions, the last thing that Lang would need was complications with an accompanying soundtrack. Especially as Ufa were insisting upon sound being added when the rocket was launched—exactly the portion of film that was going to be needed for other purposes.

A similar excuse was later to be used by NASA to explain the demise of interest in Apollo. The lack of TV images during the 'Apollo 12' turned the public away from the space program at the time and this disinterest potentially had an effect on the funding of the program. In fact, as we have demonstrated, that lack of images was actually intentional.

The circumstances surrounding Lang's company tend to lend weight to our claim that the set-up was established uniquely in order to make the film-within-a-film, a technique that was Lang's speciality. Lang certainly was always keenly interested in the factual detail that he incorporated in his films, yet even for him, *Frau im Mond* was considered to be overstuffed with details of scientific rocketry.

However, when seen in the light of the intended future use of this footage, namely to persuade the Nazi Führer that the potential of the rocket boys from Reinickendorf was worthy of investment, then the presence of an extraordinary amount of serious detailed scientific material makes perfect sense. Lang claimed inspiration for the film's plot, yet gave Thea von Harbou sole credit for the script. Either it was she that was in cahoots with rocket racketeers, or they both were.

Did this plot have anything to do with Willie Ley's hasty departure to the States in 1932? A departure undertaken supposedly because he saw the way the wind was blowing and did not want to stay in Nazi Germany? Willie Ley remained a close friend of Fritz Lang's throughout his life, yet Willie Ley was also a friend of Oberth's, who wrote to him throughout the war. And that circumstance does somewhat negate Ley's anti-Nazi motives for leaving Germany. For someone who did not like the Third Reich, Ley was also very close to WvB, both in Germany and subsequently in America, and remained so for the rest of his life.

Further, did this affair also add weight to Lang's desire to leave the country in 1933? As well as his pet monkey, Fritz Lang took with him four hundred stills of *Frau im Mond* when he departed Berlin in the spring of 1933, at a date that is difficult to determine. His immigration documentation does not tie in with the "dramatic overnight escape" story of which Lang was so fond. Indeed a departure date such as spring of 1934 would be more in keeping with various reasons and date discrepancies that we have noted from the diverse biographies available to date. Some thought that damaged pride after his divorce from Thea contributed to his departure. Considering the fact that Lang had been indulging in an extra-marital affair for a long time prior to their separation and subsequent divorce and that Thea only took a lover at the moment of their separation, what did Lang have to feel hurt about? Indeed Thea behaved with no animosity throughout their divorce proceedings and even in November 1933, there is evidence that Lang was in Germany to liquidate his marital affairs. McGilligan reports that on January 4 1934, Lang had *read and annotated* a Nazi document relating to the fate of the Jewish people. Which sentence implies strong links with the inner circle of Hitler's Gestapo and a seeming indifference towards the fate of members of his own race. Indeed it is on the 'official' record that Goebbels had told Lang personally back in March 1933 that the Third Reich did *not* have a problem concerning his Jewish origins, as he was recognised as the most famous and talented of German film directors. As many others also noted, Fritz Lang had been an ardent naturalised German since 1922, seventeen years before Hitler incorporated Austria into the Third Reich. According to the actor Willie Fristch (who had played the male lead of Wolf Helius in *Frau im Mond*) Lang was more patriotic than the most patriotic of German nationalists. Another associate spoke of how hard he was regarding people. "He behaved like a Prussian", it was claimed, which could be interpreted as being overbearingly bossy and im-

bued with his own superiority, for the aristocratic Prussians (such as Wernher von Braun) were the backbone of the higher ranks in the Germany Army.

Lang's real attitude and associations with the Nazis are open to debate. Many people in Hollywood thought that Hitler had fed pro-Nazis into the American movie industry. And the more one learns about the *Frau im Mond* plot and its perpetrators, the more one has to ask questions about those involved who left for the United States before the war. Neither Fritz Lang's accounts of that period of his life, nor his subsequent behaviour in France and America, nor the content of some of his films do anything to alleviate the suspicion that Lang was not as anti-Nazi as he proclaimed. Even though he knew that it was not his best film, Lang had an attachment to *Frau im Mond* that was out of proportion to its value, even as his last silent movie.

After the war Lang wrote to von Harbou asking her about the legal rights to all his films but most especially *Frau im Mond*. He wanted to remake a modern version of the film and a series of press interviews were arranged in which he announced this intention. None of the letters reached von Harbou—or at least she never replied to him. So why did Lang arrange these press conferences before he had confirmation from Germany? He would have wished to avoid looking foolish in public. Was this tactic to remake the film a part of the upcoming space project? And was the announcement of an event before it had happened an attempt to 'authorise' said event and help create a climate in which funding would become available? *In the 1960s* he again talked of a modern remake of the movie and it was then that he referred to his four hundred *Frau im Mond* continuity stills, stating that they showed how some of the technical problems were resolved. The same questions apply. Why try for something that was by now so patently out of date? In the event, it never happened. As we all know, it was Arthur C Clarke and Stanley Kubrik who would make the seminal sound movie about spaceflight.

190

In 1968 Fritz Lang was invited as a guest of honour to the Space Science seminar at Huntsville, Alabama. Why was he so honoured? On account of the influence of *Frau im Mond*, they proclaimed. In many ways, it seemed, they considered Fritz Lang to be the *"Father* of Rocket Science". But that was a title that many considered rightly belonged to Hermann Oberth. Which takes us back to 1946 by which time Wernher had arrived in Fort Bliss, Texas. ■

9. Preparations for a V-2 flight at White Sands, New Mexico in 1946.   ARCHIVE

1946 Fort Bliss, Texas

Although not published until the mid 1950s, von Braun wrote his work *The Exploration of Mars* during his early days of comparative idleness at Fort Bliss during 1946. Subsequently, he would write articles for *Collier's* magazine which referred to orbiting space stations, a trip to the Moon and then a journey to Mars. For his Mars project von Braun envisaged a total of seventy astronauts travelling in ten spaceships which were launched from low Earth orbit towards a space station already orbiting around Mars. Was von Braun in any way influenced by the writings of the Englishman J D Bernal who, in 1929, had also described manned space stations? Bernal suggested that men would live in spherical stations 10 miles/16 kms in diameter, and at first these would be inhabited by space navigators, then by scientists and then by a third category: "Those who for any reason were dissatisfied with Earthly conditions would come to inhabit extraterrestrial bases".

Following the documentation confiscated from Peenemünde, the United States Army Air Corps tendered contracts for an Earth orbiting satellite. This tender was won by Douglas Aircraft. By the late 1990s the first two of these three categories have been achieved—and indeed Project Apollo was particular in emphasising this structure—no scientists were written into the script until late in the program. The interpretation of category three is ambiguous and as yet (as far as we know) unfulfilled.

1946 Germany and USSR
October 12, 16 & 22

The Soviets suddenly moved their 5,000 Germans into the Soviet Union and deposited them just outside Moscow. Contrary to the American system, these scientists were allowed to take their women with them, legally wed or otherwise. They were also allowed to take all their possessions. Harford recounts how Mrs Gottrup tested that particular directive by insisting on taking her cows with their hay—and she succeeded! This freedom of action tells us much about the mutually beneficial arrangements between the Allies at the end of the war. It supports our view that the scientists were shared out between the two nations, so much for the 'race' to snatch the best scientists, for Helmut Grottrupp was a close colleague of Wernher von Braun.

The Soviets used 92 trains to move their rocket researchers from Germany into the USSR. A total of 20,000 people were moved in the first wave, 200 of whom were sent up to Gorodomyla Island on Lake Seliger, north-west of Moscow. Mr and Mrs Grottrupp were moved to the outskirts of Moscow on October 22 1946.

With hindsight, it would seem that the Soviets demonstrated a more humanitarian approach towards their technical prisoners than did the Americans. Moreover, the ways in which the technical information was passed from teacher to pupil was very different. The Soviet experts and the Germans worked side by side in the same factory, but in separate areas. Information was passed between these teams without the Germans ever meeting their Soviet counterparts. They only spoke directly to Korolëv, who was far curter with them than he had been in Bleicherode.

Further down the ladder, the two nationalities worked together until all the information had been absorbed by the Soviets.

At that point the Germans were repatriated.

1947 Moscow April 14

Korolëv had a private meeting with Stalin and informed him that the Soviet designers were quite capable of creating a better rocket than the V-2, which Korolëv now considered obsolete. They were, he stated, able to produce a more reliable launcher with a greater range. Stalin nevertheless insisted that they first learn all that they could by building an exact replica of the V-2 and launching it. These rockets were to be tested from Kasputin Yar, Astrakhan, Southern Russia. In early July at Stalin's behest, Korolëv and subsequently other Soviet scientists were sent for by the forerunner of the KGB and asked for their opinion on unidentified flying objects.[44]

1947 Washington July 26

In an exercise that combined logistics with more levels of segregation, President Truman separated the United States Air Force from the Army and also created the US Department of Defense through the signing of the National Security Act. Rocket research and the very beginnings of the Strategic Defense Initiative (SDI) via the development of ICBMs were the first steps towards the military's new defence scheme. The levels of secrecy surrounding this project were so hermetic that it is unsurprising if most of the military considered that the only reason for the development of ICBMs was the maintenance of America's superiority as world leader and the suppression of Communism (the carrot to keep them going). Having witnessed the deconstruction of the USSR in the 1980s and the current attempts at the reconstruction of the West and the East into a one-world system, it is not too far-fetched to state that the division of the world into two different ideologies was a deliberate scheme.

A Soviet joke

Question: What is the difference between capitalism and communism?

Answer: Under capitalism, man exploits man. Under communism it's just the reverse.

1947 Fort Bliss

For man's conquest of space, Wernher von Braun had formulated a list of key steps to be accomplished. Many of his projects were for the future and his more ambitious designs needed to be preceded by other, smaller projects. These early papers were written partially with the intention of bringing the general public progressively towards the idea of investing in space exploration—an area of research in which the 'bang for bucks' concept was not immediately applicable. In Autumn 1947 the US Air Force established the Department of Space Medicine under Dr. Hubertus Strughold.

1948 Fort Bliss

WvB elaborated on the necessity for a *multi-*

Rocket names—Part I

It is our contention that the codenames given to projects by the Americans reveal through word association (either intentionally or unintentionally) much about their function. The names of the rockets designed by WvB at this time were the Redstone and Jupiter. Although the old arsenal in which he worked at Huntsville was called Redstone, it is an interesting coincidence that Mars is also the red planet. Jupiter, associated with war and victory, is the Roman name for the god that the Greeks called Zeus, who was the father of Apollo.

staged launcher, claiming that the size of such a launcher did not represent an insurmountable technical difficulty, even if the cost was tremendous. Money in any case was no object, but WvB's ideas for the appropriate launcher would have to be re-appraised later!

1949 USA February 21

David Baker, space historian in his work *Spaceflight and Rocketry: A Chronology* has noted under the events of this day that the Project RAND (Research And Development Corporation) report D-405 established the principal reasons for government-run space programs and for the United States, satellites and space travel would bring about:

- A demonstration of US technological superiority;
- A device for communication;
- A reconnaissance instrument;
- An instrument of political strategy.

Baker then writes:

These were the first formal declarations of the *primary reasons* as to why the USSR and the USA would inaugurate space projects and use *ambitious goals like the Moon landing* for stimulating national acclaim (emphasis added).

Baker goes on to state that the world-wide reaction to Sputnik clearly identified this *desired link* between technology and *perceived* national greatness. In the light of the hypotheses set out in this book this is an extremely relevant entry. As a declaration of intent from the 'masters of infinity', placed discreetly on the public record and using sentences which echoed the opinions of Wernher von Braun, it could not be bettered.

10. Wernher von Braun, third from right, at the Billy The Kid Bar in Lincoln, New Mexico *c*1946—note the swastika on the sign.   ARCHIVE

1950 Texas-Alabama April 15

Wernher von Braun and his team were moved from Fort Bliss to the Guided Missile Division of the US Army Rocket Research Center at Redstone Arsenal, Huntsville, near the northern state line of Alabama to begin work on the Redstone rocket. This department known as ABMA was under the supervision of one General John Bruce Medaris. In the same year the International Astronautical Federation (IAF) was brought into being in order to provide a public 'platform' for the development of space exploration. In con-

---

Cobbler, cobbler, mend my shoe

The headquarters of the IAF Congress was in Baden, Switzerland, home of the permanent secretary, Josef Stemmer. Born the son of a shoemaker, Stemmer became a talented engineer through sheer hard work.

The first IAF Congress was held in Paris, France, September 1950.

The second was in London, England, September 1951, hosted by the BIS (q.v.).

Robert Maxwell was also strenuous in his support of the IAF, and through his dealings with the scientific press in part via Pergamon Press and NATO/AGARD, was familiar with the big names in astronautics throughout the world.

tradictory fashion the IAF tried to justify the fact that the rocket scientists who were obliged to manufacture weapons would eventually see their craft used for peaceful purposes. Given that by 1959 General Medaris would be officially pushing for the establishment of a military outpost on the Moon and that this statement was made in 1953, we question the IAF's truthfulness.

At the second symposium of Space Medicine held in Chicago, WvB presented a paper in which he recommended the construction of:

- Multi-stage rockets of a size and weight commensurate with the requirements of launching heavy loads into Earth orbit and beyond.
- Orbiting satellite stations in which astronauts could perform scientific and astronomical research—studying the *stars*. So please note, no totally-black skies in 1950!

Wernher von Braun emphasised that these *wheel-shaped manned space stations* of about 200ft/61metres in diameter should be placed in orbit around the Earth. He also underlined the fact that they would be useful as a military observation posts, as well as weapons carriers. He added: "The orbiting station will help us to reach out into deep space, well beyond the confines of our trouble-ridden home planet". This statement encapsulated much of Bernal's 'third breed' of space travellers. Reminiscent of the elitist idea of an exclusive colony far away from 'hoi polloi', it indicates that WvB did not consider himself at all accountable and responsible for the chaotic state of affairs on *this* planet.

1952 USA
The idea of manned space travel was brought to the general attention of the American public when WvB started publishing articles on the subject in *Collier's* magazine. The medical detail in these articles was provided by his close collaborator Dr. Hubertus Strughold.

1952 Soviet Union
The Soviets returned three drafts of German scientists to their homeland in January, June and November. These men had passed on all their knowledge to Soviet engineering and aeronautical students as well as to the men already working in the various Soviet design bureaux. By involving students at University level, the Soviets assured themselves of a solid base in rocketry for the future. Whereas the American students, for their part, did not acquire any practical experience until they had terminated their studies and found employment in the industry.

1953 USA
The Mars Project (Das Marsprojekt) by Wernher von Braun was published in English by the University of Illinois Press.

In the autumn the aircraft and rocket builders Glenn L Martin Company volunteered to build a space ship for a flight to the Moon, "if the defense effort of this country demands the execution of such an order". Heinz Gartzmann emphasised that the key words were "defense effort" and that rocket-launched radio-guided ballistic missiles would be the weapon of the future. Furthermore he said: "The rapid development of rocket-propelled spacecraft is bringing the space station and the base on the Moon into the realm of serious possibilities".

1954 Soviet Union
The Soviets returned the final group of German scientists to their homeland.

Dr. Donald's SFX trickery — Part Three
Both the cinema and the space program gave each other a helping hand again in 1954, when

---

New World Order—variations on a theme

"The logical outcome of interplanetary travel must be the development of a common, supra-national ethos. The International Astronautical Foundation is called upon to hasten this process."

Heinz Gartzmann

Spaceballs—really!

A version of the 'bottle suit' from the first Disney film is now part of the escape system attached to the Space Shuttle. Developed by NASA in 1976, the Personal Rescue Enclosures are 'fabric' balls some 30ins/76cms in diameter. These are to be used by the crew for transfer to a rescue orbiter, should their Shuttle malfunction while in space.

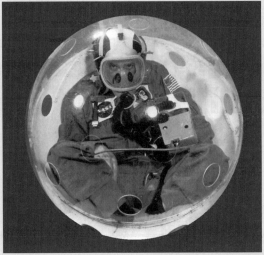

NASA

WvB acted as consultant to Walt Disney for the setting up and filming of a three-part TV series: *Man In Space, Man And The Moon* and *Mars And Beyond*. All these were designed to raise finance for the building of the Disney theme park in California as well as to enthuse the public towards space exploration.

The first film summarised the state of play as of that date and set out many of the practical problems of spaceflight. It featured parts of a space station and a lunar craft filmed on full sized set constructions at the Disney studios. The astronauts left the space station enclosed in 'bottle suits', which were miniature space vehicles with atmospheres and rocket thrusters.

Remarkably, especially in the light of subsequent events, the second episode in the series did not feature a lunar landing by astronauts but only a circumlunar orbit! Von Braun opting, most uncharacteristically, and for whatever reason for the cautious approach in this glitzy public relations exercise.

The third film elaborated on the problems of lengthy space voyages and the Disney studios built six interplanetary spacecraft to WvB's and Stuhlinger's designs. Willie Ley was also a great source of information throughout the project. The old gang were warming up, working together on film/rocket promotions for the first time since having left Germany. ■

1954 Washington

Six weeks after President Eisenhower ordered a screening of *Man In Space* for the Pentagon, the US Government proceeded with plans for the joint Army/Navy satellite known officially as Project Orbiter. Unofficially it was called Project Slug. The US Army were to build the launcher and the Navy the satellite. By the end of the year WvB had promoted the idea of space travel to such an extent that both the general public and financiers on Capitol Hill were psychologically prepared to accept the expense of such a project.

However, the Air Force were conspicuous by their lack of involvement in this project as Arthur C Clarke noted during his stay with Mr & Mrs Fred Durant in Washington in June '54. There Clarke met several members of ABMA and the Navy to discuss Project Orbiter—

including his fellow houseguest at the Durant residence, one Wernher von Braun. After some years of correspondence, Clarke had met WvB for the first time the previous year at a hotel in Manhattan, and in 1954 he also visited WvB at his home in Huntsville. It was during his stay at the Durant's house that Arthur introduced WvB to the pleasures of aqualung diving, a pastime that von Braun would declare his favourite and which he pursued for the rest of his life, often in the company of the man who became his very good friend, Arthur C Clarke.

1955 Mexico

The USA organised the 'official' immigration of the 127 German scientists by bussing them across the border into Mexico and then having them walk back across a bridge through Mexican and American immigration. Both countries co-operated in this fix-up.

The 6th International Astronautical Federation Congress, now boasting 9,000 members was held in Copenhagen. Twenty-one countries were represented, including the first appearance of the Soviet Union. Two days before the opening sessions of this IAF conference President Eisenhower announced that the United States had a satellite launching program underway. Very interestingly, two days after the *beginning* of this conference the Soviet Embassy in Copenhagen announced that Soviet satellites would also "be taking part in this sortie into space".[45]

1955 Washington Autumn

Officials in Washington told Wernher von Braun that they "were *not* in a satellite race with Russia".[46] Project Orbiter was dropped—under the pretext that the Navy's

Vanguard space craft was going to be the vehicle for the satellite launch. Despite the fact that the rocket was only on the drawing board and not a proven launcher, the US Army were told to get on with the Jupiter C rocket (a three stage vehicle capable of incorporating a fourth stage). This was ultimately tested with a 'dummy' fourth stage in place and Major General John Medaris specifically telephoned WvB to forbid the inclusion of any 'live' mechanism.[47] Given the intense rivalry between the US Army, Navy and Air Force over their respective roles in rocket development, this restraint was somewhat astonishing.

1956 USA

Viking press published *The Exploration of Mars* written together with Willy Ley. This book was an aspect of Von Braun's 'Mars Project' document and contained designs and illustrations for a martian expeditionary fleet and much data on the planet itself.

1957 Hollywood July 1

International Geophysical Year began.[48] WvB was continually refused permission to launch a satellite on the Jupiter C rocket. Even the MGM film studios offered to underwrite the expense of such an operation—but to no avail. The Vanguard rocket development was vastly over budget, yet the Pentagon continued with it—and had axed the Jupiter C project by July 15. So were the Americans fulfilling a pre-arranged plan and waiting for the Soviets to get their satellite launched first?

1957 Moscow October 4

The first Soviet Sputnik was launched. *The New York Times* telephoned WvB and asked

---

Rocket names—Part II

Juno was the Roman name for the Greek Goddess Hera. Referred to as the wife and sister of Jupiter/Zeus,
Queen of the Heavens, the mother of Ares (Mars)and patroness and defender of the cities of Argos & Samos.
(The letters S A M O S would be used as the acronym of a satellite system.)
The Romans considered her as "the goddess of the day of the new Moon".
In both Greek and Roman mythology, Juno/Hera hated the Trojans.
The sacred animals associated with her were the cuckoo, the cow and the peacock.
Ears of corn were her sacred 'flowers'—are there subtle links to the Crop Glyphs of Southern England here?

for his reaction. WvB claimed never to remember his reply because he was so shocked. He allegedly did not even know that Sputnik Zemlis had been put into orbit. With hindsight the apparent reluctance of the powers that be in the USA to take heed of the information emanating from the Soviets concerning an imminent satellite launch *could also* be put down to the fact that at the very highest level it had already been agreed that the Soviets would be first into orbit.

This sequence of events can have been designed expressly to stimulate the American Senate and Congress, who would then rally behind the vast monetary spending requests from the military forces that would be required to retain their status as leaders of the first world. The people of America—and indeed the West—would also clamour for parity having been fed the untruth that dominance of the high ground would ensure their safety. A year later, there was this from WvB's friend Carsbie Adams:

By 1958 it was evident that the USSR was engaged in a spaceflight program that exceeded that of the Western world. Despite the public front of 'astonishment', ***neither the timing nor the magnitude of the Soviet achievements came as any great surprise in informed quarters***".[49] (emphasis added)

Our own words precisely.

1957 Washington October 8

Four days after the Soviet launch of Sputnik 1, President Eisenhower inquired why Vanguard was not operational and was fobbed off with several conflicting answers by the Deputy Secretary of Defense, Donald Quarlse.[50]

- The US Army were in a position to launch a satellite in 1955 but had not done so.
  (Because they never received the go ahead from the Pentagon!)

- The Pentagon wanted to keep the satellite project under civilian control.
  (Since when has the Navy, parent of Vanguard, been civilian?)

- A reconnaissance program was already underway but Army/Air Force rivalry was retarding developments.

Now that the Soviet satellite had been successfully launched, General John Medaris now authorised the Jupiter rocket as 'go' again and renamed it the Juno, which in mythological terms was indeed most apposite.

Eisenhower ordered the Pentagon to use a 'Manhattan Project' approach to the 'problem' —thereby sanctioning 'need-to-know' compartmentalisation and secrecy. Both the Manhattan and Peenemünde Projects had shown the movers and shakers of the American Government and the Third Reich just how much money needed to flow unceasingly over many years in order to fund the realisation of their ever-increasing technological ambitions. These two projects had also provided invaluable experience in the art of running a top secret operation involving thousands of people, not all of them military, while still maintaining a high level of secrecy concerning the true nature of these projects. The fundamental understanding of the factors involved in such an exercise would find their ultimate expression in the organisation of the parallel objectives of the space program. The fact that this cover-up worked for nearly thirty years is a tribute to just how well these people learned from their experiences. Indeed Heinz Gartzmann cited Argentina, Sweden and Switzerland as examples of other countries that used the very same 'Manhattan Project' methods adopted for the development of their rocket programs by both the USA and the USSR.

Research and production were carried out in secret and the construction program separated into 'hermetically sealed' compartments so that *none but the few at the top* had any knowledge of the overall process of design and assembly.

Gartzmann also stated that *no more than a few score men controlled the rocket research and output of the world.* They controlled the "services of some of civilisation's most highly trained specialists", and they also controlled "the large funds *appropriated* for armaments" (emphasis added). Gartzmann was not speculating. As a highly proficient rocket engineer he was on the inside track, and here he was writing of the 'masters of infinity'.

Most conveniently, at the end of WWII the political globe had been divided into two—one 'public sector' in the West and one private sector in the East. What could be more simple than to exploit this division and lower the iron curtain in exactly the same way as the safety curtain comes down in the theatre. This ruse enabled the organisers of the space project to go to work in relative obscurity.

In the sense that two teams were targeting the Moon there was always a space race. In reality, the objectives were not those of competition. These two teams, while wearing different colours, were in truth on the same side. And even if many of the key players were unaware of the real script, it is likely (in our view) that at least both Korolëv and von Braun were aware of the true situation.

Well versed

The rockets go up

And where they come down

Is not our concern

Says Wernher von Braun.

Tom Lerher

The new boys with the know-how

It is also our opinion that the rocketeers, Dornberger and von Braun were expected to perform the same functions in America as they had done in Germany. Dornberger was indeed nominated as consultant on rocket ballistics upon his arrival in 1946. As was the case in Peenemünde, von Braun excelled in the tactical organisation of men and materials—if one was prepared to overlook his authoritarian, somewhat arrogant Prussian style—these skills made him exactly the right man to run the planned Apollo Surrogate program. The Aryan archetype of blue eyes, blond hair and a handsome physique combined with an exceptional talent for public relations made him an acceptable front man for the German 'Rockettes'. We suggest that despite his billing as the rocket engineering genius behind the American effort, when it came to the actual development of the

technology WvB was either not as capable as the Americans had been given to understand or that his potential was restricted—either by political or financial considerations. All of these reasons might have some bearing, and in biographies appearing in the late 1990s it is readily acknowledged that there were many people working at NASA who were more competent as scientists and engineers than von Braun.[51] As the facilitator and co-creator of highly sophisticated killing machines Wernher von Braun had played a significant part in bringing our planet nearer to the very troubles that he so ardently railed against in his lectures. Despite his protestations of innocence and his alleged desire to use rocket power for the exploration of space rather than warfare, WvB, just as he had done under Hitler, also worked with the US Army creating missiles and extolling the virtues of his future creations as a means of making war, not love. Even when later tempted by civilian industry with larger salaries and the opportunity to continue his research, he chose to stay with the army.[52]

If it is acknowledged that von Braun and Korolëv were the prime movers and shakers in the practical application of rocketry on our planet, then it can also be acknowledged that *without* their skills the path of mankind might have taken a different direction. However, as we have already seen in "Rocket Rackets", American rocket technology was well behind the standards set by Korolëv in the Soviet Union. In the USA, yet another rocket scientist would apparently be needed to actually make things work. For by 1955, WvB had sent for the eminent Hermann Oberth, who as we have seen, was the technical advisor to Fritz Lang and erstwhile colleague of WvB's from Peenemünde.

The third man—Hermann Oberth

Astonishingly, for those who have been reared on the myth that Wernher von Braun was the best of all the rocket men, and despite the fact that NASA later honoured Lang as the "Father of Astronautics", what emerges from the record is the fact that the absolute wizard of *practical* astronautics was Hermann Oberth. The assis-

11. Hermann Oberth. working at ABMA
Huntsville in 1956.   NASA

tant to rocket engineer Helmut Zborwoski and author of *Men and Rockets,* Heinz Gartzmann, considered Oberth to be the founder of the science of astronautics. Stuhlinger and Ordway described him quite simply as "a visionary genius". Born on June 25 1894 in the town of Nagyszeben, Austria-Hungary (now Sibiu, Romania) Hermann Oberth, like von Braun, was greatly influenced by Jules Verne. Initial experiments during WWI when he served in the Austrian Army (as did Fritz Lang) did not attract the attention of his superiors at the War Ministry. But in 1923, by the age of 29, Oberth published *The Rocket into Interplanetary Space* which brought him world-wide recognition. His later book *The Ways of Spaceflight* anticipated the development of electric propulsion and the ion rocket by 30 years.

Oberth was more responsible for the structure of the V-2 than was von Braun. Amongst *only some of the V-2 requirements* formulated by Oberth was the choice of propellants; the configuration of the propellant tanks; the combustion chamber pressure; the choice of graphite-stabilising fins in the exhaust stream together with the *general shape and configuration of the V-2.* Oberth was indeed the power behind the throne.[53]

The official record of Oberth's adventures post-Germany 1945 and pre-America 1955 gives a flavour of the man. After the war, Hermann Oberth was interrogated dozens of times at the Allies' 'Dustbin' holding camp but then released without making the 'A' list for the United States. Oberth was also seemingly out of range of the Baikonur 'B' list. Was he such a formidable threat that von Braun deliberately did not select him for inclusion with the 'Rockettes' at the time of Operation Paperclip? Oberth seemed to think so and said as much when writing to Willie Ley, already in the USA. He might well have been correct in this assessment. The net result was that Oberth was left to fend for himself while WvB departed for America and a new life, in the relative comforts of a land that had escaped the ravages of war.

The historical record states that the Soviets had people keeping an eye on WvB and his team, with a view to capturing them for themselves but that they were too well guarded by the Americans—allegedly. Such a big and disgruntled fish as Oberth, with no immediate prospects, was surely a catch for the Soviets but by ignoring Oberth we have yet another indication that the idea of a competition for these scientists was nothing more than disinformation. As with any smart party, guest lists are drawn up well in advance.

Hermann Oberth returned to his castle in Feucht near Nürnberg in Germany in 1943, purchased supposedly with money from his father (or Fatherland?). How he had time to buy a castle when working night and day for the Peenemünde project is not explained. Upon his return from the war he found that he had to share his castle with refugees—living conditions which he found intolerable. Due to the German currency reform of 1948 he was also apparently in dire financial straits—a position which was not improved by his "unwillingness to participate in dirty deals".[54] Forgive our cynicism, but this is the same man who was associated with deceiving Hitler (a very dirty deal) so that he could pursue his rocket research; who worked on the V-2 construction *wittingly*, while managing to "look the other way" and who then worked on the V-3, the missile with a baggage ticket labelled the United States of America.[55]

Swiss roll

Sources state that he was increasingly lonely (no mention here of his wife). This accumulation of miseries obliged Oberth to leave his castle and travel to Switzerland—a country he was 'forced' to enter illegally (no details on why *that* was necessary). Despite this 'illegal' entry Oberth found work as a consultant engineer for a year and was then a guest of the fireworks manufacture Hans Hamberger for a further twelve months. This brings the Oberth story to 1950 and for anyone familiar with the Swiss authorities' dealings with immigrants, it is barely credible. Their meticulous paperwork relating to *legal* immigrants combined with strict laws on foreigners working within the Swiss borders is further backed up by an equally strict policy concerning *illegal* immigrants. So would it have been an officially sanctioned businessman who hosted the officially welcome ex-Nazi employee Hermann Oberth?

The Italian job

The Italian Admiralty were not fazed by the problems of possible illegal entry into their neighbour's territory. They contacted Oberth in Switzerland (how did they know he was there?) and offered him a job, for which 120,000 Swiss Francs—a considerable sum of money at that time—was deposited by the Italian government into a Swiss bank account. Suddenly he was not lonely any more because his wife emerged from the background (where had she been hiding?). They both travelled to Italy where Oberth worked with a team of three other Germans and five Italians—on a rocket project that had been abandoned in Wittenberg seven years earlier in 1943. He allegedly remained in Italy for ten years, until the spring of 1953 and then returned to his castle in Germany where he held court to a continual flow of visitors, most of whom were related to the emerging rocket industry and affiliated media.

Once again we have a timetable problem: ten years in Italy from 1950 would have taken him to at least into 1960, yet all the records state that WvB had sent for him by 1955! And although not beyond the bounds of the international postal services of that time, we also have one Professor Hermann Oberth publishing an article in the *American Weekly*—on October 24 1954 entitled *Flying Saucers Come From An-*

other World. Why would the American public be interested in the views of a rocket scientist living in Germany?

In any event, the one consistency in the recorded movements of these rocket racketeers is their startling lack of adherence to any calendar with which we are familiar. Especially as in September 1951, with time off from his Italian contract obviously, Hermann Oberth was staying with the Chairman of the Second International Congress on Astronautics—Arthur C Clarke at 88 Nightingale Road in London.

His old 'partner in crime', Wernher von Braun interrupted this lifestyle therefore in the summer of 1955, three years before the formation of NASA with the urgent request that he join him in the United States. By this time von Braun was safely established as the head of his rocket team in Huntsville and had also acquired his American nationality. Was he now experiencing technical teething problems? It would be another two years before the Soviets and the Americans would discover the radiation belts around the Earth but by now Project Blossom was underway. Was NASA already concerned about the preliminary results of radiation and micro-gravity on bio-organisms? And did they need a man like Oberth because they were having trouble trying to create a *powerful enough propulsion system* to lift the required loads, or were they attempting to respond to such challenges using hitherto undeveloped technologies?

Whatever the reasons, it would seem that the genius of Hermann Oberth was the vital adjunct that the American space program required.

As it turned out, eventually Wernher would also need all the *simulation skills* that they had used when deceiving Hitler. Is it possible that as early as 1955 von Braun already had a suspicion of that requirement? Despite his previous grumbling off Oberth went, his knapsack on his back, to help out his erstwhile pal. Did he know even then that by this act he would become involved in yet another deception, but this time the target would be not one single national leader, but the entire world?

200

Pigments from our palette

We maintain that mankind's first steps to reach another world were forged and faked. What could have been a noble odyssey distorted into a travesty of the truth. It seems clear that:

- The foundations for the grand space project were laid down during WWII.
- This project was conceived and designed as a collaboration between two superpowers.
- The Cold War was a convenient cover under which aspects of this project could be implemented and hidden.
- All these machinations were orchestrated at the very highest level, with only a select *and hidden* few ever knowing *the overall objectives* of the project.
- These objectives have not yet been achieved in full. We are referring to a project that has been around at least since 1947—and it divides into several sections.
- Put another way, NASA's Apollo phase, seen by the public to be the end result of a decision made in the 1960s by President Kennedy was in fact only a small (but significant) part of a greater plan.
- Whatever humanity has so far experienced concerning the rivalries between the super powers of this world, today, at some very high but invisible level, our attitudes are being moulded to suit an agenda which does not necessarily have all our interests at heart.
- By the time that you, dear reader, have finished this book, you might wish to envisage a different outcome than that towards which these self-appointed masters are inexorably moving.

The 'masters of infinity' prepare their goals decades in advance. As we have seen, their space project has encountered a stumbling block—the natural barriers of the solar system, yet they have neither attempted to resolve these matters publicly nor have they admitted to encountering any such major problems.

QUESTION: What set of circumstances would lead to the initial establishment and maintenance of such a plan when it was clear that both nature itself and the masters' limited technical ability to deal with it would entail a longer and slower approach to the exploration of space?

QUESTION: What single condition other than the artificial reason supplied by President Johnson, could exert such a powerful attraction upon these men that they would risk nearly everything to overcome it?

These questions bring us full circle, back to our painting metaphor in an attempt to find the answer.

As a working premise, let us say that the 'masters of infinity' commissioned a space portrait depicting their intentions, which resulted in a work similar in concept to that of the Mona Lisa.

Leonardo set his subject against *two completely different landscapes,* one to the West and one to the East of her meridian. Yet this representation is not immediately discernible to the casual observer. Generally it has to be pointed out by one that knows.

Does the more recent work commissioned by the 'masters of infinity' also incorporate twin aspects? Yes, indeed it does. The USA and the USSR are the Western and Eastern backgrounds of the masters' painting of the Moon. This however, is a little known fact to the rest of the world and indeed to vast majority of the million or so people involved in the US/Soviet Space Project (400,000 USA; 800,000 USSR) to the end of the Apollo phase.

So is there a parallel to the enigmatic smile on the Mona Lisa? Yes, there is. We propose that the secret and subtle aspect in the masters' commissioned work was the certain awareness by the authorities of the existence of *extraterrestrial intelligence.*

This awareness of ET was the driving force behind their mission to land on the Moon.

However, the Moon was only a staging post to their avowed destination—a manned mission to a location on the plains of Cydonia, Mars. Once again using our restoration metaphor, we can begin to reveal the intricate details hidden under many years of dirt (disinformation), and in order to do that we must first travel to New Mexico.

201

13. The Mona Lisa, Louvre, Paris.

Part Two

MIDDLE DISTANCE

Chapter Six

Truth or Consequences

Nine Flew over the Cuckoo's Nest—Kenneth Arnold's sighting triggers public UFO awareness in America. The Roswell Incident—if we remove the disinformation can we discern what really happened in New Mexico during the Summer of 1947? Was new knowledge offered to mankind whilst an opportunity for self-realisation denied us? Had similar events occurred before? Are there links between the Tunguska event of 1908 and the New Mexico incident of 1947?

Push me, pull me

While mankind had been perfecting his killing skills, both in the air and on the ground, certain aerial activity was manifesting that was not the direct result of technological developments at that time. During the aerial battles of WWII pilots from all nations had reported seeing strange balls of light flying near their aircraft. The official records state that each side assumed that these luminosities either belonged to some weaponry of their adversaries (though they never actually caused any damage) or were natural phenomena such as ball lightning or St Elmo's fire. Tagged 'Foo-Fighters' after a cartoon character called Smokey Stover who had a stock phrase: "Where there's Foo, there's fire!" [1] Apparently, only *after* the cessation of hostilities was it revealed that personnel of every air force had seen and reported these lights—which is a little hard to believe, perhaps, given the close liaisons between the Allies. But in any case it became quite clear that these lights were not generated by any of the countries involved in

air WWII combat. So man-made objects were definitely eliminated from the equation and the investigations.

Fee, Foo, Phi, Fumb
Similar aerial events also occurred throughout the Korean war of the early 1950s and then again during the Vietnam war of the '60s and '70s but went unmentioned by war correspondents.

After the war the American military announced that the Foo-Fighters were nothing other than mass hallucinations on the part of the pilots. This 'explanation' was so obviously ludicrous that public opinion veered readily towards an alternative cause. It became generally accepted in the minds of the public that these Foo-Fighter lights were somehow linked to natural phenomena. In the post-war world ordinary people had very terrestrial priorities (rebuilding their lives for example) and for most individuals, if they heard about them at all, these Foo-Fighters were a curiosity, merely a passing wonder, much like Crop Glyphs to-

What's my line?
Ohio State and its close connections of the first kind.

On June 13 1947 Ohio State University succeeded in the first successful firing of a liquid hydrogen/liquid oxygen rocket chamber. Tests went on at this university until May 1950 with the first engine undergoing a total of 119 tests. The only other groups studying such systems in the US at that time were the Jet Propulsion Laboratory, conducting its first tests on September 21 1948 and Aerojet, with initial tests on January 20 1949.
Ohio State University, one of the platforms used by the 'Enterprise Mission' has evidently had a long-standing connection to the military and NASA.

day—those structured formations that have appeared for many years in the fields of England and elsewhere—a relevant and significant event for some, including the military, of little apparent relevance to the majority.

Attributing the previous Foo-Fighters of WWII to natural phenomena or mental aberration, both tacitly and overtly, was the obvious response of authorities who wished to maintain control of 'their' immediate environment.

Ninepins

It was in this post-war climate of 1947, just before 3 pm on June 24, that the floodgates of UFO activity were opened.

The individual who unlocked them was thirty-two year old pilot and businessman Kenneth Arnold whilst searching for a downed Mariner C46 (a marine transport aircraft) that had crashed in the region of Mt Rainier in the Cascade mountains of Washington State.

1. Cascade Mountain region.

Arnold knew that there was a reward of $5,000 for the recovery of this plane, a considerable amount of money in 1947. His own aircraft was equipped for mountain rescue, as Arnold was a founder member of the search and rescue team back home in Boise, Idaho. Cruising at an altitude of 9,500ft, Arnold flew past the south-west flank of the 14,410ft Mt Rainier. Seeing nothing he banked over the town of Mineral and returned for another scan. It was then that his attention was diverted.[2] Kenneth Arnold himself is the best person to tell us what happened next.

A terrifically bright flash hit the sky and lit up the inside of my aeroplane, lit up the wings, and it actually lit up all the area around me, almost like an explosion, only it was a bluish-white flash. Now this was in the middle of the afternoon. I'm flying at the mountain with the sun at my back; in other words, I had wonderful visibility and at that altitude the whole world below you looks like a giant swimming pool. It's very distinct, and it was a beautiful day. Anyhow, I had assumed quickly—I suppose in a matter of a split second thought —that some military boy with a P51 had dove over my nose and the sun was reflecting from his wings back onto me. And I looked all around and couldn't see anybody, and then the flash hit again, and then of course, I looked off to the left in the vicinity of Mt Baker. And here comes a chain of very peculiar looking aircraft.

They were flying rather erratically, but they were flying, I knew, at a tremendous speed. I estimated their span as being at approximately a 100 foot span at least, if not more. They were flying quite close to the mountain tops, and actually they were flying at my altitude because they were on the horizon to me, and being on the horizon, I knew that their flight path was approximately 9,200 to 9,500ft.

They were approaching Mt Rainier very rapidly in a kind of diagonal chain-like line, like geese; and there were nine of them in number. I think there were five in the lead. There seemed to be a little gap between the five and the other four. They would dip and kind of flutter and sail.

They looked, Arnold continues,

...flat like a pie pan and so shiny that they reflected the sun like a mirror, they were silver coloured on top and black on the bottom.

Kenneth Arnold calculated that the craft were aiming towards Mt Rainier. "They were flying, I knew, at a tremendous speed." Arnold estimated the speed to be at least 1,200 mph and that the chain of craft was 5 miles long. When Arnold stopped for fuel at Yakima, (situated on Indian land, north of the Oregon/Washington border and about sixty miles from Mt Rainier) he announced what he had seen. Of course, by the time he reached his final destination at Pendleton airfield many people had gathered to hear his story.

There followed a press conference which lasted in all three days! Arnold described the movement of the craft as "saucers skipping across water". It was journalist Bill Bequette who thereupon dreamed up the term 'flying saucer'.[3]

But when Kenneth Arnold subsequently drew up his report for the authorities the craft that he had sketched were not actually disk-like but *heel*-shaped.

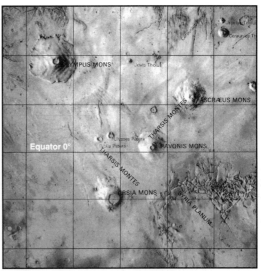

2. Olympus Mons, plus three volcanoes on Mars.

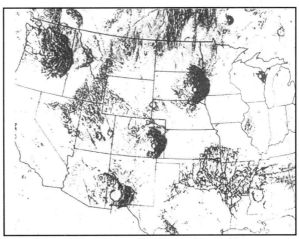

3. This US Geological Survey of the Tharsis Rise on Mars superimposed (by the Smithsonian Institute) onto a map of the United States, *drawn to scale*.

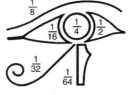

4. Kenneth Arnold's heel illustration is remarkably reminiscent of the right part of the Egyptian symbol known as the 'Eye of Horus'. This (heel-shaped) symbol of ½ was used exclusively for the measurement of grain.

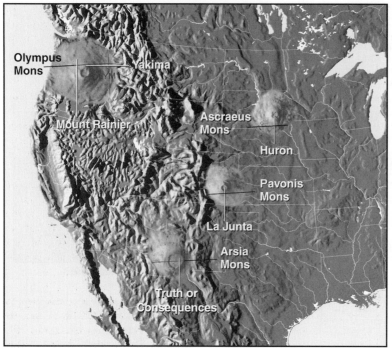

5. Full combination, Mars volcanoes and United States map.

Overlays:

Olympus Mons *Washington State* = Mt Rainier is at 47°N on Earth = 19.47°N Mars.
NOTE: 19° to 22°N or S is also the location of all the other major energy upwellings in our solar system.

Ascraeus Mons *South Dakota* = Huron 44.22°N 98.12°W = Mars 12°N.
NOTE: Devils Tower, Wyoming is located at 44.36°N 104.42°W.

Pavonis Mons *Colorado* = La Junta at 37.59°N 103.34°W = 1°N of the martian equator.

Arsia Mons *New Mexico* Truth or Consequences 33.34°N 107.16°W = Mars 10°S.

craft, together with the Foo-Fighters, were intelligently guided, and were neither man-made nor a natural phenomenon. This is a vital point. Current disinformation of the 1980s and '90s conveys ideas that the Americans are experimenting with flying discs powered by advanced technology acquired from 'Aliens' —they wish! It is absolutely certain that the Americans, the Russians—all of us— are as *incapable* in the late 1990s as we were in 1947, of using any technology for space travel other than limited variations of rocket or nuclear propulsion. Much like the Chinese back in 1232 AD, we effectively still light the blue touch paper and stand well back! It is in this context then, that with the benefit of hindsight, we can detect deliberate side-stepping by the authorities regarding the questions raised by such sightings as those of Kenneth Arnold.

Nor, as it happens, was he alone.

Cascades

The flight that introduced a new phrase ('flying saucers') into the vocabulary of the English speaking world—and brought the entire planet into a new dynamic—was not the only happening of the summer of '47. Down on the ground ordinary American citizens had been seeing 'strange lights' in the sky.

Compared with the manoeuvres demonstrated by these unknown flying objects, the state of the 1940s aviation technology was primitive. The crafts' speed had been estimated at approximately three times faster than the capability of any jet aeroplane in the mid '40s. *None* of the world's air forces at that time was capable of the technological feats witnessed by Kenneth Arnold. Even with the impetus of two World Wars, no country on Earth had had the opportunity, the technological know-how, the money or even sufficient time to develop any such flying machines.

It is our contention that the military authorities of the time fully understood that these

On that same day of June 24 there were reports of another 18 sightings in the Pacific north-west with a further 20 reports following over the next few days. By the end of 1947 at least 850 sightings had been reported around America.

With this flood of flying saucer reports the authorities needed to find a containing mechanism. This they did by adopting the explanation of 'meteorological phenomena' as the rationale for most of the sightings seen by the public. The seemingly all-encompassing label of UFO (a very military style abbreviation, meaning of course, Unidentified Flying Object) was used in reports and this term gradually replaced the very much more specific 'flying saucer'. (The magazine *Flying Saucer Review* however is still regularly published.)

Thus the way was paved for the next phase: debunk at least most flying craft sightings as natural phenomena and by extension, be prepared to ridicule the person or persons involved as being either naive or half-witted. However, should the witness not buy that particular version of events, the disinformers had another trick up their sleeves: patriotism. Information provided to the authorities by the witness would be noted—but the witness should then

become silent—the argument being that such an object *might* be an enemy craft (Soviet), a secret spying device, or a weapon. It is noteworthy that the person who planted the idea of guided missiles was a scientist from New Mexico, 'Pazzy', or Dr. Lincoln La Paz.

From our perspective of the 1990s, it is important to remember that most ordinary US citizens had been isolated from the physical theatre of two World Wars and had little idea as to the real extent of the material decimation throughout Europe. Of course that material decline included the Soviet Union, which had suffered the devastation of people and economy not only wrought by two massive wars but also by its own internal social revolution of 1917. The American people were more or less dependent upon the statements issued by the authorities. As they did not expect their own leaders to withhold the truth—that is, to *lie* to them—it was unsurprising that witnesses to UFO sightings in the 1940s tended to toe the line as dictated by the government and/or the military. If they could or would not be silenced by ridicule, they could most certainly be coerced by patriotism. Kenneth Arnold indeed

---

Containment

"By the end of July 1947 the UFO security lid was down tight"..."there was confusion to the point of panic at the ATIC" (Air Technical Intelligence Center).　　　　　　　　　　　　　Captain Edward Ruppelt *Report on Unidentified Flying Objects*

September 23 1947 ATIC informed Commanding General, US Army Air Force that they considered UFOs to be real.

January 22 1948 Air Force Project Sign Matériel Command, Ohio, received UFO reports.

August 1948 ATIC 'Top Secret' document sent to the USAF Chief of Staff concluded that UFOs were interplanetary space ships.

December 27 1949 USAF issued Project Grudge which explained away all UFO sightings to that date as delusions, hysteria, hoaxes and/or crackpot reports. Announced cessation of project.

September 1951 Captain Edward Ruppelt headed up Project Blue Book.

June 9 1951 Dr. Donald Menzel, Harvard University astrophysicist and astronomer, listed as a member of the MAJIC group, wrote an article published in *Life* magazine and stating that UFOs are "light reflections".

July 29th 1952 At an Air Force press conference in Washington DC Major General JA Stamford attributed UFOs to weather phenomena.

January 22 1953 Dr. Lincoln La Paz 'suggested' that UFOs could be a type of "strange new guided missile" used by the Soviet Union.

August 26 1953 USAF Secretary Harold E Talbott issued Air Force Regulation 200-2 containing updated procedures for reporting UFOs which included *restrictions on public discussion by Air Force Personnel.*

February 23 1954 Commercial airline pilots had been "requested" not to discuss their UFO sightings publicly. Each airline was assigned an Internal Security Specialist Officer as liaison between the airline and the military.

subsequently said that if he ever saw anything strange in the skies again, he would not tell anyone. A certain William Brazel, generally known as Mac Brazel would echo exactly Arnold's sentiments before the year was over. For during the summer of '47, something happened that would galvanise the New Mexico warmongers and start a train of events so potent that fifty years later, we have not yet reached the end of the line. We refer of course to the 'Roswell Incident'.

6. The town of Roswell, New Mexico. ARCHIVE

Roswell

What was so special about this New Mexico town of Roswell? Well, it had early links to the development of flight and military equipment. Robert Goddard, the famous American pioneer of rocketry carried out his experiments at Roswell, and some years later the astronaut Ed Mitchell lived there. The White Sands and Trinity Site proving grounds were a little further down the road and Los Alamos, home to the Manhattan Project, was just around the corner. But most significantly, it was in Roswell that the 509th Airborne Division of the United States Army Air Force was based during the 1940s: and it was the 509th Bomb Group that had the task of dropping the A-bombs on Japan.

All in all the mightiest of the American strike power was present in the state of New Mexico and it would not be an exaggeration to say that in those post-war days the town of

Roswell was the signpost at the cross-roads of our scientific evolution.

There are several versions of the 'official' Roswell Incident that have become ever more embroidered over the years. Facts have turned into hearsay, rumours have been recorded as fact so often that now they are part of the official record. Unless of course, it is more accurate to say that the 'official record' has been specifically *designed* to be such a mix of truth and lies to make even the curious give up trying to fathom it all out, and go away. We, the authors, are among the curious—and like some of the curious are also stubborn.

Some researchers have devoted much of their lives to this incident in an attempt to learn what really happened. All are united on one point: *something* happened near Roswell in the summer of 1947 *which has not yet been adequately explained by the authorities.*

The unfolding story

Once upon a time in a state far, far away from its capital city, on an evening in

7. The aircraft that carried the two A-Bombs to Japan.

early July 1947, two craft crashed into each other above New Mexico during an electrical storm of some violence and wreckage from this crash was later found scattered on the ground.

After that, this 'fairy story' gets rather more complicated. It depends upon which version you study as to where and when the crash(es) occurred; how many 'aliens' were either alive, dead, wounded or even present at all; whether they were near to, or still in the crashed craft. There are differing opinions as to the biological type, numbers of digits, height, appearance of any 'crew' of this supposed craft. Finally there are differences of opinion on the timing of this event, over the nature of the remnants found and the activities of the authorities at the time of the discovery as well as afterwards. To this day these authorities protest that there is nothing to explain, and then spoil their own rationale by publishing ever more incredible explanations for an event which did not happen—according to them. There are many sources of information available which go into this incident in very great detail, and we have listed some of these in the Chapter Notes. We have taken various points in order to delve into the mechanics of this story and have added our own comments in italics. Additionally, we have chosen to provide easily identifiable names to each of the three locations discussed, so that we do not all lose our way in this labyrinthine puzzle.

Firstly, we examine the Roswell Incident sites. Both are actually geographically nearer to Corona (north of Roswell) but it is these two: Brazel's 'debris' site and the 'skid mark' site that are linked to this "collision of two craft" story. We shall then deal with the 'mystery' crash site, which relates to another location (allegedly near Magdalena to the west of Corona) where bodies were apparently found with a craft.

In early July 1947, 75 miles north-west of Roswell, William Mac Brazel, manager of the Foster Ranch near Corona, discovered 'wreckage' scattered over an area approximately ¾ of a mile long and several hundred feet wide.

This is the Brazel 'debris' site. Some researchers say that the Foster Ranch was 120 miles north-west of Roswell and that the wreckage covered ¼ of a mile.

Information which surfaced in 1995 quoted this 'debris' site as being 30 miles north of Roswell.

The suggested dates are July 2 from researcher Timothy Good and July 4 from more recent accounts.

However, in the 1996 updated version of Timothy Good's Beyond Top Secret *there is a*

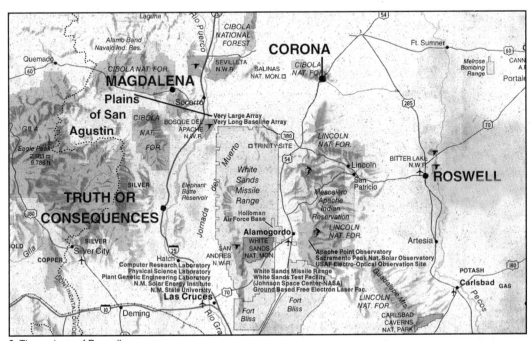

8. The environs of Roswell.

APRIL							MAY							JUNE						
Mo	Tu	We	Th	Fr	Sa	Su	Mo	Tu	We	Th	Fr	Sa	Su	Mo	Tu	We	Th	Fr	Sa	Su
	1	2	3	4	5	6				1	2	3	4							1
7	8	9	10	11	12	13	5	6	7	8	9	10	11	2	3	4	5	6	7	8
14	15	16	17	18	19	20	12	13	14	15	16	17	18	9	10	11	12	13	14	15
21	22	23	24	25	26	27	19	20	21	22	23	24	25	16	17	18	19	20	21	22
28	29	30					26	27	28	29	30	31		23	24	25	26	27	28	29
														30						

JULY							AUGUST							SEPTEMBER						
Mo	Tu	We	Th	Fr	Sa	Su	Mo	Tu	We	Th	Fr	Sa	Su	Mo	Tu	We	Th	Fr	Sa	Su
	1	2	3	4	5	6					1	2	3	1	2	3	4	5	6	7
7	8	9	10	11	12	13	4	5	6	7	8	9	10	8	9	10	11	12	13	14
14	15	16	17	18	19	20	11	12	13	14	15	16	17	15	16	17	18	19	20	21
21	22	23	24	25	26	27	18	19	20	21	22	23	24	22	23	24	25	26	27	28
28	29	30	31				25	26	27	28	29	30	31	29	30					

9. Calendar covering the June/July period, 1947.

10. Colonel William Blanchard. SMITHSONIAN INSTITUTE

report of a July 6 crash site and a subsequent July 5 crash site—pretty neat—especially when the report was allegedly penned by Rear Admiral Hillenkoetter Director of the CIA.

We hope that he means the dates *of discovering these sites.*

According to Major General Roger Ramey, Chief of Staff at Fort Worth Army Air Field in July 1947, the debris gathered from Brazel's debris site stopped over at Fort Worth on the evening of July 6 and was then flown on to Washington. He would have us know that some of the 'junk' as he called it, was in a mail pouch and handcuffed to the wrist of a Colonel Al Clark. He also stated that nobody knew what the debris was, and that they used the weather balloon cover story just to get the press off their backs. He justified this cover-up by saying that having suffered destruction on a large scale during WWII, the public were not ready to deal with the arrival of flying saucers. This—from the military who had unleashed the A-bomb on the world!

Building on the fact that nobody recognised any of this 'junk,' we can already deduce that this definitely was not the remains of an air balloon. Alternatively, given that Ramey was instrumental in the subsequent cover-up, they wanted everybody to know that this was considered to be UFO debris. The dramatic 'locked mail pouch' scenario leans toward the second option.

The consensus is that Mac Brazel did *not* immediately alert the authorities. Assuming that someone from the base would come to ascertain what had happened to their 'crashed'

material (not one mention of the word 'aircraft' which would occur years later in connection with this find) it was only on the occasion of his next visit to town that Brazel alerted the Sheriff of Chavez County, who in turn alerted the Roswell Air Base. (see Appendix)

The dating of his visit to Roswell is unclear but given that Friday was July 4th, Independence Day and a national holiday, we are led to understand that Mac Brazel only informed the authorities on Monday July 7. We do know, however, that the first report in the Roswell Daily Record *occurred on July 8 1947.*

11. Lieutenant Jesse Marcel in WWII. J MARCEL

We have also been given a date of July 7 when Major Jesse Marcel, a staff Intelligence Officer from Roswell Army Air Force Base, together with a Counter-Intelligence Corps Officer, went out to view the reported wreckage, and upon their return—a Press Statement was released—*authorised* by Colonel William

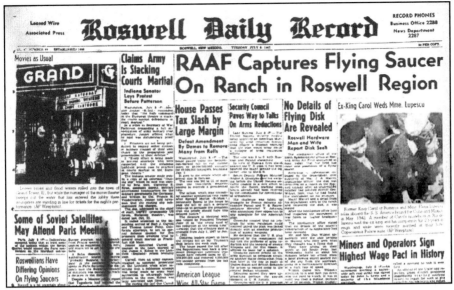

12. The Roswell Daily Record, July 8 1947.

Blanchard, *confirming* that wreckage of a flying disk had been recovered. This first press statement was headlines across the front page of the *Roswell Daily Record*.

At the time, Major Jesse Marcel categorically stated that he had found no bodies among the Corona debris. Does the later mention of bodies refer in fact to another incident elsewhere? We suspect that the July 8 1947 press statement was put out deliberately to draw attention away from an earlier crash incident, which we shall evaluate further on.

According to his recollections in 1995 Jesse

Marcel Jr remembered that his father came back at 2 am—*two* in the morning—and that his father showed him extraordinary materials, but cannot remember the date.[4] Earlier in 1978, Jesse Marcel Jr had told Timothy Good that he was unsure of the date but that it was in the late 1940s.

QUESTION: How can it be that an eleven year old boy is woken up by his father who wanted to show him pieces of a SPACE CRAFT and he cannot remember what day it was? For an event of such magnitude this uncertainty is astonishing. It ranks right up there with Jim

FLYING DISC
FIND IN U.S.

FLIMSY DESIGN : NO
SIGN OF POWER UNIT

FROM OUR OWN CORRESPONDENT
NEW YORK, Tuesday.

mander of the Eighth Air Force, with headquarters at Fort Worth, Texas, who had received the "saucer" from Roswell air base, said it was being sent by air to the Army Air Force Research Centre at Wright Field, Ohio.

BADLY BATTERED

In a telephone call to Army Air Force headquarters in Washington he described the objects as of "flimsy construction, almost like a box kite." It was so badly battered that he was unable to say whether it was shaped like a disc. The material of which it was made was "apparently some sort of tin foil."

13. The highly-respected London *Daily Telegraph*, early July 1947.

213

Lovell forgetting what year he visited the Moon! Especially, as we shall see, Jesse Marcel Jr's other memories of this event remain intact.

As a result of this conference, on July 9 a second press release was issued by Ramey, contradicting the original and stating that the wreckage was not a flying disk at all but actually a damaged weather balloon, together with its tinfoil radar target. Samples of such material were displayed at this press conference and duly photographed. Meanwhile the 'real' Roswell remnants supposedly winged their way to Wright-Patterson. Also on July 9 the *Roswell Daily Record* published an interview with Mac Brazel in which Brazel stated that he first saw the material on his ranch on June 14 but did not go and pick anything up until July 4. It was on July 5 that he first(!) heard about rumours of flying disks and July 7 when he

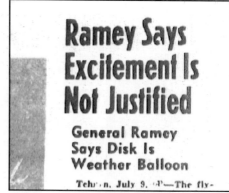

Ramey Says Excitement Is Not Justified

General Ramey Says Disk Is Weather Balloon

Tehran, July 9. (P—The fly-

15. General Ramey discounts his previous statement.

14. Young Jesse Marcel Jr in the late 1940s.

appeared in town to "sell some wool". It was then that he "whispered" to the Sheriff that he might have found some flying disk material.

This story has been received with some incredulity even by members of Brazel's own family. More especially because Brazel would not have "come into town to sell some wool". This was not how the sheep trade functioned. The description of his finding is so detailed that we find it hard to believe that the military at Roswell could have mistaken these fragments for anything other than a balloon and issued their first flying saucer story. Mac Brazel might not have recognised new balloon materials but if the argument is that the materials used were unknown to the military, it is also arguable that they would check with each

of their bases, such as Holloman AFB prior to a press release of such major importance. This July 9 Brazel interview is, in our view, the reinforcement of the fake incident sites 'debris' and 'skid mark'. Major Marcel was also perfectly capable of recognising the remains of a weather balloon when he saw them—either aloft or on the ground. Furthermore at no time prior to this July 9 date did Major Marcel mention that the wreckage was related to a balloon.

We are informed that a press wire transmitted from Albuquerque New Mexico, which had managed to escape the press embargo was interrupted—as was that of another radio station—by a message telling them to cease transmis-

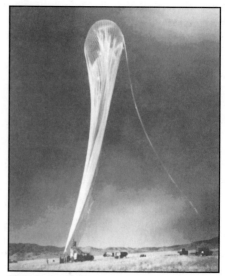

16. Instrument balloon. USAF

214

17. General Ramey (above) and Major Jesse Marcel with the radar target and balloon debris. Apparently this material was NOT what was shown to Jesse Marcel Jr.

sion as they were dealing here with a national security item.

Such an action and statement certainly contradicted the 1947 US weather balloon claim! It 'works' as a means of creating a high profile for this Roswell Incident and it 'works' for the subsequent 'solution' in 1995—the revised 'spy balloon' scenario.

After this Fort Worth conference Major Jesse Marcel returned to Roswell and *then* the Brazel 'debris' site and the attendant 'skid mark' site were stripped of every remaining scrap of debris. The 'skid mark' site had been found after the 'debris' site and was remarkable insofar as it displayed the gouging of the land over a considerable distance. Apparently this was put down to a craft hitting the ground and taking off again, as a result of the mid-air collision.

Why wait two days to strip the Brazel site of debris? Could it be that, through both the troop presence on the outlying roads and the general 'fuss' that was being created through the press releases and the radio embargo, attention was deliberately being focused on this Roswell Incident? Apart from the very obvious duplicity and confusion already apparent within days of the discovery, one of the most questionable aspects of this case is the manner in which the US forces are said to have treated civilians. According to some sources, Mac

Brazel was held incommunicado for nearly a week by the authorities and both he and his family were warned not to speak of the incident to anyone, neither then nor in the future.

QUESTION: Now why exactly was that action necessary?

QUESTION: Was Mac Brazel too honest to buy the American cover story?

QUESTION: Was it all some kind of elaborate 'fix' or 'double fix'? Including the willing participation of Mac Brazel who was subsequently kept away from the public until the excitement had simmered down?

QUESTION: Alternatively, could Mac Brazel have been the unwitting victim or fall-guy, stemming from circumstances beyond his control?

Brigadier General Thomas Dubose, Chief of Staff Fort Worth: "It was a cover story given to the Press, and anything else—forget it!"[5]

Phew! Everyone back to sleep again by July 9 1947.

There were apparently three main categories of material found at the Brazel 'debris' site:

1) Small pieces of a substance "like balsa wood" only hard, non-flammable *and* flexible! These were supposedly inscribed with indecipherable hieroglyphs.

215

18. Colonel Thomas Dubose.
SMITHSONIAN INSTITUTE

In 1981, now an MD attached to the US Army, Jesse Marcel Jr made a statement in which he said that many of the remnants had strange 'hieroglyphic' writing symbols across the inner surfaces and that he thought it unlikely that the remnants belonged to an earth-made craft.
QUESTION: How could he tell inner from outer surfaces of this material?—had he been told what to say on this point?
QUESTION: Major Marcel Senior was a security officer returning from what must have been a top security site (whether planted by the military or not). Stopping off to see his family and babbling information hardly fits such a background. Unless of course it was a pre-arranged procedure, in order to establish that these 'hieroglyphs' belonged to debris from a crashed craft—whereas in reality they were fakes planted by the military?

With the exception of a certain Robert Morning Sky (a North American Indian much in evidence in the British UFO milieu) these 'hieroglyphs' have not (to our knowledge) been translated.[6] In 1996 Morning Sky contributed to the Roswell myth by way of an article purporting to decipher these already pseudo hieroglyphs! Technically these are not hieroglyphs, at all, as they contain actual letters. The word 'video' (relating to a technology that was definitely not in general use at that time) can be seen on the published samples.

As none of the Roswell witnesses—including Jesse Marcel Jr have recognised these artistic signs and were absolutely certain that what they were shown in the 1990s did NOT correspond to the 1947 fragments, we do not consider it worthwhile quoting Mr Morning Sky's perambulations. The fact that there is an apparent discrepancy between the two sets of alleged 'hieroglyphs' does not automatically validate the first set and we judge that, in any event, all these pieces of inscribed material could have been deliberately 'manufactured'. The second set of hieroglyphs now emerging at the end of this millennium may well be part of a further unfinished scenario.

2) A great deal of 'parchment-like substance', very strong, light brown in colour was also apparently recovered. According to some sources this material, when held up to the light, displayed yellow 'flower-like' inclusions within its structure.

We find the specific *mention of this substance questionable and suggest that it was also planted by the military. This together with those 'hieroglyphics' on 'balsa-like wood' being preparation for a future debunking/ denial scenario.*

3) A quantity of 'tinfoil' was also found at Brazel's 'debris' site, the material supposedly as thin as the silver lining of a cigarette packet, yet excessively resistant and very lightweight. In fact it was reported that one 2ft x 1ft piece proved to be totally impervious to an assault with a 16lb sledgehammer. This material was also uncrushable, and sprung back into shape when released from pressure. Further, it was also said to "spread out like a liquid" when placed on a surface.

The debris at the Brazel site was said to be so smashed up that it was impossible to tell what shape the craft might have been. Thereby rather conveniently making it easier to move from one place to another.
QUESTION: Could this particular 'tinfoil' have been more fakery or was it originally from the mystery site?

It is further alleged that a welder at Wright-Patterson AFB was unable to produce a flame hot enough to melt "a piece of the 1947 New Mexico crash material". And an engineer from Wright-Patterson 'volunteered' that a gear fragment contained rare elements, in a quantity impossible to consider using on this planet for the manufacture of gears. The gear also used a 'strange' technology and was not of the cycloid design normally used.

Given the amount of security surrounding this incident, it is astonishing that these two engineering items have somehow escaped the embargo of secrecy. We suspect these various items to have been 'designer leaked'. It also sounds like preparation for a future back engineering scenario.

QUESTION: Was the engineer instructed to say that it was a gear fragment?

QUESTION: Is it not an assumption that something that resembles a gear fragment would actually be such an item?

QUESTION: Which actual crash site was being referred to by these Wright-Patterson technicians?[7]

QUESTION: If two craft had crashed in mid air, then how did one get smashed to smithereens and the other sustain very little damage? All the stories of a lightly-damaged craft sitting on the arroyo (dried up river bed) do not link up with the Corona Ranch land scenario. Another appearance of a mystery site?

QUESTION: How would they have recovered undamaged bodies from such a collision?

Which brings us to the official mystery of the 'mystery' site.

In an absolute copycat report of Kenneth Arnold's sighting, there is an interesting entry in a report picking up the main sightings for the UFO flap of June/July 1947. Published by the independent National Investigations Committee on Aerial Phenomena in 1964 (NICAP) this lists a sighting on July 4 1947 of nine silver disks, in two separate groups, seen by "a United Airlines pilot and crew".[8] Moreover, the location was Kenneth Arnold's home town of Boise, Idaho. On July 9 also over Boise, Idaho an aviation editor with a private pilot's license witnessed a daytime sighting of one dark disk which climbed and 'turned on edge'. We are referred to a previous section of the NICAP report devoted to sightings by pilots and aviation experts where we learn that the aviation editor/private pilot was named Dave Johnson and that others on the ground also saw this disk. However, there is no mention at all of the nine-disk sighting by the United Airlines crew.

Bearing in mind that Roscoe Hillenkoetter, Director of the CIA was also on the board the allegedly civilian NICAP, can this nine-disk sighting have been fed into the reports arriving at NICAP to substantiate, yet again, the importance of this July 4 1947 date? Does it indicate an attempt to overlay Kenneth Arnold's June 24 sightings with this 'more appropriate' date? If so, we can see that this ploy did not work. To our knowledge, Roswell investigators have not commented on the very particular symmetry of these two sightings.

Roswell re-runs

After Ramey's second press release of July 9

1947 announcing or denouncing the discovered debris as being a weather balloon, the Roswell Incident remained officially quiescent for decades. But it never quite went away. Several investigative books on the subject were published over the years and notwithstanding the authorities' public opinion of UFO researchers, many serious people continued to track down officials who had been at Roswell Air Field in the Summer of 1947.

Oppo-sites

A man in the wilderness asked of me,

How many strawberries grow in the sea?

I answered him, as I thought good,

As many as red herrings swim in the wood.

English Nursery Rhyme

On October 20 1989, Lt Colonel Joe Briley, at Roswell from 1946 to 1947 and Operations Officer for some of that period, told researcher Kevin Randle that he was on the base at the time of the Roswell Incident and that the story was changed and hushed up "...as soon as the people from Washington arrived". He said that the incident was treated as a hoax, "...we all forgot it immediately". He went on to explain that he was very vague about the incident because it just did not circulate. "We were in the A-bomb business...I was privy to a lot of information along that line. But on this particular thing I was completely shut out."

Walter Haut, the PR officer who had issued that first 'flying saucer' press release of July 8, also emphasised that the 509th Bomb Group was a tightly run, top security unit. Everybody on the base operated strictly on a 'need-to-know' basis. Containing an operation would neither have been considered extraordinary *nor would it have been difficult to do.*

Who, or what, was J B Foster? It has generally been inferred that Mac Brazel owned the ranch where the crash material was found, yet he is always referred to as the manager. At that time, in New Mexico, about 44% of the land that was not a national forest, park land, an Indian Reservation, or government property *was privately owned.* However, ranchers often

---

In too deep?

Dr. Foster went to Gloucester

In a shower of rain

He stepped in a puddle

Up to his middle

And never went there again.

English Nursery Rhyme

---

needed to *lease* additional acreage from both the Federal and State Governments.[9]

QUESTION: To whom did the deeds of the ranchland upon which the debris was found belong? Could it have been the Federal Government? Did Mac Brazel lease the land, or was it a Mr Foster?

On January 11 1990, when Kevin Randle interviewed Major Edwin D Easley, the Provost Marshall of 509th Bomb Group in the summer of 1947, he could not get any information from Easley, other than to confirm his position as Provost Marshall. Easley had been sworn to secrecy and repeatedly told Randle that he could not speak about the Roswell Incident.

In so doing (perhaps unwittingly) he affirmed that there was an incident meriting an enormous degree of secrecy.

He did ask Randle to whom else he had spoken, suggesting that Randle talk to "the man who owned the land, he ought to be able to tell you a lot more".

But what if Easley did not mean Brazel? We can understand that to speak to the owner of the ranch would seem to be a deviation from the essential witnesses who could throw some real light on the situation. However, Easley's remark makes perfect sense, if the owner of the land were the US Government, either Federal or State!

It also makes sense if the owner of the land was a private citizen, who had been co-opted into an arrangement with the military and allowed his land to be 'set-dressed'. A place to plant props that would not only be helpful in explaining away the incident but also be used in future scenarios.

When Brigadier General Arthur E Exon of Wright-Patterson AFB was interviewed by researcher Don Schmitt on June 18 1990, Exon told him that whenever there was a UFO investigation afoot, Wright-Patterson Air Force Base would receive a call from the Secretary of Defense or someone of equally high rank, to order an aircraft and crew.

Thus Exon unwittingly acknowledged that the Military were regularly investigating that which they denied the existence of—UFOs.

Does this comment elucidate "the thing" mentioned by Colonel Briley? Note also that Exon mentions "the guy" in the singular. While he is no doubt using the American meaning of the word, we cannot help thinking that the English version (as in Guy Fawkes of the November 5th, the Gunpowder Plot) is also appropriate.

NUTRS

The official description of a database referring to UFO activity monitored by the United States.

Military Sponsor: Air Force Database

Name: **N**orad **U**nknown **T**racking **R**eport **S**ystem.

In a continuing assertion of airspace sovereignty, it records details of all air traffic declared 'unknown' in North America and the Greenland-Icelandic-United Kingdom Gap.

Data is accessed by a wide variety of users in NORAD, USAF, Joint Chiefs of Staff, Canadian National Defense Headquarters (NDHQ) and region (sic) commanders.

Exon then elaborated on the methods employed: The Washington investigators would use a commercial airline to fly down to the nearest civilian airport, then use a military plane to travel to an air base adjacent to their final destination. There, the crews would wait for them, sometimes for a week, then fly them back to Wright-Patterson at the conclusion of the investigations. Exon recalled that it was the Washington guys who were involved in "what to do about the residue from *that*..." He then corrected himself and said *"those two findings"*. Don Schmitt naturally picked up on this important correction and Exon then said that it was "probably part of the same accident, but two distinct sites. One, assuming that the thing, as I understand it..."

He then carried on talking, but throughout the subsequent conversation as published by Don Schmitt, his sentence: "One, assuming that the thing..." was never explained nor elaborated upon. Don Schmitt informed Exon that he knew of witnesses who in the 1990s, still perceived that they must honour their commitment to stay silent.

Exon had agreed saying: "I'd do the same thing. You'd just be hazed and hassled by everybody who was trying to reconstruct *the thing and the guy* after 50 years plus".[10] (our emphasis) Exon went on to say that the government was still investigating to this day.

By 1994 the American authorities in the shape of the USAF were feeling enough pressure to make an official announcement, in an attempt to clear up the situation. This action simply perpetuated the decisions taken in the 1940s by reinforcing the balloon theory, albeit this balloon had now become a 'spy' balloon. The authorities 'admitted' that there had indeed been a cover-up in 1947 concerning the Roswell Incident and went on to 'confess' that the debris was actually part of Project Mogul, a Military program which used high altitude balloons to monitor possible Soviet Atomic explosions.

That official announcement was partly incorrect. Project Mogul existed, and according to The Roswell Report, Case Closed, *issued by the USAF in June 1997, was indeed over the skies of Roswell in June 1947. Yet the US Government was perfectly well aware that in June/July 1947, it was the only country in the world able to experiment with Atomic devices.*[11]

The 1995 official Roswell balloon 'confession' then proceeded to relay what the "odd materials" that we discussed earlier actually were: "The strange material that would not burn *was* chemically treated balsawood! The markings on the struts were a variety of flower-patterned tape made by a toy company".[12]

Trading places

The name MOGUL was the designation of top quality playing cards; published in 1842, so called because these cards had a picture of a Mogul on their wrappers.

The Oxford University Dictionary definition of *Mogul* is:

1) A follower of Genghis Khan in the 13th Century.

2) A follower of Baber (founder of the Mongolian Empire in Hindustan) in the 16th Century.

3) The Great Mogul was the European (read British) designation for the Emperor of Delhi, who ruled most of Hindustan. Mogul was therefore affiliated to the identity of a great autocratic ruler.

Using Mogul as a code name smacks of the British sense of humour and reinforces our suspicions concerning the nationalities of the principal players in this game.

This 'revelation' bears out exactly our feelings concerning the planting of materials by the military. Since when did the most advanced technology extant use toys as components. But this explanation in no way eliminates the real problem nor does the report published in the British Sunday Times *actually help. For* The Sunday Times *were mixing up the markings (hieroglyphs) on the struts with panels of flower-impressed tape.*

In a UK Channel Four TV documentary on the Roswell Incident, broadcast in August 1995, a spokesman at White Sands declared: "There was no official record of any such malfunction [of a balloon] concerning Project Mogul for the time period under question". He added that "White Sands was too far from the alleged crash site for it [the crash site] to be a likely site for a Mogul crash". Kevin Randle dealt with this subject in his *Roswell UFO Crash Update* published in 1995 and confirmed the absence of balloons in the area for any of the time periods in question.

This evidence from two sources effectively rules out the possibility of the Roswell Incident being the result of a balloon crash—whatever the USAF might now wish to say.

Additionally they state: "The oddly constructed radar targets (of Project Mogul) were found by a New Mexico rancher during the height of the first US flying saucer wave in 1947".

Well that does not accord with the July 9 revisionist text in the local paper which stated that Mac Brazel actually found these remnants on June 14, even if he only appeared in Roswell on July 7. Moreover, the 1947 flying saucer flap did not even start *until June 23/24.*

Rose red

The above details were the principal elements surrounding the initial Roswell Incident but even at that time, there were rumours of yet another, earlier crash site—allegedly near Magdalena on the Plains of San Agustin, west of Socorro, New Mexico. Magdalena is about 96 miles west of Corona and 66 miles north of the appropriately named Truth or Consequences.

Once again, there are in these reports variations of distance, with some researchers quoting a distance of 150 miles west of the Roswell site (Magdalena is in fact approximately 167 miles from the town of Roswell), but according to the USAF is 175 miles north-

---

Board change

The Joint Development Board, at that time concerned with creating a satellite launcher, was replaced first by the Research and Development Board, then in 1948 by a Technical Evaluations Group which finally assigned all future research to Project RAND.

Now called the RAND Corporation, this group and the SRI (formerly the Stanford Research Institute currently Stanford Research International) are well known among scientists and inventors as *the* places for advanced research projects. Innovators approach RAND in the hope of being able to develop their ideas.

As with NASA, the militaristic origins and connections of the RAND Corporation and SRI are not widely known.

---

west of Roswell.

US Soil Conservation Service Engineer, Grady L Barnett was purported to have seen, while on a military assignment near Magdalena in the late 1940s, a metallic-shaped disk lying on the desert floor. He saw dead bodies outside the disk, which had split open, enabling him to see more dead bodies inside. Then military personnel immediately approached the area.[13] However, when interviewed in the mid 1960s (by Colonel William D Leed II, of the US Army Reserve Signal Corps) Mr Barnett stated that he had walked around a saucer-shaped disk but was unable to enter it. No mention was made of bodies and allegedly it was only two or three days later that the US Army Air Force arrived on the scene.

Timothy Good has turned up the following story of an Army Sergeant, but failed to elaborate on the significance of his story.[14] In June 1947, i.e. *before* the Roswell Incident, Sergeant Melvin E Brown was stationed at Roswell Army Air Field base. He subsequently told his daughter that he had to stand guard outside a hangar where recovered material was temporarily stored from some crash, and claimed to have seen "at least two alien bodies".

to him while on duty with Task Unit 7.4.1. This letter went on to emphasise the 'task' by using the phrase "...the peculiar and tedious circumstances resulting from that project".

QUESTION: We ask why it was necessary to emphasise that particular project, which was shrouded in such a veil of secrecy that all related documents—when they have not gone 'walkabout'—are classified at the highest security level?

QUESTION: Is it not possible to recommend a man on the basis of character and performance without drawing attention to such a sensitive issue? A quiet word in the right place would have avoided any written mention of Task Unit 7.4.1?

QUESTION: So was it vital to mention that secret matter—in order to plant a specific date? Note that in the United States, dates are generally written: month, day, year. Thus 7.4.1 for Europeans would normally mean the 7th April—1. To an American it would mean July 4th—1.

QUESTION: Did the '1' signify that there was at least one other site, it could have referred to the 'debris' site or the 'skid mark' site.

In the 1995 information updates, there was a further attempt to muddle the sites together.

Alien sighting

Charles Lindbergh (Jim Lovell's boyhood hero)
was seen at the Roswell Officer's Club in the Company of Brigadier General Roger Ramey,
Commander of the 8th Air Force.
While allegedly not associated with the *recovery* of any object, we find the timing of his appearance and
the company that he was keeping interesting, to say the least.
Charles Lindbergh had known pro-fascist sympathies. Indeed during WWII Lindbergh was helping the Nazis to
negotiate the sale of German aircraft engines to the French. This deal was utterly phoney of course, but did it
conceal some other money-making scheme?
Lindbergh was awarded the Knight of the German Eagle by the Nazis.

While varying descriptions of alleged bodies have been given by different people, what is noteworthy in the Sergeant Brown account occurs a year later.

In 1948 Sergeant Brown received a letter of recommendation concerning a promotion. Dated May 7 1948, this letter *specifically* stated that he had performed all duties assigned

At the site the US Army called the 'crash' site (our 'skid mark' site) we were told that a damaged metallic aircraft was apparently discovered *together with* 'alien' bodies.

We trust that personnel who made this discovery were retained in the US Army during the July 26 split into Army and Air Force. The difference between an aircraft and a space

craft in 1947 was a fundamental: aircraft could not fly in space. However by 1995 Shuttle visuals and emerging technology such as Ramjets and Scramjets had muddied that definition somewhat (in the eyes of the general public at least) and thus enabled the USAF to feed off the Roswell Incident yet again. We suspect that these 'upsums' are part of the continuing soap opera, which then produced a further exciting episode: Roswell, the Autopsy.

Dr. Donald's SFX trickery—Part Four

In the Summer of 1995 a 'rare' piece of film footage was introduced to the world. It was supposed to be the filmed record of an autopsy carried out on an extra terrestrial (owning six fingers on each hand and six toes on each foot) from the Roswell 'wreckage'.

Moses in the rushes—THE movie!

The original official Roswell investigation stated that there were NO bodies at the Brazel 'debris' site. So, firstly, it is interesting that this modern documentary is linking a body with the Roswell Incident. Secondly, there were at the time unofficial descriptions of bodies that were thin, small and with fewer than five fingers (including thumb). But there were never any descriptions of figures of normal height, overblown bodies with six fingers and six toes—from any source. So this 1995 autopsy scam has to be a new act in this forever changing script.

The 1995 announcements both from official sources and from seemingly unofficial sources are as good as issuing a statement: "Business as usual, we have not, and will not, change our perspective on this scenario".

So for the authorities—no change. But for us, the public, there has been considerable change. We are less gullible than in the past and we are capable of evaluating all the (dis)information that we receive and then forming our own opinions.

Screened on British and American TV, together with other territories as part of a 'serious' documentary about the Roswell Incident which included interviews with various inter-

> **Mistaken identity?**
>
> Moses supposes his toeses are roses
> But Moses supposes erroneously
> For nobody's toeses are posies of roses
> As Moses supposes his toeses to be.
>
> *English Nursery Rhyme*

ested parties, the '1947' silent black & white autopsy film had 'bleached out' close-ups and was very 'contrasty'.

Such is not a normal characteristic for either the type or age of the claimed negative film stock. There are countless examples of far older pre-WWII footage which are not bleached out, whether B&W or even in colour.

The rolls of film had apparently been kept secret by the cameraman ever since he had allegedly shot the material—though only the purchaser and promoter of this rarity, one Ray Santilli, claimed to have met this person. Santilli commented that the footage was "out of focus" at times, as the camera was hand-held.

The scenes referred to are not actually "out of focus" at all. Such a description is the wrong terminology for what is merely a vain attempt to make the film look 'old'.

Dr. Paul O'Higgins, from the University of London, in *The Sunday Times* of July 29 1995 stated:

> The anatomy appears human though with several deformities. The large skull could be caused by fluid on the brain, often found with low set ears, hairlessness and lack of secondary sexual characteristics.
> On an anatomical and evolutionary basis I find it impossible to believe these are aliens.

Why did Paul O'Higgins use the plural "these are alien" when he was discussing only the one body? Or did he see further footage of 'other' aliens that it is claimed feature on the Santilli film footage?

For Dr. Stringer of the Natural History Museum in London, England, the bodies that he saw in the disputed film footage were so human as to lead him to believe that these alleged

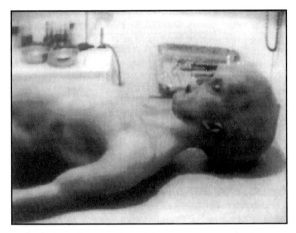

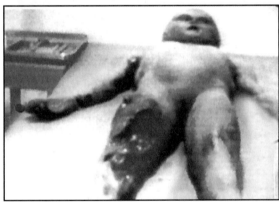

19. Santilli's autopsy body that he claimed was from the Roswell crash.   SANTILLI MERLIN

'alien' bodies were fakes, probably just modified human bodies.

Dr. C M Milroy, Senior lecturer in Forensic Pathology found no evidence of decomposition, and a general absence of injuries one would associate with having been in an aviation accident. He remarked on the six digits to hands and feet and went on to note that certain aspects of the examination suggested that it was not conducted by an experienced autopsy pathologist but possibly only by a surgeon. He could not make an accurate evaluation of organ structure due to the lack of detail, 'focus' in the close-up shots.

Top London pathologist Ian West appears in the documentary in connection with this autopsy and admits that he cannot tell for cer-

tain what he is looking at—but that he is *98% sure that the body is manmade.*

As does an SFX expert, who ventures that the film was probably not photographed before the 1960s.

Pauline Fowler, another SFX expert is of the opinion that the skeletal posture exhibited by the tension in the shoulders and the distribution of body mass does not conform to that of a prone bio-organism but is indicative of a mould having been made on a standing human.

According to Mr Santilli, in a magazine interview published in October 1995, the cameraman who sold him the film footage explained that he had been contacted on June 2 1947 and had received an order from a General McMullan telling him to go to *White Sands* and film everything that he could of a crash.[15] He was ordered to stay with the recovered material until it was dispatched *(to where?)* and he, the cameraman, had authority over and above the on-site Commander(!) The cameraman was to report only to General McMullan. We are told that this cameraman flew to *Roswell* and was then taken by road to the 'site' which he described to Santilli as being a small dried-up lake bed. In a further magazine article there are descriptions of the 'crash' happening on May 31 and defined as a Russian spyplane.

Both the cameraman's story and the film footage has been examined by several retired combat cameramen who were operational at that time. Now these are military men and they are all agreed that a) the standard of photography was abysmal and b) should have been in colour. In addition, it made no sense to them to fly someone down when there were available cameramen at the bases.

WHOOPS! Timing . . .

While Ray Santilli professes himself happy with the cameraman's story, the date of June 2 is far too early to corroborate with Mac Brazel's story of either June 14 or July 4th! Granted the circumstances were allegedly ex-

traordinary, but if this cameraman was such a hot shot that he was the official cameraman for the Army Airforce and had worked on many events (including the Manhattan Project as he claimed) and was specifically sent for, to do this job, then it is certainly astonishing that he was unable to use his camera in a professional manner. And why was he allowed to keep a 'copy'(film print) of this obviously top secret material? The film rushes, or dailies, would have had to be developed professionally in a military laboratory and would therefore either have been returned to him (most unlikely in the case of an US Army cameraman)—or he has to have permanently 'borrowed' the processed material. It is usual practice for the laboratory to retain the camera negative as it is of no use for showing on a film projector, only for making further prints—after the film has been edited, usually by others.

When we attempted to put some of our queries concerning these matters to one of these magazines, they insisted that we speak to Mr Santilli directly. We informed Mr Santilli's staff that we only wanted to verify some already published facts and that we did not necessarily need to speak to Ray Santilli himself. His staff insisted that he was the only person in a position to help us. Despite several attempts to contact him, he was always nearly, but never quite, available! In a later magazine article Santilli said that he would now love to "wash his hands of the whole affair".[16]

Stock and bond—accounts rendered

Challenged to provide an analysis from Kodak for the authenticity of the film material Mr Santilli has so far failed in this regard—merely saying that he has a gamut of likely dates for the origination of the film stock from Kodak. Originally those dates were specified as 1947, 1967, 1987, but in later interviews the year 1987 was 'dropped'.

It is known that Kodak altered the edge code marking system in the early 1970s, which might explain the disappearance of 1987 from Santilli's shopping list.

Early film stock had a tendency to spontaneously combust but by 1947 a stable film base of acetate prioponate (at the time called non-flam) had been invented. It has been alleged that the Roswell/Santilli footage is on Ciné Kodak Super XX high speed Panchromatic Safety Film. This is a high speed film designed for indoor or dim light outdoor photography. It was marketed in the early 1940s and withdrawn between 1956-57 at which time Eastman Kodak began replacing all its stock with a triacetate film base. This stock was even safer than the acetate prioponate film but required different developers. It is not possible to process pre-1956 film stock with these newer chemicals.

This does not mean that pre-1956 film stock cannot be developed or indeed simulated. It is not unknown for film stock with the appropriate edge markings to be supplied as a special prop for period film productions.

Bob Shell, who allegedly was given two strips from some footage, confirmed the age of the film and has inferred that this is film stock dating from the time of the Roswell Incident.

However, the autopsy dummy does not figure on the exciting shots of stairs and a doorway that he allegedly examined. It reminds us of Armstrong photographing a leg of the LM while Aldrin made his historic descent onto the Moon!

Mr Shell, by the way, was apparently at one time a photographic consultant to the FBI and the US legal fraternity.

Neither Mr Santilli nor Mr Shell are lying when they declare that the piece of film has been validated by Kodak as a piece of Kodak film—but that does not establish the authenticity of the autopsy footage, as it has not been demonstrated that it came from the same film batch. Nevertheless, none of these matters have prevented Mr Santilli from producing scripts backing up his claims that this footage and all therein is the real McCoy.

We ourselves suggest that:

* *The autopsy scenario broadcast on TV worldwide in 1995 was entirely manufactured in the 1990s and it very conveniently ties in with the continuing disinformation program.*

- *That the 'alien' with deformed body; subnormal-looking head; the extra digit (that used to be associated with witchcraft); and with internal organs unlike our own, was specifically designed to transmit and maintain a climate of fear, distrust and repugnance at alien life forms.*
- *The information from the declared cameraman would appear to belong to future scenarios so that even when—not if—this story is blown, items have been seeded that can be used later.*
- *So absolutely confident is Ray Santilli that his company did not make the model or shoot the film, we had the feeling, that he knew perfectly well who had really made it! A feeling that we have subsequently found to be correct.*
- *In 1996, a UK Whistle-Blower confirmed to us that the cameraman who filmed this autopsy is alive and well, and not a retiree from the US Army. We also have further information from another Whistle-Blower who knows with certainty that this creation was made at a location not more than 40 miles or so from the north of London, England, in facilities belonging a UK production company. All the details are known to us.*
- *This A N Other Whistle-Blower confirms that Ray Santilli was aware of the creation of the fake footage, including the manufacturing of the prop dummy. Apparently when the film makers realised the significance of what they were creating, they telephoned Mr Santilli, who was in the States at the time, and told him that they had realised the news value of the job they were doing. Santilli immediately dropped everything and returned to London, in order to resolve the problem in the best way possible.*

It seems obvious that the authorities, both in 1947 and to this day, are deliberately allowing, if not encouraging, *all* the rumours and reports concerning UFO activity in New Mexico to become intermingled, thus relying not only on time and human memory to do its own work

Merlin the magician

The company formed by Ray Santilli for the *distribution* of the claimed Roswell autopsy footage was **Merlin Productions**.

in muddling the truth, but also by purposefully planting disinformative rumours as and when necessary.

The disinformation, as we have tried to show, is subtle and so far-seeing that it is easy to throw out the baby with the bathwater and dismiss all the Roswell Incident and its attendant hypotheses as yet another ridiculous UFO rumour, only subscribed to by the unintelligent. Yet with the benefit of hindsight, analysis of the actual events that occurred in 1947, combined with the pattern of *continuing* disinformation surrounding the Roswell Incident, we can see that 'intention' does begin to emerge.

If *nothing* had actually occurred in the summer of 1947, then surely the denials of 1994 and 1995 would not have been necessary? Nor would the next episode in this saga, that less than glorious film (and book of the film) *Independence Day*, which provided us with yet more insights into the ways of the weird—in this case the mentality of the 'masters of infinity'—as we shall now see.

Dr. Donald's SFX trickery—Part Five

The book of the 1996 film *Independence Day* manages some very lurid and inaccurate reporting of the Roswell Incident. It fixes the date as the night of July 4 1947 and informs the reader that the entire town of Roswell was apparently on the verge of hysteria. The inhabitants spent the night gathered in the streets and restaurants to discuss the *sixty-foot* glowing object that they had seen *streaking* north-west across the sky!

In total NICAP (q.v.) lists three sightings in New Mexico for the period of June 23-July 13 1947. None of these dates cover the alleged sightings by hundreds of Roswell residents over their town:

- *On June 29, at an unspecified rocket test site, one disk was sighted by "a rocket expert" flying straight. No time given.*
- *On July 1 Albuquerque a bluish-coloured disk was seen zig-zagging through the sky by "a Chamber of Commerce Executive". No time given.*
- *On July 10 New Mexico, south at 16:47 hrs local time a white elliptical craft was reported a wobbling through the sky by "a top astronomer".*

Indie four

The writers of *Independence Day* the book obviously know something that no other researcher has ever been able to ascertain, for they tell us that on the *afternoon of Saturday July 5* Mac Brazel found wreckage of "an unusual aircraft" on his property. He then drove into town and went straight to the Roswell airfield 75 miles away.

Note, aircraft, not spacecraft. The dating contradicts all the details of the July 9 newspaper article in the Roswell Daily Record.

A squad of intelligence officers went out to the site and that same night they issued a press release! We are then given a feeble description of 'alien' mechanics and the tale of a crash with two bodies. One alive inside the aircraft and one dead outside on the *desert floor* (no mention of the Foster Ranch pastures here). The authors then infer that Mac Brazel had seen a body but that he always refused to speak of it.

So two men have become an entire squad and the Foster sheep ranch has become a desert. Deliberate site confusion again?

Independence Day, the movie, tells us that this crash happened in the 1950s which is totally at odds with the date in their own book of their own film!

Is all of this a) sloppy research b) inside information or c) simply disinformation? With the plethora of available data it is most doubtful that sloppy research could be responsible for such inaccuracies, especially from the makers of a movie having close contacts with the relevant American authorities and the use of the Howard Hughes Aircraft Company's facility for their location.

ID4

The 1996 film *Independence Day* sent the message that the planet will be invaded by aggressive 'aliens' one July 3rd and the Americans will retaliate for us all on July 4th. Through the reinforcing of July 4 as the date that something *will* happen it is clear that part of the film's message is related to the Roswell Incident of 1947 that allegedly did not happen! Could it be that the schizophrenic authorities are now seeking to reinforce phase two of their scenario?

SDI

Independence Day, the book and the film, appear to be yet another deliberate exercise in providing variable information—with intent to confuse. The book's authors avoid direct criticism by describing their book as fiction. As they are writing fantasy, technically they are right. But surely they are also morally wrong in attributing thoughts and intentions to *actual people who themselves, on the record, have given a very different version of these events?*

The writers of the book also attribute Mac Brazel with the thought that this was an experimental military *aircraft*, thereby inferring of course that the bodies would have had to *look* reasonably human for him to be able to consider that they were of American airmen.

How could Mac Brazel have recognised that these fragments of wreckage were from an aircraft? Did he find wings? On the face of it, this view contradicts everything that any previous researcher has learned about Brazel and his findings. Yet what this deviation from the usual tale does is to provide background for that 'autopsy' film produced in 1995 by Merlin Productions for our delectation. Perhaps we should expect a future scenario where writers will describe asexual cloned humans with weird insides, and heads that come off their necks, genetically engineered to fly experimen-

tal craft at altitudes and speeds dangerous for humans.

Mac Brazel's expertise in the matter of aeronautics was obviously superior to that of the top military experts—men who were only able to identify the wreckage as a crashed weather balloon with seeming difficulty and much thought. Brazel was obviously wasted as a rancher! In fact as aircraft cannot fly in space, the *Independence Day* book of the film is telling us that the Roswell Incident did not involve a space craft—which rather ruins the rest of their storyline! ■

Dummy run

The authorities, at least, could not lay the ghost of Roswell and it was in 1997 that the official USAF report called *The Roswell Report, Case Closed* was published. What the USAF had to say is highly illuminating. Here is an extract from the introduction:

> The bodies turned what, for many years, was just another flying saucer story, into what many UFO proponents claim is the best case for extra-terrestrial visitation of Earth.

This report then goes on to infer that all the witnesses to a space craft crash site and alien bodies have, over the years, got themselves into a hopeless muddle and mixed up events that took place from 1953 through to at least 1959 and then called the resulting layered confection *The Roswell 1947 Incident*. They then produce fulsome reports of anthropomorphic dummies and technology such as astronautical test equipment to explain the cause of this muddle. As this report is based upon dummies that were not used in New Mexico until May 1950, together with the insulting premise that people in New Mexico cannot remember their own past—only waste your money on purchasing a copy if you feel you must.

To believe their story we are expected to accept that adult-size dummies look the same as the very small bodies previously described; that the fingers of these dummies are forever getting lost so that people can only see four digits. And that the people who saw these dummies not only saw them from a distance so

20. Anthropomorphic dummy used for parachute drops *c*1950.

USAF

that they muddled them up with "dead bodies" but also were able to see that they had their little fingers missing. Oh yes, and that height discrepancy was explained away by the fact that the legs regularly fell off the dummies!

21. The high altitude 'dummy parachutists' displayed by the US authorities in 1997.

USAF

22. Wright Field (later Wright-Patterson Air Force Base) Ohio.   SMITHSONIAN INSTITUTE

So where did the legs disappear to? These dummies were dressed in coveralls and wearing strap-on equipment, as can be seen in picture (20) despite the set dressing in (21).

We are then given a morality lecture by the authors of this USAF report on the shamefulness of UFO researchers, credulous people, hoaxers and profiteers, who wilfully ignore the brave US research scientist's hard work which is carried out in the defence of their nation. This bunch of doubters, it is implied, demonstrate an irresponsible desire to focus on UFOs and aliens instead of the good of their country, the world leader in technology and defence, thanks to the efforts of these worthy scientists. This is a variation on the patriotism theme. In attempting to realign the Roswell Incident with events that occurred as long afterwards as 1959 not only do the USAF infer that the residents of New Mexico are mentally feeble, they also place themselves in a morally tenuous position. This pontificating report reads like the back-engineered response to a problem that refuses to go away.

Some key points to bear in mind:

- The anthropomorphic dummies brought in evidence by the USAF date from 1953.

- The technology brought in evidence dates from the mid 1960s and 1970s and nothing that even *looked like* a Viking probe (one of their examples) was made by human beings in 1947.
- The human accidents brought in evidence relating to "live alien sightings" date from 1959.
- Their signed witness statements do not emanate from people who were in Roswell in 1947.
- The US Air Force states that the witnesses, or the UFO researchers who "liberally" interpreted their statements, were either a) confused, or b) attempted to perpetrate a hoax believing that no serious efforts would ever be taken to verify their stories.

The fact that the USAF see the necessity to create this anthropomorphic report demonstrates that they are still: a) *very* confused b) attempting to pull the wool over our collective eyes and c) contemptuous of their citizens. Who is really setting up the game board? And there is a further important point. If the authorities are prepared to display "dummy parachutist" bodies in 1997, surely they are in

23. Viking Orbiter awaiting recovery following tests in 1972 at White Sands, New Mexico.   NASA

fact confirming, or admitting, that witnesses were not lying or hallucinating when they spoke of seeing bodies back in 1947? Those 1947 bodies may indeed have been dummies, however, they certainly were not made by the USAF or their contractors—on their own admission.

Here is some more of that statement by Captain Edward Ruppelt:

> By the end of July 1947 the UFO security lid was down tight. The few members of the press who did enquire about what the Air Force was doing got the same treatment that you would get today if you inquired about the number of thermo-nuclear weapons stock-piled in the US Atomic arsenal...At ATIC there was confusion to the point of panic.[17]

Truth or Consequences

Having examined the many points of discrepancy in the records of the Roswell Incident it is time to attempt a reconstruction to ascertain what might have really happened.

We have been provided additional information from an confidential source, a Whistle-Blower who was very close to the original event. Although the USAF (and no doubt others) might feel that such an exercise is a waste of time, for as far as the authorities are concerned, nothing happened. We offer them our conclusions in the hope that we could *all* move forward from this event. Our source made it known to us that the United States Government has not revealed the facts concerning its knowledge of ET and their craft. In other words it has been highly secretive in this regard.

In 1993 our source told us that:

> In 1947 there was a probe which *looked like* a saucer and which *appeared* to crash. There never was an actual operational craft and there never were any crew on board. Parts of a non-functioning craft, debris and *pieces* of 'alien' (flesh and body parts) were deliberately placed for retrieval. The body parts were designed to suggest a form for alien beings.

We appreciate that our own explanation will for many be cause for mental indigestion. But we have not reached this explanation either lightly or in a hurry, nor simply in the context of Roswell.

We suggest that what the military found, far from Roswell, were the parts of a spacecraft without its drive mechanism arranged by actual extra-terrestrials—yes, actual ETs *to look as if it had accidentally crashed.* We maintain that this material was placed on site on the *night of* Monday *June 30* 1947 between 23:00 hours and the early hours of the morning.

The realistic but *artificial* body parts placed around this craft by extra-terrestrials were designed and placed there for at least three reasons:

1) To endorse the fact that the 'survivor' was definitely from beyond this planet—in other words, that it was extra terrestrial in origin—and from the quality of this dummy it would be immediately recognised by the military as of non-human origin and therefore could not be interpreted as a crew member from a crashed Soviet or Japanese spy plane. This exercise underlined the peaceful motives of their action. These were not mischief makers.

2) The placing of these items was also intended as a metaphor which would only be understood many, many years later. The 'masters of infinity' and their cohorts are not the only ones who can plan ahead. The military were offered a choice of action and one of the consequences of the choice they made would be reflected back to them decades later.

3) The dummy that the authorities were able to examine was the foundation of what was to become known in the United States and elsewhere as the 'Gray' ET. The head was large with over-sized almond-shaped eyes and the hands displayed three fingers and a thumb—four digits.

In our opinion, one of the reasons that the 'survivor's' hands had just four digits was in order to indicate that these *really* were *dummy* parts, not those of a real being.

24. The classic 'Gray' with *three fingers and a thumb.*

C DOWELL

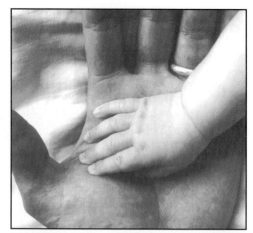

25. Hand, living = five-sided

26. Snowflake, non living = six-sided.

All living things have five-sided symmetry and the bio-organism of self-aware beings has evolved to the form of a torso with two arms, two legs and a head (= five) with hands that have *five* digits—four fingers and a thumb—and feet with *five* toes. Non living items are six-sided, as with crystalline structures—a snowflake for example. (The foregoing proposal is fully examined and described in the book *Two-Thirds).*

Dummies' run

The authorities were alerted by a radar *'blip' that we suggest was arranged by the deliverers of the gift* and which had been observed then tracked by the military for several days prior to the 'crash'. We have information from our source that suggests that this 'blip' had been detected on a course of approximately 27.2° gyro east of magnetic north over the United States and that the actual trajectory of the craft did not necessarily correspond to the radar trace

(27). The site chosen for this 'accident' was between the towns of Truth or Consequences and Magdalena. It is our conclusion that the 'mystery' (original) crash site was what is now the current location of the Very Large Array.

The military arrived on the scene and collected the debris. From the state of the evidence it would not be clear to the military *exactly* how long that craft had been there. They then had to make a choice: either to announce to the world that we were apparently not alone in the Universe, or make an attempt to contain the entire incident.

However the US military had no way of knowing whether, before their arrival, anyone had visited the scene and at the time chosen to remain silent. This possibility was something for which they would have to cover in any fu-

---

Whys and wherefores

Established in October 1981, the world's most powerful radio telescope is the Very Large Array (VLA) located on the
Plains of San Agustin, a 400 square mile former lake bed encircled by pine-covered peaks.
The location is approximately 25 miles west of the town of Magdalena.

The VLA comprises 27 parabolic antennas which are arranged in a Y shape along a distance of 23 miles.
Each antenna measures 82ft in diameter and the total collecting area is equivalent to a single 462 ft antenna.
It has a resolution equivalent to that of a single dish about 17 miles in diameter.
Would the officially unacknowledged event in New Mexico of 1947 be one of the principal reasons for
the Y-shaped arrangement and the eventual selection of *this* site for the VLA? (see Appendix)

---

ture scenario, and with the hindsight of the 1990s we can see that the authorities have done just that. It is our view that many of the witnesses to the 'mystery' site (north of Truth or Consequences) were fabricated out of whole cloth in order to cover for the eventuality of anyone at all having seen the probe before the military arrived.

The USAF in its 1997 anthropomorphic dummy report featured witnesses and interviewers, whose methodology is considered 'delicate' even by the most ardent of serious UFO researchers. Gerry Anderson, supposedly five years old at the time (yet possessing a remarkably acute memory for detail) has admitted to falsifying a document and changing his testimony.[18] Glenn Dennis (who was said to be the first person to make a drawing of the 'grey' at Roswell) whatever his purported sincerity, quite frankly, comes across as being a 'plant'. Although the USAF would no doubt say

"quite, our point exactly, unreliable testimony and a muddling of the events".

In the case of this crash event, it would be logical to have witnesses perceived as independent, yet who are intentionally seeding disinformation into the scenario. These witnesses would subsequently be revealed as 'unreliable'. This is a classic method of assuring that an event is dismissed as invalid for lack of credible evidence. Finally, all those who sincerely believe that they saw evidence of a crash at the Brazel 'debris' and 'skid mark' sites near Roswell are correct. They are only incorrect in their conclusion that the authorities *inadvertently* revealed the fact that these were events related to a flying saucer crash. They saw what they were meant to see. They read what they were meant to read in their newspapers. There were no mistakes made by the Press Officer Walter Haut. The cover-up was perfectly executed and planned down to the last detail.

27. Course of the craft 27.2° west of north.

perfectly well that they had found a craft of non-human origin. What better way to disguise and discredit this momentous event than by circulating *fake* parts from a *phoney* craft at an alternative location well away from the original site and then create an entire rumour machine around an event that they could control from start to finish?

A rather dumber run

The 509th at Roswell had its own weather forecasting capabilities and with access to accurate forecasts it was easy to establish a counter operation under cover of bad weather—electrical storm activity. The week ending July 4 gave them their opportunity (possibly not coincidentally, New Mexico at that time had one of the severest electrical storms of its history). Under cover of inclement weather (and also counting on the fact that most people would be occupied by Independence Day celebrations) the Corona sites were prepared and 'seeded' with a set piece. All the authorities had to do was to wait for Mac Brazel to come to them, like a lamb to the slaughter.

The scenario described would then explain why Major Jesse Marcel and a second Counter-Intelligence Officer were at the ready when Mac Brazel finally got to them around July 7. There are however, not enough facts available to make a decision as to whether Brazel was an unwitting participant in this staged event, or was conversely coerced into active participation by either the military authorities or by his boss. For it *is* our contention that this was done with the compliance of the owner or leaseholder of the ranch land, known as the Foster Ranch.

The military authorities had proceeded to do exactly the same thing for the public as ET had done for them. Except of course, we were not going to be given any choices. In the authorities' cover-version of the crash discovery, some far-sighted and sophisticated refinements were added: future components that would be required to establish the short term weather bal-

The implications of such a large-scale cover-up (and the subsequent even grander cover-up of what really happened regarding the lunar landings) are so far beyond the reasonable that most people immediately class any such misdemeanours as 'impossible'.

Nevertheless, we maintain that the military *did* choose the second option (that of a cover-up) and thus began the mechanics of deception. Secrecy would have been difficult (but not impossible). The best way to lie is always to tell the truth as near to the line as possible. And the bigger the lie the more believable the lie actually is. Their first concern, then, was to camouflage the fact that an extra-terrestrial craft complete with body parts had been found. We believe however that those concerned knew

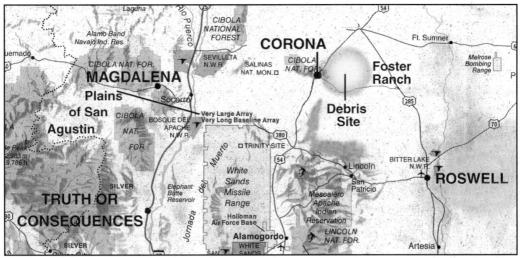

28. The 'official' Corona debris site north-west of Roswell.

loon scenario and the longer term Mogul scenario—the balsa wood-type beams inscribed with 'hieroglyphs' and a flower-decorated waxy paper.

So to summarise:

- The real timing of the first mystery crash incident is different from that of the Brazel 'debris' and 'skid mark' sites near Corona, which is the official version.
- The craft and *pieces of body parts* of an 'alien' being found at the mystery crash site were intentionally planted by extra- terres- trials as both *a test and a choice,* whilst, at the same time, providing us all with con- firmation that we are not alone.
- The set dressing of the 'skid mark' site in that area and the debris scattered on the Foster ranch site where it was discovered by Mac Brazel, was deliberately placed there by the appropriate authorities of the United States. This action was shortly after the discovery *and recovery* of the Truth or

Consequences (our mystery crash site) ma- terial, in order to *draw attention away* from that location.

- It is our contention that this operation was done with the compliance of the owner/ leaseholder of the land used for this pur- pose, whether that be J B Foster in both instances or two different parties. Some of the material used at the hoax sites *may* have been genuine debris from the original crash site. However these particular pieces would have been carefully cata- logued, collected up and speedily removed.
- The above scenario would certainly explain why a press release was officially sanc- tioned. By 'establishing' the date of the crash incident as the July 4, the original in- cident, north of Truth or Consequences is 'lost' in the public focus on the Corona site. The official 'unofficial' press release of July 8 is subsequently denounced—the Corona site is not the remains of a UFO but a weather balloon.

Indie Nile

April 5 1948 White Sands New Mexico scientists watched a disc-shaped UFO, streak across the sky—alleged to have appeared to be approximately ⅕th the diameter of the Moon.

November 7 1957 Charles Capen, scientist at White Sands said that scientists were "shook up" about the sightings that occurred over New Mexico and West Texas in the first week of November. He also said:

" It's something that hasn't happened before".

MAJESTIC 12 - MAJIC 12 - MJ12
Original structure of group as listed September 24 1947

Function	Original member
Director Central Intelligence Agency	Rear Ad Roscoe H Hillenkoetter[6]
Chairman Joint R&D Board	Dr Vannevar Bush
Secretary of Defense	James V Forrestal[1]
Commander US AAF [Now USAF] Air Matériel Cd. at Wright Field (now Wright-Patterson AFB)	Gen Hoyt Vandenberg
Chairman National Research Council	Dr Detlev Bronk
Chairman of NACA [now NASA]	Dr Jerome Hunsaker
Executive Sec. of the National Security Council	Sydney Souers[2]
Assistant Secretary to Army	Gordon Gray[3]
Chairman Dept. Astronomy, Harvard University	Donald Menzel[4]
Exec. Sec. of the Research & Development Board	Lloyd V Berkner
Commanding Officer of New Mexico area that includes White Sands & the AEC* Sandia Base	Major Gen Robert M Montague[5]

1. Forrestal resigned March '49 died May '49 (allegedly suicide) only replaced on Majic 12 council Aug 1 1950.

2. Souers was also special consultant to President Truman on intelligence matters.

3. Gray was Chairman of the CIA's very secret 'Psychological Strategy Board' which encompassed the psychological warfare implications of UFOs.

4. Menzel was also Professor of Astrophysics at Harvard. Publicly he was a virulent debunker of UFOs.

5. A classified project at Sandia was headed up by Montague, post the Roswell Incident in July 1947.

6. The CIA was established at the same time as this MJ-12 Council.

*AEC = Atomic Energy Commission, successor to the Manhattan Project.

OK. everybody back to sleep by July 9 1947. But not quite everybody, as it turned out.

The last king?

From our viewpoint of the late 1990s it is easier to see that the 'official' Roswell story has more holes in it than a fisherman's net and that much of this story bears the hallmark of having been written, edited and then staged. It is also clear that the curtain has not yet been raised for the final act. With their 1995 and 1997 statements on this matter we have seen that the American authorities are either still re-writing the script or are doggedly acting out the disinformation scenes they wrote for themselves fifty years ago.

It is however worthy of note that the story has not been allowed to die. One of the most recent departures has been the linking of a group called Majestic 12 or Majic 12, with Roswell. Do we have here what is known in show business as an 'upsum' sequence, one which provides bits of background information to the TV viewer recapping on the serialised story so far? In other words, it would seem that at some level it has been decided—officially— to give us all an unofficial wake-up call.

It would appear that the 'masters of infinity' are ready for the next phase of their endeavour. Unlike ET, they do not shake us gently by the shoulder from time to time, so that we wake up calmly and harmoniously. No, they use very loud alarm clocks in an attempt to jerk us into a state so that we rush to conclusions without thinking matters through carefully.

Stanton Friedman (nuclear physicist by profession) introduced Majestic 12 to the outside world in his book *Crash at Corona* (first published in 1992). He related that in December 1984 Jaimie Shandera, (a movie producer known to be "working with investigator Bill Moore in intelligence-related activities" as Friedman put it) was sent a roll of undeveloped 35mm film. Postmarked Albuquerque, New

Mexico there was no other information enclosed. When processed this turned out to contain photographs of documents pertaining to the formation of a group of twelve men who were, it is alleged, to deal with the Roswell Incident. These eight pages were apparently assembled on November 18 1952 for the attention of the President-elect, Dwight Eisenhower. Friedman, while finding the documents seemingly authentic was not, at the time of writing *Crash at Corona*, utterly convinced by them.

Could it be that these documents are indeed genuinely produced but that they deal with the mechanics of a hoax? That is, the establishment of the ways and means of compartmentalising and then causing to function over long periods of time—a hoaxed scenario, the like of which the world would not see until Apollo—which we suggest was run on very similar lines. It is not in essence the *specific individuals* who mattered on this Majestic 12 list—though of course they too had their importance—people would eventually die but a suitable successor would take over. The King is dead, long live the King. It is the *functions* these men fulfilled, especially their affiliation to the intelligence networks of the USA, that gave them their tickets to join this group. A careful examination of the functions held and previously held by these men (and more importantly the processes during WWII which led to the events at Pearl Harbour) would lead us to suppose that we are dealing with an organisation that has functioned in the same way since at least the 1940s.

Magic marker

The operation for the intercept of the Japanese intelligence between Japan itself and its foreign embassies was called Magic. This operation was run by Stanton Friedman's nearly namesake, William Friedmann, master cryptographer. He called his team the Magicians, hence the origin of the name.[19]

As perceived by America at that time, it would be fair to say that the Japanese were small oriental-eyed alien beings who were invading and attacking areas of the world that the Americans considered under their jurisdiction. What is the differentiator between small oriental-eyed extra-terrestrial alien beings who were perceived as invading American territory? The difference is one letter: Magic, became Majic, the codename of the nearly top level group dealing with such matters. It is also our understanding that the three codenames used by this group: Majestic-12, Majic-12 and MJ12 were not variations on the one section but denoted three different but interdependent aspects within the overall operation. Did the top secret Japanese cipher code 'Purple' ultimately become that used as a means of encrypting com-

---

A bird in the hand worth two in the bush?

Dr. Vannevar Bush established the National Defense Council in 1941, the Office of Scientific Research and Development in 1943, the Manhattan Project (development of the A-bomb) in 1943. And Majestic 12 in 1947.

Post war he was head of the Joint Research and Development Board.

In 1949 he worked on a method of linking all the US Intelligence agencies together for the Government, a request initiated by James Forrestal.

Can't see the wood for the trees

A businessman in the style of Joe Kennedy (father of JFK), Forrestal had apparently amassed most of his considerable fortune through 'dubious' Wall Street deals.

Forrestal was Under Secretary of the US Navy in 1941, and Secretary of the Navy by August 1944.

He shared many points of view with the young John F Kennedy, the latter travelling with Forrestal to Germany at the time of the Potsdam Summit in July 1945.

Forrestal was made Secretary of Defense in July 1947 but resigned from his post in March 1949 due to ill health. He apparently committed suicide two months later in Bethesda Navy Hospital where he was undergoing medical treatment.

---

munications between members of Majic-12 and their foreign terrestrial counterparts? Coincidentally the Japanese language is based on ideograms and the alleged hieroglyphs at the Brazel site were drawn in *purple*. Incidentally, Corona was subsequently the name of a spy satellite program within another satellite program, Discovery.

If Stanton Friedman could not obtain the proof that this find was an authentic document, he might be willing to consider that he has been put in the way of some mighty loud Whistle-Blowing. There is more information in the structure of those papers than in the actual words they contain.[20]

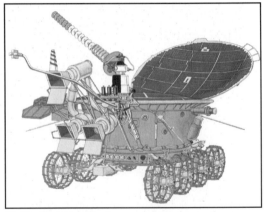

29. The Soviet Lunikhod.

Different folks, same strokes

The majority of American citizens, as well as the rest of the world, were convinced that the Soviet and American authorities were separated by the Cold War and that communications between these two super powers were strictly defined by the prevailing political conditions. With hindsight, it can be seen that from the very outset, at the very highest levels, these two 'enemies' were working side-by-side on the question of space travel, and also on information concerning ET. The official attitude propagated in the West by the American military of the 1950s was that they had far too much to do to speculate about "interplanetary voyages so stigmatised by the fallacies and exaggerations of the comic pages".[21] This, we suggest, was the exact opposite of what they actually thought and what they were really doing. Behind these words, which combine elements of both the "ridicule and patriotism scripts" with which we are now familiar, the truth was somewhat different. The scientists and engineers of the 'masters of infinity' in both countries were desperately trying to invent machines to get out into space, and these often turned out to be faithful copies of those very same comic pages!

Roswell was also on the agenda in the Soviet Union, when, in July 1947, at Stalin's behest, Korolëv was requested to attend the Ministry of State Security—the NKVD, later called the KGB. Korolëv was given a team of translators

30. Compare the Lunikhod with Jules Verne's *Time Machine*.   E Castañeda

and handed many *foreign* documents relating to UFO activity. Three days later, Korolëv met Stalin to give him his verdict on these documents, which are considered to have included details of the Roswell Incident.[22] Korolëv opined that UFOs were *not* enemy weapons, but that they *were* obviously a real phenomena. Other Soviet scientists subsequently consulted by Stalin on the foreign UFO papers also came to that conclusion. By this time, Korolëv had quasi-unlimited authority and his opinion on such matters would have been highly valued. (It has been alleged that Korolëv had been part of one of the Soviet expeditions to remote Siberia—although his

31. What a coincidence that the LM was nicknamed *the Spider* when the head of NASA at that time was a certain James Webb!

life story does not accommodate this allegation in relation to Tunguska, unless that was prior to or during his Siberian' Sharaga saga.) Scientists have always ignored the political borders, so much so, that during the Manhattan Project, American security chiefs were worried at the lack of seriousness with which some of the very senior physicists treated all the security precautions taken, including the vetoes on talking about the project.

The 39 Steppes

Thirty-nine years before Roswell, something had happened in pre-revolution Russia, during the reign of Nicholas II, that was to have world-wide consequences. This early incident is very relevant to our story but take heart! It is not in quite the same vein as the complex Roswell scenario with which we have just had to deal. On June 30 1908, seventeen minutes and eleven seconds after midnight GMT, an explosion of monumental proportions occurred over an area near the Podkamennaya Tunguska River (60° 55' N; 101° 57' E) in Siberia. The blast of the explosion had been visible from about 500 miles away from its epicentre and distant eye witnesses had seen a fireball which lit up their horizon, felt the ground tremble and experienced hot winds strong enough to blow people over and shake buildings. The vibrations from this gigantic explosion were felt in America, while in

---

The Horz whisperer

The USA has had many holographic images of ET craft and allied phenomena 'funnelled' to it.

The Soviets have been co-operating with the USA in investigative research for years.

Other countries close to these two have been aware of these matters.

This information was the result of a conversation that took place in 1990 and published in

The Only Planet of Choice (see Appendix).

We would say that the space program certainly comes under the heading of 'investigative research'.

> ### *Taiga, Taiga*
>
> In 1921 Lenin created the Soviet Academy of Sciences, and this body commissioned Leonid Kulik
> to investigate the Tunguska Event.
> He spent six years collating information and preparing for an arduous trek into the Taiga and Tundra of remote Siberia.
> Kulik was to spend more than ten years on the project and his four lengthy expeditions left Moscow for Tunguska in
> 1927, '28, '29 and '37. In 1938 aerial photographs were taken of the area and in the summer of 1939 Kulik spent a
> further six weeks at the site.
> The long gap between the third and fourth expedition was due to the years of Stalin's Great Terror. However, in that gap
> Dr. Donald Menzel, astrophycisist, astronomer, owner of Top Secret Ultra Clearances, linked to covert activities with the
> CIA & NSA, (including codebreaking) and a member of the MAJIC listing,
> led a scientific expedition to the USSR.
> In 1957 Kulik's soil samples were again analysed using up-to-date techniques and suspect fragments of iron dust were
> found. In 1958 the largest expedition to Tunguska ever mounted was undertaken—with the intention of finally settling the
> meteor theory. After 34 days during which 500 miles of Taiga was explored, no signs of meteorite activity were found
> and those iron dust fragments turned out to have come from the equipment used on
> Kulik's previous expeditions.
> Despite Kulik's personal convictions and (as we approach the millennium) the tendency of orthodoxy, for fundamental
> reasons, to cite Tunguska as evidence that we *shall* be hit by a meteorite, *NO* conclusive evidence supporting the
> meteorite theory has been established to this day. Indeed, given the plant mutations, growth details and the 'pattern'
> of the site, it is clear to any thinking person that a meteorite is definitely
> *NOT* the cause of the Tunguska Event.

England scientific instruments registered two consecutive shockwaves which travelled full circle around the planet.

In Europe there was light enough to read a newspaper at midnight, and it was too bright to enable astronomical observations to be made. In Russia, these bright nights continued for several weeks. While the meteorological effects were the subject of much discussion at the time—we can be sure that the information concerning Tunguska would have been shared amongst the scientific communities of the US and Russia—very soon everybody went back to sleep. Thirteen years later in 1921, Lenin instructed the newly-formed Soviet Academy of Sciences to research the incident. If it seems rather surprising that it would take so long to investigate such an extraordinary event, it should be remembered that politically Russia went through the 1914-18 World War and also her own revolution in 1917.

Geographically the site was far from Moscow and the conditions on the ground were diabolical. Travelling first by Trans-Siberian Railway, then horse and sledge and sometimes using reindeer in the deep snows, the party had to traverse the Taiga, the Russian name for the dense Siberian forest. Freezing cold in winter, a mudbath in the summer, hundreds of lonely miles of unrelenting virgin forest had to be hacked through before these travellers could look for a site they had never before seen. A place that until then existed for them solely as words on paper and local rumour.

On his first expedition, Kulik came upon the initial signs: over thirteen miles of flattened trees—all lying in a south-easterly direction. Following the lines of the flattened trees he finally found the epicentre of the blast. Less than a mile across, over time, it had become a marshy bog situated in an amphitheatre-like valley. Kulik then realised that the full extent of the blast—his south-east-pointing flattened trees were 37 miles away from the "the Great Cauldron", his name for the epicentre. Later he would be able to evaluate that the entire area of destruction amounted to around 777 square miles. It was subsequently evaluated that whatever had exploded, did so 5 miles above the Earth's surface.

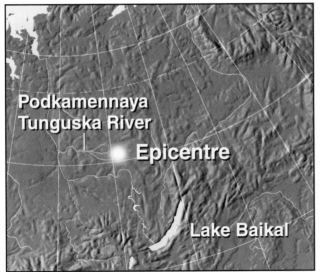

32. The Tunguska site. At approximately 5,315 ft in depth, Lake Baikal is the deepest lake on the planet. It is also the eighth largest lake occupying 12,161 square miles.

Surprisingly however, there was no trace of an impact crater and even more surprisingly the ground damage at the epicentre resembled "the outspread wings of a butterfly" (see below). So much so that this was specifically remarked upon. Kulik nevertheless deduced that a meteorite had exploded over the site. He spent the rest of his life and three expeditions attempting to find proof to confirm his theory. This eventually turned into an obsession for he would

permit no other explanation. He was to die during WWII without succeeding, for despite careful, close examination of both the territory and the trees *no meteorite fragments were ever recovered* and no proof that anything had ever struck the ground was forthcoming.

From these pre-war researches and examinations something else *was* established. Witnesses in the region of Lake Baikal enabled Russian scientists to deduce that a flying object (as nobody knows what it was, we will call it a UFO) had become visible over the lake and then followed a descending trajectory, moving across the sky from south-east to north-west. However, over 700 eyewitness in the western region maintained that the UFO had altered course. Their reports are consistent and indicate a trajectory which is at a totally different angle of approach than that seen by the witnesses in the region of Lake Baikal. This *fact* certainly eliminates the meteorite theory! We cannot over-emphasise this point.[23]

Korolёv was of the opinion that the origin of the Tunguska event was a mid-air explosion of non-terrestrial origin. With no damage to the ground other than flash burns and extensive but short-lived fires, yet with two blast waves—an

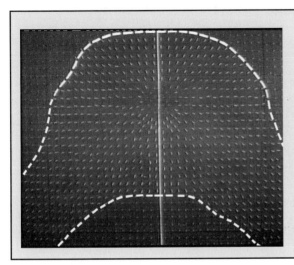

Fives
Remember that figure?
Arnold's nine craft flew in a line five miles long.
Is there also a further link here with, for example,
the five-sided symmetry of living things?
Or is this all just a coincidence?

The butterfly has landed

The butterfly-shape of the fallen trees at Tunguska.

explosion and a ballistic wave—Korolëv had some justification in so claiming. Later it was found that the new growth of saplings in the *damaged* area was more vigorous than the new growth in the *surrounding* area. (Rather significantly, a similar phenomenon occurs within the Crop Glyphs found in the UK.)[24]

The world then became embroiled in WWII, when those two highly destructive A-bombs were unleashed on Japan—a country lying to the south-east of a continent that had seemingly experienced just such an event *37 years* earlier—the traces of which were apparently radiating out for *37 miles* from the epicentre. It is hardly surprising then that the Russian scientists noted the similarities between these affected areas in Japan and Russia. Both Hiroshima and Tunguska demonstrated idiosyncratic new plant growth; single trees remained standing; objects and people were protected by ground contours, even very near to the epicentre.

Moreover, blisters that had appeared on the Tunguska reindeer were found to be similar to radiation burns found on cattle hit by the dust cloud after the first A-bomb testing in New Mexico. Mutations in the local insect world had been noted at Tunguska and it was deduced that the descriptions of the explosion could correspond to the same type of mushroom

cloud that the A-bomb produced. Therefore, after WWII, Korolëv decided that the Tunguska Incident must have been a nuclear explosion. Then some four months before the Roswell event, on February 12 1947 at 10.38 am (local time) another fireball streaked across the eastern Russian (become 'Soviet') sky, and fell to Earth on the snow-clad slopes of the Sikhote-Alin mountains. Contrary to the Tunguskan event, this meteorite did not even register on the nearest seismic station's equipment—some three hundred miles distant in Vladivostok. Nor were there any of the explosive effects witnessed at Tunguska. Geologists flown to the site found 122 craters in all, some 30ft deep and 80ft wide and the site was full of meteoric iron fragments. While providing much information on the nature of meteorites for the Soviets, it only highlighted the fact that the Tunguska event was *not* of the same nature. Much of the post-war Russian research had been led by Dr. Vasilieyev of Tomsk University. Even though radiation tests were undertaken in 1960 (fifty-two years after the event), for this nuclear explosion theory to be valid there should still have been traces. The problem is that the Russians have not found any trace of abnormal or nuclear radiation whatsoever.

During the testing of H-bombs in the 1950s, extra-bright aurora lights and disturbances of

---

Tunguskan tales—the reasons why

A mini black hole—refuted.

Anti-matter collision—disproved.

Comet strike —120 observatories *worldwide*, consulted by the Russians, produced *NO SIGHTINGS* for the appropriate time. Arthur C Clarke maintains that this lack of evidence is due to the fact that the comet must have entered our atmosphere in the daytime, when observation was impossible. Writing in his book, *Mysterious World* ACC is of the opinion that: "there is now not the slightest reason to doubt that the Tunguska body was a very small comet".

The Tunguskan event happened at just after midnight GMT and therefore observation of a comet or meteor, had there been one, *would* have been possible from one of these 120 observatories.

This event was also visible with the naked eye—it was 7.15 am local time.

Sir Bernard Lovell informs us that we *will* have a Tunguska-type event again and it surely will not be so benign as to land away from habitation.

Astronomers know that to date, no human being has ever been killed by any meteorite, so this remark is a presumption.

Furthermore, *nothing actually landed at Tunguska*.

The script is in need of a rewrite!

the ionosphere were produced in the exact *opposite* hemisphere of the Earth from the detonation.

By great good luck, during 1908 in the opposite hemisphere of the planet from Tunguska, Ernest Shackleton the explorer was camped beside Mount Erebus, the active Antarctic volcano. His expedition recorded significant displays of aurora lights—both *BEFORE* and after the event. Dr. Vasilieyev was quoted as saying: "I know of no other phenomena than the nuclear explosions that produce these displays at their magnetic opposite side of the world". Yet what *was* found was *electro-magnetic* chaos. It was deduced that an extremely potent electro-magnetic hurricane at the Tunguska epicentre had altered all the normal alignments with the Earth's magnetic field.

We feel that it is no accident that this 'explosion' occurred in a part of the world where human beings would be in the least danger. There are, for us, indications that this Tunguska event was specifically engineered and was neither nuclear, nor atomic as we understand it. Nor was it an act of aggression. Subsequent events such as the Roswell Incident, the increasingly intensive UFO activity and the current Crop Glyph phenomenon, have exposed

the *demonstration of intent* inherent in the 1908 Tunguska event. All of which goes some way to explain why the media were prompted to bring up the subject of Tunguska again in 1996. Despite the continuing evidence to the contrary some scientists, not unacquainted with certain aspects of the space program,[25] are now unequivocally stating that the Tunguska event was due to a meteorite exploding in the atmosphere.

Yttrium is found as a result of meteoric impacts and apparently the post-war expeditions to Tunguska found tiny particles of magnetite and silicate buried within the soil and the trees which, by their composition, have been established as being extra-terrestrial. The nickel content of the magnetite was too high for Earth and it also contained elements rare on Earth, such as yttrium. The effects at Tunguska were *not* caused by meteorite impact and have neither been understood nor explained in the context of present day physics. If you will forgive our cynicism, the 'finding' of this element, combined with the 1996 re-attribution of the Tunguska damage to a meteorite impact theory, lead us to conclude that this information concerning rare yttrium deposits is part of another scenario now beginning to taking shape.

If we were to replace 'meteorite' with 'ET',

A REbus?
Mt Erebus is 12,448 ft/3,794 m high and last erupted in 1989. Coincidentally or otherwise, this was the year when the first Crop Glyph with a diagrammatic floor lay was activated in England.

Winterbourne Stoke Crop Glyph, August 1989.   F TAYLOR

then we would have a far better insight into the authorities' real concern.

Dr. Donald's SFX trickery—Part 6

In December 1947, just six months after the Roswell Incident, Dr. Bernard Heuvelmans sent Herge, the Belgian creator of Tintin, a Moon adventure storyline for Tintin, set in the United States.

Cell mates

Dr. Bernard Heuvelmans, was a scientist and author of *L'Homme Parmi les Etoiles (Man Among the Stars)* but Herge found that however much he might like the authors of such material, he was unable to restrict himself to the confines of a predetermined plot. However, he continued to collaborate with Heuvelmans on technical matters and on November 29 1949 Herge wrote:

> I think it is time to send Tintin to the Moon. Since the question of such a journey first arose I have felt a nagging impatience...could you get me information on the subject?

Why it took Herge two years to succumb to this "nagging impatience" is hard to say, since he had already started thinking about this adventure by September 1947, at least. Although *Destination Moon* was copyrighted 1953 and *Explorers on the Moon* 1954, Tintin's Moon adventures were published in the *Tintin* magazine in episodes which started in the spring of 1950. Then: "Following the publication of *Explorers to the Moon in 1954*, the Commission for the International Geophysical Year canvassed the launch of artificial satellites from

Earth".[26] In 1957 both the Soviet Union and the United States were off on their 'space race', only of course it was Laika the real dog and not Snowy the cartoon character who was the first dog in space.

Coincidence corner

We are informed that much of the intrigue in the Tintin story comes from *the rivalry* between two camps. *Destination Moon* shares its title with the film produced by George Pal at the same time, 1950. Not only that, but in the Tintin stories there is a hero-villain by the name of Frank Wolf. This *last* name was the *first* name of the hero Wolf Helius in the 1927 Fritz Lang film *Frau im Mond* as you will no doubt recall. By introducing a grey area of morality, it is this Wolf character that alters the clear-cut good/bad morality prevalent *in all other* Herge stories. We also have the launch of Tintin's rocket from a space centre with an Eastern European name—The Sprodj Centre in Syldania. And the first person to step onto Herge's cartoon lunar surface is—a civilian. Albeit Herge's astronaut is untrained. This is another case of life imitating art. However, in a glorious example of a fool rushing in, an anecdote from *The Making of Mission to the Moon* recalls that: "The Americans were not so bold, the astronauts were all servicemen".

As a final aside on that subject, to the CIA operatives, the changing of a military pilot into a civilian for the purposes of a mission, is known as "sheep dipping".[27]

Where Angels fear to tread

This comparative analysis of these two space adventures Apollo and Tintin notes that Tintin

---

Beginnings

Buzz Aldrin described the Moon as "magnificent desolation". So did somebody else, and he too was describing an imaginary scene.

When Tintin arrived on the lunar surface in his red and white chequered V-2 lookalike, had climbed down a ladder not dissimilar to the LM's and surveyed the scene before him he exclaimed:

"It's a nightmare land, a place of death, horrifying in its desolation. Not a tree, not a flower, not a blade of grass. Not a bird, not a sound, not a cloud. In the inky black sky there are thousands of stars".

Tintin saw more than any of us—he got to see the stars shining around the Moon.

Just like Tintin, the Apollo adventures to the Moon by the named astronauts, was just a story for the children—us.

and his crew wore goldfish-bowl helmets through which it is possible to see the astronaut, whereas the helmets of the Apollo astronauts completely inhibited that degree of identification.

The story of the development of these Tintin adventures raises several interesting points. Up until then Herge had not been known for rigorous attention to scientific detail, and in 1950 just when *Explorers of the Moon* was appearing in *Tintin* magazine the Studio Herge was founded. We are then told that this was the time that one Robert de Moor began working with Herge. Allegedly it was de Moor who was responsible for the technical detail of the backgrounds and the rockets in these drawings—yet the story was already being published, so how can that be right? As this technical detail is deemed to be an "important contribution to the credibility of these adventures", then we must assume that Robert de Moor was in fact, unofficially working on these adventures well before the official inauguration of his employ. Why should that be necessary, unless Herge was not interested enough to come up with that type of detail?

We are given to understand that Herge was uncomfortable with this world of precision and research and critics of these lunar adventures have said that: "However well the storyteller's intentions are fulfilled, his imagination is more constrained in these two books than in almost any of the *Adventures of Tintin*". And again:

"The importance attached to the dialogue, the technicality of the drawing and the requirements of verisimilitude, impede the flow of the plot". Herge himself said, "It was a tricky subject...interplanetary travel, for me, it is an empty subject". To which comment we must ask why he wanted to write the lunar adventures in the first place? And why in 1969 he took up pen again to draw a cartoon version of the 'Apollo 12' mission for *Paris-Match*, a publication very well disposed towards the Americans. ■

Tintin's lunar adventures refer to principles, in our view, specifically designed to reflect the momentum of the space program and to focus the public—primarily the Europeans—on the idea of a 'space race'. Guaranteed an audience, especially of future citizens of a world in which the space program would be ever present, was Herge either wittingly or unwittingly the vehicle through which this message was transmitted?

The foundations of beating the Soviets in a 'space race' were being laid down, the starter's gun fired in public when we all witnessed the placing of the first ever satellite Sputnik. The authorities have certainly not given the public the full or true facts leading to that event, nor to those which followed. Both as scriptwriters and film makers, these people have singularly failed in this regard.

Apropos the Roswell Incident, it is, however, no longer necessary for any 'official' to say

---

Further containment

November 12 1953 The Canadian Government announced Project Magnet, the installation of an observatory near Ottawa, dedicated to the observation of UFOs.

December 1 1953 The US set up cameras using diffractor gratings to analyse UFO light sources.

December 24 1959 Air Force Inspector General's brief issued to Operations and Training Commands: UFO investigating officers to be issued with Geiger counters, cameras, binoculars and 'other' equipment.

August 15 1960 USAF secretary sent policy letter to Commanders in which he stated that "the USAF maintains continuous surveillance of the atmosphere near Earth for unidentified flying objects—UFOs".

August 25 1960 Grumman Aircraft Corporation photographed "mystery satellite" over a period of several days.

December 5 1960 Public debate on US television between UFO investigator Keyhoe and USAF spokesman.

December 14 1960 The Brooking's Report on the implications of ET interaction with humans was published.

December 5 1963 The National Academy of Sciences issued a report (pub # 1079) that the search for extra-terrestrial life "be proclaimed the top priority scientific goal of our space program".

whether the original Roswell story is 'true' or 'false'. It has endured for so long that it has now become the stuff of legend—which was the ultimate intention of ET. A legend that would resurface when the time was ripe.

No-one can ignore the *fact* that the locations of these 'crashes' were adjacent to the top security sites of American airborne defence systems. Our contention is that these sites were carefully selected by ET and an opportunity was offered to the US Government to learn and to reach an understanding regarding human-

kind's place in the greater scheme of things.

On that day in June 1947, we, the *children* of the Universe, were presented with a doll and a space craft from beyond, and subsequently it has emerged that those who found these items were unwilling to share that gift with the rest of the world.

Given the choice between truth or consequences, they chose consequences.

They chose poorly.

Two for the price of one

The timing of the Spruce Goose maiden voyage has recently come into question. In the 1996 biography *Howard Hughes the Untold Story*, authors Brown & Broeske claim two dates for the test flight: November 2nd 1947 and November 2 1947, (which *might* be attributable to a printing error). Then in 1998 a British TV documentary *The Secret History of Howard Hughes* stated clearly that this test took place on July 28 1947, during the very publicised Senate Hearings in which Hughes was charged with corruption over the $18m Spruce Goose had cost the US Government. Hughes issued counter charges against a Senator Ralph Brewster and the hearings came to a 'Mexican stand-off' and were closed.

If Hughes had used the Spruce Goose maiden voyage to swing the public behind him, it certainly worked.

It is alleged that 'rent-a-crowd' tactics were adopted and progress of the Goose from Hangar to test waters was a very dramatic and much publicised affair. Following his brief adventure Hughes was declared a hero and 'Hughes for President' clubs sprang up all over the nation!

Quite frankly, given Hughes' standing with the government and the continuing work with its many agencies, this entire trial script looks rather like a storm in a teacup—designed to remove the attention of the public from other matters of the time. Interestingly, although the Goose was never to fly again, she was not scrapped but kept in storage, costing $1m a year to preserve in pristine condition. For such an investment, this aircraft surely has a greater significance than even Hughes had stated, as he had staked his residency in the US against its ability to fly.

If the July 28 1947 timing of this event is correct, then it suggests that the lumbering wooden Spruce Goose was enlisted in the effort to banish the 1947 UFO flap, Roswell's flying saucer and rumours of ET bodies from the American press as well as the minds of the American public—for decades to come as it turned out. As investments go, it was no doubt considered cheap at the price.

Chapter Seven

Distant Horizons

We examine the organisation of NASA and details of Project Horizon. Unmanned probes and alleged manned missions notwithstanding, the origins of the Moon and its relationship to Earth are in no way properly understood by Earth scientists. We look at the orthodox theories concerning the Earth/Moon relationship. Then we take some geology 'lessons' from the named Apollo astronauts and listen in on some of their conversations. As a result we are able to learn even more about their parents — NASA.

Under control

For those who cannot cope with or will not accept the hypothesis that extra terrestrials really exist, there is yet another reason why the 'masters of infinity' were eager to get out into space: power. For as President Johnson knew, those who controlled the leading technology of the day would dominate the planet. Space was the future arena for all leading technology, whether used for war or peaceful purposes. Arthur C Clarke had foreseen the use of satellites for all means of communication very early on, and while not being the *inventor* of such satellites as is often claimed, he recognised the potential use of outer space. While Clarke continues to adopt a fence-sitters attitude on the subjects of UFOs and ET, we suggest that, like the masters, ACC was fully cognisant of the inconsistencies surrounding the Tunguska event in Russia, the Foo-Fighter lights in Europe, the increase of UFO sightings worldwide and also the Roswell Incident. As a scientist with many contacts throughout

the space club, no doubt Clarke would have been well aware of the necessity to establish surveillance satellites, as these events combined to push the space explorers into action. So each arm of the 'military octopus' had various and diverse reasons for pursuing the space program, depending upon the level of 'need-to-know' attributed to that particular arm, the same principals applying to the individuals involved. The military, both East and West, wanted to get out into space *fast*, in order to find out where, who, or what the ETs are. For everyone involved, the Moon was the logical first stop-over in this endeavour.

For the public it was to be the focus of exploration and the major prize in an artificial race *designed* to create the necessary tension that would ensure patriotic public support for the continual vital funding. With all these events in mind, the development of rocketry was the necessary first step in venturing beyond our atmosphere for a first look. In order to avoid the inevitable world-wide debates, confrontation and panic over the subject of ET, it was going to be necessary to carry out much of this research in relative privacy, behind closed doors. So it would be "absolutely essential" to draw the curtains and conceal the real reason for the exploration of space from the gaze of the world.

Western audiences were to be presented with the painted picture that decorated this iron curtain. A glamorous image of peaceful scientific space exploration would be depicted and ultimately paid for by this audience.

The Soviet Union had enough land to carry out space research without attracting the attention of its population. Communism as a regime, in conjunction with a leader such as Stalin, was enough to ensure that those involved would have little means or desire to share any inappropriate information that they might acquire. Korolëv had already served time in Stalin's prisons and would not wish to return to such a life. The Communist structuring of the USSR meant that the Soviet leaders did not need to justify their motives to their peoples. Nevertheless, the American political system had to pay lip service to public opinion. It would be necessary to establish the conquest of space as something with which the public could identify.

To this end in the US, NASA was promoted as a civilian space agency—an impression that many people retain to this day. NASA de-

> ### NASA questions
> Question: "What's the most difficult part of the flight?"
> Answer: "I guess the part between lift-off and landing."
> *Astronaut Gus Grissom*

volved from the National Advisory Committee for Aeronautics (NACA) which was established by Congress in 1915. *Space Age,* the companion volume to a PBS TV series produced in collaboration with NASA and the National Academy of Sciences stated that: "The Eisenhower administration called a halt to the arguments between the various branches of the military and research laboratories such as JPL as to who did what in space when it created NASA . . . *a new branch of the government".* (emphasis added) Its job would be: "To concoct a space policy out of the witches brew of these [the aforementioned squabbler's] plans."[1]

So it is clear, that NASA is the *result* of the gradual evolution of aeronautics in America—it was not simply conjured up out of thin air in response to the Soviet space activities—as is generally assumed and indeed asserted by many authors and space historians.

Never A Straight Answer

The National Aeronautics and Space Act of 1958, Public Law # 85-568, 72 stat. 426 was signed by the President on July 29 1958. Far from being a genuine civilian agency, the 1997 Encyclopaedia Britannica records that the National Aeronautics and Space Administration of the USA is an independent US Governmental Agency, established in 1958 "for the research and development of vehicles and activities for the exploration of space both within and outside the Earth's atmosphere". Quite how a government agency can be truly independent is a very interesting question!

NASA has five publicly-defined basic areas of research:

Aeronautics & Space Technology.
Space Science & Applications.
Space Flight.
Space Tracking & Data Acquisition.
Space Station Development.

The proponents of the civilian agency theory claim that due to the highly sensitive nature of many of its programs, NASA *collaborates* with agencies such as the Department of Defense (DOD), the National Security Agency (NSA) and the Central Intelligence Agency (CIA) as well as others. Statements from the enabling legislation of NASA indicate that the definition of "civilian agency" is not quite as clear-cut as people have been led to believe. In fact page 11, section 1, of the enabling legislation contains a sentence that is in direct contradiction to this notion:

The administration (NASA) shall be considered a defense agency of the United States.

Then, in later sections we find:

Section 203...3. [the administration (NASA) shall] provide for the widest practicable and appropriate dissemination of information concerning its activities and the results thereof.

This reads acceptably, until one realises that the definition of what is, or what is not practicable and appropriate is relative to the question of whether this agency actually has a civilian or defence status.

Section 206 (a). The administration [NASA] shall submit to the President for transmittal to Congress, semiannually and at other times as is deemed desirable, report [as] to its activities and accomplishments.

Section 206 (d). No information, which has been classified for reasons of national security shall be included in any report made under this section, unless such information has been declassified by, or pursuant to authorization given by, the President.

Section 304. The administrator shall establish such security requirements, restrictions and safeguards, as he deems necessary in the interests of national security.

The definition of NASA's purpose as an agency is once again of great interest.

Section 102 (a). The Congress hereby declares that it is the policy of the United States that activities in space should be devoted to peaceful purpose for the benefit of all mankind.

How do the projects 'Star Wars' (SDI) and HAARP fit with that statement?

Section 102 (b). The Congress declares that the general welfare and the security of the United States require that adequate provision be made for aeronautical and space activities.

There is the allocation of those millions of dollars. These constant references to security also hardly fit with the 'peaceful purpose' of the previous section.

The Congress further declares that such activities shall be the responsibility of, and shall be directed by, a civilian agency exercising control over aeronautical and space activities sponsored by the United States,

Do these salaries constitute sponsorship for the civilian agency, or does this mean that the person(s) providing the adequate provision /control for this agency shall be civilian?

Except that activities peculiar to, or primarily associated with, the development of weapons systems, military operation, or the defense of the United States (including the research and development necessary to make effective provision for the defense of the United States) shall be the responsibility of—and shall be directed by—the Department of Defense;

And here is the Department of Defense and the DOD men.

And that determination as to which such agency has responsibility for, and direction of any such activity, shall be made by the President, in conformity with section 201(e).

And that is a masterly example of how to have every which way covered!

Other sections of the enabling legislation published on July 29 1958 are also relevant to this issue. Section 206 (a) has the clause: "The

Administration [NASA] shall submit to the President, for transmittal to Congress, semi-annually and at other times as is deemed desirable, report [as] to its activities and accomplishments". However, further on we read (206 (d)): "No information which has been classified for reasons of national security shall be included in any report made under this section". In their innocence, the public have understood that the often-quoted clause "provide for the widest practicable and appropriate dissemination of information concerning its activities and the result thereof" actually *means* that NASA will convey whatever it learns. The two key words in this statement (from section 203 of NASA's enabling legislation) are "practicable" and "appropriate". The interpretation of both depend solely upon the decisions of the policy makers who govern the agency.

1. *Destination Moon* Produced by George Pal.

Dr. Donald's SFX trickery—
Part Seven

Before arriving in the United States, George Pal, born in Hungary in 1908, was trained as an architect in Budapest. Subsequently he worked as a set designer in Berlin before going to Eindhoven in Holland where he created animated advertising films for the electrical giant Philips. This company would be the inventors of, among other things, the audio cassette, the video cassette and the CD.

NASA's best Pal—America 1943

One of the pioneers in the field of stop motion photography, George Pal's combination of a yen for fantasy coupled with technique was an irresistible cinematic combination. George Pal's expertise in stop motion photography earned him a special Oscar in 1943, two years after his arrival in Hollywood. Pal went on to produce inventive sci-fi features using extraordinary special effects. Best known for the Oscar winning *War of the Worlds* in 1953, he also won Oscars for *Destination Moon* in 1950; *When Worlds Collide* in 1951, *Tom Thumb* in 1958 and *The Time Machine* in 1960.

The twin-like similarity of certain images in *Destination Moon* with some of the early NASA photographs is inescapable. In those days few people knew of Pal's close contact with what we now call NASA, but looking at Pal's choice of subject matter—mayhem and exploration in space, one cannot but help draw parallels with the outpourings of the 1990s in both cinema and TV: *Armageddon, Asteroid, Independence Day, Mars Attacks, Millennium,*

TechnoSpeak

Stop motion photography
is the art of filming scale models
against backgrounds which result in the model
looking 'real' and as if it is moving in a real setting.
This is done by filming one frame of the film at a time.
24 frames make up one second of the finished movie. The
technique requires a great understanding of model making, plus
perspective, scale, photography, the art of lighting . . . and patience.

248

Dollars

60 miles south-west of the Prague border of Czechoslovakia and Germany,
the Erzgebirge Mountains (the name means ore in English) have been mined for ore since the middle ages.
In 1516 a silver lode was found in the region of Joachimsthal, and Count von Schlick, the owner of the land,
immediately appropriated the mine.
Three years later he struck the first silver coins and called them the Joachimsthaler.
By 1600 the English version of that name had become shortened to 'dollar'.
The US dollar descends from the silver mines of Joachimsthal.

Destruction

In 1789 pitchblende was found in these mines and named uranium by its discoverer, Martin Klaproth.
In 1921 Robert Oppenheimer, then aged 17, visited the mine on a prospecting trip.
The nuclear bombs of America and the nuclear-powered space probes of NASA descend from
the silver mines of Joachimsthal.

GREED

In June 1943 General Groves of the Manhattan Project, believing that uranium ore stocks were extremely rare,
proposed that the USA attempt to acquire the rights to all known uranium ore deposits worldwide.[2]
Uranium ore is actually present in millions of tons of the Earth's crust.
All the silver dollars in America could not buy what they really wanted—total control of the world via nuclear force.

Stargate and so forth. It is the same old story with an updated picture on the cover. ■

The foundations of Camelot

The United States was the only nation in the post-war era that could possibly be seen to afford such a high budget operation as a manned space program. But the results were going to be worth every dollar, for if the Americans succeeded they would also have complete military domination of this planet and all its peoples. From that situation would flow enormous economic and political influence. All of this effort was directed from behind the scenes by the self-appointed masters. Just below the summit the monetary 'carrot' and the competitive 'stick' working at every level of this pyramid-style organisation.

Prior to the establishment of NASA, much thought had been given to the ideal structure for such an agency. An analysis undertaken by Kurt Stehling, a rocket research engineer for Bell Aircraft Corporation, Buffalo, New York concluded that the American space program personnel could be split into various groups. His views were presented at the Innsbruck International Astronautical Congress in 1954 by Frederick Ordway as Stehling was 'unable' to attend. We have added our own titles.

'knights of yaw'

The Stehling analysis began by summing up the potentials of the alliance between the American people and the 127 German rocket scientists.[3] This was one of the groups. There were problems associated with the incorporation of such a large group of top men from the most ruthless war machine to have roamed the Earth since Genghis Khan stormed across Asia. In many cases, the mostly ex-enemy German technicians and scientists had been the leaders of their discipline in their own country. The influence they exerted in the realm of advanced technology obviously would be considerable but there was concern that their managerial and political attitudes might leave something to be desired. After all, these scientists were used to wielding *absolute authority* and could be considered inclined to impatience when functioning within a democratic system that worked hand-in-hand with a public relations system.

So consequently, the recommendation was to employ these scientists but keep them out of sight, with the notable exception of Wernher von Braun, organiser and public relations man par excellence.

The American part of the rocket engineers and scientists could also be broken down into four groups.

'knights of roll'

The first group was the already established American aircraft engineers, designers and managers. Considered to be mature types, they were adept at co-ordinating complex multi-facility projects between the industrial aeronautical giants of the US and less given to impatience. As such they would exert a powerful influence.

'knights of pitch'

These men were elected to the ranks of the knights of pitch for their capabilities as promoters of the space program and it was from their ranks that the eventual successors to the knights of roll would be chosen.

Apart from their public relations role, were some of these men also "manipulators and appeasers"? Remember the situation during NASA Administrator James Webb's reign?

'knights of the log table'

The third group consisted of the younger engineers and physicists already working in the fields of rocket and jet propulsion research. These youngsters tended to be impatient with the slowness of public opinion and the principles of political expediency. However, their technical know-how meant that they would eventually emerge as the single most important group within the program.

Less inclined to hypocrisy and despite their innate belief in the possibilities of manned space travel, would all that change as their mentors from the first group prepared them for taking their place in the hierarchy? With the passage of time it would seem that this group has been absorbed by their elders.

'princes of the tower'

This fourth group consisted of future engineers and technicians who were still at school and college in the 1950s. By dint of their generation they considered space flight utterly achievable within their lifetimes and many of these students would become the theoreticians of the future.

Unfortunately, there are indications that many of these people by the 1990s, have suc-

Leg ends

Camelot. FOSS

Originating in the Arabic as a name for a costly Eastern fabric containing camel hair, by mediaeval times 'camelot' was used in Europe as a descriptive of substitute stuffs (firstly wool, silk and hair; later cotton and linen) used to SIMULATE the original Arabian fabric. In France to this day the word is used to describe rubbishy junk.
Also used as a slang word for merchandise.
"Faites voir votre camelote! = Let's have a look at your stuff!" The implication here being that the merchandise in question will not be up to much.

cumbed to the status quo of the academe of their respective sciences, which obviously played a major role in their educational development.

'peasants of the realm'

Finally, Stehling considered that the most significant group of people to be involved in the space program would be the American taxpayers—who would ultimately be paying for the trip! The public image promoted by the space program as a whole would be *the single most important factor in the development of space flight*. Therefore the more that budgetary allocations were in favour of the space program and the more that taxation increased as a consequence of the space program, the more the "advantages and possibilities" of the program had to be emphasised to the public.

Ostensibly then, NASA rose phoenix-like from the ashes of NACA. However, in the transferral process from military to civilian authority the accounts department seemed to have been left behind. On July 30 1958, the day after the enabling legislation was passed, President Eisenhower requested $125 million to initiate the National Astronautic Space Agency. On August 27 1958 he signed Public Law # 85-766 which included $80 million allocated to NASA:

$50 million for R&D;
$25 million for construction and expenses;
$ 5 million for salaries and expenses.

Whether the August figures are in addition to the initial $125 or instead of that July request is unclear. But we are speaking of a possible total of $205 million.
QUESTION: How many civilian or private sector corporations receive government funds for salaries and expenses?
QUESTION: If these budget requests were initiated a quarter of the way through a financial year and NACA was absorbed into NASA, what happened to the remains of NACA's funding for the financial year of 1958?

The kings were in their counting houses, counting out their money

The introspection generated by Stehling in the 1940s as to the structure of the American space program was a part of the bigger question of the day: who would be responsible for the construction of the vehicles that would eventually achieve orbital and space flight? At that time there seemed to be four available alternatives:

(1) The Army—managed as a continuation of the existing missile program.
(2) All services jointly—but run in parallel to the missile program, operating as a military program.
(3) A special agency—established specifically for the purpose (as was the Atomic Energy Commission for the nuclear industry, post Manhattan project). In the late forties, this possibility was considered less likely than the first two options.
(4) A privately capitalised operation— funded from a number of foundations,

industry, or even individuals.
Considered as a possible, but least likely option.

As it turned out, Stehling was not in the ball park. While the final definition of NASA appears to have been choice number 3, in fact most, if not all of these options have been exercised over the last fifty years. We suggest that as with the real purpose of the space program, perhaps no more than two dozen people worldwide would ever know precisely all the sources of the financing arrangements that were going to be necessary to support this new agency.

Swiss rolls

The analysis of the monetary juggling that went on across the planet at the end of the last war is worthy of a book in itself, and indeed several have already been written on this subject. Is it significant that in the 1990s, we have learned that funds deposited in the Swiss banks during WWII by Jewish and other individuals including refugees, corresponds to the amount of money that was spent by the American Apollo space program? Is it significant that when challenged for settlement by the rightful inheritors to these sequested accounts, the Swiss banks, after years of refusals, non-negotiation, denials and obfuscation have finally agreed to the principles of a settlement— but (at the time of writing) with the proviso that half the monies be spent in Switzerland?

Apart from the about-turn on the denial that this cash ever existed in their banks in the first place, this last condition surely reveals a vital point. The only way that the Swiss banks can fund a settlement is by making sure that the much of the cash remains within the Swiss economy—and *that* requirement surely indicates that the original monies have already been 'spent'. Were all these funds secretly dispersed during the war, on Hitler's projects? Or were some of them used to finance the beginnings of either the USA's or the Soviet's post-war rocket development program? The attitude of a majority in the Swiss Government during WWII was a clear demonstration of their abiding loyalty to *currency,* über alles. The Midas principle in Switzerland as profoundly entrenched as their bank vaults. So the fact that the Soviets had been fighting alongside the Allies, while the Swiss were supplying the Axis powers, would not have been an insurmountable ideological problem in the post-war period.

But the Swiss banks do not bear the guilt on their own for complicity with the Nazis. The Bank for International Settlement (BIS) worked with German money throughout the war. Moreover, its Assistant General Manager was a Nazi.[4] This bank had links with the Swiss National Bank through a chairman, Ernst Weber, who worked for both banks. The Swiss National Bank was the prime conduit for looted Nazi gold. Winston Churchill was well aware that there were British employees working in the BIS but Chamberlain chose to ignore the Germans' particular use of the BIS as a conduit for looted gold.

Bankers from America, France, Belgium, Italy and Japan were also involved in the BIS. A bank that ironically was originally set up to co-ordinate the financial reparation of *First* World War funds *from* Germany to the Allies, it is now emerging that British banks were also guilty of appropriating money from foreigners who had placed their savings in Britain before the war. At least £700 million has been frozen since 1945. After the war, refugees attempting to recover their funds were told that it had been confiscated. Indeed some of that money was 'given' to companies who had lost funds throughout the war years. Bankers are generally more concerned with money than morals but this sheer abuse of human rights, business *moeurs* and the trust between banker and client are almost beyond belief. Given such behaviour it would be unsurprising if some of this war loot, or the dividends thereof, did not eventually finance the on-going projects of the masters, either directly or indirectly.

Alternatively (or additionally) the gold available in the USSR could also have contributed to the funding base for the Soviet Moon space program in terms of buying-in technology that may be lacking in their country, for example computer equipment. Hidden from the public

and funnelled through the ultra-private facilities of the Swiss banking system, the allegedly neutral territory of Switzerland would be ideally placed for such money lending arrangements. Russia had always been at the top of the gold-producing table until the Californian gold rush of 1848. Stalin began an expansive gold program in 1927 and by 1937 the Soviet Union was the second major player in the gold-producing league. During the 1960s and '70s the true amount of gold produced was pretty much a state secret. If Soviet gold *was* used in part to finance or supplement their space program, then it is a supreme irony that their Chief Designer, the one man who could have achieved their objectives, was one of Stalin's slave labourers at the gold mines. Unlike the deep mining of South Africa, Russia's richest gold fields are mined by using enormous dredgers with mining procedures similar to those of Alaska.

Gold fingered

The solid fuel of the space program was in the spotlight in 1963 owing to a row between the London bullion dealers Samuel Montagu and the CIA.[5] What was significant about this conflict and why was it relevant to the space program? Samuel Montagu and the CIA were, at the time, arguing about a one-off year of gold production, and basing their conclusions on previous experience of Soviet gold mining. With the hindsight of the 1990s, a pattern is revealed that linked the movement of gold to the space programs of both the USA and the USSR.

Despite Lenin's opinion that gold should only be used to line the walls and floors of public toilets, Stalin and his successors used their gold production to buy foreign technology and also supplementary wheat when their own harvests were poor. The Soviet Union was the only non-aligned country in the world able to influence the free market price of gold through substantial sales. The West estimated that their gold production increased steadily over the decades, with a record high of 500 tons in 1957 (the year of Sputnik for those who like coincidences). Yet it was in 1963 that the CIA announced, rather contrarily, that Soviet production for that year had been reduced to the levels of 1940. The CIA had received their information from a spy who had allegedly advised Kennedy throughout the Bay of Pigs crisis—Colonel Oleg Penkovsky.[6] His information demonstrated that the Soviets were not merely selling their gold production but dipping into their reserves, as well. The end result was that gold sales to the West were halted in 1965 and not resumed in quantity until 1972—the intervening years, it is suggested, having been used to rebuild gold reserves back to acceptable levels.

Samuel Montagu, the London bullion dealers who worked closely with the Soviet gold market, disagreed and published their opinion on this CIA statement. There was an exceptional period of trade in the nine years between 1957 and 1965, during which time the Soviets sold almost $3 billion through the London, Zurich and Paris gold markets—a period which coincided with the main push of the space program. And within these nine years there were two other peaks in 1963 and 1965. Montagu's findings concluded that these sales were based on newly-mined gold.[7]

So what are *we* to conclude? Firstly, both pieces of information work together. The CIA *took it upon themselves* to alert the gold markets via their bulletin, that the Soviets were digging into their reserves. If we are correct about the level of complicity taking place between the two superpowers, were we meant to think, thanks to the CIA and Oleg Penkovsky's 'designed data', that the Soviets were using their gold production to refill their own reserves? This would ensure that nobody would enquire as to what had become of the gold that normally would have been produced over these years.

If Samuel Montagu are right, and clearly they would not take the trouble to fight publicly with the CIA over these results if they were not confident of their analysis, then the Soviets were exchanging vast amounts of gold at the very time that they required massive amounts of foreign technology to incorporate into their space program.[8]

It is our oppinion that these peak years of 1963 and 1965 reflected the changing nature of this program, thanks to Soviet scientific conclusions concerning radiation in space and their subsequent problems with the stability of their launchers. It is estimated that in total around $40 billion was spent by the USA on their own program (Apollo) and an equivalent amount of around $41.25 billion by the USSR—plus or minus $3 billion or so.

Pocket money

How NASA was meant to *generate* enough income from space projects to supply their needs is unclear and it is therefore absolutely logical that the agency should be funded by the government. But this then makes the NASA civilian agency profile absolutely redundant and explains the fact that Wernher von Braun's salary was paid by the US Government. WvB professed not to care about money, being devoted only to his rocketry, yet he found his government salary insufficient to supply the needs of his growing family. He supplemented this government income by allocating himself time from NASA to act as a consultant, journalist, speechmaker, and public persona, all of which activities commanded fees. And woe betide anybody who failed to pay WvB on time, they were soon informed as to their duties regarding prompt remuneration by the man who professed to care little for money. The publicly-popular WvB became so busy with these extra-curricular activities that NASA administrator James Webb had to step in and restrict the amount of time von Braun spent on these sidelines.[9]

Fool's gold

It is considered naive business practice to put all of one's own wherewithal into a new venture, more so if that venture has a high risk factor. A wise procedure is to persuade others to invest as well by selling them the 'idea'. The principle behind the funding of Apollo therefore was to extract much of the money from the American taxpayers via the Senate and Congress. Consequently this 'idea' of space travel had to be skilfully marketed and well

promoted, as Kurt Steh-
ling had already noted in
his analysis of the space
program. The key words
appear to have been:
"glamorous", "sexy",
"thrilling" and "relevant".
When NASA was ready to
put on the show, they
went public in a big way.
President Kennedy's May
1961 speech started the
countdown on a project
that had been covertly in
preparation for years. It
was time to up the stakes
and focus the interest of
the nation and the world,
on NASA.

President Kennedy's

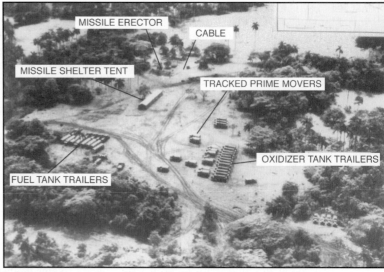

MISSILE ERECTOR
CABLE
MISSILE SHELTER TENT
TRACKED PRIME MOVERS
OXIDIZER TANK TRAILERS
FUEL TANK TRAILERS

2. Cuban crisis—overview of the missile site. CIA

now famous (one day per-
haps to be infamous) speech contained the often quoted words: "I believe that this nation
should commit itself, before this decade is out,
to landing a man on the Moon and returning
him safely to Earth". More significantly this
speech also contained these words, which are
less quoted: "No single space project in this
period [the 1960s] will be more exciting or
more impressive to mankind or more important for the long-range exploration of space..."
And here is the part of that sentence that is
hardly ever quoted: "...and none will be so
difficult *or expensive* to accomplish".
(emphasis added) And there you have it in a
nutshell. Hereby in effect NASA warned its
countrymen of *its insatiable appetite for
money.*

Showtime!

This situation having been accepted by both
politician and taxpayer, in September 1962 at
Rice University, Kennedy enlarged on his challenge of the previous year. He outlined the
need to be seen to be the best, to beat the 'enemy' (the Soviet Union) and to rise to the challenge of space exploration 'just because it was
there'. A week later, the tenor of this message
was reinforced when the script, or the 'dictates

of fate', brought about the Cuban missile crisis, thereby underlining the danger and the
closeness of the Soviet threat and the aptitude
of Kennedy's words.

Many mortals in the West at that time felt,
rightly or wrongly, that the survival of mankind was in the balance. While we all held our
breath and truly *knew* the precariousness of life,
with hindsight, *we never really knew if there
was actually anything beneath those 'missile'
shelter tents . . .*

Was this crisis just a show choreographed for
Western audiences? Oleg Gordievsky (the KGB
officer who spied for the West while in Moscow), during a 1985 interview, alleged that this
Krushchev/Kennedy confrontation was "barely
reported" in the Moscow press. And Penkovsky asserted that he had kept Washington up
to date at every stage of the Cuban crisis, thus
enabling Kennedy to act with confidence.
Surely more play acting. For if Moscow was
truly having a stand-off with the Americans the
Soviet press would have been profiting from
the occasion to remind their citizens of the
decadence and hostility of the West.

It is our assessment that these exercises were
mere window dressing, designed to emphasise
the East/West 'split' and to reap considerable
political and financial benefits. Proud of the

gung-ho stance their young President had taken towards that wily old fox from the Soviet Union, Nikita Krushchev, the patriotic American taxpayers (and the West in general) would warm towards the idea of beating the Soviets at *everything*. After this Cuban scenario, the embarrassment of the early space failures would be forgotten, the tardiness of the American response to Sputnik forgiven and public enthusiasm for the 'space race' would be assured. It is our understanding that the 'masters of infinity' were in fact not at all surprised at the early Soviet successes. These masters no doubt had calculated that successive shock waves of discovering that the 'peasants' had repeatedly beaten the American's space targets, followed by the subtle squeeze that would be added by accelerating political pressures of the Cold War, would ensure the necessary funding and motivation of an otherwise indifferent majority for the American space program. In their haste to catch up and even beat the Reds in this, as we believe, entirely staged race, the innocent guardians of America's wealth would unlock the lids of their financial coffers without any further ado.

Each country had items without which the space program would have been unsuccessful: the Americans their computer technology and modern materials; the Soviets their gold mines and their superior ability to put heavy loads into space in addition to the capability of functioning in quasi-privacy. As Clive James wrote in 1979: "The Soviet Government was able to isolate the space programme so that the genuine co-operative effort it entailed could not become too infectious".[10]

Arthur C Clarke said: "If there had been no confrontation between the United States and the USSR, and space technology had been driven by purely scientific and commercial considerations, the first landing on the Moon might still be decades in the future".[11] We could not have put it better ourselves. Create the tension required in order to stimulate the financiers into providing the funds to resolve matters. After all, nothing significant ever occurs without a situation of creative tension preceding the action. The outer face of the program was beating the Soviets to the "military advantage of the high ground of space". The inner face of the program was getting out to the Moon as the initial stage in reaching Mars—and this first phase of getting to the Moon had to be achieved *at all costs*.

Ironically, during the 1940s the Germans had thought the Americans too technically primitive to be capable of assembling an A-bomb. One decade later the Americans adopted a similar attitude towards the Soviets. Despite the fact that from the early 1950s the USSR was turning out two to three times more engineers and scientists than the American educational system, the Americans thought that a nation of 'peasants' could not achieve any major scientific breakthrough. Was this evaluation simply national arrogance, or was it a deliberately cultivated idea designed to reassure the populace—along with the majority of scientists—of the proponents' technological superiority? In any case, how does this arrogant attitude square with the apparent advance that the Soviets held over the US in the early post-war days of space exploration?

How could we, the authors, ever suggest that the Soviets and Americans were working together on this space program when they were in the throes of a political war, allegedly and potentially every bit as deadly as the World War which had preceded it?

The official Cold War between the USA and the USSR was started almost immediately after WWII and we have suggested that one reason for its inception was the need for deep cover for the space project. The idea of a 'space race' was of course further enhanced by the very deliberately competitive structure within the program. Within their own countries there was perpetual

---

The 1996 buzz word

"We must leave behind the Cold War mentality about space, when it was about beating the other side. I believe the Apollo program did actually help end the Cold War by proving that America's freedom allowed technological innovation that would always be denied the Soviets. However, space exploration must now be strictly commercial, not political."

Buzz Aldrin Focus magazine August 1996

competition for contracts. In America NASA operated as the arbiter of these matters. The Soviets attributed different tasks to different design bureaux and then set tight deadlines for producing the goods. Sometimes they also set different design bureaux onto the same project without indicating which bureau's efforts would eventually be selected.

Internationally, each country was then spurred on by ostensibly competing to be first in achieving an objective such as the "first man in orbit". Most of the administrators, scientists, engineers and technicians were not to know that at the very top, this 'race' was being monitored by the masters and that the pace was dictated by money. Using cash alternately as carrot and then stick, it was possible to keep both halves of the space program striving to achieve their next step. At the very highest level of the political tree there were hardly any barriers at all, while at many levels of the military structure there was indeed real enmity.

Within the scientific academe of both countries the barriers were positioned according to the 'need-to-know'. For the rest of the planet, the permanent threat of Armageddon in the post-war years was maintained by the warmongers and the sawmongers who thus kept all of us very much under tight social and economic control. For an alternative view on scientific relations between the two super powers the situation down south in Antarctica offers us significant insights.

While the rest of the world was frozen in the metaphorical icy grip of the Cold War, the scientists in the literally icy wastes of the Antarctic were pursuing joint studies into such realms as the ionosphere (the electrically-charged band which ranges from 40-60 miles above the Earth's surface). Even in those early years of the Cold War, the relations between the scientists of both nations were both cordial and frank and became increasingly so year on year.[13] These Antarctic studies were essential for the success of future space travel, be it with manned or unmanned craft. Not only would the Apollo phase benefit, but this information would provide some of the background to the DOD projects of the Strategic Defence Initiative (SDI, 'Star Wars') and Project HAARP.[14] Why should the situation have been any different because the information pertained directly to the space project?

Land ahoy!

It has been said that Eisenhower was more interested in space for peace rather than space for defence purposes. The use of small satellites such as Explorer 1 (discoverer of the Earth's radiation belts) was put forward as an example of such peaceful endeavours. The Americans claimed that such research was the exploitation of space "for all mankind"; and that they shared all of the relevant data with the scientists of the 1958 International Geophysical Year. Did the subsequent realisation regarding the true depth of the radiation belts therefore fall under the heading "irrelevant data" to such an extent that it has been generally suppressed to this day?

In fact Eisenhower was thoroughly briefed as to the importance of space in terms of reconnaissance satellites (Spysats) by an intelligence sub-committee led by the Harvard physicist and Nobel prize winner Edward Purcell. Also sitting on this committee was Edwin Land.

Land had been a personal advisor to every President from 1955 through to 1970. Why?

Watching the box

Through a series of technical developments in the UK, Europe, the Soviet Union and the USA, television had reached a state of technical feasibility by 1931.

TV had been broadcast post war on a regular basis from 1952 in the USSR (UK and USA in 1946).

Ten years before the West was allegedly able to broadcast over a comparable distance, the USSR was using satellites to link 6,836 miles/110,00 kms of its territory. The West's Telstar satellite was only activated in 1972 yet the West had launched enough military and NASA satellites to possess the capability for such a public service satellite well before 1972.

Apparently the will to do so was lacking. Why?

Was it necessary to wait until the end of the Apollo program before turning the public's attention on to the potential of satellite links?[12]

What did a manufacturer of polarising sunglasses (later to develop the Polaroid camera) possess that rendered him invaluable to four Presidents—namely Eisenhower, Kennedy, Johnson and Nixon?

Did the conditions of space photography necessitate a special camera that could *successfully take and develop pictures* in unknown territory when well away from home base? Remember the strange, unclarified references to the use of *polarising filters* on the Hasselblad lunar camera? There is of course nothing wrong with using a Polaroid camera but there is something wrong *if this was done*—as it has not been listed among the Apollo photographic equipment that was flown. Why not? Yet another commercial opportunity gone to waste this time by the Polaroid Corporation?

Purcell's special intelligence sub-committee formed one-third of a group which included a committee on *offensive* forces and another on *defensive* forces. This triumvirate was chaired by James Killian, the president of Massachusetts Institute of Technology (MIT) and was initially called the Surprise Attack Panel (SAP). The group was then given the more covert, stinging title of the Technological Capabilities Panel (TCP).

Land and Killian delivered the results of their findings to Eisenhower personally and, for security reasons, some of it only verbally.[15] The fact that their recommendations were followed by subsequent White House administrations can be seen by analysing the satellite programs in detail. (Which would take up more room than we have at our disposal here.) How closely then were these recommendations of the offensive and defensive committees followed? Even after the formation of NASA late in 1958, the armed forces of the United States were still battling amongst themselves for supremacy in the internal race for dominance of "the new frontier"—"the high ground of space", to employ the clichés used at the time by the space industry and their politicians. None of the services had won the battle for space—officially. The public perception of the new space agency as civilian *implied* independence from the armed forces and secret services.

Far horizon

Over at ABMA in Huntsville, where WvB and his team were still ensconced, a feasibility study that was to be later known as Project Horizon was undertaken at the instigation of von Braun's superior General John Bruce Medaris on March 20 1959.[16] The primary objective of this incredibly ambitious plan was stated to be nothing less than the establishment of a military outpost on the Moon. Project Horizon proposed that: "Space, or certainly that portion of space encompassing the Earth and the Moon (sic) will be treated as a military theater". And in the establishment of this plan, what, might we ask once again, happened to the proviso made only a year before, "that space shall be used only for peaceful purposes"?

In January 1963 some of the named astronauts at NASA were given specific duties over and above their standard training. When we look at these duties combined with their designated Apollo mission an interesting picture emerges. We see a program concerned with testing various stages of a space project in which the objective of walking on the Moon is a mere detail set against the overall objective of reaching Mars and claiming "The Golden Fleece".

The fact that the Moon was just a staging post in the process of getting to Mars, is yet another reason why mankind has not attempted to return there since the days of Apollo. As for our satellite the Moon, it is poorly served by the very people who attempt to wax eloquently over the exploration of our solar system. The Treaty on Principles Governing the Activities of States in the Exploration and Use of Outer Space was signed by over 60 countries during LBJ's Presidency. Among the conditions established by this treaty were the guaranteed safe return of any astronaut to the "country of origin *designated by his spacecraft*"—which leads to some interesting thoughts on the equivalence of the 'Panamanian flag syndrome' prevalent on our terrestrial seas; no land claims would be allowed on any planet, including the Moon; outer space would always be a non-military zone; no country would declare any part of any orbital zone around Earth as its own territory.

In his novel *3001: The Final Odyssey* Arthur C Clarke describes using the Moon as a dump for dangerous viruses, both bacterial and mechanical. Given the paranoid nature of the military, surely at some stage the area between the Earth and the Moon would be considered as a zone in need of protection. In much the same way that the scientific communities are choosy about who goes to Antarctica, the need to 'protect these dumps' would require a defence mechanism. In this way space and the Moon would in fact become a militarised zone in direct contradiction to the Space Treaty. A Whistle-Blower, close enough to the military to require anonymity, has informed us that using the Moon as a waste dumping ground is *still being considered very seriously.* Indeed, with the subsequent alleged behaviour scripted into the Apollo missions, it is obvious that officially, it is perfectly all right to dump rubbish (including nuclear reactors) in Earth orbit, elsewhere in the magnetosphere and on the Moon. And it may not have been written into

Astronaut task assignments—1963		
Program/Function	Astronaut	Apollo mission
Mercury		
Pilot phase	Cooper	
Pilot phase	Shepard	'Apollo 14'
Gemini		
Pilot phase	Grissom	Apollo 1 decd.
Apollo		
Pilot phase	Glenn	
Flight Control Systems	White	Apollo 1, decd.
Elec & Mission planning	See	Plane crash, decd.
Lunar Excursion training	Carpenter	
Launch Vehicles	Borman	'Apollo 8'
Recovery Systems	Lovell	'Apollo 8' & 'Apollo 13'
Guidance & Navigation	McDivitt	Apollo 9
Communications	Stafford	'Apollo 10'
Trainers & Simulations	Armstrong	'Apollo 11'
Cockpit Layout	Conrad	'Apollo 12'
Environmental Control & Survival Equipment	Young	'Apollo 16'

Project Horizon dated March 20 1959 *Staging posts*	*Projected timeline*	*Realised timeline*
1) Unmanned satellite projects by	1900s (mid)	1950s
2) Ballistic flights with animals on board by	1950s	1950s
3) Ballistic flights with astronauts on board by	1960s	1960s
4) Satellites with astronauts on board by	1960s	1960s
5) *Space rescue* systems established by	1970s	1970s
6) Simple orbiting stations by	1970s	1970s
7) Shuttle-type Earth to orbit transport by	1970s	1980s
8) *Unmanned* flights to the Moon by	1960s	1960s
9) *Manned* landing on the Moon by	1965	1969 (alleged)
10) *Lunar outpost* deployed on the Moon by	1966/7	Annulled
11) Elaborate space stations in orbit by	1980s	Late
12) Expeditions to Mars (unmanned) by	1960s	1970s-'90s
13) Expedition to Mars (manned) by	2001	Annulled

this treaty but tacitly, it is obviously acceptable behaviour to dump rubbish throughout the solar system. It should not be the thought of meteorites smashing into Earth that keeps NASA and its counterparts awake at night. It should be the fact that by the time they have learned to get out into deep space safely, they will have virtually barred the way with their own ever increasing space-junk belt.[17]

The military principles of Project Horizon were hidden within a program of planetary exploration, and although Project Horizon was not *officially* adopted as an army program, it *is* up and running, for this is the twin package that became the American space program, or more accurately this planet's space program.

The secondary objective of Project Horizon was to achieve the actual go-ahead for the establishment of their Mars outpost and thus retain an active US Army interest in space exploration. By extension it was hoped that this would keep the services of the von Braun 'Rockettes' uniquely within the US Army's structure. Apparently WvB's tactics during the inter-services battle for supremacy reflected his personal ambitions rather than any moral disapproval of army outposts on the Moon. Yet it has been said that he kept his distance from Project Horizon, although that must have been quite a feat, for several reasons.[18] Firstly, von Braun was not the sort of person who would let such a major issue slip out of his control.

Secondly, it embraced nearly all of his own theories concerning space travel. And thirdly, the project was being created by members of his own team, Dr. Hermann H Koelle and the Future Projects Office staff, assisted by the Army Technical Services, the Army Ordnance and the Army R&D departments.

David Baker states that Medaris' plan drew heavily on WvB's thinking and that it read "like a compendium of WvB's articles published in *Collier's* magazine in March 1952".[19] In the 1997 book *The Day After Roswell* by Colonel Corso we are given a peek at some fifty-four pages from a four volume document of 808 pages. From which we see that the main thrust of Project Horizon was the requirement of 149 Saturn rockets just to build the lunar outpost and then, from 1964 through to 1967, a further 229 Saturn launchers would be needed to ferry the equipment and provisions to a lunar base designed for twelve men.

If we look at this plan and compare it with what has been presented to the world, we can see that the program appeared to begin slowing down as soon as it reached stage ten—which is of course, when NASA & Co. experienced problems that remain unsolved to this day. The seed of Project Horizon *must* have been sown by the late 1940s. In order to arrive at stage ten it was necessary to pass through stages 1-9. Unfortunately this acorn has not produced a mighty oak, for in the 1990s these manned

---

Silence is golden

Project Horizon (US Army) was dated March 20 1959.
Conceived under the aegis of General John Medaris and Lt General Arthur G Trudeau, Chief of R&D,
it stipulated a budget of $6bn over 8 ½ years.
Project Horizon was declassified on September 21 1961,
only to be *reclassified CONFIDENTIAL* on June 13 1962.[20]

---

mission problems remain unresolved, as we have seen. It has *only* been possible to leap-frog to twelve—because bio-organisms are not required on the trip.

Back at the ranch

The internecine plotting and planning continued and the third motive for proposing Project Horizon seemingly failed when, in the summer of 1960, President Eisenhower removed von Braun and his 'Rockettes' from the Army Ballistic Missile Agency and dispatched them to NASA. Not that they actually had to move shop, they simply changed the sign over the door.

Outranked by the Secretary for Defense, von Braun's Redstone team worked under the new banner of NASA's Marshall Space Flight Center. WvB, however, did not go quietly in the direction of the good life. Having already won one battle to keep his Huntsville team within the US Army's structure, he was furious at being obliged to re-address this issue. However, that was probably more huffing and puff-

ing, for although space technology R&D had effectively been put into the hands of NASA, in practical terms this step tied NASA to the DOD men and von Braun's team continued to play an active role in army missions.[21] Outwardly there was a difference—for they were now obliged to wear civilian clothes. More double standards to co-ordinate with the double breasted suits of these men in black. The space historian Heppenheimer commented on the makeover with a significant and beautifully crafted sentence: "von Braun himself would now report to officials in mufti for the first time since joining the Reichswehr in 1932"—yet he would continue to draw a government pay check!

Before we get carried away by these conflicts of interest, it should be remembered that in America these policy makers only had one group of people capable of manufacturing the rocket hardware necessary for *both* programs: Wernher von Braun and his team. The separation of NASA from the ICBM program was not only an exercise in public relations but also a desire to keep the ICBM program on track. Consequently the cosmetic removal of these people from ABMA to NASA was just that—cosmetic.

The reading room

At the time of Sputnik, there was some suggestion that the Americans 'surprise' at the advance of the Soviet space effort was due to a lack of awareness of the advanced state of Soviet technology as evidenced by the technical literature emanating from the USSR during the late 1950s and early '60s. There were few Russian translators

3. Wernher von Braun and his German Mercedes at NASA in 1961.   NASA

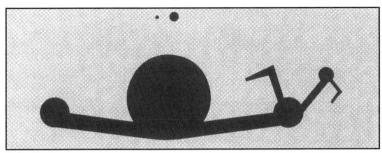

4. Snail's Pace.
Representation of the 1992 snail Crop Glyph, activated in Alton Barnes, England. DODMAN is the Old English word for snail. Langley is the USA home of space and spies—the Department of Defense are DOD men!

Korolëv was most certainly pointing out two major problems that had been encountered by both the Soviets and Americans—the difficulty of launching the required weight into space from the Earth's surface and the exceedingly difficult procedures surrounding both entry into lunar orbit and tsubsequent re-entry into the Earth's atmosphere.

and even fewer scientists in the West could read the language. The number of Russian-language journals subscribed to by the US Library of Congress numbered 2,000 in 1957 but only 30 of these were ever translated. During the same period the Soviets were monitoring 8,000 journals worldwide, of which 1,500 were from America and 1,000 from Britain. The in-depth discussions on the challenges of space travel featured in these Russian journals was often the result of years of research by highly qualified experts. The sheer quality and quantity of these articles were light-years ahead of the Western scientific press.[22]

Indeed the nation of 'peasants' were not quite so cabbage-like as they were green looking, for in October 1957 plans for a 1,700 ton Earth-Mars spaceship together with all the necessary calculations on the travel timing of such a craft had been established. Even before the Soviet lunar project, Korolëv had developed a plan to launch a cosmonaut to orbit around Mars. Korolëv intended to create an artificially low gravity, and use a closed-loop life support system for the cosmonaut's 24-36 month journey. In one paper a certain Professor K Sergeyev had also stated that whilst it was technically feasible for the Soviets to undertake a Moon program, he felt that permanent space stations in Earth orbit and methods of re-entry into the Earth's atmosphere were of higher priority at that time. Professor K Sergeyev was actually the pen name of Sergei Korolëv. Whether or not he was publicly reiterating the role of the USSR within in the masters' space program,

Digging deeper

Apart from the photographic evidence discussed in the preceding chapters, there are only two other categories of evidence supporting the complete success of NASA's manned return trips to the Moon. These are the geological samples supposedly gathered from the lunar surface and the moonwalkers' personal statements. This testimony consists of the sound (allegedly transmitted with the 'live' TV images back to Earth) and their 'post-lunar' statements. We have demonstrated that the photographic material as such can be pre-created or simulated and that alone, is not irrefutable proof that the named Apollo astro-

---

Apples and pears

The Soviet news agency TASS provided that nation's news. Non-communist party members were not allowed to work on Soviet TV news programs.

The Soviet news broadcasts were always designed to reflect a 'positive' attitude in order that people felt happy (thus keeping a tightly controlled society 'up' through a sense of its well being).

This approach was in high contrast to the Western news services which were (and still are) generally of the 'doom and gloom' variety (thus tending to keep an apparently free society 'down').

The results of these two methods are exactly the same: manipulated world opinions controlled by governments via their media.[23]

---

nauts ever arrived on the lunar surface. We have also offered overwhelmingly practical reasons as to why these Apollo mission records may have had to be faked. With nearly thirty years of hindsight, it would be hard for us not to suggest that the entire lunar exploration program has been limited to the installation of several pieces of scientific equipment on the lunar surface and the return to Earth of some soil and rock samples for analysis—all of which could have been handled by unmanned probes. The Soviets have more than adequately demonstrated the possibilities of both surface and sub-surface automatic soil extraction and both the Soviet and American space agencies have seemingly mastered the art of sending unmanned probes to the Moon and Mars.

Rocks on the box

Prior to the latter-day space program, no human being had ever wittingly seen or handled a mineral from our satellite, the Moon. Therefore whatever NASA produced as such would tend to be accepted as the genuine article. As NASA and its Soviet associates were (and still are) the only people able to collect lunar samples we simply had (and have) no other means of comparison.

As geologist Sir Malcolm Brown wrote:

Recognition of the significant advances in our understanding of the Moon must be tempered by an awareness of their limitations. We have only scant knowledge of the subsurface structure and of the surface compositions beyond the near-side equatorial region. Knowledge of the cratering and volcanic events and their time span is *chiefly based on analysis of the returned samples*.[24] (emphasis added)

As is the case with the photographic images and the TV coverage, the only information in our possession concerning the nature of the lunar surface is what NASA *chooses* to give us. Again, as all their *imaging* has demonstrated manipulation, then what are the odds that this further information has either been compromised or faked?

Sir Malcolm penned his observations at a time when NASA had cancelled the unmanned Lunar Polar Orbiter mission, formulated in 1972. He confidently expected that the interest expressed by the USA, the USSR and Japan in exploiting the possibilities of unmanned orbiters and lunar landers was genuine. Innocent in the ways of the space agencies, he expected them to continue their lunar research and eventually establish a manned base on the Moon. Sir Malcom wrote further:

Man has the knowledge, experience and facilities to inhabit an accessible environment beyond the Earth—that environment is the Moon. It is still an object of controversy and therefore still an object of interest.[25]

Whatever the scientific community's hopes and opinions, NASA dropped the Moon from its list of missions to accomplish rather like the proverbial hot potato. After 1972, its part in lunar exploration outwardly ceased. The Soviets, in the meantime, continued to send probes to the Moon, officially as late as August 1976. It is our opinion that Sir Malcolm, along with the rest of the world, has been duped concerning the capacities of NASA and its scientific teams. For it is *certain* that during the run-up to Apollo the masters had realised that none of them had the knowledge or facilities to safely visit and return from, let alone to inhabit, its nearest neighbour in space.

Humpty Dumpty and the fall

As late as 1964 the Moon was little understood and even now, with the benefit of more than thirty years of space research, scientists have no wholly satisfactory theory to explain the origins of the Earth/Moon system.

Before 1969 most American scientists were divided into two camps, known as 'Cold Mooners' (supporting the 'impact' theory of origin from deep space) and 'Hot Mooners' (believing that the Moon's features had been formed by volcanic activity). By July 1969 most geologists involved with Apollo were taking positions that accommodated both impact and volcanism. They did not, however. acknowledge this state of affairs by calling

suggests that they are considerably older and of different composition to those on Earth. The Moon contains about 50% more iron and about 50% more refractory elements than the Earth's mantle.

The *capture theory* stated that the Moon was formed somewhere else in our solar system and somehow became drawn into Earth's gravity. This theory gained increasing favour among scientists. Such a captured body however, would need to have been uniquely placed for 'Earth seizure'.

... this is now

But never fear, NASA is here! We are informed that after analysis of samples returned from the Moon by the Apollo astronauts (or by remote probe) scientists concluded that no proof existed to support *any* of the three theories we have outlined and came up with yet another explanation. In another giant leap for mankind they called it the *giant impact theory* (GIT). By the 1990s, most scientists have either been won over, succumbed to peer pressure or have even been nagged into accepting this new theory as the 'official' version of how the Moon came to be.

This GIT theory very conveniently solves the angular momentum problem which invalidated the fission theory. The GIT theory states that a body with 0.1 the mass of Earth but the size of Mars (4,224 miles diameter) had a near tangential impact with the Earth. The enormous amount of energy liberated by this impact vaporised and crushed the surface of both bodies. This dual surface debris was ejected into space

themselves the 'Lukewarm Mooners' They sat astride the two theories while secretly expecting their opponents to be smashed by the weight of evidence to be returned from the 'Apollo 11' mission.

So let us look at some of the scientific thinking on the Moon's origins.

That was then ...

The *binary planet theory* stated that the Moon was formed at around the same time as the Earth and that it consisted of flying space debris consolidated into a mass. Since the analysis of actual measurements from the Moon this theory became less popular. For it to be wholly viable the Earth and Moon would need to possess the same *density*—and they do not.

The *fission theory* first proposed in 1879 by the mathematician, Sir George Darwin, stated that during its early formative time, Earth was spinning so fast, that part of the equator 'broke' off, settled into orbit and became our Moon. This theory has been shown to be invalid because:

1) The orbital details of the Moon do not correlate to this model, the *angular momentum* of the Earth/Moon system does not support rotational fission.

2) Analysis of returned of rock and soil samples, purporting to have come from the Moon,

Physics—2 out of 12

Al Bean of 'Apollo 12' wondered what the function of the Moon was.

If it was just to make the tides, he thought that the Earth would probably get on fine without them.

This unfortunate comment shows a complete lack of understanding of even the basics of our solar system and a quasi-total ignorance of the place to which the named Apollo astronauts allegedly travelled.

But we cannot blame him,

he was only a rocket rider after all.

and remained in orbit around the Earth. Eventually the two kinds of debris combined and thus formed the Moon.

A computer simulation of this event has demonstrated that between 10% to 20% of the impacting body would be engendered by the *Earth's* mantle, the remaining percentage would belong to the *impactor's* mantle. It was also estimated that this moon would be formed from the hot debris in about 20 hours and would in fact be mostly molten, as would the impacted crust of Earth.

The fact that this proposal is based on an analysis of rocks and soil taken from a very limited portion of the Moon's surface is, in our opinion the shortcoming of this theory. These rocks are not necessarily an accurate representation, or sample, of the entire lunar body and the soil-sample probes (Soviet) have dug, at the most, about two metres into the surface. Is this enough to give scientists an accurate analysis of the entire lunar sphere?

QUESTION: As we have samples of lunar material containing elements completely unknown on Earth and of ages far older than our planet and indeed older than the entire solar system, how did this initially molten, mixed together, ejected material manage to sort itself out into neat and distinct packets labelled 'Earth' and 'Moon'?

It is interesting to see how the NASA version of lunar geology has varied over the years during which the GIT hypothesis was taking hold. Let us take the example of Moon quakes. Based on data obtained from NASA, the first reference books published following the Apollo

missions, and revised in 1993, indicated that rare moonquakes occur some 31-186 miles below the surface of the Moon. These quakes are strong but less intense than Earthquakes. There are also numerous moonquakes at a depth of 496-620 miles, seemingly triggered by lunar tides occurring at perigee (the Moon's nearest orbital position to Earth). This NASA data apparently provided information for the structure of the Moon's interior:[26]

- A dry, porous lunar crust of around 37 miles depth.
- A mantle of at least 682 miles.
- A core approximately 745 miles in diameter. This core is considered by some scientists to be partially molten.
  (Others do not think that the Moon has a core at all.)

However in 1995, the science writer for the UK *Daily Telegraph* and columnist for *Astronomy Now* advises us that the Moon is utterly silent and inert with no seismic readings whatsoever. Of course we must assume that Adrian Berry is accurately reporting the information available to him when he writes:[27]

Experiments left behind by the Apollo astronauts showed that, seismically, the Moon is absolutely quiet. There are no 'moonquakes' to disturb the ground.

Now that is indeed interesting. Ignoring (for the moment) exactly how said experiments were set up on the lunar surface, either NASA is supplying two totally different accounts concerning the activity of the lunar sphere; or the Moon has entirely stopped emitting quakes *of*

Nots landing

In 1996 on the *Art Bell* radio talk show in the US Ed Mitchell of 'Apollo 14', was keen to describe his landing spot on the lunar surface.[28]

"Let's pin down *exactly* (his word our emphasis)...if you look up at the full Moon, right in the centre (both vertically and horizontally centre) and just to the left and down (left 15° down about 3°) you get the area that we are talking about.
We were just to the east of the Apollo 12 mission, *we were a couple of hundred miles apart, or maybe a little more.*
Our area of investigation was about a mile (or maybe a mile and a half long) and maybe a hundred yards wide."
As Ed Mitchell must remember, the 'Apollo 14' designated landing site was 17°28′ W and 3°40′ S. It was 5°55′ to the east of the 'Apollo 12' designated landing site and to within 29′ of the same latitude. The distance between the two landing sites is just over 100 miles *NOT* 200 hundred plus. So much for Ed Mitchell's accuracy.
But then, Ed Mitchell also said that even in 1971, he couldn't remember what it *felt like* to land on the Moon.[29]

any sort since the era of Apollo, indeed since 1993!

Volcanic rumblings

We are also advised that the *mare* basalts had shown that the lunar mantle had once been geologically alive but that these maria only covered 17% of the lunar surface and that the samples returned to Earth covered *a very limited portion* of the Moon's timescale. So they agree with us that the sample area is tiny. However, if NASA asserts (as they do) that they have rocks nearly as old as the solar system's age of 4.6 billion years; if they also assert (as they do) that this is a 'very limited portion' of the Moon's *timescale*—then there is a very important deduction to be made: NASA is aware that the Moon is much, much older than our solar system.

QUESTION: Why have NASA not openly announced that the Moon is older than the solar system? For the agency to know this information, they must either:

• Already have in their possession (or be aware of Soviet lunar analysis) rocks and/or soil which *are much older than 4.6 billion years.*

• Or, they know this fact by some other means.

Others as we shall see, claim that NASA have rocks at least as old as 5.3 billion years. Yet, instead of discussing this matter, their scientists have established a theory—GIT—based on, by their own admittance, very limited data.

As the backbone of this theory is that the Earth was impacted by a very large celestial body, it is interesting to observe in the late 1990s the ever-increasing media emphasis relating to meteorites and other perceived threats from 'out there'. Hold that thought!

The mare (or maria) are large dark basins on the near side of the Moon which have been flooded by internally generated basalt lava. They contrast vividly with the pale-coloured highland regions, which consist of feldsparic-breccia (mountains of pulverised rock). The far side of the Moon has very few mare regions. Sir Malcolm Brown considers that this effect is due to the crust being thicker on the far side (63 miles/101kms) compared with the near side thickness of approximately 41 miles/66kms. But instead of this difference of 22 miles between hemispheric crusts, NASA states there is a difference of only six to nine miles!

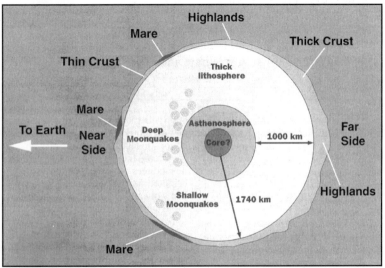

5. Interior of the Moon depicting variations in Crustal thickness between near and far sides.

The *regolith* of pulverised boulders and dust that make up the surface of the Moon, has apparently yielded only three components[30]

1) Primitive highland crusts.
2) Mare basalts.
3) Extra-lunar meteoritic particles.

Interestingly, Malcolm Brown records that:

Considering the amount of cratering on the near side, the meteoritic particle contribution is remarkably low, at about 1-2% of the fine-grained regolith.

Brown concludes that larger meteoritic bodies were vaporised on impact and lost, due to the low gravity of the Moon which allowed any remaining particles to escape.

Cratering sizes range from circular basins, thousands of miles in diameter, to micron-sized pits which cover all the upper rock surfaces. There are also very interesting twin craters; two craters of a fairly uniform size which occur, over and over again, looking nearly like figures of eight.

Andrew Chaikin writes that they *did not find* what they wanted to find (the volcanic rocks). What they discovered were rocks that turned out to be "clods of dirt that fractured in their hands and in the sample bag". The script indicated that John Young "almost tripped up over a white rock that sparkled in the sunlight...*it was certainly not volcanic*". This was certainly very clever of him. How would he see the "sparkle" with his gold visor down? And if he almost tripped up, then the rock was right under his feet. As the astronauts could not even look down to see the camera lens on their chests (according to Hasselblad) then how could he see down to his toes, with all his gear on?

The Rocks they allegedly found on that trip were "breccia, and more breccia". Mattingley (allegedly in the CM) "looked at the bright highlands and *didn't feel* that they were volcanic". All that training for such a *nice, non-scientific* statement! "But he knew that cameras didn't make mistakes and that the *true* story would be in the pictures". (emphasis added)

Willard White's crock of rock

The named cast of 'Apollo 17' were also credited with photographing and sampling North Ray Crater. We saw the TV camera pan around

6. Claimed lunar rock sample.   NASA

7. Whitewash, or House Rock near to the location picture (8) where Schmitt was photographed walking towards the 'sun'.   NASA

8. Off to see the wizard? Schmitt, strolling near the NASA
House Rock location. While he was filled-in with extra light,
the foreground rocks were left unlit.

the eastern rim of the crater and it was near there that they found what came to be called 'House Rock'. This was a boulder as high as a four storey house, and twice as long as it was high. Apparently, it was this particular discovery that killed the volcanic thesis stone dead. We could also surmise that this was dubbed 'House Rock' as it thus reflected the in-house policy—whether that of the White House or NASA's HQ, is your choice. We have chosen another name for this piece of set dressing and called it the 'Whitewash' Rock (7).

From the information gleaned from the author Chaikin however, we could conclude that the 'Apollo 17' script was *specifically written* to scotch the theory that there had been any volcanic activity on the lunar surface. After all, no volcanic rocks on the surface, means no volcanic activity has taken place on the Moon. Which point contradicts the opinions of eminent geologists such as Sir Malcolm Brown.

A Horz complex

In 1995, we were informed of caverns under the lunar surface. NASA scientist Frederick Hörz, thought that caves caused by lava

flows could serve as shelters for future lunar bases. Most caves on Earth have been created by the action of water, but some, such as those in Iceland and Hawaii, are volcanic in origin, like the Moon's caves, despite the specially-written 'Apollo' 17 script. In fact another NASA scientist Bevan French, affirmed that the Moon has had a volcanic past and that to-day the signs of this activity are evident even upon the surface in the form of twisting channels—called lava tubes or 'Rilles'.[31]

QUESTION: The Lunar Orbiter craft, whose program ran from August 1966 through to January 1968, had already imaged these lunar caves. So why then did NASA go to such pains to write the No Volcanic Rocks script back in 1972?

QUESTION: Did the timescale that these volcanic caverns indicated contravene the 're-quired' 4.6 billion years age of our solar system?

QUESTION: Was there photographic evidence (such as artificial-looking craters) that indicated that the Moon was *not* a 'virgin' never-before-visited-planet?

QUESTION: Why did NASA's tune change between 1969 and 1972 and then again since 1972, concerning this vulcanism?

The prop department

The NASA probes (and allegedly the named astronauts) are said to have brought back a total of 838lbs/380kg of rocks and soil samples from the lunar surface. These samples are said to originate from the sites at which the Apollo missions officially landed.

At various NASA facilities there existed simulated lunar surfaces, created by trucking in appropriate quantities of several types of dust and soil. Interior sets, one appropriately called

Rocks in the box			
'Apollo 11'	47.7 lbs:	Sea of Tranquillity	Jul 16/24 1969
'Apollo 12'	075.7 lbs:	Ocean of Storms	Nov 14/24 1969
'Apollo 14'	094.4 lbs:	Fra Mauro	Jan 31/Feb 9 1971
'Apollo 15'	169.0 lbs:	Hadley-Apennine	Jul 26/Aug 6 1971
'Apollo 16'	208.3 lbs:	Descartes Highlands	Apr 16/27 1972
'Apollo 17'	243.1 lbs:	Taurus-Littrow	Dec 7/19 1972

'The Moon Room', were also filled with moon-type rocks.[32]

NASA certainly had access to facilities for the manufacture of simulated Moon materials. Laboratories that specialised in the study of such matters as high-speed impacts, would have been able to employ their technology to simulate the micro-meteorite bombardment of the lunar surface. By the mid 1960s in fact, the University of London, England had already simulated lunar surface materials. Obviously their information was from a source other than the Apollo astronauts.

In 1977, Whistle-Blower Bill Kaysing viewed documentary material on the NASA Ceramics Laboratory. From what he learned, it was evident that such a facility would have been *ideal* for the creation of any amount of extra-terrestrial geological specimens; be those 'moon rocks' or 'martian meteorites' for that matter.

A few months before his untimely death in 1978, the well known American investigative journalist Paul Jacobs, interviewed the Head of the US Geological Survey Department in Washington DC. Jacobs asked him for his views on the Moon landings in general and the lunar rock samples in particular. When he reported his interview to Kaysing, Jacobs said that he received some very cryptic answers. The geologist had assured him that the rocks were real. But when Paul Jacobs said: "If they weren't real and you were in on the hoax, you would still attest to their reality, wouldn't you?"—the geologist just smiled.

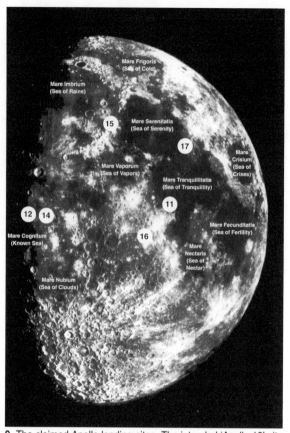

9. The claimed Apollo landing sites. The intended 'Apollo 13' site was identical to the 'Apollo 14' location.   LICK OBSERVATORY

University challenge

Members of the production team on *200:1: A Space Odyssey* visited the laboratories of the University of London in Mill Hill, Hertfordshire UK (a short distance from the studios) to obtain advice on models of the lunar surface. There they inspected the lab's simulated lunar surface materials.

Continuity and make-up

According to the seemingly 'authorised' accounts of the Apollo record, some of the biggest problems for the NASA scientists concerning the analysis of the rocks and soil from the Moon missions were that:

- Many of these rocks did not meet with the expectations of the geologists, either by their composition, or their age, or indeed the places in which they were found. In fact, we are advised that when the scientists recovered material from one specific site, they were astonished that the expected type of rock was conspicuous—only by its absence!

- Some of the maria (seas) turned out to be astonishingly uniform in their levels: varying by only 490ft/149m in height over distances of 370 miles/595 kms.

- The highland rocks were rich in aluminium and calcium, while the maria appeared to be richer in titanium, iron and magnesium.
- The lunar samples contained neither water nor any trace of organic material. While they did contain more *titanium* than a comparative basalt rock from Earth, they also contained less sodium and other elements of the volatile type.

All this information could be obtained from unmanned probes. If one were subsequently manufacturing rocks to order, one could create whatever model was required, and to adjust the compositional balance would be a reasonable possibility—thereby allaying any suspicion from Doubting Thomas and his friends that these samples were faked.

The discovery of unexpected anomalies in the lunar geological sampling of the 1960s threatened all the currently received theories concerning the genesis of the Moon. Instead of engaging in public debate by detailing these puzzle pieces, it appears that NASA has elected to keep their problems 'in house'—thus depriving many scientists throughout the world of a chance to contribute to a genuine debate.

NASA officially recognised the oldest Moon rock to be no more than 4.5 billion years BP.[33] Yet according to the reputed astronomical periodical *Sky & Telescope,* the Fourth Lunar Science Conference held in March 1973 revealed that one of the Moon rocks had given a reading of 5.3 billion years BP.

That is astonishing enough.

But the potassium-argon dating system (the isotopic dating system accepted by science as being the most accurate at that time) gave a reading of between 7 billion years and 20 billion years for some of the Moon rocks from the 'Apollo 12' samples.

That span is *four times* the age of our solar system.

NASA did not, to our knowledge, comment publicly on the facts set out by the scientists, namely:

- That rocks lying side by side could have greatly differing ages.
- That these ages would again differ from

the soil and/or dust samples in which, or upon which, the rocks were found.
- Even single rocks were sometimes inconsistent within their individual structure.
- That the area around the Sea of Tranquillity ('Apollo 11') supplied rocks rich in titanium and other highly refractory elements. The samples were conversely poor in low melting point elements, such as sodium and potassium.
- That the area explored around the northern part of the Ocean of Storms ('Apollo 12') and the Aristarchus area had a unique chemical composition: the samples contained more than twenty times the amounts of uranium, thorium and potassium found in all the other lunar samples.

This Ocean of Storms sample can only be considered unique in relation to the limited number of samples returned from the Moon as a whole. It is not necessarily a unique event until the entire surface has been sampled and analysed. Unless, of course, it was one that was made earlier!

With regard to the soil, what is fascinating (but NASA does not seem to think so, as they have again made no comment) is that most of the 'Apollo 11' rock samples were around 3.6 billion years old—but found resting on soil that was 4.6 billion years old. Which means that the soil had to have come into existence one *billion* years earlier!

10. The Whistle-Blowing pre-fabricated rock, part of an image NASA
allegedly taken on the Moon. Note unenhanced 'ground C'.

'Apollo 12' as it happens produced the same results—the soil samples read out at 4.4 billion years old, while the rocks strewn about on it were dated at 3.3 billion years. More bewilderment occurred when the chemical analysis of this soil showed that the lunar dirt did not itself come from the on-site rocks but from elsewhere. Without having first analysed every part of the Moon's surface our scientists cannot easily find answers to these problems.

It is possible that all the rock/soil samples designated 'Apollo lunar samples' do not necessarily come from the named Apollo sites or have arrived back on Earth directly to the USA. And, of course, if the rocks were manufactured rocks, with soil brought in from different places, the results would be the same. Similarly, if the rocks came from one place (on the Moon or elsewhere) and the soil from another, the results would also be the same. We are not necessarily accusing NASA of any of these stratagems, indeed these findings could be the result of a totally different scenario, which we shall explore later.

While NASA no doubt recognises the problems raised by the specifics of the Moon rocks' composition, they do not make any comment on the discrepancies of age raised by several independent experts. Their on-going official stance on the Moon material is that the lunar rocks do not all have the same composition as those of the Earth and that the oldest so far analysed is 4.6 billion years old. A most convenient position to take as that is the scientifically accepted age of our solar system.

More to come

Let us look at some further problems that NASA & Co. certainly do not want to discuss.

As already emphasised, there are examples of lunar rocks containing certain isotopes which indicate that some are far older than anything in our solar system.

The American scientist Dr. Harold Urey was awarded the Nobel Prize for Chemistry in 1934 for his discovery of the heavy form of hydrogen known as deuterium. A key figure in the development of the A-bomb, he was a supporter of the 'capture theory' as the means by which the Moon came to be present in our solar system. Urey had originally suggested that the rocks on the lunar surface might date back to at least the beginning of the solar system and maybe beyond that.

In the journal *Chemistry* Urey stated:[34]

> Moon rock has been shown to contain xenon isotopes from fission of plutonium 244, which are not found on Earth and [which also] indicate that the Moon is much older than [Earth].

But despite this evidence, most scientists feel that the capture theory is unlikely. Some samples from the Moon have never been found on Earth in their natural forms.

At the Third Scientific Conference held in Houston, the Argon International Laboratory reported that they had found Uranium 236 and Neptunium 237 in lunar samples from the 'Apollo 12' & '14' missions—elements never previously found in nature.[35] The outer surface of the Moon contains titanium, zirconium and yttrium in:

> Amounts higher than present estimates for either our planet or for the elemental abundance of these materials *in the universe.* (emphasis added)

We should all reflect on that statement!

In *Science News*, August 16 1969 and January 10 1970 we were told that lunar scientists had found a new mineral.[36] It was a titanium-

---

TechnoSpeak

Isotopes are produced as a result of nuclear fission.

Our Sun is not producing isotopes of the age of some of those found on the Moon, and will not do so for many aeons to come.

(Isotopes have the same number of protons but differing numbers of neutrons; e.g.: hydrogen has 3 isotopes:
normal hydrogen = 1 proton; deuterium = 1 proton +1 neutron;
tritium = 1 proton + 2 neutrons and is radioactive.)

iron-zirconium silicate with concentrations of calcium and yttrium together with lesser amounts of eight other elements, including aluminium and sodium. Are there more things in heaven and Earth? On the face of it, it would seem that we do not know very much about the composition of our Universe. For if, as it is reasonable to suppose, our estimates for the amount of these materials present on Earth were based on what we thought were relatively accurate data pre-Apollo, then the fact that the Moon apparently gives us readings that wildly surpass our estimates would indicate that our present understanding of the Universe is very sadly lacking.

To formulate the hypothesis that all these extraordinary rocks have been made to order is one thing. But the question is—by whom? Were they laid out on the Moon to provide further insights into the existence of other intelligencies, *by other intelligencies?* Or had all these rare elements been assembled into 'moon rocks' by more down-to-earth means. Had these rocks been intentionally manufactured to support the Giant Impact Theory, which in turn supports the American military's SDI requirements that were planned for the turn of this millennium?

NASA has not announced finding any precious metals on the Moon. Perhaps it has 'found' elements that are just as rewarding in its quest for space travel, as the agency sees it. Could these be used as a carrot to provide the means to request further funding in an eventual endeavour to mine the Moon for such elements? Granted, this did not appear to happen in the years following Apollo but the program is very long term and formulated over decades.

Whomever supplied the initial data that formed the basis of the information revealed in the scientific journals, it might just be that the outside world has not yet seen the end results of this geological aspect of the Apollo program. Especially when one relates this information to the Tunguska yttrium findings.

Brighton rock

We do not question that geological samples were obtained from the Moon by unmanned probes. In stating that astronauts have been to the Moon on several occasions, NASA is not necessarily making an erroneous claim. Such a statement would be correct if any *surrogate* astronaut from Earth had set foot on the lunar surface—without necessarily surviving the return trip. Alternatively, "going to the Moon" can also mean walking onto any one of a number of the specially created 'moon' sets on an interior or exterior stage used for the photography and creation of the 'live' TV recordings.

At the same time, NASA could have taken genuine information and used it in a *disinformation* campaign.

For example, we are aware that Crop Glyph formations in the UK—certainly a very real phenomenon since the 1980s—have on occasion been man made and *in some cases* have received additions introduced by various interested parties. We know first hand from Whistle-Blowers that such a circumstance has been engineered (by an individual in authority) in order to discourage serious researchers from pursuing their investigations; and to foster the idea among the general public that *all* of these Crop Glyphs are hoaxes. The clear intention here is to promote the idea that serious research is not worthwhile. Regretfully, by and large, these tactics have succeeded.

We suspect that this is exactly the type of disinformation campaign that NASA has conducted with regard to their lunar findings. Their pre-'Apollo 11' data, their limited supply of soil and rock samples returned from the Moon (via both USA and Soviet probes) produced anomalies of age and composition that could not be wholly suppressed within the scientific community. By manufacturing rocks that fitted their needs they were able to steer scientists in the direction that they wished. In this particular instance it was *away* from the problems that the Moon posed. And by mixing the components of any given rock into a glorious muddle of age and elements, the agency diluted the effect of the genuine samples. This action created so many problems for the received thinking of orthodox science that the majority of researchers turned their backs on the whole problem of the Moon. By stating that their astronauts did not always have time to label the location from which they obtained their samples they invalidated any research as the methodology was sloppy and incorrect from the start. Chemically, any type of lunar environment required can be created. After all, some of the scientists who 'predicted' what would be found on the Moon were the very same scientists who would be examining the 'lunar' samples! How many geologists have truly examined the genuine article and how many more have been served up with a specially-created rock?

According to the late Dr. Paul Gast, chief of the Planetary and Earth Sciences division at Johnson Space Center during Apollo, rock number 12013 from the 'Apollo 12' November 14-24, 1969 mission was "a mess, a marble cake", due to its assortment of differing components and ages.[36] It was also chemically different from any rock found on the lunar surface up to that time, containing at least ten times as much uranium, potassium and thorium and possessing a significantly higher level of radioactivity.

But we have already been advised about another rock from this mission that apparently had *twenty times* as much potassium—are we in a muddle or are they? Is this the same rock? The 'Apollo 13' scenario is hard on the heels of this incident, and is highly suspect as you will find out later, so forgive us if we view their catalogue number: 'ROCK 12013' with some cynicism! Do we register another subtle but nonetheless clearly audible whistle?

QUESTION: Why draw attention to such a rock when they seemingly do not to want to discuss (or wish to discredit) the very interesting subject of rocks older than our solar system?

QUESTION: Do we have here a manufactured red herring? Does NASA wish us to fixate on the interesting *radio-active* components and forget the dating?

QUESTION: So is this a quest for further funding or was it more serious than that?

QUESTION: Is NASA trying to establish in our minds the fact that the Moon is in some

way 'designed' and possibly a danger to humans? While this view may sound over dramatic, is it any less dramatic than the fact that NASA has apparently found rocks *older* than the solar system on a satellite of Earth and *are not prepared to discuss this astonishing finding? Instead it fostered a hypothesis which does not quite work but nevertheless hoped that everyone will return to sleep.*

Does the agency regard us all as GITs?

Astro not moon rocks

On their first day of rock exploration, the named 'Apollo 12' astronauts noticed that the soil under their feet was light grey beneath the dark outer surface. They gathered a sample of the two dusts and carried on. Most rocks they said, looked identical, hidden by the all pervading dust, but closer inspection revealed glints of olivine crystals or white grains of feldspar running through the rocks.

QUESTION: If the astronauts could not see the stars through their gold-tinted visors, how then, could they see these glints of olivine, a dark green colour, let alone a differential of subtle greys?

Apparently, the Moon rocks are so precious that stringent precautions were taken to avoid contamination by Earth bacteria. All personnel were required to wear protective clothing, including sterile gloves, when handling them.

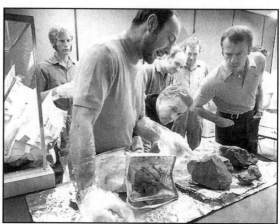

11. 'Apollo 14' Mitchell, Shepard, Roosa—here's one we prepared earlier!   NASA

12. The Lunar Receiving Lab, Building 37 at Houston.   NASA

QUESTION: If the astronauts are carrying out 'closer inspection' in the LM then how are they reproducing the sterile conditions of the lunar rock facility back on Earth? Are they wearing the *appropriate* protective clothing in order to protect these rocks from their own bacteria?

In 1996, we all saw images of technicians handling the supposed Mars meteorite in even more stringent conditions than prevailed in the 1960s, and recent footage of the Mars Path-finder probes also depict NASA technicians kitted out in face masks, sterile gloves plus head coverings and body coveralls.

So what had happened to these 'stringent precautions' in 1971, when the cast of 'Apollo 14', Astronauts Shepard, Roosa and Mitchell visited the laboratories, hands in pockets and not a sterile gown or mask between them? (11)

13. 'Apollo 16' Dave Scott looks at the 'Genesis' Rock. NASA

Chaikin tells us that from a geological perspective the 'Apollo 14' show was the low point of the scientific program. Mission commanders set the tone of the expedition and Al Shepard was said to be not interested in geology at all.

If these astronauts were not interested in geology, what were they doing in the lab in the first place? If this was a publicity and promotion opportunity, it flies in the face of reason. Whether such stringent precautions were worth taking with regard to the Moon rocks is one thing, but this single photograph of the 'Apollo 14' team demonstrates that during Project Apollo, NASA forgot their own script. Either that, or some Whistle-Blower mounted yet another telling photograph into the album.

Between several rocks and some hard places

In the late 1990s much is made of the fact that the first visits to the Moon were for the purposes of gathering scientific data. The sampling of as many different geophysical places on the lunar surface as could be achieved within the limited time of each lunar exploration. Grand words. However in the 1960s that did not appear to be the masters' principle concern. NASA claimed that the candidate astronauts with the required scientific qualifications simply did not match up to the physical and technical constraints of the astronaut training program.

QUESTION: If these rocks are so irreplaceable, why have they been offered for auction in the sale rooms? Moon rocks—*Soviet* Lunakhod rocks—were auctioned at Sotheby's New York for the dollar equivalent of over 2.6 million French Francs in December 1993.[37]

Whistle-Blower Kaysing tells us that many lunar rocks were shipped to Switzerland.[38] There are three possibilities:

• Were they, like gold, very precious?
• Was it because these rocks were inconveniently *too old?*
• Or were they masquerading as real lunar rocks and required a secure, central location.

QUESTION: Did Switzerland revive the role it played during the WWII and serve as a transit route and/or a repository for goods travelling between two régimes?

Could it be that the only people to have the real rocks were the Soviets, because these samples were returned from the Moon to the Soviet Union. The Soviets then shipped them to Switzerland from whence some of them found their way to the USA. It is said that the USA had copious amounts of lunar dust and that those who requested samples of lunar material were in fact sent some of this dust.[39]

QUESTION: Why are the majority of these alleged Moon rocks only in museums?

QUESTION: Why have some of the core samples taken during the Apollo period not been analysed to this day?

The waste bin

Back to Earth, with a bump. Antarctica is a prime hunting ground for meteorites. Apparently these pennies from heaven are highly visible, sitting patiently on the surface of that stark, white landscape. Also, compared with other deserted areas upon which these meteorites fortuitously land, there are more people to spot them in Antarctica. Teams of scientists have regularly examined the surface of that polar wasteland for meteorites. In documentary footage on Antarctic meteorites, scientists have been filmed creating flurries of snow as they ride their snowmobiles.[40] Then such scenes cut to close ups of a rock lying on a perfectly still white surface. How they are able to spot these miniature stones through the snow flurries is difficult to tell. Perhaps in much the same way that the astronauts could see through the smoke they did, or did not generate when landing on the lunar surface. Here is an extract from the *National Geographic* magazine, of September 1986:

> *Surprisingly* four of the Antarctic finds are believed to have come from the Moon—rocks hurled into space by lunar impacts. Their chemical and mineralogical make-up *closely resembles* that of samples collected on the Moon and is unlike that of other meteorites. (emphasis added)

It is not difficult to resemble something closely of course, if one is a copy of the other.

> ### *Practice should have made perfect*
> "We take endless photographs.
> The photographs, it seems to me, provide us with a testament that transcends time,
> for we may be photographing the distant past of our own planet."
> *Dave Scott, 'Apollo 15'.*
> But more than likely the *near present* of our own planet ![41]

On the other hand this also confirms the fact that genuine models *did* exist on Earth for anyone wanting to produce additional 'moon' rocks prior to and during the Apollo missions.

And later on, in 1996, an insignificant meteorite found in the Antarctic some ten years previously and filed away under 'uninteresting', would be fortuitously rediscovered just before the first of a number of probes were due to leave for Mars. This little rock would become NASA's PR fund raiser par excellence, for lo! the intervening years with NASA had conferred upon it the title: "Rock containing *life*, made on Mars".

The dogs do bark!

On February 8 1969, in spite of not having said a proper "thank-you" for our 1947 gift near Truth or Consequences, just five months before 'Apollo 11' was scheduled to leave the launch pad, humanity received another 'gift'. It was a very large and rare type of meteorite. Totalling nearly four tons of material it covered more than 100 square miles of open desert in an *elliptical* pattern. The meteorite was named 'Allende' after the nearest town to the crash site. This place was Pueblito de Allende, in Chihuahua State, Mexico. Elibert King, NASA's Johnson Space Center Curator, was counting the gamma-ray emissions from this Allende meteorite within four days of its arrival. *When analysed it was found to be of an extremely rare type, of which only seven other examples had been found to date. Overall, about 4,400 lbs (nearly two tons) of material was recovered. It consisted of carbonaceous chondrites* **4,566 ± 2 million years old.** *This dating made the meteorite virtually 20 million years older than any rock on Earth.*[42]

Interestingly, there are no records of any meteorite ever having killed a human being (although the Nahkla meteorite which fell in Egypt did kill a dog (not a Chihuahua though). It is also rare that solid fragments survive the entry through the Earth's atmosphere. The total number of meteorites known is no more than a few thousand, and of those, a very small percentage are recovered. It is only very occasionally that such large meteorites as the Allende arrive on Earth. The positioning of the Allende on NASA's doorstep and the timing of its arrival can be considered to be apposite—or remarkably coincidental—to say the least. From the information released both by NASA and independent scientists, we are acquiring evidence that suggests that the Moon has been cosmetically 'set dressed'. But precisely by whom? Perhaps the loose surface dust was not originally from the Moon at all! As even *we* do not think that NASA would wish to point the finger at itself quite so blatantly, it is our *tentative* conclusion that Earth's satellite does indeed have disparate rocks upon it and that some of these rocks have been brought to Earth. This situation has a parallel within the Great Pyramid on the Giza Plateau, as we shall see.

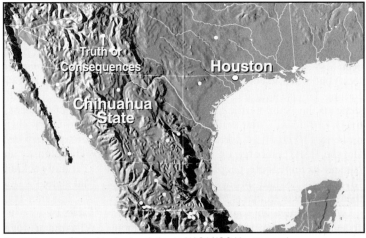

14. Chihuahua State, Mexico in relation to NASA/JSC Houston and Truth or Consequences.

The Zzzzzz files

Most people are not particularly interested in the geological composition of a given piece of moonrock, what they *really* want to know is—did the astronauts find any signs of extra-terrestrial activity (read intelligent ETs and/or their artefacts) on their visits to and from or during their stay on the Moon?

As far as the subject of ET is concerned, NASA generally reflects the establishment ambivalence towards the subject, and in 1959 a specially commissioned study *The Brookings Report* was circulated. This report referred to the possibility and consequences of discovering either extra-terrestrial intelligent life or artefacts attesting to the existence of same, during space exploration. It contained studies to determine the emotional and intellectual understanding and attitudes of mankind towards this possibility.

The ramification of such an event was evaluated by the Brookings Report as being deeply disturbing to global civilisation. Such a discovery was deemed likely to undermine all the structures of authority on this planet: religious, social and military. Interestingly, the report concluded that the people who would be most disturbed by the affirmed reality of ET intelligence would be the scientific and engineering community.

From observation of the behaviour of our governments it is easy to see that they have taken this report to heart and moulded their policies in such a way that their scientists and engineers avoid the deep trauma of confrontation with such intelligence. In 1994 an ex-NASA consultant stated that the authorities did not intend to be dictated to by public opinion, led by the illiterate and the semi-illiterate, for whom the idea of ET was very exciting.[43] No change there then. This attitude prevails publicly to this day, despite a continual increase in

275

sightings (only by the illiterate, the semi-illiterate or the lunatic fringe, naturally!).

Concerning the lunar regolithic findings and the vagaries of their lunar images, NASA have been less than forthcoming (to the public at least) but when it comes to conversations concerning UFOs and ET, the astronauts, and some of the Apollo officials, have been positively garrulous. After reading "Truth or Consequences", you might ask why that should be. Did the USAF embargo on talking about such matters exempt these people? As it applied "even unto civilian airlines and their crews", then the answer to that is obviously "no".

Let us indulge in some apparently extreme speculation. If it were the case that the Moon had somehow been specifically and intelligently placed in its orbit in this solar system for the *benefit* of planet Earth, and/or the surface of the Moon had been specially designed with soil and rocks of disparate ages to enable us to arrive at such a conclusion, then we would of course have to open the door to the 'problem' of extra-terrestrial intelligence and our general relationship to such matters. The very reactions of NASA to the results of its exploration of the Moon—the lunar surface and its environs—reduce the chances to a minimum that we are indulging in pure speculation.

In an information sheet published by the US Government in February 1978 the following further statement was made:

> NASA is the focal point for answering public enquiries to the White House relating to UFOs. NASA is not engaged in a research program involving these phenomena, nor is any other government agency (USA). Reports of unidentified objects entering the United States air space are of interest to the military as a regular part of defense surveillance. Beyond that, the US Air Force no longer investigates reports of UFO sightings.

• The wording '*no longer* investigates' is interesting, given that the 'official' existence of UFOs has always hitherto either been ignored or denied—but then as we have already stated in the previous chapter, the definition of UFO as natural phenomena and UFO as fly-

ing saucer is an ambiguity which, we feel, was established by the authorities themselves as part of their policies for controlling information on this taboo subject.

• Any *unannounced* flying object entering US airspace is rather obviously an unexpected guest. This little masterpiece of doublespeak actually means that the authorities are as interested as they always have been, but they are not prepared to admit that interest openly!

• The phrase "any *other* government agency" certainly acknowledges their own governmental status!

Title 14

Why did a government that denied the existence of extra-terrestrial intelligent life and its artefacts need to pass a law stating that any US citizen coming into contact with an ET and/or its spacecraft, could be heavily fined or even imprisoned if said person did not follow the protocols set out by the head of NASA—*sole judge* and arbiter in the definition of such protocols. That is a considerable position of power for a 'civilian' chief executive! With no preceding public debate whatsoever this legislation was quietly adopted onto the Code of Federal Regulations, Section 14, subsection 1211 on July 16 1969—the day that 'Apollo 11' was launched.

Disclosed encounters

One of the messages from Kubrick and Clarke, via astronaut Bowman in the film *2001: A Space Odyssey* is that we are searching for higher consciousness in the wrong place—out there in space, when we only need to look inside ourselves. This particular interpretation of higher consciousness would appear to be rather more related to the noetic concept of intellect without soul. Over the years, rumours have persisted concerning the astronaut's alleged conversations with Houston. The designated 'Bowmans' of the 'Apollo' program have divulged some of their thoughts concerning their alleged travels to the Moon. Much has been made of code words and sightings that apparently took place on nearly every trip to and from the Moon. Now, when considered from the viewpoint that we may not have gone to the Moon *with these particular astronauts*, the alleged conversations take on a completely different slant.

Most of the situations in which these named astronauts found themselves therefore did not necessarily exist at all.

Let us examine some of these 'official' extracts from this point of view and see what happens. There are records of UFO-related comments connected to various NASA personnel which date from 1962, but they are outside the domain of this book. The transcripts reproduced here are concerned with the experiences that NASA personnel *might* have experienced while on or in orbit around the Moon.

According to the author Don Wilson, who interviewed Dr. Farouk El-Baz of NASA on the subject of some of these transcripts, Dr. El-Baz admitted that not every discovery had been announced by NASA. This statement does not, of course, necessarily refer to the possible presence of ETs. Yet it is surely contradictory to NASA's official statement *that the findings of lunar and space expeditions have never been kept secret from the public.* This sentence might more correctly read "the findings of lunar and space expeditions are not discussed if *we* can't deal with them—or if we decide not to publish them". However, Dr. El-Baz further suggested to Don Wilson that sometimes codes might have been used to impart information from the Moon to Earth.

QUESTION: Why would it be necessary to use codes, if there is nothing to hide?

QUESTION: Do NASA and/or the government agencies involved with that agency wish to keep us all in ignorance of certain data and information?

QUESTION: Or does the very fact that El-Baz *volunteers* to Wilson that codes were in use, *implant* an idea that NASA wishes us to 'buy'? Dr. El-Baz being very much a company man, was certainly not blowing any whistles.

The famous comments from Neil Armstrong regarding ETs allegedly made on an alternative channel during the 'Apollo 11' landing have gone down in history. Yet Farouk El-Baz is implying, surely, that there was *not* an alterna-

tive channel. If there was, why use code? The astronauts only speak directly to Capcom and anyone in the control room has to speak to them via Capcom. That person is always carefully selected, and generally a fellow astronaut.[44]

Maurice Chatelaine was an expert in radar, telecommunications and telemetry. At North American Aviation (NASA contractor par excellence) he was instrumental in the development of the data-processing and communication system for the Apollo Program. Here is his version of Armstrong's 'Apollo 11' communication:

> These babies are huge, Sir. Enormous. Oh my God! You wouldn't believe it. I'm telling you there are spacecraft out there, lined up on the far side of the crater edge. They're on the Moon watching us.

Chatelaine specifically said that all the Gemini and Apollo flights were followed either at a distance or at fairly close range, by space vehicles of extra-terrestrial origin. So not *unidentified* flying objects then! What an amazing admission. Mission Control was apparently informed on each occasion and a complete silence was then observed. When an astronaut says he hasn't seen any UFOs he isn't lying. He has, according to this statement, only seen IFOs—identified flying objects.[45]

Former space program member Otto Binder maintained that the 'Apollo 11' astronauts were surprised by what they saw on the Moon. Binder claimed that Armstrong grabbed

Aldrin's arm and exclaimed excitedly: "What was it? What the hell was it? That's all I want to know". Then followed another version of the much-quoted exchange between Houston and Armstrong:

> Houston: What's there? malfunction....
> [garble] ...Mission Control calling
> Apollo 11..."
> Armstrong: "Oh God you wouldn't be-
> lieve it! I'm telling you there are
> spacecraft out there...lined up on the
> far side of the crater edge...they're on
> the Moon watching us.

So between these two versions we have lost seven words, one, 'my', has been lost from between an otherwise perfect copy of a sentence. If this story was valid the text would be identical, because it is a matter of record. On magnetic tape! Otto Binder was awarded an honorary degree by NASA for his services as a science writer (of fact or fiction?).

Incidentally, this situation was further backed up by the Soviet scientist, Dr. Aleksandr Kazantsev, who claimed that Buzz Aldrin took colour film of the sighting *from inside the LM* and then took more images when both astronauts had descended to the lunar surface.

Another Soviet, a physicist and Professor of Mathematics at Moscow University, Dr. Vladimir Azhaza claimed Armstrong told Houston (in a message that was immediately censored) that two large mysterious objects had landed near the LM. These objects then left the scene *just minutes after* the astronauts came out onto the lunar surface. It is our contention that this exchange (allegedly recorded by radio hams) was intentionally planted by NASA.

Please remember we, the authors, are claiming that Armstrong and Aldrin were not there! Also even in the script, the 'Apollo 11' astronauts did not step onto the lunar surface at the same time. According to the timeline for the EVA, Buzz Aldrin did not commence his exit through the LM's hatch until approximately 26 minutes after Armstrong, and Aldrin did *not* have use of the Hasselblad surface camera immediately on descending the ladder. He only picked it up for a while to take some photographs after Armstrong had been using the

camera for some time. Thereafter, Armstrong used it until the termination of the EVA (see also Chapter Two "Photocall").

In 1995, another source stated that: "Armstrong walked on the lunar surface for *nearly an hour* before Aldrin left the LM"—history is being officially re-written, again.[46] Always and always there are conflicting statements. So did the sighting of the mysterious object occur 26 minutes after Armstrong's descent or six minutes after Aldrin's descent? The answer is—neither. A time interval of twenty minutes does not constitute "just minutes". So if these 'craft' left just minutes after the arrival of Armstrong on the lunar surface, then Aldrin could *not* have taken snaps of them from the lunar surface with the Hasselblad.

Apparently, the only way that anyone in the public domain could be aware of such messages is through the work of *unnamed* radio hams bypassing the NASA broadcasting outlets during the landing in July 1969. These radio hams allegedly called the Judica brothers of Turin (which title smacks of an in-joke) have themselves never come forward to settle this controversy and we know of this incident *thanks to* Messrs Binder and Chatelaine, both heavily associated with NASA.

Researcher and author Timothy Good reports a conversation between Armstrong and a professor at a NASA symposium that was apparently overheard and reported by another guest at the same function. In substance, Armstrong was asked what had really happened on the Moon. He replied that they had been "warned off" by the very size of the craft that they saw. He went on to infer that the incident had put the lid on the question of there ever being a space station on the Moon.[47] It also establishes a dramatic reason a) for abandoning further manned flight to the Moon, and b) establishing the need for SDI. Hearsay is not evidence but it is somewhat surprising to find Armstrong the Taciturn, standing in a public place, discussing—loud enough to be overheard—the most taboo subject in NASA's book. Unless of course it was *intended* that the words that he uttered should be spread around.

Now why would that be?

We suggest that the seeding of this later (dis)information was designed to endorse the authenticity of that first alleged transmission. In fact, even if this story is completely apocryphal, it has still produced the specific and we suspect, required, effect. It establishes that ETs are dangerous and to be feared through the use of very emotive words, "Alien ships...far superior to ours both in size and technology"..."big and menacing"..."we were warned off."

When questioned about the fact that despite these warnings, several other missions had supposedly been to the Moon, Armstrong had allegedly replied that it had really been "a quick scoop and back again" *(sounds more like probes, does it not?)* ..."that NASA were committed..." and..."couldn't risk a panic on Earth".

Armstrong initially confirmed to Timothy Good his "cocktail party conversation" but at a later date, told him that his (Good's), sources were unreliable and that no objects other than those of a natural origin were reported, found or seen, on any of the Apollo flights.

Considering the rigours with which NASA pre-scripted as much as they could of Apollo, it is obvious that amongst themselves the question of ET would have been addressed in detail, whatever was said in public. After all, it is in NASA's enabling legislation that it should be prepared to find signs of life when exploring the solar system. Therefore, if it were *really* necessary to "not cause panic on Earth" the astronauts would either have *not said anything at all* or relayed a pre-arranged and *undetectable code* back to Houston. El-Baz who also does not have to speak out, hints heavily at such codes. But before we all get frightened at this sinister turn of events, we should step back and look carefully at these stories. Are they genuine Whistle-Blowing, or are they the deliberate seeding of disinformation?

B-minus

In 1994 Buzz Aldrin, who currently uses his astronaut status in commercials, features in PR for space fiction on American TV and develops

15. Buzz Aldrin.   NASA

ideas for future space transportation systems, was quoted as saying:

> I participated in what will probably be remembered as the greatest technological achievement in the history of this century. I travelled to the Moon but the most significant voyage of my life began when I got back.

Aldrin does not believe that we have been visited 'from anywhere' and thinks that the continuing questioning by the public in this area is misguided and 'misleading in the falseness'—whatever that might mean. Reading Aldrin's answers makes you glad that he had a co-writer on his book *Encounter With Tiber,* which he tells us to read if we want to know what he thinks. As this space fiction novel is *very much* concerned with past and future colonising spacemen, and not necessarily all of them from planet Earth, we detect answers here from the school of 'Never A Straight Answer'. Buzz seems to be attempting the impossible—to blow a whistle while at the same time trying to hold his breath![48]

Phony home

Do we have other instances of Apollo astronauts talking to Houston about possible ET contact? Here is 'Apollo 16' on April 21 during their first EVA moonwalk, wherever that really took place, for all these Apollo dialogues sound rather pre-arranged; Houston feeding

279

them their lines and providing us with a tempting little exchange:

Houston: "OK Just a question for you, John. When you got to halfway, or even thought it was halfway, we understand you looped around south, is that right?"
Young: "That's affirm. We came upon—Barbara."

This conversation transcript was reported by Joseph F Goodavage who then made an appointment with Dr. Farouk El-Baz.[49] On being asked what the 'Barbara' remark could possibly mean, El-Baz replied that he really could not say, perhaps it was code.

Here is another conversation concerning 'Apollo 16'. We are supposed to think that Ken Mattingley is circling the Moon in the Lunar Orbiter—the conversation is between Houston and Charlie Duke on the surface of the Moon:

Houston: "Hey, fellows, Ken was just flying over and he saw a flash on the side of Descartes—he probably got a glint of you?"
Duke: "Oh sure, that's us. Men of miracles. We're dusty."

Well they really must have been men of miracles, in the majority of pictures that have been published, they are not very dusty at all.

Mattingley is reported as having seen another rather large flash disappearing behind the Moon while he was orbiting in the Command Module. El-Baz commented on this sighting during a discussion on cosmic rays and he emphasised that Mattingley had seen something beyond his CSM. El-Baz entertained three possibilities: a powerful cosmic ray, a piece of dust suspended in front of his window and a micrometeorite travelling towards the Moon. Then he said that none of these fitted the facts and Mattingley's experience had to remain in the category of a UFO.[50]

El-Baz went on to emphasise that neither the Russians nor the Americans had spacecraft capable of moving at the speed of this flash of light and when *Saga* journalist Goodavage remarked that it had already been said 'officially' that there have been no ET landings

on the Moon, El-Baz disagreed, remarking:

- "The Moon has not been as thoroughly mapped as some people think!"
  (Did they not obtain good data with their photographic equipment then?)
- "The best resolution that has been achieved is of one or two miles, which means that the smallest objects that can be spotted measure a mile across".
- "We cannot possibly rule out that extra-terrestrial objects may be on or under the lunar surface".

Here El-Baz belies the other official statements made about the resolution capabilities of NASA's space cameras, and he is certainly planting information, whatever the content! A resolution of one or two miles sounds more like typical resolution from *Earth telescopes* to us. We add this item to our growing collection of evidence suggesting that NASA is a regular supplier/generator of confused information and disinformation.

Here is Mattingley again in the CSM Caspar, orbiting around the Moon:

Mattingly: "Another strange sight over here. It looks—a flashing—light—I think it's 'Annbell'. Another crater here looks as though it is flooded, except that this same material seems to run up the outside. You can see a definite patch of this stuff that's run down the inside. And that material lays [sic] or has been structured on top of it but it lays [sic] on top of things that are outside and higher. It's a very strange operation."

This is a completely non-technical and ungrammatical description from a man who is supposed to have had a considerable amount of specific geological training! Although virtually incomprehensible, the speaker seemingly conveys the impression that whatever he is looking at is manufactured. And remember "Barbara"? Is she a relation of "Annbell"? A day that was to have been spent studying the surface of the Moon from Caspar was forfeited. The astronauts thought this was due to "nervousness on the part of Houston" and no explanation was forthcoming.[51] We are obviously meant to conclude that something had thrown Houston into a flap. This is a neat piece of script writing that goes towards consolidating the 'scary ET' scenario.

Here is some more from 'Apollo 16':

Duke: "Orion has landed. I can't see how far the [indistinct]...this is a blocked field we're in from the South Ray—tremendous difference in the albedo. I just get the feeling that these rocks may have come from somewhere else. Everywhere we saw the ground, which is about the whole sunlit side, you had the same delineation [that] the Apollo 15 photography showed on Hadley, Delta and Radley Mountains."
Houston: "OK Go ahead."
Duke: "I'm looking out here at Stone Mountain and it's got—it looks like somebody has been out there ploughing across the side of it. The beaches—the benches—look like one sort of terrace after another, right up the side. They sort of follow the contour of it right around."
Houston: "Any difference in the terraces?"
Duke: "No, Tony. Not that I could tell from here. These terraces could be raised but of [indistinct] or something like that."

For people who have supposedly undergone extensive training in the recognition and reporting of geological phenomena this report is nothing less than totally inarticulate. But what they lack in geological description they make up for in artistry. They heavily infer that the scenery has been "artificially manipulated".

The night before Christmas

"Please be informed that there is a Santa Claus."

When the 'Apollo 8' crew uttered those words during the first sortie around their Moon, remember who was their Capcom? It was Ken Mattingley who replied: "That's affirmative, you are the best ones to know".

While most people connected this comment to the circumstantial date of Christmas Eve 1968, there were many who felt that the remark had a deeper meaning.[52] Or so Timothy Good would have it. He went on to recount that

Walter Schirra first used the expression "Santa Claus" during his Mercury 8 sighting but this had not been noticed by the public. This is hardly surprising, the Mercury missions received far less publicity than the Apollo flights. Good then takes the trouble to point out that Walter Schirra was referring to unidentified flying objects around his craft. Jim Lovell then used this same expression at the most dramatic and most attention-getting moment of the 'Apollo 8' mission—the re-emergence of the CSM from the far side of the Moon.

Having been nicely 'prepared' by these events, we have John Young inserting a dramatic pause before the word "Barbara", and in case we have all missed the point, El-Baz tells us that they might be using code. One that is rather evidently past its sell-by date. Are we *meant* to be making connections?[53]

In the light of the fact that we *affirm* that these named Apollo astronauts did not go to the Moon, we must ask:

- Why it was necessary to 'transmit' these messages?
- Either these events have a basis in reality, in which case NASA, by denying them and the manifestations of extra-terrestrial activity, appears to be lying to us.
- Or these events did *not* happen and NASA and their associates are participating in rumour mongering and/or the creation of disinformation or untruths.

Granted NASA had to write some sort of script to accompany and flesh out the alleged lunar missions. But why this particular script? We seem to be witnessing an underlying campaign that has been created here—at home—by humans. A campaign designed to generate fear of ET among the general public. And one that also implied that ET inhibited our named astronauts from exploring the Moon. Note the quantity of 'events' during the penultimate 'Apollo 16' mission of April 1972, towards the end of the Apollo program. In fact the majority were either at the beginning or the end of the program, times when the most audience attention could be guaranteed. We could be

---

Star Wars

The Gulf War served, of course, as a useful arena for testing some of the 'Star Wars' hardware, such as Patriot missiles.

Unfortunately for the Pentagon, the 'Star Wars' laser technology was not up to the job.

The Patriots were either a total failure, or at best had a very poor success rate. Clearly, the difficulties involved in getting lasers to operate in an atmosphere over long distances had not been overcome!

The opinion on their performance varies, depending upon the source of information.

Generally, these missiles were passing the oncoming Scud's path rather than intercepting it.

Their computer systems were incapable of accurately evaluating the moment of impact due to the exceedingly fast approach speeds of both missiles.

Since the passing of the Reagan administration the 'Star Wars' project has gone quiet.

Officially the program has been cancelled—but unofficially? In the late nineties there have been breakthroughs in the use of laser aiming techniques through an atmosphere.

The British ex-Prime Minister Margaret Thatcher reiterated the necessity for such a system in 1995.

---

forgiven for perhaps thinking that these dialogues were engineered in order to excite Congress into the continuation of funding. As we shall see by the end of this book, over time, several reasons have surfaced which explain these conversations. In 1998, NASA were talking about a return to the Moon (with more probes) so it is clear that we have not yet seen an end to this storyline.

Title 14—the comeback

At the time of Pearl Harbour, the 14th and completing portion of Japan's coded messages to its embassies was delivered well after the preceding thirteen code blocks. And so it was with that 1969 piece of legislation relating to ET encounters. It was to be another thirteen years before this piece of legislation became public knowledge when Dr. Brian Clifford of the *Pentagon* announced the existence of Title 14 *at a press conference* held on October 5 1982.

QUESTION: Why use a press conference to announce a piece of legislation such as Title 14 unless you wish to *specifically* draw attention to it by gaining maximum or efficient coverage? (Remember Sergeant Brown from Roswell?)

QUESTION: Why wait until 1982 to announce a thirteen year-old legislation which at first glance, would ensure that from henceforth, few American citizens would report any UFO sighting for fear of the consequences. To our knowl-

edge, that 1982 statement concerning Title 14 has not been questioned or investigated and most of the public (including a few of our Whistle-Blowers) are still unaware of its existence. So we could conclude that the UFO-watching public were not the target of this piece of legislation but that it was necessary to have it on the public record. The press conference was therefore mainly for benefit of the cognoscenti.

At second glance, it is obvious from its date of July 16 1969 that we are *meant* to conclude that this legislation was 'designed'—to cover any eventualities arising from the Apollo landings.

If the general public heard about this Title 14 at all, it would trigger the response: "Well, *that's* why the astronauts can't speak about their endeavours on the Moon—they *must* have met ET and they're bound by the NASA version of the Official Secrets Act. All those rumours are true, then. Neil Armstrong *did* see craft on the side of the crater when he landed at Tranquillity".

Decades of 'education' by our governments plus an innate desire not to face the unknown, would then ensure that most of us turn our backs on ET as a reality and continue on as before. There would be no more questioning of the validity of the lunar program and NASA. The Whistle-Blowers would be condemned to the dungeons of Conspiracy Castle. Watching such programs as *The X Files* from the safety of our armchairs we could enjoy a delicious shiver of fear as we remember Armstrong's description of "those menacing craft" that allegedly warned the American astronauts away from the Moon, safe in the knowledge that our parents will look after us.

Now it looks as though in 1982, the Pentagon was joining in *officially*—and in so doing, implying that NASA took special precautions in 1969 against ET. As it was not *necessary* to say anything about ET in the first place, we suggest that the aim of this confusion goes well beyond the need to establish excuses for closing down the lunar exploration program, indeed one reason for waiting all those years becomes clear: in June 1982 NASA launched the Shuttle *Columbia* containing an unspecified Department of Defense payload.[54] Was Title 14 duly aired publicly four months later as a lever, to convince the Americans of the *need* to commit financially to the development of a Strategic Defense Initiative? In an eerie echo of the Kubrick/Clarke *2001* scenario, the 'Star Wars' script concept was largely driven by a committee of science fiction writers among whom Larry Niven was prominent. They were proud to have been so forceful in the driving of government policy.

By March 1983, when President Reagan officially announced the setting up of the $100-200 *billion* SDI program, Dr. Clifford and his colleagues from the Pentagon had a period of five months to reinforce the lobbying of those still uncommitted to SDI. While publicly using the Soviet Union as the scapegoat for this project, the examples of ET 'announcements' that you have read in this chapter could then be used discreetly to add weight to this leverage.

The 'masters of infinity' could target the White House, the Senate, their congressmen, their contractors and the public with the reason most appropriate for the person or people they were targeting. By promoting their own scripts, they neatly avoided the truth—their aspiration to exercise their self-appointed right to rule over our planet and eventually the entire solar system.

It is time for us all to *WAKE UP!* and look at the reality. We have seen that the source of the "ET on the Moon" rumours are NASA astronauts and associates such as Chatelaine, Binder, El-Baz, Hoagland and other researchers, wittingly in some cases, perhaps unwittingly in others. Notwithstanding the conversations cited above, NASA & Co. have denied that anything ever happened relating to ET during their missions. From this evidence alone, we must conclude that these Houston-Apollo conversations were pre-scripted. The authorities are perfectly well aware of the manifestations of ET existence and all our governments are perfectly aware that ET is not a *defence* issue per se.

Indeed, all have repeatedly said so.

Their awfully small adventure

What about the named astronauts in all this? During the early days of NACA/NASA the men who were to become the first astronauts were selected by the USAF for the purpose of manned MILITARY space missions.[55] So we are referring to a breed who were already highly trained service men *hand picked* for the very qualities that would enable them to deal with even the very extraordinary in a controlled and logical fashion.

There are many space history books that review the lives and post-Apollo careers of all the astronauts concerned. The issues that we discuss here involve Neil Armstrong and Buzz Aldrin both of 'Apollo 11', together with Ed Mitchell of the 'Apollo 14' cast.

Portrait of the astronaut as a young man

NASA Administrator, Bob Gilruth wrote, in January 1965, that the astronauts came to NASA as post-graduates.
Most of them had obtained degrees in science or engineering before taking flight training and then spent time as jet pilots. Many had also qualified as test pilots.
They all possessed excellent health, emotional stability and the ability to maintain coolness under pressure.
The subsequent reclusive behaviour of many of these men is, therefore, astonishing.

16. Armstrong, Aldrin, Collins in the quarantine vehicle.　NASA

Andrew Chaikin informs us that it was an open secret among the astronauts in training that many of them were not especially interested in the 'moon' as anything more than a place to fulfil *'THEIR'* mission which was going to be *'THE'* perfect mission of the whole program. Scientific research was apparently not the astronauts' idea of priority. (Which is another way of telling scientists that scientific methodology was also not a priority).

QUESTION: What then *was* the priority of the lunar missions for the named astronauts?

As we have never actually been told, we can only conjecture that in true military fashion and in accordance with their job description at induction, *THE* perfect mission is *one that is executed according to the book.* A controlled exercise in getting from Point A to point B and back while incurring minimum casualties,

---

Extinction—distinction

The Dyna-Soar project began in 1957. Severely wounded by a change in direction on St. George's Day, April 23 1959, this beast lumbered on, eating up vast amounts of cash until late into 1961. What a predestined name—though possibly less of 'the Pterodactyl' and more of 'the plane that would not survive' lay behind that choice?

Awarded the Uncle George Medal.

---

be they of men or equipment. Unless, of course, you were on the 'Apollo 13' set, where the criteria were slightly different—being an 'exercise' in crisis handling. All of which, for an actor, is much the same as remembering lines and hitting the marks.

Look carefully at this photograph of the triumphant 'Apollo 11' astronauts. They have just returned to Earth and President Nixon (out of frame) is congratulating them on their achievement—do they look comfortable with themselves? Look at their eyes. Are these the expressions of men who have just stepped back onto their home planet after the adventure of a lifetime? Does the subsequent behaviour of many of the named Apollo astronauts, their demonstrated relationship problems, the reclusiveness, the yearning (by some) after spiritual values, denote any kind of inner discomfort?[56]

Only the astronauts themselves or again NASA, can say what really happened to these men. Hardly any of them are talking with any enthusiasm about their missions so they must have been sworn to the essential requirements for safeguarding the National Security of the United States of America—absolute silence and total secrecy. From our observations of their behaviour these men have surely been put under tremendous and continual pressure by their masters. With the designation of the astronaut's jobs as military missions, the *public* description of the Apollo missions as a scientific exploration to the Moon (carried out for all mankind) and the definition of the Moon as a place for peaceful exploration it is clear that NASA have mislead the public. At least from the time of their induction into the program, these men appear to have been obliged to collaborate in the withholding of information. Unless of course, from the astronaut's point of view, the initial reason for these manned missions was clear cut, reasonable and in the interests of the United States and their masters. Should that have been the case then patriotism and the necessity for silence would no doubt

284

have been considered acceptable. In our view, whatever the United States opinion of itself as the representative of all mankind, these actions have disqualified it from such a position.

At the beginning of this program we suggest that that there would be no reason for any putative astronaut to think that, beyond security silence on the real reason for these flights, there would be any other constraint upon their consciences. Very possibly it was only once these men had reached a certain level in their special training in the early 1960s that more and more of the plan was revealed to them. Stroke by stroke the surrogate 'solution' started to add splashes of colour to the picture taking shape on the canvas. At the point when it became impossible to see how they would accomplish these missions in the manner originally described by NASA, it would have been far too late for them to retire from the project. The fact that *they* would not actually be travelling beyond the Van Allen belts, but that they would still be required to act as though they had been to the Moon, might well have been a bitter pill to swallow. Remember that all these astronauts were military-trained personnel, and although some may have been willing participants, it would have been totally impossible to ignore orders. No reward on Earth could compensate these men for the harm done to their lives through the execution of their diets during the Apollo segment of the space program.

'silent knight'

Neil Armstrong has gone down in history as being the civilian astronaut of 'Apollo 11'. In fact, Armstrong earned his pilot's license at the same time as his automobile driver's license. He became a Naval Cadet in 1947 and then flew 78 combat missions in the Korean War (1950-'53)—receiving two medals. In 1955 he became a test pilot at Edwards Air Force Base, clocking up more that 1,100 flying hours working for the National Advisory Committee's Aeronautics High Speed Flight Station (NACA later to become NASA).

The X-15, a rocket-powered aircraft was built by NAA for NACA/NASA in the late 1950s and Armstrong was named as one of the very

few pilots qualified to fly it. Armstrong was selected by the US Air Force as one of the first six candidate astronauts on March 14 1962. These men were chosen for general manned military space missions without affiliation to a specific program. (The next batch were selected for the same purpose but assigned to specific programs, initially, the Dyna-Soar). Neil Armstrong transferred to NASA on September 17 1962. Therefore, even if Armstrong was then sheep dipped—designated as a civilian test pilot on the 'Apollo 11' flight, his entire career had been within a completely military regime and it is difficult to see how that definition of civilian fitted anything other than the clothing regulations and political requirements of NASA. After all, NASA was and still is a government agency, its chief executive appointed by the President of the United States.[57]

As far as talking about his experiences on 'Apollo 11', Armstrong is virtually a recluse. On Neil Armstrong, HJP ("Douglas") Arnold comments: "He has always kept himself to himself. During the various celebrations he has tended to appear, you might say, as limited as decency would allow." Indeed, one hapless American TV journalist who dared to approach Mr Armstrong at his home to ask some questions about his lunar exploits was shown the door with the promise that if he ever came back he would be removed by the police. He *did* return, he *was* removed and the accompanying film crew recorded the whole incident.[58]

Remote views

Of his travels in space and the 'Apollo 14' mission, Ed Mitchell has said that he experienced a feeling of euphoria, and great peacefulness combined with a sense of understanding. He felt that the Universe did not function at random. He felt something of the order of the heavens, the harmony of the individual components that made up the solar system, the galaxies. He felt a part of it all and he knew that he had been enlightened, and in the years to follow, that would come to mean more to him than having been on the Moon. Andrew Chaikin reported these observations. However, Ed Mitchell is another astronaut with a very

17. Ed Mitchell.   NASA

interesting background.

In an American Radio debate on the *Art Bell* coast-to-coast talk show of May 15 1996, Ed Mitchell claimed that as possessor of a PhD and also being a *SUPER RATIONALIST* he did not think the question "what did it feel like to be on the Moon?" germane.[59] He emphasised that he did not start to explore the non-local (as he and the military PSI researchers put it) intuitive, more mystic side of himself until 1972.

Yet from information recited by all the NASA historians we are asked to believe that it was this very same, self-proclaimed super rationalist who was responsible for carrying out an extra-sensory perception (ESP) experiment during the 'Apollo 14' mission—*unbeknown to the rest of the crew*. Mitchell had apparently organised this independent thought transference experiment very privately, a few weeks before his 1971 flight with the intention of investigating the nature of consciousness.

It is known that for a time Mitchell had an interest in Scientology. He was not alone, many of the researchers at the Stanford Research Institute (SRI) in California were Scientologists. The laser physicist Hal Puthoff had also been a member of Ron Hubbard's cult until the mid-'70s, after which he became very 'anti'. Referring to this incident in the lives of Mitchell, Puthoff *et al.* Jim Schnabel, author of *Remote Viewers* suggests that Scientology

offered a particularly appealing combination of "Eastern religious themes of reincarnation and retrospection with Western themes of *predestination,* ethical rigor and self-improvement through science and technology". Schnabel, (himself a Catholic) sums up scientology as "a severely mutated form of Protestantism, gone amok in the machine age". While Schnabel thought that Scientology appealed to both spiritual and technologically-minded people, it seems to us that most science-minded people would class a belief in predestination right up there with "new age crankiness".[60]

Open all hours

After his stint in the Apollo program, Ed Mitchell was involved with the organisation of a US Government-based research program into consciousness. And it is more than likely that the experiment during 'Apollo 14' was also organised with the knowledge of the government, even if his colleagues were in the dark, as it were, as to his activities. It was Ed Mitchell who 'sponsored' the admittance of Uri Geller to the United States for the testing of Geller's paraphyschological abilities in a PSI research program that was set up at—yes, the Stanford Research Institute and directed from 1972-1985 by one Hal Puthoff, formerly of the National Security Agency. From 1972-1982 Puthoff's assistant was the laser physicist Russell Targ.[61]

In May 1972 Ed Mitchell had met Andrija Puharich in Chicago and arranged that he, Mitchell, would have the rights on the first US-based research of Uri Geller's abilities.[62] Allegedly, the 'contract sponsor' was interested in Geller. Uri Geller relates that Puthoff and Targ had meetings with the Israeli Secret Service, Mossad, prior to his departure for the United States. Did Mitchell also have secret ties with the American secret services by then?

At that time, the USA was not alone in wanting to investigate Geller. The Munich-based Max Planck Institute for Plasma Physics was also interested, but *"Puharich had already committed"* to the USA. This is the language of contracts and arrangements, not of a private individual. Despite Puharich's arrangements,

Geller records that he *did* work with the Max Planck insititute.[65] In another biography *The Geller Effect* Uri Geller tells us that he first worked in a series of laboratory experiments with the SRI in November 1972, the first running for six weeks which coincided with the alleged timing of 'Apollo 17'. He then did a further eight days in August 1973 supervised by laser physicists Harold Puthoff and Russel Targ. In 1972, the Chairman of the Physics Dept. of Kent State University, Ohio, tested Geller's abilities to alter metal. In 1973, research physicist Eldon Byrd of the US Naval Surface Weapons Center in Maryland tested Geller and subsequently learned to bend metal and taught others to do the same. These tests were under the aegis of the US DOD and *not* held on the Maryland premises.

So for all the sceptics out there, it should be noted that the authorities were obviously taking a great interest in such matters, while pretending not to do so. Readers of this book should be getting used to that attitude by now!

All the spyboys of the space age wanted the psiboy Geller on their team, though not necessarily too visibly! The practise of doing their tests after hours or in remote locations seemed to have been the norm. Additionally, SRI and the Lawrence Livermore Laboratories, just up the road from Stanford in California most certainly conducted experiments with Geller.[66] When Ed Mitchell had witnessed one of Geller's experiments demonstrating the mental interaction possible with computers he observed that *everything* in America was stored on computers. Interestingly, in August 1972

Ed Mitchell arranged a meeting between Wernher von Braun and Uri Geller.[67]

After Apollo, Ed Mitchell established his Noetics Institute dedicated to the exploration of PSI. An alleged 'goodbye' to the super rationalist? Not really. The word noetic means "of, or pertaining to the mind or intellect". Noetus was a native of Smyrna and presbyter of the Church of Asia Minor in about AD 230. A follower of Noetus excluded the Son and the Holy Spirit from the Trinity. As noetics propounds a science of the intellect, philosophia tends to be ignored.

The leopard does not change its spots, and Ed Mitchell may well research the effects of ESP, remote viewing and whatever, but then so does the American Government.

To be unable to respond to a question about his trip to the lunar surface because he was "out of touch with his feelings" is rather sidestepping the issue in our view, unworthy of someone with such a grasp of the potentiality of the mind. A man who prizes intellect so highly could surely conjure up an adequate phrase in response to *THE* question. Of course, that might be harder to do if one has not truly had the experience. In case you might think that little tour of PSI irrelevant to the issue of the Apollo Program, the very fact that Ed Mitchell and the US think tanks are so involved in such matters indicates that on the contrary, it has a great deal of relevance.

Buzz-words

Whether these astronauts were wittingly or unwittingly dragged into what appears to have been a massive deceit, they certainly exhibited behaviour patterns contrary to their job qualifications. The extent of their problem is epitomised by this anecdote from Buzz Aldrin. After his involvement with the 'Apollo 11' scenario Aldrin had experienced increasingly severe bouts of mental illness. In his autobiography *Return To Earth* Aldrin writes that from the time he left the quarantine headquarters until he went into a psychiatric hospital, he spent nearly two years in varying degrees of depression interspersed with the odd moment of optimism. In June of 1971, under medication but reintegrated into the USAF and working out of Edwards Air Force Base, California, Buzz Aldrin felt strong enough to accept a public invitation. He was to participate in an informal question and answer session at an after dinner gathering (which included Aldrin's Base Commander) of the Lancaster Chamber of Commerce.

Increasingly apprehensive as the day came nearer, he met the presenter and was told that the questions would be easy and that no preparation would be necessary. However, the first question asked was the one that he dreaded most and had never known how to answer adequately: "What was it really like on the Moon, Buzz?" He tells us that he carefully picked his way through a reply, and that he thought that all the test pilots would be laughing at him.

Now why should they do that? Is it because the unemotional pilot of the right stuff does not like sharing his feelings? Or is it because it is virtually impossible to describe a momentous event which never occurred—or only 'occurred' as a cover version of an allegedly real event?

Aldrin goes on to tell us that he remembers little more of this interview. What his audience did not see was Buzz, on leaving the gathering with Joan, slip into a side alley immediately next door to the venue and silently weep his heart out—until Joan took him away for a very strong drink.[68]

The psychologist Stan Gooch has observed that this anecdote demonstrates the signs of a deeply disturbed psyche and that the severe guilt associated with such circumstances could certainly cause two years of depression.[69]

Six years later in 1977, Whistle-Blower Bill Kaysing was invited by CBS Television to appear in a debate together with Buzz Aldrin. It was the intention of the moderator, Truman Lafayette, to finally settle the issues that Kaysing had raised concerning the authenticity of the lunar landings.

Aldrin did not show up. Bill Kaysing was obliged to continue the show alone.

Later in the mid 1990s, Aldrin appeared on a British TV talkshow hosted by Frank Skinner during which he gave the impression of being utterly detached from anything to do with 'Apollo 11'. For example, when asked where exactly he had landed, he did not reproduce Ed Mitchell's enthusiasm (albeit inaccurate) for latitude and longitude but pointed casually and without interest to the large map of the Moon suspended above the set. Finally, when Skinner asked Aldrin to comment on the speculation that they never went to the Moon, Aldrin's face was a study.[70] Yet when this show was repeated in a 1996 compendium of the best moments from the Frank Skinner series, that question had been edited out from the interview. Who made the decision to edit and if there was nothing to hide, why was this particular moment cut?

Tee total

When golfer Peter Alliss played golf and spoke with 'Apollo 14' astronaut Alan B Shepard he asked him about his feelings concerning his visit to the lunar surface. Shepard said that: "It was a beautiful quiet place while I was up there on the Moon and it's a beautiful quiet place down here among these rocks" (referring to the mountains which he could see from the balloon in which he was being interviewed). He said that it was a very satisfying part of his life and that "he had been rather hard and unpleasant" during the six years between his flights (May 6 1961 and 'Apollo 14' 1971—his walk on the Moon as he called it) but that he had matured in the process. Well he certainly had not learnt to count, that makes ten years, not six.

When asked why he thought that many of the astronauts had returned from their Moon missions and become totally different people, Shephard acknowledged the questions as valid and asserted that the unique cause for such changes was their inability to deal with the publicity and their role as 'national hero'.

He insisted that these behavioural problems were *nothing to do with their having been on the Moon,* "that was a totally different process". *(our emphasis and we could not agree more!)* Shepard then went on to say (twice) that although becoming a 'national hero' *had* been the problem, it was no longer so, as all the astronauts concerned had overcome such reactions. We have to comment that the behaviour of Armstrong and Aldrin does not corroborate his remark.[71]

As Whistle-Blower Kaysing has said: "If I am wrong in my claim that we did not go to the Moon with Apollo—any of these astronauts, with their hands-on experience and technical knowledge of the event—would be able to demolish my theory within five minutes of discussion".

Although Kaysing is still waiting and still happy to debate the matter with any of the Apollo astronauts, so far, there have been no takers. According to David Wise, the author of *The Politics Of Lies,* at least 25% of the American population also think that the Moon landings were faked. There has been a further Mori poll that concluded the figure was nearer to 30%. When the 'Apollo 11' astronauts were given a parade of honour in Sweden, Aldrin particularly noted that the people, while polite, were less than enthusiastic.[72] Major Dutch newspapers openly questioned the authenticity of the event, but this European point of view was, somewhat naturally, not taken up by the American press.[73] Moreover, during an interview in 1994, Aldrin said that he first heard of the concerns regarding the veracity of the Moon landings—*in May of 1994!* [74]

Who dares—sins

If you had achieved the most extraordinary accomplishment in human history—to be among the first to ever walk on another planet—after the event, would *you* not be enthused, become emotional and desirous of sharing that experience with your fellow men, and in some considerable detail, however rigorous your military training? After all, think of war veterans and their stories; of those who have miraculous escapes from death. All those who fulfil outstanding sporting achievements, such as breaking speed or endurance records. When humans have something extra ordinary happen to them, they try to convey something of that experience to their fellow humans. Such attempts contribute to the growth of civilisation.

We appreciate the suggestion that this business of visiting the Moon is so "out of the range" of most people's everyday lives that it could be difficult to convey the breadth of such an experience. However, that does not appear to be the problem. Here is a band of men, who were hand picked from the best (the bravest and the most intelligent) that their country could offer.

From the behavioural patterns of many of these astronauts in the post-Apollo era, it would appear that the Moon had the singular ability of draining all such qualities from its visitors!

Where is the *EMOTION*, the *PASSION* of the never-to-be-forgotten experiences and achievements of the named Apollo astronauts? Although we can comment on the apparent effects of the Apollo flights on these men, none of us are in a direct position to judge the astronauts and their behaviour. These men have no doubt lived their personal hell and heaven many times over. We have to ask ourselves what exactly would we have done if faced with similar circumstances? What power or influence does NASA or any other government department exert that results in these people conveying little or nothing of their amazing exploits?

However, it would appear that the technicians directly involved with this deception, and who were equally powerless to take any direct stand, were so outraged at the massive fraud involved that they managed to conceal and/or encode within the NASA official record the Whistle-Blowing clues that we have discovered and documented in the present book.

Chapter Eight

Servants of Circumstance

More trials and tribulations for the masters' class. Why both Project Horizon and the Apollo lunar program seem laden with obstacles. We examine the conflicting reports regarding the first man in space, setting a precedent for the Apollo scenario. NASA as well as the Soviets run into serious difficulties. Inconsistencies surface in connection with the Apollo laser ranging experiments.

Gridlock

The Project Horizon proposal put forward by General Medaris had recommended its concept for a military lunar outpost to accommodate a company of twelve *soldier-astronauts*. Two men would precede a second group of seven and finally a further three astronauts would land, bringing the total to twelve. No surprise then that the Apollo missions demanded a total of twelve men designated for the lunar landing and that these men should proceed two-by-two.

The most favourable location for such an outpost was considered to be bounded by 20° latitude and longitude of the optical centre of the Moon.[1] The high proportion of the probes

from the Ranger, Surveyor, Apollo *and* Luna missions landing in this sector indicate that the same overall target area was adhered to by *both the USA and the USSR.*

Coincidence? Surely not.

We suggest that this arena formed the basis of a cohesive lunar exploration program undertaken by both nations. The necessary restriction to this 20° lat/long arena was dictated by accommodating "a number of technical reasons" of which rocket vehicle energy requirements and temperature were cited. At first glance, this is a strange choice of location for the equatorial region is the *hottest* place on the lunar surface. Unless equipment is set up in the

---

Rocket reasons

The Greek god Apollo was often linked to the origins and defence of civil order and to the founding of cities (or lunar outposts!).

Saturn, eventually adopted as the name of the launcher for Project Apollo, was the Roman name for Cronus, associated with limitation and time.

The Greeks considered Cronus to be the god of Agriculture—

which in turn forms an interesting link with the Crop Glyphs of Southern England.

---

permanently shadowed areas on the lunar surface, there will be thermal strains due to the variation in daytime and night-time temperatures.[2] What the Project Horizon report carefully omitted was the crucial fact that the centre of the visible disk of the Moon is the only arena from which a radar echo is efficiently returned. To elaborate on this important point we leave the ABMA HQ, Huntsville, Alabama and cross the water to Cheshire, England, home of Sir Bernard Lovell and the Jodrell Bank radio telescope.

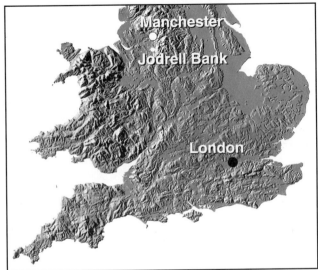

1. Location of the Radio Astronomy Laboratories, Jodrell Bank, England at 53°14′ N, 2°18′ W.

The Cheshire cats—Part One

In the pursuit of Project Horizon and the Apollo Surrogate Program, the radio telescope at Jodrell Bank under the direction of Sir Bernard Lovell had its role to play. All this had started in the early post-war days when Lovell, together with his colleagues and other scientists around the world, wanted to establish the correct Earth/Moon distance and were attempting to bounce radar off the surface—the 4/7ths of the lunar disk that is permanently turned towards our planet. After an initial success in 1949, significant scientific results were achieved at Jodrell Bank in 1953. Using long pulses lasting 30 milliseconds on a 2.5m

wavelength, strong echoes were returned to Jodrell Bank after a delay which varied from 2.4 to 2.7 seconds, depending upon the orbital position of the Moon.

At Jodrell Bank the brilliant John G Evans estimated that the Moon reflected radar waves in a different manner to light waves. The entire lunar disk reflected light waves but it was only a region in the centre of the lunar disk with a radius ⅓rd of the lunar radius of 1,080 miles/1,738 kms that reflected the radar waves. This was an effective target area with a diameter of 720 miles/1,158 kms.

John Evans had concluded that the effective depth of the Moon *would enable it to be used in a communications circuit* with modulation frequencies of up to 1000 cycles/Hz per second. That would be *"just sufficient for intelligible speech and could be used for transmitting teletype".* Sir Bernard Lovell considered this to be *"a remarkable conclusion that would have been of vital importance* had it not been for the development of communication by Earth satellites".[3] (emphasis added) On the other hand Arthur C Clarke, who had been an RAF radar instructor at Yatesbury, England during some of WWII (in hut Number 9, for those who note that sort of detail), opined that "the Moon was too distant and too bad a radio-mirror to be of any use".[4] Why two such diametrically opposed viewpoints? And why did ACC attempt to diminish the importance of these experiments?

Despite Arthur C Clarke's reservations, lunar experiments at Jodrell Bank would be pursued. Was there a hidden agenda? Sir Bernard Lovell conceded that post-war research scientists were operating with a set of attitudes formed from their association with the armed forces and industrialists—probably the providers of both motivation and money. Certainly the 1947 events in New Mexico would have made the construction of the Jodrell Bank radio telescope even more relevant.

> ### De witt to woo
>
> **1946 January 24 Washington USA**
>
> It was announced that Lt Col John De Witt, working on US Army Signal Corps research—*Project Diana*—and using army radar equipment on a wavelength of 2.6 metres had finally detected (on Jan 10) variable strength radar echoes from the Moon. Apparently this experiment was considered of little scientific value by the Americans. An opinion that would not be shared by Sir Bernard Lovell. Setting the tone for PR policy relating to space, the USA only announced this experiment 14 days after it had *actually* taken place.
>
> **1946 February 6 Budapest Hungary**
>
> The Hungarian scientist Zoltän Bay reflected radar signals off the Moon for thirty minutes.
>
> **1947 April & November Shepparton, Australia**
>
> Australian scientists examined the problem of variable-strength lunar radar echo.
>
> **1949 July Jodrell Bank UK** Sir Bernard Lovell's first successful attempts at obtaining radar signals from the Moon.
>
> **1959 May 14 England-Moon-USA**
>
> Jodrell Bank bounced an intercontinental transmission *via the Moon* to USAF Cambridge Research Center, Bedford, Massachusetts.
>
> **1959 June 3 USA-Moon-Canada**
>
> Millstone Hill Radar Observatory, Westford, Massachusetts *bounced a recording of President Eisenhower's voice* via the Moon to Prince Albert, Saskatchewan Canada.
>
> **1959 August 25 England-Moon-USA**
>
> The Royal Radar Establishment at Malvern, England bounced signals off the Moon and over to the University of Texas.
>
> **1961 June USA & England-Moon-England & USA**
>
> Transmissions were received at both Jodrell Bank, Cheshire and Sagamore Hill Observatory, Massachusetts during mutual lunar visibility. Knowledge regarding ionosphere irregularities was greatly augmented through this collaboration.

Taking the MIC

The apparent spontaneity of the events associated with the functioning of Jodrell Bank, described in Sir Bernard's autobiographies, owes more to a certain style of writing than a lack of awareness. Lovell recounts that on one occasion he went to play cricket instead of observing the launch of a Soviet space probe. He was not merely being an insouciant Englishman enjoying his favourite sport, despite the American hourly phone calls for progress reports, as is inferred. He must have known that he had the time to spare until the Soviet craft was trackable by his dish. Which leads us to suppose that he knew of the launch coordinates and pointing data before he left for his cricket match, and not upon his return, as is implied in his text. While this soft, 'friendly scientist' style makes for good dramatic writing, it cannot disguise the fact that Sir Bernard Lovell has been at the cutting edge of scientific development in the fields of both

radar and radio astronomy in England, and has always been in contact with those who direct the UK's defence programs.

Whether or not all the participants were aware, those that Sir Bernard referred to as the armed forces and industrialists (which we would now term the Military Industrial Complex) were absolutely fundamental to the establishment of Jodrell Bank. It is therefore evident that the role of go-between that was apparently 'foisted upon' Jodrell Bank during the American/Soviet space program was, in reality, a deliberate policy and vital adjunct to that program. For despite the space historian T A Heppenheimer's insistence to the contrary, Sir Bernard Lovell himself has always been quite clear that he and his team *were* actively associated with both the Soviet and the American space programs from the late fifties onwards.[5]

In October of 1957 Lovell's Jodrell Bank radio telescope was still the only dish *in the entire world* capable of tracking the carrier rockets that would launch the Soviet Sputnik satellites into orbit—what a surprise. Prior to this launch, necessary work that would normally have taken months was completed within 48 hours. A demonstration that the British at least were taking the announcement of an imminent Soviet launch seriously, something which the Americans were publicly dismissing—safe in the private knowledge that the British would be tracking the Soviet craft.

Lovell and his team were successful in tracking both Sputnik carrier rockets and returning the technical information to the Academy of Sciences in Moscow. The Americans were successful in pretending that they had been totally surprised by such feats and the necessity to "beat the Commies into space" was tightened a notch. Was this why Heppenheimer has downplayed Jodrell Bank's link with the Soviets in his writings? Could it be that the Americans were (and are still) not keen to let it be known publicly that they were working together with a British observatory that was closely connected to the Soviets—their claimed Cold War enemy?

Why might we conclude that?

Well, in April 1958, a funny thing happened on the way to the Moon when the US Air Force in the shape of the American Colonel L, paid a secret visit to Sir Bernard Lovell.

Open secret
Upon his arrival at Jodrell Bank Colonel L requested that Lovell close all the doors and windows to his office and thereupon proceeded to talk in such a near whisper that Lovell had to strain to hear. It turned out that the United States Air Force needed Lovell's help in tracking their Moon rocket launch, planned for mid-August. The Americans intended to send a small team of technicians and a large trailer full of tracking equipment over to England from the Los Angeles Space Technology Laboratories.

About one month before the launch, Lovell had to ensure that he would be able to connect their equipment to the telescope. This project was so hush-hush that nobody at Jodrell Bank was to know about it until a few days before

the launch. Unable to consult the British authorities before agreeing to the deal with Colonel L—due to this intense secrecy—Lovell said that he accepted the commission after deciding to incorporate it into his International Geophysical Year experiments, in this way he avoided the need to consult with either the M or the IC.

QUESTION: How can it be that Bernard Lovell's DSIR colleague Hingston had a meeting with the British Foreign Office *just two days prior to the launch?* Allegedly exasperated by the events taking place, the Foreign Office had suggested to Hingston that the US Embassy knock together the heads of the USAF, the PR organisation and his own. In relating this incident, Sir Bernard reveals that the Foreign Office were a part of this PR exercise all along. So why pretend otherwise?[6]

QUESTION: Having taken so much trouble to maintain secrecy, why did the Americans then send (through some narrow roads in north-west England) to Jodrell Bank their very large trailer emblazoned with the words *JODRELL BANK —US AIR FORCE—PROJECT ABLE* in large letters along its sides?[7]

QUESTION: How exactly did it come to pass that the science correspondent of the respected *Manchester Guardian* newspaper just *happened* to see this trailer arriving at Jodrell Bank and wrote a remarkably informed piece for the next day's edition of this major national newspaper?

Whether the real reason for all this secrecy was to steal a march on the US satellite launches, thus securing a strong foothold for the USAF in the space program, or to impress the American and British public and use the go-between to inform the Soviets of their progress, it was all to no avail. The United States Air Force's Project Able was unable to either show the Soviets, or their tri-service rivals, the American Army and Navy, that they were 'go'. Launched by an Atlas ICBM rocket carrier on August 17, Able exploded 80 seconds after leaving the pad, long before it came within Jodrell Bank's jurisdiction. Oh well! It lasted 20 seconds longer than that other PR exercise, Howard Hughes' *Spruce Goose!*

1958 October 11

Jodrell Bank picked up the next experiment from the USA, Pioneer 1, ten minutes after its launch from Cape Canaveral. The radio telescope was able to fix the direction to within *half a degree* and signals indicating the rocket's speed, encounters with micrometeorites and the measuring of their ion content were returned to Earth. Over a hundred accurate fixes of the probe's position were made and all the telemetered data from the probe was then returned to Los Angeles for computation. We are emphasising the accuracy with which Jodrell Bank could pick up these space launches—for the very good reason that on two significant future dates, there was to be a remarkable *lack of information* available at Jodrell Bank.

Over the following months the USA plodded through varying forms of failure in the early launches of the Pioneer program and the Soviets were heard to comment that they would only attempt a lunar rocket when they could guide it accurately.[7] What is of significance in this comment is the fact that the Soviets did not have a radio telescope of any appreciable size until February 1961, by which time they had built the Crimean deep space tracking station with a 140ft/42m aperture (Jodrell Bank had a 250ft/76m aperture). Previously they had compensated for this lack by using very powerful transmitters in their Lunik probes which their smaller dishes could pick up. It also needs to be said that for a rocket to reach the Moon and inject into lunar orbit, a tremendous amount of precision is required in designing the trajectory through the Earth's gravitational field. At this time the USA were apparently very pleased if they could get to within 50,000 miles of the Moon. The Soviets on the other hand, despite their observations on guided rocketry, *were* masters in the art of accurate rocket guidance.

If any of us were lunar rocket riders, surely we would rather travel with the bus company that actually stopped at the intended destination, particularly so if that destination also happened to be the last stop on the route to infinity!

First there

Soviet superiority in space was underlined again in September 1959 by the launch of Luna 2, and using Soviet-supplied data by arrangement with Korolëv, Jodrell Bank tracked the craft. The American contingent were *still* hanging out in their trailers next to the radio telescope—why? Were they waiting for the launch of Luna 2? Less than one hour after launch, Moscow telexed Lovell the precise co-ordinates of the probe and its predicted lunar impact time of 22 hours 01 minutes BST the next day, Sunday. At 22 hours 02 minutes 23 seconds, to within 83 seconds of their prediction, the Soviets had placed the first man-made object on the Moon. Richard Nixon, then Vice-President to Eisenhower, questioned whether it had really struck the Moon. And surprise, surprise! Lovell, the 'go between' was able to establish the validity of the Soviet attempt. Lovell's colleague J G Davies, proved conclusively that Luna 2 had succeeded by measuring the Doppler shift during the last 60 minutes of the rocket's passage through the Moon's gravitational field and all the way down to the surface. Davies had also compared the frequency of the received signal on the 19 megahertz equipment, with a standard in the control

---

Communications

Hermes, the Greek name for the Roman god Mercury, was the son of Zeus and thus the brother of Apollo.

Supposed protector of cattle and sheep he was also associated with Pan and fertility.

Protector of thresholds and inferior to Apollo, he was also nominated

the god of deceit.

Hermes covered the preliminary stages of space research, the ICBM program.

The Mercury program (stage 1 of the manned flight phases of Project Horizon) was ostensibly aimed at getting a single astronaut into orbit around the Earth and communicating successfully with Mission Control.

Were they also attempting to get communication satellites into operation *around the Moon?*

---

room. This comparison was crucial in formally establishing the general region of impact. Lovell stated that this was the first time such measurements had been made—it then became a technique that would be refined and used "in all subsequent Moon experiments to establish the motion of rockets under the gravitational field of the Moon". A month later, in October 1959 Jodrell Bank were working with the Soviets again, when the data and recorded tapes collated (relating to the Lunik III probe which photographed the far side of the Moon) were sent to Moscow by Diplomatic pouch.[8]

For what we are about to receive ...

On 11 March 1960 the American solar probe Pioneer 5 launched from Cape Canaveral became the first probe *to receive transmitted instructions from Jodrell Bank*. Prior to this event Jodrell Bank had only received signals *from* space vehicles. Their dish was still the only telescope in the world with enough strength to command a probe's functions at a distance of some thousands of miles. Their first job was to separate the rocket carrier from the payload by signalling to the probe when it was at a distance of 5,000 miles from Earth. After which Jodrell Bank monitored and maintained contact with Pioneer 5 throughout its journey through the inner planetary region of our solar system. Jodrell Bank was equipped with powerful military transmitters during the early 1960s, while the Fylingdale early warning system radio dishes were under construction. This was ostensibly so that the observatory could serve as part of the West's anti-ICBM warning system. Supposing that to be the false Cold War reason—as at the very highest levels scientists and engineers were working together on the same project—the space program—then what would the extra power enable them to do? Was it a necessary addition to their already powerful dish, in order to send those signals to Pioneer 5 perhaps?

... may we be truly grateful

It was apparently only following this last exploit that Lord Nuffield and his foundation 'rescued' Jodrell Bank from the remainder of its debts and thereafter the telescope facility become known as the Nuffield Radio Astronomy Laboratories. However, the reality is that the 250ft/76m telescope at Jodrell Bank was partially funded by the Nuffield foundation from its very beginnings, and remembering the MIC, might we not conclude that this observatory's site and the size of this dish had always been considered as a prime and integral part of the space program by the self-styled 'masters of infinity'? The PR-friendly "Jodrell Bank rescue from financial ruin and worry" by the Nuffield foundation looks more like a matter of ongoing space program policy—whereby the unofficial story is regularised by an enactment of the reality some years after the event.

In his biography, Lovell says that Jodrell Bank continued to play a "significant role" in the space programs of both the USA and the USSR *throughout the next decade*, but then somewhat contradicts himself by stating that Jodrell Bank's contribution had fallen off notably by July 1969, as the USA and the USSR had acquired their own tracking stations.

While this information gives added credence to our proposition that Project Able had been a PR exercise, elsewhere Lovell records that the USA possessed very powerful defence transmitters *as early as 1958* and that they were using these transmitters to complement their smaller telescopes—a process that enabled them, for example, to pick up signals from Venus, nearly 100 times further away from Earth than the Moon.[9]

Reserved parking—management only!

When taking the lunar unmanned landings as a whole—not as the result of two nations racing to the Moon—one can see quite clearly that the selectors of the Project Horizon manned lunar base landing sites had obviously taken John G Evan's radar target area into account as an important communications detail. Taking a 30° x 30° grid as the very outside limit, we can see that Ranger 4 landed within these parameters, albeit on the far side of the Moon. On the near side, Rangers 6, 7, 8, and 9 also met this criteria, as did all the Surveyors and the Soviet Luna. The variants on these parameters were

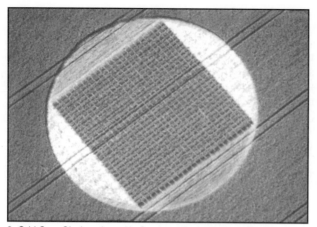

2. Grid Crop Glyph activated in Southern England, July 30 1997.

S ALEXANDER

Russian real estate—who bought the farm?

In Moscow a request authorising the launch of a human being into space in December 1960 had been granted and signed on September 19 1959 by the Central Committee of the Communist Party in conjunction with Korolëv and five other designers of the space program. Despite a horrific ballistic missile explosion on a launch pad at Baikonur on October 24, which killed 165 people, the manned space program continued undeterred. Two years later, on April 12 1961 Moscow announced the successful orbital flight of Yuri Gagarin, and the space program entered into its most serious phase—the test run of public opinion.

the landing sites of the Luna soil diggers and the Lunikhod rovers. If one wishes to leave prospective landing sites uncluttered and unsullied, it makes a lot of sense to practise soil sampling and lunar roving capacities outside the intended landing grid. Could the Luna craft sited on the weaker transmitting areas of the western and eastern limbs really be a matter of uncoordinated chance? We think not. Were they there to bump up communication capacity?

As with Sputnik, the Western world was supposedly taken aback on hearing of the Soviet's technical first. Wernher von Braun was awoken by a phone call from a journalist who asked him what he thought of the news. When WvB found out what that 'news' was, he professed later that he was so astonished he never could remember the reply that he had given.[11]

The sites specifically designated as Apollo manned landing sites were nearly all within the 20° x 20° parameters, allowing a leeway of 6° latitude ('Apollo 15') and 10° longitude ('Apollo 17') which nevertheless kept them within the 30° x 30° arena. And note that in the Sea of Tranquillity target areas numbers 1 and 2, there were unmanned probes well within the vicinity of the alleged ultimate 'Apollo 11' landing site. It is worth noting that landing site No 1 at the Sea of Tranquillity was not originally earmarked for 'Apollo 11'—so for what was it destined?

Was it the intended parking place for the Soviet Luna 15?[10]

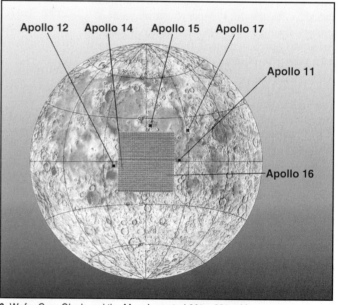

3. Wafer Crop Glyph and the Moon's central 20° x 20° grid.

Others within the NASA agency, in the throes of preparing the Mercury launch of Alan Shepard, were also alleged to have been ignorant of this flight until after the event. President Kennedy, thanks to the American intelligence networks, is said to have been well aware of the imminence of the flight. And Pierre Salinger is alleged to have prepared a press release in advance for him.[12]

In Moscow rumours abounded. The British aristocrat Lord Bruce-Gardyne, at that time foreign correspondent to the London *Financial Times*, arrived in Moscow in the spring of that year on business.[13] He toured from Leningrad to Siberia and returned to Moscow some six weeks later on April 6. The capital was awash with stories that the Soviets were about to launch their first manned space flight.

Bruce-Gardyne left for London on the morning of April 11 1961 and during the trip to the airport his remarkably well-connected Soviet minder informed him that the *manned space flight had already taken place.* Bruce-Gardyne said his minder had this information officially from the Chairman of the Soviet Committee of Sciences *who confirmed that this flight had been successfully completed.* When the somewhat astonished Bruce-Gardyne asked why there was no official announcement, his minder replied that the cosmonaut was undergoing post-flight checks, after which the news would be broadcast. On breaking his journey in Warsaw, Bruce-Gardyne communicated this news to the *Financial Times* office back in London, indicating his reasons for believing it to be accurate. But when changing planes in East Berlin on April 12, Bruce-Gardyne heard the airport loudspeakers announcing that Gagarin was orbiting the globe *at that very moment!*

Later, Bruce-Gardyne was able to establish that although *NASA had initially denied all knowledge of such a flight,* this "erroneous statement" was subsequently corrected by the White House—who confirmed that the flight had been tracked on the morning of April 12 after all! By whom? The records of the time state that the American radar and electronic detectors had not picked up any signals of such a flight on April 12 1961 and that it was only

well after the event that they *eventually concurred* that the flight had taken place.[14]

While mentioning the space programs of both countries generally, Sputnik I and II specifically, and some aspects of the space program in great detail in his memoirs of that period,[15] Sir Bernard Lovell makes no mention *at all* of the alleged Gagarin flight. This is most certainly an odd omission, when one considers that this landmark event was supposed to be the flight of the first human being into space. Unless of course, Jodrell Bank radio telescope *had also failed to pick up any signal—BECAUSE THERE WAS NOTHING THERE TO PICK UP.*

By 1998 the storyline had changed. The Doran & Bizony (D&B) Gagarin Biography *Starman*, published in March 1998 on the 30th anniversary of Gagarin's tragic death relates:

> American radar stations recorded the launch of an R-7 rocket and fifteen minutes later a radio monitoring post in the Aleutian Islands off Alaska detected unmistakable signs "of live dialogue with a cosmonaut".[16]

Later to become an economics adviser to Prime Minister Margaret Thatcher, Lord Bruce-Gardyne was an upstanding figure of the British establishment. We have been told on good authority from someone who knew and worked with him, that it would have been completely out of character for him to have made up this story as 'a joke' for his newspaper for, in his experience, Bruce-Gardyne was not possessed of a sense of humour.[17] Further, this story of a previous flight is apparently corroborated by a man who was hardly biased in favour of the Western establishment. At the time Dennis Ogden was the official British Communist Party journalist and Moscow correspondent for *The Daily Worker*. Ogden reported on the Gagarin substitution for the original cosmonaut in the first manned spaceflight.[18] This second independent account seemingly corroborated Lord Bruce-Gardyne's report. As we shall see, near enough is not good enough, and seemingly is not actually!

The inevitable conclusion that we are *led* to consider by this rumour fest is that the Gagarin

297

flight was nothing more than a show—the real event having taken place previously.

Incidentally it was at around this time that Wernher von Braun referred to the choice of the Moon as the immediate objective of the space program by stating that: "Everybody knows what the Moon is, everybody knows what this decade is and everybody can tell a live astronaut who returned from the Moon from one who didn't". A remark which needs some explaining—unless, for example, despite his apparent surprise at the news of Gagarin, *he was fully aware of what had actually happened during the first attempt at manned space flight.*

My name is Bond . . .
Valentin Bondarenko

James Oberg, in his research into Soviet space matters, unearthed the story of Valentin Bondarenko, a Soviet cosmonaut who is alleged to have died on March 23 1961. Victim of a pressure chamber experiment which went wrong, twenty-four year old Bondarenko suffered such severe burns that there was little skin left upon his body, his eyes were burned out and he was literally scalped. Yet he was still alive when he was admitted to hospital. The only way that Dr. Golyakovsky, the emergency surgeon at the prestigious Botkin hospital, could insert pain killers was through the soles of the victim's feet. Golyakovsky was told that the cosmonaut was 'Sergeyev' a 24 year old Air Force lieutenant. James Oberg says that Bondarenko was to live for sixteen hours before his body gave up the fight for life. According to the authors of *Manned Space Flights in the Soviet Union* and the space historian Brian Harvey he was to survive for only eight hours.[19] The dead cosmonaut was buried in his home town of Kharkov in the Ukraine far from his wife and five year old child—his name not mentioned in the annals of space-flight for 25 years. Why?

Chinese whispers

We are told more about this accident by various researchers. Bondarenko had been in the pressure chamber for ten days (the Oberg ver-

sion) and towards the end of the test period had removed the sensors which were attached to his skin, then wiped his skin with cotton soaked in alcohol! This he had *carelessly thrown on a burner,* which had (not unnaturally) ignited. The pressure chamber was filled with pure oxygen and it had been impossible to stop the fire or release the cosmonaut quickly.

Brian Harvey informs us that Bodarenko was in the chamber for three days, Oberg tells us it was for ten days and in 1998 the D&B version of events states that Bondarenko's test went on for fifteen days. This disparity of information is not necessarily to be laid at the door of the Soviet political system. However, the amount of *time* spent in the chamber does not alter the results—the accident. So this variation of the length of time spent by the cosmonaut within this chamber, reveals that a principle flaw in this story relates to the time factor. And why should that be so? Before we attempt to answer that question we need to unpick the various strands of this Bondarenko affair, for there are more fundamental flaws to be found.

We are given to understand that the isolation chamber in which Bondarenko was working was at the Institute for Medical and Biological problems near Petrovsky Park under the direction of Oleg Gazenko. It is inferred that the facilities at the cosmonauts training school in Star City, some 25 miles north-east of Moscow were incomplete when the first twenty cosmonauts were recruited. This does not mean that by March 1961 the facility was still unfinished. The chamber was a large sealed tank in which the cosmonaut lived while the doctors raised or lowered the air pressure according to the criteria of their experiments and these sessions ran from between one and ten days—although the cosmonauts never knew how long the tests were going to last at the outset of each experiment. The experiment was meant to simulate the conditions of being alone in a spacecraft that was possibly going to experience delays in returning to Earth, thus exposing the cosmonaut to the tensions of not knowing when the journey would be over. Contact between controllers (doctors and technicians) and subject (the cosmonaut) were kept to a minimum.

For those with an interest in such matters, the Petrovsky Park simulator *had no windows*. The cosmonauts were given no visual stimuli, did not know what time of day it was and the interior electric lighting was switched on and off with no regard for their circadian cycles. Yet supposedly, the controllers could observe the astronauts through a thick plate glass window, or a porthole, or a TV screen, take your pick, each source of information is different!

In an aside which has relevance to this, the cosmonaut Titov once persuaded his controllers to let him take a book into the chamber with him. This was strictly forbidden but eventually Titov convinced them, saying that he only wanted it as a good luck talisman. He already knew the contents by heart, he said. Of course this was a lie and Titov says that he spent a lot of time reading his book during his stint in the chamber.[20]

Which raises the following points:

All the cosmonauts knew that if they did not go through with the chamber and perform well, they would not get into space. Titov, a proud and clever man was, like all the cosmonauts, success driven. Together with Gagarin, Nikolaev, Popovich, Bykovsky and Nelyubov—he was one of the Sochi Six. The equivalent of the USA's Mercury Seven, these six cosmonauts were selected out of the initial group of twenty for the 'first flight' training. Bondarenko was the youngest of the twenty. The odds on him ruining his chances by being caught out at such an exercise were virtually zero. If he knew he could get away with reading his book in forbidden circumstances, it was because he knew that he was not under *visual observation* during that experiment. After all, if the cosmonauts needed to practice space conditions, so did the technicians on the ground. And there would be no large windows for them to observe their cosmonauts when they were in their windowless tin cans in space. There would be only a TV camera, taking pictures for the medical doctors. Perhaps Titov managed to read his book out of view of the camera!

As the cosmonauts had to eat to survive, within this sealed tank there were rudimentary necessities for cooking! A saucepan, water and cans of tinned food together with an electric plate were the extent of this luxury. The pre-packed meals that the American astronauts would eventually squirt into their mouths were apparently not yet available in this simulation of space conditions experiment. This is odd, for on the Vostok that took Gagarin into space twenty days later, all the food was of the American-style prepacked space food sqeezy variety. As for the practicalities of heating food in such a chamber, this would only have been possible within two parameters:

- That the controllers de-pressurise the chamber at designated times for meals, which signifies complete co-ordination of activities between the two parties.
- That the mixture used for the tank was of nitrogen/oxygen. The Vostok space capsule had been built to use an 80% nitrogen/20% oxygen mix, almost the same as that experienced on Earth.

Living in the pressurised tank with that mixture would be to all intents and purposes the same as living in a submarine. Any problems with the nitrogen/oxygen mixture would only occur if a cosmonaut had to leave his ship *in a hurry* and use the portable pure oxygen supply, without first having vented his lungs of residual nitrogen—such an exercise can give a cosmonaut the 'bends'. The Soviets had chosen the nitrogen/oxygen mix for their manned space craft not only from the point of view of crew functionality but also from the safety aspect. Which fact means that they were perfectly aware of the fire risks attendant to a pure oxygen environment—well before March 1961.

Voluntary best servants

Now the one consistent theme to the Valentin Bondarenko saga is that he was living in the dangerous environment of a pure oxygen atmosphere. Had they been experimenting for a future project with this air mixture, they would not have been using Bondarenko but one of their testers, the military volunteers who were the unsung heroes of the Soviet space program. And had that individual been a tester, he would have been quietly buried and there would have been none of the subsequent stories and directives from on high.

The 1,200 testers who worked on the space project from 1960 through to the 1990s always had the choice of saying "no thank you" to any particular test, yet none did, for they *wanted* to contribute. Recruited from the military and offered a significant chance to make a contribution to the space program they were medical guinea pigs. Tested to the limits of physical endurance and having all the 'right stuff' they were just as keen to be the best and bravest in their accomplishments as were the more privileged named cosmonauts in their own domain.

As an example of the differences between the levels of difficulty experienced by these two groups of space pioneers, in testing for gravity tolerance the named cosmonauts had to endure up to seven Gs for two or three minutes and twelve Gs for twenty seconds. In their efforts to establish the parameters of human endurance, the Soviets pushed their 'volunteer testers' to up to forty Gs for a fraction of a second, twenty-seven Gs for a short time and ten Gs for up to seven minutes at a time. The doctors were considered to be ruthless, a trait they seemed to share with some of their Americanised colleagues. The testers' mortality rate of 50% overall was very high, bearing in mind that the negative results of some of their experiments (no doubt including radiation research) would only manifest later in their lives. Despite the great sacrifices they made for the advancement of space technology and humanity, these men were never publicly acknowledged, their work was undertaken in secret, the tragedies and the triumphs known only to themselves and their colleagues. Clearly, there is no exploration into new territory that proceeds without risk. The sadness is that those who took the greatest risks were hidden from view. D&B are to be congratulated for having revealed this aspect of the space program, and it is most fitting that the immense contribution to our understanding of space travel made by these men can now be recognised. It is our

opinion that the sort of tests that Bondarenko is said to have undertaken, actually would have been carried out by one of these unknown men. However, there are some points arising from D&B's story:

- Under pure oxygen conditions, there is a pre-existing highly combustible configuration. There would certainly not be *any form* of radiant heat liable to ignite flammable material functioning in the pressure chamber. Nor would there be any known flammable materials such as alcohol.
- A cosmonaut performing under test conditions would be unlikely to remove his equipment by himself before the test chamber had been depressurised.
- By the same token, Bondarenko, performing under test conditions, would have had permission from the technicians outside the chamber (who could read the pressure levels) before even touching his stove.
- In the identical conditions of an oxygen-rich atmosphere within a sealed capsule, it took only four minutes for the three American astronauts to die. How then did Bondarenko survive for thirty minutes, and survive well enough to be able to speak when they got him out?
- It is our preliminary conclusion that the cosmonaut Bondarenko did suffer from severe burns but that these *were not incurred as a result of a pure oxygen session in the isolation tank.*

Resolutions

On his arrival at the Botkin hospital, Dr. Golyakovsky had been told that his accident victim was named 'Sergeyev'. It is our opinion that the burnt cosmonaut was given the alias 'Sergeyev' because he was from Sergei Korolëv's cosmonaut team. This avoided the specific naming of a person. (Remember Professor K Sergeyev, alias Korolëv?) It also tells us that Korolëv was involved with this accident and that says to us Baikonur, not the medical Institute. Dr. Golakovsky stated that while the cosmonaut 'Sergeyev' was dying, a nameless army officer sat by the telephone in the corridor. This man had supplied him with the details of the accident and the man's name. Golakovsky would later recognise that officer from his photograph in the Soviet press. *It was Yuri Gagarin.*[21]

Orders from on high

"The family of Senior Lieutenant Bondarenko is to be provided with everything necessary, as befits the family of a cosmonaut."
Special order by Soviet Defence Minister RD Malinovsky
April 16 1961.
And Classified *Top Secret.*

The above edict was passed four days after the 'official' Gagarin flight; but a full 24 days after the March 23 'Bondarenko incident'. Given the importance of the statement, its security classification and the dramatic death of a cosmonaut, which time frame seems more logical? Surely, in a regime which prided itself on taking care of its citizens, the needs of the family concerned would be dealt with sooner, rather than later? And if we agree on that point then we need to take another look at the dating of this event. We have established that the circumstances of this incident are highly suspect and that a clue lies in the timing.

We therefore propose that the said date of March 23 1961 was not the final day of Bondarenko's test, instead let us try it as the date of commencement. According to the three accounts of this event, we have a choice of dates:

March 23 + 3 days = March 26, a Sunday
March 23 + 10 days = April 2, a Sunday
March 23 + 15 days = April 7, a Friday.

Given that Yuri Gagarin, albeit incognito, was with this patient as this man was admitted into hospital, either Yuri Gagarin was at the isolation tank when the incident occurred, or he flew with this man back to Moscow from the launch site in Baikonur. The cosmonauts disliked the medical tests in general and the isolation chamber in particular. We should remember the Soshi Six were the cream of the elite. At the other end of the scale, Bondarenko was the junior. There was no particular reason for Gagarin to be at the isolation chamber when another cosmonaut was in training there. If the accident occurred at the medical facilities, why send another cosmonaut to accompany the victim to the hospital rather than one of their own medical staff? On the other hand, if there was need of a cosmonaut at Baikonur, to assist the elite, then Bondarenko was their man; the top of the list would do the actual flying, the bottom of the list would provide back up.

On March 26 Gagarin was apparently at home in Star City.

On April 2 Gagarin is not recorded as being away from Star City.

On April 7 Gagarin was at the Baikonur launch pad with Cosmonaut Titov and the overall head of the Cosmonaut Training School, General Kamanin, in order to rehearse *what to do if a fire broke out while a cosmonaut was sealed in the capsule.*

In principle, under such conditions the ejection seat would fire the unlucky cosmonaut into the air. Should that operation fail there was a back-up system instigated by the control room. If that failed the cosmonaut would have to fire the seat himself. Ejection seats containing dummies had been tested under such conditions but on that day, April 7, the test was the 'real thing'. Who was doing the 'real thing' is a matter of conjecture for there is no indication that either Titov or Gagarin ever actually attempted the escape procedure themselves. There was a talk-through concerning procedures, much discussion over viability and expressions of confidence in 'the plan'.

Indeed in his diary Kamanin had noted that the cosmonauts had not made a training ejection from an aircraft and that Gagarin was seemingly "reluctant to do this".[22] It must be noted that Kamanin had not made up his mind as to whom would be on the first flight, Titov or Gagarin. And that on April 6 he was still in favour of Titov. The decision as to which cosmonaut would be chosen out of the six candidates was made by the State Committee in another area of Baikonur that same day, April 7th. As Kamanin was still appraising the responses of the two prime candidates during the fire test, we can only conclude that this decision was made after that test. Did the final choice of Gagarin have anything at all to do with the fact that at some point during the April 7 safety lecture and demonstration Titov had expressed his worries concerning the automatic firing system? Perhaps Kamanin did not have to make a choice. Perhaps the circumstances dictated his decision. In his diary for April 7, Kamanin had noted that: "He [Gagarin] did well today. Calmness, self-confidence and knowledgeability are his main characteristics".

To Bondarenko, with love

It is our opinion that at a date so close to the final decision for a public manned flight, these two cosmonauts Titov and Gagarin only *witnessed* run throughs covering the procedures for ejecting from a Vostok invaded by fire. These run throughs were performed *for them* by a cosmonaut—Valentin Bodarenko. Either the simulation of a fire condition got out of hand or when Bondarenko attempted to release the ejection seat, it failed or got stuck, and the ensuing fire gained control. It is our view that the cabin mixture was the normal nitrogen/ oxygen mix used in the Vostok. This factor enabled Bondarenko to survive but by the time they were able to remove the hatch Bondarenko had suffered the severe burns that would soon cost him his life. Bondarenko kept repeating: "It was my fault. I'm sorry, it was my fault". If he had fluffed releasing the ejection seat, then he would be attempting to tell the ground team that *he* had made a mistake, that the seat itself was probably functional.

We suspect that Gagarin either elected, or was asked (being Korolëv's favourite cosmonaut and at that time possibly still number two as the choice of first flight cosmonaut), to fly Bondarenko to Moscow (or be flown) and provide the cover story of the isolation chamber for Bondarenko, now labelled 'Sergeyev'. Yuri Gagarin was utterly loyal to the space program and would, some five days later, happily corroborate the fabrications that were recorded concerning his landing procedures.

This hypothesis cannot be dismissed out of hand. Cover stories should always stick as close to the truth as is possible and in this one there are indeed elements of truth.

In summary:

- We suggest that the entire Bondarenko story was lifted from an event that occurred at an earlier time period, (perhaps March 23 1960).
- Which fact would explain the discrepancy over the type of food used, and the use of the Moscow Institute.
- We suggest that the Soviets did actually test an oxygen environment, both in an attempt to be compatible with the American system and for their own decision-making processes.
- We suggest that it was a volunteer tester who died in such a test, not a cosmonaut.
- The Vostok nitrogen/oxygen supply was designed to last for ten days, and the orbit was designed in order to be able to take advantage of natural atmospheric friction that would slow the craft down over a few days, should things go very wrong. Whether this natural aero-braking would occur before the cosmonaut ran out of air and food was an unknown. This timing is the factor that conditioned the isolation chamber's ten-day time limit. Should the controllers have experimented with this unknown then the fifteen days mentioned as the length of stay in the chamber gives us even more reason to believe that such an experiment would have come under the heading of 'voluntary best servant, for the testing of', as the military would describe it.

The Ilyushin Illusion

Returning to the rumours that abounded prior to the Gagarin launch, in Moscow it was thought that Vladimir Iluyshin, son of the famous aeroplane designer, was also a cosmonaut and that he had used his famous father to pull strings to secure him as the first Soviet man in space prior to the Gagarin departure on April 12. Journalist Edouard Bobrovsky named the cosmonaut as *Sergei* Ilyushin returning him from space half dead and in a coma, writing that he subsequently had to be permanently hospitalised. Dennis Ogden's report for *The Daily Worker* named the cosmonaut as *Vladimir* Ilyushin.[23] James Oberg states that

> ### April 7 1978
> The Japanese launched a *broadcast* satellite called Yuri. Did the space club name it 'Yuri' in commemoration of an
> event that resulted in Yuri's trip becoming just a Soviet *broadcast* on April 12 1961?
> The society of masters thereby acknowledging the sacrifices made "in the name of the game"?

Vladimir Ilyushin lived in the same building as Bondarenko and was coincidentally in a car crash at the time of the Bondarenko event and that these crash injuries were the cause of the rumour about the space flight. There is no trace of Ilyushin in any of the published cosmonaut records and his presence on the space program has neither been confirmed nor denied. In fact, there is no trace of Ilyushin *at all*. He is non-existent. If he was not on the space program, why not publish a photograph and attempt to disprove this rumoured account? The D&B *Gagarin* biography relates that Ogden's story was published on April 10, and although a minor detail, it does not correspond with Bruce-Gardyne's timetable. In Moscow from April 6 through to the morning of April 11, it is extraordinary that neither he nor his Moscow minder mentioned it when backing up their own assertions.

Dennis Ogden's political and professional standing guaranteed that his position would be seen to be pro-Soviet by the West. Thus any revelatory topical story from his paper, such as a cosmonaut flight, would be taken as being highly likely to be true. This happy circumstance would enable him to print and pass on anything that the Soviets wished to be known in the West. And the same applies to Lord Bruce-Gardyne. He was known to be a newspaper man, and he came from the other end of the British political spectrum to that of Dennis Ogden. By planting different details but essentially the same story on the unwitting Bruce-Gardyne, the Soviets bedded down the rumour and enabled it to become a seedling, which would eventually grow into a tree. This in its turn would become a forest of rumours within which it would be impossible to dig for the true account.

These already inaccurate rumours were then officially exposed as being inaccurate. Wrong name of astronaut, wrong time, wrong circumstance. All the stories of a launch prior to that

of Gagarin are rumours. The rumour mongers are ridiculed for evermore and Gagarin is iconised as having been the first man into space after all. Everybody goes back to sleep! In the meantime back by the Baikonur 'drome, there had been a bad accident prior to the first attempt to get a man into space. What they 'wished' to be known and disseminated to the West via the two British journalists, was a double-bluff in the 'Roswellian' style. And why not? The same brains were running this Eastern version of the magician's show.

'chosen one'
And was Kamanin writing of the odds or was he Whistle-Blowing for posterity when he wrote in his diaries for that period April 6/7? "It's hard to decide which of these two men [Gagarin and Titov] should be sent to die and which of these two decent men should be made famous worldwide".[24] The day after the April 7 events, the Soshi Six were assembled in an allegedly spontaneous ceremony for the decision as to who should fly the first mission. Kamanin had already informed Gagarin and Titov of the selection, so that when Gagarin stepped forward as the chosen one this was, to all intents and purposes, a set-up. Gagarin made a supposedly off-the-cuff speech of acceptance and this fake ceremony was filmed by the official photographer, who ironically ran out of film. The play stopped, the actors waited in place, and when Suvorov had reloaded with fresh stock, the principal boy recited his lines all over again. Titov says to this day that he was convinced that he was to be the one, right until the moment that Kamanin enlightened him.

Dr. Donald's SFX trickery— Part Eight
Four days before the committee's decision as to who would be the 'chosen one', on April 3 1961 both Titov and Gagarin had been to a full

dress rehearsal, which was also filmed for posterity.

Total fabrication

Both these men took it in turns to make their farewell speeches at the bottom of the gantry, but as the rocket was then lying on its side, there are no clear photographs of it. The interior shots of the capsule sealing procedures were *completely staged* in another area of the launch hangar with the launch pad operators, *miming* for the camera. But this film was not just for the Baikonur historical record. This 'record' was for all of us. Vladimir Suvorov never got near enough to the actual launch to be able to film clearly this small matter of just what was going on in and around the capsule, when and exactly how. Nothing wrong with that, of course. Except that subsequently the Soviets cut the faked footage into the final shots of the actual launch and presented it to the world without *telling anyone* of that fact. World-wide, viewers were presented with a mostly fake event pretending to be a totally real event. And before we all go, "Tut! tut!— typical of the Soviets at that time", please remember Chapters One and Two of this book!

From this methodology, and given the number of technical problems that were unresolved,

4. The orange space suit similar to that which Gagarin wore, Moscow.   AULIS

5. Gantry with an A-1 rocket (full size replica), Moscow.   AULIS

it is easy to imagine that the Soviets could well have totally stage managed the actual launch on April 12 1961. And there was enough time to remove Gagarin and send up an empty capsule with a tape recorder in it—for lo and behold, just as the hatches had been battened down, Korolëv pronounced that the sensors for the door seals were not showing up correctly, although back at the pad, nothing had been signalled as amiss. Korolëv not only insisted on reopening the hatch, and starting again, which cost the launch a minimum of 30 minutes delay (there's that time period again) but also informed the staff that he alone would apprise Gagarin of what was happening. Now it would have been at this precise moment that Gagarin was instructed to leave the capsule.

Oleg Ivanovsky recalls that it took himself, the Chief Test Pilot Mark Gallai, the Chief of Rocket Troops Vladimir Shapalov, plus two juniors to seal the capsule and check the procedures. Thirty-two bolts had been screwed down in sequence around the circumference of the 100 kg hatch. But Ivanovsky tells us that only six hands were used for the resealing. Having gained at least a half hour break, and lost at least two men, another decidedly odd incident then occurred.[25]

The blockhouse had continued their count-down as if there were no delays at all and at T minus 40, the gantries and walkways began to swing away from the sides of the craft, even though the three men were still working at the hatch. How could the blockhouse do that, when Korolëv was in there co-ordinating the launch (and notably supplying music to Gagarin while he waited)—thereby creating opportunity for his exit from the capsule? Korolëv was in total charge of the blockhouse and he *knew* full well that the men had not finished their job. D&B record that there was a "moment of awkwardness" while the block-house was telephoned and the gantries swung back to the rocket again.

What sort of a "moment of awkwardness"?

Was it a *cosmonaut change* "moment of awkwardness"? In any event, if anything went wrong during the flight they would certainly need a body. Was one of the 'gantry juniors' actually Grigory Nelyubov, who, before coming to an untimely end, always maintained that he had served as Yuri Gagarin's back-up? And did another 'gantry junior' escort Gagarin off the rig during that "moment of awkwardness"?

Of this launch Titov said:

It was strange to hear Yuri's voice...we were sitting together just half an hour ago, and now he was up there some-where. It was hard to understand. Time somehow lost its dimensions for me. That's how I felt.[26]

Well, he's right on the button there. Because over two hours had elapsed since their fond farewells in the bus that had delivered them to the pad and the departure of Vostok.[27]

Such a scenario as we have just outlined would have been made totally possible through the extreme loyalty of all those involved in the project of getting a man into space. By care-fully selecting his team, Korolëv had sur-rounded himself with such high quality people that a deception of this nature would have been difficult—but not impossible—to pull off. The technical side of it was "in the can" as they say, for the necessity for faking the film of the event was an already accepted propaganda pro-cedure, as we have seen. The Soviets had first perfected the art of capsule-to-ground commu-nication by using taped messages in their ma-chines and there is no guarantee at all that the film footage of Gagarin inside the capsule was not shot pre-flight, as was the case with the other sequences associated with this attempt.

If our reconstructed scenario for the death of Bondarenko on April 7 is correct, then this flight planned for April 12 had to go ahead, indeed that previous incident would not have been considered as part of the main launch on April 12 at all. Although very sad, the April 7 incident was nothing more than an accident during routine rehearsals, and as we all know, the reason for rehearsals is to iron out any kinks, which is why they did not put one of their top guns into the Vostok capsule that day. It is also why Bondarenko was the first of the *cosmonauts* to die in the line of duty.

On April 12 1961 did Korolëv and his team take out insurance against any possible technical hiatus that might occur, thereby as-suring the practical future of the entire space program? ◼

Every dog has his day

No matter how the actual mechanics of this event were played out, permission *had* already been given to fly a cosmonaut by the end of December 1960, and dates are what this recon-struction is all about. Human nature is com-petitive and once the green light had been given, the race was on. Both Sputniks 9 and 10 carried what were designated as a dummy and a dog. Why fly a dummy when one can fly a man? What is a dummy going to reveal about the psychological reactions of a human being in space?

In March 1960 one capsule containing two dogs was the subject of an intense search by a plane load of search and rescue people plus two bomb disposal experts, themselves the subject of a KGB search and rescue mission which extricated those who had been doing some se-rious relaxing in a number of night-clubs. They were very drunk, but had plenty of time to sober up during the journey to save the space dogs, as the capsule had landed near the

1908 Tunguska site. Yes, we know, another tidy coincidence. Why should there have been such haste and panic? The craft had been primed to detonate within sixty-four hours, thus blowing the dogs to bits. As the Soviet space program had been allegedly sending dogs into space for some time without any conscience, why should this suddenly become a matter for the KGB *et al*? Could it be that this capsule contained testers? The thought of these human guinea pigs being blown up within their craft on Soviet soil was perhaps too much to bear? As many testers died as a result of their trials, it is perhaps more realistic to assume that this entire exercise had nothing to do with concern over the dogs' fate but more to do with the fulfilment of one of the compulsory items on the Project Horizon "things to do" list—an exercise in space rescue systems.

So at this stage we have reached several conclusions:

- By April 1961 the Soviets and the Americans were both hard pushed to get their hardware ready to put a man into space and bring him back alive and well. Although many may have died in space travel research, neither side could safely announce that they were going to put a man into space and guarantee returning him in a fit state to represent his nation.
- We consider that the rumours that a flight had already been tried were both true and false at the same time. Many testers may well have died and many flights which allegedly carried either dogs and/or dummies may well have had human beings on board. However, it is our feeling that with an abundance of military testers from which to choose, none of the top twenty cosmonauts would have been exposed to such dangers. Only when it was considered politically expedient would a named cosmonaut be introduced into the process.
- We feel it is *unlikely* that Bondarenko was actually attempting to leave the planet in a secret attempt to travel into space and back successfully, thereby endeavouring to get ahead of the Americans. An idea not only stemming from the rumours seeded into the

media by those running the space program but also a result of our Western thinking, which was entirely conditioned by the Cold War "climate of the day".

- Down at Baikonur the Soviets *were* private and any sharing of information via the American Turkish-based listening posts was quite voluntary. As one of the guidance experts said, "each side was *pretending* not to know the other's business".[28]

Gagarin gagged?

In Gagarin the Soviet people were given the image of a wholesome young man with whom they could identify, just as the Americans were given the apple pie image of the perfect family man for their astronauts. Korolëv listed the qualities of patriotism, courage, modesty, iron will, knowledge and love of people as the requirements for the mission of first man in space. However in our opinion, the qualities most required by Gagarin would be a silent tongue and utter loyalty to the space program and his government, because we suspect that Gagarin *actually went nowhere* at that time.

Indeed, Gagarin's "calm, self confident manner" were qualities evident throughout his career as the Soviet Union's authentic hero /cosmonaut/diplomat—until towards the end of his life, when the stupid and unnecessary death of Komarov would lead Gagarin to become saddened and angry with the space program and the system which had ultimately let him down. After April 12 he had already had his wings clipped, being too precious a national asset for his life to be endangered by flying. Gagarin was loyal to his people and his country. He simply did what he was asked to do, defend the technological reputation of the Soviet space program against all odds. Were the circumstances of April 1961, reawakened by the stupidity of Komarov's death? If Gagarin knew things about those days which were better left unsaid this made him a powder keg at the end of a fuse which had suddenly got much, much shorter.

So when did that fuse actually come in touch with a taper? Was it in April 1967 when Komarov died, or was the final explosion on

March 27 1968 the result of a slow burning fuse that had been lit on April 7 1961?

The sound and light show

The only people who needed to be duped by these space dramas were in fact us, the general public throughout the world—and to varying degrees (depending on their 'need-to-know' status) certain space program employees. With the connivance of their American counterparts, who had been instructed to acknowledge the first manned orbital flight by their 'masters of infinity', did the Soviets succeed in pulling off the first real-time space hoax, as opposed to the purely filmed version? With hindsight it would appear that the mechanics of the Gagarin flight were the way out of the technical impasse into which the space program was heading.

By delivering a mixture of fact and fiction, reality and play acting, filmed with accompanying audio tracks, the sound and light show was the gold-plated insurance cover in the face of technical uncertainty and political insecurity. Such actions would assure the backing of the public, the politicians and the bankers. The magician's trick of focusing attention on one place while the real business goes on elsewhere would be practised, like a fractal, endlessly repeated in the same way in different-sized versions of itself.

Although April 12 1961 would establish the way of the future, this was the honeymoon period in the marriage between man and space. So naturally the cake had already been cut at the wedding reception. The Soviets were always going to get the credit for putting the first man into space in the recognition of their very real technological superiority and the fact that they would be the hosts to the actual business of 'getting out there'. The Americans were always going to be first to the Moon in the recognition of the skills that they enjoyed best—showmanship, the organisation of the cover story and the supplying of the very costly hardware components required by their colleagues and contractors, facilitated through money and research. The April 12 scenario became necessary because Korolëv and his crew were obliged to obey a timetable that was set not by themselves, not by their technology but by their masters.

If you want to achieve any challenging task, fixed-date deadlines always produce results. The end justifies the means. However, nature was not playing the same game. Despite the prepared timetables, everybody was finding space travel far harder than had been envisaged.

Project Argus

Prior to the 'Gagarin' flight, on August 8 1958, the highly secret US Operation Argus had been launched. The first of three nuclear devices to be exploded was detonated at high altitude. How high? 300 miles up, just below the Van Allen belts. Where? above 49.5°S, 08.2°W; the second on August 27 1958 was above 38°S, 11.5°W. The third on September 6 was above 48.5°S, 09.7°W. The results were monitored by the Explorer IV satellite, and Eisenhower was informed that:

- X-rays from such explosions would penetrate craft and disable electronic control systems.
- High energy electrons could generate radio noise.
- Delayed radiation due to fission could block radio communications.

Operation Argus was only reported in the American press seven months later, in March 1959, at which date the American authorities admitted to these tests and furnished further details. The bombs had been of one to two kilotons and were exploded over the South Atlantic. The results were *"in a sense* mostly scientific and as far as military use was concerned, somewhat negative"*. (emphasis added) But according to Sir Bernard Lovell and his colleagues in both England and America the truth of the matter was that these "scientific results were somewhat alarming".

In fact:

- The Earth's ionosphere was temporarily disrupted.
- There were artificially-induced aurorae, magnetic storms and a fadeout of short wave radio communications.

Probe	Orbit/miles	Inclination	Launch Date	End Date
Remember, remember . . .				
Sputnik 1	141 x 581	65.10°	Oct 4 1957	Jan 4/Feb 25*'58
Sputnik 2	131 x 1031	65.30°	Nov 3 1957	April 14 1958
Explorer I	225 x 1594	33.24°	Jan 31/Feb 1*'58	Mar 31 1970
Explorer III	117 x 1740	33.50°	Mar 25 '58	June 28 1958
Sputnik 3	135 x 1158	65.18°	May 15 1958	April 6 1960
Operation Argus				
Explorer IV	163 x 373	50.10°	July 26 1958	
Ist test			Aug 8 1958	
2nd test			Aug 27 1958	
3rd test			Sept 6 1958	
Explorer IV				Oct 10/23*'59

*Depending on source

March 25 1961

The USA *Explorer X* satellite was launched into the Van Allen belt regions—
the first satellite to supply detailed measurements of the outer radiation belt.
Shortly after 48 hours in orbit, due to excessive radiation in the outer belt, transmissions died, before the probe
had completed half of its projected trip.
This failure occurred at the equivalent distance of approximately one quarter of the way to the Moon—
i.e. between 59,500 miles/95,730 kms and 63,000 miles/101,370 kms from Earth.

- The electrons trapped in the magnetosphere produced an *artificial radiation belt* so intense that it was comparable to the Van Allen belts already *in situ*. Although the American official history asserts that the effects of this belt were extremely short lived, in fact it was still detectable after a further three months, according to David Baker.
- During a press conference at NASA on December 30 1959, Explorer VII scientists admitted that *sporadic bursts of radiation could influence manned space flight.*
- NASA's Space Task Group based at Langley, Virginia, stated that sounding rocket data indicated that by the time of the Mercury mission of October 1962 the Project Argus belt had dissipated.

Starfish Prime

Despite the fact they had signed a pact declaring that no group had the right to alter the Earth's environment in any significant way *without full international agreement and accord* the Americans announced their intention of repeating the Project Argus process in 1962. Except, that this time, they were going to use a megaton bomb—*one thousand* times more powerful than the Argus bombs. The scientific community were understandably outraged. For as well as flaunting the existing Russo/American scientific agreement it was considered, and quite rightly so, that such a detonation would seriously affect the Earth's radiation zones. Their protests were to no avail, and Starfish Prime turned out to be more catastrophic than even the most pessimistic of the scientific communities' predictions.

On July 8 1962, at 09:00 hours GMT this megaton bomb was exploded 19 miles from Johnston Island in the Pacific Ocean at a height of 248 miles/400 kms.[29] Sir Bernard Lovell stated that the effects were "cataclysmic". The upper ionosphere level around the Earth was broken up, causing severe disruption to long distance radio communications. Auroral displays and magnetic field disturbances were evident. The EMP (electromagnetic pulse) from this explosion sent massive electrical currents through the power lines in Hawaii, especially in the Honolulu area, some 800 miles distant, where 30 strings of street lights were burned out, circuit breakers damaged over a wide area

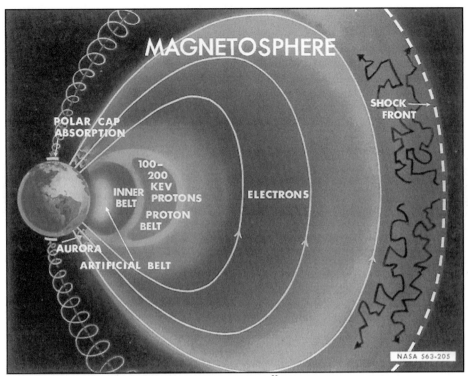

6. NASA's depiction of the *artificial* radiation belt around Earth.[30]

NASA

and several hundred burglar alarms triggered. And these were only the immediate or deterministic effects of this detonation. On August 20 1962 the Atomic Energy Commission, the DOD and NASA issued an official report in which it was noted:

- The solar cells of several satellites had been damaged and within three days of the explosion the British Ariel satellite had ceased functioning altogether.
- Measurements made in Peru calculated that the rate of radiant decay would be slow and that 10% of the excessive *radio noise* would still be present in two years time.
- More than one hundred trillion, trillion electrons from the fission product decay had been trapped by the Earth's magnetic field and *an entirely new radiation belt* had been formed at an altitude of 2,484 miles/4,000 kms. This zone had an intensity *over a hundred times greater* than any of the naturally existing radiation belts.

- The NASA Space Task Group report stated that this newly-formed artificial belt was 400 miles wide and 4,000 miles deep.[31]
- From the rate of decay already observed it was estimated that the *half-life* of this belt could be as long as 20 years.

The length of a half life is of paramount importance, as Professor John Davidson has pointed out.[32] Essentially it continually slows down, which means that the artificially-induced radiation created by Starfish Prime would be dropping to a half of its original quantity by 1982; to a quarter by 2002; to one eighth by 2022; and that even by 2042 we would still be at one sixteenth of the original amount of radiation. As the original dose was measured at 100 times *in excess* of the natural radiation levels, this means that by the end of this millennium this artificial belt still contains a level that is descending from between 50 to 25 times the already intense background levels of that region of the Van Allen belts.

309

Project Argus—BIS

During the early 1990s, co-ordinated by Ralph Noyes (ex-UK Ministry of Defence), the *Project Argus* team of American scientists visited the fields of Southern England, looking for radiation effects in the Crop Glyphs.
Despite their relaxed image it would seem likely that this project was in fact instigated by the military.
We are pleased to report that at least one of these scientists went home with a different world view, following his highly-enlightening experiences in the Crop Glyphs of England.

From Clive Dyer's evaluation of at least a 500 rem dosage in the belts,[33] then this artificial belt would have originally engendered thousands of rem in the 1990s *over and above the background levels.*[34] This space agency artefact of a radiation belt still features in a 1996 book written by the well-respected English astronomer Dr. Patrick Moore.[35]

Brute force and ignorance

Having seriously damaged our environment, on September 13 1962 President Kennedy announced that any further tests would be reduced. In the event, no further high altitude explosive tests were carried out. At the end of this millennium, when the doom and gloom soothsayers have yet again pronounced destruction for our planet, it might be worth remembering that representations from the British and American scientific community, the British Government and the general public had absolutely no effect whatsoever upon the misguided military or the masters concerning the devastating effects that the explosion of this megaton bomb could and probably would have on planet Earth. These people were determined to control nature and they were also prepared to lie about the outcome of such crazy experiments. Such complete disregard for the environment and the consequences of their behaviour demonstrate either desperation or utter idiocy. The White House had announced that the decision to conduct further high altitude tests was "based on military requirements".

As they had already discovered the disabling effects of intense radiation on space probes and equipment, we suggest that Operation Argus and Starfish Prime were attempts to *force an entryway* through the natural Van Allen radiation belts in order to be able to enter and exit the planet with a minimum of disruption to

their rocket riders and their electronics. The timing of these experiments makes this hypothesis very likely and is no less stupid than the manner in which these people ignored the advice of their own scientists and of foreigners such as Sir Bernard Lovell. In the event, through Starfish Prime the Americans created another glass door which all astronauts venturing to the Moon and beyond would have to avoid running into. In fact they *increased* the problem of leaving Earth safely.

THE 64,000 dollar question

Two years after the 'Gagarin' flight the Soviets were postponing their plans for a manned lunar landing because the gain-over-risk was not a valid equation. They were unable to deal with radiation in space and this they knew was a problem for all manned space flights beyond LEO. It was in the summer of 1963 that Sir Bernard Lovell had informed Hugh Dryden of NASA about the results of his meetings with the Soviet scientists. So having discussed the matter with James Webb on September 18 1963, why did President Kennedy propose to the United Nations, on September 20, that the Soviet Union and the USA go to the Moon together? As it was obvious that nobody was able to beat the radiation problem, was he going to propose the 'fake and make' deal? (This was the year in which the Soviet's Lunik Moon probes became the Luna probes.) Why was this step necessary, was it going to be easier on the American ears as a co-operative venture? It is also significant that on October 6 1970, only sixteen days after Kennedy's UN speech, Dr. James Van Allen was one of two scientists who supported four Senators, one of whom was William Proxmire, in their attempt to eliminate the manned space program. Officially Van Allen argued that *unmanned pro-*

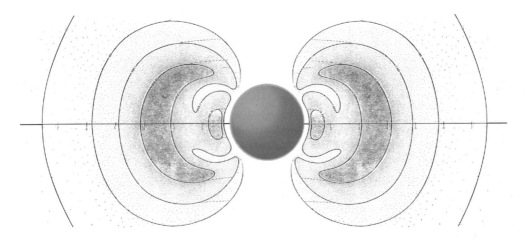

7. A reminder of Dr. James Van Allen's original illustration in 1958 of the radiation belts around the Earth showing the extent of radiation—as far as eight Earth radii and continuing beyond.

jects would bring a higher return of scientific information for the money spent. As we are well aware, Van Allen (the discoverer of the radiation belts) knew of the full implications of radiation on manned flight and he had already informed NASA that their aluminium shells of their spacecraft were insufficient protection against the dangers of radiation. As early as March 20 1959, he had informed NASA that the intensity of radiation would prohibit astronauts from spending long periods within the belts—and that was before the military made matters even worse with their Project Starfish bomb.

When we asked Sir Bernard Lovell for his comments about the American and Soviet attitudes towards radiation he replied that he was astonished at the different attitudes prevalent in the two countries. This is the complete letter referred to in "Radiant Daze". We have reproduced his reply in full, as his choice of words is most revealing.

Dear Mr. Percy,
I am replying to your letter of June 15th about the Soviet attitude to the effects of solar radiation on cosmonauts. In the 1960s I was a frequent visitor both to the United States and to the Soviet Union and I was surprised by the attitude to this danger by the authorities in the two countries. In America one of the principal medical advisers to NASA was unconcerned and dismissed the idea that there should be a concern for the relative short cosmonaut flights to the moon then in prospect. The Soviet attitude about radiation danger and, indeed, to the whole problem of the safety of cosmonauts was in marked contrast. If one asked about their manned lunar plans the response was always that they will attempt a manned lunar landing when they were confident of securing the safe return to earth of their cosmonauts. At the time of the first American landing on the moon the Soviets attempted to land a device that would return lunar rocks to earth by rocket. That Lunik crashed within hours of the lift-off of Armstrong and Aldrin from the moon. Months later the Soviets succeeded with their automatic system of securing lunar samples without involving human life on the moon. If, in 1969, the Soviets had succeeded and the Americans had been stranded on the moon, then the repercussion in the two countries and on world opinion is not difficult to imagine.

The whole American manned lunar landings of the 1969-70 era was a technological and logistical triumph. They expected, and were prepared for some fatalities (and Apollo 13 nearly was a disaster), whereas the Soviets were not then prepared to risk tarnishing the immense internal and external impression of Soviet technological ability created by the 1957 Sputnik.

I hope the above comments answer the question raised in your June 15th letter. My response applies to the 1960 epoch and not to more recent attitudes. Since that time the long duration flights of men in space will have made possible a far more realistic assessment of radiation dangers than was possible in the 1960s.

Yours sincerely,
Sir Bernard Lovell, O.B.E., LL.D., D.Sc., F.R.S.

Dr. Donald's SFX trickery— Part Nine

We stated earlier that film images are often doctored for political, sociological and propaganda purposes which leads us to another aspect of the movie business. Film and TV can sometimes be used to convey hidden ideas or concepts that cannot be stated at the time in any other way. We would describe it as advanced seeding—a variation of Whistle-Blowing. Writers, painters and artists are generally very sensitive to the 'ambience' within which they work and are open to the general cultural atmosphere of the times in which they are living, incorporating images or ideas, either wittingly or unwittingly, into their creation—for example those brilliant film makers responsible for such classics as the *Star Wars* series, the *Indiana Jones* trilogy, *Close Encounters of The Third Kind* and *E.T.*

Before that era, the producers of the Bond films had already inserted another level of information into seemingly innocuous adventure stories encoded by Ian Fleming. Indeed, this information is so near the truth, that those involved with the *James Bond* stories in both publishing and film had to have the content of Fleming's work cleared at high levels. In a letter dated June 5 1959, Frederick Hyar-Miller of the British Foreign Office wrote: "There are no security objections to any of the books about James Bond which have been published". And that: "There would be no objection to any film or television broadcast based on material in them". But these stories are not

as innocent as some might believe, for they are all heavily encoded with matters of considerable importance. Fleming himself called his books the "serial biography of James Bond" and emphasised the fact that he consulted many experts in their various field, undertook detailed research into both the technical and geographical aspects of his books and that as a result Bond's adventures had both "solidity and integrity". To presume them uniquely as fantasy, he thought, was either an indication of the critic's ignorance of what was apparent through simply reading a newspaper or that said critic had not noticed the "revealing peaks of the great underwater iceberg that is secret service warfare", as he wrote in 1962.[36] One example of such encoding occurs in *Diamonds Are Forever*. Here we have a significant scene featuring a lunar film set—for anyone wishing to check their own video copy it occurs about forty minutes into the movie. Bond, fleeing from a pursuer, breaks into a film studio where apparently a Moon landing scene is being created. Here follows a reconstruction of the scene:

JAMES BOND penetrates W Techtronics, a US Government establishment in the Nevada desert. The most prominent building on the site is a dome situated just beyond the main gate.

BOND is five floors underground by the car park elevators when he encounters a young German—who speaks with an American accent.

KLAUS HERGERSCHEIMMER: "I'm from G section.... I'm checking radiation shields for replacement .....where's yours?"

BOND professes to losing his and waiting for a new delivery.

KH: "Lucky for you I carry spares."

KH pins a green badge onto BOND's breast pocket.

KH: "Now you keep that on, you can't be too careful about—radiation!"

JB: "Absolutely. I feel much safer with this on!"

BOND then enters a lab where a delivery of diamonds have arrived. He pretends to be KH the G section man. BOND uses a German accent.

JB: "I'm here to check Radiation Shields."

BOND having seen all that he needs to see, is thrown out by the apparently German lab head. BOND exits by one door as the real radiation shield man enters through another door.

KH: "I'm Klaus Hergerscheimmer..... checking ...... radiation ...... shields?"

Everybody, including KH look around and realise they have been 'had'. CUT TO interior moon set with an astronaut walking slowly across the foreground, part of a lunar rover to the right and the US flag in the left background. BOND is hiding behind the flats running across the background—until discovered.

SECURITY GUARD: "There he is, behind that rock."

BOND makes a run for it, avoiding the astronauts and leaping for the rover. Three men are above the set in a control booth, equipped with reel-to-reel tape recorders and computer machinery. One of them yells.

CONTROLLER: "What the hell is this—amateur night?"

BOND climbs into the rover and starts it up. CUT TO more views of the control gallery.

CONTROLLER: "Get him off that machine, it isn't a toy!"

BOND careers across the set in the rover and exits below left of the control booth by crashing through the wall. CUT TO exterior. Revealed that the set is within the dome which we saw at the commencement of the scene, in full view of all visitors to W Techtronics.

The British Foreign Office letter obviously covers the book *Diamonds Are Forever* originally published in 1956. However the film, first screened in 1971, a year before the end of NASA's Apollo program, conveys the general plot from the book, but uses other location set-ups, such as this lunar moon set, to drive the action. Seen by some to be out of step with the rest of the film—it is certainly a curious and quite deliberate insert—this entire sequence makes sense when seen against the background of the *RADIATION* dangers that we maintain plagued the Apollo program. ∎

The arthurised version—Part One

Arthur C Clarke, writing in 1966, expressed alarm at the fact that the Apollo manned space flights would be getting underway at the worst time of the solar cycle.

The astronauts would be travelling "under the worst possible conditions", he wrote. Should solar flare activity occur the astronauts would start to die of radiation problems "in a few hours", he opined. At the time of writing Clarke thought that the astronauts should travel only when the Sun was quiet. However, as we have already seen from the information in *Radiant Daze*, it is possible to experience solar activity even at a low point of the solar cycle, and therefore the only guarantee of protection from SPEs and other radiation is through adequate protection of the spacecraft itself. Clarke was fully aware of that fact and suggested astronauts "stay within the shield of the Earth's atmosphere". Clarke also made this rather misleading statement: "A careful watch for solar flares will always give us a day's warning of an approaching storm, *this will be no handicap for lunar travel, for flights to the Moon will last no longer than this*". (emphasis added)

By 1966, Clarke had been thoroughly immersed in research for *2001: A Space Odyssey* and as an astronomer and space expert to boot he knew very well that, with the rocket technology available in the 1960s, the travel time

Some 1963 space-related events	
May	President Kennedy alleged to have met George Adamski secretly at the Willard Hotel near the White House.[37]
May	Cooper completed 22 Earth orbits in Mercury capsule Faith 7.
June	Bykovsky completed 81 Earth revolutions in Vostok 5.
June	Tereskova completed 48 Earth revolutions in Vostok 6 (launched 2 days after Vostok 5, the first woman in space).
August	J A Walker qualified as astronaut in an X-15 by exceeding 50 miles altitude!
September	Gagarin spoke at the Congress of Astronautical Federation in Paris, told delegates that the Soviet Union was developing techniques to assemble components in Earth orbit, including propellant transfer, because it was impossible to launch vehicles "of several scores of tons" directly to the Moon.
October	Kruschev speech, referring to the Americans: "We will see how they fly there, and how they land there and most important, how they will take off and return".
October 4	Sixth anniversary of Sputnik 1, Gagarin delivered speech.
Dec 10	US FX-20 project dinosaur, sorry! Dyna-Soar was abandoned. Was it ever meant to go anywhere?
December	Soviet Union launched meteorological satellite Cosmos 23.

to the Moon was a minimum of three and a half to four days. Which made a round trip minimum of seven to eight days, and that is without stopping off to stretch their legs!

Indeed by 1970 in *Beyond Apollo* Clarke acknowledged as much—although he had modified his response to "a few hours flight time away from Earth, one can always come home in a hurry", which is still totally inaccurate.

Dr. Donald's SFX trickery—Part Ten

In his references to the making of *2001: A Space Odyssey* Arthur C Clarke informs us of several interesting facts. As well as a writer of science fiction, an early member of the British Interplanetary Society and very closely involved with all aspects of space—he was, and still is, a consultant to NASA and has been so for many years.

ACC wrote in the Spring of 1964: "The lunar landing still seemed psychologically a dream of the far future. Intellectually, we knew it was inevitable, emotionally we could not really believe it..." He tells us that the first Gemini flight was still a year away and, "that argument was still raging about the nature of the lunar surface..."

We rather doubt that last statement—given the level of co-operation that we suspect was taking place between the Soviets and Americans. By then the Soviets had crash-landed

Luna 2 and would have obtained information as to surface conditions, if not of sub-surface conditions.

Clarke continued: "NASA was getting through over $10,000,000 *EVERY DAY!* but space exploration seemed to be marking time". (Arthur's words, not ours.)

In reality, by then, the Americans themselves had crashed Ranger 4 and Ranger 6 (allegedly no photographs). As for the rest of 1964, it was choc-a-bloc with American endeavours, which can hardly be described as "marking time" in the pursuit of an attempted lunar landing.

8. Arthur C Clarke during a TV broadcast at the time of 'Apollo 11'.

Was it synchronicity that the classic *2001: A Space Odyssey* had been conceived in the *spring of 1964*—at which time Stanley Kubrick, who had just released *Dr Strangelove*, contacted Arthur C Clarke requesting "ideas that would create *the* proverbial (i.e. still nonexistent) good science fiction movie"? He remembers how Stanley Kubrick met him at Trader Vic's, the well known American watering hole, on the April 23 1964 (St George's day in England) to discuss the project of making a movie about mankind's place in the Universe. They went on to construct their film which would take Kubrick (working in the MGM studios in Borehamwood, North of London) until 1968 to bring to the screen. As we all recognise, this film is still regarded as one of the most influential movies of all time. Even so, using 65mm special motion picture cameras and equipment, taking four years to produce this epic was rather pushing it. But if you want the movie released on a specific date, so that it is fresh in the minds of your audience by the time the Apollo missions are staged, then of course that length of production time can makes sense. Especially if your moviegoing experiences have to keep pace with the unfolding of the 'real' space program.

Methinks he doth protest too much ...

Stanley Kubrick and Arthur C Clarke privately called their film *How the Solar System was Won* and they were given every assistance to produce the film to look as realistic as possible. That meant among other matters visits to NASA's contractors—including Grumman, the builders of the LM.

Even at this early date, the film production team received charts of vast areas of the lunar surface and detailed photographic data from several sources, amongst which were: Lick Observatory, Mt Hamilton California; Lowell Observatory, Flagstaff, Arizona; Mt Wilson and Palomar Observatories and the California Institute of Technology. The University of Manchester's Department of Astronomy in England supplied them with photography of the Moon, as did the Pic du Midi observatory in France. They had large scale models of the Tycho and Clavius craters, as well as charts and maps of many lunar sites. Two consultations were held, one in Manchester and one near London, concerning the surface characteristics of the Moon, the nature of the lunar regolith and the appearance of celestial bodies such as Earth and the stars when viewed from the Moon. Yet, in 1997 Mr Clarke wrote that

---

April 23rd and Uncle George

For anyone interested in symbology, St George speared the dragon/drakon
to the ground without *seeming* to notice that it was not a fierce beast but the lady's pet.
Arthur C Clarke's *seeming* penchant for symbology, might well have something to do with the choice of this date.
In his *3001: The Final Odyssey*, Clarke tells us that dear old "Uncle George" owns a collection of vintage
videotapes and science fiction magazines.

when they started filming at the MGM Borehamwood Studios on December 29 1965, they did not even know what the lunar surface *looked* like at close quarters. Poetic license there, surely!

Apart from the sources listed above, the Soviets supplied them with images from Luna 9. This information was sent to the filmmakers via the Soviet Embassy in London—so much for the Cold War when it came to space and Hollywood.[38] This piece of information appears to render Mr Clarke's 1997 protestations of ignorance rather superfluous.

Mr Clarke is a very intelligent man. If, as he professes, his book, his movie and the real space program got mixed up in his *own* mind, surely this was also the intention for his target audience of cinema goers, readers and the public in general? Indeed he actually says that the Apollo, Skylab and Shuttle flights do not look as convincing as Stanley Kubrick's version of such matters. He usually accompanies his TV interviews with either a very sardonic twinkle, or a basilisk stare (his description) and he manages to sit very comfortably on the middle of the wall when it comes to making statements for or against the ETernal question concerning *OUT THERE.*

In the introduction to the 1990 paperback edition of *2001* Arthur wrote that: *"2001* is often said to be based on his own short story *The Sentinel*, a mood piece about the discovery of an alien artefact on the Moon". He stated that some of the material also came from a short story called *Encounter in the Dawn* (copyrighted 1953 & also titled *Expedition to Earth)* plus four other short stories. This collection, together with a lot of brand new material, resulted in the film that we all know. However,

in a TV program on the life of Kubrick, transmitted in the UK in 1996, Mr Clarke denied that *2001* was ever more than the material from one short story, that the others were never used. Interesting discrepancies! Film buffs can consult the literature on this subject, where they will find several other parallels with the post-Apollo space program and Mr Clarkes' creative output. Here we are specifically concerned with the possibility of actual cinematographic links to NASA's Apollo program.[39] Arthur Clarke again tells us that: "The film *2001* lies behind one of the great divides in human history, created by the moment when Neil Armstrong and Buzz Aldrin stepped out onto the Sea of Tranquillity".

If it is indeed the untruth that it would appear to be, then he is absolutely right, it is the great divide between the dictators of history and the dictated to—all of us.

Clarke then went on to say: "History and fiction have become inexorably intertwined; the Apollo astronauts had already seen the film when they left for the Moon".

More accurately, the public already knew what to expect in terms of beautiful, perfect science-fiction cinema and therefore were preconditioned to accept black and white fuzzy images and visual inconsistencies as much more likely to be the 'real' thing. ■

The Cheshire cats—Part Two

When we initially requested information from Jodrell Bank radio telescope concerning the Apollo flights, they advised us that although they *had* picked up very poor quality TV images once the Apollo missions had reached the Moon, they were never able to track the craft during the trajectory, because the Americans

---

Far horizons

Twenty-one years before the birth of Project Horizon and forty-two years before 'Apollo 11',
The First World Exhibition of Interplanetary Apparatus & Devices was opened in central Moscow in 1927 and
proved extremely popular with the public.
Using photographs, drawings and *models set against a lunar landscape*
behind which *planet Earth rose on the horizon* it summarised the work of
Goddard (USA), Valier (Germany),
Oberth (Transylvannia/Austria) and Tsiolkovsky (Soviet Union).

---

did not give them any pointing data. We asked Bob Pritchard of Jodrell Bank for further clarification, and on this second occasion he informed us that in fact they *had* been able to pick up these craft but only once they were "near to the Moon".

Bob Pritchard explained:

The Moon probes were observed with a 50ft radio telescope which at the frequency used (2300Mhz) had a beam width of ⅝ths degree.

In round terms this allowed us to pick up signals from up to about 1,000 miles above the Moon's surface, although small corrections had to be made to the pointing as the probes orbited the Moon.

Voice signals (of good quality) were received from both the orbiting spacecraft and the Lunar Lander but television signals were only picked up from the spacecraft on the surface of the Moon.

As we were not actively involved in the tracking of these spacecraft, we did not track them after they had left the Moon. And with regard to Apollo 10, I have no details of any observations, after all this time—the reason [for that omission] escapes me.

This about-turn reminded us of the USA situation with the 'Gagarin' flight. No record one minute then five minutes later "Oh yes! sorry, of course we picked it up!" Had someone at Jodrell Bank mislaid their copy of the script? We asked Bob Pritchard for even more precise data, which he kindly supplied. Jodrell Bank received fuzzy TV pictures direct from the Moon displayed on one TV monitor, and on a second monitor a much better picture

(from the BBC) *but delayed by about six to eight seconds.* Bob Pritchard assumed that NASA were giving themselves a delay framework of a few seconds, within which they could react "if anything went wrong on the Moon".[40]

Not only that, but the signals they received from the spacecraft to Earth were apparently good. Yet they discovered that the Earth to CSM uplink seemed to be *re-transmitted* from the spacecraft-back to Earth. When attempting to receive signals from the LM they told us they could not get enough bandwidth and the signal-to-noise ratio was very poor. Which translates as bad fuzzy pictures.

Home phone?

Back in 1958, when selected extracts from that *Manchester Guardian* article appeared in Sir Bernard Lovell's book, some interesting and relevant facts were omitted.

- The Jodrell Bank telescope is uniquely suited to the task of following the broad outline of a rocket on its way to the Moon and equipped with a radio transmitter due to:

   1) Its high sensitivity.
   2) The ease with which it can be turned towards different parts of the sky.

- These two assets combine to enable this dish to locate rapidly within *a fraction of a degree* the position of *even weak* radio transmissions as far away as the Moon.

- If the radio detection devices are to work at full sensitivity they need to be used at night, when terrestrial sources of radio interference are less intrusive.

. . . the dish ran away with the spoon

In a detailed, extended article on 'Apollo 11', *Time* magazine on July 25 1969 confirmed the fact that Jodrell Bank tracked not only Luna 15 with their 250ft radio telescope but also the 'Apollo 11' mission,

and quoted Professor Bernard Lovell who said they were:

"Listening to Apollo with one ear and Luna with the other".

However, in September 1997, Jodrell Bank told us there was neither the interest

nor the possibility of following 'Apollo 11'

as NASA had not supplied them with the pointing data.

TechnoSpeak

The way to delay TV images (and this goes for sound as well) is to record the signal
and play it out again a number of seconds later.
This requirement establishes the need for a video recording/replay facility.
Forget for a moment our claim that all the programming was pre-recorded.
It is little known that the 'live' Apollo pictures from the Moon were actually coming off tape.
Very few people know that *the only way* to assemble the signal from the Apollo colour TV camera was to
record it onto tape, and then play it back on another machine![41]

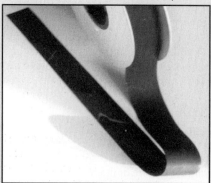

We have firmly established that there were **motives** for
perusing a cover version of events. By virtue of having
access to 'legitimate' video record/replay equipment there was
also the **opportunity** for the 'masters of infinity' and their
associates to manipulate the entire Apollo historical record.
(see Appendix)

Two inch video tape similar to that used for TV recording and playback on Ampex equipment during Apollo.

We must point out that at the time of 'Apollo 11' the Moon was just coming up to first quarter when the craft arrived there. In fact these missions left Cape Canaveral when the Moon was in sight of the Atlantic for the *least amount of time* and full Moon occurred only two days after the 'rocket riders' had sailed into home port again.

Jodrell Bank informed us that there was not *the urgency, money or interest* in using their large 250ft dish to track 'Apollo 11', and then said that they could not get a wide enough bandwidth for receiving the LM on their other dish. As we are talking about mankind's very first footsteps on a planet other than his own, we find it very hard to believe this statement. Bob Pritchard actually worked on the space program during the Apollo period but he had apparently forgotten Sir Bernard Lovell's

---

Clear reflection

At full Moon over the Atlantic, the Moon is within sight of
short wave radio from Earth for the
greatest amount of time.

---

statement that the 250ft dish *was* used for the USA and USSR space program throughout the 1960s, and that the amount of dish time used did not inhibit the radio astronomy research being carried out with the British telescope.

The answers we received were raising ever more questions but we did learn that if we did not use exactly the right wording when formulating our questions we would not get a direct answer!

The fat lady sings

According to the official record, communication procedures for 'Apollo 11' within the zone of the Van Allen belts and during Earth orbit were handled by eleven 30ft dishes, four tracking ships and a support fleet of eight Boeing KC-135 jets. These Apollo Range Instrumentation Aircraft (ARIA) were equipped with a 7ft antenna in the nose of the aircraft and a crew trained for tracking communications. The 85ft dishes sited at Goldstone, USA; Canberra, Australia; and Johannesburg, South Africa were used to connect with the spacecraft beyond Earth orbit and the radiation belts—one of these three locations always having 'line of

9. DSS-14, the Mars antenna Goldstone, California as it is today.   AULIS

dent of a small Western Australian town. Nearly thirty years later, on hearing of our hypothesis concerning Apollo she contacted us with a very interesting story. We went to see Una and she told us how, for her, the reality of the space program had become altered forever.

Having decided to stay up and watch what she believed to be live images of the 'Apollo 11' EVA direct from the Moon, she was more than astonished to see a *Coca Cola* bottle roll across the lower right quadrant of the TV screen! The incident lasted only two or three seconds at the very most.

"It's a fake—it's a set up—it's not on the Moon at all!" she cried out. "Look at this... there's a *Coca Cola* bottle!"

But nobody else was in the room at that moment.

"The TV picture I was watching was extremely fuzzy, you could just about distinguish the movements of the astronauts, but when the *Coke* bottle rolled across the screen it was totally visible, in complete contrast to the fuzz, it was as sharp as anything. Everyone knows the distinctive shape of a *Coke* bottle—the design was *completely* clear."

Una Ronald continued to watch the Moon landing broadcast, while ruminating on why such an incident should have occurred. If it was a fake set-up, then how could those responsible allow such an obvious mistake to have been made? Phoning friends and acquaintances, Una was able to establish that none of them had seen the *Coca Cola* bottle but all agreed to watch the scheduled repeats being broadcast the next morning on daytime TV. By which time the *Coke* bottle was only conspicuous by its complete absence.

sight' on the Moon/craft, despite the rotation of the Earth on its axis. In other words, the baton was passed from one dish to another. 'Apollo 11' also benefited from two 210ft dishes from the DSTN. Some researchers include Madrid, Spain in their deep space tracking network of the 1960s, although it did not have a 210ft dish until 1974.

Prior to the 'Apollo 11' mission, NASA stated that the TV signals transmitted from the Moon would be picked up by a 210ft diameter radio telescope at the National Radio Astronomy Observatory in Parkes, Australia. The signals would then be transmitted from Parkes to Sydney by microwave link where they would be converted to a standard US TV picture and then sent on to NASA's Mission Control in Houston via the Intelsat III Pacific satellite.[42] From Sydney these images would also be converted into PAL signals for Australia and elsewhere. (see also Appendix)

Linked to this process we have discovered an Australian Whistle-Blowing incident of great importance.

Message in a bottle

Una Ronald, a perfectly ordinary, normal and delightful lady now living in England was, in July 1969, married to a businessman and resi-

At this point, with no witnesses, you might well think that this incident was nothing more than a trick of the light, or the tired imagination of a wife and mother at the end of a long winter's day down under—but Una Ronald is extremely rational and quietly convinced as to what she saw. Rightly so, as it turned out.

"I then believed that it had been edited out" she went on, "but about a week to ten days later, I saw that several letters mentioning this *Coca Cola* incident were published in the West Australian Newspaper, and I looked forward to the ensuing discussion or debate that should have followed, but nothing happened. Perhaps the newspaper *did* receive more correspondence but felt—or was advised—not to print anything further on this matter?"

We subsequently contacted this newspaper requesting information on the subject of the *Coke* bottle letters but despite several enquiries they have declined to respond; which gives them less points than the American Embassy in London, who at least fobbed us off with a courteous reply![43]

Una had more to say about these letters:

"Seeing and hearing no more of this incident I thought that perhaps those who had written to the newspaper, rationalised the incident in their minds—'of course I didn't see a *Coke* bottle, I must have imagined it'. Or 'it could have been quite genuine activity filmed on some other occasion'. People will invent all kinds of solutions to things they don't understand. But I didn't invent any solutions. For me, after that, the Moon landings were a fake. I don't believe that this *Coca Cola* bottle was part of the astronaut's rubbish discarded on the Moon. I think it had to have been filmed on Earth, somewhere private, and secluded, probably in America."

Wizards in Oz

Contrary to the established pattern set up by Parkes observatory together with NASA and Australian Television, the images of 'Apollo 11' destined for Western Australia were not sent via satellite, neither was there a broadband link from Sydney. The moonwalk had to be retransmitted from Perth to the relatively small population of that region. At the time of Apollo, and even at the time of this interview, none of us knew of this important difference in methodology (we were to learn of it later during e-mail correspondence with Parkes Observatory). However, this technical fact makes Una Ronald's observations even more pertinent. For it demonstrates that there was a unique technical *opportunity* at some stage of this transmission, for an unknown Whistle-Blower to add the *Coke* bottle incident to the broadcast. The choice of Western Australia for this unscheduled *Coca Cola* commercial ensured that it would go out undetected by those in control at Houston, who were receiving their images from Australia's east coast via satellite.

The *motive*? In our opinion it was designed to place a protest marker "on the record" by sending a one-off whistle-blow alerting those who saw it to the fact that the 'Apollo 11' Moon landing as claimed by NASA was nothing but America's best-marketed fizz.

The fact that this story was virtually ignored by the press (both at the time *and to this day*) would indicate that this incident was *not* merely the work of a bored technician making a mockery of the real event. Una had not felt the need to write to the newspapers on this subject, wishing to observe proceedings from the sidelines. Did the *Coca Cola* Whistle-Blower also participate in a follow-up by sending a letter, or letters, to the press as a back-up toot on that whistle? And why to this day does the West Australian newspaper wish to ignore this subject?

Shadowy lands

Una Ronald went on to tell us of other things that she felt were not quite right with this broadcast.

"These I had perceived even before the *Coca Cola* bottle appeared on my screen," she said. "I first became uneasy about the lighting conditions. The lighting seemed odd, I felt that they must have set up some sort of illumination. I didn't get the feeling that these men were 'alone on the Moon', and as the shots changed I became confused as to the whereabouts of the 'cameraman'."

320

> ### *TechnoSpeak* *The Early Bird gets the worm*
>
> **Intelsat Generation I**
>
> *Early Bird* over the Atlantic at 27.5°W live: April 4 S live: June 28 1965
>
> 1 x B&W TV channel or 240 voice circuits. *(Jodrell Bank link?)*
>
> **Intelsat Generation II**
>
> Commercial traffic between Australia/Japan/Hawaii/Washington State.
>
> Military traffic between/Hawaii/Philippines/Thailand/Japan.
>
> Intelsat F2 over Pacific at 178°W live: Jan 11 S live: Feb 4
>
> Intelsat F3 over Atlantic live: March 23 S live: April 7.
>
> Intelsat F4 over Pacific at 174°E live: Sept 28 S live: November 4.
>
> **Intelsat Generation III**
>
> Capacity: four TV programs at one time or 1,200 voice circuits.
>
> Intelsat F2 over equator E of Brazil (South Atlantic)
>
> live: Dec 18 1968 S live: Dec 20 1968 (in time for 'Apollo 8').
>
> Intelsat F3 a) over Pacific then moved to b) over Indian Ocean
>
> live: Feb 6 1969 (in time for 'Apollos 9' & '10').
>
> Intelsat F4 over Pacific. (This satellite completed the global circuit.)
>
> live: May 22 1969 (in time for 'Apollo 11').
>
> Two more Intelsat IIIs were successfully launched within this phase:
>
> Jan 15 and April 23 1970 (in time for 'Apollo 14').
>
> **Intelsat Generation IV & V**
>
> Intelsat generations IV & V were launched between 1970 and 1978.
>
> Intelsat IV was capable of carrying twelve TV channels
>
> or 9,000 voice circuits.

"The shadows weren't right."

"The planes of illumination disagreed with each other in some subtle way."

"But as I am not an expert on the lighting conditions on or around the Moon, I was quite happy with all these oddities until I saw that bottle roll across the screen with my own two eyes."

"For me, that *Coke* bottle was the final straw and I then began to consider those other niggles that I was seeing and feeling from a different viewpoint. Why should it have been done? Why was this set up? I knew that it would be difficult to find the truth of this matter and although I didn't care to speculate on what the reasons for such a hoax might be, I put it 'on the back shelf' of my mind."

Until now. We were given permission to quote her story of this incident, as long as she remained incognito. She joins our Whistle-Blowers under an assumed name and we hope that her contribution will enable all of us to unravel what really happened amidst all these inconsistencies.

Intelsat and Apollo

The Intelsat satellites were constructed by Hughes, under contract to COMSAT and the first of these was launched on April 4 1965, although it was only on August 20 1971 (a belated seven years later and 13 days after the 'return' of 'Apollo 15') that the final agreements setting up Intelsat as a world satellite communications system were signed at the US State Department.

Nicknamed Early Bird, the first Intelsat used gold protective covering for its camera and film and allegedly became operational just over two months after launch, on June 28 1965. Early Bird had then been switched off in January 1969, or so the record states.[44] Despite the fact that Intelsat II F3 was in operation over the Atlantic, Early Bird was then switched back on, between June 29 1969 and August 13 1969, in order to handle the 'Apollo 11' TV traffic. Which of course infers that the existing network was insufficient, or in some way inappropriate to cope with the communications demand. Was Early Bird actually needed for TV/voice traffic superfluous to official TV/voice link-ups? And why did NASA need to continue heavy TV/voice traffic so long after 'Apollo 11's termination in July 1969? Was there lunar activity, either manned or unmanned, which continued well after the 'Apollo 11' splashdown?

David Shayler asserts that the Mars Antenna at Goldstone was used to talk to the LM when it had separated from the CSM Columbia. Clearly it was perfectly possible to separate the main elements of CSM comms and LM comms into controllable sectors. Another important factor of controllability was that the

---

Doing the dishes

By the 1960s NASA's deep space tracking network (DSTN) consisted of Goldstone, USA; Canberra/Parkes, Australia; and Johannesburg, South Africa until 1974— whereafter the latter location was replaced by Madrid.

Washing

Set up by technicians from DARPA and NASA, all three sites were equipped initially with 85ft dishes.
Then 112ft antennae were added.
The 210ft dishes were built in the USA in 1966, Australia in 1973 and Madrid in 1974.

Rinsing

Johannesburg was dedicated on September 8 1961.
Goldstone, one of the most powerful and largest space tracking stations with the Mars 210ft diameter antenna operated by JPL, was only officially inaugurated into the DSTN in April 29 1966.
Canberra/Parkes only inaugurated its 210 ft telescope on April 13 1973.
The third 210 ft telescope was set up in Madrid in 1974.
So from 'Apollo 8' through to 'Apollo 15' only the USA's Goldstone 210ft dish was available.

Drying

On October 28 1981 it was decided to close down the 85ft telescopes at Goldstone, Canberra/Parkes and Madrid, but retain the 112ft and 210ft dishes at these three sites.
The 85ft dishes had provided 30% of the DSTN coverage but the shutting down of these dishes made vast economies in the overall budgets.

All washed up

One could be forgiven for wondering why, with their considerable tracking experience and powerful 250ft telescope, Jodrell Bank was not *officially* part of all this activity! No doubt at the time it was occupied with another, more private, aspect of Project Apollo?

---

relatively feeble signal relayed by the Intelsats could only be picked up by multi-million dollar Earth stations equipped with antennae of a *minimum* 20 metres diameter.

This means that *the only people* with the capability of picking up these signals were those using government-controlled installations. For this very reason alone, it suggests that those 1960s rumours concerning astronauts 'UFO' conversations on the link from the CSM to Earth, that we looked at in "Truth or Consequences" cannot have been picked up by radio hams. Which clearly tells us that these 'conversations' were very probably sponsored by the authorities.

The facility at Parkes in Australia was set up in 1959 and used an 85 foot telescope, as was the case at Goldstone in California. The United States and Australia signed an agreement on February 26 1960 but it was to be nearly a year later on February 10 1961, that Goldstone celebrated the *inauguration* of Canberra/Parkes

into the DSTN by bouncing a transmission off the Moon over to Canberra/Parkes. This belated official demonstration (par for the course it seems) demonstrates that bouncing signals off the Moon does indeed work!

Shaken but not stirred

The named Apollo astronauts were credited with placing LR^3's at the 'Apollo 11', '14' and '15' sites on the lunar surface. NASA's Brian Welch, with no prompting from us, had thrown down the gauntlet over the question of these LR^3's and his "you tell me how, then I'll tell you what, why and when" led us to examine more closely the manner of the placing and the functioning of these laser retro-reflectors.

NASA might wish that Brian Welch had not issued this challenge, for en route to answering the question we learned many other interesting facts which we would like to share on this voyage of discovery. (see Appendix)

TechnoSpeak
Laser daisy stitch

1958: 1st paper published describing laser principles: *The Optical Maser* (Townes & Schawlow). This equipment was the optical adaptation of the microwave amplifying device the maser, which Townes had developed in 1951 (Nobel Prize 1964).

1960: Dr. Theodore Maisman of Hughes Aircraft Company developed the first ruby laser using synthetic ruby (they had used sapphires initially but found that rubies were better).

Spring 1960: IBM asked ISOMET to make a rod of calcium fluoride doped with samarium. This crystal was used to make a laser.

By 1966: The most powerful pulse laser was made by Westinghouse and it could concentrate 750 trillion watts onto 1 square centimetre.

Facts

A direct hit in the eye can cause instant blindness even reflected laser rays can burn holes in the retina.

Many laser labs paint their walls a dull black to cut down on reflections.

Gas lasers give off continuous beams of coherent laser light.

Ruby lasers give off sharp pulses of coherent laser light.

Tiny semi-conductor lasers will work at supercold temperatures.

Made of such material as gallium arsenide these may be especially useful in computers for transmitting signals where densely-packed electrical devices leave little room for wire connections.

Many lasers are pumped (tech term) by light.

Others may be made to lase by radio waves, by electric current or by chemical reactions.

In Sacramento, New Mexico at the Air Force Systems Commando, a ruby laser keeps watch for missiles and satellites.

It can fire a searching laser beam hundreds of times narrower than radar, pick up the reflected signals with an optical telescope and measure the distance to the target. As with microwave radar, the time that the pulsed signal takes to go and return automatically reveals the distance.

The A Factor

There is one major hurdle: *rain, snow, smog and dust all interfere with the output of most lasers.*
The Earth's atmosphere is the challenging factor.

The secret of a laser's power lies in the fact that it produces light of essentially one colour. Being of only one wavelength it is always in synchronisation. This beam, technically called coherent light, can travel over long distances with minimal spread and therefore retains its power (or strength) for longer. By 1966 it had been discovered that if this beam was first transited through a telescope operating 'in reverse' it could then be focused.   This reduced the beam's divergence by as little as a third of an inch per mile of travel, enabling it to retain its power for an even greater length of time.

As a measuring tool between the Earth and Moon, how does a laser work? *Ordinary* incandescent light is of different colours (as in a rainbow).   It therefore produces a different

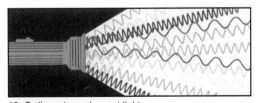

10. Ordinary incandescent light.

11. Coherent laser light.

323

wavelength per colour and each wavelength has its own pattern, hence the technical name incoherent light. When this incoherent beam travels over long distances it spreads out and the greater the spread the faster the dissipation of its power.

Jerry and the laser rangers

In order to respond to the challenge set before us, we needed to find out more about the process of measuring by laser between the Moon and the Earth (laser ranging as it is called). So taking Brian Welch's information as a starting point, we contacted McDonald Observatory on Mount Livermore near Ft Davis, Texas, and Jerry Wiant together with his colleagues kindly responded to our enquiries.

Jerry corroborated the fact that the Soviets used specially made French laser reflectors on both their Lunikhod roving vehicles in order to provide two LR^{3}s for measuring the precise Earth/Moon distance. These Lunikhod reflectors were built higher up on the chassis than the cameras that returned over 80,000 images, and both cameras and laser reflector had protective dust covers. Lunikhod 1 arrived on the Moon in November 1970 by which the time the Soviets, who were highly skilled at remotely controlling their vehicles, had acquired enough data on the properties of the lunar surface to be prepared for any dust movement.

So how can it be the case, as Jerry Wiant informed us, that the LR^3 on Lunikhod 1 was unusable because it had become covered in dust from the wheels? It is also of interest to note that dust in a vacuum would spurt up and away

---

The liver birds

In thinking of Livermore
the mind is drawn to the Lawrence Livermore Laboratories, California, one of two nuclear research laboratories in the USA,
much associated with the CIA, SRI, Uri Geller, the military's remote viewing program, and laser work.
In 1972 Uri Geller was involved in Puthoff and Targ's remote viewing project at SRI and Livermore which were, in part, related to lasers.

---

from the wheels of a vehicle *in an arc* (generally termed a 'cock's tail, see page 328) and not mass around the vehicle in a cloud, which is the case within an atmosphere. A dust 'cloud effect' on the Moon can only be caused by massive displacement of the lunar surface by activities such as landing and take-off, where rocket engines are involved, or again upon impact, whereupon vast clouds of dust can be displaced for miles.[45] Jerry Wiant also confirmed however that the Lunikhod 2 (which arrived on the Moon in January 1973) worked better than Lunikhod 1.

12. Lunikhod with its 'Jules Verne style' lid in the open position—the adjustable LR^3 to the front of the craft lid is circled. FACTS ON FILE

As well as these Soviet LR^{3}s, Jerry Wiant told us that his observatory used the three American LR^{3}s, situated at the 'Apollo 11', 'Apollo 14' and 'Apollo 15' designated landing sites. So we should have five LR^{3}s in service, in chronological order of arrival on the Moon these would be:

'Apollo 11'	July 1969
Lunikhod 1	November 1970
'Apollo 14'	November 1970
'Apollo 15'	July 1971
Lunikhod 2	January 1973

QUESTION: If the reflector panels *were* placed on the Moon by the named Apollo astronauts in 1969, then why were the Soviets so desperate to get the Lunikhod 1 working? After all, they could have accessed the Apollo panels with or without permission from the Americans. Perhaps the remote viewing pro-

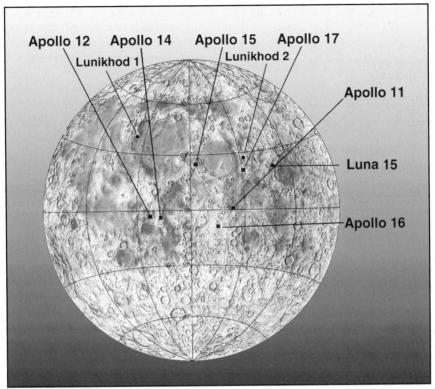

13. Designated landing sites of Lunikhod, Luna 15 and the Apollo missions.

gram set up at SRI in the early 1970s had something to do with this problem. Geller is on record stating that they were particularly concerned with laser experiments.[46]

We were informed by Jerry Wiant that four laser reflectors, (three from Apollo plus Lunikhod 2) were still being used in 1997 by the MLRS at McDonald Observatory in Texas, although the signal received from '*Apollo 14*' was higher (i.e. better) than that returned by 'Apollo 11'. This, Jerry added, was considered to be due to the scattering of debris onto the retro-reflector during the LM Eagle lift-off.

However:

• The *National Geographic* of December 1969 in a report on the 'Apollo 11' EVA claims that the seismometer was placed about 60ft/18.3m away from the LM and that the LR[3] was set up "nearby, where they would presumably not suffer from the blast of the ascent engine".

• The official NASA site plan of the 'Apollo 11' site indicates that the 'Apollo 11' LR[3] was sited 40ft/12.19m away from the LM.

• In the photographs of this set up it is quite clear that the LR[3] is *nearer* to the LM than is the passive seismometer. Yet according to historian David Shayler the LR[3] was placed 10ft/3m *further* away than the passive seismometer which itself was at 80ft/24.38m from the LM. A discrepancy of some 20ft with the *National Geographic* account.

The NASA site plan clearly indicates the location of these instruments (14). Therefore it *ought* to be the *result* of the mission and was obviously what NASA wished to be regarded as the record. Yet Shayler's research has also been undertaken with data supplied by NASA. And the *National Geographic* article was written with the active participation of Houston. If the LR[3] was placed on the Moon during this mission by the named 'Apollo 11' astronauts

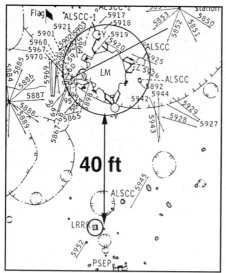

14. Close proximity of 'Apollo 11' LM in relation to the laser ranging reflector (LR³) marked LRRR. NASA

there can only be one position for it. Neil Armstrong and Buzz Aldrin should have been able to inform their PR office as to its precise place or at least the *only* place. In other words—assuming that the astronauts had actually been to the Moon—there should only be one LM-LR³ measurement. And any article or reference work quoting 'Apollo 11' data thereafter should cite this same distance!

QUESTION: If the distance LM Eagle to the LR³ has such variants, is it just carelessness?

QUESTION: Has NASA authorised the dissemination of divergent information concerning the same event in order to confuse?

Perhaps the astronauts cannot tell us where the laser reflector is located because they did not place it there in the first instance. Which docs not necessarily mean there is not an LR³ at the site designated 'Apollo 11'.

The reflector at that site was stated to be a 24 inch/61.9cm square panel (according to Baker or an 18 inch square frame according to the *National Geographic)* into which were set 100 fused silica prisms, each one being about as wide as a silver dollar. Each prism was the corner of a cube which reflected laser beams from Earth back to ground stations because the light striking one face bounced off two other faces and back from whence it came. Despite

the accuracy of these prisms, and the efficacy of coherent light, this was still a gigantic task due to the attenuation of the beam during its round trip of approximately 500,000 miles. Of the 10 billion, billion photons sent out from the laser only 10 photons returned to the detector. Too few for the eye to see but discernible by instrumentation. By taking into account the speed of light (as understood by present day science) and timing the distance (2.7^2 seconds approx. for those 500,000 miles) to an accuracy of one billionth of a second it was possible, allegedly, to refine the measurement to within a six-inch margin of error.[47]

According to the *National Geographic* of December 1969:

> As soon as Neil Armstrong had put the reflector in place and carefully aimed it at Earth, scientists began firing powerful pulses of Ruby laser light at it.

Allegedly, at the time of 'Apollo 11' the 120 inch optical telescope at the Lick Observatory on Mt Hamilton in California and the brand new 107 inch telescope at McDonald Observatory were used to concentrate these beams. At a distance of around 250,000 miles the span of the laser at this point was approximately 83,333 inches = 1.32 miles/2.12 kilometres.

However, the above record of when the laser(s) was/were first fired turns out not to be quite in order. Jerry Wiant informed us that the McDonald Observatory was unable to obtain any readings from the lunar surface until "mid-August 1969". Why? Well, Jerry says that there were too many clouds in the local Texan sky that Summer. So to check this claim, we contacted the relevant American meteorological office and interestingly their weather data for the area recorded:

> Clear skies with temperatures averaging 88°F and no precipitation from July 18 thro' August 25 1969![48]

However, the *National Geographic* had a different reason for the lack of success in reading the 'Apollo 11' LR³. According to them, no detectable light was returned as the brilliance of reflected sunlight obscured whatever laser light might be returning (those 10 photons worth, apparently). One would have thought that the astronomers could have worked out that problem of ambient sunlight prior to July 20 1969. *Shortly before* lunar night, the 120 inch telescope at Lick Observatory was picking up signals and since then McDonald Observatory has detected them repeatedly. Lunar night occurred on August 13, so shortly before means whenever they like before that date, which hardly concurs with Jerry's mid-month date which we take to mean August 15 or so.[49] If one were to provide a *scientist* with such vague terminology for a specific scientific experiment, one would not be taken at all seriously. Yet it seems to be acceptable for a scientist to provide the *public* with such vague replies and expect to get away with it to boot. However, in the hope of obtaining something more precise, we put some further questions to Jerry Wiant who then sent us this reply:

> The Apollo pictures show the reflectors angled with reference to the local horizontal. If the astronauts had landed at the Moon's equator I believe the reflector panel would have been flat to the surface. The [sun] angles were known prior to landing and so the astronaut made an alignment with the sun to get a local azimuth. Then he looked at a carpenter's (type) level to get the panel (bottom plane) level.[50] [sic]

But Jerry, 'Apollo 11' did land at the equator! At 0°41′E latitude, according to the NASA record. Yet the reflector was tilted a full 28° to the horizontal, not flat on the surface. How can that possibly square with Jerry Wiant's statement.

David Shayler advises us that Armstrong had difficulty in levelling the LR³:

> The instrument refusing to display the spirit level type bubble level in a tube [sic] so he walks away. On his return he found the instrument perfectly aligned![51]

Magic! This account is clearly a total impossibility. A carpenter's spirit level is not a 'read out' but is literally a bubble in a tube. In order for the bubble to display 'LEVEL' the base of the instrument to which it is attached must be

15. The 'Apollo 11' LR³ depicting an approx. 28° angle of tilt—when *according to the McDonald Observatory* the reflector should have been flat.   NASA

perfectly horizontal. In order for the base of this reflector to become perfectly horizontal it is necessary *to adjust* it manually.

Dust to dust

The *pretence* that the lunar surface was completely unknown and that nobody knew what landing conditions would be like before the first crash landings of the 1960s is just that—play acting. As early as 1949, Australian radio physicists had penetrated the surface of the Moon to about one metre and demonstrated that there was solid rock underneath a thin layer of dust.[52]

QUESTION: Why did NASA choose to publicly ignore such findings, while anxious scientists such as Dr. Thomas Gold—who held that the Moon was probably covered in deep blankets of dust—were given much publicity?

QUESTION: How can anyone seriously position the 'Apollo 11' reflector at a minimum distance of only 40ft/12m away *from a rocket engine that they knew was going to scatter vast clouds of lunar dust over a wide area at take off?* A location that, by their own admission, would become *so badly covered in dust and debris that the reflector would be rendered virtually useless?*

Their foreknowledge of the lunar dust conditions combined with their pre-Apollo probe information should have alerted the experts as to the best placing for the 'Apollo 11' LR³. But then, we are advised that the ascent stage of the LM when fired, *"did not create any dust"*.

In *Moonshot* astronaut/authors Deke Slayton and Alan Shepard inform us that the 'Apollo 14' ALSEP site was some 250 paces from the LM. With a generous 27 inches per pace that is approximately 563ft, some fourteen times further than the 'Apollo 11' LR^3 position. Which would correspond with Jerry Wiant's statement, "that on later landings the astronauts were asked (and they did) to walk further away from the LM before setting down the retro-reflectors". However, the Fra Mauro region was apparently excessively dusty. Shepard and Slayton wrote: "Fra Mauro was thicker and deeper in dust than the sites encountered by earlier Apollo landings" and "as they approached the site for the ALSEP experiments, some 250 paces from their landing ship, the two men seemed to be sinking into some great bowl of Moon dust". And further, "Shepard laughed as he waded through thick layers of the Moon's topsoil". So how much of that dust would have been blown about had their LM really ascended?

Despite the fact that McDonald Observatory tells us there is an LR^3 at the 'Apollo 14' landing site of Fra Mauro, finding any mention of this LR^3 making up part of the scientific instruments flown on this mission in the many sources to which we have referred is hard, and finding explicit reference to its deployment on site by the astronauts even harder. In his 1981 *A History of Manned Spaceflight* David Baker refers to the positioning of both the 'Apollo 14' and the 'Apollo 15' LR^3s. But then in his very detailed 1996 *Spaceflight and Rocketry: A Chronology* the laser reflectors are conspicuous by their absence from these missions' listed equipment and ALSEP packages.[53]

QUESTION: Why choose Fra Mauro, allegedly the dustiest site of all the selected locations for an LR^3?

Apparently NASA used a reflected beam of laser light from the 'Apollo 15' LR^3 to ascertain that the Moon does indeed have a bulge. According to NASA the far side is between six to nine miles higher than the average of the near side, which itself had an intriguing depression. Laser light is *bounced* back off the surface off the Moon. How do you get a *laser* light to tell you the crustal *thickness* of a hemisphere which is hidden from Earth, and therefore not in the line of laser light? Surely the laser had to be bounced off the far side surface from a probe already in orbit on that side? Which adds another apparent porky to their ever-lengthening catalogue of Never A Straight Answer(s).

McDonald's other farm

The University of Maryland's Professor Carroll

Dusty evidence

Rover producing <u>clumping</u> of dust (circled) as would occur in an *atmosphere*—first observed by American researcher Jim Collier.

As with the Lunikhod, the dust plume caused by the Rover wheels should arc into a 'rooster or cock's tail' but in all the 16mm film shots of the Rover's movements the dust plume does *not* arc, it falls away as it would on Earth—*clearly indicating it was photographed in an atmosphere and not in a vacuum. An atmosphere affects dust, just as it affects the performance of lasers.*

Alley Jr was the co-ordinator for the laser measurement experiment during Apollo, and while he has mentioned the necessity of taking simultaneous measurements from separate sites on Earth, in Europe and the Americas, he did not mention the necessity of a reception triangle of LR^3 sites on the Moon. Professor Alley estimated that using two or more ranging sites on Earth would enable scientists to determine whether the Earth's continents were slowly drifting apart, for an increase in distance between the two observatories, as determined by these laser readings over a period of some years, would support that possibility.

Professor Alley did however expect that within ten years the laser experiment would help scientists establish by how much the Moon was receding from the Earth. Which is a pity, because even though McDonald Observatory uses these LR^3 reflectors to this day, Jerry Wiant was unable to advise us as to how much the Moon is moving away from Earth.

Jerry wrote: "The number I remember (sometimes I cannot trust my memory) is 4 millimetres." We were astonished at this professional's memory lapse, because it is generally acknowledged that the Moon is moving away from the Earth at a distance of approximately 4 *centimetres* per annum. We had asked that question in order to ascertain the accuracy level of the information returned to us. Did Wiant's response infer that as we are not scientists known to Wiant this was a tactful(ish) way of putting us off? Did Wiant not value our questions? Or did it mean that he simply did not know? Jerry Wiant said that McDonald personnel "are not skilled in analysing the data" and that "McDonald do not use the data from these LR^3's but send it up to archives in Maryland for other scientists to access". Wiant explained that their data is "analysed by geo-physicists and used by a large variety of scientists". But how can it possibly be that an astronomical observatory is *unskilled* in understanding the lunar data returned by their own laser measurements? We asked Jerry Wiant to elaborate on some of his responses to the questions engendered by his initial communication.

> **Observation**
> *Question:* What would be the best optical instrument for studying the Moon?
> *Answer:* A hand held magnifying glass—you just have to get close enough to use it.
> *Walter Cunningham astronaut*

- We asked for confirmation of the *exact* day that the observatory had picked up the laser reflector on the 'Apollo 11' site, together with the Earth/Moon distance measured at that time.
- We also asked for more precision concerning the rate of movement per annum and to specify whether his "4mm" was a constant.
- We requested that he inform us what were/are the furthest and nearest distances McDonald personnel have measured since 1969.
- And to stipulate if those distances were expressed as centre-to-centre, or surface-to-surface.
- We also asked him if the Lunikhod 2 reflector was considered to be as good at returning their beams as the 'Apollo 15' reflector.
  - Was it perhaps even better?
  - How many reflectors did it actually have?
  - And when did they first try it?
- We pointed out that 'Apollo 11' was sited virtually *at the equator*, to be precise at 0° 41′E latitude.
- So could he tell us why the LR^3 needed to be angled at about 28° or so, or *were the NASA Apollo photographs wrong* on this highly crucial matter?

No reply. So we sent Jerry Wiant a nudge requesting that he confirm having received our communication. Bullseye! we had a response within hours.

"Yes, I did get your last note, but it is beyond my knowledge. I forwarded your questions to Pete. I will ask him if he got them." Jerry signed his message with a small 'j' and fled from our questions. The mysterious Pete never contacted us, despite requests for further details.

Had we—have we—seriously set the cat among the pigeons?

For pete's sake

Following this exchange, on December 18 1997 the London *Daily Telegraph* published a positively rhapsodic article exclaiming over the fact that astronomers can measure the distance between the Earth and the Moon. Yes! A feat which these professionals find 'extraordinary'. Has it really taken nearly thirty years for the scientific community to wake up to this scientific prowess? We do not think so, in fact having spoken to astronomers in France, America, Australia, England and Germany, we know that is not so. Had our cat got the pigeons flying?

The *Daily Telegraph* article stated that the precise distance between Earth/Moon had been measured by using the mirrors (plural) placed on the Moon by the Apollo astronauts and telescopes that fire lasers. The observatories taking part in this laser ranging work—Texas, Hawaii, France, Germany and Australia—bounced off one (singular) LR^3 (no mention of whether or not it was the Linikhod 2) on the lunar surface. An international group of scientists (based in Munich) discovered that the distance, as measured on the afternoon of November 24 1997, was 15,654,023,458 inches (which is approximately 247,065 miles). Naturally, a spokesman informed us all, as the Earth and the Moon are both constantly moving in their own elliptical orbits, this is accurate only for the moment at which it is taken. And it is now claimed that the Earth/Moon distance can be measured to *within an inch* rather than the six inches accuracy range of 1969.[54]

That is very impressive is it not? A little more precise than the "shortly before lunar night" and the "around mid-month" responses that we received from McDonald. The significant thing is—this information also came from the McDonald Observatory, "from where the November 24 measurement was made", as the *Daily Telegraph* reported. The spokesman at McDonald was a certain Dr. Peter Shelus. No doubt he was Jerry Wiant's 'Pete'. Perhaps we were meant to read this article and shut up. As nobody from McDonnald seemed keen to communicate with us further, we can only surmise the answers to these questions.

OK, so we did read the article,but we are sorry, it failed to lull these cats back to sleep!

Never say never

Faced with virtually insurmountable technical problems, the instigators of the space program still needed to maintain control of the situation. They still wanted to get out into space, fast and discreetly. On the one hand they had to be seen to be carrying out a totally successful project (in order to secure funding continuity) while on the other hand they could get on with the job of pursuing their aims without needing to pay homage to public relations, or indeed public opinion. Efficacy was not going to be the neat pictures of daring, debonair astronauts flying through space with the greatest of ease.

In reality it would be exactly what one would expect—long periods of trial and error, building on the small successes of yesterday in order to add another step today to the ladder that would lead to a possible Moon landing tomorrow. This procedure would involve technicians and engineers and all the ground staff working under rigorous schedules, and on problems that had never been addressed before by human beings. It would involve astronauts and cosmonauts working under excruciatingly difficult conditions and it would involve the inevitable loss of life that occurs when anyone explores a totally new and untried medium.

Space travel will always be problematical until the controllers alter their concepts and cease using the rocket technology and fuels that go with it, and that statement includes the use of nuclear power. As far as manned space travel goes, with their limited and blinkered understanding of conditions in space and their effect upon the human organism, the chances of the guaranteed survival of any pioneering expeditions from Earth to the Moon together with a guaranteed safe return were about as unlikely as winning a national lottery—time after time. In this book we are looking at the Apollo missions but thirty or so years later space technology still cannot produce an answer to the problem of radiation and therefore man cannot travel safely any distance in deep space.

Not to the Moon. Not to Mars.

Is it any wonder that NASA and their counterparts were going to have to make some alteration to their game plan after all these preceding events. The year 1963 was a watershed in the Apollo phase of Project Horizon. But the show had to go on. And once more the end would be considered to justify the means.

That 'giant step' was probably grammatically correct after all. In fact if you take Neil Armstrong's words as being *exactly* what he wished to say, then that "small step for man *was* a giant leap for mankind". Perhaps that was a way of signalling that the small step onto the 'lunar surface' truly was a giant step for us all—into confinement and whose guardians are masquerading as our benefactors under the NASA flag.

Your starter for 6
Did this exchange actually take place?
Can you <u>guarantee</u> that:

- Our guys are going to make it?
- The rockets are powerful enough?
- You can protect our astronauts?
- They will not be seen live on TV being very ill or even dying while on the Moon?
- They are going to get off the Moon again?
- You can bring them all back alive and well?

You can't give me that guarantee?
Well, these criteria must be *seen* to be fulfilled.
We're committed and we're going,
somehow—so sort it out!

Chapter Nine

Slaves of Limitation

We take a detailed look at the recently-published Apollo transcripts. We visit the parallel universe of the Apollo Simulation sites. We pass through the looking glass, only to find that 'Apollo 13' and the 'accident' is surrounded by yet more anomalies and inconsistencies. Dr. Donald pays a house visit and based on the evidence available to date, we explore in greater detail the Dark Moon scenario.

Web master

On March 7 1967 James Webb testified to the United States House Committee on Science and Astronautics:

If we get this done by the end of 1969 we will be very, very fortunate. The prospect of doing all the work necessary is less this year than it was last. And I testified at this table, last year, that it was less at that time than it had been the previous year.

For those who do not understand NASA-ese this translates as: "We are getting further from the target, not nearer, and the chances of succeeding are diminishing". As far as Apollo goes, nearly three decades between the events and our questions as to the validity of the Apollo record might well mean those who have to respond to researchers are out of touch with the fine detail of the historical record—other than "NASA went to the Moon in the 1960s". In an exercise of 'plausible deniability' it would seem that these front-of-house spokespersons have been left to their own devices to a large degree and are working within an organisation run on the 'need-to-know' only principle.

The amount of evidence unearthed as a result of our research has obviously rattled various departments and contractors that were associated with Apollo. It may well be that all these good people, like our contact at the McDonald Observatory, were seriously disturbed at the results of what started out as a routine enquiry into their records. Are they only realising the discrepancies within Apollo at the same time as everybody else—*now?* Or is it that they do not like being 'found out' after all this time? If there is still another reason for their uneasiness, only they can tell us. Therefore it is no wonder that we are accused of talking "nitpicky clap-trap" by a NASA spokesman.

Despite such demonstrative responses, based on the evidence available we have reached a completely different conclusion as to what really might have occurred during the unfolding of Project Apollo. Unlike our fellow researchers we do not declare that NASA *did not* send astronauts to the Moon.

On the contrary:

NASA did go to the Moon

but neither in the manner that NASA have claimed as set out in the historical record, nor with the individuals named in the historical record.

Surely for a journey from E to M undertaken by the company men in company vehicles run by company officers and surveyed by company officials, the *detail* of what the company men did and *how* they did it should correspond in the historical record, whether filmed, photographed, written or spoken?

Frankly my dears . . .

Our questions first arose as a result of studying photographs that were released by NASA itself. Even if the realisation that there was an encoding of information in the Apollo photographic record might be as much of a surprise to many at NASA as it has been to others, the time has now come for those who know to explain the discrepancies that we have exposed through our research into the supposedly *real* events of the Apollo era, namely:

- The divergence of information regarding the what, when, where, who and why on all published data.
- The anomalous, faked lunar surface photographs.
- The faked TV coverage from space as well as alleged 'live' transmissions from the lunar surface.
- The continuity errors between the still photographs and the TV transmissions.
- The suspect record of extremely low radiation counts for the named Apollo astronauts, despite known radiation levels and the unpredictable, severe radiation hazards in deep space—'American Solar Flare Roulette'.
- The dangers of the trapped radiation in the Van Allen belts and the reason for suppressing their true extent.
- The apparently wrongly-angled laser reflec-

tor (LR^3s) as pointed out by McDonald observatory and confirmed by the photographic record of 'Apollo 11'.
- The Moon/Earth data, the TV transmission/reception details and inconsistencies.
- The inability and/or refusal of scientists and contractors who worked on the Apollo program to respond adequately to investigative questioning.
- NASA's general refusal to be accountable for its actions.

This is not a complete list of problems and we shall discover still further inconsistencies in the coming chapters.

During that August 22 1997 Sky TV interview with NASA's Brian Welch, an attitude of co-operation was not forthcoming. In his response, Brian Welch exclaimed:

> You are coming to NASA which is the organisation being accused by this person [the authors] of having put together the most monumental hoax in the history of humanity. Don't come to us. If you don't believe we went to the Moon, don't ask us, go ask the scientific community.
> The fact of the matter is that we *did* go to the Moon. And it is not just NASA saying so, the scientific community worldwide says so. If this person [the present authors] or any people believe they have some stunning, Earth-shattering scientific finding that proves we did not go to the Moon, don't bring it to us. Take it to the scientific community. Take it to the Royal Academy. Frankly, we don't have time to deal with their claim.
> I had a chance to look over the points this person was making and I didn't understand them. I don't understand why we should go off and do the research to prove to people that we went to the Moon.

Firstly, as a comment on this rather emphatic retort, Brian Welch assumed that we are point-

---

"Frankly, we don't have time to deal with their claim. We mounted this expedition—
the *expeditions*—to the Moon almost 30 years ago."

Brian Welch NASA HQ Washington

ing a finger at everyone in his organisation, NASA. We fully realise that the vast majority of those involved at NASA and the space program as a whole were entirely ignorant of what was going on at the highest levels. This is no crazy statement. For precisely that state of affairs existed during the Manhattan Project. Very few of the thousands of individuals involved knew at the time that they were contributing to the creation of a nuclear killing device, the A-bomb. The diverse plants working on the different elements were spread around the country and military-style management and compartmentalisation discouraged cross fertilisation between the various lines of development. As in a large corporation with its many small companies and various divisions within those companies, the entire space program was also conducted on a 'need-to-know' basis only. Any one department would not necessarily have any meaningful information concerning the activities of another. The division of work and the objectives, the subcontracting to the many smaller firms involved with the construction processes and the spreading of tasks over the many bases, centres and offices of NASA & Co., would all combine to render the whole program as impermeable to the curious as a storage warehouse of identical crates, numbered but not named.

As the real perpetrators of this "monumental hoax", the self-appointed and self-styled 'masters of infinity' are out of reach, we must necessarily address our enquiries to Brian Welch. For he is the man that his organisation has placed at stage front. We would also point out to Mr Welch that the more we do ask the scientific community for validation of these events the more they become tongue-tied to the point of inarticulation. They can see the problems yet they cannot answer the questions. Despite his protests, Mr Welch had obviously taken the time to do some research in the NASA history department at least, for he had this to say concerning the photography:

> We used the best film and technology that we could afford and get a hold of in the late 1960s and early '70s. And the proof is in the photographs.

Is Brian Welch's statement a credo of faith in the historical record, or is he attempting to reverse the situation by claiming that the photographs looked good, therefore all must have been well? Or was it actually a very carefully-worded response? Because his reply can be interpreted in various ways.

As we have already discussed in "Photo Call" the best film stock they could afford, according to their official supplier Kodak, was quite simply regular Ektachrome 64 ASA and 160 ASA emulsions on a thin base.

Should Brian Welch be a master of the obvious then we need to re-read his statement. Money was no object for NASA at that time, so *if* they were using the best film and technology available, was that the *publicly announced* official suppliers—the Kodak and Hasselblad technology? Or did they "get a hold of" another type of film and technology from an unofficial supplier?

This brings us back to Edwin Land and his invention—the Polaroid camera with its special film. Since its public launch in 1947 this technology had enjoyed plenty of time for experimentation and improvements—all of which might not have featured on the models available to the public in the 1960s—especially as certain new technologies can be retained for assessment by the military well before being released to the open market.

Mr Eric Jones and the Apollo transcripts

Remembering our earlier observation that eventually one's sins will find one out, Brian Welch and the other inheritors of NASA's 1960s space policy are now beginning to realise that our questions and those of others are becoming rather more than awkward.

Is this because the agency has only a few pages remaining of the original script? Is this why detailed and updated transcripts from these missions have recently started appearing on the Internet? At the time of his interview, was Brian Welch aware that NASA was preparing transcripts for publishing on the World Wide Web that would attempt to respond to at least some of our awkward questions? Or have the editorial comments on this particular web site been *backdated or even back engineered* as a result of these probing enquiries? Any of these questions might be partially accurate, but being somewhat cynical as to the capacity for NASA to admit to such a hoax, we feel there is probably a more prosaic reason for the appearance of these web transcriptions. This 1998 web site could be an example of 'carry on regardless!'

NASA knows that it is only when real people are involved in actual spaceflights that the energy of the taxpayer is truly harnessed. As NASA stokes up the funding for the long haul to Mars and the last phases of Project Horizon, it is essential to re-involve the public in the original space program. Despite the fact that the agency is many years away from being able to provide a safe environment for a Mars-bound astronaut, and that the job of the Shuttle astronaut has all the charisma of a pilot with engineering skills, the agency has the International Space Station to build but this project has not yet caught the public's attention fully. Though at $50 billion and counting (at the time of going to press) it has certainly caught the attention of Congress. In order to convince us all that manned space flight is still 'go' has NASA been obliged to recall the boys of yesteryear? Or is there another reason for this refocusing on Apollo at this time?

Can it really be a coincidence that the notes accompanying these transcripts have had two 'updates' in 1995 and 1997, during which several astronauts, including Armstrong and Aldrin, have allegedly gone through their 1969 notes and recalled varying phases of their missions with the diarist Eric M Jones? Even taking into account the passage of time, the astronauts' recollections are astonishingly vague concerning the record. Then again, exactly what is an astronaut expected to remember that was not already noted in the debriefing sessions immediately after the event? May we suggest that these transcripts target all the principal problems levelled at the Apollo record by researchers such as ourselves? And taking this new material into account together with *The Daily Telegraph* article cited in "Servants of Circumstance", concerning the November 24

1997 lunar measurement, is a pattern emerging? For example the Jones works were updated on November 24 1997—so we certainly see the same day, month and year of action! Is NASA attempting to respond to the problems raised by investigative researchers without being seen to so do? Thus avoiding the need to acknowledge any of the ever-increasing number of inconsistencies—all of this a mere thirty years after the event!

During our research into the subject of lasers and radio communications from the Moon during the Apollo period, we had contacted JPL/Goldstone and been assigned an appointment with remarkably, another Bill Wood who was the USB Lead Engineer during Apollo. However no Whistle-Blower he, for despite his retired status, Goldstone's Bill Wood was now the man dealing with questions at Goldstone.

Goldstone's Bill Wood showed us the Mars antenna and the Apollo station used for tracking during the missions, and followed up our on-site exploration with an interview during which he elaborated on the way that the communications were passed between the Apollo craft and Earth. He e-mailed vast amounts of highly technical data both prior and post our visit. Indeed while we were there, without a prompt from us, Bill asked us if we were aware that Eric Jones had a web site offering information concerning the Apollo lunar missions. You could say that he was the most helpful of NASA officials. You would be absolutely right. Yet as we drove back to Los Angeles Airport that evening, why did we have the same persistent feeling that there had been an attempt to 'blind us with science'? Bill Wood had made the point that Jones' Internet project had been sponsored by NASA itself. So the fact that these Apollo/Jones transcript updates are headed up with copyright "Eric M Jones" is very interesting. If he wished to copyright his *own comments*, then Eric Jones has not made this clear.[1] For surely, the mission pictures, sound tapes and transcripts therefrom are, like all other NASA material, in the public domain.

Did Bill Wood carefully point us in that direction because the Eric Jones transcripts are

NASA's latest attempt to respond to the growing number of critics and questioners of these thirty-year old lunar missions?

Here is an example from these updated transcripts in which we discover Armstrong's and Aldrin's totally amazing vagueness concerning supposedly *the* most extraordinary day of their young lives. They are referring to the rope and pulley arrangement that they used for hauling their rocks from the surface of wherever they were into the LM.

> Armstrong: "It was a piece of equipment that did not exist—was not planned—until we were someplace in the middle of our training cycle. And we were not confident about our ability to transfer articles to and from the cabin and the surface. I can't remember who devised this idea, but it was devised collectively by our EVA planning group. It was a jury-rig that we collectively devised."

This is an incorrect use of the term 'jury-rig'. Correctly used, 'jury-rig' refers to temporary or makeshift rigging improvised *during a voyage* to *replace original* rigging that has been damaged. The word jury having its origins in 'aid' or 'remedy': Another example: 'jury-mast' is much used in the Navy.[2]

> Aldrin: "I guess one problem was that it tended to carry up dust? It didn't have a pulley, you just lifted at the top. Or did it have a pulley?"

> Armstrong: "It was a flat nylon strap, as I remember..."

> Aldrin: "Didn't it just go through the AOT guard, or did it have a pulley?"

> Armstrong: "I don't remember. It may have been some kind of a cylinder with a hook."

Really! They can't remember? Is this the 'jury-writing' of a new ship's log? Perhaps space travel affects the memory, selectively! But these two astronauts were not alone. While the method of hauling some of their equipment from the 'lunar' surface to the LM cabin did not vary from 'Apollo 11' through to 'Apollo 15', none of the other six astronauts had any clear memory of the way that the rope

and pulley system was attached to the LM. Our assiduous Mr Jones has been unable to find any drawings of this lunar equipment conveyor mechanism. Perhaps it was all a dream? More practically, perhaps these particular astronauts never really used such an item? Having had no actual practice they therefore have no memory of this matter.

On reading these transcripts one gains the growing impression that these men are *totally* unfamiliar with many of the systems about which they are talking. Surely had they actually performed these lunar EVAs they would have lasting memories of them? However, had they merely learned their lines from a script and been filmed acting our their parts in a studio, then we suggest *that* would be the reason why they have little recall of these alleged events.

The evidence revealed in this book suggests that we need to radically review a historical record that appears flawed beyond belief. The current generation of NASA personnel, without knowing the full extent of the Apollo misrepresentations, find themselves in the hot seat—but they cannot fail to be aware that their agency will eventually have to provide adequate answers to these questions.

Down the rabbit hole

If all that were not enough, we then discovered still further problems associated with the LMs, and especially the presentation made to the

1. 'Ribbed' lining to LM tunnel (TV frame).   NASA

2. No ridges on LM tunnel in the Smithsonian.   J COLLIER

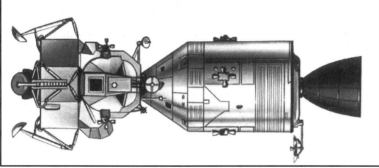

3. LM/CSM combination.

public of the 'Apollo 13' LM Aquarius. These LMs were production-line models, therefore all similar in design and the Aquarius was numbered by Grumman as LM7. Yet there are seeming inconsistencies between the LM on display in Washington's Smithsonian and Aquarius, the LM that featured in the NASA recorded TV coverage from the 'Apollo 13' mission. According to researcher Jim Collier in the 'Smithsonian LM' the tunnel connecting the LM to the CSM is perfectly smooth on the inside. In the TV coverage, however, the tunnel between 'Apollo 13' CSM Odyssey and LM Aquarius is totally different, giving the appearance of being ribbed on its interior surface.

When seen from the inside, even the configuration of the tunnel *appears* to be different in design. The connection to the LM from another space craft seems to be at *right angles* rather than the linear connection demonstrated in all official illustrations of the linked CSM/LM.

The watch chain

In order to double check Jim Collier's theory, we tracked down another LM and were most intrigued to find that its home was in the land of clocks and banking—Switzerland. We were intrigued, but not surprised. Then like Alice, we were off, chasing after the white rabbit who held in his paws the instrument of another Apollo mystery, as Omega claim that without their Omega Speedmaster Professional watch on board the 'Apollo 13', the crew would have been "unable to return to Earth". Omega maintains that Jim Lovell, having switched down all power circuits, used his trusty Speedmaster chronograph to time the firing of the secondary rockets that took the LM out of lunar orbit and into a free-return trajectory for Earth.

Lovell's version of 'reality' is very different.[3] Apparently not all the systems were disabled and the course correction to a free-return trajectory was carried out on April 14 at 2.43 am CST (Central Standard Time) by the computer, utilising its countdown display. Guidance control was set on 'primary guidance' and thrust control was set to 'auto'. The secondary rockets (as Omega describe them), sprang to life 7.5 seconds before ignition. This is a process called initiating Ullage. At this point Lovell writes that he still had his eyes *clamped* on his computer display. The only time that Lovell ever mentions looking at his watch was just before the end of this course correction.

We cite the above incident because unless Omega had built the computer countdown display, theirs is a rather inaccurate claim, even in the interests of publicity. And if this account is inaccurate, then what *else* has been exaggerated in the claims of Omega? The company

states that NASA historian Alan A Nelson summed up the incident with the following words: "This [watch] contributed not only to saving the lives of the crew but the vessel as well". Omega do not put that speech in context so that we are unable to tell whether NASA is referring to Lovell overseeing the trajectory correction or Lovell glancing at his watch.

Somewhat disharmoniously Omega also consider the Apollo program as "the triumph of technology and willpower over nature". But then Omega, like Hasselblad and so many of NASA's contractors, make no secret of the fact that the company had been a supplier to the military since the Boer War of 1899. Their customers include the British, French and American aircraft industries—and the major airforces of the world including Canada and Sweden.

4. Omega Speedmaster watch with Velcro strap. OMEGA

Turning back the clock

Mindful of the downturn in the industry at the end of the First World War, Omega had formed an alliance with Tissot in 1930 and were joined by Lemania in 1932 to form the *Societé Suisse pour l'Industrie Horlogère* (SSIH). Tissot's best market had been with the Russians but this had largely collapsed thanks to the Russian Revolution. Lemania, like Omega, was a specialist in chronographs and stop watches. This fortified triumvirate, with contacts in both Russia and America, was thus in a good marketing position when WWII started. During that conflict the British Ministry of Defence purchased 110,000 Omega watches, and the US Army was another good customer. At the end of hostilities Omega was able to think of enlarging its premises at Biel. In 1957 their creative genius Albert Piguet gave birth to the Speedmaster chronograph and in 1958 after three years in construction, Omega were ready for the space watch contract. What excellent timing!

Winding us up

The following years were spent in perfecting and fine tuning this watch. However, well before it had passed all the NASA tests, the Omega chronograph was up there in LEO with Wally Schirra on October 3 1962 during the penultimate Mercury flight. Gordon Cooper wore a Speedmaster during the last Mercury mission on May 15 1963. NASA selected it for space use 'officially' in March 1965 when the Gemini crews took it into orbit within their craft, then Ed White wore a Speedmaster on the first spacewalk in 1966. It was only after White's EVA that the word Professional was added to the title of this watch and although hard to believe—it was apparently another six months before news of its 'dazzling' performance during the White flight reached Omega headquarters! Omega continued to make adjustments to the watch through to 1968. But by the end of 1967, this watch had not been tested on the long haul of a return trip to the Moon which would mean a journey of around 500,000 miles! Although NASA had apparently subjected it to the most demanding tests that they could organise—in the environs of LEO we should add—the testing of this relatively simple mechanical watch, as you will read, was somewhat less than adequate, given the conditions prevalent in the radiation belts and beyond.

Here we have a *manual, wind-up* yes wind up, watch which never needed any adjustments to life in space—apart from having extra long wristbands in order that the astronauts could wear them strapped around the sleeves of their spacesuits. Obviously they always remembered to wind their watches before they put their gauntlets on!

Yet: "NASA chose the Omega because it was the only watch to flight-qualify for space and thus earn their [NASA's] unbounded confidence", Omega informed us.

The account of how NASA came to select Omega is almost the same 'down on the farm' story as was told about the Hasselblad lunar camera. Towards the end of the Mercury missions, NASA officials bought five different watches from a store in Houston and subjected them to tests designed to select the watch most likely to survive—being on the arm of an astronaut during an EVA in space and when on the lunar surface.

During the Apollo missions an efficient and calculating Public Affairs Office was instrumental in engineering a publicity campaign designed to specifically respond to each phase of the project. When it was politic for public attention to be diverted from the manned space program, this PR machine deliberately, in our opinion, created a sense of public boredom. That incident with the 'Apollo 12' camera was a case in point. It is hard to imagine a more efficient way of switching off your television

audience than to offer them a blank screen. Did this Omega watch just have to survive the publicity of being on the arm of an Apollo astronaut? Surely this was an example of tying in ordinary people to a yet another piece of equipment which they could also own, thus helping them to be a part of the program and capturing their enthusiasm.

Getting warmer

We took a look at the tests that NASA asked Omega to perform on the Speedmaster and found that somewhat oddly, although NASA advised Omega that the surface temperature on the Moon would fluctuate from between -320°F to +248°F (-195°C to +120°C), the Omega testing would be nowhere near those temperatures. Nor would they correspond with earlier data established in 1965 and 1966 by NASA's Bob Gilruth—he had finally settled at the general and conservative ±180°F mark. Yet remarkably this watch was tested at Biel in Switzerland to the *highest* temperature of only +200°F/+93°C and to the *lowest* temperature of only 0°F/-18°C. These less than the true extremes of temperature were as far as they were asked to test despite Omega having the capability of pushing the watch to greater limits in their altitude chamber and their space simulator facilities.

Interestingly, the range on the altitude test chamber went as far as 360,000 feet, or 68 miles/109 kms. While this distance technically qualifies as space, it is nowhere near the conditions that astronauts would endure on EVAs even below the Van Allen belts—or *was* it? The paucity of these two tests in particular leads us to ask if that was as high as this watch ever flew during the claimed Apollo missions?

5. Astronauts' sleeve with watch (circled in black) strapped over outside of suit.   NASA

'Apollo 11' EVA:

111:34:43 Aldrin: "I think my watch stopped, Neil."
111:34:46 Armstrong: "Did it?"
111:35:01 Aldrin: "No it didn't, either..?...second hand."

Omega states that shortly after touchdown on the lunar surface, Aldrin *noticed* that the LM *clock* had stopped! (our emphasis and astonishment!) Neil Armstrong is said to have left his Speedmaster behind in the LM for safety's sake, and thus it was only Aldrin who wore his Speedmaster to the surface. Is this not the same scenario as leaving a Hasselblad just inside the porch of the LM and only using one camera for photography on the surface of the Moon? Is anyone attempting to convey that only one astronaut ever touched the surface of the Moon? Omega and Mr Jones are the only sources we have found describing this Speedmaster watch story.

Aldrin's watch was later stolen from him, never to be recovered—apparently.

Oh, my ears and whiskers!

We have become used to seeing synchronistic patterns during the course of this research. However, this virtual repeat of the Hasselblad saga both before and during the mission, is astonishing. Given the connections that Omega had with the US agency, the more likely explanation might well be that these stories are

PR utterances to disguise the very structured military operation that is truly NASA. One could be forgiven for enquiring if Omega was responsible for the timing of *every* aspect of the Apollo operation, after all they were—and are—the masters of their art at the timing of specific events and the co-ordination of image and clock. From being the official timers for the 1909 James *Gordon Bennett* Racing Trophy balloon race in Zurich, (that's where that expression comes from!)[4] they developed the photofinish techniques adopted for the Olympic Games and details of the elapsed timing of an event whilst it is still taking place. They were the originators of timing touch pads; the integration of data processing with a timing device and display board; and an electronic video which continually scans a pre-determined spot—generally the finish line. Why not run the mission elapsed time schedules for NASA and their counterparts as well?

Whip out those rulers!

The CEO of Omega apparently enjoys very close links with NASA. Nicholas Hayek has purchased a model of a LM from Spaceworks Inc. in Kansas, the company that supplied the models for the Hollywood film version of the 'Apollo 13' story. This LM is an exact reproduction scale 1:1 and we are grateful to Omega who allowed us to visit their head office at Biel and crawl all over the component parts of their dismantled spider (or collapsed wigwam) during which time we noted its vital statistics.

The principle and most interesting measurement that we took was the size of the hatch through which the astronauts are alleged to have exited backwards, wearing a PLSS backpack. (Their Hasselblad camera(s) were passed down separately to be subsequently clipped to their chest brackets).

There has been some confusion among researchers about the exact dimensions of the LM's hatch.

However, our trusty tape measure records that *the aperture of the LM is only 32¼ inches wide (by 29⅝ inches high).*[5]

(see LM dimensions in Appendix)

sion in a rather more fun-filled way! He had simulated the space available under his kitchen table, donned a volume equivalent to the suit and PLSS and then attempted to extricate himself from under his table. The scene hardly bears thinking about! He has made many laugh with his very amusing description of this reconstruction and we are happy to confirm the results of his cordon bleu studies with our measuring stick. Despite the fun, this is a

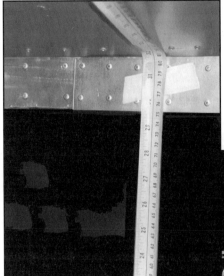

6. LM vertical hatch measurement 29⅝″ high by 32¼″ wide on a 1:1 replica.   AULIS

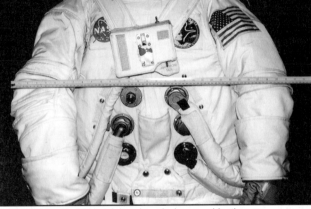

8. At 32 ¼ ins the LM hatch is only an inch or so wider than an *unpressurised* space suit!   AULIS

Surely, it would be very difficult for a pressurised, spacesuited astronaut, fully loaded with his PLSS and *measuring about 31 inches in width* to exit through such a small and awkward aperture. It would seem to be rather a challenge to say the least. Yes, we are being sarcastic and we also remember Ralph René, another sceptical researcher who had come to the same conclu-

serious problem that NASA need to explain—but probably will not wish so to do. As exiting through such an opening is clearly impossible, we ask if that is the reason why some sources state that the width is 42 inches?

There follows an account of Armstrong exiting the LM taken from Eric Jones' journal with our comments in italics. We have then patched in Aldrin's exit. This sequence starts with a reference to the Hasselblad cameras. Having been set up by a remark from Aldrin suggesting that the camera went down with the astronaut, Mr Jones has already marked our cards by noting that it was impossible to get through the hatch with a camera strapped to his chest. Armstrong then commented that he didn't know if it would have been a tight fit or not!

Why not? Perhaps he had never practised egress fully dressed either—with or without a camera.

7. Hatch (indicated) on a production LM.   GRUMMAN

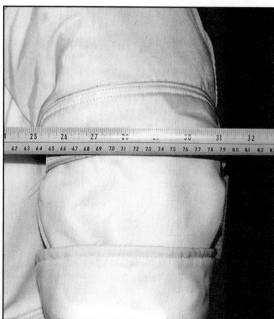

9. Apollo space suit width—close up of (8).   AULIS

believe that in a mission allegedly timed and paced to the nth degree, *absolutely no written instructions were provided as to the best and speediest procedures for achieving the contorted and torturous exit through the LM's hatch?*

109:16:49 Aldrin: [to Armstrong] "Okay. Your back is up against the purse (stowage bag). Allright. Now it's on top of the DSKY panel (Data Storage & Keyboard). Forward and up, now you are clear. Little bit toward me. Straight down. To your left a little bit. Plenty of room. Okay, you're lined up nicely. Toward me a little bit, down. Okay. Now you're clear. You're catching the first hinge."
109:17:26 Armstrong: "The what hinge?"

Armstrong is facing the rear of the LM and backing out in a kneeling position inch by inch following Aldrin's instructions in order to clear the overhang of the hatch with his backpack. He cannot see very well because of his visor and if he is not careful he is going to bang his helmet on the ascent engine cover. So how is Aldrin going to do this bit on his ownsome?

109:17:29 Aldrin: "All right. Move...to your...roll to the left. Okay. Now you're clear. You're lined up on the platform. Put your left foot to the right a little bit. Okay. That's good. Roll left. Good."

When asked why only one Hasselblad was used on the lunar surface Aldrin made a joke about skinflint tourism and Armstrong stated that there were two in the LM but that they only used one, and they had left the camera body on the surface. Aldrin said he remembers the "gnashing of teeth about leaving a valuable Hasselblad on the surface—and that was to save weight".

Valuable in relation to what? And why should there have been anguish at the execution of a simple order which had been planned months previously? And what is the price of a Hasselblad compared to the irreplaceable photographs that they were meant to have taken? Or even compared to the cost of Apollo?

Armstrong then changed his tune and hesitated as to whether they had left a camera or just a spare magazine in the LM.

Having 'justified', 'back engineered' or muddied the waters still further as to why only one Hasselblad was used throughout this significant mission we can move on to the egress procedure. Note that in the flight plan there were no written orders from this point until they were standing on the ground. Can you

The Jones transcripts then note that in the 1969 Technical Debrief it had been said that the most important part of training for this egress was "that our simulation work in both the tank and in the (1/6G) aeroplane was a reasonably accurate simulation. They were adequate to learn to do the job and we didn't have any big surprises in that area".[6]

Simulation of what? The 'vomit comet' and the tank did not produce sustained 1/6G conditions, rather zero G or micro gravity conditions. The wall at Langley and the Peter Pan rigs were used to reproduce 1/6G. The comet and the tank would teach them to move slowly as a simulation of the 1/6G lunar environment and to that extent Armstrong's statement is accurate.

Armstrong went on to say that he had learned about body positioning and the amount of clearance required to get through the hatch, then stated that he had checked that he could return through the hatch before finally setting off down the ladder.

109:17:54 Armstrong: "Okay. Now I'm going to check ingress here. (Pause) I'm right in position (on the porch) and now I'm going to have to go back, in a check, maybe, of just clearance going through the hatch. That's what I think it is."

Was it not rather late to find out if everything really worked 'live, on location'? Had they not had any LM exit training in the preceding months before the final act, or was Armstrong's knowledge only theoretical?

109:18:05 Aldrin: "Okay. You're not quite squared away. Roll to the...Roll right a little. Now you're even."
109:18:14 Armstrong: "Okay, that's okay."
109:18:15 Aldrin: "That's good. You've got plenty of room to your left. It's a little close on the (garbled)."
109:18:28 Armstrong: "How am I doing?"
109:18:29 Aldrin: "You're doing fine."
(Long Pause)
109:18:51 Aldrin: "Okay. (Do) you want this bag?"
109:18:53 Armstrong: "Yeah. Got it."

Mr Jones tells us that Armstrong took a jettison bag which contained empty food bags and other things they no longer needed as they did not want to have to use up fuel taking them back into orbit. After getting the jettison bag from Buzz, he dropped it to the surface and later he pushed it under the descent stage to get it out of the way.

And that action gets those footprints we saw under the cowling of the descent engine (at the start of the EVA) out of the way as well! And also gets rid of the discrepancies that have occurred in all the accounts of the throwing out of trash prior to their departure. These varying stories of their departure and the manner thereof have created enormous prob-

lems as to timing, air locks and the plausibility of this event over the years. The evidence suggests that NASA's engineering did not get their named guys to the Moon, furthermore it has not worked as back engineering either. But we suspect the agency already knows that.

Tunnel vision

Concerning those discrepancies relating to apparent right-angled tunnel connections, visible in the NASA footage of the 'Apollo 13' LM Aquarius—could it be that the LM was using a different connecting tunnel, possibly designed to behave as a collapsible airlock and to connect to something *other* than the CSM? The Soviets had developed a collapsible airlock which they had used successfully with their craft.[8] Was there a necessity for creating a physical link between the American LM and the Soviet Soyuz? Would such a link only have been brought into play if the 'Apollo 13' accident/incident had gone *very* wrong, docking the LM to an orbiting Soyuz craft and then transferring the astronauts back to Earth via the Soviet Union? And was this variation unique to the 'Apollo 13' LM or was it an optional modification for every LM?

In asking these questions we are obviously inferring that the adaptation of the Apollo-Soyuz craft may have been executed five years before the official ASTP demonstration link-up of 1975. This idea is not as outrageous as it might seem, since we know very well that the whole business of Soviet/American space co-operation had been under sporadic official discussion *since 1961* and that President Nixon and James Webb had discussed the ASTP demonstration in July 1969 on *Air Force One*, during their flight to meet Buzz and Neil upon their return from "...there and back, to see how far it was".[7]

Higher maths
"The collaborative whole is greater than the sum of its parts."
Jim Lovell to Jeffrey Kluger the author of
The Apollo Adventure: The making Of The Apollo Space Program and the movie *Apollo 13*.

10. Soviet Soyuz airlock (note its right-angled connection to the craft).

Dr. Donald's SFX trickery—
Part Eleven

The 'Apollo 13' mission had an extremely interesting and relevant connection with *2001: A Space Odyssey*. When the spacecraft's computer HAL reported the failure of the AE35 unit, the phrase he used was the fictional line: "Sorry to interrupt the festivities, but we have a problem". The record of the 'Apollo 13' mission states that the crew of the 'Apollo 13' Command Module *Odyssey* had just concluded a TV broadcast and signed off with the famous music *Also Sprach Zarathustra* (another key link with the film *2001*) when an oxygen tank exploded. What did they say? "Houston, we

have a problem", in tones borrowed not from the automated voice of HAL but from Mr 'right stuff' himself—Chuck Yeager, the rocket-powered Bell X-1 pilot who broke the sound barrier on October 14 1947. (A fact which was kept quiet by the military until June 1948—again par for the course!)

Come in number 13, your time is up!

In the 1994 movie *Apollo 13*, the music played just before the explosion is *not Zarathustra*. There is a line in the script which explains away this anomaly as 'a change of program'. It certainly was! But why should that substitution have been necessary? Were they afraid of the parallels between *2001* and this film, in an age when more and more people are openly questioning the authenticity of the Apollo record? 'Apollo 13' astronaut Jim Lovell, collaborated with Jeffrey Kluger on a book published in 1994 with the title *Lost Moon: The Perilous Voyage of Apollo 13*. Officially, the movie *Apollo 13* was based on this effort. Yet the movie was released in 1994, which means that it was made during 1993/4 and the business deals would have had to have been done in parallel or before the writing of the book.

This reads just like the timing of the origination and release of *2001*. The use of the old fashioned word 'perilous' in the title of *Lost Moon* is very Arthurian in tone, very evocative of the grail, and of course, using the name Odyssey for the CM reminds us of epic voyages and links up with the 'Voyage' of the book title.

Back seat bus drivers

The full comment made by Lovell to Houston was:

"Houston, we've had a problem, we've had a main B bus undervolt".

Main B bus was one of the two main panels that distributed power to all the CM's hardware. With Main B down, 50% of the spacecraft's systems could be lost.

Why—in a country which is so superstitious that the hotels do not generally have a *thirteenth* floor— do they name a space mission 'Apollo 13'?

What is the statistical probability that the mission will go wrong on *Mo(o)nday April 13*!

Either there are no buses at all, or they all come along at once

---

Home-Ur?

Lovell professes that he chose the name 'Odyssey' for the CM because he liked the sound of it! He supposedly found a dictionary definition which described it as "a long voyage marked by many changes of fortune". Our Oxford English dictionary defines the meaning as "a long wandering or series of travels" which is not quite the same thing. He chose the LM name Aquarius from the Egyptian mythological meaning of the water carrier who brought fertility and knowledge to the Nile Valley.

It is our opinion that the number 13 motif with its attendant superstitious connotations was deliberately seeded into the original script. The date of departure from Houston was April 11 1970. Lift-off was scheduled for 1.13 pm Houston time, which was 13:13 hours. The region in which the 'accident' occurred—the equigravisphere which, as we shall see, is an all-important factor in the Apollo missions—would be reached on Monday April 13. We know of course that Monday means 'the day of the Moon'.

A knowledgeable researcher in the field of electronics and stored gasses informed us that:

The alleged explosion would have blown the CSM/LM combo to smithereens.[8]

But that outcome would not help towards getting the 'rocket riders' back safely after their 'accident', would it? That this accident should become a successful failure was an integral part of the scripted plot, a guarantee to revive media interest in NASA's attempts to get to the Moon and back. Needless to say, it worked. Immediately after 'the problem' occurred, the TV networks sprang into action, having turned their backs on NASA during the staged 'Apollo 12' TV no-show. At the time of the 'Apollo 13' mission in April 1970, apparently NASA was not at ease with the Nixon administration. The war in Vietnam was the focus of public attention and their budget was the tightest since 1961. Space exploration appeared to be in jeopardy. What better moment to launch a rescue package labelled *Dramatic Escape* specifically designed to stimulate the public, cure their apathy and re-focus everyone's attention back to NASA?

Know any good scriptwriters?

When NASA administrator Thomas Paine sent Arthur C Clarke a report of the 'Apollo 13' mission, he wrote on the cover:

Just as you always said it would be, Arthur.

QUESTION: Did Arthur C Clarke get a report of *all* the Apollo missions or just this particular lucky strike?

Clarke is either blowing a whistle or his own trumpet when he wrote:

I still get a very strange feeling when I contemplate this whole series of events—almost indeed, as if I share a certain responsibility.

Maybe he does, and ACC said it first.

Both these films became big hit movies. However, the film *2001: A Space Odyssey,* whatever the reasons for its origin, is a work of art which will endure forever—unlike *Independence Day* and *Apollo 13*. We call the script of 'Apollo 13' in evidence that the whole of the Apollo cover version was scripted and played out in a film studio, and furthermore, we suggest that this script is not even original. Obviously both stories are about space journeys but three specific points in the 'Apollo

---

This is the house that Jack built

It is another coincidence, surely, that it was the unfortunate Jack Swigert, who was the switched astronaut who toggled the switch that caused the explosion and was, to boot, the thirteenth astronaut on the Apollo program.

Then again, surely it was synchronicity that *2001: A Space Odyssey* was timed to release in the USA in 1968, the year before the departure of 'Apollo 11'? And that the movie of the *'Apollo 13'* saga, was released on the 25th anniversary year of the first Moon landing, timed to rekindle the glory of NASA?

From Falcon via Spruce Goose to Aquarius—an odyssey

In April 1970, a pre-'Apollo 13' launch party was held on a yacht off the Florida coast. to celebrate
the Hughes Aircraft Company's contribution to the mission.
The absent host was Howard Hughes, his company had built
"a lunar observer which sent messages to Earth from the lunar surface".
Given our findings concerning Odyssey/Aquarius, we ask if this party was more of
a 'post-launch' celebration of the Apollo objective? In military and espionage electronics Hughes was the King—
by 1953 the CIA alone had acquired a quarter of a million dollars worth of spy technology
so advanced that even today the details are classified.
Was the Hughes contribution to Apollo more in the nature of a 'post office' facility?—
providing the ability to send messages to Earth from elsewhere,
messages incorporating the *timing delay* equivalent to the Moon/Earth distance for example?

13' script were lifted directly from the movie *2001: A Space Odyssey:*

- The music, *Also Sprach Zarathustra.*
- The name of the craft, Odyssey.
- The line of script "We have a problem".

If the memorandum from NASA to Arthur C Clarke which penned those words, "just like you always said it would be", was not a credit for the screenplay, then perhaps Mr Clarke should take legal action for plagiarism!

Designer dress—cue mission #13

The full space project as originally envisaged by Wernher von Braun was never restricted to simply visiting the Moon. Perhaps NASA believed that with evolving technology the problems unresolvable in 1969 might well become resolvable a decade or so later, for that reason alone it has been absolutely essential to keep the momentum of the space program going. This is a most reasonable point of view, for once lost it would be difficult to return to such high levels of investment, and the next stage of Project Horizon would require an even more massive investment—the Space Shuttle. But NASA had a another problem. Unprepared to discuss the difficulties encountered during their research and experimentation in deep space—and

equally unprepared to lose their livelihoods together with the funding that the manned space program engendered—they apparently made the wrong choice. Instead of being courageous and perhaps accepting that the pace of exploration would be slower than they wished, they chose to maintain the tempo of research and development and give us all the impression of success through *simulating* that with which they could not deal. This choice would encompass 'Apollo 13', a mission that appears to have been deliberately designed to serve three specific purposes:

1) To provide an excuse for the Apollo program to be officially terminated earlier than 'planned';
2) To fulfil the phase "space rescue drills" of Project Horizon;
3) To demonstrate the superb ability of NASA and its astronauts to deal with a crisis within the environment of space.

The cumulative result of this exercise on public and political opinion would enable NASA to maintain a high research profile and hopefully assure funding for the next phase of Project Horizon. This scenario was to reinforce not only the dangers and the expense of space travel but also the fragility of man in such an environment. Space was difficult but not impossible, and it was necessary to keep— exorbitantly—"boldly going" but especially remember the "where no man has gone before". Perhaps coupled with a limitation of funds from Congress if all went badly with public

minutes and 53 seconds into the flight—8 minutes after a TV transmission which, in 1970, had included that piece of music as used in the soundtrack of *2001*. At the time of the explosion, the LM/CSM combo was well on its way to the Moon, some 178,000 miles from Earth,[9] and yet in the TV pictures through the LM spacecraft

11. 'Frames from the TV transmission just minutes before the 'Apollo 13 accident'. NASA Port and starboard views with BLUE visible through the windows—where there should undoubtedly be **BLACK**.

opinion, we consider that the ultimate aim of this scenario was to supply NASA with an excuse for dropping manned space flight beyond the VAB's from its list of things to accomplish. Deep space manned missions were to be "scaled down". A euphemism for "dropped altogether". Thus the objectives of 'Apollo 13' would then have been be accomplished! Ex-astronaut Jim Lovell backed this horse when he stated that it was the 'Apollo 13' accident that finished off the program![11]

However, the best laid plans . . .

Careful study of the evidence from 'Apollo 13' suggests that NASA's recorded TV images demonstrate yet another space *simulation*— nothing more than a practice rescue operation, a real-time exercise *carried out in its entirety right under our noses in low Earth orbit!*

Mist before our eyes

That 'accident' occurred not only under all those coincidental 13s but also at 55 hours 54

windows we see the impossible—not Homer's wine red sea, nor NASA's unrelenting blackness of a starless space—*but the colour blue!* Yes, blue (11).

How can this situation possibly be real if they were approaching the Moon? It is extremely difficult to fill the entire window with unrelenting blue 'sky' and at the same time have the crew weightless. When in orbit such an expanse of blue is only available *near the Earth.*

We estimate that for this situation to pertain, the 'Apollo 13' LM/CSM was flying a few hundred miles up in a low Earth orbit. As we see this expanse of blue out of both windows, the combo was probably rolled 'pointing down' towards the Earth's surface when this TV transmission was made—and we repeat, this transmission allegedly took place just *minutes* before an explosion that was supposed to have taken place at least *178,000 miles from Earth.*

According to NASA itself, the view through the windows should have been inky-black!

This very serious 'error' would appear to us to be one of the loudest toots yet on the 'game's up' whistle.

This apparent blue could be argued as being the result of ice crystals or other particles collecting on the outside surface of the LM's windows. Such crystals, when backlit by the Sun, might show up as blue (bearing in mind that the TV images were balanced for interior tungsten lighting). However, as picture (12) illustrates, ice crystals or any other deposit on the windows would *show up as such* since the TV camera focus was set for objects just a few feet away. No such artefacts are visible on the LM windows whatsoever.

The LM *Odyssey* of 'Apollo 13' cannot simultaneously be approximately two-thirds of the way to the Moon *and* in low Earth orbit—enabling the view through the craft's windows to be filled with blue! Whether or not Lovell was aware of this damming whistle-blow we cannot say—he may well decide to remain silent about the matter. We can only report our findings.

12. Close up of clearly-visible ice crystals on an aircraft window.   AULIS

However, there was little point in carrying out these 'real-life' simulation exercises if everybody was in the know. So it is highly likely that the fact that this mission was taking place entirely in LEO was totally unknown to the majority of NASA personnel at Houston, or elsewhere. Again, as it would be a requirement that the astronauts perform in optimum reality conditions, it is entirely possible that while cognisant of their actual whereabouts, the astronauts of 'Apollo 13' were unaware that their mini 'accident' was the rehearsal for a major space disaster as was suggested by WvB many years previously. And in any case, our information is that this exploding-tank theme is totally implausible.

There is very loud whistle-blowing in this scenario because according to an experts on gas

---

Blank space

"This white, grey-white Moon, it contrasts with the black sky just like everyone's reported. The black's about as black as you have seen in your life—its a solid, straight, dull black."

Alan Bean

Sky (of any colour) is the result of an atmosphere and our sky stops at the exosphere, the outer layer of the atmosphere some 500 miles up.

Space is the name for the expanse beyond our atmosphere. Deep space is certainly beyond the VABs.

NASA states that space starts at around 50 miles up! This is the height at which it is necessary to use rockets rather than jet engines.

Between 53 and 60 miles up is actually the coldest part of the atmosphere.

vacancy filled

pressurisation, it could not have been *a main oxygen tank* that exploded during the 'Apollo 13' flight. An oxygen tank exploding in space (a vacuum) *would not just cause damage* to a flimsy module. As we have already emphasised it would destroy the craft completely, killing the astronauts in the process. Moreover, the resultant damage might well have extended to the entire manned space project itself.

'project sterling'

Jim Lovell stated that the LM Aquarius had been equipped with more oxygen than the LMs used by the 'Apollo 9', through to 'Apollo 12' crews. This generous supply of oxygen was apparently necessary because the 'Apollo 13' crew would be doing *two* EVAs on the Moon and would therefore need to vent and repressurise the LM cabin atmosphere twice.[10]

Objections to that claim:

- In the 'Apollo 11' official-as-you-can-get record we are informed that having repressurised the LM Eagl*e* once, Buzz and Neil subsequently *reopened* the hatch in order to throw out their unwanted trash. This action would have required the depressurising of the cabin. They would therefore have subsequently needed to repressurise their LM but according to Lovell they could not have done so, as they did not carry sufficient oxygen. (Note, the official NASA timeline did not specify this second repressurisation which rather dilutes Mr Jones efforts to regularise this situation.)
- 'Apollo 12' allegedly did perform two lunar EVAs and therefore *would* have needed to repressurise the LM twice. Which means that there should have been adequate oxygen on board for such requirements.
- Either the 'Apollo 11' and '12' LMs described in the official records were never used on the lunar surface *by the named astronauts* in the manner described—in which case the actual quantity of oxygen for each mission did not matter anyway;
- Or Jim Lovell does not know what he is talking about, which as a NASA astronaut with the 'right stuff' surely cannot be the

case. And if he *does* know what he is talking about, then Buzz and Neil could not have done what they claim they did, and the 'Apollo 12' crew may not have been able to carry out their two EVAs on the surface of the Moon.

The only way that the above statement of Lovell's makes any sense—and it then makes a *lot of sense*—is as a justification for having *extra* oxygen on board the 'Apollo 13' LM Aquarius. The mission scriptwriters knew that they would need extra oxygen for this mission as they planned to *use* a substantial amount up at the time of the 'accident'. In this way, after the mishap, the three astronauts would still have enough oxygen during their 'rescue' operation. In other words, this data is either evidence that the 'Apollo 13' 'accident' was pre-planned, and/or is a very loud whistle-blow by Lovell. But given Lovell's low opinion of certain Whistle-Blowers, we are inclined towards the first option.

Night sites

A further highly significant piece of evidence relates to the 'Apollo 14' designated landing site. 'Apollo 14' was assigned the exact same landing site as that originally designated for 'unlucky Apollo 13'—Fra Mauro. This fact has been emphasised and repeated ad nauseam by NASA over the years. It is important to recall that all the Apollo landing sites *were stated to be in the sunlight* at the time of the alleged landings for obvious reasons. This was a requirement for the 'live' TV transmissions as well as for all the still photography—and remember, no lights were taken to the Moon. Indeed, 'Apollo 14' duly landed in sunlight.

At the time of the 'Apollo 13' 'accident' on April 13/14, 1970 this Fra Mauro site was actually a *considerable distance into the unlit side* of the terminator. This is such a crucial point that we sought verification on this circumstance from Dr. Percy Seymour, astrophysicist and Principal Lecturer in Astronomy at the University of Plymouth, England. Percy confirmed that this was in fact the case and kindly supplied us with his own computer

Intended 'Apollo 13' landing site

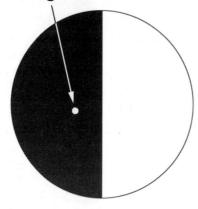

13. The selected 'Apollo 13' landing site on the Moon for April 13/14 1970 at the time of the 'accident' would have been completely in the dark.

print out illustrating the position of the terminator at 23:30 hours GMT on April 13 1970.[11]

The Fra Mauro landing site would remain in darkness for the entire time that 'Apollo 13' was scheduled to be orbiting around the Moon and would not be in sunlight until nearly 88 hours of the mission had elapsed. By which time 'Apollo 13', at a distance of over 19,000 miles from the Moon, would be some nine hours into its homeward journey.

In the NASA-approved feature film *Apollo 13,* the astronauts inserted into lunar orbit and went behind the far side at a height of 136 miles from the surface. In the 25 minutes they were screened from the nearside, the actornauts commented on the lunar sites that were unfolding beneath their gaze. 'Haise' was credited with being able to see their Fra Mauro landing site, 'Swigert' spotted the Tsiolkovsky crater, they commented on the Mare Imbrium to the north, and came out from around the farside over Mare Smythe before leaving lunar orbit.

But actually, neither Fra Mauro nor the Mare Imbrium would have been visible to them. Moreover, much of the Mare Imbrium would have been in the dark as well!

Jim Lovell recounted that at some 86 hours into the mission, Fred Haise told Houston that he was staring at the left-hand corner of the Moon and he could barely make out the foothills of Fra Mauro. This is not at all surprising as they were still in the dark! Contradicting the later muddling movie version, Haise added that he *did not* get to see the Fra Mauro landing site when he was up close. Lovell stated that the Moon was only in shadow on its western edge (when viewed from Earth), which is completely incorrect for the 'Apollo 13' scenario and only just about correct for 'Apollo 14'.

Why was it necessary to adopt/adapt 'Apollo 14' terminator co-ordinates? Why have blatantly incorrect versions of lunar geography and solar mechanics been presented here? Whistle-Blowing by setting yet more booby-traps?

After this revelation, how can anyone ever believe the published details of the other lunar missions with the named astronauts?

Over to you and your masters at 'mission control'. Roger and out.

Casting spells

Orson Welles once said that the camera was unique, in that it registered on film something that was only vaguely discernible to the naked eye, and that was the transference of thought. Or put another way, by the process of filming the actor, the quality of consciousness is in some way transmitted.

Straw, final, short, for the use of — two words, 2 and 5

'Apollo 13' would appear to be the final straw in the pretence set up for the world that we went the Moon with the named Apollo astronauts. The Apollo TV coverage and films are drama-documentaries purporting to be a true record. They are beyond doubt as fake as that staged lifeboat rescue on Wimbledon pond. The argument put forward by some researchers, and indeed entertained by us at the beginning of our quest, namely that the conditions in space do not allow for good promotional photos, does not stand up to scrutiny as a *reason* for hoaxing these images—and the missions.

350

While this is doubtless true in terms of physics, if that were the reason for faking these photographs, NASA could have justified their actions very easily, in a manner that would have been acceptable to everyone: "We cannot provide very clear images from the Moon, due to prevailing conditions in space, therefore the photographs, film and TV coverage that we are making available to you are from practise runs done on Earth: as was the case with the entire Soviet space program".[12]

SFX is the artificial creation of imagery for the screen. It is the simulation of an event, be that real or fictional. *Film faking* however, is the creation of images intended to be used as a *substitute for actual footage* of a real event, it is not the true record of an occurrence, but falsely pretends to be such.

How could it be that we were all taken in? What was the technology that enabled NASA to pull the wool over *our* 20th Century eyes for so long? What was *added* to the manipulation of audio and visual special effects, at which Hollywood was already so adept after decades of practice?

If the conjuror will not tell us how he did the trick, then all we can do is make an educated guess. To do this we have taken the official record of Apollo including the Apollo-Soyuz test project (ASTP) link-up of 1975, together with facts that we have either unearthed ourselves or which have been presented to us.

Parallel universe

Given that the 'art' of hoaxing events by the media has been common practice since photography was invented how did this major production, featuring the Apollonauts, actually get made, without it becoming an international scandal at the time?

We start by looking at what material NASA had available that would be of use in the process of generating this hoax. The agency needed scriptwriters, actors, directors, props and of course sets. It had astronauts, spacecraft and simulators for every activity it would undertake during its exploration of space. NASA also had the advice of their colleagues across the way, for the Soviets had already pulled off the 'Ga-

> ## *Ptomkin Village*
> During the reign of Catherine the Great of Russia,
> an entire village was erected out of wood,
> (as we build film sets today)
> in order to convince the Czarina that her country was
> indeed prosperous and her peoples happy.
> She travelled through this make-believe village
> without acknowledging the fakery.
> Parallels with the Apollo Simulation/Surrogate
> Program (ASP)?

garin' launch using the very cinemamatic and simulation techniques that NASA would now put into practice in a truly Apollywood style.

We start by looking at the simulators.

NASA built simulators for many aspects of the space program, in order that the astronauts could learn to use each piece of machinery and equipment before attempting to fly in space. Here we will mention the simulators that would have been helpful in the faking scenario, leaving aside others, such as the centrifuge, which contributed directly to an astronaut's rigorous training program. In passing, this training program included survival courses (in case these lunar travellers missed the ocean on the way home and landed in the Amazon) which taught the men how to eat off the land—iguana for example. The Soviets packed a gun into their cosmonaut's survival pack. This was ostensibly to be used as a defensive weapon against the wildlife, not the natives! Did the Americans do the same thing? These programs provided excellent publicity for NASA's tough boys, and their sponsor's magazine, the *National Geographic,* featured these survival courses for the future space travellers in one of their publicity articles. The astronauts were photographed next to an Amazonian tribesman, tastefully kitted out in a hat and necklace *colour co-ordinated* with the astronaut's overalls and hats. And of course, in the interests of preserving their readership's blushes, the tribesman's naked lower half was carefully airbrushed. Picture (14) is probably therefore as authentic as American Cheddar cheese.

14. Astronauts in training with an Amazonian tribesman.   NGS

This tribesman is showing trainee explorers how to survive. The brotherhood of man—American 20th Century technology rubbing shoulders with the way we all used to do things. A great script, but not the slightest use in terms of surviving on the Moon of course. And surely in the event of a crash-landing on return to Earth, The military would have tracked the descent of the CM, flown to the point of impact and if they were not already dead, got these adventurers out before they used up their emergency chocolate bars?

Apollo elevenses

Buzz Aldrin reported to Andrew Chaikin that upon his arrival on the Moon he wanted to evaluate the various paces that one can use for travelling across the lunar surface. He started by taking off in a slo-mo trot towards the TV camera. Then he bounded 'kangaroo' style. He thought he must look like a science fiction version of Eadwearde Muybridge's turn of the century film sequences showing the human figure in motion. Aldrin fully expected that engineers would use the videotape to aid future moonwalkers, by making careful measurements of his motions, much as Muybridge had done (albeit in a different medium) so long ago. "Instead", Chaikin writes, "they would be content simply to hear him tell about it (sic)".

Did they blow a whistle when it was time for elevenses? Is Buzz actually trying to say something about the studio techniques used to simulate the lunar gravity on a film set?

Tall storeys

The lunar temperature simulator was housed in a nine storey building at the Manned Spacecraft Center in Houston. A chamber 120 feet high enclosed a full-sized Apollo capsule. This simulator exposed the practising astronauts to the temperatures of space by filling the chamber walls of the simulator with liquid nitrogen, creating the -280°F/-173°C to be experienced in the lunar shade. Yes, well that is what Dr. Robert R Gilruth stated in January 1965 and the capsule simulator created the intensely hot sunlit temperatures by using racks of glaring searchlights as heating to bake the craft at +260°F/127°C. (Sounds very much like powerful TV studio lighting!) As the Director at that time of the Manned Space Center near Houston, surely he should know!

However, by 1966, the lunar surface variants had warmed to -235°F/-148°C and +235°F. Then in February 1969 it was even warmer +243°F/117°C and five months later, in July the Moon had become *much warmer* in the *unlit* areas—because we are told that the night time lunar temperature was now only -180°F/-117°C!

Over those years the Moon also managed to become *much cooler* in the sunlight, as by 1969 the maximum daytime temperature had reduced from +260°F down to +180°F/82°C. That is a massive drop of 80°F.

Full of beans

NASA's Robert Gilruth: "What did the survival training teach you, Al?"

Astronaut Al Bean: "I learned that the best thing to do is to try very hard to keep from coming down in the Jungle."

These variations in surface heat certainly imply at least a lack of co-ordination in the dissemination of basic information from NASA, and most certainly to contractors such as Hasselblad and Omega. Jan Lundberg of Hasselblad said that NASA knew *exactly* what temperatures they were dealing with well before 1969. Given the confusion over the lunar temperatures in the various and diverse statements, we have to suppose that either the agencies were not getting consistent information from their probes and/or that these variations on a theme were designed to befuddle the curious. One could even say that these temperature extremes were 'massaged' to more manageable levels.

A twist of lemon

This section title is a tribute to Gus Grissom, who hung a lemon from the Apollo 1 capsule as a non-verbal indication of the low esteem in which he held it. We would agree that the LM deserved a lemon award. One of the first completed LM models was adapted as a full scale simulator, and this was illustrated in Gilruth's *National Geographic* article of January 1965 with the accompanying credit:

> First full scale mock-up of Apollo's LEM; Lt Comdr Charles Conrad Jr, a life support pack on his back, dangles on the end of a Peter Pan Rig, a pulley device that simulates the Moon's gravity. He descends a knotted rope while his mate waits inside.

The original concept of descending from the LM on a rope was soon abandoned, if it had ever been a serious contender. In a pressure suit, it was totally impractical. There is a good deal wrong with the original caption of picture (15). Firstly this is not a photograph, but only

15. Illustration of a full scale mock-up of the LM.   NASA

an *illustration* or drawing. Secondly, the astronaut dummy could be Tom, Dick or even Harry, but it certainly is not a live person. And if that is a simulation with lifepack, where *is* the pressure suit? The name 'Peter Pan' wire rig is the term used by stunt artists for the harness used by actors to simulate flight around a stage or a film set, *wired* from the roof space (as we will show shortly). The rig illustrated has a pulley device that provides the ⅙th gravity environment.

QUESTION: Why was it necessary for Dr. Robert Gilruth to write fiction as fact? What was wrong with presenting the concept as an artist's illustration?

QUESTION: Was it because they did not want to admit that the LM development was at the time behind schedule?

However, over at NASA's Langley Research Center in Virginia the astronaut was strapped into a harness and walked a wall, the angle of this wall effectively taking away from him ⅚ths of his weight.

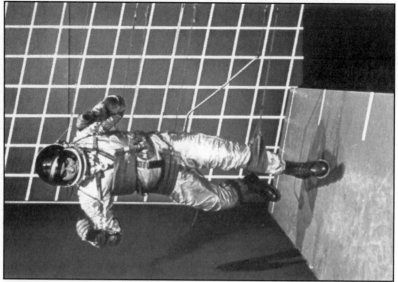

16. The ⅙th gravity simulator at Langley Research Center, Virginia.   NASA

Wire flying—how it was done?

Using 'Peter Pan' wire rigs where necessary and the slow-motion capability of the video record/replay machines, the studio engineers could easily produce hours of plausible recordings ready for each mission's 'live' TV coverage.

In order to make any performers 'fly', it is necessary for an actor/actress to wear a special harness under outer 'normal' clothing. Attached to this harness is the fixing for wire(s) and the wire(s) in turn connect to a rig attached to small wheels and tracks, well above the action. The wires are strong, but thin and invisible to the camera when appropriately lit by the studio lighting. These rigs can be very sophisticated, allowing considerable lateral and vertical movement, depending upon the length of the wire, and the tracks which are in the studio roof space or gantry over the set. Counter weights are used on the other ends of the wires to take the load, or (with the assistance of a skilled operator) even hoist the performers well into the air—as in *Peter Pan* or *Mary Poppins*.

In the case of simulating a lower gravity in a studio however, it would only be necessary to *partially reduce the weight* of the per-

former—which simplifies matters somewhat. An example of a situation of apparent over-eagerness by a wire operator is to be found with the 'Jump Salute' of 'Apollo 15', which we discussed in "Photo Call" picture (63). In the TV recording of this event, just prior to this famous jump, the astronaut is seen to have nearly all the weight taken off his feet—the soles of his boots are virtually 'tickling' the ground—just prior to the main jump!

At McDonnell Aircraft Corporation a training simulator existed for the Gemini/Agena docking procedures. Interestingly, these facilities were later moved into Houston's Manned Spacecraft Center.

Pandora's rocks

Together with the indoor LM simulator which was suspended from a gantry, Ellington Air Force Base owned another very interesting dark studio, called the 'Moon Room'. This was an interior reconstruction of the lunar surface, where astronauts, in pressure suits, practised 'moon rocking'. Ellington also had a geology classroom which contained sample collections of rocks, minerals, crystals, large globes of the Moon and models of lunar terrain.

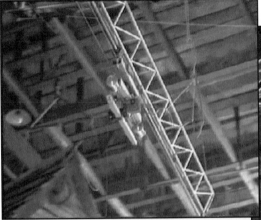

17. Gantry rig for actor's wire movement.

18. Multi-directional rig shuttle.

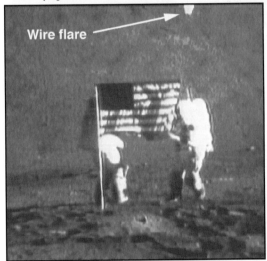

Wire flare

19. Flare on wire caught by the 'sun' above astronaut.　NASA

naut on the Moon will say, 'Hey, this reminds me of Houston!'" said Dr. Ted H Foss of NASA's *special* geology team. The astronauts were sent for geology training to the Grand Canyon, and also to the Rio Grande. Sunset crater in Arizona was used for practice walks over lava flows.

To conform with all other stages of their program Houston kept asking the geologists for a mission script so that Houston could know in advance what the astronauts would say. Rather engagingly these innocents refused, reminding Houston that nobody knew exactly what Aldrin and Armstrong would find and so they were unable to oblige with pre-scripted comments.

Geologists 1, Houston 1.　Match drawn, because Houston probably made it all up in advance anyway!

By 1964, an area of the Moon had been simulated at an exterior location in Texas by reconfiguring two acres, and trucking in volcanic rocks and cinders. As the Ranger, Surveyor, Lunar—and probably Luna—programs returned information, it was planned to upgrade and improve the location. "We hope to perfect our simulation to the point that the first astro-

A simulated lunar surface existed at Kennedy for training and practice, as well as rehearsal facilities at the Manned Spacecraft Center in Houston Texas. Interestingly, in the picture by Ralph Morse for NASA (23), the astronaut has no fill light, therefore *WE CANNOT SEE ANY DETAIL* of his torso on the shadow side.

Alice in thunderland

The KC-135 jet, popularly known as the 'vomit comet', was the flying zero-gravity simulator. Much vaunted as a facility used for some of the *Apollo 13* sequences they were able to film for *just half a minute* at a time.
Talk about stop-motion movie making!

20. Astronauts training.

21. Cernan and Schmitt practice at a simulated lunar surface site at Kennedy.

NASA

Pictures 20 & 21 above were exteriors originally taken with a daytime sky—we have substituted a dark sky to demonstrate the similarity to the lunar surface photographs as seen in "Photo Call", even without artificial sunlight.

22. Armstrong (on right) and Aldrin practising in Building 9 at the Manned Spacecraft Center Houston—April 1969.
23. Training to use a seismometer on the Moon at Houston. (Notice how dark the figure looks without any additional fill lighting, the prime source of light is clearly behind the subject.)

NASA

A further lunar surface rehearsal site located in Arizona, was prepared by the US Geological Survey. They blasted away at the volcanic soil to produce realistic craters spanning up to 80 feet wide and 25 feet deep. No loose surface dressing or rocks are evident in picture (24) below, creating a rather bland look.

Through the looking glass

These then were the principal training simulators and facilities that were known to the *400,000* people who helped the first named Apollo astronauts to step off the LM's ladder, directly into the history books. Instead of being grouped together at one or two locations, these simulators were spread across the United States and the astronauts were obliged to travel from place one to another.

An example of this administrative compartmentalisation is cited by Whistle-Blower Bill Kaysing who recounts the story of the "Lost Tribe". A group of staff got 'left behind' in a staff move within Rocketdyne, California. These people enjoyed a relatively carefree time for six months before they were rediscovered and reintegrated with the rest of their group. Paperwork and administrative 'need-to-know' had kept them safely out of the spotlight. In the same way, the fragmentation of the space program made it impossible for anyone involved to be cognisant of what was going on throughout all NASA's bases at any one time.

The advantage of such an arrangement was that the various components of the jigsaw were kept separate. The astronauts, if not present at one base could be assumed to be elsewhere and no questions asked. Without the full picture it would be difficult for anyone to 'see' what was really going on. The people at each simulation site would observe a succession of astronauts being trained, videotaped or filmed on a daily basis. Every move repeated 'a hundred times' in order to achieve the robot-like perfection that should minimise the unexpected, when in the strange environment of deep space and on another world.

It is more than likely that a high percentage of the simulated Moon voyage was carried out under the very noses of largely unsuspecting employees over a long time period. After all, they had most of the latter part of the sixties to create these recordings and generate the still photographic images. Astronauts spent 50 hours a week for two to five years training for a single mission. By January 1965 the astronauts totalled fifty in all.

It was not even necessary to use the same astronaut or even any particular mission's named astronaut for these recording sessions. In a pressure suit with the gold visor *down*, all astronauts of the same height and build look the same!

Reels within reels

We can assert that it was the utilisation of early videotape recording machines, deployed long before this technology was generally used (and a decade before domestic video recorders or VCRs were widely available) together with the computational power that was out of reach to all but the largest corporations at the time, that enabled the pre-recorded 'transmissions from the Moon' to be produced.

24. Rehearsal site in Arizona prepared by US Geological Survey prior to dressing. NGS

Assembly of a colour TV picture, and especially the generation of a few seconds delay, required the use of what today we call "write before read" technology, located somewhere in the chain. Ampex 1100 four-head two-inch video recorders were used during 'Apollo 11' and on later missions Ampex VR 660 helical scan machines were used (more than ten years before helical scan machines were generally available). The converted signals were recorded onto such video equipment. So after transmission and arrival at the receiving station, the TV signals (purporting to emanate from the CSM and from the lunar surface) would have been placed into a series of two tape recorders for the purpose of presenting a usable colour TV picture. This was accomplished by recording the information—as it occurred—on the first of two tape machines and driving the second machine in a special mode which corrected the first tape machine's speed for any errors.[13] According to Larkin Niemyer (the engineering manager of the Apollo TV camera program) this process only incurred *an approximate 10 second delay* from input to output as an NTSC television signal. (See also Appendix)

Regarding the transmissions from the lunar surface, remember that Bob Pritchard in charge of the unofficial tracking at Jodrell Bank in the UK had told us that he was able to see the official BBC broadcast alongside his poorer quality 'unofficial' TV signal. And apart from a better picture, the main difference was that timing delay of six seconds or so in the BBC transmission. Did Pritchard's approximate six second delay correspond to Larkin's approximate 10 second delay?

The key point here is that the Apollo support equipment *legitimately* required the utilisation of Ampex videotape machines. The *opportunity* was therefore available to play out pre-made television transmissions during Apollo.

In summary:

- We propose that the full *lunar surface scenarios* including the lunar EVAs were prerecorded in the specially-equipped studios—the very same sets that were used for creating the still photographs.

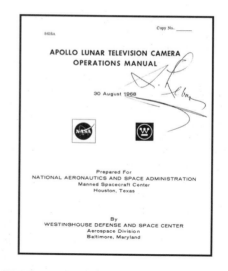

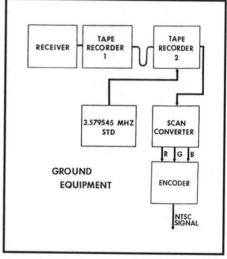

25. 'Write before read' circuitry, the 2" tape machine set up used to assemble the colour TV pictures.

- The programs for any Apollo lunar surface 'live' transmissions would therefore have been played out from videotape. And no doubt back-up copies of these 'live' transmissions would have been made prior to each mission.
- These 'live' transmissions could then have been fed to the key facilities of the DSTN via Tetra, Early Bird or the Intelsats as well as designated secure broadband links. Thereby the TV images 'from the Moon' could be

'received' at one or more of the three affiliated tracking stations.

- It is absolutely certain that a number of personnel were aware that two-inch video recorders were actually in use at many of the NASA/JPL facilities around the world.

- All the TV transmissions, allegedly 'live' from the Moon *were recorded* (again! as they were 'received') by technicians *at each DSTN location* and simultaneously they were being sent out to Houston.

- Goldstone's incoming TV signals were sent to Image Transform in California in order that the pictures could be electronically 'cleaned up' before onward retransmission to Houston—incredible, but true!

- These previously-produced recordings would have been the source of what we all saw when Armstrong stepped off the ladder and into history, believing it to be 'live from the Moon'.

- So at the time of the lunar EVAs, this 'live' TV would be transmitted from Goldstone or wherever, *eventually* ending up at Mission Control, Houston. Virtually all of those present having no idea whatsoever that they were being fed a pre-recorded deal.

- *Thereafter* this 'live' TV coverage was made available to the world's TV networks.

- *Simulated display data* (as was supplied during the many technical rehearsals and tests) would have been the source of information appearing on various monitoring screens in Mission Control.

- We suggest that one video play out was delayed by a number of seconds for the benefit of both amateur and professional astronomers who might have attempted to track and receive 'Apollo 11' to and/or whilst on the Moon. The second signal would have been for the benefit of locations like Jodrell Bank and their Soviet colleagues, or indeed anyone who may not have been officially 'in the loop'.

- Operated in conjunction with 1969 state-of-the-art networked computers the *timing and synchronisation* of this entire operation was accomplished. Technically it was possible to dupe the entire world—and it appears that this is what the masters and the military actually did.

Studio procedures

The astronauts were photographed in the various NASA studio locations, and *videotaped* onto special video recording machines as described above, over the period of time required for the preparation of their missions. We were

26. Part of the control room at Goldstone much as it would have been during Apollo. AULIS

27. One location where very bulky Ampex VR 1100/660 two-inch video recorders once stood at the Apollo Station, Goldstone, California. AULIS

28. Two-inch tape cases similar to those used to store the Apollo video recordings.   AULIS

Bill Wood is showing us where video equipment was located during the Apollo period.

- As the recordings had to be 'slowed down' on replay to complete the simulations, the astronauts' dialogue would obviously have to have been added afterwards in a later post-production phase. This procedure, known in the industry as dubbing or looping would have been a relatively easy exercise as no one could see the astronauts' lip movements through the gold visors.

- We know that the astronauts rehearsed the many scenarios that might come their way during any 'lunar flight'. The named astronauts were the leading players. The others enrolled into the astronaut program may have unwittingly contributed without ever being aware that the sessions would be used as a substitute for the real thing.

- We must emphasise once again, as it does seem so incredible, that pulling off many aspects of this cover version *would have actually been easy*—because most of the action happened as a part of ordinary NASA day-to-day training and was kept secret because ostensibly there was *no* secret. The perfect three card trick—a variation or extension of Project MOGUL!

- We maintain that only a very few people (perhaps a hundred or so and not necessarily within the program) would have known the *complete* truth of the real script. Most of the employees and their affiliated contractors were no doubt totally innocent and unaware of the real agenda.

informed that when the LM trainers were being used up at the Cape, the flight controllers in Houston were linked up to the simulator room and that these Earth/Earth communications incorporated the Moon-Earth time delays of approximately 1.3 seconds in each direction.

Yet from time to time the supposedly 'live' TV coverage did not incorporate any time delay at all between *Houston and the astronaut's replies from the Moon.* How can that circumstance be possible?

During our visit in 1997, Goldstone's Bill Wood allowed us to see some of the other equipment used to process these signals. Of course it all looks very dated today. In (27)

Ride a rocket horse

The National Geographical Society, sponsors of NASA over the years, have already been the victims of hoaxed explorations. These also involved the realities of undiscovered and out of reach territory.

In the 1920s the editorial board of *the National Geographic* were so impressed by explorer Walter E Traprock they invited him to lecture to their society in Washington DC.

Traprock had written a book *The Cruise of the Kawa,* purporting to be about the discovery of the Filiberts a new group of inhabited islands in the South Pacific.

It turned out to be an elaborate piece of fiction but Traprock completed two volumes of his adventures before being rumbled.

If such specialists in exploration can be duped, what chance do the rest of us have? Have the National Geographical Society and their magazine staff been taken for yet another ride, on a rocketship rather than a sailing ship on this occasion?

The Cheshire cats—Part Three

When Bob Pritchard first told us about the "lack of urgency, interest and money, to warrant Jodrell Bank's telescope following the 'Apollo 11' mission" we were still doing our research and it was only later that we realised that Bob had given us a perfectly truthful answer—if their 250 foot dish was in fact being used to track the more urgent and interesting Luna 15 craft. This solution also made sense of the limitations incurred by using the smaller 50 foot dish for keeping track of 'Apollo 11', otherwise adequately covered by the DSTN.

29. The 250ft Jodrell Bank Radio Telescope.

So having covered urgency and money, did Bob's answers to our questions square with the position of the Moon at the time of the lunar walk? Well no, they did not, for NASA would appear to have run the 'Apollo 11' mission at a time that would create optimal confusion for futureresearchers.

While the story of the supposed named astronauts of 'Apollo 11' landing on the Moon is known to everyone in the West, the *parallel existence* of the Soviet Luna 15 mission is far less well known. Jodrell Bank reported that Luna 15's signals were of a 'new type' which they had never heard before, nevertheless they apparently tracked Luna 15 all the way to the

Sin* chrono city

July 15
Luna 15 was at the halfway point of its journey.
July 16
'Apollo 11' was launched from Cape Canaveral.
July 17
Luna 15 settled into its lunar orbit.
July 19
'Apollo 11' entered into its lunar orbit.
Moscow stated that the
Luna 15 craft was selecting its landing site.
July 20
'Apollo 11' touched down on the Moon.
The Moon's position at 24hrs GMT was 25° Virgo and 9.28° SW of SPICA—just below the equator and 10° below the ecliptic.
Luna 15 continued to descend towards the surface.
July 21
Luna 15 allegedly crashed onto the lunar surface to the north-east of 'Apollo 11' site.
This event was ignored (or at least not commented upon) by the astronauts, the seismometers on the lunar surface and Houston.
*Sin is an ancient name for the Moon.
Chrono means time.

Moon. The Soviets stated that the probe might try to take lunar soil samples or even attempt a return from the lunar surface. It is unclear whether the Soviets meant the entire lander or just a soil sample that was to be brought back to Earth by rocket.

30. Radio telescope and military aircraft.

'source' *all* the time as they purport to have done? If Jodrell were *not* able to receive from the Moon then these signals would have to come from another telescope somewhere in the DSTN network and be *relayed* to Jodrell Bank at that time. In which case Jodrell Bank know that fact—a 99% probability—and are being very economical with the truth concerning 'Apollo 11'.

If this turns out to be the case, then Luna 15 could only have be tracked intermittently, and the area of impact only 'calculated'—not seen, which is claimed to be the case, according to the official record—and therefore again confirms our view that all was not well in this regard.

Would that explain why Jodrell Bank told us that they did *not* track 'Apollo 11' until it was near the Moon? And if it does, why did they say that: "They could not track the US flight because they did not have the pointing data from NASA"? Let us remember that they had a dish capable of doing a sky search and tracking a feeble signal to within a half a degree, as well as all the way to the Moon at the farthest point of its orbit, some 252,760 miles away from Earth. Jodrell Bank stated that the Soviet probe was on a slow course "to economise on fuel", and as they were in touch with both the Soviets and the USA their word ought to be authoritative.

However, Jodrell Bank had only a one in three chance of seeing the Moon at any one time. How could they be viewing the lunar EVA TV transmissions directly from the

Lifters

As we have seen in "Rocket Rackets", with their better grasp of rocket technology, the Soviets had built machines for space travel that were ruggedly functional but hardly the sexy-looking machines created by the space engineers based in America. The Soviet's powerful wide-bottomed green rockets were topped with a heavy, bug-like spacecraft that looked remarkably similar to the lander in Spielberg's classic *E T.* The overall impression was of an aggressive, armour-plated boiler-like machine designed to do a dirty, difficult job. The designations of the Soviet craft did not necessarily describe their type or function. In a successful ploy to confuse observers as to the exact specification and ultimate function, the Soviets used different identifying names for the same type of craft.

Ley lines

Willie Ley, who had risen to become the curator of the National Air and Space Museum in Washington, died just before the launch of 'Apollo 11'.

Not long before that, Fritz Lang who referred to the Moon as "his personal location set" had asked Ley if he ever thought that man would get there. Ley replied: "We *will* be there".

Surely Ley, close to the centre, should have been more certain? Unless of course he knew of the problems that NASA were experiencing. The other partner in the *Frau im Mond* hoax, Hermann Oberth (who had returned to Germany in 1958) was invited by NASA to the 'Apollo 11' launch as a special guest.[14]

This was light years away from the people-friendly glossy image of spacecraft presented to the American public—who were also told that the exploration of space was for peaceful purposes only. The American launcher was a glamorous, relatively slim-line rocket, girdled with a black and white chequered belt (the Nazi's idea for better visibility) and emblazoned with the words 'United States'. Visually it appeared to have been tailor made especially for the American taxpayers—who would need a lot of "bang for their bucks'—as well as for the media-infused Western audiences generally. Hidden within the Saturn V was the LM, the folding wigwam of the Apollo tribe. Above the LM perched the cone-shaped command module sheltering three white-suited knights of Camelot who could lie on their backs and think of the payoff. This set piece was the real life version of *2001: A Space Odyssey* spaceflight, Apollo-would style. These adventure toys had fun names like Gumdrop, Spider, Charlie Brown and Snoopy which not only rendered them distinguishable but made them user-friendly and helped to 'sell' the costly concept of space travel to the American taxpayer. The names of birds (viz Eagle, Kitty Hawk, Falcon) being another popular source of inspiration for both the USAF, NASA and the CIA. We leave you to ponder upon the symbolism inherent in the choice of these names when linked to their specific mission.

Ultimately as neither the Soviets nor the Americans were able to protect their astronauts adequately from the radiation present in the Van Allen belts, from solar particle events and galactic cosmic rays, as well being unable to resolve the problems incurred during re-entry, who could lift how much weight into space for the trip to the Moon was academic. However, well before those major problems had been discovered, we maintain that the military and certain criteria of the 'masters of infinity' had determined that those in the Eastern arena of the space program were going to give it their best shot while the Western arena provided the cover version. The unofficial link between the two being those in the island of the looking glass. Working on the premise that politics is

perception, we estimate that the honours in manned space flight were (and are) intended to be *perceived* by the public thus:

First Human into space   Soviet Union
First Human onto the Moon   USA
First Human on Mars   1. Russia*
                                  2. USA*

*A Joint venture but in this giant stepping order!

As the technology necessary for the creation of a plausible sound and light show existed within the military and industrial R&D arena, all that was needed was a way of actually pulling off the magician's trick in front of a world-wide audience. Judging by previous form, the manner in which the military have run their operations pre- and post-Apollo, NASA was not going to perform in public what they could not guarantee as a perfect realisation of the announced script. And although the Apollo program in general was given the PR hype, the public's attention was not so much on the vital preparatory steps so much as waiting for the 'big one'. Which was just as well for the party planners. Because having understood by 1963 that the real event was not going to take place within the required time frame, those supposed preparatory circumlunar missions 'Apollo 8' and '10' cannot actually have occurred in the way that NASA announced them to the public.

One year before the end of their self-imposed deadline, the 'Apollo 11' show was proclaimed to be the 'big one.' Our research indicates that the very public lunar landing of 'Apollo 11' went ahead in parallel to the very private lunar landing of a manned spacecraft. A landing made in tandem and with full co-operation between the Soviets and the Americans and in order to substantiate this claim we will present our suggested reconstruction of how this could have been practically executed. We have based this on the evidence available from the historical record of the Apollo events; the published space data both from NASA and the Soviet Union; information emanating from official recent sources (American and Russian among others); and of course, the Whistle-Blowers of the past and present. For the sake of convenience we have referred to a Soviet space craft as the Soyuz and in order to avoid a boring repetition of phrases such as for "evidence suggests" or "allegedly" we present it as the real event, rather than the hypothesis that it is at this time.

A script for the 'lost boys'

During the period that 'Apollo 11' was orbiting the Earth, the Soviet Luna 15 was proceeding to the Moon. Allegedly competing against the 'Apollo 11' journey, *it was in fact* doing *the 'Apollo 11' journey!* How could this situation come about? The Saturn V launcher containing the three named Apollo astronauts left American soil as announced by NASA on July 16 1969 and reached its orbital path in LEO—at which point the space train was supposed to carry out a checklist with Houston, extract the LM from the Saturn, reconfigure the CSM+LM combo, prepare for its dash through the Van Allen belts and then continue on its way to the Moon.

However having reached the low Earth orbital distance specified by the mission planners, we propose that the 'Apollo 11' CSM Columbia remained there. The three astronauts safely ensconced for a LEO flight that would last until the scheduled time of re-entry. Meanwhile, A Soviet 'Soyuz' craft had left Baikonur (on July 13 officially) and was orbiting in LEO waiting to hook up with the American craft. It was the Soyuz and not the CSM which would take the

31. Actual photograph of the Apollo-Soyuz Crop Glyph activated in   P DELGADO
Chilcomb, Southern England in 1992.
This Crop Glyph had the CSM component located entirely within the 'double brackets', *which suggests the two van Allen belts, indicating that the CSM remained below the Van Allen belts and never left Earth orbit. Note the Soyuz (right) is beyond the belts.*

32. Visualisation of the Apollo-Soyuz Test Project link-up demonstration that   NASA
took place in 1975.

LM to the Moon, and all the expertise acquired during the endless simulations of the Gemini/Agena phase of the Western arena's space program came into play in the transferral of the wigwam from tribe to tribe. This wait in LEO was the equivalent of Luna 15's slow trajectory referred to by Jodrell Bank, but in giving the impression that these two craft were on very separate time scales the public were kept read-

364

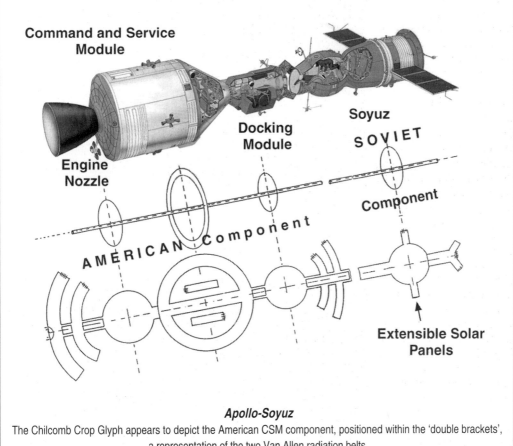

Command and Service
Module

Engine
Nozzle

Docking
Module

Soyuz

S O V I E T

AMERICAN Component

Component

Extensible Solar
Panels

Apollo-Soyuz

The Chilcomb Crop Glyph appears to depict the American CSM component, positioned within the 'double brackets',
a representation of the two Van Allen radiation belts.
Compare illustration on page 86 of the two belts and their relative sizes.
This glyph therefore indicates that the American CSM remained *below* the Van Allen belts **and never left Earth orbit.**

ing the 'competition' script between the two space craft, and any idea of a joint venture was thoroughly eliminated. The train that actually left for trans-lunar insertion and the Moon consisted therefore of the final stage of the rocket, the Soyuz craft and the LM.

As to the crewing of the lunar train, we propose that within the Soyuz was one cosmonaut 'taxi driver' and one lunar-bound astronaut, whether called a surrogate astronaut or more simply a 'voluntary best servant'—a tester, as the Soviets called them—only those who know can tell us. And which nationality these two men were, only those in the know can say, but in this scenario we have assumed that the taxi

driver was Soviet and the lunar walker an American. In any case, the lunar walker would have had to board the Soyuz in the Soviet Union, for there was no room in the CSM for a fourth astronaut. Everyone looks alike in a space suit and there are plenty of ways of travelling from the USA to the Soviet Union (either over or under the oceans) without being detected by observers.

Having departed upon its lunar trajectory we suggest that the combo, perhaps designated the Apollo Soyuz Project, was in principal communication with the Soviet Union and tracked by the appropriate stations of the space program's DSTN.

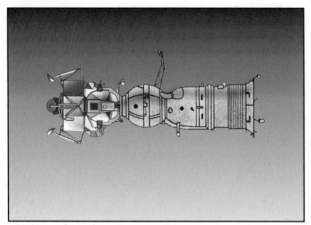

33. Linked Soviet Soyuz/American LM combination.

Linkers

Upon arrival at the point where the LM must separate from the Soyuz to descend to the lunar surface, the lunar walker would have transferred to the LM.

This scenario supposes that there was a period of adaptation in an airlock between the two craft, as there was in the 1975 ASTP link up. This action was necessitated by the different life support breathing mixes on each craft. (See illustration above which does not include the optional airlock.) In a perfectly normal procedure in the aerospace industry, the docking adapters and airlocks for such manoeuvres would have been already manufactured as a part of R&D for the ASP program—to be 'officially adopted' six years later for the realisation of the 1975 demonstration that perhaps should have been called the Apollo-Soyuz Termination Project.

Alternatively, the solution to the problem of adapting the astronaut's organism via an airlock, would be to use *the same mix in both crafts*. Should the initial idea have been for the Soviets to adopt the American's choice of a pure oxygen environment, then we have the reason for that Soviet tester dying of a pure oxygen fire at the medical Institute in 1961. The Soviets still exploring the possibility of mutual air system for the future lunar train, used their inexhaustible supply of 'voluntary best servants' to help them make their deci-

sion—the circumstances of this death hastily 'adopted' a month later when cosmonaut Bondarenko accidentally died on the pad at Baikonur during the Gagarin/Leonov fire practice demonstrations. Did the Soviets back off from this method, even for the short hop to the Moon, and decide to stay with the nitrogen/oxygen mix for all their trips? Or had it always been decided that the long haul team, learning to travel over long periods of time and space in preparation for the Mars voyage, would adopt this nitrogen/oxygen alternative? After all, the Soviets were building the craft that they thought would serve for voyages lasting perhaps years. The months spent in the Earth orbit space stations were (and still are) the testing of technologies and methodologies for the real business of getting to Mars. However these decisions were reached, the fact remains that the Soviets decided to stick with the nitrogen/oxygen mix for all their manned craft. It was then necessary to build the aforementioned adapters for the lunar train combo.

For the Americans it would have been rather more difficult, but not impossible, to have tanked up the LM with the Soviet mix, with its attendant modifications, although it might have spread the 'need-to-know' base of the operation a little too thinly for safety.

Landers

The Soyuz cosmonaut may have orbited around the Moon until the LM had landed, but we suspect that he returned on his Earth-bound trajectory as soon as was feasible. On arrival on the lunar surface, the surrogate astronaut exited the LM—*connected to an umbilical life support line*—just as they do today during EVAs from the Shuttle. Having no PLSS backpack, exiting through the small hatch of the LM would have been relatively easy.

Which probably explains why the two named astronauts could manage neither the exit from the hatch nor the very small space of the LM's interior with ease. Although the LM *could* fly two people in the restricted space, it came into its own as a vehicle for one astronaut. As a

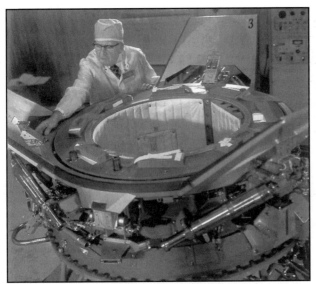

34. The ASTP docking module under examination by an   NASA
American aerospace expert at the Space Research Institute of the
USSR Academy of Sciences. This module allowed transfer from the
Soyuz to the US craft—the LM.

have seen in "Servants of Circum-stance" how the stories differ as to the reality of that event, but surely the presence of a man on the Moon was vital to the success of both these in-strument tests? He would have been able to establish between Earth and the Moon that these processes were work-ing correctly. Seismometer tests run while there was an astronaut on the lunar surface would have enabled scien-tists to establish the difference between a readout where internal lunar activity was evident, and the vibrations of feet walking upon Selene's grey and silent slopes.

As we have seen, according to the re-cords and the scientists involved, both the seismometer and the LR^3 on the 'Apollo 11' mission were too near the craft to be useful, and both would be blasted to relative uselessness by the ascent engine. Our reconstruction actu-ally *permits* these problems to really exist and again we must emphasise that we have determined this scenario from actual evi-dence obtained and not as a justification for our suggested final script. Lunar rock and soil samples could have been returned to Earth by the Soviet rocket technology, allegedly only perfected by September 1970.

A la 'din' land

Most important of all, the surrogate would have had to take some good souvenir pic-tures—and why not with a specially-protected version of Edwin Land's invention, the Polar-oid Land camera? Photographs which could have been fired back to Earth along with the soil samples, using the Soviet method.

We have discussed in "Distant Horizons" the connection that the inventor of this camera had with the US Presidency and Intelligence Community. We are informed that he was the man who rubbed the magic lamp and released the genie from the bottle. We are given to understand that a Polaroid film system was in place within the probes well before the advent of the manned mission to the Moon and that

bonus the surrogate had the advantage of life support supplies officially established for *two* people. He would therefore be able to spend twice as much LM-supported time on the lunar surface, and unhindered by the PLSS backpack, he would be able to employ his resources to a maximum. Given the fact that the astronaut might well be working in conditions totally unlike those that we have seen on the official record, to say nothing of the trauma of the journey itself, he would probably have needed that extra time to complete even the simplest of tasks.

The length of the life support feed would dic-tate the distance that the astronaut could travel. Apparently the TV cables unwound to around 60 feet, which might well be the indication of ambulatory limit but not necessarily the indica-tion of the exact distance our lunar walker would actually manage. The life support feed was no doubt accompanied by a strong life line attached to a motorised winch to assist the astronaut in his return to the LM in case of partial incapacitation.

Did our surrogate astronaut also establish an ALSEP, as well as a LR^3 (laser reflector)? We

this film was suitable for registering the extra-terrestrial conditions relative to the space environment. The Polaroid system would also reduce the time between exposure and development of the film to the point where much of the disabling fogging could be avoided. Was it Polaroid images from probes in the perilunar environment that (in part) had initially confirmed the need for the simulated TV, film and stills scenario?

When the voluntary astronaut best servant did arrive on the Moon, the Polaroid system would enable him to be able to readjust exposures and development time and retake any shots that did not 'work'. That intelligence tool and patented, advanced research asset— E Land's Polaroid camera—could provide the masters with the real photographs of the lunar surface that very few human beings would ever see. However, much of what these privileged few would see, they could not explain. These images would provide other useful data. It would register any anomalies of gravity and light that were present, either visible or invisi-

35. Commercially available Polaroid camera, 1968.   POLAROID

ble, at the time of exposure.

It is our information that a number of authentic lunar photographs have ghost-like effects upon them. Some of which are not unlike the Aurora Borealis; others are misty; others shadowy, as if they were double exposed; some—as

36. Distortions in a Crop Glyph, due to various temporal anomalies, demonstrate the possible problems   J HOLMAN
encountered during genuine lunar photography. (More details on this phenomenon in the next chapter.)

in picture (36)—with the appearance of dragging or distortion of the objects imaged. None of these effects created publishable results for *National Geographic* magazine—or anyone else. Within the range of their knowledge of physics, NASA scientists could neither explain these effects, nor could they adapt them and produce better pictures, for these anomalous results were beyond their capability for enhancement.

Through a glass darkly

In addition to the stills, Westinghouse developed a special low light lens for the TV camera. As all the official Apollo sites were in the sunlit area of the lunar surface we must ask why this special lunar night lens was necessary. The only obvious answer is that there was a requirement for images from a dark area of the lunar surface and that the surrogate astronaut was expected to organise the transmission of TV pictures from such a location. This could have been *anywhere* on the lunar surface on the dark side of the terminator or it could have been at the bottom of a crater or even within a lava cave.

The TV camera lens for photographing in the dark on the lunar surface was called the *Lunar Night Lens.* It had a maximum aperture f/1, and could operate with a minimum of 0.01/5.0 foot lamberts, in other words, in *very low lighting conditions.* Where was there ever a need to take TV pictures under such conditions in the lunar night during the official missions? Goldstone's Bill Wood stated that this lens was used to take the images of the astronauts

37. Lunar Night Lens for the Apollo TV camera.
WESTINGHOUSE

descending to the surface in the *shadow side of the LM* where visibility was nearly impossible, it was so dark.[15]

Comment: If that was so, then how could the still photographs have been taken, when the maximum aperture available was f/4, totally inadequate to take such low-light photographs operating with a shutter speed of 1/250th second? Armstrong and Aldrin both admit to the murkiness of the shadow side of the LM.

But Eric Jones suggests otherwise. Here is an extract from the specially-annotated version:

109:27:13 Armstrong: "Okay. It's quite dark here in the shadow and a little hard for me to see that I have good footing. I'll work my way over into the sunlight here without looking directly into the sun."

During the 1969 Technical Debriefing, Armstrong is reported to have stated that it was very easy to see in the shadows after adapting for a while. On first coming down the ladder he was, of course, in the shadows, and he could see everything perfectly. It was walking out into the sunlight and then returning to the LM shadow that created a sight problem. Aldrin stated that when first moving from the sunlight into the shadow, the sun was still shining on the helmet and creating a reflection in their faces as they 'traversed cross-sun'. It was impossible to see anything in the shadow but as soon as they got their helmets into the shadow they began the dark-adaptation process. He recommended that future astronauts avoid moving back and forth between these two regions of light and shade because it would cost them 'some time in perception ability'.

What an explanation! More attempted justification. Our 'perception ability' prompts us to note that despite the fact that their helmets had been equipped with double visors against the Sun's glare they were then still incapable of seeing in the shadows. And we do not have the 'perception ability' to understand how they then proceeded to take near-perfect photographs and with no loss of dark-adaptation time, under such visually difficult circumstances.

Then one minute and four seconds later:

109:28:17 Armstrong: "Looking up at the LM, I'm standing directly in the shadow now looking up at Buzz in the window. And I can see everything quite clearly. The light is sufficiently bright, *backlighted (sic and emphasis added)* into the front of the LM, [so] that everything is very clearly visible."

In contradiction to the opinion of NASA/Goldstone's Bill Wood and Armstrong earlier on, but in justification for the excellently-lit still photographs of the 'Apollo 11' EVA, Mr Jones interprets this remark as meaning 'that there is enough sunlight reflecting off the lunar surface onto the LM that Neil can see the shadowed LM surfaces'. We have already had a conversation about this with Hasselblad. But then, as Bob Dylan didn't quite say:

Because something is happening here
And you know what it is
Don't you, Mister Jones.[16]

Hands up!

To return again to our suggested scenario, we consider that any surrogate astronaut—as with any military personnel—would surely have been *armed*. If these men were armed just for returning to their own planet, then you can be absolutely sure that this would have been a prerequisite of this voyage. Whether anything the military had at the time would work satisfactorily in space is a different matter.

It must not be forgotten that this endeavour sprang from the loins of Project Horizon. A military operation designed for the exploration and eventual domination of totally virgin territory. Arming the individual would have been normal procedure and would be another very good reason for a surrogate explorer not being seen 'live' on global TV. Whilst possibly useless as weaponry in the face of any extraterrestrial's technology, it *is* possible that any new weapon system under test involved experimentation in the vacuum conditions of space and with the specific conditions on the lunar surface that could never be accurately replicated on Earth.

Homeward bound?

We can have no way of knowing the physical state of this surrogate individual. It is entirely possible that by the time that he had reached the neutral point between Earth and Moon he was already in a weak and depleted state due to the distance travelled from his home planet in inadequate conditions.

His efforts on the lunar surface, as we have discussed, might have been a real struggle for him. And if he did manage to leave the surface and return to Earth he may not have survived the accumulated effects of deep space radiation and another passage through the Van Allen belts for very long. So, perhaps near to the end of his usefulness and his life support supplies, possibly this astronaut then returned to the LM and prepared to depart from the lunar surface. Only those that know can say whether it was ever intended for him to return. Only NASA can say if there was an orbiting craft still waiting for him and if he succeeded in rejoining it for the journey home. Indeed, as we have established earlier, there are doubts as to whether the LM contained enough fuel to return to lunar orbit and rejoin the orbiting craft. Whatever happened to that LM, in order to support the claimed scenario, and be there for any future lunar explorers to locate, the descent stage would be required to remain on the Moon. It would be reassuring to think that our unnamed hero returned together with the Soyuz cosmonaut back to the USSR. But the odds are against it. Most spacecraft have a detonation system that can be activated from Earth, allegedly in order that a craft can be destroyed if it goes wrong or lands in 'foreign territory' where the secrets of the craft's technology might be at risk. Would the LM have been an exception to that rule? The Moon would certainly qualify as foreign territory.

Even if his LM *was* capable of leaving the lunar surface, did the Americans really want him back? Was it worth the effort of returning to the States in order to study his progress in the months to come? Along with all the other species that had submitted to NASA's space medicine radiation research had they not already tested out enough human guinea pigs?

Several scientists told us that most of NASA's named astronauts had received doses of radiation on Earth during their training, but unfortunately it appears that the deep space radiation data circulating throughout the scientific community has been 'doctored', or adjusted downward (see radiation dosimeter chart on page 376). Therefore it is highly likely that the unknown surrogate lunar walker (whether alive or dead) would be hastily removed from circulation and miss the welcome home that he truly deserved.

However many people returned, we suspect that they, or he, died within 237 days. The Soviet craft were always fully automated, previous experience having demonstrated that rocket-riders (due to the effects of deep space travel and radiation) would become incapable of action sooner or later.

Our findings suggest to us very strongly that the Soviet cosmonaut Belyayev would have been the Soyuz 'taxi driver'. Officially, he was in training for the lunar mission 'that never happened'. According to the record, Belyayev died on January 10 1970 following an operation for an ulcer which resulted in peritonitis. These circumstances were so similar to those of Korolëv's death that we conclude that if one were closely associated with the rather more delicate aspects of the Soviet space program one should never submit to the surgeon's knife, sterilised or otherwise.

Contrary to general custom, cosmonaut Belyayev was not cremated, but was buried with full honours in Moscow's most exclusive cemetery. Of all the graves of *all* the cosmonauts, his is the most splendid, with a magnificent statue, evocative of a man who has truly voyaged through space—and possibly returned alone.

How sad that the American lost boy had no acknowledgement from his fellow humans. Or was that toy astronaut placed by the named Apollo actornauts on their 'lunar surface' in reality a symbolic gesture to the unspoken side of the space program?

The haunting and powerful novel *Omen Ra* by the leading young Russian writer, Victor Pelevin, is rich in metaphor. It was, of course, written in Russian yet a single verse was originally written in *English* (see overleaf). The English translation does not mention this significant fact but the author kindly told us so, when we met with him during a visit to Moscow in 1997. Victor also told us that the story of *Omon Ra* was conveyed to him by the "Internet without wires". Interpret that as you will, there *are* several meanings.

Victor Pelevin's story is of a manned lunar mission. A cosmonaut had landed *on his own;* needed a light to see his way for he had landed *in the lunar night.* (In writing of the criteria necessary for lunar exploration, WvB had suggested that the astronauts would need a light on their helmets.) He had to carry a gun and he was to kill himself once the mission was accomplished—except that Pelevin's cosmonaut did not follow instructions and 'came to' in a photographic studio, only to find that the whole thing was a staged simulation. He was then . . . but you will have to read his book to learn the outcome.[17]

38. The unique grave of cosmonaut Belyayev in the prestigious Novodevichy Cemetery, Moscow. AULIS

371

Omon Ra

We're spaceward bound tomorrow
But there's no grief or sorrow
Alone in the sky
The Moon's riding high
You ripe ears of Barley, goodbye.

Victor Pelevin

Crop Glyph in Barley, activated in Wiltshire, England August 1991. P DELGADO

Bring me the heads of those of Garcia . . .

Our outline hypothesis deals with an actual lunar landing but what of the named astronauts, whom we left in LEO at the beginning of this scenario? Although still dangerous, returning men from low Earth orbit is a far safer procedure than the mechanics involved in returning from a deep space lunar trajectory. It is our understanding that these men re-entered from their orbiting 'line shack' when it was time to land back on Earth according to the mission timeline. Whereupon they were immediately placed in quarantine. This no doubt would have been for the psychological protection of both themselves and the others involved as well as the 'big one'—the gross inexactitude to be reported by the space agency.

An idea suggested by other researchers is that these men actually returned to Earth almost immediately after leaving it, their launcher doing a parabolic hop across the horizon and that on landing these men were harboured in secret (perhaps on an island in the Indian Ocean) then taken up with their CM by air and dropped out of their capsule into the Atlantic

ocean for their timely 're-entry'. For this to be so the space program would have been in an even worse shape than we maintain it was! It would mean that by 1969 they were *still* incapable of returning men safely from Earth orbit. We offer you this alternative theory because in the mess of potage that is the Apollo Space Puzzle, every detail is worthy of attention, whether emanating from NASA and Co., or from others who have found cause to be suspicious of Apollo.

Practice makes perfect

Whether parallel trips to the Moon using *unnamed surrogate astronauts* continued to take place through to 'Apollo 17' is another question NASA probably will not answer. Having pulled the wool over everybody's eyes, the further Apollo exploits were scripts that stayed strictly within the designated limits of the ball park. While carrying out various aspects of space research as set out by the Project Horizon guidelines, that particular ball park ended where the radiation belts begin. It is our contention that the 'Apollo missions 8-17' contained the overall sum of the Project Horizon objective, and that in reality these objectives were all met by the one and only manned craft to actually land during the 'Apollo 11' slot. These Project Horizon mission objectives were then incorporated into the scenario for each 'mission script', in order to add 'authenticity':

'Apollo 8' Arrives at and orbits Moon;
Apollo 9   Tests out LM in Earth orbit;
'Apollo 10' Approaches in LM and tests mascon interference etc.;
'Apollo 11' Lands, deploys LR^3 and ALSEP, collects lunar dust/rock;
'Apollo 12' Takes photographs;
'Apollo 13' Tests space accident/recovery drill;
'Apollo 14' Tests use of small handcart;
'Apollo 15' Tests Rover;
'Apollo 16' Tests modified equipment and technology;
'Apollo 17' Idem.

It is easy to see that it would be entirely possible for one manned craft to fulfil the majority of these criteria within a single mission, as we have described. However, one person cannot visit all the sites that NASA have named as Apollo landing sites. It is our information that while July 1969 was indeed the mission operation time slot, the actual landing site was that of Fra Mauro, west of Sinus Medii. The craft was called Luna 15. Whether there was a rover on board that flight, engineered ahead of its official date, or whether there was a handcart, or another shelter for this astronaut, perhaps delivered earlier, only NASA can say.

Anyone for blackmail?

Some individuals have proposed that if the manned Moon missions had involved some kind of hoax or covert plan, the Soviets would have given the game away, and that they were in a position to score countless points over the US in the Cold War 'space race'. But in our view, the Soviet tracking people would *not* have blown the whistle on the United States for several reasons. Firstly, all involved would have been acting under the same masters' in-

---

Large dose of salt

During a US talk show in May 1996 Astronaut Ed Mitchell said that the Soviets stopped their race to the Moon after receiving images from their unmanned probes, "just before the Apollo 8 flight." (1968). He stated that the Politburo intervened and "stopped the cosmonauts from going into lunar orbit". Was Mitchell giving us a load of old flannel—hinting at ET threats—or was he inferring that there were cosmonauts on board this craft?

aids digestion and sprinkled liberally

Mitchell also called the Soviet cosmonauts *"our partners"*, then as if to correct himself added, "or protagonists or antagonists".

stops slip ups

---

structions. Secondly, this was a very real *team* effort. The Apollo-Soyuz link-up capability, as we have proposed, could easily have been a reality years before the 1975 public demonstration. And thirdly, the Soviets said nothing because, as reports have indicated, the Americans had been their accomplices—accessories after the fact—following the true details of the first manned flight into space—officially that of cosmonaut Yuri Gagarin.

The Aero-Space Project—a summary

Why?
- We consider that decisions to explore space urgently, at whatever the cost, were really founded on a hidden agenda—the need to deal with the 'ET problem'—which had manifested practically, from WWII onwards.

Who?
- The space program was always designed to be played out in two parts: the cover script, written and conceived in the USA, and the real record, achieved with the help of those back in the USSR.

Where?
- The 'Rockettes' from the Peenemünde troop reflected the decision to run two versions. As it was never going to be necessary for the American craft to go much further than Earth orbit, Wernher and his pals went West. Their brilliant front-of-house skills, allied

The sound & light show
According to the experts at Jodrell Bank,
radar signals can be transmitted only from the centre of the Moon back to the Earth from
a 30° x 30° lat/long arena.
The signal becomes weaker and weaker, the further one bounces from that central arena.
Light of course can be transmitted from the entire surface of the Moon (as with sunlight).
The grid occupies a surface area of 230,400 square miles/1,340,964 sq. kms centred on Sinus Medii.
As this area curves off somewhat to the edges one could liken it to a great lace covering, rather than a grid.

Crop Glyph activated in Southern England, August 1994. S PATTERSON

with competent rocket building techniques enabled Apollo to be seen to be functioning as planned.

When?
- We consider that the decision to *fake the record and simulate* would have been taken by *1963,* when the Soviets had told the British (who officially told the Americans) that they could not cope with solar radiation and GCRs in deep space. However, it is our contention that from the Sputnik data in *1957,* the Soviets already had a very good idea of the problems ahead of them and that, in liaison with the Americans, they continued to research and attempted to overcome the problems that radiation posed—research that continues to this day.
- It is also our conclusion that the necessity to fake and also the decision concerning the future of the Apollo manned lunar program was affected by the discovery of many more ob-

stacles than had been anticipated. Some of these problems were not even *understood* by physicists.

What?
- The amount of lead/aluminium protection from the dangers that lurked within and beyond the Van Allen belts would have been commensurate with the amount of power that could be coaxed from their launchers.

- Maximum power requires high-performance materials and fuels. Maintaining the program required millions of dollars on a regular basis. We suggest that considerable funding was handled through Switzerland. Further, in order to facilitate communications between the two leading protagonists of this Cold War 'space race' it was also necessary to have a technical and scientific messenger service, for which the British were ideally placed, both geographically and ideologically.

- The American-Soviet/Apollo-Soyuz/Apollo-Surrogate/Aero-Space Project did indeed send missions to the Moon.

How?

- These lunar trips were a mixture of unmanned probes and manned flights using surrogate 'rocket riders' not featured on the published crew list for the scheduled Apollo missions.
- The named astronauts, flying in LEO for the duration of the mission and wearing medical bio-sensors generated the radiation data subsequently used to provide the 'official' figures that backed up the NASA claim that these men travelled safely to the Moon and back—thus establishing that with no further protection from radiation than that already provided, space travel is safe for bio organisms and thereby contradicting the original 1958 recommendations of Dr. James Van Allen. The feat of apparently travelling without incurring any physical problems effectively silenced Dr. James Van Allen. In an interview with researcher Jim Collier in the late 1990s Dr. Van Allen, first stated that he stood by his research of the 1950s, his radiation belt findings *were* correct and his estimation of the shielding required by the astronauts valid. When asked then how could it be that the Apollo astronauts were still alive and well, despite the inadequate shielding of their craft, Dr. Van Allen then replied there had to be some fundamental flaw in his research. We find it inexpressibly sad that a man of the scientific calibre of James Van Allen be obliged to deny his outstanding work and insightful conclusions in this area. The reported figures cannot be correct for legitimate lunar missions through and beyond the Van Allen belts but they *are* consistent with dosimeter readings for low Earth orbits.
- This data also had the effect of persuading the general public *to this day* that deep space travel is safe.
- Today it is implied that anything dangerous in space *lies beyond the Moon's orbit.* This single fact is most useful to NASA who can admit with impunity that travel to Mars is a 'little tricky' without tarnishing the Apollo record.

- Scientists attempting to evaluate the dangers of radiation for a trip to Mars are, it would seem, working with flawed data, designed to support the notion that we could travel to the Moon and back safely.

Here is an authoritative prediction (a NCRP report issued in 1989) of likely "radiation exposure to personnel for a future manned lunar mission":

A round trip mission to the Moon, assuming a four day total transit time to and from the Moon plus a 84 day stay on the lunar surface, would involve a total dose equivalent to the bone marrow of (7.4 rem) 74 mSv. This total dose equivalent is comprised of: (a) (4 rem) 40 mSv from transit through the radiation belts, on both legs of the journey, (b) (0.3 rem) 3 mSv on the journey from beyond the magnetosphere to the lunar surface and (c) (3.1 rem) 31 mSv on the lunar surface. The total dose equivalent for a mission that does not encounter an anomalously large solar particle event would be (7.4 rem). 74 mSv.

After all the data and information on radiation and its dangers presented so far in this book, how can anyone take the above prediction seriously?

Communications

- The TV recordings, having been made over the period of the astronaut's training, together with DAC 16mm film footage and the still photographs for all the Apollo flights were 'in the can' well before the scheduled dates of the missions.
- The orbiting Command Module was no doubt on a separate uplink/downlink with 'base'—via specially equipped US communication vessels at sea and/or US aircraft airborne during the missions until the CSM's scheduled re-entry and splash down.[18]
- All the TV transmissions and other data purporting to come from the named astronauts *apart from when on the lunar surface* were all actually being returned from Earth orbit. This would have covered everything that apparently occurred on the way to, whilst orbiting, and the return from the Moon.

Dosimetry data from US manned space flights

Flight No	Duration (days)	Apogee-perigee (km)	Mission dose (mGy)	Daily dose (mGy)
Apollo 7	10.83	229-306	1.60	0.15
Apollo 8	6.12	lunar orbital flight	1.60	0.26
Apollo 9	10.04	197-249	2.00	0.20
Apollo 10	8.00	lunar orbital flight	4.80	0.60
Apollo 11	8.08	lunar orbital flight	1.80	0.22
Apollo 12	10.19	lunar orbital flight	5.80	0.57
Apollo 13	5.95	lunar orbital flight	2.40	0.40
Apollo 14	9.00	lunar orbital flight	11.40	1.27
Apollo 15	12.29	lunar orbital flight	3.00	0.24
Apollo 16	10.08	lunar orbital flight	5.10	0.46
Apollo 17	12.58	lunar orbital flight	5.50	0.44
Skylab 2^c	28.00	alt = 435	15.96	0.54 ± 0.3
Skylab 3^c	59.00	alt = 435	38.35	0.65 ± 0.5
Skylab 4^c	90.00	alt = 435	77.40	0.86 ± 0.9
ASTP	9.00	alt = 220	1.06	0.12

1mGy = 100
ASTP = Apollo-Soyuz Test Project
Doses quoted for the Apollo flights are skin doses
^{c}Mean thermoluminescent dosimeter doses from crew members

Reproduced from NCRP Report 98
based on NASA data

39. How can the claimed Apollo lunar orbital flights deliver average daily doserates (0.49) *lower* than those of Skylab? Skylab remained permanently in Earth orbit. Whereas Apollo was subject to trapped radiation in the Van Allen belts as well as GCRs and solar radiation/SPEs plus the totally unprotected conditions on the lunar surface.
The figures in this table are actually non-comparable as they were collected from readings taken from entirely different situations. The daily dose in this table is expressed as the total dose for the mission divided by the number of crew members. This 'mission dose' is then divided by the number of days in the mission to provide the 'daily dose'. However, a dosimeter reading taken from a spacecraft's dosimeter is hardly indicative of a biological individual's reaction to the same amount of radiation. In the table above only the Apollo missions were specifically indicated as having readings taken from personal dosimeters. (see also Appendix)

- Re-entry from orbit and splashdown were as billed—routines that were well tested. The Service Module and the Command Module having separated, the Service Module was jettisoned and the CM returned to Earth as per the scripted scenario.

A SET PAPER

A multiple-choice set of questions. Any configuration is workable.[24]

- During the time of the surrogate lunar landings, were the surface EVAs run from the specially pre-recorded two-inch video tapes produced in the secret TV studio facilities? —Yes.

- Were these pre-recorded TV images and sound played off machines that were computer controlled to synchronise precisely with the entire mission presentation? —Yes.
- Were these pre-recorded TV images and sound played off machines and then transmitted directly to orbiting satellites?—Yes.
Or:
- Were these pre-recorded TV images and sound for the 'Apollo 11' moonwalk *bounced off the Moon* from one of the Deep Space Network dishes located in California, Madrid, Johannesburg, Canberra/Parkes, or even Jodrell Bank? —No, probably not.
Or:

- Were the pre-recorded TV images and sound received by the tracking stations via designated *secure broad band links* for subsequent treatment *as if they had been transmitted from the Moon 'as billed'?*—Yes.

This last suggestion is a result of information from a technician at Goldstone during the Apollo period. Our Whistle-Blower claims that he had reason to believe that at the time the signals arriving for processing by his department at the Goldstone Stations were coming in by secure *broadband link..* This West-Coast insider, now retired, of necessity insists on complete anonimity.

Packing up

Over the years, associates of NASA and space historians have cited various factors to explain the demise of the Apollo program. The Vietnam war, American home policy, the Nixon administration, Watergate, the 'Apollo 13 accident' and a general lack of interest in space travel by the American people—all have been blamed for the speedy cessation of manned space travel beyond the radiation belts. The specific items cited obviously affected the nation's mood and consequently the budget available, so the above reasons do have *some* validity, but only make up part of the picture.

Once a mission has achieved its major goal then clearly it becomes a challenge to maintain the focus and enthusiasm of the research teams. As far as the majority of the public were concerned, NASA had convincingly demonstrated that mankind could travel to the Moon and return safely—point made. Through this alleged demonstration, NASA had of course inferred that astronauts could exist safely in deep space as well as on the lunar surface. Yet having apparently done so well, any ideas of establishing a lunar manned base or even an observatory on the Moon were abandoned. Using mainly budgetary excuses, the Apollo 18, 19 and 20 missions were cancelled in 1970 and with the shutting down of project Apollo any chances of astronauts venturing more permanently into deep space evaporated.

However, the continuation of the hoax *was* necessary in order to maintain funding levels. The Command Module allegedly destined for Apollo 18 was actually used for the Apollo-Soyuz Test Project of July 1975. But remember that NASA generally does not risk missions in the public gaze without having tested them thoroughly first. This use of a part of the Apollo program not only 'officialised' the collaboration on the project it was also *guaranteed to work* as it would have been tried and tested during the covert operations of Apollo. The US and the USSR space technology came together in a near replica of how it might have been done, thus making the cover version that much more bearable for those who would have to live with it for the rest of their lives.

Excuses, excuses

In a 1994 interview the current NASA administrator, Dr. Daniel Goldin, stated that for the 1972-2002 period the original plan had been: "For the United States to go back to the Moon and then go on to Mars, at an outlay of a half trillion dollars over thirty years". He went on to state that now the Russians were not there "to compete against", this was no longer an acceptable policy. In other words, the vast sums spent on the official "beat the Soviets in the space race" had been *justifiable expenditure* for that very reason.

We should point out that (in any published history of space that one cares to examine closely), in policy terms the Moon objective was a 'done deal' by the time that Armstrong and Aldrin landed back on Earth. The 'official' get together with the Soviets was prepared and then officially brought into public awareness between July 24 1969 and May 24 1972, when, a month after 'Apollo 16', the co-operative deal was officially signed and sealed. The actual Apollo-Soyuz demonstration took place in Earth orbit during 1975. As the Cold War only (officially) melted away in the late 1980s, Goldin's statement is a somewhat dextrous muddling of the facts and a sad reflection on the political manipulations within the program.

> **Mantric buzz**
>
> NASA received its orders from the executive branch.
> This executive branch of the President's Office
> was financially supported by Congress.
> Congress distributed funds according to
> their interpretation of the will of the people.
> *Buzz Aldrin's reason why manned lunar*
> *exploration stopped.*

Boldly, going, going, gone

In 1996 NASA appeared to have made a trajectory correction concerning the spin that it is now putting on Project Apollo.[25] During a speech to the American Association for the Advancement of Science, the administrator Dan Goldin, referring to future manned missions to Mars, was adamant that NASA:

> Was not going to set up a multi-hundred billion dollar manned mission to Mars, whose sole purpose is to plant a flag, strut around importantly and then forget Mars.

If we were to replace the words 'Mars' with 'Moon' then do we not have hindsight and insight into NASA's attitude towards the Apollo program? This statement in any case recognises the *importance* NASA attaches to the erecting a national flag on the target planet, despite the fact that the official international intentions of the Space Charter expressly stipulate that no planet shall belong to any single nation. The United States insisted that the flag in their lunar photographs of their official record of Apollo should only be the Stars and Stripes. Surely this chauvinistic attitude is totally incompatible with the credo "for all mankind" which was devoutly chanted while the pictures were apparently being taken—although it is totally compatible with the militaristic aims of Project Horizon.

Goldin's statement propagates the myth that the Moon is at the end of the park, when of course, it is beyond the rings of the Van Allen belts. It assumes the capability of a 'rocket rider' to function fully after having played a game of 'American Solar Flare Roulette'. Furthermore Goldin's statement recognises that NASA had little intention of returning to the Moon after having determined what they needed to know in terms of landing a craft and humans on another planet. However perhaps not unsynchronistically, over the last two years the notion of 'water on the Moon' has swung into action—enabling NASA to maintain the mythos that we can go back to the Moon when we like, it being only a matter of priority and of course, finance.

The auf wiedersein set

After 'Apollo 11', the Americans began disbanding their German scientists, finally doing what the Soviets had already completed by the mid 1950s. Many of the resentments concerning Wernher von Braun's somewhat authoritarian behaviour resurfaced. It was said by his friends and biographers, Ernst Stuhlinger and Frederick Ordway, that von Braun did not encourage or enable younger American engineers to reach the forefront of his team, and that under intense pressure, WvB left for Washington and NASA headquarters. Following his departure from the front line, the NASA administration immediately rectified the promotion problem by disbanding his team of German and Eastern European engineers in favour of an all-American nucleus.

QUESTION: If that is a true account of how things were within NASA, then how did it transpire that von Braun's place was taken by his ex-Peenemünde colleague Eberhardt Rees? Surely that appointment made a nonsense of the reasons given by Stuhlinger and Ordway for the removal of von Braun? Yet these biographers must have realised this glaring contradiction and surely blew a whistle by even stating these two facts. So what were they trying to say? Did the truth lie elsewhere?

Sergei Pavlovich Korolëv and Wernher Freiherr von Braun were largely responsible for bringing mankind into the regions of space travel that we are now investigating. These were men who were clearly in the right place at the right time, and all of us have much for which to thank them. If the flaws in their characters have been reflected by the dismissive and ruthlessly mendacious attitude of their employers, seen and unseen, then we can but comment that birds of a feather actually flock together.

In the last two chapters we have explored something of the inner space aspect of the Project Horizon/Apollo phase of the project and the outer space aspect of the cover-up. If any-one still finds it a challenge to accept the findings presented thus far, then we leave the reader to think about the implications inherent in the following words uttered by Wernher shortly before his death. He was speaking to Neil Armstrong:

"By the prognosis of statisticians, you should be dead in space and I should be in jail on Earth."

Wernher von Braun

Part Three
BACKGROUND EXPLORATION

Chapter Ten

Essentials

How are we to travel beyond the magnetosphere of our planet safely? Are hyperD physics and what we refer to as the Spinning Disk the way to go? Are we trapped here until mankind develops these highly-advanced concepts? Will all this result in a paradigm shift requiring our re-appraisal of such fundamental matters as the speed of light and gravity? We explore these issues and find some surprises that so far apparently have eluded the school of accepted scientific thought.

To fly . . .

Many men of both religion and science have been against the notion of man taking to the skies in flying machines. These critics of aviation's inventors and dreamers, preached the vision conjured by the folly of Icarus, rather than the farsightedness of Leonardo Da Vinci.

The American Bishop Wright, once thundered: "If God had wanted men to fly he would have given them wings" —no doubt considering the desire to fly presumptuous and possibly blasphemous. Simon Newcomb, Head of the US Naval Observatory's Nautical Almanac Office, published an article on October 3 1903 in which he predicted

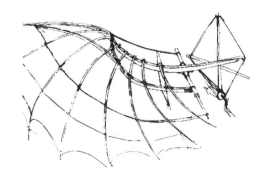

1. One of Leonardo's concepts for a flying machine.

that man would never learn to fly: "...aerial flight is one of that great class of problems with which man can never cope..."

Two months later would he regret his prophecy? On December 17 1903 the Wright brothers of North Carolina made their first successful powered flight in the Kitty Hawk. Great embarrassment for these critics! The scientist Newcomb was demonstrably of closed mind

US Presidents 1900-1998 and flight events worldwide		
1901-1909	Theodore Roosevelt	Wright bi-plane 1903
1909-1913	William H Taft	Bleriot flew English Channel 1909
1913-1921	Woodrow Wilson	
1921-1923	Warren G Harding	
1923-1929	Calvin Coolidge	Lindbergh flew Atlantic 1927
1929-1933	Herbert Hoover	
1933-1945	Franklin D Roosevelt	DC3 aircraft 1935
1945-1953	Harry S Truman	
1953-1961	Dwight D Eisenhower	Comet Jetliner 1952
		Sputnik 1957
1961-1963	John F Kennedy	Gagarin orbited Earth 1961
1963-1969	Lyndon B Johnson	'Apollo 11' 1969
1969-1974	Richard Nixon	Boeing 747 Jumbo Jet 1971
1974-1977	Gerald Ford	Apollo-Soyuz Test Project 1975
1977-1981	James Carter	
1981-1989	Ronald Reagan	Space Shuttle 1981
1989-1993	George Bush	
1993-	William J Clinton	

... and the first shall be last

"If ever there was an enterprise where your first mistake becomes your last—space travel is it."

Carsbie C Adams
President of the National Research and Development Corporation
Author *Space Flight*, 1958

and out of touch with the realities of his time. The Bishop on the other hand was out of touch with his family, for Orville and Wilbur Wright were his nephews!

These two men were expressing the point of view of their respective disciplines. Currently it would appear that science is leading this age-old two-pronged effort to influence (even manipulate) the general population. In practice these two disciplines are akin to Janus, the two-faced god—part and parcel of one and the same ideology, expressed from diametrically opposed viewpoints.

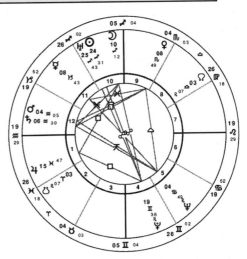

2. Distinctive astrological chart at the time of the flight of the Kitty Hawk—December 17 1903.   KEITH MAGNAY

Janus

From the Roman pantheon of gods.

Guardian of thresholds, then of gateways and ports. The month of January was named after this deity.

When the Romans incorporated the Greek pantheon of Gods into their own, there was no equivalent god, so the status of Janus was transferred to Saturn who became the god of boundaries and limitation.

In the translation, the idea of thresholds was somewhat lost.

Today, to call someone a Janus is to imply that they are a hypocrite.

From our standpoint of the late 1990s, it is easy to forget that the evolution of flight and its attendant militaristic potential has been breathtakingly fast. The development of flight from the Wright brothers' debut in 1903 through to the Apollo show of July 1969 took a mere sixty-six years. This rate of progress in itself is an astonishing achievement and one of which mankind can be proud. Although sadly, until now, much of the development in aeronautics and astronautics has been as a result of a *creative tension* stimulated by war. As we reach the end of the 20th Century, there are signs that the majority have at last attained the awareness that the way forward for us all is through the mature understanding that creation's processes respond better to constructive, interactive, creativity and co-operation, rather than aggressive competition. This principle also applies to the future of astronautics. We maintain that the advanced technology that will enable us to reach out and return from beyond our planet in safety is accessible only to a mature species, one that is in harmony with itself and its environment.

This situation then poses a problem for our planet's governments, the secret services, the military and the space agencies and they need to consider their response to the following:

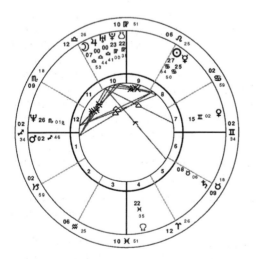

3. Astrological chart for late July 1969.   KEITH MAGNAY

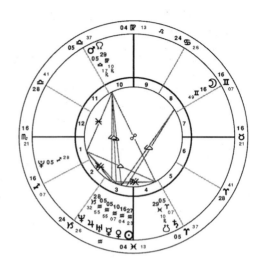

4. Astrological chart for February 16 1997.   KEITH MAGNAY

QUESTION: Are *you* mature enough to be able to invest in astronautical development for the sake of peaceful exploration of our surroundings, rather than the need to wage war on fellow citizens of this planet or elsewhere?

It is clear that the space agencies in particular need to find and use a more economical and humane method of propulsion in order to be able to proceed around and about with the minimum of cost, noise and pollution, without continuing to damage our planet through the continual extraction and burning of fossil fuels. And further, without endangering all forms of life and the physical environment both within our atmosphere and beyond, through the use of nuclear processes. Most particularly, we need a means of propulsion that will, due to its design, adequately protect a crew from the dangers of radiation and other harmful effects.

Keith Magnay is editor of the well-respected *Aviation Informatics* magazine, and is both an aviation and computer journalist with an special understanding of astrology. According to his studies and charts, there is an interesting parallel between the state of the solar system in December 1903 at the time of the first flight of the Kitty Hawk, July 1969, and the advent of an era in which an entirely new method of propulsion would be realised. He estimated that the shift towards this research would have its beginnings in February 1997.

Stephen Hawking has said that: "The eventual goal of science is to provide a single theory that describes the whole universe". This attitude of "we have the ability to deliver the one and final answer" prevails very much to this day, especially within the scientific community. He went on to say that only then "shall all—philosophers, scientists and just

still eludes the scientific community. While it may not be accepted thinking now, we consider that soon it will be acknowledged that all of creation: basic matter, living things, self aware beings—indeed, the entirety of the three-dimensional Universe—functions along one set of principles, namely patterns within patterns within patterns within patterns. In other words, we will eventually come to realise that *everything works in precisely the same way.*

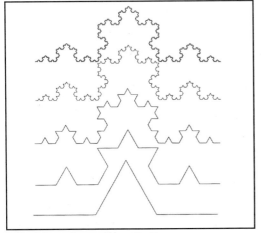

5. Fractals—patterns within patterns.

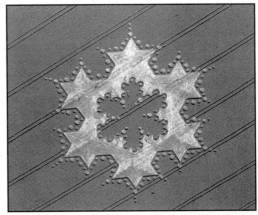

6. Six-sided fractal Crop Glyph activated at Alton Barnes, England, August 1997. (see also Appendix)   L PRINGLE

ordinary people—be able to take part in the discussion of the question of 'why it is that we and the Universe exist'". Further, if *that* question were answered, "it would be the ultimate triumph of human reason—for then we would know the mind of God".

Whatever our calling in life, we certainly do not need to be *dictated* to as to how, when or what to think by our scientists—who number relatively few and are by no means an elite team of super brains. This statement of Hawking's is an example of scientists behaving in exactly the same way as the organised religion they so outwardly despise. Science for the most part does not acknowledge a creator at all, preferring, as Hawking infers, to triumph over such a concept with human reason. Which reminds us of Scientology and takes us full circle back to the Stanford Research Institute and those pioneers of laser research and matters spatial, Ed Mitchell, Hal Puthoff and Co. It is hardly surprising that the *Theory of Everything*

Naked before creation

In an article on space science written in 1987 the authors made a promise to the future astronaut.[2] "The human crew of a spacecraft on a long mission will have protection as good as the Earth's atmosphere and magnetic field," they wrote. Bad luck on anyone on a short mission then, they had no option other than to play 'American Solar flare Roulette'. Perhaps these authors would like to explain *how* they think the lunar travellers of 1969/72 survived? For whoever they were, they certainly did *not* have that quality of protection.

- How *can* anyone venture beyond the Earth's protection and not be subject to the effects of radiation?
- How *can* we bring the accomplishment of long missions to distant planets into the present day and not consider it a far future project?

- How *can* we travel in harmony *with* our environment rather than pushing and shoving at it with the 'brute force and ignorance' of relatively primitive rockets?

Before we can even contemplate alternative forms of space travel one thing is quite clear. Whatever their past history of pulling the wool over our eyes, if NASA & Co. are serious about sending men and women on interplanetary explorations it is time to draw a line under past behaviour patterns and start over. Admitting that the agency's scientists and consultants do not know everything about the workings of the Universe in general and the manner of travelling through it in particular, might stick in their craw, but it is the way forward.

- If they continue to pretend that we can travel successfully beyond the Van Allen belts in the manner that they are currently adopting while secretly knowing that they do not have the answer;
- If the masters continue to pin their hopes on rocket fuels, ion drives or nuclear-powered craft to get them over long distances fast (and they hope safely);
- If they maintain the pretence that they have the answers to the Universe and everything:

Then they will be stuck in LEO forever whilst we, as a civilisation, will start to lose our societal courage.

As a civilisation we have begun our exploration of space, whether the stick-on-the-Earth's like it or not, for once the threshold has been crossed there is only one way to go—and that is forward. We are presently being held up by the very people who are so keen to get out there. Full of pride and misplaced 'right stuff', out of harmony with themselves and their solar system, they cannot bear to admit that they do not know how to do it! So we, the non-scientists, would like to help matters along by asking them to reconsider the fundamentals.

Unsurprisingly, the answer to the problem of travelling safely into deep space is under our very noses: we need to imitate the structural mechanics of the environment in which we are most protected—our spaceship Earth. We have already used the analogy of the womb for our situation on our home planet, and it is worth repeating here in this discussion of our future essential travel arrangements.

All living things on planet Earth are protected from solar and other forms of space radiation by the rotation and revolution of the planet spinning at the 'ideal' speed. For these motions generate the conditions which have resulted in the creation of our sophisticated, multi-layered atmosphere, together with the outer protective shield of the planet, the magnetosphere.

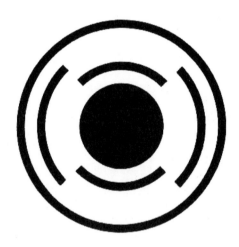

7. Representation of a Crop Glyph activated in Southern England, June 1990.

The expression "in a shirt sleeve environment" is a space agency favourite! Does it not make the dangerous business of space travel seem familiar, comfortable and relaxed?—rather like commuting to the office in ones car. However, if the amount of protection we have described is the minimum necessary for us to be able to live here on Earth in a "shirt-sleeve environment" then how can we expect to travel beyond the protection of our planetary 'womb' into deep space and still expect to live happily

---

Newtonian notes

Sir Isaac Newton calculated that the force exerted by the rotation of the Earth to throw us off into space was 1/3,600th of the force of gravity keeping us to the surface.

Newton also asked himself what would be the force that would drive the Moon to recede from its gravitational relationship with the Earth and this he found to be 1/4,000th of the force of gravity at the Earth's surface.

This value he decided was only approximate to the value of 1/3,600 that he had expected—having used 60 Earth radii 3,963 X 60 = 237,780 miles) as his basis of mean Earth/Moon distance.

Newton decided to leave that idea.

It is our contention that this result is not unrelated to the hyperD component of gravity, of which more later.

---

ever after? This is blindingly obvious: if we *could* live in space *without* this protection, then we would not require any such protection when living on our planet! Surely if we travel beyond the protective facilities of the planet, we must *emulate* the environment that we enjoy on our beloved home.

This point is born out, albeit unwittingly, by the ex-NASA astrophysicist Andre Bormanis, who has worked in the private sector as a consultant to *Star Trek*. Responsible for injecting scientific realism into the show, and researching a dramatic medical storyline, he once asked an associate how best to transfer a baby from the womb of one mother to another. He was told that the *entire* foetal complex must be moved (including the placenta). This is *exactly* the point that we are making. To remove ourselves from one planet to another we must take our entire environment with us and moreover maintain that environment during the voyage. We include here the 'nourishing placenta'. Unfortunately, those who are entrusted with the task and the problems of safe space travel apparently do not recognise this requirement. Nor do they seem to be fully aware of the exact composition of our 'nourishing placenta'.

Planet Earth is special in so many ways and most of us probably do not fully appreciate this wonderful blue-green planet for which we are all responsible. Our thinking is that it really is *totally* different from virtually *all* the other planets in this galaxy. It seems that many planets do not have the same natural rotational speed as Earth. And it is *certainly* a fact that no other planet in this solar system has a retrograde precessional period of 25,920 years. Our planet revolves around the Sun, rotating as it

goes. It is this spin that makes everything work. However, before we deal with what we call the three Rs—rotation, revolution and retrograde precession, we need to consider gravity—**BIG G**.

Gravity, Macavity, gravity

Before we discuss the dynamics of simulating the way in which our planet generates gravity—for possible application in our future travel in space—we should look at the propulsion system that drives our planet.

Some scientists are proposing that anti-gravity systems might be the most appropriate form of propulsion for future space travel. However, the attempt to create anti-*matter* has so far proved both expensive and ephemeral, as has been demonstrated at CERN, Geneva.

The way forward, in our view, is much simpler, more an exercise in harmonics, frequency

387

8. CERN super proton particle accelerator ring, Geneva.   CERN

plicity's sake we describe the amount of gravity acting upon us here on Earth as '1G'. When an astronaut is launched skyward, the speed of the rocket progressively increases—and so does the amount of pressure or G-force on the astronaut and the vehicle.

Every action of course has an *equal* and *opposite* reaction.

So to climb into a rocket and then accelerate *fast* enough to generate enough force to lift the rocket off the ground and then escape the Earth's gravitational pull creates a lot of Gs, which have the effect of flattening the human body against the nearest available surface (usually the astronaut's couch) thereby severely stressing the entire bio-organism.

Arthur C Clarke wishes that there was a term, other than 'Gs', for this effect of 'artificial' weight engendered by such acceleration. Although 'Js' (for strawberry jam) springs to mind, we will not need to worry about Gs when we adopt Spinning Disk technology, because such a method of travel will eliminate that effect.

We have all become used to astronauts talking about zero G for weightlessness when travelling in orbit around the Earth. Technically this term is a misnomer and the more recent term of microgravity has also been adopted by astronautics as being far more accurate.

and balance—emulating the natural physics of the Universe. We could call such a system *pro-gravity*. A gravity *generation* method. The concept requires, we maintain, the voluntary participation of focused consciousness which leads to a different way of thinking and therefore acting. It leads us to the technology of the Spinning Disk and the practical realisation of quantum theory.

Despite Sir Isaac Newton's best efforts, even today, we have minimal understanding of how gravity actually works. It is the most important 'stuff' in the Universe—for example it is gravity that holds us to the planet's surface. Yet we know relatively little about it.

We measure gravity in reference to the Earth as 1. Scientists have calculated the gravity of all the other planets in our solar system *relative* to this evaluation — which is fair enough, as Earth is the only place we really know. For sim-

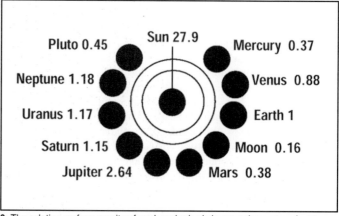

9. The relative surface gravity of each major body in our solar system (not to scale) from a Crop Glyph activated in Southern England in 1990.

The Moon's gravity is ⅙th of the Earth's and this is the reason why everything weighs less on the lunar surface. To get an idea of that—a jump of 1 foot/30 cms into the air on Earth, would become a jump of around six feet on the Moon (and three feet on Mars—which has a gravity ⅓rd of Earth's). Interestingly, *none* of the Apollo 'astro-nasts' attained anything approaching a six foot leap—even when attempting such feats specially for the camera!

Now why would that be, do you think! (10). The lunar gravitational pull is so mild compared with that of Earth that it was apparently 'difficult' for the astronauts to tell exactly where the vertical was. Also, in order to counter the weight of the PLSS, the astronauts were obliged to lean forward at an angle that—on Earth—would have resulted in their "falling flat on their faces". But there are no photographs or recorded TV incidents that show any astronauts adopting such an ungainly angle. In the recorded TV coverage everybody moves around with ease—despite those 'heavy' back packs and suits which are supposed to be so pressurised that their stiffness should have made movement extremely difficult.[1]

LEO & GEO

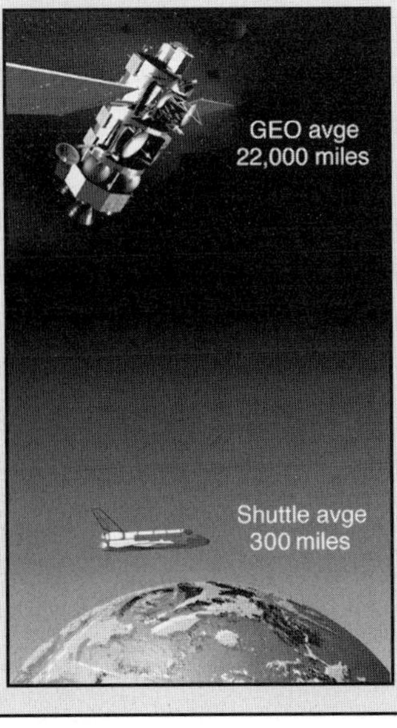

GEO avge
22,000 miles

Shuttle avge
300 miles

GEO

The 'Clarke orbit ring' or the geostationary ring as it is also called, is 22,300 miles up and that is where most of our satellites orbit.

LEO or low Earth orbit, is where the Shuttle and the space stations operate and these orbits are generally around 250-350 miles up.

389

10. The 'Apollo 16' 'jump salute'. Astro-not even able to jump one-third his own height! NASA

- The point between two planetary bodies where the gravitational 'pulls' between the two bodies *cancel each other out.*
- Once this point in space is passed, a craft is no longer affected by the gravity of the planetary body which it leaving but is now progressively under the influence of the planetary body towards which it moving.
- In this book we will be concerned with the Earth/Moon trajectory so this means that on leaving the pull of Earth's gravity—for a *fraction of time a craft reaching this equigravisphere or neutral point, is no longer affected by either Earth's gravity or the Moon's gravity*—before it falls under the influence of the Moon.

From now on, we are going to use the term neutral point. It is easier on the reader's eye and more descriptive of the effect this area of space has on travelling spacecraft. Please note that although here we are discussing flights of craft going to the Moon, under the designation, 'Apollo 8' or '11' etc., we have not recanted on the past nine chapters! It does *not* mean that the named Apollo astronauts were necessarily sitting inside these craft or indeed that these specific named craft were those that went to the

Neutral Point neurosis

There is a significant phenomenon concerning the alleged outward journey to the Moon during 'Apollo 11' which has to our knowledge never been elaborated upon, explained, or indeed mentioned in relation to any of the subsequent Apollo 'trips'—a phenomenon which may have assumed gigantic proportions for NASA and the space scientific community. So much so that (as far as we can tell) it has been 'locked down' in an attempt to sweep any discussion or knowledge of it under the carpet.

To what are we referring?

It is the neutral point, which is also called the equigravisphere. This location is just what it says it is:

Apollo flights			
Mission Number	Arrival date	Distance Earth/Moon	
		Miles	Kilometres
'Apollo 08'	24 12 1968	234,611	377,796
'Apollo 10'	22 05 1969	251,416	404,857
'Apollo 11'	20 07 1969	246,322	396,654
'Apollo 12'	18 11 1969	235,162	378,683
'Apollo 14'	04 02 1971	237,389	382,269
'Apollo 15'	30 07 1971	253,015	407,431
'Apollo 16'	20 04 1972	238,235	383,632
'Apollo 17'	11 12 1972	247,083	397,880

Crop Glyph representing Earth/Moon activated in Wiltshire, England in 1991.

Moon. We are using these 'accounts' in order to discuss this very specific problem of the neutral point.

Whip out those rulers again!

The Moon's orbital distance from Earth, according to our 20th Century experts, now varies from a minimum of 221,086 miles to a maximum of 251,140 miles. (Or to a maximum of 252,700 miles, Chaikin; or 253,000 miles, Smithsonian Institute; or 253,475 miles, NASA.) Is it not interesting that no sources agree on the exact distance of the Moon's orbital path?

Speaking of the elementary Earth/Moon distance centre-to-centre at the time of each Apollo mission, we have found no mention of this in any published accounts of these exploits. Nor is it easy to ascertain accurate Earth/Moon trajectories of each spacecraft. We asked Dr. Percy Seymour for precise Earth/Moon distances at the time of each alleged trip.[3]

QUESTION: Why is it difficult for NASA to confirm an accurate distance for these mission trajectories, which must have been known to the last inch?

QUESTION: When these figures exist they vary according to the source. Why? For example, two different sources cite the trajectory of 'Apollo 11' with a difference of nearly 4,000 miles.

QUESTION: Why is the Earth/Moon centre-to-centre distance missing from the published Apollo information? Where one can find the craft's trajectory, the Earth/Moon distance is often missing or vague. Where one can locate the Earth/Moon distance, the craft's trajectory is often missing or vague.

QUESTION: Could it be that the inconsistencies in the published data were intentional and designed to inhibit investigation?

QUESTION: Is there a good reason why this information is so difficult to obtain?

Yes, it would appear there is!

Space experts at NASA or elsewhere, do not state whether they are using planetary surface-to-surface or centre-to-centre measurements. Nor do they always state whether they are using nautical miles or statute miles. Nor do they stick to any one system, in fact they sometimes use miles (unspecified) and sometimes use kilometres. The only consistency in the Earth/Moon measurement scenario is the inconsistency of the data emanating from official sources.

Whatever measuring system is being used, differences of between 1,560 to 1,860 miles (unspecified) for the Earth/Moon maximum orbital distance *on a specified date* are very significant discrepancies.

Given that NASA maintains that by the time of 'Apollo 11' in July 1969 it was possible to

---

Earth

Using the 360° system to establish a grid for navigation north and south of the equator brought about the designation of *Latitude*.

Using the prime meridian at Greenwich as a starting point, these same degrees, minutes and seconds were then measured out as *Longitude*.

180° east or west of the prime meridian became the 'International Date Line'.

Time

The *Nautical mileage system* is a combination of time with planetary measurement. There are 360° around any planetary sphere and 60 minutes in each degree. Multiplying degrees and minutes together: 360° x 60 = 21,600.

This is the total number of nautical miles around the equator of *any given planet*.

The nautical mile is ⅚ths of the Earth's retrograde precessional period.

Life

⅚ths is also a metaphor for the balanced relationship between non living (six sided) and living things (five sided—living things which, over time, on Earth have evolved into self-aware beings, thanks to the Moon generating off-centre rotation and the retrograde precession of 25,920 years.

The significance of miles

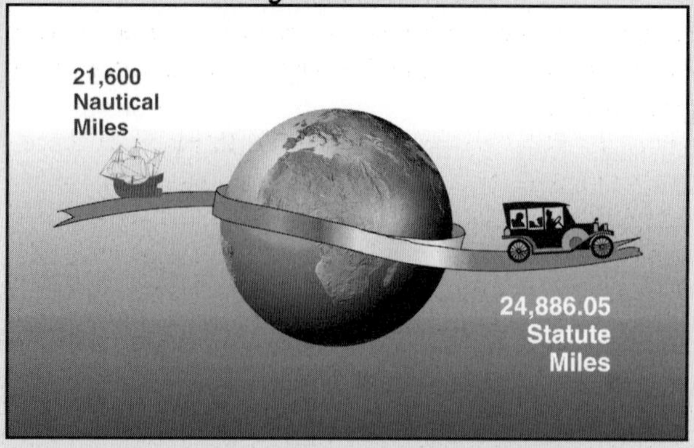

21,600
Nautical
Miles

24,886.05
Statute
Miles

The word *mile* is ancient. In Old English it was mil.

Miles interrelate with our 24 hour clock and 360° measurement system. The kilometre does not relate to time at all.

69.13 X 360° = 24,886 statute miles at the equator (7,921.476 miles diameter).

69.13 Statute miles = 1 equatorial degree lat/long.

60 Nautical miles = 1 equatorial degree lat/long.

60 : 69.13 = square root 2 divided by 3, or as a metaphor, ⅔rds.

60 x 360° = circumference of a planet at its equator in nautical miles =

21,600, *no matter what* the physical size of the planet.

21,600 : 5 x 6 = 25,920 in years, this is the length of the precession of a planet like Earth.

As a ratio 5:6, or as a metaphor, ⅚ths

measure the Earth/Moon distance to an accuracy of *within six inches* through the use of lasers, these discrepancies are inexcusable.

The great mystery of NASA and the Neutral Point

Before mankind ever dreamt of sending probes to the Moon, Sir Isaac Newton had calculated the mean distance of 238,900 miles to the Moon with great accuracy and his evaluations concerning the equigravisphere between the Earth and the Moon were part of his Law of Universal Gravitation. This neutral point was considered to be at an *average distance* of 215,000 miles from the Earth and 23,900 miles from the Moon.

Without Newton's preparatory work, NASA's scientists would not have been able to make the necessary calculations to get to the Moon and back with their probes. During the 1960s, according to the majority of references (which were still using Newton's mean Earth/Moon

distance of 238,900 miles) the neutral point occurred:

- At a *mean* distance of 215,000 miles from the Earth and 23,900 miles from the Moon.[4]
- This calculates to a lunar gravity of 0.167 or ⅙th of the Earth.
- We repeat—the neutral point is the location where the attraction exerted by the Earth is equal to that exerted by the Moon.

We underline once again that these earlier calculations were not just theoretical figures—the Moon's gravity is indeed ⅙th of the Earth's. Otherwise none of the space agencies' slingshot trajectories would have been accurate and the return of the Soviet probe containing samples of the regolith would not have taken place. Additionally, we have it first hand from a space rocket scientist that the gravity on the Moon is indeed 0.167 of the Earth.[5]

- In the late 90s, the precise figures for the *mean* Earth/Moon neutral point are consid-

Not as the crow flies

- In 1969, at the time of the 'Apollo 11' mission, *Time* magazine reported that: "**43,495 miles from the Moon** lunar gravity exerted a force equal to the gravity of the Earth, then some 200,000 miles distant". Which gave a total distance to the Moon of some 243,495 miles.
- The 1981 edition of Baker's *Space Technology* gives the 'Apollo 11' distance to the Moon as 253,475 miles.
- In 1989, *Apollo 11 Moon Landing* cites a total distance of just *under* 250,400 miles.
- Then in 1996 Baker's *Spaceflight & Rocketry: A Chronology* provides different neutral point figures and Earth/Moon distance to that of *Time* magazine in 1969. Baker states that 'Apollo 11' reached the neutral point 38,925 miles from the Moon, and 214,550 miles from Earth, thereby giving the Moon an orbital distance from Earth of 253,475 miles! This distance is at least consistent with his previous 1981 publication, but then that book did not give any neutral point data at all!
- Additionally, a highly-qualified rocket scientist assures us that the neutral point for 'Apollo 11' *is correct at 43,495 miles* from the Moon.[5] So we have from this data alone, two identical distances yet two *divergent* neutral points!
- Simply put, there *cannot be more* than one distance between the Earth and Moon on the same date and time; and there should only be *one* figure for the distance from a given planetary body at which the calculated neutral point (CNP) occurs.

ered to be 214,895 miles from Earth and 23,959.5 miles from the Moon respectively.

The bottom line regarding these neutral point discrepancies (as in the box above) is this:

The calculation using the Universal Newtonian Gravitational Constant (UNGC) for the neutral point (CNP) is different by a factor of tens of thousands of miles compared to the experienced neutral point (ENP) when a craft actually went to the Moon. It was not expected that the *theoretical* as opposed to the *experi-* enced neutral point between Earth and the Moon would vary to any significant degree, if at all. Actually, the variation was so unexpected to our knowledge, that the anomalies inherent in the 'Apollo 11' data have not been generally discussed since July 1969!

The correct centre-to-centre distance for the Earth/Moon at the time of 'Apollo 11's arrival was 246,322 miles. This figure corresponds closest with the information from *Time* magazine of 1969 (see box above) but there is a discrepancy of 7,153 miles with the 1996 figure from David Baker, who is seemingly attempting to fit the standard UNGC calculation to this trajectory. The lunar orbital distance of some 253,475 miles did not appear in the Apollo mission data—until 'Apollo 15'!

Question time

All the figures quoted appear in publications that have received input from NASA scientists, historians or advisors.

- So why did NASA permit these figures to be published whilst failing to explain or

11. NASA craft leaving the Earth's gravitational field.

comment on the enormous discrepancies?

- Is there some factor (or factors) affecting the measurement and calculations that are being ignored or swept under the carpet?
- Was NASA allowing disparate figures to be published in order to drown the very real discrepancy of the 'Apollo 11 neutral point'?
- Did the agency hope that researchers would give up asking questions about this conundrum and eventually go away?
- Did the NASA & Co. think that by 1996 (Baker data) sufficient time would have elapsed that new distances for 'Apollo 11' could be published?
- Did the article in *Time* on July 15 1969 accidentally blow the whistle on this discrepancy between the CNP (at the time of 'Apollo 11' (24,736 miles from the Moon) and the ENP (43,495 miles from the Moon)?

An unaccounted-for difference of nearly 19,000 miles!

Or was this ENP of 43,495 miles deliberately supplied to *Time* magazine? Their article appeared in print only the day after the return to Earth of 'Apollo 11', so this data must have emanated from NASA but from whom in that organisation? The only other mention of this 43,495 mile figure (pertinent to the *Time* article date) occurs in the 1969 reprint of *History of Rocketry & Space Travel,* originally published in 1966. Would the authors of this book have been in a position to reveal this new information? By 1969 only one of them was still working at NASA—a exceedingly accomplished spokesman and publicist for the space program, dubbed the Crusader by his friends, his name was Wernher von Braun.
(see also Appendix)

Private eyes . . .

Could that *Time* magazine article in which the specific question of the 'Apollo 11' experienced neutral point was mentioned, have anything to do with Wernher von Braun's somewhat hasty departure for pastures new? The indications are that the data and information in that article was of such significance that it would eventually have an adverse effect on

NASA. And it might well have contributed to the distancing of WvB at least from the *visible* portion of the NASA iceberg that emerged from the sea of space politics.

Six months before the end of the manned lunar program on May 26 1972, Wernher von Braun resigned completely from NASA and became Vice President of Engineering and Development at the makers of the Intelsats used during the Apollo missions: Fairchild Industries, Germantown, Maryland. Two months later, on August 29, his friend Ed Mitchell brought Uri Geller to meet him. WvB was most impressed by Geller's talents and considered that any fakery in his case was impossible.

Two years later in 1974, WvB was influential in getting a satellite dish delivered to his good friend Arthur C Clarke so that he could link into the Fairchild ATS 6 satellite. Von Braun suggested to Arthur C Clarke that of the several thousand satellite installations being installed in Indian villages, one be 'siphoned off' to ACC. (Bad luck on the Indian village which would have to go without!) WvB pulled the correct strings and on the August 12 1976 the *Ceylon Daily News* announced that the planet's only privately owned satellite station had been installed on the island. But that Indian village did not have to miss out on education and information after all—because Sri Lanka was not on the beam centre. It had not been possible to 'siphon off' this equipment from the production line. In fact a 50% larger dish and a special low noise converter had to be tailor-made for Clarke. After it had been kindly installed by six engineers from the Indian Government, Clarke subsequently found it a rather expensive present as he was expected to provide liquid hospitality to the many visitors who wished to inspect the installation.

. . . and knowing looks

Following his departure from NASA WvB had become President of the National Space Institute and whenever he was asked for a souvenir photograph it was sent under the aegis of this society. As it happened there was something not quite historically correct about this particular photograph (12) and close up (13). We do

12. WvB in his souvenir 1975 photograph of the Saturn V.   NATIONAL SPACE INSTITUTE

13. Cut-away revealing the Lunar Excursion Module.

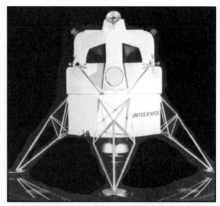

14. The *1963* Lunar Excursion Module.

not know why NASA failed to notice it, but then again it is an infinitely small detail, and we wonder if you would have spotted it?[6]

Objections

From the disparate published data there are indications that the *experienced* neutral point might be at odds with the calculation according to the UNGC. At the relatively primitive stage that we are at in our space exploration, surely it is necessary to ascertain what is causing this discrepancy?—certainly not to ignore the problem and/or attempt to confuse the issue by permitting diverse figures to be published. Though it must be said that perhaps NASA is aware of what is causing this difference and wishes not to announce the fact.

It has been postulated by at least one researcher that the gravity on the Moon may not be the UNGC calculation of ⅙th, and that the cited neutral point variations are indications that the gravity is perhaps different.[7]

Taking the *experienced* (and in that sense confirmed) neutral point of 43,495 miles, the Moon's gravity *ought* to be 0.666412 of Earth —which is almost *four times* that of the actual value of 0.167, (or ⅙th of Earth).

That value for the gravity for the Moon cannot be right—(or can it be right for another reason?—see calculations in the Appendix.)

Well, we say it cannot be right because, as we have already pointed out, NASA and the Soviets used the Moon's ⅙G as part of the calculations for their successful slingshot manoeuvres around the Moon and also for the calculations relating to energy requirements for their crash lander and soft lander probes, including those that actually returned samples to the then Soviet Union. If the evaluation of the lunar gravity had been incorrect, then surely none of these manoeuvres would have been successful? We can also see (from the 1996 information provided by Baker concerning the 'readjusted' neutral point for 'Apollo 11') that NASA (and its colleagues in the military) are continuing to use this UNGC calculation for its post-Apollo lunar probe trajectories such as Clementine.

Lemmings

The escape velocity required to leave a gravity four times greater than that expected would be correspondingly increased, and consequently the fuel requirements for the LM would also increase.

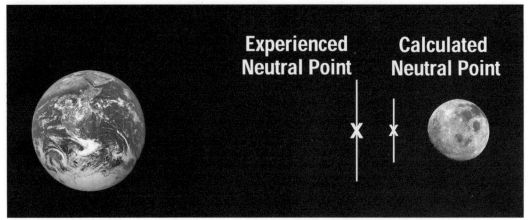

15. Representation of the experienced vs. the calculated Earth/Moon neutral point.

There is little advantage to be had in concealing the discovery of a different gravity for a planet one is visiting for the first time. By its very nature, exploration *is* a voyage of discovery. And to announce such a major finding would have given NASA bonus points rather than anything else. It would have been the perfect dramatic news headline:

NASA's New Moon—Newton's Downfall

The very fact that *nothing* was and publicly announced is significant. On the principle that UNGC calculation is correct at the time of the 'Apollo 11' mission, the place at which the neutral point between Earth and the Moon occurred was found to be around 19,000 miles *nearer* to Earth than expected. If the gravity of the Moon is a constant at ⅛th, (which we have established) and the value of Earth's gravity is 1 (which we know it to be) then *something else* is altering the distance at which the neutral point is experienced *and* we need to establish what this 'something else' might be.

WE MAINTAIN IT IS THE UNDERSTANDING OF THIS FUNDAMENTAL PROBLEM OF THE *EXPERIENCED* NEUTRAL POINT THAT HOLDS THE KEY TO OUR SUCCESSFUL NEGOTIATION OF DEEP SPACE IN THE FUTURE.

Considerations

It appears to us that we have just about got to the end of the usefulness of Einsteinian physics. And even with the limited amount of knowledge that has been gleaned from our space exploration, we suggest that NASA and Co. must by now be aware that some of Einstein's principals *ARE NOT WORKING OUT.* If things do not work in practice, we need to go back to the drawing board and start again from the point where they started going wrong.

We present the following hypotheses, as we believe they offer solutions to the problems now being encountered by our quantum physicists, astronomers and cosmologists. We hope that the upholders of these disciplines will have the grace to consider, improve upon, or at least debate our suggestions, however unorthodox they might seem. It is our understanding that as a result of our accumulated knowledge of physics gleaned from Newton to Quantum via Einstein, we are now capable of learning and applying another branch of physics. Given that this branch of physics deals with differing dimensions we have adopted the term transdimensional (or transD) physics.

The charge of the light brigade

We find that we cannot discuss the implications of gravity without involving light, or the electro-magnetic force as it is conventionally called. Nor can we discuss these two forces

---

TransD—the way to be!

Firstly, we need some definitions.

Dimension: of or pertaining to measure.

Hyper: beyond.

Trans: across.

Three-dimensional: 3D our experienced, measurable physical Universe.

Hyper-dimensional: hyperD (also referred to as 4D) is that which is outside our experienced three dimensions; but has an *effect* on our 3D Universe.

Trans-dimensional physics: The combination of hyperD (4D) and 3D working in harmony— both together and with their environment.

Putting this another way,

TransD physics is also the combination of consciousness and technology working together in order to achieve the required result without damage to the environment, whether that be physical, mental or spiritual. This branch of physics is fun and all of us can 'get it' because it involves the way that everything works. We need transD physics for space travel—for without it we shall not go any further than the patio of our planet and the rest of the garden lies within and beyond the radiation belts.

---

without incorporating consciousness and so we are back to the metaphysical aspects of quantum mechanics. Wigner (1905-1995) suggested that the *consciousness of the observer* made a difference to the experiment being undertaken—not liking the implications of such a statement, science took agin it! Indeed, one might deduce that Einstein's theory of relativity was formulated in response to this problem and succeeded for a while in holding off the quantum theorists.[8]

16. Albert Einstein.   PHOTOPIA

Much later, CERN scientist John Bell challenged Einstein's PER paradox experiment and his tests were in turn challenged by the American Clauser in 1978 and Aspect in France in 1982. All these tests correlated with each other and from which it was concluded that:[9]

- In spite of the local appearances of phenomena, our world is supported by an invisible reality which allows communication faster than light—even instantaneous communication.

During these tests they established that the interactions observed did have three particular properties:

1) They were constant in that they did not become weaker over distance.

2) They could—and did—travel faster than the speed of light.

3) These interactions occurred without travelling through space—at all.

When something is inherently 'right' after it has been expressed it will not go away, and will eventually become common knowledge. While agreeing with points one and two we understand point three to mean that these interactions trans-dimension out of three dimensions via the fourth dimension and back again into three dimensions. In this way the interactions can virtually instantaneously affect the particle (or 'other location') within 3D space.

Given the ramifications of this theory, mainstream science quickly produced enough statistical analyses to swing the balance of scientific opinion away from Bell Clauser and Aspect—even though a few scientists cautiously conceded that Extra Sensory Perception (ESP) *might* be a manifestation of this 'invisible reality' at work. While not quite closing the door on them, science has kept the door marked PER paradox wide open. And it is the authors' opinion that the statistical research currently underway is being sustained by those who have a vested interest in maintaining Einstein's special theory of relativity.

By denying the implications of Bell, Clauser and Aspect's work, mainstream scientists may be keeping us prisoners on our planet, prisoners within our solar system and consequently prisoners in a limited understanding of ourselves and our place in the Universe. John Wheeler, Emeritus professor of Physics at Princeton University, has said: "We have no right to ask what the photons are doing during their travel". Yet he also upholds the Anthropic Principle whereby: "Observers are necessary to bring the Universe into being".[10] With all due respect to John Wheeler, we have *every* right to be curious about all aspects of creation and our role within it. Surely, to be ordered otherwise is yet another example of scientific arrogance? Wheeler's statement attempts to keep us in our place, but neatly avoids the issue of non-local effects. As a result of the developments within quantum physics, it is now necessary that we re-examine the validity of orthodox science's strict adhesion to the basic insistence that nothing can travel faster than the speed of light. Until we remove Einstein from the pedestal to which he is so firmly glued (saying of course

"thank you" for what he has done for our progress as we do so) then we shall stagnate and only create for ourselves the *illusion* of progress via sterile discussions on the Internet.

Let the floodgates be opened

Researchers have been exploring the idea of working with theoretical higher-dimensions, making geometrical 'higher' dimensional models of three-dimensional geometric shapes, postulating that a higher-dimensional Universe might be more complex than the physical Universe and therefore contain more energy. We would respectfully suggest that the complexity of such a Universe is identical to that of the third dimension. It is only human beings themselves who complicate matters. In fact, the basic principles of the Universe (which consists of both three dimensions and four dimensions) are probably similar throughout.

We maintain that everything in the physical Universe is based on *spin*.

It is the mechanics affecting the rate of spin which dictates to what extent a celestial sphere can rotate at the *right* speed, and in so doing, open a 'gate' through which the 4D energy can spill down into 3D—in much the same way that water from a dam is released.

Until the beginning of space exploration we had only one place, planet Earth, from which to evaluate our surroundings. When the *unmanned* probes went to explore space during the late 1950s and early '60s, no evidence emerged—in the public domain—to suggest that any data provided by these probes altered our understanding of this fundamental Einsteinian principal. However, in our view Einstein calculated incorrectly that the speed of light is a *constant* and that gravity *bends* light.

Two-Thirds

It also has been established that all stars generate energy by means of nuclear fusion—a process which emits radiation and particles. Among these particles is a zero rest mass particle called a neutrino. Nuclear fusion produces a set number of neutrinos. However, during evaluation of the quantity of neutrinos streaming from the Sun of our solar system only one-third the expected amount of neutrinos was found to be present.

Thus it should be concluded that ⅔rds were either retained by the Sun or are 'missing'.

Where are they?

Does this situation not infer that nuclear fusion is only responsible for *a part* of the Sun's energy generation process?

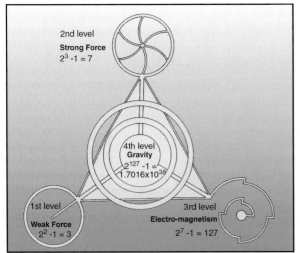

2nd level
Strong Force
$2^3 - 1 = 7$

4th level
Gravity
$2^{127} - 1 = 1.7016 \times 10^{38}$

1st level
Weak Force
$2^2 - 1 = 3$

3rd level
Electro-magnetism
$2^7 - 1 = 127$

17. Representation of the tetrahedral Crop Glyph (depicting the four forces in a combinatorial hierarchy) activated at Barbury Castle, Southern England, July 1991.

The problem was, of course, that he made his calculations and measurements were taken here *ON EARTH*—and it was *assumed* (mistakenly in our view) that the speed of light is the same everywhere throughout the Universe.

Another measurement made from here on Earth, the November 24 1997 laser ranging experiment (mentioned in "Servants of Circumstance") was carried out "by scientists [some connected to NASA] with an interest in Einstein's theory of relativity and what it has to tell *about gravity*". Their conclusion? All is well. "Relativity's predictions *seem* to be correct" said Richard Teske, Professor Emeritus of Astronomy at the University of Michigan, USA. Thereby *"reinforcing beliefs* that his [Einstein's] theory is the best description we have for how nature operates". (emphasis added) Well! That's all right then, if they don't measure the Earth/Moon distance too often, they will sleep more easily at night.

When analysed it turns out that the good Professor is speaking in a rather unscientific manner: "seeming to be correct" is not necessarily "actually being correct" and a "belief" is not necessarily a scientifically proved fact. Indeed the scientific community are fond of asking those who profess to a *belief* in God to *prove* His existence! We shall be interested in their comments, if any, on our hypothesis, for that statement is rather more an announcement that nothing has changed publicly as far as Einsteinian physics is concerned—and specifically in regard to the findings relating to the equigravisphere and the speed of light.

They are both right and wrong at the same time, as we shall see.

Gravity and light—our hypothesis

- The speed of light is complementary to the prevailing force of gravity.
  Simply expressed — little gravity equals a higher light speed; more gravity equals a slower speed.
- There is a resulting hyperD component (4D) which can be discerned.
- The prevailing force of gravity has a hyperD component, three-quarters of that 3D component affects not only the speed but also the *characteristic* of light.
- Three-quarters of gravity has a 4D component.
- It is this 4D component of gravity that stops light from travelling at an infinite speed.
- If it were not for this 4D component of gravity, light would be drastically bent due to refraction. Instead, the 4D component of gravity (acting strongly from within a solar system) counteracts almost all such refraction.
- 4D gravity—together with three of its four manifestations in 3D: the weak force, the strong force and the 3D component of gravity—holds the physical 3D Universe together.
- Working together, 3D and 4D gravity are sometimes strong enough to even *stop light* due to the coalescing of an enormous amount of extremely dense matter—as in the collapse of certain types of stars found in the centres of galaxies ('black holes'). These celestial bodies are of such extreme density that their gravity traps and draws in *all matter* that comes near them so that nothing, *not even light* can escape. (Both visible and non-visible light together with the energy emitted by the matter drawn towards these 'black holes' have been detected.)

399

- Despite the hints inherent in the fact that it is *gravity* that is preventing the light from escaping—literally *stopping it in its tracks*—the academe of science is slow to recognise or admit *the converse*, that light might possibly *speed up* when beyond the gravitational effects of our, or indeed any, solar system.
- As the distance between matter increases the strength of both 3D and 4D gravity decreases at the same rate.
However,
- The initial strength of 3D gravity is weaker than that of 4D gravity.
- The ability of 3D gravity to govern the speed of light decreases before that of 4D gravity. Simply put, if you were leaving a planet, 3D gravity would release its hold over a craft and its occupants before the hyperD component of gravity released its hold.
- Due to the fact that galaxies are actually close enough together throughout the physical Universe, 4D gravity never entirely loses its ability to govern the speed of light.
- The invisible 'bits' of gravity are called gravitons or preferably should be called *gravitrons.*
- In 4D, *gravitrons* are 'something' but in 3D they seem to be 'nothing' but we nevertheless benefit from their effect in our 3D, physical existence. (Postulations concerning the properties of anti-matter, anti-gravity and the expectations of magnetic-related propulsion systems are simply demonstrations of a lack of knowledge with regard to the potential harnessing of *gravity*. In our opinion, the existence of the detected unexplained 'dark matter' in deep space is a demonstration of the 4D component of gravity.)
- The physical 3D Universe is held together by 4D gravity along with the weak force, the strong force and the 3D component of gravity. (Three out of the four manifestations of hyperD in the 3D Universe.)
- The fourth manifestation of hyperD in the physical 3D universe—is light.

Bill Odun

In order to gain a better grasp of how gravitrons actually work, here is a story from the book *Two-Thirds,* which encompasses the principle of gravitron-driven craft.[11] The narrator is a talking to an indigenous being of a planet, in a galaxy far, far away . . .

"We are not from this planet, but we are prisoners here now because we have been robbed of our flying craft.

"We come here not by magical means, but by flying craft from beyond the confines of your knowledge. Nevertheless, you will be able to understand," she began to explain.

"Instead of using wind to fill our sails—as you do to propel your ship across your seas—we use the gravity that holds you to your planet to propel our craft across the great 'seas' [space] you can see from your ship at night. It is really very simple how we use this force of gravity but you must first think of gravity as bits of stuff, just as you know a beach is made up of bits of sand.

"We have figured out how to make gravity work for us. Think of it this way, Bill Odun. You know that your ship goes forward through the water because the wind is filling its sails. In our flying craft we make bits of gravity into a stream, and we thrust those bits of gravity out of holes in the sides of our flying craft.

"Can you picture that, Bill Odun?"

"Yes, I think so," I replied, though I could not.

"Good," she continued. "Then now think of what happens to the wind itself when it fills those sails."

"Well, it fills the sails," I suggested, repeating her words.

"I have put it badly," she responded with an enchanting little pout that turned into a smile as she suddenly thought of a new way of trying to explain something which was obviously very simple to her, but which was very difficult for me to understand.

"What would happen," she asked, "if your ship was stoutly moored to a pier, all sails set and a hurricane began to blow?"

"The sails would be torn to shreds!" I replied proudly, finally realising I was getting somewhere.

"That is correct," she answered. "What would happen though if those sails were so strong they would not tear, and the masts so stout they would not break? What would the wind do then?"

I thought for a moment, befuddled. I had never thought this process through so completely. "The wind would have to bounce back on itself, I think," I finally ventured.

"Exactly!" she shouted with glee. She walked over, gave me a hug as I sat in the chair and kissed me on the lips.

"Now we are making real progress, Bill Odun," she added. "This is difficult, but you are doing fabulously. It took us billions of years to figure just this much out, but you have done it in less than an hour. I know this is tiring, but we must finish it quickly, so I will carry on.

"There is a principle of physics which we know as the following: for every action, there is an equal and opposite reaction. When the wind fills your sails, they billow out and push the ship forward. Action: wind pushing on the sails. Reaction: ship being pushed through the sea..."

"But," I interrupted boldly, "those actions and reactions are in the same direction."

"Very good, Bill Odun," she replied, quite excited by my insight. "It would seem thus, but let me go on and you will see why they are really opposite.

"If the ship is stoutly moored to the pier the wind would bounce back—as you yourself said—if the sails did not shred, and the masts did not fall. The reason the wind has to bounce back is because the ship can't move forward as it wants to.

"The bounce back is the reaction. The reaction when you are under way at sea is not 'necessary' because the forward movement of the ship alleviates the requirement for the specific reaction. However, your ship is actually reacting to the original action of the wind filling the sails.

Do you understand, Bill Odun?"

"Yes," I replied honestly.

It really was beginning to make sense now. I clearly understood that if the ship did not move forward due to the wind pushing on the sails, something else had to give, and that was the wind—if the sails and masts were strong enough; otherwise it would be the sails and masts that had to give way.

"The situation with our flying craft is very similar," she went on. "Except we create the 'wind' *within* those flying craft. The 'wind' is the streams of bits of gravity, and we thrust those streams very rapidly out of the holes of the flying craft.

"The equal and opposite reaction is..."

I could not help but finish her sentence, so I interrupted her again, "the craft going forward...very rapidly..."

She was delighted and I got another kiss, but there was more to learn.

She went on to tell me how the craft worked, and it was merely a process of thrusting the bits of gravity. There are nine different thrusters used in various combinations to make the craft go rapidly in different directions. The thrusters swivel so they can be pointed up and down, so the craft can go up and down as well.

I have seen birds fly, but I had never expected to do so myself. I never did—but later I saw her fly away and . . . leave.

The process of creating these little bits of gravity was really quite simple but also complex, she explained. They simply flew off a rapidly spinning disk.

I knew about spinning disks. We threw disks for sport, and they became spinning disks as we threw them.

But, she explained, her spinning disks spin much more rapidly than our spinning disks.

When she had finished her explanation, I thought it all through and offered my own summary of what she had told me.

"You have now told me that you have a rapidly spinning disk in your craft," I said, "from which bits of gravity come flying off and that you then vent these bits of gravity very rapidly through thrusters in order to make your craft fly very rapidly."

She smiled her beautiful smile, and I got another kiss.

Then she added: "There is something else I need to tell you. The bits of gravity are only somewhat like the grains of sand on the beach, the grains of sand are made up of something. The bits of gravity are made up of nothing, but they still cause an equal and opposite reaction when they are vented through the thrusters, because they *act* as if they are made of something. We don't know exactly why, but it has to do with the interaction between the different densities of the Universe.

"You know about three of these densities because you have length, width and breadth. None of us can see, touch or even measure the fourth density, but we know it is there because the fourth density interacts with the first three densities.

"We think the reason why bits of gravity do what they do is because of this interaction between the three and the four.

"I know this is getting a little complex, so I won't say any more except that the energy we use to spin our disks works the same way. That energy is also apparently made up of bits of nothing, which thrust against grooves in the spinning disks and make them spin—very rapidly."

A bicycle made four three!

Gravitrons are powerful because (just like the circle described by retrograde precession) they have off-centre rotation, and a backward wobble. We maintain that the untorquing of these counter forces in the gravitrons as they thrust, releases *phenomenal propulsion capabilities.*

However, the main composition of a planet's gravitational field does not consist of gravitrons. Gravitrons are the *result* of mass spinning. This statement includes the spinning of gravitational fields. So gravitrons behave like bits and pieces of gravitational fields. Gravitrons are emitted by rotating celestial bodies.

However, gravitrons return 'home' because many of these particles leaving rotating celestial bodies are recaptured—due to gravity.

As a result of the increasing inability of 3D gravity to govern the speed of light, our research suggests that when correctly ascertained, scientists will find that there are *three, greatly differing* speeds of light.

These *three light speeds* are dependent upon how far light is from large amounts of matter, or in other words, gravity. We cannot say why light changes speed suddenly as it gets farther and farther from large amounts of matter rather than gradually, but it appears that the Universe tends to immediate action rather than dissipated action.

1. *Solar system light speed* is approximately 186,282 miles per second and extends well beyond the immediate limits of any given solar system.
2. *Interstellar light speed* is the speed of light between solar systems. Interstellar light speed is hundreds of thousands times faster than solar system light speed, begins well beyond the limits of a solar system and extends well beyond the fringes of galaxies.[12]
3. *Intergalactic light speed* is seven times faster than interstellar light speed.[13] Intergalactic light speed is the speed of light in the physical Universe well beyond the fringes of galaxies.

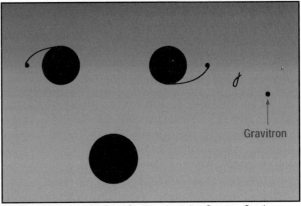

18. Representation of a Crop Glyph activated at Overton, Southern England, June 1992, which appears to depict the process of releasing gravitrons from a rapidly Spinning Disk.

402

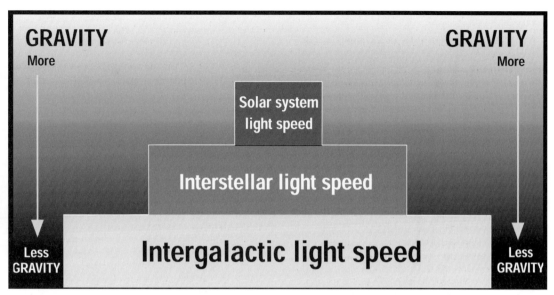

19. The authors' suggested model for the real interrelationship between gravity and light.

This is an appropriate moment to mention time (sometimes described inappropriately as the 4th dimension). Physical time is affected by the speed of travel: slower speed results in faster time; faster speed results in slower time. The rate of physical time is determined by the total speed component of the observer.

The full realisation of these principles clearly brings true deep space travel into the realms of achievable reality for living beings. It also means that *out there* is actually *right here!* Our scientists' general unwillingness to take the blinkers off and consider relinquishing some of Einsteinian physics is possibly hindering mankind from even starting the task of testing these ideas. It is also hindering those same scientists (and many others) from understanding that there are almost certainly other planets in existence supporting self-aware life. For many, this idea may appear to be both inconceivable and scary. Yet the number of UFO sightings that are witnessed is growing, year on year. Small wonder the Roswell Incident was hushed up. No wonder the scientific community is unwilling to even consider the dethronement of Einstein. We need reconsider the way light behaves and look closer at the interrelationship between gravity and light. Recognising the obvious and demonstrated problem of the neutral point would be a start.

The amount of mass and gravity within a given system dictates the speed of light. Thus:

C^1 *solar system light speed* = slowest light speed within a limited arena.

C^2 *interstellar light speed* = faster light speed within the region *between* solar systems in any galaxy.

C^3 *intergalactic light speed* = the fastest light speed in the space between galaxies.

A whistle was blown when the *speed of light* Crop Glyphs were activated in Southern England during July 1991—along with the encoded non-metric data derived from these glyphs.

. . . Darkness ruled

Despite being fully aware of variations in the speed of light within this solar system[14] the scientific community has agreed among themselves to *lock the speed of light* to that irrelevant,[15] recently-created unit of measurement— the metre.

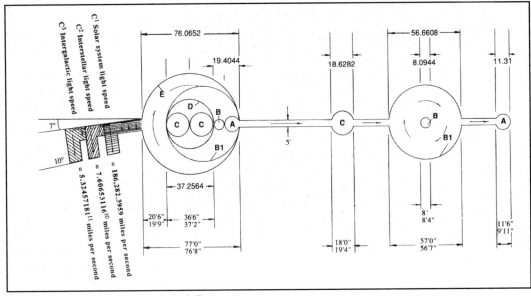

20. *Our decodings from these two glyphs indicate:*

C[1] solar system light speed   186,282.3959 miles per second.

C[2] interstellar light speed 7.60653116^{10} (186,282.3959 x 408,333.333).

C[3] intergalactic light speed 5.32457181^{11} (7.60653116^{10} x 7) miles per second. (see also Appendix)

Testing, testing, one two three

How can it be good science to take measurements *within the system being measured* and assume that the result applies everywhere, throughout the entire Universe? But we maintain, as we have shown, that there are faster light speeds than that which academe has (misguidedly in our opinion) tied into our metre-based measurement system.

The way to put these predicted figures to the test would simply require a probe to be sent beyond our solar system with the appropriate technology on board to evaluate the light speed once well away from the gravitational effects of our Sun.

Patterns within patterns

In simple terms then, we have three distinct speeds of light which are all part of the whole but apply in different situations. You could say that Einstein was right in stating that there is only one speed of light—but that such a conclusion only applies in the *one* set of circumstances.

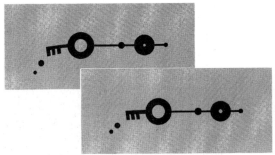

21. Representation of two 'Keys to the Kingdom' Crop Glyphs, both activated in Southern England in July 1991, and encoding (among other information) the three speeds of light.

The principal speed of light is intergalactic light speed. This speed is then affected by gravity and *slowed down* to become interstellar light speed within a galaxy; then *slowed down yet again* by the celestial bodies in a solar system to become the light speed with which we are familiar.

Now we can take the above principle and see that it becomes a microcosm of the macrocosm: even *within* our solar system, the speed

Interstellar
light speed

22. Interstellar space within a galaxy, between stars.

of the system. The positioning of this approach point is directly in proportion to the total mass of the system. For our solar system the approach point is situated at 800 million miles from our Sun. Which places it between Jupiter and Saturn at 69.28 million miles from Saturn's orbit; and tells us that the total mass of our system is related to 1,200 million miles of distance.

The light fantastic

As a result of the interaction between the celestial spheres and the environment within which they function, light also varies *in characteristic* or *quality*. Lots of gravity means slower light speed. It also means very intense, clear light.

of light is variable within the paradigm of 186,282.3959 miles per second, because the amount of mass and therefore the gravity also varies *within* our system. The slowest speeds of light occur around the inner planets. From Saturn outwards there is less mass and greater distance between the planets and therefore light can, *and does,* flow slightly faster there.

Thus the progression of light throughout a solar system could be depicted as a series of steps, with an entryway ⅔rds of the way out

On our blue-green planet, the light is crystal clear, despite our atmosphere and we can perceive the visible colours in the light spectrum. If you were to progress outwards from our planetary system, we suggest that you would find the quality of light alters. Losing the individual colours, you would experience from clear light (the whiter shade of pale) in the so-

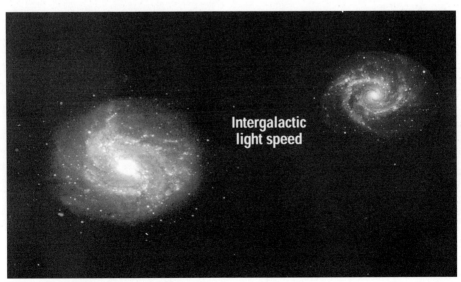

Intergalactic
light speed

23. Intergalactic space, between galaxies.

lar system through to medium-thick 'grey misty' light (the grey scale) in interstellar space, through to thicker light (the deep black) in intergalactic space.

The body in the library

Now we can clear up the *great mystery of NASA and the neutral point*. Although this solution will no doubt be unwelcome to some, as it is already an issue within quantum physics, we would like to mention it here: the effect of human consciousness upon an experiment.

- We propose that the craft that collected this experienced data contained human beings and that either one or both experienced the 'jolt' and the attendant momentary surge that accompanied the effect. This occurred at 43,495 miles out from the Moon or 202,827 miles from Earth.
- Not knowing what this effect actually was but being informed of the 'jolt' NASA probably put it down to the neutral point interface.

- We contend that the previously-established neutral point as calculated is absolutely correct and is still valid. This is the *physical* site of the neutral point. Beyond *this location* any *unmanned* craft would steadily gain in speed on its way to the Moon. We suggest that this fact is borne out by the continuing activity of unmanned probes to the Moon and the subsequent 1996 attempt by NASA to re-establish the 'Apollo 11' data according to the UNGC calculation.
- In July 1969 the CPN (calculated neutral point) would have occurred at a distance of approximately 24,736 miles from the Moon's centre. And would have been at 221,586 miles from the Earth's centre (see 24 below).
- The *experienced neutral point* is the location at which the 4D component of gravity takes over from the 3D component. This interface occurs well *before* reaching the calculated neutral point between planets. In the case of the Moon—on July 20 1969—this was nearly *19,000 miles adrift* from the previously accepted CNP.

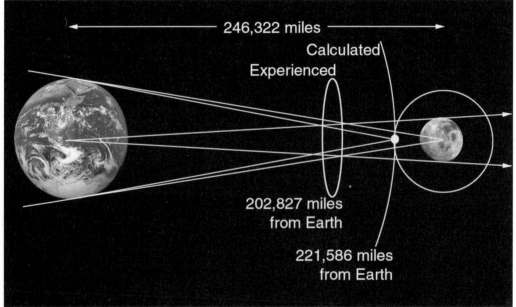

246,322 miles

Calculated
Experienced

202,827 miles
from Earth

221,586 miles
from Earth

24. Modelling of the interfacing 3D/4D arenas of the Earth/Moon gravity system. Note that the 'Apollo 11' experienced neutral point occurs well before the calculated 3D point, because the experienced neutral point is where the two planet's 4D arenas cross-over each other. It is this exchange of the hyperD component that causes a self-aware being to notice an event undetected by probes. The Earth's 4D component of gravity actually continues far beyond the Moon.

As the Earth's 4D component of gravity extends well beyond the Earth/Moon system, the *entire lunar surface* falls within the influence of the Earth's gravity.

- We maintain that the discrepancy between the experienced and calculated neutral points is due to the *four-dimensional (the hyperD) component* of gravity.
- The 4D component of gravity *only shows up at interfaces*.

In other words, the neutral point between the gravitational fields of any two planetary bodies, is affected by this 4D component of gravity. And from the point of view or experience *of the traveller*, the manifestation of this point occurs at a different location to the calculated point.

- We contend that at mankind's current stage of technological development in space, the experienced neutral point would only be revealed by the presence of a self aware being.

An unmanned probe, or a probe containing living organisms other than human beings, will traverse this interface without registering an effect—but *will* react to the physical effects of the calculated neutral point. Travelling to the Moon, human beings will be affected firstly by the *experienced* neutral point *and then* at the calculated neutral point locations. In other words, the presence of *consciousness* reveals the presence of the 4D or hyperD component of gravity. In due course the necessity for a totally different type of spacecraft will become fully realised. A craft that works in harmony with the environment of space which is quite unlike any rocket and/or module combination that the space agencies are currently using.

We are assuming that NASA and Co. truly have not understood what actually occurs at such interfaces. If, on the other hand, the agency has already grasped the ramifications of its 1969 neutral point discrepancy then the situation could be far more serious.

Until those in the driving seat come to understand the interrelationship between gravity and light they will never have the ability to measure accurately between planets and we

would suggest that this lack of understanding concerning 3D/4D gravity and its manifestations might be playing a part in many of the problems currently encountered by NASA. during its exploration of our solar system. Having chosen to do things its own way with Apollo, the agency and its masters has created its own haunting—and has no need to lay any of its problems at the feet of some 'galactic ghoul' seemingly lurking 'out there'.

By emphasising the length of the *trajectory* allegedly flown by the Apollo craft on each mission—at the expense of the actual *distance* between the Earth/Moon spheres, NASA has cleverly side-stepped the implications of the neutral point discrepancy. Given that these Apollo trajectories were established well in advance, these figures would have revealed—before the 'event'—the *exact* position of the CNP for each mission. In the case of 'Apollo 11' this information would subsequently have been found to be incorrect and NASA could have immediately been at the sharp end of some potentially awkward questions concerning 'Apollo 11'.

No-one had publicly commented on the CNP/ENP differential before July 25 1969. Although the mission was allegedly the third occasion that men had gone to the Moon, it is not beyond the bounds of possibility that astronaut 'testers' had already been sent moonwards, whether or not they actually arrived on the lunar surface is a matter of conjecture.

The fact that the 'Apollo 11' data published after the July 1969 event replaces the calculated neutral point is surely evidence that:

- There were no more *manned* missions to the Moon after the 'Apollo 11'/Luna 15 event.
- It occurred in *parallel* to the announced 'Apollo 11' mission.
- This parallel flight contained astronauts unannounced to the world (and could have been codenamed the Apollo Surrogate Probe).
- This craft did not carry any of the three named astronauts: Armstrong, Aldrin or Collins to the surface of the Moon (which was then orbiting at a distance of 246, 322 miles from Earth).

WvB—the ultimate Whistle-Blower?

In the 1960s there was no public debate over the neutral point discrepancy. In the 1980s NASA ignored the questions raised by the book *Moongate* in which the author raised the question of the revised neutral point figures.[16] Will, in the 1990s, NASA respond to the questions raised in this book, or are we going to continue into the next millennium in the same vein? If NASA and its counterparts continue to ignore transD physics they will have signed their own short term lease through an inability to send man into deep space safely. They will have thwarted a dream started by the very man who helped the American space exploration program (and therefore NASA) come into being—Wernher von Braun. In 1969 when he published the new neutral point data he may not have known what its significance was but he would certainly have sensed its importance to the future of space flight. In so doing he has performed a service to humanity which has gone some way towards rebalancing the disservice that he also performed in the pursuit of his objectives.

Mascons on the Moon

It is our contention that the massed concentrations of gravity found on the Moon are *demonstrations* available to us, perhaps even *prepared* for us (the first visitors from Earth) as a practical demonstration concerning the principles brought about by changes in mass and therefore of gravity. Analysis of the Lunar Orbiter's motion around the Moon during the 1960s identified regions with gravitational anomalies. These mascons, as they have been named were particularly apparent in relation to the lunar maria. For the space agencies these mascons, as far as we can ascertain, are still a subject of debate. Indeed in 1998 NASA released a new map of the mascons revealing two areas that allegedly were unmapped in the 1960s. It would appear that no conclusions have been reached, or if they have, the 'need-to-know' principle is at work, yet again, and we the public, obviously do not need to know!

Both NASA and the Soviets had problems in the 1960s with these regions. When flying

above an area of mascons their space probes were pulled downwards and *tugged about momentarily* during their orbits. This effect also occurs on Earth, only generally it is not recognised. When flying above or near the cones of volcanoes more gravitational differentials are in evidence, aircraft have been known to lose power and fall, sometimes this effect is recoverable sometimes not. The interface of an aircraft or a helicopter at the location of this anomalous field creates a 'jolt' and momentarily can interfere with our electronics and computers.

> **MASCONS**
> "Gravitational anomalies
> on the Moon
> have been
> swept
> under
> the
> table."
> Whistle-Blower T O M
> **MASsive CONSequences**

Problems, problems!

This planet upon which we are slowly growing up provides an environment that is virtually perfect for us. We enjoy a gravity that is suited to our physicality and a magnetic field which enables us to maintain our atmospheres—both physical and hyper-dimensional. When anyone leaves the planet's surface and passes the neutral point, they leave behind their native physical arena in which they were in balance and harmony and from henceforth they are out of 'tune' with the physical arena of any planet upon which they tread. In the case of the Moon they will still be 'surrounded' by the 4D component of their home planet as this extends beyond the Moon's orbit. *BUT* as this arena is also home to a gravity of ⅙G a human being on the surface of the Moon will have the interesting experience of being in a physical gravity ⅚ths less than his native gravity.

When people step onto the lunar or any other 'alien' surface they find themselves in an envi-

408

ronment which, because of its different gravity is not in harmony with their physicality. It is precisely these differences between our two planets that enables visitors when in the vicinity of the Moon, to *actually perceive* the effects of the interplay between 3D and 4D gravity.

We suggest that NASA has experienced *light variations* at the interface between the horizon and space, around any being or object 'alien' to the lunar surface and at certain sites on the lunar surface, for instance where the crust is thinner than the prevailing area, and the mass variable. These anomalies should register on imaging devices and film emulsion including those developed by Edwin Land. They might also affect any object orbiting around the Moon.

These gravitational anomalies are the principle reason that spacecraft experienced disturbances when orbiting the Moon. We also suggest that these disturbances are particularly prevalent around the equatorial regions of a planet, and are equally applicable to our own planet. This would also explain the 'jolting' that the astronauts talk of on leaving Earth itself. Restricted by their technology, they are thrusting straight through the least appropriate departure region of our planet, rather than spiralling outwards on a completely different but preferable trajectory.

NASA and the Soviets were 'lucky' that they cut their space exploratory teeth on the Moon, because when approaching a planet of significant mass and gravity, larger spacecraft could be seriously shaken about—even damaged—if inadequately built. It is possible, if space scientists were to continue to ignore such matters, that their major probes and manned craft of the future could have a tough time when approaching a planet such as Mars. And it could explain some of the problems (including electrical and other failures) probes actually have experienced when in the vicinity of Mars. Its not that ubiquitous 'galactic ghoul', unless of course you wish to call hyperD physics by such a name— which indeed some may wish to do!

Quality control

It is difficult to forget NASA's faked photographs. We have already postulated that the anomalies we are discussing may well have *contributed* to the decision by NASA to present pictures of lunar adventures that were not taken on the Moon. Unable to understand why the agency's early, real lunar images were so shrouded in haze, distorted, and/or double-imaged, it therefore resorted to recreating (or rather pre-creating) its Apollo TV material and photographs under controlled studio conditions on Earth, where everything would be 'normal'.

We suspect that the effects in question could be picked up by cameras on Earth as well as on the Moon, although these anomalies would vary in photographic terms because a bio-organism within its own environment is at least in physical *harmony* with that location. When we are on Earth, the effects cannot generally be perceived with the naked eye even in areas generating an artificial gravitational anomaly, such as that created by certain ancient stone circles—unless the observer is highly sensitive. Many people do however *sense* these anomalies and are aware of feeling 'something' different about such areas. Others sense these places subliminally and by varying degrees, depending on their overall constitution.

Serious Whistle-Blowing!

In order that we can all learn the lessons from our Moon, and if we care sufficiently to look, another source of information is available to us.

The U NIT

"Now reason, investigate and contemplate this thoroughly.

All that has been sent into space from Earth is being reflected back,

so that those on Earth may understand that when you create a situation that might be catastrophic, it may then

impress upon the minds of the people the effect that one unit can make on all."[17]

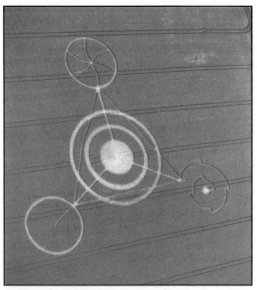

25. Photograph of the Barbury Castle Crop Glyph F TAYLOR
activated in Southern England, July 1991.

what they really are principally because (as already stated) the scientific community has no intention of disturbing the status quo by looking afresh at Einstein's conclusions, for to do so probably would bring the house of cards tumbling down. Secondly, what is not understood is generally feared and then either ignored, ridiculed or scorned as magic, witchcraft, the paranormal and, in our epoch, millennium fever or 'new age mumbo jumbo' by those who wish to remain as the masters of nature and 'the *only* ones who know'.

Photo finish

The 'Anomaly' Crop Glyph (26) was also called the Dolphin, the Whale, or the Fish. It was activated in wheat in the early hours of Tuesday July 30 1991 near Lockeridge, Wiltshire, England. This glyph made many people feel "as if time was standing still". The photographer, John Holman, thought that he was

Since the late 1980s there has been an artificial additive to our scenery, which is demonstrating, beyond reasonable doubt, many of the anomalies that we have postulated. This additive is the crop circle or Crop Glyph, found predominantly in Southern England. Within these Crop Glyphs—activated by off-planet Whistle-Blowers, researchers have recorded many instances of *interference* with their sound, film and TV recording equipment. Many people have had experiences of accelerated or prolonged time.

Part of the message in the Crop Glyphs appearing in our fields therefore concerns the manifestation of the hyperD physics that clearly we need to get to grips with, in order to travel through deep space successfully. These effects have not been formally recognised for

26. Central part of the 'Anomaly' Crop Glyph (see also page 368). J HOLMAN
Note the distance between the two dark figures—these images are of the same person!

taking a picture of his three friends standing within the glyph. When the film was developed and printed to his astonishment, he saw that each of his friends featured in two different positions—a technical impossibility.[18]

This photograph and the camera with which it was taken have both been examined and the film analysed by Kodak. No faults whatsoever were found with the camera, despite it having been completely dismantled during the examination, and the film had not been tampered with nor had the photograph been altered at any stage of its processing. To this day John Holman and these experts have not come to any conclusion as to the real causes of the anomalies present in this picture.

It seems fairly obvious to us that in this image something happened to the speed of the light reaching the camera lens. The photographer took a wide-angle photograph of a field featuring a recent glyph with his three friends standing inside this glyph. The *centre region* of the resultant image, however, has an almost vertical *displacement* of both the glyph and the treeline, but the people have been displaced in a manner *inconsistent* with the principal displacement. We seem therefore to have two speeds of light operating at the same time in the area of the glyph:

A) *Speed 1,* registering immediately with the camera—has provided the main image including the *stronger, sharper* record of the people.
B) *Speed 2,* which has registered *above and below the feet* of the people has apparently displaced the other components of the image in the region of the glyph with *less strength.*
C) Further, there is a secondary image of these same people—standing in different positions and with even *less strength*—which is also displaced above and below the feet.

More and less

We propose that A) *Speed 1,* is the normal speed of light experienced on Earth outside the region of the glyph, with which the camera has coped normally, as can be seen on the *outer areas* of the photograph.

B) *Speed 2,* is the speed of light prevailing locally inside the glyph, causing the anomalies that are apparently manifesting as the vertical displacements of the areas in the vicinity of the glyph.

Yet this is still not a wholly satisfactory explanation.

As the interior of the glyph has registered at a different rate, or speed, than the exterior, it has created an interface at which the whole glyph was at a different harmonic than the extended environment. This registration has affected the skyline.

The people were also recorded at a different rate than the interior of the glyph and this situation has resulted in the manifestation of their consciousness—*it has become visible.* Not only that, but as thought precedes action, these people knew that their photograph was being taken and they knew that they could 'unfreeze' as soon as John had finished. They were already *thinking* of what they would do next, and it is this *thought process* that has manifested as the secondary image. As this action had not yet taken place, it is of much less strength than the 'basic stance' image, itself less sharp than the 'earth-based image'.

We are of the firm opinion that this particular glyph was designed principally in order to demonstrate the fundamental relationship between gravity and light.

By affecting the gravity inside the Crop Glyph, the local light speed was *automatically altered* resulting in the demonstration of the relationship between gravity, light (and, yes, consciousness too).

Now this is where quantum physics joins with eastern philosophy, and where western science cries: "Oh, no! spare us!"

Today's mantra therefore is:

"Less is more."

Less gravity means a faster speed of light. The presence of participants at the interface results in a different characteristic or 'quality' to the light, namely a secondary image.

No wonder that we, the authors, maintain that any gravitational irregularities on the Moon might produce similar results! We are of the opinion that this type of anomaly would manifest when a human being *takes a photograph* on the lunar surface—just as we have seen in this Crop Glyph demonstration. If such anomalies were somehow anticipated prior to the scheduled Apollo landings there would have been sufficient time to take the appropriate corrective measures resulting in the 'credible' photographs needed for the scheduled missions. In simpler terms, NASA and Co. had to have suspected well before July 1969, that as far as getting clear pictures were concerned, the lunar photographs were going to be a catastrophe.

This data and information, it seems, concerning the relationship between gravity and light is accessible to anyone who *wishes* to know. Interestingly, it would appear that the information is not primarily intended for NASA, the UK Government, or any other official organisation. Through the medium of the encoded Crop Glyphs it was and is literally being placed at the feet of ordinary people, so that anyone interested might ask "why".[19]

The little dog laughed to see such craft

Today there is a growing feeling that the much needed and long awaited *alternative energy* is almost to hand. Clearly we cannot go on indefinitely raping our planet, burning crude fossil fuels and polluting our environment. Throughout Part One we demonstrated to what extent the space agencies need to develop a more economical and viable method of propulsion in order to be able to proceed around and about, both on and off the planet, with minimum noise and pollution, and without reliance

---

Not the once and future king . . .

"If we ever do invent a 'space drive' it will surely depend upon some new fundamental discovery in sub-atomic physics,
or [in] the structure of space time.
Until then we are stuck with rockets
—chemical, electric or nuclear."
. . . but author Arthur.[20]

---

on conventional fuels. Even those entrusted with handling our 'modern' nuclear energy generation are not managing the by-products of nuclear fuels correctly. These are a permanent hazard. We feel therefore that it is time to take heed of other new proposals, that use *non-pollutionary elements,* working *harmoniously* with the natural order of things to provide our future travel needs.

Blueprints 1

So where should we start? Firstly, by replacing those long, thin rockets, those stubby pencil shapes that were the 'command modules' and those flimsy 'wigwams' that were the lunar landers. The Soviet's spherical craft were actually more compatible with the dynamics involved, Korolëv having observed the fact that planets are spherical. We can no longer expect to travel beyond our planet's protection in a *Tintin* rocket powered by 'blood and thunder', born out of the ignorance associated with the early stages of our spaceflight efforts. It simply will not do! Furthermore, the method does not work for deep space return journeys if we wish to return home alive.

In "Truth or Consequences" we wrote of our conviction that the military set piece called the Roswell Incident conceals the fact that the authorities actually found a spacecraft that was deliberately, carefully (and we believe lovingly) placed to provide us all with the basic idea of a form and structure that would transport and protect astronauts while travelling in space. Our research suggests that this gift (for it was the equivalent of placing a toy in a child's Christmas stocking while it sleeps) has been analysed to the best of the US Government and NASA's abilities. Having studied such a craft, it *ought* to have been clear to those involved that attempting space travel in the *nose cone* of a rocket, would impose severe limitations on how far human beings could travel *and on their ability to return home safely.*

The authorities have seemingly realised that the fundamental design, construction materials and method of assembly of that craft differ very considerably from our primitive rockets, whilst copying some of the principles inherent in the *structure* of such a craft, they have been totally unable to reproduce the method of propulsion—primarily because the gift they received did not contain any recognisable propulsion system. After all, we do not give our children a toy that is way beyond their age of development—not if we want them both to learn and enjoy themselves at the same time. The major restrictions of having to use rocket propulsion have consequently limited the choice of *form* for our present space craft—including the design of the LM.

So what would be the appropriate shape for a space vehicle that intended to emulate the way in which our planet functions? If Korolëv had pushed his thoughts a little further and recognised that our planet is not an exact sphere, then he could have come up with the ideal shape: an oblate spheroid. If he had then installed inside it a large Spinning Disk, with a

capability for generating gravitational and magnetic fields—then he could have been in business, as they say.

A viable means of propulsion is required that will, among other matters, automatically protect a crew from the dangers of radiation and bone loss. We believe the way forward is with *Spinning Disk* technology.

Our own research suggests that we should be using a system which has *already* been tried and tested—it is probably the standard power source used by other self-aware beings in civilisations elsewhere. How can we possibly know that? This understanding is mainly the result of the painstaking Crop Glyph decoding that has been undertaken over the last nine years or so.

Therefore for affordable, safe, manned space travel beyond the confines of our planet's protection, we propose that the Spinning Disk is

---

Said Simple Sigh man

Robert Oechsler is a man who claims to have worked as a NASA mission specialist from 1974-'77. He also claims that the US Government does indeed have craft that meet the description of UFO reports— and that he worked on these craft. In 1989 he asked a question

to the Spi man

Admiral B Robert Inman, Director Naval Intelligence and the National Security Agency (NSA), Deputy Director, Defense Intelligence Agency (DIA) and the CIA:

let me see your wares

"Would any of the recovered vehicles become available for technological research, outside military circles"?

said the Spi man

"Honestly I don't know....whether as time evolves, if ever we become more open...it is a possibility."

The Viking probe
Looks the part on the outside, but certainly is not the part on the inside.
For neither Simple Sigh man nor the Spi man understand how ET craft actually function.
In 1996 *Janes Defence Weekly* published an article on anti-gravity propulsion systems in which it was mentioned that Admiral B Robert Inman became President of *Science Applications International Corporation* in San Diego California (SAIC).
Clearly, the penny hasn't dropped yet!

28. The wheel.

powered by a Spinning Disk are various and diverse. These matters are discussed in detail in an earlier work, *Two-Thirds.* Here we will just take a look at some of the key aspects of the Spinning Disk, which is the prime component of what we call the Gravitron Drive.

The information that we have gained suggests first that the disk has to be spun at many hundreds of thousands of revolutions per minute. The disk itself is fabricated from a very solid heavy concrete-like material of a specific size, weight and thickness, according to the craft in which it is to be placed. It has steel-like radials and is also banded around the rim (where it is appreciably thicker) in order that it should not fly apart when spinning rapidly.

the solution, and that in the future this Gravitron Drive propulsion system will be even more significant to the furtherance of our civilisation than was the invention of the wheel. In a sense, a Spinning Disk *is* of course a wheel—rotated through 90 degrees. However, the means of making this gravity generation system function is slightly different! We must emphasise once again that ours is not an anti-gravity concept. In fact, it should be described as a *gravity generation* and propulsion method.

The components and configuration of a space craft

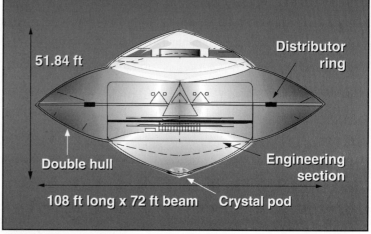

29. Side view of craft with Gravitron Drive. Note the double hulls and crystal pod.

Joke in the box

Currently, some scientists are studying various other means of propulsion,
pinning their main hopes on anti-matter as a solution.
Such a theoretical anti-matter propulsion device would work, it is claimed,
on the principle that a particle of matter is of a positive charge
and that if one can divide this particle and recover the opposite atom, that will have a negative charge.
Then by collecting enough anti-(or negative particle) matter and banging that together in a controlled manner with
particles of (positive) matter,
scientists think it will be possible to create a propulsion system that does not rely on liquid fuels.
To date, and at great expense, the particle accelerator at CERN in Switzerland has produced a very limited
amount of anti-matter,
which only *existed* for a few moments before being annihilated.
We maintain that his system will *never* work satisfactorily because it is still *forcing* energy instead of flowing with
the harmonics of the way things work naturally.

The windmills of our whirled

Our Crop Glyph research indicates that all things in nature work in essentially the same way.
Therefore it must be possible for us to study the way that our planet itself works, and then *extrapolate* from our findings a way in which we can model what is really occurring as the planet rotates, revolves and processes.
Our planet travels around its Sun at a rotational speed of 66,000 miles/106,194 kms per hour. This planet revolves on its axis at over 1,000 miles/1,609 kms per hour (measured at the equator) turning from west to east throughout its 23 hour and 56 minute sidereal day.

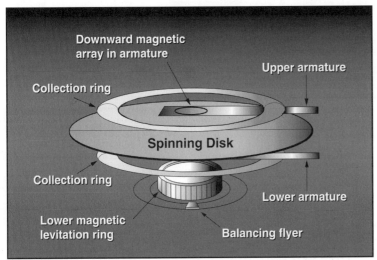

30. The Spinning Disk concept that forms part of the Gravitron Drive (isometric view).

These gravitrons are conduited to the gravitron *distributor ring.*

In order to support the base of this disk while it is spinning, our research has led us to realise that a ring of magnets at the bottom of the rig is required in order to levitate the disk. Another ring of magnets pressing *down* on the disk holds it into position. So the disk is supported free of any contact with any surface by a magnetic field.

During flight a computer-controlled balancing flyer orbits *around* the disk on a track (30, 31 & 32). This essential balancing

At a point two-thirds of the way from the centre of the spacecraft's disk, at an angle of between 19.47° and 22.48°, massless particles of gravity are emitted from the surface of the disk. These massless particles are what we call *gravitrons.*

Due to the fact that the disk works in exactly the same way as our solar system, or indeed a galaxy, then we should know that a Spinning Disk is actually a simplified version of a planet (which, when spun at the right rate also gives off similar 'bits' of gravity—gravitrons).

When revolving at the correct spin rate the disk starts to lose apparent mass, and as loss of mass equals loss of gravity, the gravitrons fly off the disk by virtue of its spinning at the 'right' rate. These energy vortices of gravity are collected by rings placed above and below the disk (see 30).

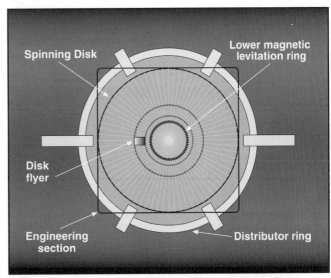

31. Top view of the Spinning Disk and the Gravitron Distributor Ring.

415

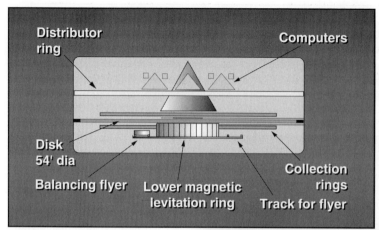

32. Side view of the Gravitron Drive.

suspended, free floating—but in the case of the disk, suspended between magnets. Two armatures hold in place the two sets of thrusters that spin the disk.

On a much larger scale, the *nine* thrusters around our spaceship Planet Earth/Moon can be likened to the orbital paths of the Sun, Mercury, Venus, Mars, Jupiter, Saturn, Uranus, Neptune and Pluto.

flyer is necessary to keep the disk 100% level at all times (in relation to the supporting magnets and the armatures) no matter what the angle of orientation of the craft.

Now where have we seen something like that before? We have a demonstration of the same basics in our solar system. The Earth/Moon system is just like such a unit, with the Moon acting as the flyer to the spinning disk that is Earth.

The Moon in fact rather like the Earth's balancing flyer. This disk, *just like our own planet*, is

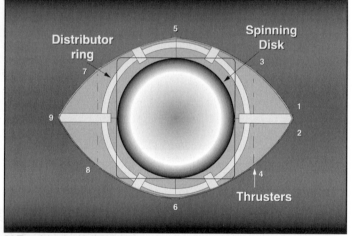

34 Top view of craft with distributor ring and thrusters. In a space craft it is the release of the gravitrons through specially-designed narrow openings which give them their outstanding thrusting capabilities.

33. The solar system.

We firmly believe that this revolutionary technology will be at the heart of future craft, whether destined for use within atmospheric conditions or for deep space travel.

The same principles inherent in this technology are the quintessence of our planetary system, our solar system, our galactic system, and the Universe too. They are also at the heart of our physical bodies, and indeed manifest throughout everything there is.

Odunside	Starboard
Our findings from Crop Glyph research suggest that the Gravitron Drive is *the* propulsion system used by other civilisations and it is to be *the* propulsion system for us all on this planet. Although these 4D gravitrons are actually made of 'nothing', in 3D they *act* as if they are made of 'something' and thereby propel the craft very rapidly.	
Port	Seaside

One might ask at this stage, why is it necessary to use these energy particles, these gravitrons in this propulsion system?

Well, a correct amount of *gravity* (usually equal to that of the planet from which one has departed) is a necessity to provide the basis of the essential environment for passengers and crew on board such a craft. Gravity is also used to prevent the occupants from becoming 'strawberry jam' when the craft is accelerating rapidly, or making abrupt turns.

If we were to be sitting inside such a craft when it suddenly accelerated, we would not feel any sensation, due to the computer-controlled distribution of gravitrons (maintained between the inner and outer hulls of the craft) which create an *induced gravitational field*. These gravitrons are directed to the appropriate parts of the craft to compensate for acceleration and changes of direction.

Occupants do not even need to use seat belts!

—it is so sophisticated.

Re-volution of a species!

What on Earth has the site of Stonehenge got to do with this Spinning Disk technology? Accepted thinking states variously that this stone megalith was an observatory, a clock, a temple, and a place to hold celebrations. Traditional mythology (and there is actually a great deal of information to be obtained from such stories) has it that the structure was also erected by magical means, by Merlin, the power behind the throne of the once and future King of Britain—Arthur.

Establishment archaeologists maintain rather fixed attitudes towards the dating of ancient sites such as Stonehenge—mostly, because they do not want to have to rethink their existing paradigms. This mental inertia is backed up by the fear of losing face and of being considered foolish or 'non-scientific' by their peers. Cowardice, in other words. Of course they will tell you, it maybe all right once they retire, they can then 'play' as they no longer feel the need to maintain their reputations or to respond to peer pressure to quite the same degree. During her or his career, however, the 'expert' expends much energy thrashing all who dare to question the 'facts' laid down and maintained by the academic establish-

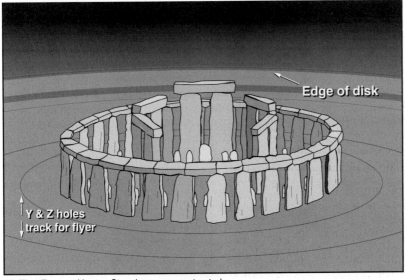

35. That Famous Henge, Stonehenge reconstructed.

---

sTONEd CIRCLES

As one archaeologist said to us, while laughing at theories concerning encoded information in the layout and siting of megalithic sites: "I don't believe such hypotheses. However, I must say, what no one has been able to tell us, is why these places are built *precisely* where they are".

sCORNed CIRCLES

---

ment. What a pity that so much effort could not be put to better use.

While it is not within the capacity of everybody to envisage, for example, the possibility that interplanetary visitors moved into place the megalithic stones of many of our monuments, is it too much to ask that we all keep an open mind on such matters? Especially since, if we are honest with ourselves, there are still many questions concerning these places that have, so far, not been inadequately answered. Given this *lack* of knowledge concerning much of our archaeological heritage, 'alternative' proposals, should not be automatically excluded from consideration and experimentation.

Archaeology has yet to find an appropriate dating system for these megalithic sites—the dating of artefacts or soil that is nearby an ancient standing stone is *not good enough*. For example, the sight of a representative of the archaeological profession standing in front of Stonehenge on British TV, waving antler horns in a 'digging' motion and telling the public: "We couldn't date the stones themselves *of course* (our emphasis) but we dated these horns to 5,000 BP using the very latest radio-carbon dating system. We know that they dug the holes for the stones with these antlers because we found them in the ditch nearby—so we know that's when Stonehenge was built!"

This kind of approach is either an insult to our intelligence or an indication of the mental cul-de-sac into which at least some academics have walked. If the situation was not so appalling it would be laughable. If an archaeologist in the far future finds an artefact such as a glass *Coca-Cola* bottle (thrown away by a 20th Century person while visiting an ancient site) will they be daft enough to attribute the age of the *site* to the time scale of the attendant arte-

fact? Worse, to imagine that the site was *constructed* to promote the artefact?

This is exactly the process being followed by such analysts today. Having little understanding of either mythology or coding, they link objects together that may well have something to do with each other but not necessarily within the same time frame. One might suggest that when they can see yet another use for which Stonehenge was constructed, they will truly have their eyes opened.[21]

A is for...

Alternative is another 'A' word to place next to 'A for Atlantis' on the shelf of prohibited words in Academe. When scholars learn the true significance of our very ancient history they will realise that Academe is also an 'A' word, when viewed from a certain perspective.

...Apple

Blind dates

If these present-day high priests of our heritage are not dating the stones themselves—and even such dating of course will only tell them the age of the stone and not when it was put there—then these archaeologists are making assumptions mostly based on their professions 'boggle factor' capacity (very limited) and of course the degree of accuracy of their dating systems. Modern archaeology persists in ignoring the most simple facts, for example:

- Many of the human skeletons discovered and dated to the time it is claimed these ancient sites/monuments were constructed show signs of osteoarthritis.
- These megaliths are huge at Stonehenge: a significant part of each stone is set well beneath ground level, yet they were allegedly dragged from their original sites and floated up rivers then rolled on tree trunks to the Salisbury Plain. The nearest point of the River Avon to Stonehenge is at Amesbury. It

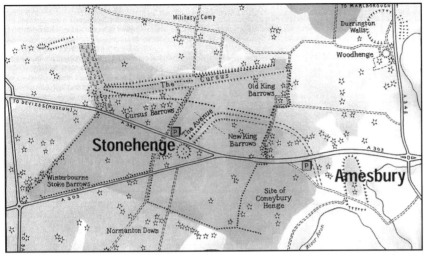

36. Stonehenge in relation to Amesbury.

ENGLISH HERITAGE

sized tree trunks would have been needed in order to get these very large stones moving.

We are all expected to believe that these trees were felled then stripped of all their bark and branches, then made smooth enough for rolling by small, sometimes arthritic people, equipped with flint-axe heads! (Axe heads which have recently been demonstrated to be of rather less use than the flints used to make them, but that's another matter).[26] The surrounding earthen rampart and ditch was supposedly dug by people using antler horns as picks and oxen shoulder blades as shovels, filling willow baskets with the material they were moulding and moving. We are assured that this was also the method of construction for Avebury Circle and Silbury Hill, nearly 18 miles away, where the total amount of earth moved was far greater than at Stonehenge.[22]

It has been stated that it would take 700 peo-

is then a long haul uphill, a steep descent downhill and another sloping haul uphill again, a distance of over a mile across country from the river to the site.

There have been several present day reconstructions attempting to explain how human beings could have constructed Stonehenge. These use relatively slim mechanically-prepared logs and state that people of that time would have used the stripped tree bark twisted together to make a pulling rope, and that they would have used the equivalent of these modern ropes to attach and pull the stones. Here, in documentary TV clips we see tall, fit and healthy youths of today heaving one megalithic-sized stone (made of concrete) a few hundred yards over a prepared flat surface free of any undergrowth, trees or hindrances. The 'experts' then pronounce this a valid contribution to research and consider such an exercise proof enough that Stonehenge could have been assembled in precisely the same way! And everybody goes back to sleep! Contrary to such a scenario, large quantities of substantial

37. Typical misguided (in our view) portrayal of the construction of Stonehenge.

ENGLISH HERITAGE

419

ple ten years to build Silbury Hill. Imagine how many individuals would need to be living in these areas around 5,000 years BP, that this scale of project could be manned for such an extended period, and still time be left to provide for growing families. And how large were their herds of animals, that they could kill such numbers in order to use the shoulder blades to dig earth, but still maintain food and breeding herds? Oh, and when did all these people get the time to go hunting for deer, in order to acquire either fresh antler horns or seek cast-off antlers.

The truth is that archaeologists *assume* that these megalithic sites were prepared using antlers, due to their *proximity of the find* relative to the site. Interestingly, antler horns are primarily made of hair, and represent regeneration and rebirth. They are both dead and living at the same time—as are human beings, until they come into balance of both physicality and spirituality. Archaeologists can envisage no other solutions than correspond with their 'mind set' and have woven all the understandings of how megaliths were put in place around such pre-assumptions. Being 'rational scientific types', they have eliminated speculation and are not prepared to admit that there is much that they simply do not know.

Why not? What is wrong with calling a spade a spade—and not a shoulder blade? What is wrong with having the honesty to say: "Currently we simply do not have any means of accurately assessing when or how these stones were assembled, so we shall have to keep an open mind, maintain a sense of wonder and exploration about the subject"? That is surely a far more intelligent and honest response than to offer explanations that a child could see through. The Emperor is still wearing no clothes!

Senseless censoring

To demonstrate our points with regard to 'established ideas' we have an amusing episode to relate

that concerns the current custodians of Stonehenge—English Heritage. After nearly six months of deliberation their purchasing committee agreed to stock the book *Two-Thirds* in their Stonehenge shop, for a trial period—*to see if it would sell*. Their first order of twelve copies sold out in less than ten days, which pleased the on-site staff, not unnaturally. However, the stock replacement is activated by a central ordering department. No follow-up order was placed. When asked why they did not wish for more copies of what was obviously a good seller, English Heritage stated that they would not re-order the book "as it did not fit in with their policy on Stonehenge". Perhaps such a non-commercial decision was *made for them* rather than by them? Whatever the source of such an irrational commercial decision, English Heritage have declined the publisher's request to state their reasons for destocking in writing but they attempted to justify their actions twice during subsequent telephone conversations.

We offer this incident as an example of censorship exercised in the interests of preserving academic *bias*. The fact that such an action overrides any commercial interest demonstrates that the maintenance of 'the party line' concerning one of the most important archaeological sites on the planet is a prime consideration—even paramount. Is this perceived im-

38. Stonehenge as it is today.   AULIS

420

portance of the academic status quo strictly limited to the official guardians of our ancient sites or are others equally concerned that we all remain in a permanently lethargic state?

Unlike mainstream archaeologists English Heritage & Co., we do not totally refute other researchers opinions as to the function of Stonehenge. It is quite likely that over time, this megalithic structure has fulfilled all of the functions that are attributed to it. After all, if everything works in the same way, as we claim, one should *expect* a piece of harmonious technology for air and space travel to *interface* with a means, for instance, of monitoring the heavens; known as a place of communion between heaven and Earth; and be subsequently adopted as a temple for that very reason. Nevertheless we believe that there was a more fundamental and central reason for the design of this monument.

Stonehenge was constructed primarily for the period we find ourselves in *now* in order to demonstrate to us, at a time when we have grown mature enough as a species to travel beyond our planet, and when we have begun to realise that rockets are not the answer to such logistics, that we would be able to see—from a fresh perspective—that which was previously 'mist before our eyes'.

We should, for the first time ever, now begin to see that these stones and the workings in the ground are the *detailed blueprints* of a scale model of the Spinning Disk, together with the magnets of the Gravitron Drive.

Firstly, it is worth remembering that Stonehenge comprises an *earthen rampart and ditch* as well as the famous standing stones themselves. The earthen rampart and ditch are vitally important and mark the edge of the disk itself, the thickness of the edges of this ditch representing the thickened, reinforced rim of a real disk, essential to prevent the disk from flying apart when spinning very rapidly. But when viewed from *above,* the effect is the same.

Incidentally, the word henge means to suspend. *In particular reference to Stonehenge: something hanging—or in suspense (OED),* or hanging in the air, and that can also mean waiting for something to happen!

All the sarsen stones depict *magnets.*

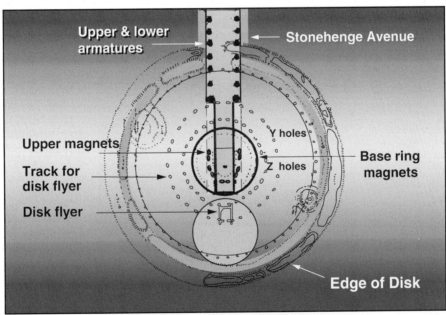

39. Stonehenge as a *scale model* of the Spinning Disk—top view—compare (30 & 31).

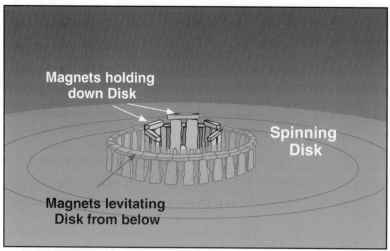

40. Stonehenge with the sarsen stones representing the levitating magnets located above and below the level of the disk.

the prime trigger for this realisation and subsequent 'unveiling' of the monument.

This then required the ground plan of Glastonbury Abbey (located to the west of Stonehenge). The 'blueprints' all came together when these groundplans were combined. This exact three-way matching of plans could not in any way be attributed to pure chance and was the corroboration of our findings at Stonehenge.

In this modelling, the Avenue, part of the Stonehenge complex, and the Mary Chapel of the Abbey represent the upper and lower armatures of the Disk. The stones at Stonehenge have a range of four different heights, to convey the essential information that the Spinning Disk avails itself of 4D (or hyperD) energy and the total of 75 sarsen stones are a reminder of the 750,000 rpm operational spin rate.

The various heights of the stones are also relevant. The central horseshoe represents the magnets that hold 'down' the disk. These stones are *taller* than the sarsen ring surrounding them because on the Gravitron Drive these magnets are located *above* the disk and are attached to the upper armature.

Confirmation of all this reasoning has come in the form of the Chilcomb May 1990 Crop Glyph—(41), the light grey area—which was

Two out of three

In our view, using a Spinning Disk inside a future spacecraft will provide the appropriate gravitational field for the astronauts and enable the passengers and crew to move around naturally in the environment within which they are travelling. It is clear that a craft powered by a Spinning Disk would be *the* ultimate reusable space craft that those (including NASA) who are anxious to develop a har-

41. Glastonbury Abbey groundplan and Chilcomb Crop Glyph (May 1990) combined.

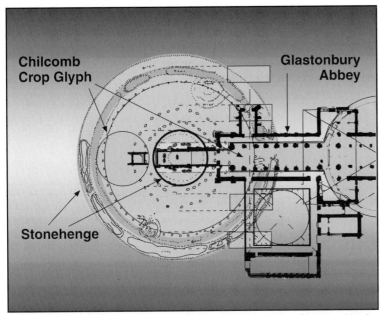

42. Stonehenge, Glastonbury Abbey groundplan and Chilcomb Crop Glyph combined.

was indicated by that 1997 astrology chart.

In September 1996 there was an announcement from Finland that a group of scientists had built a small piece of equipment that manifested an effect that apparently defies gravity. They themselves described it as an anti-gravity device.[23]

Most interestingly, this model is a very simplified version of our Spinning Disk concept. In our opinion, however, in order for a Spinning Disk to release gravitrons the disk has to have considerable *mass* and spin at hundreds of thousands of revolutions per minute.

The experimental device in Finland comprised a rapidly spinning ring (not a solid disk) of superconducting ceramic material that was suspended in a magnetic field and enclosed in a low-temperature container.

This ring was then spun at approximately 5,000 rpm. Even though it was only a *ring,* and was only spinning at a relatively slow speed, it did reduce by four and a half ounces a

monious, safe form of deep space travel are seeking. It will be interesting to see who is far-sighted enough to truly understand the implications of this technology enough to step forward and start development work.

Will it be a multi-national corporation, one of the established aircraft manufacturers, or a *private* far-seeing individual? Lets start turning things around—let's get spinning!

master mind

Scientists with Scandinavian connections appear to be leading the way forward. Will they survive the censorship of the 'masters of infinity'? At the time of writing the answer seems to be no, but that's another matter. Once an idea is verbalised it enters the planetary consciousness and is 'on its way'. So despite the reactions of orthodoxy, the process of change has begun, and right on cue as

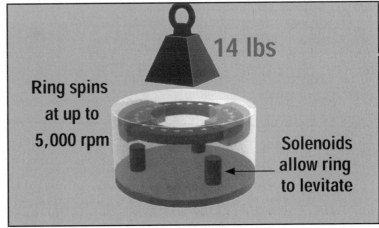

43. The spinning *ring* experiment at Tampere University, Finland.

423

Dick 'n Ed

Apart from Ed Mitchell's stolid denial of the usefulness of hyperD physics, the last word on this must come from one Richard Hughes of the Los Alamos National Laboratory and a member of the Greenland Experimental team:
"There are only four forces in nature. *Read my lips.* No new forces."
Sounds like Bishop Wright and Simon Newcomb have resurfaced!
Are these famous last words?

14lb/6.35kg weight suspended over the device, a reduction of approximately 2%.

Because our Spinning Disk is fabricated with steel radially imbedded into the disk, and *electro-magnets* are used for levitation, supercooling of the base ring of magnets is not necessary. And of course, our disk is then spun at *very high* speeds.

Once again, for either commercial or industrial/military reasons, or both, the possibility of debate with regard to the preliminary findings of the Finnish scientists has been denied us. NASA have not commented on their own possible interest in these findings, despite rumours that they had immediately 'snapped' up the scientists and their discovery. But there were very bizarre circumstances surrounding the responses from the Finnish science department at Tampere University. Following the announcement of their forthcoming paper due to be published by the Institute of Physics, this paper was withdrawn at the last minute, the research team members were allegedly either not at the University at the time of the experiment, or were currently unavailable for comment, and the general impression was not unlike the hullabaloo emitted by the American government during Roswell: issue a statement and then deny it immediately afterwards, then create confusion until everybody shrugs their shoulders and forgets about it. In the meantime all the available information is contractually secured in a desperate attempt to be first with this technology.

We believe that NASA (even if fully encouraged by their masters) will not be able to make such a disk function anywhere near sufficiently well for their needs, for three reasons.

Firstly, the disk has to be solid, fabricated from the correct materials. A *ring* is not in any way suitable, *as it has grossly insufficient mass for the job.*

Secondly, the disk has to spin at a precise rate, because *only at that particular speed does the disk acquire its match in 4D* and thereupon release gravitrons. *Any other speed will not work.*

And thirdly, the 'sting': established scientists will not like the only means by which the disk can be spun—the application of consciousness energy, via thrusters, to the ridges in the disk. Thrusting in this manner is the only way to achieve the incredibly fast spin rate necessary.

Even though only partially viable, these early experiments in Finland are certainly a conclusive demonstration of a *principle* and clearly this is only the beginning. Hopefully, and sooner rather than later, the Finnish experiment will draw attention to *hyperdimensionality,* and propel us towards looking into the 4D realm of the Universe, the part that hitherto scientists have not seriously studied.

Would it not be truly wonderful if the linear thinkers among us were enabled to make an about-turn, without losing face?

We've started so we'll Finnish

The Spinning Disk however is only one-third of the technology that humanity will need to understand and develop before we can travel successfully into deep space. The next third consists of a computer that is fast enough to deal with the *virtually instantaneous* calculations necessary when travelling at light speeds faster than we have ever experienced to date. And although the idea of quantum computers is being explored, that is not it, either!

Now a few details of that 'sting'—the final third. We only intend to touch on the subject of consciousness energy here, as the matter is already covered in great depth in our earlier work *Two-Thirds.*

These two essential pieces of hardware, the Spinning Disk and the hyperD computer are powered by one item of software, the human brain. This statement does *not* mean that human beings are to be treated like cyborgs, robots or slaves in the pursuit of generating this energy. We believe that what we are calling *consciousness energy,* once collected and harnessed, can be focused and contained to provide all the power that will be needed by mankind in the future. This is also an environmentally non-pollutionary energy that not only can fulfil our present planetary needs, but will provide the essential energy component for our future travels in space.

The complete theory can be publicly debated as and when the basic principles of the Spinning Disk have been openly accepted as a possibility by interested parties. For until the scientific community can free itself of such relatively minor matters as the limitations of a single universal light speed (with the narrow concepts of time that accompany such theories) then they will obviously find it nigh on impossible to take on board *consciousness energy* as a means of power.

For those who are currently ready and willing to look at our inherited structures on this planet from a new perspective, everything we need in order to bring forth that which we already know has been laid out before us to examine. We, the authors, have blueprints for the Spinning Disk as represented at Stonehenge and we have a modelling of the hyperD computer (to be found in Egypt). Both of those items are non-functional models, built in stone for longevity. As is the final third, the oldest Whistle-Blower on Earth, the metaphorical representation of consciousness energy on this planet is patiently waiting for us to start working it all out—our Great Sphinx.

- The Spinning Disk is modelled by Stonehenge.
- The hyperD computer is modelled by the Great Pyramid.
- Consciousness energy is represented by the Great Sphinx.

These were also gifts to us all—as indeed was that craft at Roswell.

Three
"By relying solely on three dimensions
the future beings of Planet Earth will come to a seeming dead end.
They will continue to try to figure things out
but their explanations for 'how things are' will get more and more complex
to the point that no one, not even themselves,
will understand those explanations!"

Two-Thirds August 1993

Two
"We will get the equation for everything, and when we do
it will be so complicated that nobody will understand it!"

An American Scientist, Autumn 1996[24]

One
"Certain Ideas have been accepted as true
without sufficiently careful thought."

Dr. Carl Sagan 1970

Go!

Chapter Eleven

THE Triangle

We look further at the origins of the Moon and discuss why none of the theories regarding its origins really address the current state of scientific knowledge. We discuss why an understanding of the role of the Moon in our existence is of major importance to our inter-relationship with everything, including future manned space travel. We present our own hypothesis for the introduction and positioning of the Moon in the solar system. Dr. Donald prescribes a smaller dose of medicine. Finally, NASA breaks the silence barrier.

ASPrin

Sir Isaac Newton

"The Moon is the only thing that has ever given me a headache."

Sir Isaac Newton

High diddle diddle

"Maybe the Moon is the Stonehenge of the solar system, but not the Rosetta Stone. It tells us a great deal, but there are still many mysteries."

These are the words of Dr. Farouk El-Baz, the respected geologist, formerly of NASA and the Smithsonian Institute whom we encountered in "Distant Horizons". We believe he was unwittingly voicing much more than he realised, insofar as Stonehenge is a non-functioning modelling of the principal components of our past and indeed, our future technology—the Spinning Disk. Moreover, as all celestial bodies are also highly sophisticated spinning disks, the Moon is indeed the Stonehenge of the solar system, Dr. El-Baz is quite right.

However, we maintain that the Moon *is equivalent to* the Rosetta stone. By understanding the relationships between the Moon and the Earth, our Sun and the other solar system planets, we can unveil the links between our understanding of physics as we apply them today, and the technology resulting form the new physics that hopefully we are going to be developing in the near-term future.

An awareness of the significance of the Moon has been instilled into human beings since the dawn of time. Its movement, phases and topographic details are inscribed in the legends of every culture.

As early as 150 AD, the size of the Moon and its distance from Earth had been fairly accurately measured. We are all familiar with endless lists of figures, accounting for the size, mass and general characteristics of our satellite planet. Apart from informing us of the Moon's physical properties, could it be that these details have other significances or relationships

The Rosetta Stone

The piece of inscribed stone that we know today as the Rosetta Stone, (named after the site at which it was discovered) weighs three quarters of a ton and measures about 45 inches in length, 11 inches in breadth and 28.5 inches in width.

It was found to be inscribed with three texts:
Egyptian Hieroglyphs occupying the upper third,
an unknown script occupying the middle third,
Greek occupying the lower third.

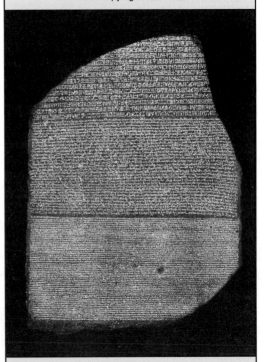

1. The Rosetta Stone.

The unknown script was given the name 'Demotic', its structure demonstrated a kinship with the Egyptian hieroglyphs, but it lacked the cartouches (lines that enclosed groups of hieroglyphs) that were present in the upper third.

> ## Connections
>
> Spinning and weaving are associated with the Moon in many cultures worldwide—among which are the Jewish people, the Ancient Egyptians, the Greeks, the Mexicans and the North American Indians.
>
> Ancient Greece gave us the mythos of Athene and Arachne, wherein Arachne wove a zodiac of thirteen divisions in a competition with Athene.[1]
>
> The American Pawnee Indians call the Moon 'Spiderwoman' to this day.
>
> This mythos can be confusing, especially as many peoples have an unreasoning fear of spiders, yet the Moon does not seem fearful in itself.
>
> However, when we make the connections between the symbology of the spider's web and consciousness, and when we truly understand how important the Moon is and how important are strong networks between those who care (as are the strong networks of web chords for the spider, who is dependent upon them for her source of nourishment and habitat) those realisations will cause a dramatic shift in our thinking and allow us to work more in harmony with each other, as individuals and as nations.[2]

that provide us with additional information when viewed from a philosophical perspective?

Our Moon is smaller than eight of the other planets in our solar system with a diameter of 2,160 statute miles in relation to the Earth's diameter of 7,926 statute miles.

Although the Moon is locked in orbit around us, which technically qualifies it as a satellite of Earth, many astronomers consider it to be rather too large for such a function and consider it to be a planet, orbiting in a binary system.

Distances between planets are always measured from the centre to centre of each celestial body, however the barycentre, or actual centre of gravity of the Earth/Moon system lies off-centre *within* the Earth, approximately 2,918 miles/4,700 kms from the Earth's centre. This particularity produces an effect known as 'off-centre rotation'. Note that in our solar system, although Pluto and its moon Charon are also locked into a barycentric system, their barycentre is *between* the two planets and therefore in

> ## Spinning spirals
>
>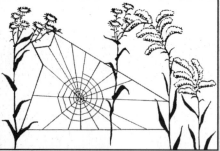
>
> A spider constructs her web by making a framework of threads to define the area in which she is interested, then constructs the radials which all connect at the centre.
>
> After which she spins an anti-clockwise (W-E) spiral of dry thread from the centre outwards.
>
> Upon reaching the outer defining framework that she laid down in step one, the spider retraces her steps, towards the centre spinning a clockwise (E-W) circle using a sticky thread.
>
> During this return trip, the original dry spiral is removed by the spider, sometimes by ingestion. Individual strands of a web are relatively weak but the net formed by all the strands is very, very strong. When spiders were taken up on the Space Shuttle, the first webs spun were completely messy, the radials were disharmonious and the spirals were equally unbalanced. Bur after a few days in space the spiders began spinning perfect webs again. However, a spider that was restrained from spinning a web for the first few days subsequently created a perfect web at its first attempt.

2. Spiders Web Crop Glyph activated at Avebury, Southern England 1994.   S PATTERSON

that instance there is no off-centre rotation.

The proportions displayed by our planet and its satellite are unique in our solar system. The Moon's diameter is 27.27% the size of the Earth. It circles the Earth at an average speed of 22,289 miles per hour in an elliptical orbit and is 'tugged' at by the gravitational fields of both the Earth and the Sun. The Moon re-

volves around the Earth in the same direction as Earth's revolution around the Sun (west-east or anticlockwise) and also spins around its own axis within exactly the same time-frame of 27.3 days. This is called synchronous rotation and it is, as far as we know, unique in this solar system. This synchronous rotation is the reason why we only ever see about 58.9% of the Moon's surface. However, thanks to its elliptical orbit we do get glimpses of up to 17.80% of the far side that occurs at the terminator (the line between lit and unlit portions of the Moon) which leaves 23.3% that remains hidden from an Earthbound observer. For Earth observers, the Moon rises just over 50 minutes later each day.

The Moon bears little compositional resemblance to the majority of meteorites, our inner rocky planets, or the other planetary satellites of our solar system. The Moon has no liquid water and no atmosphere. Erosional processes are limited to meteorite bombardment, constant effects of the solar wind, together with galactic cosmic radiation.

Most of us have a general idea of Earth's location in orbit around the Sun, but there are so many things to address in our everyday life, that unless it is part of our job or profession, we tend not to connect with the greater and

3. The Earth/Moon, with the barycentre located *inside the Earth*.

Moon notes

THE satellite of Earth; a secondary planet, whose light, which is derived from the Sun, is reflected to the Earth—*Oxford English Dictionary* definition.

"Once in a blue Moon"—
this expression was current by the early 16th Century.
A blue Moon is the name given to a second full Moon within a specific period of a month, a rare event which occurs approximately every 48 months.

"You would have us believe that the Moon is made of green cheese."
This expression was common usage by the 16th Century and used in response to a statement generally held to be beyond the bounds of possibility.
The relative newcomer to our solar system (as we will demonstrate later) has been described in terms that we use for young cheese!
Blue and green happen to be the colours that characterise planet Earth when seen from space.
Approximately ⅓rd of our planet is green (land) ⅔rds of our planet is blue (water).

---

more detailed picture. It is rather like living in a very large house and only using a few of the rooms in one wing. And just like a bird that has had the flight feathers of one wing clipped, without a greater in-depth understanding of the true mechanics and nature of our solar system, we too, are 'grounded' on our own home planet.

27.2 cents # THE DAILY FLYER

The Moon and the Numbernauts

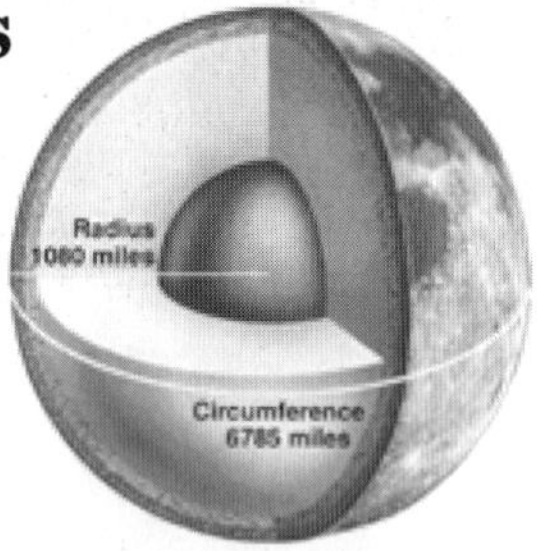

Circumference:	6,785 statute miles
Radius (mean):	1,080 statute miles
Diameter:	2,160 statue miles
Distance from Earth:	
Farthest (apogee):	252,946 statute miles (+14,092)
Mean:	238,854 statute miles
Nearest (perigee):	225,546 statute miles (-18,768)
Variation in distance therefore:	31,054 miles
Surface area:	15 million square miles
Mass ratio:	Mass Earth/Mass Moon = 81.3015
Surface gravity:	⅙th of Earth
Average orbital speed:	2,289 miles per hour west-east (anti-clockwise)
Sidereal period:	27 days, 7 hours, 43 mins
Synodic period:	29 days, 12 hours, 44 mins, 2.9 secs
Mean daily motion of terminator in longitude:	11.49°

Radius 1080 miles

Circumference 6785 miles

"The quantity of matter is a measure of the same, arising from its density and bulk conjointly."

Sir Isaac Newton

The Moon's mean orbital inclination to ecliptic:	05°08'43"
Moon's mean inclination to lunar equator:	06°04'00"
Inclination of Moon's equator to ecliptic orbit:	10°35'00"
Moon's mean eccentricity of orbit:	0.0549 (Earth's: 0.0617)
The Moon's density:	3.34g/cm^3

The Three Rs

We move through space because planet Earth works on the two basic and fundamental principles governing all celestial spheres:

- Rotation
- Revolution

and as our planet has a Moon of the required size, Earth also experiences

- Retrograde precession
  Earth is the only planet in our solar system to function this way.
  That is why we have named these three processes *the Three Rs.* All the other planets in our system work on the first two-thirds of these principles.

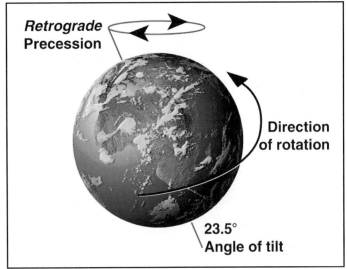

4. Rotation and retrograde precession of planet Earth.

5. The planets with their respective axial tilts.

Rotation

The planets of our solar system are principally spherical celestial bodies. Due to the various magnetic and gravitational influences exerted upon them and their orbital path around the Sun, they have tended to become rather more oblate—slightly squashed at the poles and bulgy around the equator.

As a planet moves through space around the Sun it spins on its axis, this motion is called *rotation*. This axis is an imaginary 'line' drawn vertically through the centre of the planet, and the rotating or spinning of the planet around this axis provides some of the momentum for its journey through space. Mercury is the only planet in our solar system with a virtually vertical axial tilt of about 2°. It is our view that a planet with the potential to bring forth life requires an axis at such an angle to its Sun in order that all its surfaces will benefit from the Sun's rays by varying degrees throughout the solar year. This situation gives rise to a cycle of seasons. Earth has an axial tilt of approximately 23° 45′. When our north pole is slanting towards the Sun the northern hemisphere has its summer and the southern hemisphere experiences its winter.

> ### Two-Thirds again!
> ⅔ rds of the planets in our solar system rotate from west to east,
> whilst
> ⅓ rd of the planets have a *retrograde* rotation, east to west.

Equinox

These are two instants at which the Sun in its apparent annual motion (from an earthbound viewpoint) crosses the celestial equator: from south to north at the vernal (spring) equinox, then crosses again from north to south at the autumnal equinox.

Autumn was not acknowledged as a 'season' in very ancient times. Thus the seasons were a triad of spring, summer and winter, with the fourth aspect autumn acting as a bridge between the culmination of life inherent in summer and harvest, and the regeneration inherent in winter and dormancy, prior to the rebirth of life in the spring.

Epona

In our solar system, the two luminaries the Sun and the Moon spin from west to east as do Mercury, Mars, Earth, Jupiter Saturn and Neptune. The other three, Venus, Uranus and Pluto rotate in the opposite direction—from east to west. This is *retrograde* rotation.

Our Sun is *rotating* in about 28.5 'Earth' days and taking about 221,546 years to make one *revolution* around our galaxy, the Milky Way. And naturally it takes our planet and the rest of our solar system with it.

Earth has a rotational period of 23 hours 56 minutes, which is of course, the basis of our day and night system of 24 hours.

This 23 hours 56 minutes period is called the sidereal day and it is calculated against the fixed stars; the 24 hour period is called the synodic day and is calculated against the Sun. Affected by various phenomena including earthquakes, as well as external influences such as the Moon, this rotation of ours does not proceed at a uniform speed, but increases or decreases, though by very small amounts at irregular intervals of time. These variations of speed can only be determined by observation *after* the event. Measured at the Equator, planet Earth is rotating at a speed of about 1,080 miles per hour. Recognise that figure? *It is also the radius of the Moon.*

Pluto in the doghouse

Since the early 1990s Pluto has been 'redesigned'. The *Scientific American* of May 1998 informs us that "some scientists call Pluto the largest object in the Kuiper Belt." (The Kuiper belt is populated by bodies considered to be too small for planetary status plus comets that approach the Sun every 200 hundred years or so.)

This claim is very interesting, as these academics are totally ignoring Pluto's very distinctive orbital motion and its binary system with its moon Charon, and are perhaps planting an idea for future use, as they recognise that many scientists still consider Pluto to be a planet. We suspect that the re-allocation of Pluto's status has much more to do with future 'Invasion Earth' scenario's than anything else.

More from the *Scientific American:* "Most astronomers still consider Pluto to be a planet. Although its mass is only 1/400th that of Earth, it is still easily the largest object in the Kuiper Belt. Also, Pluto seems to be more reflective than the other bodies in the Kuiper Belt."

Tradition may also have something to do with it, Pluto has been regarded as a planet since Clyde Tombaugh (who also claimed to have seen UFOs on two occasions) first discovered it in 1930. Astronomers everywhere will no doubt be pleased to know that instead of taking the criteria of daily motion into account, *reflectivity* is now the criterion for the designation of a celestial body as a planet.

QUESTION: How many other objects in the Kuiper Belt display daily motion to the same degree as Pluto, possess a moon *and* relate to that moon as a binary system?[3]

There is, as yet, no good reason to change the planetary status of Pluto. Especially not from the evidence presented in the *Scientific American* of May 1998.

Revolution! current

The time that it takes for a planet to complete one circuit around the Sun is called the period of *revolution* and varies according to the planet's size and its distance from the Sun. For example, taking an Earth day as the unit of comparison: Earth currently has a revolution period of some 365⅓rd days. Mars has a present revolution period of about 687 days.

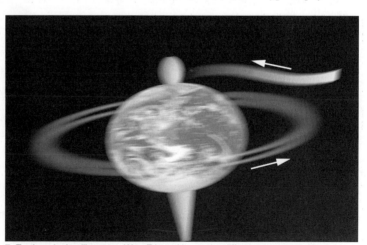

6. Earth/Mars orbits (not to scale).

Retrograde Precession

As they rotate about their axis, certain planets (and Earth is one of them) oscillate like an old-fashioned spinning top—but here on Earth this wobble is in the *opposite direction* to the rotation.

This spinning movement is so slight that it takes just over 25,920 years for the oscillation to complete a 360 degree circle. Nevertheless, this effect is also extremely potent, spinning in a wave-like motion rather than being perfectly smooth.

These waves stream out in the opposite direction to that of the axial rotation which is why it is described as *retrograde*. And scientists call it *precession* (that which precedes) because it causes the equinox to occur about 50 seconds of arc *earlier* each successive siderial year. Because this oscillation interfaces with the rotation, this will eventually result in the fact that our northernmost star will change over time. Currently the axis is inclined towards Polaris and we call this star the Pole Star. However, these processes are not quite as three dimensional as would seem to be the case, and one reason why the retrograde precession of our planet is so little understood is due, in our opinion, to the prevailing lack of awareness of hyperD physics.

7. Earth, spinning like at top W to E but with a major difference—*retrograde precession*—the precessional wobble represented by the ribbon flaring E to W.

Two-thirds dancing

If one thinks of Rotation, Revolution and Retrograde precession as being three dancers, then these three dancers are holding hands—with Retrograde precession standing between Rotation and Revolution. The dance consists of Rotation and Revolution gyrating around Retrograde precession (who while seemingly doing nothing is actually the strongest of the whole team). Therefore:

- Rotation and Revolution are physical 3D processes. The resulting interface of these two processes produces a 4D effect which manifests in Retrograde precession.
- The *only* way that this Retrograde precession is produced is by Rotation and Revolution, dancing to a specific tune at a specific tempo.

8. Onwards and upwards: The egg in this visual metaphor represents the Earth and the snake represents the spiralling motion of the planet's *retrograde* precessional journey.

- The only way that these three dancers can perform their dance is by virtue of their dance band (the solar system) providing the precise configuration to produce the right dance tune and tempo.
- The leader of the band that produces the correct dance tune and tempo is a Moon of the appropriate mass and gravity orbiting around its planet at the precise distance that will provide the right rate of Rotation and Revolution and induce the Retrograde precessional period of 25,920 years.
- The retrograde motion of the Earth's precession is analogous to the revolution of a gyroscope, weighted at one end and balanced in the middle. The circuit described by the Retrograde precession wobble, relative to the angles of the planet's axial tilt and ecliptic, is around 47° of arc.
- While every part of the solar system is interdependent and contributes to the whole, in this analogy, the Moon is really the beginning and ending, for in order for a planet to bring forth life, the circumstances need to be exactly right. Without our Moon Earth, we claim, would not have produced life, in turn leading to self-aware life—us.

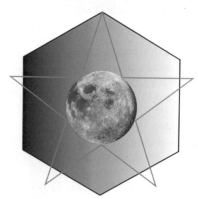

Travelling man

So, to recap, we are living on a space vehicle, revolving around its Sun from west to east at nearly 67,000 mph and rotating from west to east on its axis at around 1,080 mph as it does so. This rotation results in an off-centre, wave-like motion which 'travels' in the opposite direction from east to west. This retrograde

434

MGD

MASS is the quantity of matter that something contains—everything has mass, including people. The *amount of mass is in proportion to the gravitational field* in which the object finds itself.

GRAVITY, the more mass a planet or a body has, the stronger the gravitational pull. Gravitational attraction weakens with distance. Within a solar system solar energy in the form of solar winds combine both gravity and magnetic fields as well as the individual gravitational pulls of the planets.

DENSITY is the way that the mass of an object is *packed*. The more density the tighter packed the contents.

QED

---

precessional movement is so nearly imperceptible that it takes 72 years to affect the rotation to one degree and 25,920 years to affect it through to 360°. The Universe loves waves—they are the carriers of all material matter.

The principles of the relationship between a moon and its planet are not only of measurement (representations of both distance and time) but also of the resulting harmonics generated by the precise placement and movement of these celestial bodies. The diameter, mass and orbital inclination of our Moon is of vital importance in producing the specific retrograde precession of 25,920 years. We propose that this is the only length of time that contains within it the elements necessary to create the *tension* necessary for the bringing forth of life, emerging to self-aware life.

Without the necessary components of an orbiting satellite of the correct size operating together with its primary planet as a system, we believe life beyond blue-green algae would never have evolved on our own planet. This claim is not acknowledged by orthodoxy.

Park End

The original primitive atmosphere of the Earth has changed from the volcanic outgassing of its beginnings (which would have been mainly composed of carbon dioxide, sulphur dioxide and some nitrogen) through to the atmosphere that we have around us today. The insertion of the Moon (see later in this chapter) altering the revolution and rotation of this planet, facilitated the creation of the atmosphere as it is now and enabled the trace elements of other gases such as helium, argon, neon and krypton to be held by the Earth's increasing magnetic field. This atmospheric cycle has evolved over time and was created by the geophysical and resulting harmonics characteristic of the planet.

This new atmosphere gave rise to differing forms of life that adapted to the prevailing circumstances. These, in turn, *contributed* to the atmosphere via their biological life support systems, together with their behavioural patterns dictated by the level of their mental evolution—and so the cycle continues and evolves.

Despite attempts by the scientific community to ignore this phenomenon, the processes of mental evolution and physical evolution go hand in hand in much the same way that a fully-evolved self-aware being needs to be both a linear and a creative thinker (symbolised by the left and right sides of the brain). The Western world's educational system desperately attempts to keep these two processes in separate boxes, but that compartmentalisation can only result in a long term developmental cul-de-sac.

All systems interact in accordance with universal laws and with the advent of the blue-green algae on this planet the process of photosynthesis began (that is, the use of sunlight to produce energy for growth and survival). This booster then gave rise to a proliferation of plant life and then animal life. Current studies of the environment show that an atmosphere is significantly affected by the physicality of the life forms that live within it. Today, due to inappropriate, industrial, military and agricultural activities we are continually altering our atmosphere, as environmentalists are at pains to inform us. We are of course also altering the physiology of our planet and potentially endangering all life, including our own.

An alternative meaning for the often misused word 'karma' lies within the concept that en-

---

Jack in the box

Priscoan Period

5.0 bn-4.5 bn years BP (before present): birth of the solar system.

4.5bn-3.9bn BP: oldest terrestrial rocks dated, found in Canada and Greenland. Oldest minerals found in Australia.

The atmosphere devoid of oxygen.

Archaean Period

3.5bn-1.6bn BP: oldest prokaryotic microfossils. These are detected as bands of rock which have been formed from primitive ocean bacteria. Towards 1.6bn BP eukaryotes (cells containing compartmentalised genetic material) appear.

The atmosphere towards 2bn BP contains 4% carbon dioxide and 1% nitrogen.

Proterozoic Period

1.5bn BP: first blue-green algae appear.

1.3bn BP: oldest multicelluar fossils found.

1.0 bn-950 million years BP: oldest *signs* of worm-like animals (their burrows) are found. The atmosphere at this period contained 21% oxygen, 78% nitrogen and 0.036% carbon dioxide.

750 million BP: large soft-bodied animals such as jellyfish. Oldest animal fossils.

Phanerozoic Period

572 million BP: insertion of Moon into solar system—the HIP hypothesis. (see later in this chapter)

432 million BP: the greening of the planet begins. Oldest plant fossils.

200 million BP: dinosaurs evolved.

065 million BP: dinosaurs devolved, having disappeared by this date.

---

ergy has both a physical and a conscious dimension. As thought precedes action so are all our actions weighted with a portion of the consciousness that created them and this is 'imprinted' within the physicality of the arena in which those actions occur.

More gain

As can be seen from the arguments concerning the validity of the ozone layer threat, there are some who will not only manipulate the facts in order to accumulate material benefits but also manufacture latent *fear* by threatening us all with the consequences of the greenhouse effect, as manifest on Venus. Naturally, through not completely understanding the principles of the

---

Land truths

Before 572 million years ago

About 9/10ths of this planet was covered in water. Now 2/3rds of the planet is covered in water and 1/3rd makes up the land surfaces.

Of the energy transconverted by the planet, 2/3rds is retained by these landmasses and 1/3rd is recycled by the oceans.

sea changes

---

transD physics by which Venus functions, there are also some who are genuinely concerned about the ozone layer problem.[4] In practice, we maintain that the planet Venus is behaving as she has been designed to do by the geometric relationships between Earth and the Moon and herself. Venus is not *suffering* from her greenhouse effect due to planetary warming but is acting as the 'glass roof' *of our own house* by absorbing the energy excesses from this planet thus enabling Earth to come into balance—an essential contribution to the support of all life forms that exist upon it.

Until now, our scientists cannot have been expected to understand the real reason for the behaviour of Venus. Although anything that brings anyone into greater awareness of our symbiotic relationship with Earth is a good thing—there is no need to operate from a basis of fear and destruction. Calculated pollution on a global scale (such as the destruction of our rain forests) is driven by the desire to benefit the few at the expense of the many. But much of our pollution is mental pollution which is in as urgent need of cleansing as the oil-laden lakes in parts of Russia or our own coast lines after a tanker spill.

436

Out of mind

Most of us are aware of the effects that one person in a bad mood can have on a group of friends. The majority try to cajole the individual into being happier in order that the atmosphere becomes more harmonious.

Natives who 'worshipped' the elements were manifesting the same principle.

out of balance

Having for the most part lost touch with the principles of creation,

some of our scientists are poking and prodding at our protective shell,

through the intermediary of their experiments around our north and south poles, HAARP and via the military aspects

of the space program

—about which matters we are told hardly anything.

Studying the Shuttle flight lists makes interesting reading,

as one of our close to NASA Whistle-Blowers told us,

"You can tell when something of a military nature is going on, by the number of 'bigwigs' that are on the flight list

and by the relative non-communication as to the purpose of the flight".

out of sight!

We maintain that essential components of *our* atmosphere are the very components that, over time, would have become too rarefied for the metabolism of the dinosaurs. However, *we* adjust or diddle with our atmosphere at great peril to ourselves. None of us has yet a good enough understanding of the basic principles involved in celestial mechanics. Until those who should know have grasped the importance of *all* the ramifications of the three Rs and the functioning of the Moon/Earth/Venus relationship, no-one is in any position to play with our house.

A scientific speculation

Before we elaborate on just how *we* think this placement of our Moon came about, please open your mind and let us invite you to contemplate an idea, which was published in the respectable British *Astronomy Now* magazine. This serious theory was proposed by Lorne Whitehead, Professor of Physics at the University of Columbia in Vancouver, Canada.[5]

Professor Whitehead has considered the problems that our descendants will have in escaping from the increased heat of the Sun in around 1,500 million years time (6.1 billion years from the origin of our solar system). And he has worked out a solution.

"The most practical idea will be to move the Earth", Professor Whitehead suggests. Briefly, his rescue plan involves the *intelligent ma-noeuvring of the Moon* into an ever-widening orbit around the Sun, to be performed by our descendants. He reasons that due to the Earth/Moon gravitational 'lock', Earth should go along for the ride. Professor Whitehead envisages that this Earth/Moon combo would eventually break free of the Sun's influence altogether.

Moreover, we are told that as the Moon has the same apparent size in our sky as the Sun, we could increase the reflectivity of the Moon and make it shine as brilliantly as the Sun did in the 1990s. Whitehead goes on to address the problem of extreme cold in the interstellar space that we would be occupying in this future scenario. For all this he proposes that our descendants place on the Moon a trillion high-pressure argon arc lamps to simulate this sunlight. Finally, Professor Whitehead calculates all this on the assumption that our descendants will be using rocket power to move the Moon.

Taking this scenario at face value several comments arise:

- To escape the influence of the Sun surely means leaving the solar system!
- If we have not evolved beyond 'lighting the blue touch paper' technology at the time he describes, by then we shall be beyond hope as a civilisation!
- As the Sun increases its heat, conditions will surely get warmer further out into the solar system?

437

- Why bother with arc lights at all? All that would be necessary to increase the current average 7% reflectivity of the Moon would be to cover surfaces that are at present relatively dark in colour with a white material, such as chalk.

- A solar system functions as a complete unit and each planet contributes to the benefit of the whole system. Each planet therefore is required to be where it actually is, in order to fulfil its function within the system.

- If we were to move the Earth/Moon combo, then the rest of the solar system will need to be adjusted to compensate for such a move.

- Argon is not the only component of sunlight and living things require the full spectrum, *all* the ingredients of sunlight, not just one. If this were not so, sunlight would be composed uniquely of argon.

moon of the appropriate size or composition working with any of these inner planets. A Moon was introduced into orbit around the third planet from the Sun—Earth *by design*.[6]

In order to realise the positioning of the Moon into its orbit around Earth, adjustments had to made to the entire solar system and more specifically to the inner planets, none of which possessed any moons, either. These adjustments could be the basis of much of our species' memories which have subsequently been interwoven into our mythology.

In geological terms, we contend that this event occurred about 572 million years ago and that the Moon was *placed* into a stable *circular* orbit at a distance of 221,546 miles around the Earth. At that time our own planet's surface was mostly covered with vast expanses of ocean. Primitive life was in existence in these oceans. Shortly (in cosmic terms) after the

---

The revolution of Mars

The position of Mars in relation to Earth actually assists Earth's orbital revolution around the Sun. Revolutions can be war-like. If Mars is responsible for creating either 3D or 4D tension required for our orbital mechanics then this might well have given rise to the naming of Mars as the 'war-like' planet. Warriors *FACE* up to each other—behind their shields. Then again, without recommending it as a way of life, but understanding it as a process of refinement through which as a species we have travelled and now finished with— war produces a tension and a sense of urgency that tends to bring forth the creation of ideas and technologies that we otherwise might not realise for centuries.

The exact placement of Mars in relation to Earth is somewhat like a drive belt—
too slack and the engine won't work at the right rate,
too tight it snaps and the engine won't run!

Hip Hip Hur-Ra

In "Distant Horizons" we looked at the *current* theories concerning the origin of the Moon—none of which can satisfactorily provide answers for the 'problem' discoveries. Here we offer our own hypothesis, which attempts to *address* these problems, rather than ignore them. We have named this the *Hypothesis of Intelligent Placement* (HIP).

Firstly, we contend that our solar system, born nearly 5 billion years ago, originally contained four inner planets and four outer planets, revolving around its relatively young Sun. However, life forms *beyond* blue-green algae would never have emerged spontaneously on any of the inner rocky planets as there was no

event just described, there was a literal explosion of life, first in the great oceans and then later, on the *emerging* land masses.

Science fiction? The mathematics and physical clues set out in this solar system say not. Interestingly, our world mythology and legends appear to lead us to the same conclusions.

So if what we are claiming *could* be science fact then why should the placing of a Moon have been necessary? Do we really need a dead planet encircling us?

Lets start by imagining the unimaginable.

The astronaut's who said: "If the Moon just makes the tides, we could probably manage without it," was wrong. We could not manage without it. We would not be here without it!

438

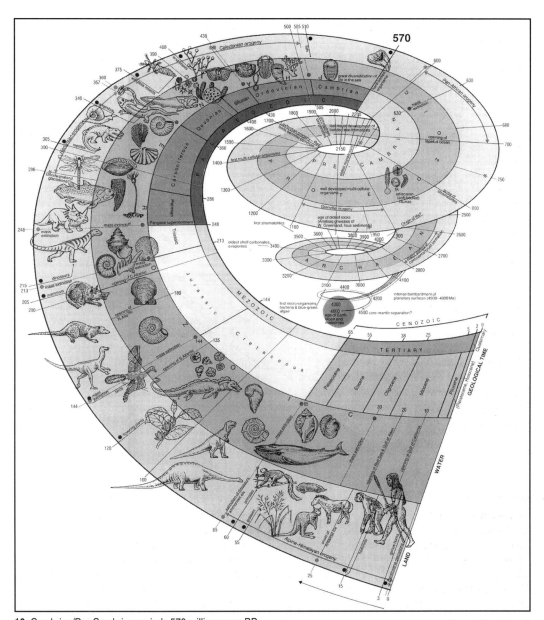

10. Cambrian/Pre-Cambrian periods 570 million years BP.

HarperCollins *Cartographic*

The cat and the fiddle

We fully realise that to ask you to accept that our Moon could be the result of intelligent placement, is to once more "imagine the unimaginable", but we would ask you please to try to do just that! Our Moon scenario really does not require any more indulgence on your part than does Professor Whitehead's. In fact it is *the same scenario*, in reverse.

About 572 million years ago, intelligent beings from life's distant past—deploying Spinning Disk technology—placed a planet that was to become our Moon in exactly the right

439

orbit around Earth in order that life could also evolve here. The ultimate intention being the establishment of the appropriate environment so that a linear and creative thinking self-aware being would eventually emerge. Before that event could take place, adjustments had to be made to other components of our solar system, the latter being 'tweaked' in order that the mass of the Moon could be inserted whilst maintaining the system's overall balance. We are of the opinion that Mars was also reconfigured to its present size of 4,223 miles (average) equatorial diameter and somewhat redesigned for both for physical and philosophical reasons.

Before being brought into this solar system:

- Our Moon's diameter was reconfigured to 2,160 miles.
- The mass of the Moon was redistributed.

And once in position within the system:

- The surface was cosmetically dressed with material of vastly differing ages—by *billions* of years.
- The orbital inclination of the Moon was fixed.
- This orbital inclination resulted in the alteration of the *Earth's* rotational speed.
- The Moon's period of *revolution* was synchronised with its axial *rotation* in order that only one hemisphere would ever face Earth.[7]

We maintain that our planet was previously spinning at a slower speed than the 23 hours 56 minutes (per sidereal day) that is necessary for evolution to occur. We suggest that this planet was rotating at about 24 hours 37 minutes, as Mars does now.

We are fully aware that this view goes against current scientific thinking, which considers that

Earth was spinning very fast at one time. (It is our contention that it is technically possible to *increase* a planet's rotation but it may not be possible to slow a planet down.)

No matter what the planet's diameter, it is absolutely vital that the axial rotation be adjusted to 23 hours 56 minutes, as this adjustment results in the generation of the required *magnetic field* capable of supporting the appropriate atmosphere. Further, such a rate of rotation facilitates the 'gating' of the necessary planetary energy—which is *hyperdimensional* (hyperD) i.e. beyond length, width and breadth, beyond three dimensions. We suggest that in any solar system into which a moon is inserted, it is necessary to maintain its orbit in an (artificial) circular path until the emergence of self-aware linear-thinking beings—whereas the moons of 'seed planets' (planets that *naturally* have a moon of the correct size and position) are in virtually unchanging circular orbits. That is because the latter are already in place as a result of the physics of the Universe. We also contend that *only* solar systems containing a natural 'seed planet' system would have planets in circular orbits. The planetary orbits in all other solar systems would be elliptical, whether they contained planets colonised by self-aware life or not.

We have concluded that *any* period of rotation *other* than 23 hours 56 minutes will result in the slow physical decline and eventual death of the self-aware beings living upon the planet. This observation applies to *all locations* be they spacecraft, deep space stations, or planets colonised either temporarily, or permanently.

So near and yet so far

The side of the Moon visible from Earth is very different to the far side. For example, the far side of the Moon has *fewer* maria ('seas') than the near side.

The imbalance between the farside and the nearside in terms of crustal thickness is part of the demonstration that our Moon was artificially dressed. No doubt it was hoped, when our technology had sufficiently matured, that we would investigate our satellite, and be advanced enough in consciousness to be aware of

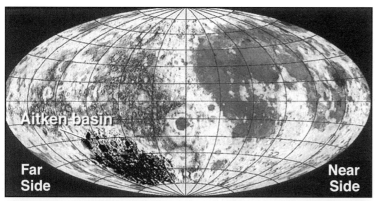

11. The Moon—emphasising farside/nearside hemispherical topographical differences.

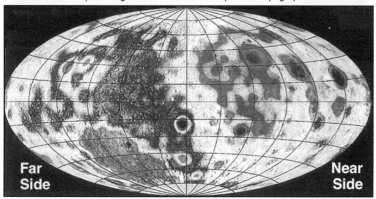

12. The Moon—emphasising farside/nearside hemispherical crustal thickness differences.

Clementine data JOHN HOPKINS UNIVERSITY

but also about our essential information concerning the nature of the Cosmos and more specifically our own connection to the Universe. A society that develops one-sidedly, will surely be disadvantaged. We suggest that NASA and others have indeed registered these anomalies, they just are not prepared to admit to that fact.

Suppressing these findings could ultimately bring about a reappraisal of NASA's role.

The official position upheld by sources including Encyclopaedia Britannica as in the box below could be described as somewhat contrived, particularly if the Moon is older than the Earth! Rather, these findings could also indicate *intelligent dressing of the Moon's crust.*

our surroundings and spot the *obvious artificiality of the situation on the lunar surface.* Realising the seemingly impossible differences between the two hemispheres we would start asking questions—not only about the Moon

With regard to impacts, any object from deep space on a collision course with the Moon is more likely to strike the Moon's far side rather than the 'protected' near side. Furthermore, any

---

Lots of data

During the early period in the solar system's history, there were many more small asteroid-sized chunks of rock than there are today.

Some of these objects when colliding with the side of the Moon *facing the Earth*, ruptured through the crust, allowing molten material from below to fill the resultant craters and surrounding low-lying areas.

It is accepted thinking

that the reason that maria are lacking on the far side of the Moon is because the outer and lighter weight molten surface material of the young Moon tended to flow outward from the Earth side to the far side, as the Moon swung around the Earth in its tidally-locked position.

The crust became thick enough there to sufficiently reduce the chance of crustal rupture by a colliding asteroid.

Encyclopaedia Britannica

apparently little knowledge

such object en route to collide with the Earth/Moon system is even more likely to be drawn towards the Earth, rather than the Moon, due to the former's greater gravitational pull, which is yet another reason why fewer craters should be present than there actually are on the Moon's near side.

Isolated isotopes

Whenever small amounts of information escape the invisible security net, ordinary citizens inevitably start to ask probing questions—not so for the establishment!

Consider the following:

- There are *certain* isotopes (the number of protons and neutrons in the nucleus of each atom) on the Moon that apparently have *not* occurred as a result of radiation from the Sun of this solar system.[8] These isotopes are a result of aeons of nuclear fusion. At an age of around 4.6 billion years, our Sun is too *young* to have produced such isotopes—and will not be able to do so until far into the future. This situation clearly implies that the material on the surface of the Moon, indeed even the Moon itself, may have come from a much older solar system or galaxy than ours. Nothing has been publicly discussed on this particular matter by NASA and its counterparts.

- Do these findings suggest that these isotopes could only exist if the lunar surface had been exposed to an star *of greater age than our Sun?*
- Do such findings infer that the Moon itself originally did not belong to this solar system?
- Has this isotopic 'problem', combined with the disparity of soil and rock sampling, tempted our scientists into constructing their GIT theory (Giant Impact Theory)?
- Do NASA and the scientific disciplines involved lack the courage to discuss intelligent placement as a possibility?

The Moon, due to many factors (including its composition), appears to be an all-encompassing geology lesson, providing unique data (not available on Earth) about our relationship to our galaxy, transD physics and our origins. Such oddities of geological information combined with the precision of the Moon's placement, indicate to us that those who find the implications hard to accept are determined to bury any evidence, and create new scenarios. The fact that these unworkable scenarios are as full of holes as a fisherman's net, is preferable (in their eyes) to this extraordinary conclusion:

Our Moon has been intentionally and lovingly placed within our solar system.

Box of tricks

The greatest variations in height are to be found on the farside of the Moon. There, the highest land is in the mountains north of the Korolëv basin, while the lowest is in the South Pole Aitken basin,

with an average depth of 7.5 miles/12 kms.

In contrast, the floors of the mare are extremely level with a slope of 1-in-1000.

The average crustal thickness on the farside is about 42 miles/68 kms compared with 37 miles/60 kms on the nearside—figures which are at variance with NASA's data.

And the Moon's *centre of mass* is offset on the Earth side by 1.04 miles/1.68 kms.

Astronomy Now March 1995

QUESTIONS:

- Why has so little mention been made of the age of these isotopes?
- Is it because that circumstance seriously upsets current theory concerning the overall age of the solar system?

Eventually the self-aware beings of this planet would become advanced enough to start exploring space. Unfortunately it is now evident that although we have become capable of sending probes to the Moon (albeit using limited and near-obsolete technology) the organisations linked to such exploration are apparently intellectually incapable of responding posi-

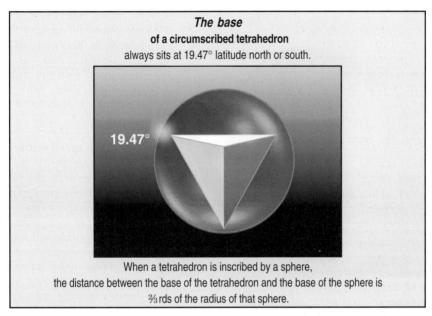

The base
of a circumscribed tetrahedron
always sits at 19.47° latitude north or south.

19.47°

When a tetrahedron is inscribed by a sphere,
the distance between the base of the tetrahedron and the base of the sphere is
⅔ rds of the radius of that sphere.

tively to the evidence set before their eyes. This incapacity has seemingly led them to write their own sets of accounts and promote their own version of events, a version that is literally light years away from the truth.

Upwellings

With most planets, by virtue of their rotating, there is always a 3D, *physical* upwelling of energy that invariably occurs at between 19° and 22° latitude in the northern or southern hemisphere of the planet. This latitude coincides with the base level of an imaginary tetrahedron placed inside the planet. The 'top point' of this pyramid would always be at the pole of the planet, either north or south. The region around the three 'base points' are always situated at 19.47° either north or south of the planet's equator. For Earth, imagine a clear sphere with this tetrahedron upside down inside it. The 'top point' is therefore at the south pole and the three 'base points' occur at the northern 19.47° latitude and are 120° equidistant.

These upwellings on the various planetary bodies are a result of the planet's size, composition and spin rate which together create enormous amounts of angular momentum. A spinning body with a liquid core causes vortices to form in that liquid, which then try to rise to the surface. These vortices quickly coalesce into one single vortex which organises itself at this northerly or southerly location between 19° and 22°.

This phenomenon has been clearly established by research into vorticular fluid flow.

- Spinning celestial bodies generate energy.
- A spinning tetrahedron models the way that the hyperD and the resulting 3D physics devolve from these processes.
- A planet's physical upwelling invariably occurs in the hemisphere which receives the inflow of the magnetic field.
- The apex of the imaginary tetrahedron always occurs at the point of *outflow* of the magnetic field.
- The 'base' of this tetrahedral pyramid invariably occurs at *19.47°* and is the site of the 3D manifestation of the physical upwellings.
- Single and interlocked spinning tetrahedra are the basis of both transD and hyperD physics.
- The physical manifestations of this geometric model drive the physical Universe.

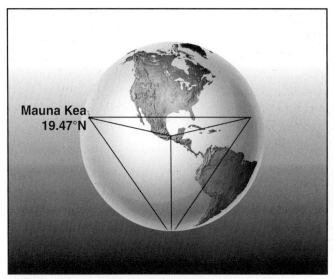

14. Earth with its prime physical upwelling point located on Hawaii.

the arrival date (1947) of the probe near Roswell, marking the second permanent insertion of an extra-galactic object into our solar system, and as with our dead satellite the Moon, there was no actual living thing associated with this gift.

The right environment

A self-aware being requires the necessary environment in which to thrive and that means more than having the right amount of water, food and air to breathe. The hyperD energy that self-aware beings specifically require exits via the *pole point* of the imaginary tetra-hedron in the rotating planet. On Earth, where the energy upwelling is in the north, then the hyper D energy out-flow is from the south polar circle. It then circulates over the surface area of the planet and re-enters via the north polar circle—the planet's magnetic field keeping the flow near the surface. *Two-thirds* of this energy is retained by the planet, *one-third* escapes out into space.

Does the reason that the Roswell Incident occurred in *1947* begin to make even more sense? Coupled with the fact that this event was precisely in the *middle* of 19 (point) 47!

19.47° and our planets

There are energy upwellings located between 19° and 22° at *Olympus Mons* on Mars; at the *Great Red Spot* on Jupiter and at the *Great Dark Spot* on Neptune. On planet Earth, the energy upwelling at is found at the Hawaiian caldera and geologists call it a prime 'hot spot'.

The Hawaiian islands were created by volcanic action and these produced the most powerful volcanoes on Earth. They also contain within their group the largest shield volcano on the planet, the now extinct Mauna Kea, situated on north central Hawaii main island at 19.5° latitude. Mauna Kea rises 13,796 feet/4,205 metres above sea level and descends to the ocean floor for another 18,200 feet. Totalling 31,996 feet/9,752 metres, this is also the highest individual mountain on the planet.

On Earth the upwelling at Mauna Kea has an encoded relationship with

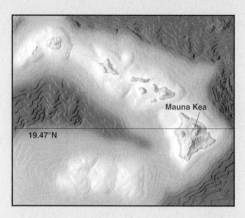

19.47
Site of the 19.47°N upwelling in the Hawaiian chain of volcanoes.

Mauna Kea rises to a total of 31,966 ft from the *ocean floor*.
Darker = deeper sea levels.

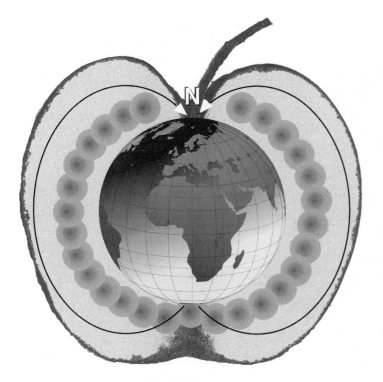

16. The hyperD energy flow (from the pole point of the imaginary tetrahedron—the South Pole) over the planet's surface re-entering at the North Pole with the planet's magnetic field.

The cow jumped over the Moon

Returning to our HIP hypothesis, when the 'implantation' of the Moon into our solar system increased Earth's speed of rotation to 23 hours 56 minutes and altered its angular mo-

mentum, the orbital position of the Moon, in relation to Earth, together with the speed of rotation, affected the Earth's magnetic field. The effects of bringing the Moon into our back-yard therefore caused the build-up of a vast amount of energy. Without drawing off this new excessive energy, Earth would have suffered from such volcanic activity that the planet would have become too hot for comfort and cer-tainly unsuitable for the emergence of any form of life—ever.

An inner planet of an equivalent size was needed as a 'heatsink' to draw off this extra energy. In our solar system, Venus would become the channel or 'heatsink' for the extra energy gener-ated by the Earth/Moon off-centre rotation. Much of the excessive energy would be ab-sorbed by Venus virtually instantaneously (hy-perdimensionally) via the Moon. As a result Venus would act as a fire bucket, and be trans-formed from a watery world—perhaps very similar to Earth at that time—into a fiery planet of vulcanism that could never harbour life. In other words, in such a situation the second planet from its star (or sun) acts as a *giant attractor* of this excessive energy from the third planet/moon unit.

In a solar system capable of bringing forth life *naturally,* we maintain that the second planet from its star would be intimately con-nected with both its *seed planet* (the third planet from its star) and *the natural moon* of that third planet. The required combination of such planets and a moon may be a very rare

445

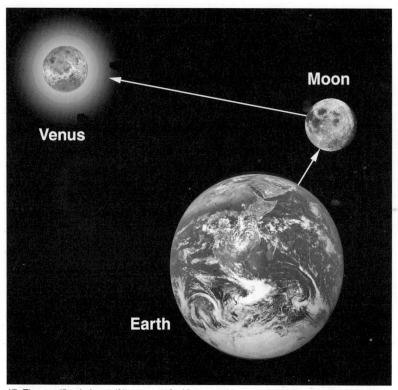

17. The sacrificed planet, if it were not for Venus acting as a 'heatsink' for the Earth/Moon system, it would not have been possible for life to have emerged on planet Earth.

creatures adapted to swamp-like conditions. As we now know, it is not like either of these, but Venus is still somewhat of a mystery to conventional scientists—in spite of the results from over twenty space probes: Mariner, Pioneer Venus from the USA; the Soviet Venera probes; and then again from the American Vega, Magellan and Galileo space probes —all of which have returned vast amounts of hard data.

However, our scientists are still puzzled as to why this planet *behaves* as it does. And they *do not understand* the mechanisms that maintain this planet's climate.

event and by no means necessarily occur in every solar system or even every galaxy. However, in the case of a solar system so equipped, the orbiting moon of a specific ratio creates the *stresses* and *tension* on the seed planet that both provides the environment for life to evolve and, at the same time, inaugurates plate tectonic movement on that planet.

The sacrificed planet

Named after the Roman goddess of love and beauty, springtime and flowers, Venus has an equatorial diameter of 7,521 miles. Due to her orbital position Venus is brighter than any other celestial body, apart for the Sun and the Moon. And like the Moon, Venus has *gibbous* and *crescent* phases. *Transits* across the Sun's disk are rare, the next occurring in 2004.

Early scientific thought considered that Venus was very like the Earth. Science fiction writers populated this planet with primitive

It is clear that Venus has changed from a sphere which resembled our Earth in its early days, to a living example of 'hell's kitchen'. On the surface of the planet the temperature at 860°F/460°C, is far higher than on any other planet in our solar system. The increase in the Sun's radiated heat from our third position to a second position planet is about 122°F/50°C, so the planet's location alone does not explain this excessive temperature. We suggest that the retrograde rotation of Venus' axis is the result of locking with the Moon and Earth's orbits. The atmosphere around Venus rotates in the same direction as the planet itself but sixty times faster than the planet. The resulting winds moderating to around six mph at the planet's surface. We maintain that by acting as a heatsink, Venus sacrificed her own ability to harbour life, out of what could be described as a kindness towards the future beings of Earth.

Venus

Falling towards Venus, a probe would experience sulphuric acid clouds then solid particles which break down into water, oxygen, sulphur dioxide and other sulphur compounds.

Thunder and lightning would be frequent events.

Then the probe would suffer heavy atmospheric pressure before landing on a rocky and sandy surface.

This pressure of 91 times that of Earth's, plus temperatures hot enough to melt lead, would rapidly destroy the probe—two hours has been the staying power of our toughest probe before succumbing to a surface pressure equivalent to being 3,274 feet under our ocean.

Venus has a rocky mantle and crust with a nickel iron core. Its density is slightly less than Earth's. Its atmosphere consists of carbon dioxide, 3% nitrogen very little oxygen, if any. Its mass is ⅘ths of the Earth's. Venus has no oblateness and no magnetic field of its own, although a magnetic field is found in the ionosphere. (This is thought to be due to the solar wind.) There is a huge hollow in the clouds over the north pole of Venus, which is currently estimated to be around 621 miles wide.

The winds on Venus vary with altitude, moving from around 32 mph at the surface to 224 mph at the top of the clouds which form three distinct layers.

Venus is the second planet from the Sun and the second fastest orbital planet in our solar system, moving in its nearly circular revolution at an average orbital speed of 21.75 miles per second! However, its very slow retrograde rotation about its axis means very long periods between sunrises—the equivalent of 116.8 'Earth days'.

Venus has a minimal magnetic field, as in our view, without a 23 hours 56 minutes rotation, no significant magnetic field can be generated by any planet.

Pancake day

Imaged very briefly in 1975 by Soviet space probes Venera 9 and 10, before they were crushed by the intense pressure of the venusian atmosphere, the landscape turned out to be a stony desert. Radar mapping by Soviet Veneras 15, 16 and the American Pioneer, 'Venus' defined this landscape as comprising a *basalt* or *granite* composition. The Magellan probe mapped virtually 100% of the planet and Venus was estimated to comprise 65% rolling plains, 27% depressions and 8% highlands. These highlands were concentrated into two areas called Ishtar and Aphrodite Terra.

It is possible to tell the length of time that this planet has been subjected to this change from an Earth-like environment into a 'hell's kitchen' by examining the impact craters. The *shield* volcanoes are mostly located on top of the highland areas. There are also volcanic domes, or pancake craters as they are called, that are unique to Venus. Less than 0.6 of a mile in height and about 39 miles/63 kms in diameter, these pancakes are formed of viscous lava. (A thicker, stickier lava than the material that generally emanates from the larger shield volcanoes.) Some 936 impact craters, *distributed in a totally consistent way across the planet* have been identified by the Magellan probe. This distribution is unique in our solar system.

Running a computer program known as a Monte Carlo Simulation, Professor Robert Strom and Dr. Gerald Schaber have demonstrated that the impact craters are entirely randomly and evenly scattered over the entire planet.[9] They could not tell the difference between the simulations and the actual surface of Venus. Nor could many other geologists. This crater population is the same age, there is no "new cratering" nor any "old cratering", it is all the same. Strom and Schaber stated that: "Venus has turned itself inside out!" And have asked: "How did she do that?"

- From the comparison of the craters with their surrounding terrain and by evaluating

---

Gambler's guess

The Monte Carlo Simulation is a statistical procedure which is used to obtain numerical solutions to mathematical problems by means of random sampling.

---

their quantity in pro to the remaining surface, it has been possible to evaluate when the conditions on Venus changed.

- Geologists have calculated the changeover time to have been around 500 million years BP and they admit that they do not understand why the event should have happened.
- We suggest that they will find the exact time to be nearer to 572 million years BP, at *the time the Moon was locked into orbit around the Earth.*
- We theorise that the craters were formed by meteorite impact during the period when the surface became molten. This was before the planet rapidly built up a thick atmosphere that subsequently prevented larger objects from striking its surface. Thus, all the impact craters are approximately the same age!

Our propositions for the causes of Venus's physical state are not only plausible but are borne out by the dynamics revealed by sensing equipment aboard space probes.

18. The planet Venus. NASA

The cosmic fire bucket

Now while Venus has the same average age as Earth, and a nearly similar density it does not demonstrate continents of old rock and expanses of young sea floor, as Earth does. There are no plate tectonics at work because Venus does not posses a moon 27.27% of its size, as does the Earth.

It is our contention that the plate tectonics present on Earth can only occur when there is a planet/moon relationship of the same proportions as our Earth/Moon system. So while we do not believe that Venus ever had plate activity, the planet appears to have been functioning initially as Earth before the Moon was put in place some 572 million years ago. This would indicate a vast amount of water present over the surface of Venus at one time in its history. So where did all the water go? Scientists do not know how, or even if, Venus lost its water. We propose that most of the water evaporated into space during the gating process described above.

Some scientists have stated that they suspect the event that caused the described upheaval to Venus that (in their estimation) occurred some 500 million years ago to be *cyclical.* Running computer simulations for a further 500 million years might of course demonstrate a cycle, but, with an example of one, that conclusion is not good science. Scientists are making assumptions which they will not be around to either prove or disprove. However, promoting the cause of venusian activity as being due to a runaway greenhouse effect is useful in terms of project funding, for this same discipline is predicting a similar fate for this planet too.

While we would like to think that this misunderstanding is due to a lack of information about how our Moon affects our solar system, we have to wonder. It is our contention that "cyclical" is the wrong word but rather as a result of its function as our heatsink, Venus has a climate that is in a *steady state.*

The breaking of the plates

Varying from 31 to 62 miles in thickness, the surface of the Earth is composed of eight large plates and eight smaller plates which together form the lithosphere. The lithosphere rests on and slides over, a weaker layer of hotter, partially melted rock called the aesthenosphere.

The boundaries of the lithosphere's plates are the arenas within which the principal structuring of the Earth's surface occurs: earthquakes, volcanism and orogeny (the deformation that forms mountains) all begin at these *interfaces.*

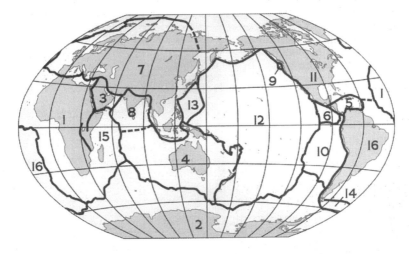

19. The sixteen plates as they are today: NGS *CARTOGRAPHIC DIVISION*

1) African 2) Antarctic 3) Arabian 4) Australian 5) Caribbean 6) Cocos 7) Eurasian 8) Indian 9) Juan de Fuca 10) Nazca 11) North American 12) Pacific 13) Philippine 14) Scotia 15) Somali 16) South American.

Plate rates

Our tectonic plates are currently estimated to be moving at about 3.14 inches per annum, when they are sliding past each other freely.

However, this rate gets slowed to about 2.09 inches when there is subduction occurring and slowed again to around 1.04 inches where subduction is hindered by a continental shelf such the Himalayas.

It is currently estimated that the Atlantic is growing gradually wider and that Africa is on the move upwards, narrowing the Mediterranean.

The Himalayan mountains are the result of two plates colliding, the southern plate embedding itself into the northern plate until it can move no further. When this 'orogeny' occurs, movement is held up for a period of time until a part of the blocked line gives way to the built-up pressure.

These plates are moving relative to each other and interact at their boundaries either by diverging, converging or slipping harmlessly past each other. The plates are named after the locality in which they are found.

The sea floor crust and the continental crust of planet Earth are of differing compositions

449

20. Earth's plates 540 m years BP;   240 m years BP;   and today.

and thickness. The continental crust is of a granite composition and has a thickness varying from 18.6 miles through to 24.8 miles. Recognise those figures? They are related to the length of a solar cycle and the length of a solar day! The sea floor crust is of a basalt composition and from 3.75 to 4.32 miles thick. The boundary between the crust (oceanic and continental) and the mantle has been clearly defined by seismic study and is called the Mohorovicic discontinuity.

We propose that it was the installation of the Moon, 572 million years BP that instigated the cracking of the planet's lithosphere into these re-

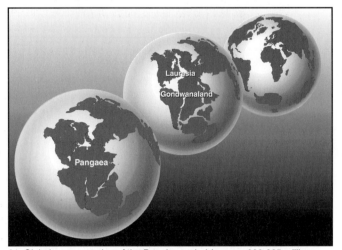

21. Global representation of the Permian period (approx. 280-225 million years BP) and the intermediary positions of the Earth's plates.   After LOVELOCK

gions that we describe as plates. The positioning and the orbit of the Moon was responsible for the emergence of land from the oceans (or the receding of water from the land if you will) and the movements of the landmasses of this planet from initially a single body Panagea, into the division of Gondwanaland and Laurasia, and then into our current continental system.

It is our understanding that the Moon orbited Earth from approximately 572 million years BP through to 237,000 years ago in the same circular orbit, 221,546 miles distant from Earth.[10] This orbit replicates the ratio between the surface area of a tetrahedron and the sphere that circumscribes it, 2.72 to 1.

A slice of Pi

The surface ratio of a tetrahedron to a sphere that circumscribes it is 2.72 :1. This full figure of 2.720699046 is then multiplied by the paradigm length of the retrograde precession which is 25,920 (years) and then by the universal constant, which is Pi, (using the precise figure of 3.141592654). Here we have one of the principles of transD physics relating to all celestial bodies, whether they be planets or advanced space craft.

Namely: 2.720699046 x Pi x 25,920 = 221,546 miles from Earth.

450

Bi-cycle clips

During a total eclipse of the Sun the Moon is just the right size to cover the Sun. This fact is so remarkable that to comment on such a coincidence and then pass on by without thinking what the circumstance might *mean* would be truly astonishing! The Moon and of course the Earth are at precisely the distance from the Sun so that when viewed from the Earth, the Moon *appears* to be the same size as the Sun. In reality, the Sun with its diameter of 864,000 miles, is 400 times larger than the Moon's diameter and 109 times larger than Earth's diameter. But the Moon is 400 times nearer the Earth than is the Sun.

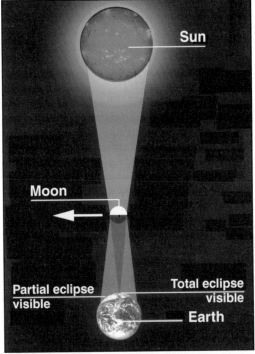

22. A solar eclipse.

Now given that the Moon is apparently moving *away* from us but that these proportions are remaining the same—the Moon is still covering the Sun in exactly the same way—then the Sun must be *either getting smaller or moving in pro with the Moon* to retain this eclipse phenomenon. Which ought to mean that gradually we are getting left be-

hind by these two bodies but that is not so, for when Earth causes a lunar eclipse when passing between the Sun and the Moon it is possible to see that the proportions of the Earth and the Moon are still exact.

So either the Earth and Moon are moving away from not only the Sun but also each other at a speed which might render Professor Whitehead's future Moon moving activities superfluous—or our measuring system is totally inaccurate.

We are fully aware that scientists are using laser measurements (and therefore the speed of light) to establish the amount by which the Moon is moving away from us. However, as they seem reluctant to *commit* to the precise distance per annum that the Moon is moving away from us we offer three reasons as to why they may not be forthcoming with an answer:

Their laser ranging will return varying measurements due to *the variation in the speed of light* in accordance with the Moon's position in relation to the varying gravitational pull of the planets in the solar system.

Chaikin has penned an interesting account of the return journey of 'Apollo 12'. He tells us that on the last day of their mission, November 24 1972, they spent over an hour flying through the shadow of an Earth ringed with sunlight. These astronauts had apparently become the first humans to witness such an eclipse of the Sun by the Earth. This fascinating bit of information has not been included in the main text but features in the author's notes. Why? Chaikin is very precise in his descriptions and seemingly familiar with astronomy, yet he uses the word "eclipse" which is actually incorrect in this instance.

Douglas Arnold has told us that the Apollo astronauts apparently experienced the sight of Earth exactly covering the Sun, when viewed from space—and he was certain that they were not on the Moon when they saw this event. We think he is referring to 'Apollo 12' and that his is a far more accurate if discreet way of expressing matters.

The definition of a solar eclipse, which occurs naturally every 18 months, is when the Moon passes *between* the Earth and the Sun, thus enabling the normally invisible corona of the Sun to be seen. Just before and just after totality, a 'diamond ring' effect caused by drops of sunlight can be seen around the Moon. This period is very brief as a total solar eclipse never lasts longer than 7 minutes.

Supposing this 'Apollo 12' scenario to be true, what we have is not a natural solar eclipse (there were neither lunar nor solar eclipses in November 1972) but *an occulting* of the Sun by the Earth, seen as a result of their trajectory.

Given the relative sizes of the Sun and the Earth, for the crew to see such an occultation it would be necessary for the Earth to be in an entirely different *orbit* (three quarters of the distance further from the Sun than the Moon when in an eclipse position), in order to compensate for the 73% difference of Moon/Earth size. And if that were not enough, *if* the astronauts were in the *shadow* of the Earth, how could they possibly observe pink and pale striped clouds in the detail that has been re-described by Chaikin?[11]

This account leads us to conclude that either Chaikin or rather *one of the 'Apollo 12' astronauts,* might be Whistle-Blowing by detailing an event that can *easily and scientifically be demonstrated as being incorrect.*

Dr. Donald's SFX trickery— Part Twelve

Our HIP hypothesis for the *intelligent* placing of the Moon may not be accepted in toto by scientists, academics and others keen to retain the status quo. But by maintaining that there *is* only one speed of light, such individuals, institutions and their masters thereby conceal our connection to all that is. They reason that even *if* ET existed (based on the currently-accepted universal speed of light) the length of time that it would take to travel around the solar system, let alone the galaxy, would preclude visitors.

Fast forward into fear

The masters are fully aware that the speed of light fluctuates and that physical remnants of ET craft are in their possession, therefore they are withholding facts and information. And withholding information is the same as lying.

23. 'Diamond ring' effect during a solar eclipse.

Notwithstanding the question of ET, in their desperation to avoid the realities of the *physics* of our Universe, discovered through exploration of our solar system to date, they are prepared to cover up and fake the physical reality in favour of maintaining their positions of warrior-scientists intact. A policy for which we, the public, have not been asked to vote upon.

To quote another commentator:

Science must begin to understand that it does not hold within it the power to dictate to the rest of humankind, but that it is only a portion of humankind. In its elitism, science has discarded the other echelons of humankind. Science has become the religion that manipulates and controls, and those who lead science must now begin to accept their responsibility.[12]

In denial of the accumulated evidence for the existence of extra-terrestrial intelligence, the 'masters of infinity' continue to encourage 'scripts' that are not only designed to fool, mislead and manipulate the general public but also provide the DODmen with excuses for continuing their expensive development of disharmonious technology designed to maintain their own status quo. This fear-based program does not restrict itself to plots concerning ET. Through the spate of 1990s mega-movies—including *Asteroid, Avalanche, and Meteorite*—the masters via the DODmen and it turn the film studios are attempting to suggest that we should be afraid of nature. This could result in our alienation from nature and thus we will give our powers of judgement and decision over to our 'protectors'—the DODmen. In reality the DODmen do not want us to realise that which they already know, that their self-appointed role as leaders of a warlike planet is no longer a viable option. Whilst entertaining, these movies serve a dual purpose, they promote the idea that if ETs exist, they are unfriendly, our planetary environment inhospitable, the solar system environment unreliable and mankind is isolated here on Earth by the very nature of the workings of the Universe.

In other words we are sitting ducks for whatever happens to target us. If collectively we do not wake up, this could well be true when it comes to our own military and space agencies and it is time that we request some accountability. For this type of duality that enables something (such as the subject of ET) which has always been officially denied, to be aired, whilst *remaining* denied—until it is deemed (by the masters) to be appropriate for the public to know a little more.

The TV series that promote the idea that we are vulnerable to attack from either unfriendly ETs and/or malevolent asteroids—*Dark Skies, Millennium, Babylon 5, Space World etc.*—are all included. The first and most notable of these was *The X Files.* Both *The X Files* and *Dark Skies* had story lines that involved an American Crop Glyph. One of these show biz glyphs was a very bad attempt at imitating a most significant Crop Glyph activated at Barbury Castle in Southern England in 1991,[13] some time between 9pm on Tuesday July 16, and 9 am Wednesday July 17, when it was discovered by a an aircraft pilot named Nick Bailey.[14] Is it any coincidence that this glyph (which among other encodings, holds one of the keys to transD physics) was activated on the twenty-second anniversary of the departure of 'Apollo 11', which also took place on a Wednesday? These dramatic plotlines endeavoured to imply that these Crop Glyphs were dangerous to those who entered them. On the other hand this effort was not at all convincing for any of those who had the experience of standing in the Barbury Castle glyph.

Moreover, as an example of media manipulation, the way that this series came about is edifying:

Chris Carter, creator of *The X Files*, said that he sensed a gap in the market for a *"truly frightening* series". (emphasis added) He was certain it would work—when he 'found' a US survey relating to the number of Americans who believe they have been abducted by Aliens. *"The X Files* producers felt that the resurgence of interest in UFOs and unexplained phenomena, and the conspiracy angle, neatly *reflected millennial paranoia."* (emphasis added) So stated author Jane Goldman.[15] We feel that the truth of that statement would be better expressed as:

> *The X Files* producers feel that the resurgence of interest in UFOs and unexplained phenomena and the conspiracy angle, *will best be dealt with by* neatly *linking them* to millennial paranoia.

Indeed Carter subsequently created the TV series *Millennium,* which dealt with a form of remote viewing.

Apart from those already mentioned, there have been numerous American space-driven series on the UK networks and more high budget series are in production. Each conveying a different message about ET and all reflecting paranoia as to the viability of communicating with any other race of self-aware life—unless one has a defensive weapon, or a whole space fleet, near at hand. The list is endless and the analysis of this phenomenon the subject of a book in itself. Briefly, the message of the majority of these scenarios is that ET is ALIEN and that means dangerous. People or ETs who use consciousness, in terms of telepathy, remote viewing etc. are to be viewed with suspicion, kept at arms length, not to be wholly trusted and if you look at them closely appear to be generally worn out (either mentally, physically or both) by the wearisome burden of their abilities. If you don't get the bad guy, IT will get you. And IT might get you anyway by invading your body or your mind. In short, whether it be the 3D reality/4D implications of ET; or the 3D use of consciousness, as far as the masters and the DODmen are concerned 'out there' is hostile and when 'out there' turns into 'arrives here' it will consume us all.

Is it any wonder that as far as they are concerned, hyperD physics are "off the picture"!

We suspect that these media manipulators are playing for real and they are upheld psychologically by the 'masters of infinity' through the Military Industrial and Religious Empire. This *MIRE* has a vested interest in keeping our attention on fear. Fear of each other, fear of the unknown, fear of the elements that surround us, fear of deprivation and fear of annihilation.

Paradoxically the *MIRE* are reflecting their own fears, for without us to support their system, they realise that they have no wherewithal and will therefore die. And so via the media they present us with the mirror image of their own fears, manifest as repulsive, unpredictable, insidious, all-invading ALIENS.

Much of the unrest on this planet at the end of this millennium stems in fact from populations who are tired of being cheated, lied to and treated as unworthy of consideration by their own leaders. Some of these leaders have been appointed by the very people who are unhappy. Some have appointed themselves. What is disturbing is the sense that we are being manipulated and coerced into a state of disharmony which is utterly alien to our nature.

'Trust no one' is a divisive, isolating and unkind order. Unkind to ourselves. Surely we should trust ourselves and our innate ability to be in harmony with our surroundings and each other? From such understanding we would find that we have tolerance of the strange, including our neighbours!

Our planet floats amidst a glorious, shining filigree of stars, a vibrant network of energy that sustains and connects us to all that is throughout the Universe. We are not alone and we never have been. When we trust our own judgement and cease to rely on those who have repeatedly demonstrated their lack of accountability for the responsibilities that have been offered them—then we shall find that we can trust—unconditionally.

The dualistic aims of the masters via the US Government have always been the same: the scientific program of exploration presented to the public as the cover under which the military plans would flourish. As was the case during the secretive Manhattan Project, if the investors did not see results for money already invested, then there would be no more research grants forthcoming. The greater the investment, the more impressive the results had to appear—even if they were not real. 'Bangs for bucks'—and we have come full circle, right back to the principles behind that first space hoax back in 1927, *Frau im Mond,* in which science, politics and the arts were combined into an eternal triangle of greed, power and SFX. ■

Almaz are forever?

The masters' dualistic aims were not confined to the USA, in the Soviet Union a similar state of affairs existed, as Alexander Sabelnikov recounts in his book based on the diaries of his famous Uncle, Vladimir Suvorov:

"Manned space flights—*including the American Moon program*—were rather propagandistic shows during the Cold War." The primary meaning of such shows was to "hide the actual main goal of getting an advantage in the space arm's race". (emphasis added) The author of these words did not have the advantage of hindsight to see how much of a 'show' the Cold War was! Given that this 'war' was itself in part a cover for other activities, Sabelnikov's next morsel of information is most significant: he tells us that in the 1970s the Soviet Defense Ministry ran a space program called Almaz (meaning diamond) and that:

- The launch on April 3 1972 of *Salyut 2* was actually *Almaz 1, a military spy station and it contained a 23mm quick-firing Nudelmann gun!* Perhaps intentionally (bearing in mind this book has been edited by English speakers) the English phrasing of the text often leaves a lot to the imagination, nevertheless the inference here is that Nudelmann gun is a weapon and not a reconnaissance camera! According to Sabelnikov's text, Almaz 1 "left the radar zones of the survey and *disappeared* somewhere in space. The subsequent search was unsuccessful." (emphasis added)

- Jos Heymann's spacecraft tables lists this flight as occurring on April 3, and makes no link to the Almaz military spy stations. Nor does Heymann record any failure during orbit, merely listing its return to Earth on May 28. However, he *does* record a launch on April 22 which failed to orbit but provides no clues as to what that flight actually was.[16]
- Interestingly David Baker indexes the name Almaz as "remote sensing" so perhaps we should call the military's remote human viewers "rough diamonds"! Baker attributes the failure of Salyut 2/Almaz 1 to an electrical fire that broke out during an on-orbit test and which caused the hull to *split apart*. He states that the Soviets tracked 24(!) parts of the craft after its *partial* disintegration and that it finally decayed from its 134 x165 mile orbit on May 28, some 55 days after launch.
- Brian Harvey records the orbit of this craft as 215 miles then 230 x 260 miles, and after another burn the orbit was raised again to 261 x 296 miles, in 89.9 minutes. This he estimated to be high for a proposed rendezvous in space but then notes that the Salyut/Almaz was signalling on untrackable frequencies—military frequencies as it later turned out. Harvey tells us that this electrical fire broke out *even as* rocket riders Popovich and Artyukin (assigned to the Almaz military program) were on the launchpad, preparing for rendezvous with the military station—how dramatic! And naturally the disappointed(?) cosmonauts were stood down, as the expression goes. No date is given for this fire, but by cross referencing several sources we can conclude that as the Soviets publicly announced the end of the test on April 18 the fire took place on the day of the only available launch window—April 14.
- According to Harvey, Soyuz only *punctured* its hull and depressurised, no mention here of those 24 bits of craft sailing around in orbit. Instead Harvey has the *whole thing* neatly failing to burn up during re-entry and dropping lock, stock and punctured barrel into the Indian Ocean on May 28.

QUESTION: Only two days after this alleged fire, the 'Apollo 16' astronauts were entering Earth orbit prior to departing for their 'moon'. When any piece of space debris is an extreme danger to a manned craft, exactly how likely is it that the 'Apollo 16' astronauts spent 2 hours 22 minutes in an arena possibly littered with 24/25 chunks of traceable but unmanageable space station that would make a micrometeorite look friendly?

These varying accounts for the same event are par for the course with regard to the way that the space agencies work, whether Soviet, Russian or American. However, they do put the most recent 1997 Sabelnikov account into the ball park for the most likely explanation for the 'demise' of Almaz 1. It would seem to be that either the agencies truly do not know what happened to their first Almaz tooled-up military station or they do know, and do not wish to divulge that fact—unless of course it is that 'galactic ghoul' again!

- June 25 1973 saw the launch of Almaz 2/Salyut 3 into the "designated Almaz military station orbit" of 219 x 270 miles. Which was then visited by cosmonauts travelling in the Soyuz 14 spacecraft.

We are advised that these ex-fighter pilots, Popovich and Artyukhin, (yes, they finally got to visit an Almaz) were "excited and enthusiastic" about the station's capacities. Could these two men get such thrills from the Earth resource tests they were supposedly carrying out during their stay in space? Knowing the lack of enthusiasm manifest by their American counterparts we doubt it. But then the public record had no details of this station's ambivalent militaristic role.

- Baker tells us that the Almaz 2 station was in a 165 x 171.5 mile orbit when the cosmonauts docked with it on July 5, two days after their launch from Baikonur. More conflicting reports or simply space mechanics?
- Soyuz 21 took cosmonauts Volinov (from the Almaz military team) and Zholotov

(from the original lunar flyby team) to visit Salyut 5/Almaz 3 on July 6 1976.

- Harvey tells us of a series of unusual procedures: instead of staying in space until September as scheduled, the two cosmonauts returned to Earth on August 24 *only two hours* after the sudden announcement of their return. These radio announcements were usually made six days or so before the actual landing. They also *very exceptionally* landed close to Baikonur and *equally exceptionally* they landed at night.
Very curious!

At the time, according to the newspaper *Izvestia,* this incident was attributed to "sensory deprivation", but this reason does not match the excuses of "illness and acute fatigue on the part of Zholotov" which were circulated years later. Returning from space and closing down a space station is not like leaving home and catching the local bus. Either the planning for this return occurred well before the Moscow radio announcement, or perhaps that other galactic ghoul 'Comrade Solar Flare' had turned up unexpectedly and the cosmonauts had to leave for home in a great hurry? Was Zholotov outside the craft at the time? Did he catch a dose of something cosmic?

Whatever had happened, just under a year later, on August 8 1977, the Almaz 3 station was "sent a suicide note from Earth" as Sabelnikov put it. That August, forty seven solar flares were officially reported. Perhaps it was a case of 'alien vibes' which scratched forever the Diamond that was Almaz 3?

The Almaz military spy station program was closed down in 1981—allegedly. We wonder *if* this program ever actually closed. Sabelnikov wonders *why* the program was closed and if there were any connections between this Diamond program and the attempted Reagan Star Wars initiative. Then, while not expecting the military to stand up and answer him, he also asks if the Almaz program was a "forerunner for future space wars or just the accidental creation of the paranoiac imagination of some military bigwigs?" The experiences that we had during the years of researching and writing this book would indicate that in the domain of space planning there are no accidents.

Perhaps one meaning of the code name Diamond reflects the means by which this spy technology was financed—a thought that brings us full circle—back to Ian Fleming and the encoding of serious sensitive information into seemingly simple entertainment.

The arthurised version—Part Two

At the launch of 'Apollo 11' one TV commentator, when pressed for his opinion of the event averted his eyes made the curious reply: "It is a hole in history". Who's statement was that? Well, coincidentally, it was Arthur C Clarke. In 1994 ACC expressed the opinion that "when the history of the space age is written it will be seen that the Apollo space program was a major anomaly caused entirely by political considerations". No doubt this is one of the justifications that NASA will use to excuse the fact that it has duped us for nearly thirty years.

Clarke went on to say:

> The decision to go to the Moon was the reaction of the United States—specifically of President Kennedy—to the series of technological humiliations beginning with Sputnik and Gagarin and culminating with the Cuban invasion. It was the product of the Cold War, a chapter of history which is now ended.[17]

QUESTION: Mr. Clarke's statement here infers that President Kennedy was the scapegoat of the Moon program. Was this situation a deliberate policy or the outcome of circumstances which got out of control?

QUESTION: Were these "political considerations" rather more related to the mutual retention by the USSR and the USA of power over their respective nations in the face of a perceived threat to their status as governments?

If Mr. Clarke has appointed himself as spokesman for the space program, then we consider that this imperious pronouncement from the island of Sri Lanka will not suffice to reply to the many and diverse questions raised by the present book.

Dan Dare

If NASA considers its history of the past 30 years to be a political issue that is no longer extant, then why do does the agency not take this golden opportunity to 'come clean' now that the game is up? After all, the decisions made concerning project Apollo were not the responsibility of the *current* heads of NASA. To label the people who ask questions as 'conspiracy theorists' and belittle their questioning by the clever use of ridicule and scorn does not mean that there is no such thing as a conspiracy. We should really point our fingers at the 'masters of infinity' as being responsible for the conspiracy of silence concerning the physical realities of our Universe—realities that ultimately inspired the anomalous Apollo images. They leave us with no alternative other than to suggest that NASA itself instigated the conspiracy to fake the Apollo record. Until those realities are addressed then NASA & Co. will continue to use technologies that only allow them to creep around on the edge of space. However, to use the appropriate technology for safe and efficient space travel requires a highly integrated attitude, one that appears to be lacking within NASA. The manifestation of the Apollo transcripts on the web in 1997 underlines the fact that NASA is going to continue as before—as does the appointment of the most recent NASA administrator.

Prior to replacing Richard Truly as Administrator of NASA in 1992 Dr. Daniel Goldin was relatively unheard of within the business. He had preceded his NASA job as the low profile VP and General Manager of Thompson Ramo Woolridge, more usually known as TRW, a company which specialises in working with *classified reconnaissance satellites.*

The qualifications of any NASA Administrator tend to reflect the nature of the job expected of them while occupying the post. The previous incumbent and his deputy were experts in the field of manned near-space techniques (i.e. below the radiation belts). Richard Truly had been an astronaut himself, within the Military's Manned Orbiting Laboratory Program. Other senior positions within Truly's administration were also occupied by ex-astronauts.

In other words, the whole directive of NASA from 1987 through to 1992 was turned towards development of the Space Shuttle and the role of human beings within the near space program. Preferring to gloss over (or being totally ignorant of) the fact that these men are merely reflecting the dictates of powers greater than themselves, several of NASA's observers and critics are prone to describe the outcome of the agency's policies as if they were actually *instigated* by these administrators and deputies. Thus, it has been implied that these outgoing administrators were only committed to costly programs such as the Shuttle and the Space Station and they were virtually held responsible for the vast sums of money that their administration consumed. Utter hypocrisy when in fact, they were doing exactly what they were put in place to achieve.[18]

If the manned space program had been abruptly halted at the end of 1975, after the ASTP demonstration, then the world might well have taken notice, thereby endangering the anomalous record of Apollo. It has long been known that since its inception the Shuttle has been s supremely wasteful program. Costing around $500m per launch, the allegedly 'recoverable' boosters have sunk without trace many more times than they have been collected and re-used—a detail that is generally not known outside the space industry. But what were they to do? The Saturn V was obviously incapable of heaving the Shuttle craft aloft, otherwise why abandon a proven rocket launcher (which had already been through development, manufacturing and testing) in order to build a far less cost-effective replacement?

Goodbye Columbus, et al.

Generally the changing of the guard at NASA's palace would appear to indicate that a phase of the overall program has been completed. The next phase was then inaugurated by the new boys. With Dr. Goldin's announcement that he expected to revert to expendable launchers rather than the 'reusable' Shuttle, we might confidently predict the relatively imminent retirement of the Space Shuttle. The intended replacement for the current cash-devouring

Shuttle is the Lockheed Martin X-33. This new rocket (which will also take off vertically and land conventionally) will not discard part of the launch vehicle each time it goes into orbit and should only cost about 10% of a current Shuttle launch. By removing the Shuttle as the people carrier it was initially marked out to be, space is quietly being returned to a mode in which clandestine operations, carried out by small groups of selected and more than likely military or intelligence personnel, will have access to both LEO and perhaps deep space. This is the mode in which the true exploration carried out by the Apollo surrogates was achieved and it is a mode to which terrestrial man will probably have no access. With Dr. Goldin at the helm the focus is thrown towards Mars. Do the qualifications held by the new 'Dan Dare' now begin to make more sense?

For those who have not had the benefit of reading the adventures of Dan Dare we should add that this space age hero of the 1950s-'60s appeared as the lead story on the front pages of an upmarket British boy's comic called *EAGLE* (how apposite!). Week in, week out, the intrepid astronaut Dan Dare and his well meaning co-pilot Digby faced the challenges of the Mekon and his cohorts. The latter, though painted a tasteful green colour, resembled to a 'T' the current image of the 'Greys' now prevalent in the UFO press of America and Britain of the 1990s.

Who is the copy cat? Like Dr. Goldin, 'Mr' Mekon favoured a smaller cost-effective form of space travel. Unlike Goldin, his preferred form of transport was a form of flying disk! The figurehead of NASA as portrayed by Dan Goldin has much in common with Dan Dare. If anyone spots a similarity between the Mekon and Arthur C Clarke, then its not surprising either, because along with Chad Varah, whose chief job on the *EAGLE* was as the scientific and astronomical consultant, Arthur Clarke also contributed to the Dan Dare stories.

Faulty towers

In 1994, as Administrator of NASA, Daniel Goldin categorically stated that humans were not ready to leave Earth orbit. He managed this tour de force without batting an eyelid or mentioning Apollo and stated that there were three reasons for this inability.[19]

Dan Goldin:

> They—the space authorities—do not know how people can live and work safely and productively in space. Hence the space station.

Our comment: How true that statement is. After thirty five years the authorities have still failed to cope with prolonged spells of weightlessness and space sickness, and these are just two of the many problems. Michael Foale, after only four months in the MIR space station during 1997, was unable to walk upon landing on Earth and had suffered significant bone loss. Yet it is *surely* somewhat remiss of Dr. Goldin to ignore the fact that twelve men are supposed to have gone through the rigors of deep space travel during the Apollo phase, albeit for less than a total of four months.

Indeed, back in 1965 it was found that only a *four-day* Gemini IV mission was long enough to cause *serious* bone-demineralisation for the astronauts.[20] With so many of these problems still prevalent today, it is simply not good enough to dismiss the early manned Apollo missions as "a political necessity" and thereby avoid any reference to the severe medical ramifications of such adventures. Can we surmise that in order to avoid such issues NASA's PR department are currently fostering the "don't mention the war" attitude, now that as we are officially friends with the Russians? The gang at *Fawlty Towers* would see this process for what it is—a device used to avoid facing the real, actual, unavoidable problems of space travel for human beings.

Dan Goldin again:

> We have to learn how to work together in international co-operation. Hence the joint venture in building the space station.

Our comment: That is a good point, except that both nations had learnt how to do that fifty years ago during WWII. Now that the USA and Russia are *officially* working together should they not perhaps be re-named ARSA—the American/Russian Space Administration?

Dan Goldin's opinion of manned space travel was that "it is much too expensive and it takes far too long". (We cannot say if he was referring to preparation time, travel time or return on investment.) Goldin went on to say that getting to the Moon and Mars was now a project to be shared, at less cost and within a time limit of eight years. Then he covered himself by adding that the objectives of NASA did not *necessarily* lie with Mars or with the Moon but could be directed towards the installation of a manned space station on an asteroid! Dream on Dan Dare! The asteroid belt is way beyond Mars, but never mind that detail, because Goldin is scrupulously avoiding the vitally important 'R' word—radiation.

Dr. Goldin stated that the budget during Apollo was in the region of $70 billion. He was comparing it to the 1994 annual NASA budget of $14 billion. Yet breaking the $70 billion (at 1994 values) into a conservative five years between 1968 and 1972, the years of Apollo, then this 1994 figure is exactly the same level of expenditure as it was then. He may have been obfuscating the issue by comparing a yearly budget with a project's overall budget. However, in comparing years with decades and Federal budgets with gross national product Goldin successfully avoided supplying valid information. NASA-ese again. The upshot of all this is, that according to Dr. Goldin the *barrier* to space travel is cash rather than radiation. The very high cost of access to space (getting the hardware off the ground) and the fact that the system is not 'routine' like an airline are the excuses to which Dr. Goldin clings. He ignores words like those of the space radiation experts, that "radiation is a show stopper". In scientific and political circles a 'show stopper' is something that requires

far too much money to resolve, *even if* one has the know-how.

Dr. Goldin then finally returned to the subject of manned space stations in LEO and emphasised the studies that needed to be made concerning our own planet. Thus enrolling the "let's invest the NASA budget in our planet" environmentalists. To this end he specifically cited the proposed examination of the sources and sinks of carbon dioxide around the Earth. Goldin stated that the belt of twenty miles of air around our planet belongs to us all. (Does he then wish to infer that space itself does not belong to us all?) We should add that given the propensity of many scientists to communicate to a wider audience only what they want others outside their circles to know, and the propensity of NASA to be economical with the truth, it is vital that NASA come to understand that despite past performance, today we all wish to receive honest answers in our dealings with the space agencies. Will political and commercial interests always take precedence? In, passing, we hope that for all our sakes, Dan Goldin (and his space agency) leans more about the actual workings of the planet upon which he lives because then those concerned may come to understand how to travel beyond it.

An early 1990s survey of US citizens suggested that a high proportion of those polled regarded NASA too expensive to run. Goldin said that the poll was taken when the nation

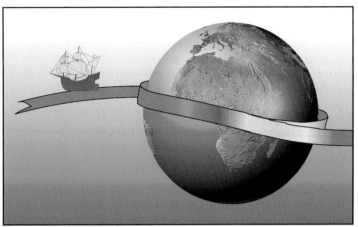

24. "As idle as a painted ship upon a painted ocean."

The Ancient Mariner Samuel Taylor Coleridge

was at 'the height of the doldrums'—again accuracy of language seems not to be Dr. Goldin's forté.

The Doldrums is the mariner's name for the area of ocean near the equator known as the Intertropical Convergence Zone. Here the trade winds neutralise each other—so that in the days of sailing ships it was possible to become becalmed in the *middle* of the doldrums for weeks on end. Dan Goldin chose the wrong adjective but the right analogy, for NASA is trapped in their very own version of the Doldrums—at the convergence of the Van Allen belts and our atmosphere, until they are prepared to openly address their problems and start to develop the totally new and necessary technologies for future space travel.

Captain Hook or Tinkerbell . . . what's in a name?

According to the *public's* expectations of US Government employees' behaviour, one of the prime movers behind Project Horizon, General Medaris was unorthodox in his methods, to say the least. When the US Army's satellite project Orbiter was cancelled, Medaris secretly kept it alive by siphoning off funding from other projects into Orbiter, apparently without the Pentagon's knowledge.[28] It is therefore unsurprising that it is alleged few people outside Medaris and his army colleagues were aware of Project Horizon. Even fewer people knew that attaining Mars and finding ET was (and is) the heart of the masters' space program. Even fewer again were aware of the name for the heart of this project. The technicians working on the photographic simulation of the lunar EVAs would not have been aware of the real name of their part of this project. To them and to their colleagues it was always the ASP. Together with the variations scattered throughout this book here are some alternative meanings, to be added to at will:

Apollo-Soyuz Project

American Soviet Program
American Space Program
Astronaut Surrogate Project
Aero Space Project

Arthur C Clarke has written that *his* motivation in life is simple and he considers that he has got what he always wanted: power without responsibility.

He would like his epitaph to read:

He never grew up, but he never stopped growing.

Clarke might wish to be likened to Peter Pan, but as he publicly does not believe in fairies or extra-terrestrials then perhaps he would be more at home with Captain Hook and the Pirates?

Bearing in mind the overall involvement of Arthur C Clarke throughout the space program, the Crop Glyph data, the desire to stop ET from visiting earth, the hook-up between the Americans and the Soviets in order to achieve their aims, the necessity of producing artificial lift in order to simulate the low lunar gravity during the studio mock-ups, the capability of specialist *wire flying technologists*—and all the other SFX required—maybe we should now ask another question. Did one group of cabalists have a closely-held secret name for the

25. Crop Glyph depicting *two hooks* meeting, Cherhill, Southern England, activated in 1993.   R RUSSEL

460

Apollo Project? Perhaps the secret services involved with remote research subjects (including those conducted at Livermore) will recognise the name:

OPERATION PETER PAN

They have rearranged the scenery by 'adjusting' the figures relating to radiation and the Van Allen belts, subjugated their scientists, and attempted to convince the public and their sponsors of the many reasons for remaining within low Earth orbit. Up until now this ploy has been a successful. But in our view it will not suffice for the next phase of manned space exploration.

We sincerely hope that the discussion points raised by this book will open up the debate and enable us all to progress in a greater understanding of our environment so we can face the future with pride.

> "A government is not free to do as it pleases. The law of nature, as revealed by Newton, stands as an eternal rule to all men."
>
> *John Locke, Philosopher*

Newton 3 — Einstein 1

Newton is a candidate for the title of the smartest person who ever lived— he was three times smarter than Einstein.

Einstein attained one great thing scientifically:

- Relativity

Newton attained three great things—each one of which was probably more important than relativity—he gave us:

- The modern theory of gravity
- The modern theory of light
- Calculus

Although a very smart man, Newton once said:
"I can predict the motion of the heavenly planets but not the madness of human beings".

Chapter Twelve

Prints of Mars

We examine NASA's photographic record of Mars, particularly the region known as Cydonia. Our own findings indicate that features within this region of Mars exhibit encoded data, which in turn leads to the finding that these specific martian structures are replicated on Earth, in Southern England and Egypt. We discuss the possibility that the positioning of the structures on Mars is the work of an advanced intelligence that is capable of modifying an inhospitable planet and maintaining a base in order to live there.

NASA

Coward's way

For millennia, the red planet has been a source of inspiration to Earthbound humans. Increasingly, Mars is becoming a focus of fascination for many people—artists, writers and scientists as well as military and political leaders. The Soviets (now the Russians) have always had a yearning towards the red planet. The primary exploration of Mars, especially NASA's, has most certainly revealed that martian fact is stranger than any science fiction, although neither space agency has admitted any such thing to date. Despite NASA's stated intentions of "going to Mars to search for life", we see little evidence to suggest that NASA is willing to respond to the challenges of Mars in a completely open and honest fashion. On the contrary, there is much to indicate 'a holding back' regarding certain martian data.

One-Third/Two-Thirds

The entire surface area of Mars is exactly equivalent to the land area of Earth, which is one-third of our planetary surface.

Mars has a surface gravity one-third of Earth's and twice as much as the Moon's gravity.

The geological composition of Mars:

Silicon	15-30%
Iron	12-16%
Calcium	03-08%
Aluminium	02-07%
Titanium	0.25-1.5%
Aluminium	traces

Orbiting at between 35 and 224 million miles/56-377 million kms from Earth, the fourth planet from our Sun is 4,214.72 miles in diameter, crater-strewn, misshapen, with a bulge at its equator.

The northern and southern hemispheres are distinctly different in appearance. The south is old and heavily cratered while the north is younger and more lightly cratered. There is, on average, a two mile drop in altitude from south to north.

Mars boasts the biggest volcano and canyon yet discovered in our solar system—
Olympus Mons and Valles Marineris respectively.

Now dry, hot and dusty, with winds of up to 300 mph, there is however, evidence of polar icecaps which advance and retreat seasonally.

These consist of frozen carbon dioxide in the south and frozen water in the north.

The atmosphere on Mars
as evaluated by the Viking 1 lander at 22.38°N, 47.49°W:

Carbon monoxide & dioxide	95%
Nitrogen	$2.5 \pm 0.5\%$
Argon	$1.5 \pm 0.5\%$
Oxygen	$0.1 \pm 0.4\%$
Helium & other gases	traces

Rotation

Mars rotates once every 24 hrs 37 mins 23 secs,
just 41 mins and 19 secs slower than our own rotation.

Revolution

Mars has a slower orbital speed than Earth and a larger orbit giving it a revolutionary period of 687 Earth days (1.88 Earth years). Average orbital speed is around 54,000 mph. The axis tilt is 25°20′ compared with our tilt of 23°45′.

Precession

While the rotation and revolution of Mars create a precessional wobble, *this is not retrograde* and is therefore not capable of generating the conditions required for self-aware life to evolve naturally. This, together with the fact that Mars does not have in orbit a single moon of the appropriate size, suggests that self-aware life *did not and cannot* evolve naturally on Mars and therefore any artificial constructions found there are the work of a species that *was not native to Mars.*

Mars/Sun/Earth

From Mars the Sun is two-thirds the size that we see from Earth.

Never A Straight Answer seems to be the order of the day once again.

Mars is traditionally considered to be the bringer of war and indeed current ideas and scientific thinking indicate a determination that this notion should be maintained. The doom and gloom brigade are upholding Mars as a planet upon which meteors have wreaked havoc destroying any life that there might have existed there. With Venus and its runaway greenhouse effect on the one hand and Mars having been destroyed by a 'big one' on the other, we

463

earthlings are being advised by scientists and space agencies alike that we do not really have a chance of survival in this unfriendly Universe. In our view this situation is not the case at all.

The solar system functions in such a way as to protect the self-aware life that has evolved on this planet. Students of quantum physics may wish to remind the doom and gloomers that all experiments are affected by the observer. The comet and meteorite impacts with Earth occurred *prior* to the establishment of man, despite the current thinking that attributes the Tunguska event to a meteorite (when it has been demonstrated scientifically not to be the result of such an event, as we saw in "Truth or Consequences").

The 1994 Jupiter comet strike (upgraded to a *meteorite* strike by the 1990s Deep Impact merchants) in which twenty one fragments hit the planet Jupiter was not entirely what it seemed. For example, one of the pieces on course for Jupiter split into two—and then actually joined itself back together again! A report from Los Alamos/NASA entitled Project Gabriel 'B' stated that:

- 20/21 'objects' are travelling [towards Jupiter] at a slower speed than the standard meteor velocity of 8 kilometres per second.
- Each object is 2.5 minutes apart incurring an unnatural mathematical resonance.
- Approximate delay between impact of objects is exactly 16.66 minutes.
- These objects appear to be either being 'pushed' or 'pulled' given the mathematics of the resonance fields and the unnatural rectangular plume.
- Redlight and Pounce operations should proceed with great caution due to unstable S3/4 interlocking and unstable electro drive characteristics.

No mention of this anomalous activity was, of course, made in the media and by 1998 the event had become a full-blown example of "what will happen to us". There follow more comments from a document that gathered together the recommendations of JPL, Caltech, the CIA, the NSA, the Jason Group, NASA

and scientists Yeomans, Sekania & Chodas, among others. Included is this most interesting observation on the ozone layer:

- Generally speaking, an increase in received UV may be expected, which may extend over a considerable period (2 or more years). This is over and above the alleged ozone depletion, *which is largely a myth* as the ozone levels are mainly governed by seasonal intensity of light and the 11 year sun cycle (emphasis added).
- An opportunity occurs to use this deep motivational drive to bring together a greater world unity . . .
- This is likely to herald a time of great changes which will last a number of years. People will be deeply affected and this will not pass quickly but will become part of the race cultural memory.
- The correct and appropriate political and security agency response is vital . . .

And most chilling of all:

- Despite the planned program for the advent of the year 2000 (31/12/99) nature seems to have stolen the stage . . .

What planned program? What do these people have in mind for us as a New Millennium gift? Are they innocently referring to the human festivities, are we all invited to a party celebrating the opening of, perhaps, their new Space Station? Or are they preparing a corker of a doom and gloom scenario, of which all these manipulations and predictions currently surfacing are an essential element. And is it for all of us, or is it aimed at the defence of the planet against their paranoia, and number one problem—ET?

If you cannot wait to find out, send a note to NASA, the CIA or the NSA and ask what the above remark really means and if their intentions are honourable. If you receive the same answer from each agency it will be a start. But in all probability, you will not get an answer at all.

We should point out that this Jupiter event coincided exactly *to the very week* with the 25th anniversary of the first Apollo Moon landing. These 'objects' proceeded to collide with Jupiter in an orderly fashion from July 16 (launch day for 'Apollo 11') through to July 22. There were also 20 to 21 'objects' and these numbers correspond to the two days that 'Apollo 11' was allegedly on the lunar surface. How clever of nature to have an exact calendar of our political/sporting events!

We consider that this occurrence was a visual demonstration that a solar system works together as a whole, to protect and nurture each and every aspect of life within it. Jupiter, a gas planet with a gravity 2.54 times our own, is capable of protecting the solar system's planet with self aware life—Earth—by attracting and absorbing any incoming space debris travelling into the solar system, rather like a giant magnet or attractor. We suspect that this event occurred around the time when the planned program dictated the activation of a "fear of impact for Earth" scenario. Now, in the late 1990s, this policy is really getting into gear for the self-appointed masters want us all in to be in a (subconscious) state of distrust and fear by the dawn of the next century.

Either NASA & Co. were offered a choice with regard to publishing the anomalistic data they had acquired concerning this event, or they may have 'fabricated' the anomalistic data in order to use it at a future date as evidence of aggressive ETs. So far, they have elected to incorporate it into their scare scenario with no mention of ET involvement as yet. However, given that NASA & Co. are not capable of creating an illusion at a location as far away as Mars, let alone Jupiter, and given the metaphorical information contained within it, we consider that one might wish to regard this event as a *wake-up call* to those who persist in ignoring the fact that we are not alone.

A kind of an advanced twenty one gun salute!

Wolpe's ways pack a wallop!

The effect of such fear mongering regarding our "imminent destruction" only serves to keep human beings in bondage—and perhaps this is truly the result that the masters are after. For they are the driving force in the propagation of this nonsense either through total ignorance or the desire to continue with their private agenda.

To have a world population depressed and dependent upon NASA & Co's technological expertise to prevent 'danger' from the big bad Universe 'out there' is to maintain their status quo, reinforce their own hunger for power and enable them to extract the funding necessary to 'get the job done'. But actually meteorite detection and destruction might not be the specific task they have in mind!

As these objects were obviously not what they *appeared* to be, then is this not a hint from outside our planet that the Moon landings were not all they *appeared* to be either? Would such embarrassing details be part of the reason why the Jupiter event received relatively little coverage in the popular press?

In our view this show was for the benefit of NASA and its counterparts and more especially for us the public, so that with hindsight we could see through the dissimulations of the masters who will subsequently realise that they chose poorly, yet again.

On the other hand, if NASA & Co. are truly unenlightened, then we can surmise that their predictions regarding the quasi-imminent arrival of a meteorite are based upon:

- Past history and events that occurred prior to the full establishment of our atmosphere and magnetic fields.
- Ignorance of this planet's evolutionary path.

Conversely, if these scientists *were aware of the minimal chances* of such an event happening to this planet, even within the long time spans that they are considering, then their calculations are also based upon:

- The compartmentalisation of data and the withholding of information.
- The deliberate withholding of knowledge—which is the same as lying.

It has been alleged by US Congressman Howard Wolpe that NASA had the remit to employ diverse methods in order to circumvent the Freedom Of Information Act.[1] So, you will probably be interested to learn that in order to side-step its responsibilities and remain unaccountable to its public, or indeed anyone else, NASA has been directed, in writing:

Martian missions 1960-1975	
USSR probes Mars & Cosmos 14 attempts—**USA** probes Mariner & Viking 8 attempts:	
1960	
Mars	launched October 10 failed to achieve Earth orbit.
Mars	launched October 14 failed to achieve Earth orbit.
1962	
Mars	launched October 24 failed to achieve Earth orbit.
Mars 1	launched November 1 flyby at 120,000 miles but contact lost March 21 '63 before mid-course correction.
Mars	launched November 4 failed to achieve Earth orbit.
1964	
Mariner 3	launched November 5 failed to leave Earth orbit.
Zond 2	launched November 3 flyby at 930 miles but contact lost spring '65 before encounter.
Mariner 4	launched November 28 successful flyby.
1969	
Mariner 6	launched February 24 successful flyby.
Mars	launched March 27 failed to reach Earth orbit.
Mariner 7	launched March 27 successful flyby.
Mars	launched April 10 failed to reach Earth orbit.
1971	
Mariner 8	launched May 8 failed to reach Earth orbit.
Cosmos 419	launched May 10 failed to leave Earth orbit.
Mars 2	launched May 19 orbiter/lander component achieved objective and orbiter returned data to Sept 1972. Lander failed to return data.
Mars 3	launched May 28 orbiter/lander component achieved objective and orbiter active to Sept '72. Lander failed to return data.
Mariner 9	launched May 30, first Mars orbiter. It was placed in orbit around Mars in November 1971 and operated until October 1972. Returned a wide variety of spectroscopic, radio propagation, and imaging data. Some 7,330 pictures covering 70% of the surface demonstrated a history of widespread volcanism, and ancient fluvial erosion. As far as NASA is aware the dead probe will continue to orbit Mars until the year 2012.
1973	
Mars 4	launched July 21 orbiter missed Mars, returned flyby data.
Mars 5	launched July 25 orbiter successful return data, periaxis 807 miles.
Mars 6	launched August 5 orbiter/lander returned some 2.5 minutes of unreadable data during descent.
Mars 7	launched August 9 orbiter/lander premature separation, missed Mars by over 800 miles.
All of these 1973 failures were blamed on a faulty computer chip in the craft, which had been known about shortly before launch! Rather than replace the chips, it was deemed that a success rate of 50% was good enough to launch. The success rate turned out to be a modest 25%. Mars 5 returned pictures similar to those taken by Mariner 9.	
1975	
Viking 1	launched August 20 1975—Viking 1 orbiter and lander component arrived June 1976.
Viking 2	launched September 9 1975 —Viking 2 orbiter and lander component arrived March 1976.

1) To minimise any adverse impact by the rewriting or destroying of documents.

2) To reduce contents in importance by mixing up papers or disguising handwriting.

3) To 'facilitate' all possible cases for exemptions from the Freedom Of Information Act—"enhance the utility" is the phrase used.

Way 1) was used in the Roswell disappearing documents scenario many of which have been "unaccountably destroyed"—allegedly.

Way 2) was allegedly used on the Majestic 12 papers and most certainly has been used in the (mis-)classification and (mis-)filing of the irreplaceable Mars images—as we shall see.

Way 3) merely requires that NASA, under the terms of its constitution, declares or organises its actions so that they fall under the aegis of the Defense Program, as was the case with the Clementine Moon mission.

It would seem that the very pressing and present desire to continue to invest in SDI technology—backed publicly by President Reagan—and pursued unofficially thereafter—is not motivated so much by the threat of an approaching meteorite, but military fear of ET. It is entirely apropos this that Reagan dubbed this technology "Star Wars".

As Graham Hancock has astutely observed, "NASA is the disturbed child of two dysfunctional parents: paranoia and war".[2] We suspect that master NASA's mother is a paranoia dating from 1947 and its father the attitudes and technology of Nazi Germany's space scientists. Yet the frustrated child of this union is incapable of taking action because such an inheritance combined with its inappropriate technology is utterly inadequate for the realisation of its underlying ambitions. NASA will have to grow up smartly and behave like a responsible adult, at which point it could acquire the adequate technology, although to date this infant is still displaying every sign of sulking in the nursery and scribbling on the wallpaper.

Twin peeks

Notwithstanding the many science fiction stories featuring Mars, and notably the writer Edgar Rice Burrough's hero John Carter and his adventures in the mighty empire of Helium on Mars, the human exploration of this planet full of wonders dates from the early 1960s. Not surprisingly, the reality of martian explora-

Mastering Mars

Mariner 4 took 21 images at a resolution of two miles from a distance above the planet of 6,118 miles. Mariner 6 made its closest pass to the red planet on July 31 1969, at a distance of 2,131 miles, and took 76 close images with a surface resolution of 950 feet.

The Great Galactic Ghoul, that cosmic scapegoat dreamed up by individuals at JPL, was accused of adversely affecting one of Mariner 7 batteries. But eventually, NASA was able to stabilise the probe and the craft made its closest pass on August 5 1969. (The probe took 126 pictures, 33 close-pass images at wide and narrow angles, and 93 images at far encounter phase.) Mariner 8 failed to achieve Earth orbit and ended its life the day after launch in the Atlantic Ocean some 224 miles north of Puerto Rico.

tion would turn out to be as gripping as any of these science fiction stories. Surprisingly, it would also turn out to be as full of plots, clues, suspects and detectives (both professional and amateur) as in any well-constructed detective story.

The Soviet Union and the United States commenced active probe launches to Mars in the early 1960s and the sharing of space in this regard is interesting reading. The US were, of course, somewhat occupied with the Apollo Showcase Premier throughout the 1960s and by 1970 their Mars program had extended to Mariner 8. Despite the maintenance of a competitive 'space race' attitude—that was prevalent in the record of that period—author Brian Harvey wrote in 1988 (and allowed it to remain in the '96 reprint):

> When the American schedule for the year became available it was clear that America's Mariner [number 8 or 9 not specified] would arrive in martian orbit just before Mars 2, 3, and 4. Accordingly the Babakin Bureau was ordered to produce an orbiter without a lander, which although it would leave Earth a day after Mariner 8, would overtake Mariner 8 and reach Mars first.

This the Babakin Bureau apparently did, although Mars 1/Cosmos 419 was the result.[3] As with the lunar scenario, the *reality* rather than the record was to be very different. Not having been in a true 'space race' in the first instance, their collaboration was so close that they even scheduled the launch of two probes to Mars on exactly the same day (March 27 1969)—the same year that the Americans and Soviets were officially but quietly discussing the 1975 Apollo-Soyuz link-up. Of course the American schedule made the order of arrival on the red planet clear, it was on both space agencies' timetables. These most interesting exploratory orbiters of the 1960s through to 1973 were followed by the launch of the two American Viking probes in August and September 1975.

Once the majority of the technical challenges of getting there had been overcome, the return of photographs from Mars increased steadily. The record suggests that it was the first of the Viking probes that imaged structures on Mars that remain the subject of contention over twenty years later. Looking at the details of the Mariner and Mars 2 & 3 orbits, one could conclude that the Viking orbiter/lander missions were partially designed *in response* to data *previously acquired* by Mariner. A closer examination of timetables, orbiter functions and discrepancies within the NASA account clearly demonstrates that such conclusions are justified.

Storm in a tea cup

Mariner 9 was destined to fly to within 800 miles of Mars. It arrived at the planet on November 16 1971 and was set into an orbit of two revolutions per Earth day so that the tracking stations on Earth, particularly Goldstone in California, were able to pick up the Mariner data transmission at exactly the same point in its orbit each day. Mariner 9 took literally *thousands of photographs* of the martian surface which were carefully pieced together onto a large globe to produce a detailed photographic map of the planet. Mariner 9 sent its final signal on October 27 1972 after completing 698 orbits of Mars and returning 7,329 images of the red planet's surface.

Most accounts of the Mariner 9 adventure stop there, but we decided to look closer at this mission. Initially everyone had to wait for the weather, for Mariner 9 was welcomed to Mars

1. Goldstone Mars antenna (DSS-14) at the time of Apollo.
NASA

by a dust storm of mega proportions, which completely obscured its surface, with the exception of four hazy spots. These turned out to be the areas above the four large shield volcanoes: Olympus Mons, several hundred miles to the north-west of Ascraeus, Pavonis and Arsis, the other three shield volcanoes on the Tharsis Montes.

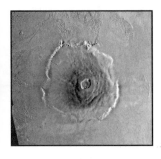

Olympus Mons is the largest volcano in our solar system. More than 10 miles high and 370 miles across, this giant volcano is located in the northern hemisphere at 19.47°N, 140°W. It is the site of the primary physical 3D energy upwelling on Mars and as we have seen in "Truth or Consequences", this entire volcanic area, known as Tharsis Montes (or ridge) can fit over the United States of America.

This martian dust storm had been forecast by Flagstaff Observatory back in February 1971, some three months prior to launch. It duly began on September 21 1971, over seven weeks before Mariner 9's arrival—but the record states that it was "just before the arrival of the craft" and that it "would persist through January 1972". Despite that inconvenient dust storm, good 'ole Mariner 9, in true 'right stuff' fashion, *was* able to do some planet-wide reconnaissance, while it waited to do full-scale mapping (although other researchers maintain that it did nothing but wait out the storm).[4] Eventually, the dust storm showed signs of weakening by December 30 and mapping cycles began on January 2. So much for "persisting through January 1972"—how well do the inaccuracies of language serve inaccuracies of action?

Babakin's alleged decree—that the Soviet probes for the 1971 favourable launch window: Mars 1, 2 and 3 be made lighter and faster, by reducing them to orbiters—eventually only applied to the unfortunate Mars 1 (renamed Cosmos 419 when

disaster struck). For when the Soviet craft Mars 2 of May 19 and Mars 3 of May 28 were actually launched, they *did* consist of an orbiter/lander combo designed to collect soil samples. Therefore there is no question of Mars 2 ever *overtaking* Mariner 9, as is implied by the 'race to Mars scenario'. These two Soviet craft therefore arrived at Mars just after Mariner 9 and it is at this point that we turn the page to find a remarkable storyline similar in every respect to the Apollo script. Just as the death of Korolëv allegedly sent the Soviet manned lunar mission into a tailspin, on August 26 1971 Georgi Babakin, the chief designer of the Mars probes died and it has been inferred that the Mars project then hit trouble.[5] Allegedly the Soviets could not alter the programming of their computers and thus the craft could not be commanded at a distance.

In September the US and Soviet craft were in place around Mars sitting out the sandstorm, except that the two lander components of the Soviet craft were programmed to descend whatever the weather, and descend they did. According to Brian Harvey, both landed successfully but failed to return any data. Well actually, Mars 3 returned 20 seconds of data and then stopped. Which gives first *landing* on Mars to the Soviets and thus conforms to the agreed division of planetary conquests that we consider was an integral component of the entire space program. Their orbiters, allegedly,

2. Representation of a Mariner craft approaching Mars.   NASA

only returned images of the storm to the USSR.

We are advised that it was the flexibility of being able to be commanded at a distance that enabled Mariner 9 to be the *only* successful mission. In our opinion the Soviets were building lunar probes that were commandable remotely from Earth in the 1960s (albeit with the help of their friends at Jodrell Bank) it is highly unlikely, notwithstanding the greater distances involved, that their technology *had regressed* when dealing with Mars probes in the 1970s.

The idea of a USSR/USA Mars race is equally untenable for the very good reason that by the launch date in 1971 the officialisation of the Apollo-Soyuz link-up was already in progress. How likely is it that the martian meteorological problems were not discussed between them? Far more likely that both agencies were carrying out the usual 'Mutt and Jeff' routine while sharing out their pre-sliced cake of space agendas. And quite likely that the real picture of the Soviets was not of such helplessness as has been portrayed. How many unpublished images of Mars do they possess that they have never needed to justify? The problems encountered by the Soviet probes sound like more "tales from the Mars side".

Mars 2 was orbiting the red planet once every 18 (Earth) hours; Mariner 9 once every 12 hours 34 mins (twice a Mars solar day) and Mars 3 every 11 days. According to Brian Harvey Mars 2 was orbiting at an inclination of 64.3° and Mars 2 at 48.54°. Harvey lists Mars 3's inclination as n/a, though whether not applicable or not available he doesn't say. It is here that we have some discrepancies with Baker, who tells us that Mariner 9 was orbiting at 800 miles at periaxis and at 37° of inclination—this is far nearer to the distance and inclination of Mars 2 and one might ask if some of the images generally attributed to Mariner 9 were not from Mars 2 at all. For even though the landers were defunct these orbiters continued to send back information and images to the Soviets until September 1972. Mars 5 also managed to send images back to Earth through to 1974.

Tales from the Mars side

The completion of Mariner 9's imaging mission on March 8 infers that all the photographic objectives had been achieved. After a pause of nearly four weeks the extended mission commenced. Note that this was not designated the 'secondary' mission, even though we believe that NASA meant the designation to mean: "continued on, due to what had been found on the primary mission". Furthermore, considering that the four/five weeks pause was the time needed to both process data acquired by March 8 and decide on a plan of action, there were remarkable differences in the *map four* cycle which could certainly merit the title "extended".

The small section covered by this *map four* session took 133 days to record. This is a timescale over *five times longer* than the mapping cycle of *map three* and *twice as long* as three primary mission mapping cycles, which took a total of 65 days to cover an equivalent latitudinal section of the planet. The most significant factor in this extended mission mapping cycle is the area of overlap that occurred between the primary mission, *map three* and the extended mission *map four*—both covered the region (from 40°N to 45°N).

What was of such apparent interest in that area for NASA?

There are two major aspects:

1) Cydonia is exactly one-third of the way around Mars, one hundred and twenty degrees eastwards from the 19.47° upwelling Olympus Mons. It lies in a region about 30 by 15 miles in extent/48 by 24 kms, making a total of some 450 square miles (about the size of Southern England). This region is located at 40.8°N and it is in trigonometric relationship to the 19.47° 'base' of an imaginary tetrahedron placed within the planet (see "THE Triangle").
2) It is within the region of Cydonia that a five-sided structure (named the D&M Pyramid or the Tor) plus various and diverse geometrical structures are located.
3) It is at Cydonia that the Face on Mars is to be found.

In 1974, supposedly following the Mariner 9 imaging, a brief comment on pyramidal and polygonal structures found by Mariner 9 in the region of Elysium appeared in the professional journal *Icarus*.[6] Then, in 1980, the well known astronomer Dr. Carl Sagan published pictures of four apparently tetrahedral pyramids from the region known as Utopia (at 40°N and nearly half way around the planet from Cydonia) in his work *Cosmos*, (the book of the eponymous TV series). Dr. Sagan *made a point* of emphasising that while resembling pyramids larger than those seen in Sumer, Egypt or Mexico these structures were no doubt natural but that they "merited another look".

Mariner 9's imaging timetable
Primary mission

January 2 *map one:* 20 day cycle covering latitudes 65°S to 20°S.

January 22 *map two:* 19 day cycle covering areas between latitudes 30°S and 20°N.

February 10 *map three:* 26 day cycle covering areas between latitudes 20°N to 45°N (includes the latitude of Cydonia) and then to 60°N.

March 8, the primary mission was completed in just over two months.

Extended mission

April 2 various Earth and solar occultations were carried out.

June 5 *map four* the region between 40°N and the north pole was mapped *AGAIN* on October 16.

This extended mission was completed
the occultations having taken just over two months—
the imaging having taken just over four months.

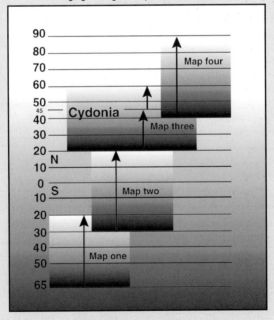

The Mars imaging program.

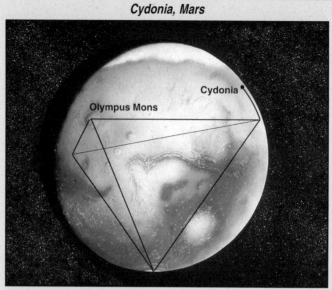

Cydonia, Mars

Cydonia in relation to Olympus Mons.
NASA, or the 'masters of infinity', either wittingly or unwittingly, have reflected something of themselves in the choice of name for this location.
Cydonia is the name of the quince apple. This is golden when ripe and reminds one of the three golden apples of Greek mythology.

Kydonia, Crete

It was also the name of a town in Crete (now called Canae).
The meaning of the word *Crete* relates to verse characterised by a particular metrical foot of one short syllable between two long syllables.
Built in north-western Crete by a colony from Samus, Kydonia was considered to be the place of residence of King Minos
who ordered the construction of the Labyrinth in order to secrete the Minotaur,
offspring of the Cretan bull and Minos' wife Pasiphae—
a liaison that had been set up with the help of Daedalus.
Daedalus was father of Icarus
(who melted his waxed wings by flying too close to the Sun).
Which makes the choice of the scientific journal *Icarus*,
as a conveyer of information regarding Mariner's pyramids, even more apposite.

It is our information that in both these cases, the images were deliberately inserted into the record in order to preclude the eventual discussion that might emerge concerning artefacts on Mars. By implying that such geometric 'structures' existed at other sites on the planet, should the Cydonia region ever start to pose a 'problem', the evidence was already on record to back up the dismissal of the Cydonian region's artefacts. By two different regions 'appearing' in two different types of publication, a professional journal and a populist book, the latter by an astronomer who, like Arthur C Clarke, and Humpty Dumpty generally sat on the wall when it came to ET intelligence. All bases were covered, if you will forgive the pun. *Icarus* and *Cosmos* were published pre and post the Viking mission information respec-

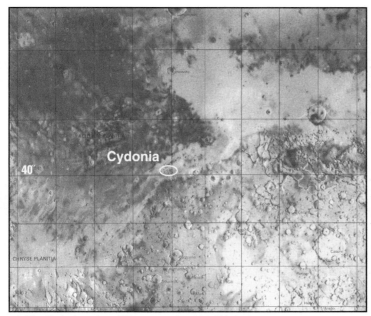

3. The Cydonia region of Mars centred at 40.8°N latitude.

tively. Moreover, it is notable that NASA was sensitive to the issue of artificial structures even *before* the 1995 departure of Viking 1. This reinforces our contention that the *Viking missions were specifically designed for investigating the Cydonia region as a result of the data received from 1972 Mariner 9 and very probably the 1972 Mars 2 and 1974 Mars 5 imagery as well.*

We are certain that the two media insertions to which we have referred went a long way towards stalling any serious discussion on the issue of artificial constructions on Mars. Scientific and academic establishments endorsed these artefacts as being the result of some peculiarity of the martian weathering processes, obviously "standard all over the planet". This prepared the terrain(!) so that when the great unwashed—the relatively 'non-scientific' general public, especially the ET and New Age crankies were to emerge with their questions, they would be silenced by such pre-packaged 'evidence', hopefully!

Indeed researcher Richard Hoagland stated that the images listed in the catalogue for the Elysium region actually turned out to be in the opposite hemisphere—and that therefore the images of the 'Elysium pyramids' are either missing or mis-filed. More hokum? How can these items have 'moved' half way round the planet? Or is this another case of following the second of Wople's Ways for avoiding the Freedom Of Information Act? For these images had been *deliberately mis-labelled* and moved around in the classification system.

Red faces all round!

Bearing all this in mind, we then looked closer at the historical record of the Viking orbiter/landers and while most of us are familiar with the squat, leggy landers, we are less familiar with the orbiters. These bear a striking visual resemblance to the traditional UFO-type spacecraft profile that NASA and the USAF have spent so much time and energy publicly denying.

The Viking orbiters' imagery improved *only slightly* on the standards set by Mariner 9

4. Viking Orbiter on special transporter during 1972 tests.
NASA

which, according to Carl Sagan, was able to image features down to 300 feet/90 metres across.[7] This is a very significant point, as all these probes were performing at comparable distances from Mars, so in reality, there would be no immediately discernible difference between these images, other than their mission name. The Viking images were sent back to Earth in digital or binary form (coded numbers) which corresponded to varying scales of grey initially registered from

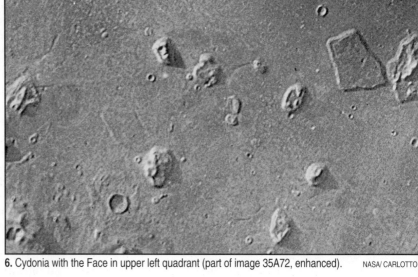

6. Cydonia with the Face in upper left quadrant (part of image 35A72, enhanced). NASA/ CARLOTTO

5. Typical Viking binary (digital) image and data. NASA

the martian surface.

These coded numbers were received by Earth-based antennae and recorded as impulses on long reels of magnetic recording tape. These were then duplicated onto smaller reels of tape. By running these duplicate reels through a computer, the numbers were reconfigured as a photographic image, either in negative or print form. The images could then be further enhanced in order to 'clean up' the transmission data, and achieve a greater degree of clarity for analytical purposes.

While the Viking 1 pictures contained much to fascinate astronomers, geologists and meteorologists there was nothing to excite followers of other disciplines. Or so it seemed at first. When the Viking orbiter images of Cydonia were released, the absolutely remarkable was found in great abundance.

It is in the region of Cydonia at latitude 41.19°N see (7) that we find the centre point of what has become known as the Face on Mars, also known as the martian Sphinx.

If NASA thought they were going to get away with exploring pyramidal structures and keeping matters quiet then they were in for a big surprise. At the time of the Mariner probes NASA had a choice, would they tell the truth about the variety of seemingly artificial structures discovered by the Mariner and Mars probes in the Cydonia region? For it is our information that the *only* artificial and mega-lithic structures on this planet are in or near that region *alone*.[8]

From the agency's actions during 1972 through to 1975 it was clear that once again NASA would not tell the people of planet Earth, who they represented, what had been found. It is our contention that the Face on Mars (like the Great Sphinx on Earth) had been partly covered by martian dust at the time of the Mariner 9 imaging—and that NASA's sur-prise was complete when it later picked up the images of the Face with their Viking probe.

No wonder NASA had to make a choice con-cerning the dissemination of the Mariner 9 information and, once more, it chose poorly.

Now there was yet another chance for the agency to make things right by disclosing its interest in this area.

But we are getting slightly ahead of our-selves, for at this point the plot thickens. As with the lunar data we shall have to pick our way carefully through a minefield of half-truths. Nevertheless, the principles that NASA applied to the Apollo Spoof Plot turn out to have been adopted by their martian plotters.

The Face that launched a thousand spaceships

The 1975 August 20 launch from Cape Canav-eral of Viking 1 achieved martian orbit by June 20 1976, and on June 21 established its final orbit of 941 miles at periapsis (closest pass) by 20,381 apoapsis (furthest point of orbit). The first images were transmitted back to Earth from the orbiter that same Sunday.

Over a month later on July 25 1976, five days after the Viking 1 lander had been set down on the martian surface, Gerry Soffen the Viking project scientist, held a press conference for over a thousand journalists wanting an up-sum on NASA's search for extra terrestrial life. It was during that conference that a photograph classified as 35A72 was presented to the press and at this point the disinformation started with a vengeance. The folklore surrounding the presentation of the Viking images, including image 35A72 of the Face, is considerable. Generally it is said that this image was first spotted by Toby Owen, at that time a NASA imaging specialist, who had discovered this frame in a search for a suitable landing spot for Viking 2's lander, then on its way to Mars. He had exclaimed: "Oh, my God, look at this!" After several more comments such as "isn't that weird!" the image had been 'ignored' as being, "too weird, so obviously not a real-ity"—allegedly!

This version of the 'discovery story' appears in Richard Hoagland's *The Monuments of Mars*. Indeed Hoagland esteemed that Toby Owen's reaction to the Face was perfectly nor-mal as, "One does not expect to find a human face on Mars, and certainly not one that is a mile long".[9] On the face(!) of it this was a somewhat astonishing comment to make when one considers that NASA had specifically stated that the Viking missions *were searching for signs of life on Mars*. What a wonderful

---

V 1 King, a creature of habit

The Viking 1 lander finally arrived on the surface of Mars at 12 hrs 12 mins 07 secs UT (Universal time/GMT) July 20 1976, thus memorialising the 'arrival of Apollo 11' on the Moon some 7 years previously.

The Viking 1 press conference presided over by Gerry Soffen, occurred on another anniversary: July 25 1976, during which the awkward problem of the Face on Mars was placed on the record and then dismissed as a trick of the light. July 25 1969 was the day that *Time* magazine raised the awkward problem of the Earth/Moon Neutral Point discrepancy which was placed on the record and then studiously ignored. It has taken nearly thirty years to slowly unravel the mythos of the manned lunar missions. Concerning the martian Sphinx it took only three years before NASA were put on the spot by researchers, yet a further twenty years on, we are no nearer a frank exchange of views between the people and the space agency concerning Cydonia and its artefacts. The day originally scheduled for the official landing of the soft lander component of Viking 1 onto the martian surface had been 4th July—of course!

if July 4 is 'invasion day' in the diaries of these traditionalist masters—is July 25 'spin doctor day'?

---

surprise to find an anomaly that had such marked correspondence to our own biological characteristics. Apparently NASA did not think so. For it only wanted to talk about possible basic signs of very *primitive* life the Viking lander experiments were undertaking and either ignore *potential* signs of *intelligent* life—or rather keep that information to itself, according to the agencies' officially 'unofficial' brief. Interestingly, at the time, Richard Hoagland was working on the Press Corps at the Jet Propulsion Laboratories, so perhaps we should think carefully about his earlier comment.

Given the number of people involved at some level with the Viking project, and given the fact that eventually this image would emerge, no doubt it was safer to get it 'out in the open' rather than to wait for someone else to ask awkward questions, for when Gerry Soffen produced 35A72 of Cydonia and the Face, he did not ignore the image, or pass it off within a series of aerial shots, he *drew attention* to the Face by saying, "Isn't it peculiar what tricks of lighting and shadow can do?" Having examined NASA's Apollo photography in some detail we most certainly agree with him!

"The Face", they were told by the friendly and trustworthy Dr. Gerry Soffen, "is just a trick, the way the light fell on it". He added that in an image taken "a few hours later, it all went away". Graham Hancock writing in 1998 stated that this photograph was actually taken on July 25 and from a distance of 1,162 miles.[10] NASA would not have had time to receive the image on July 25, process it and also have "one taken a few hours later" in the can by the time of the conference. And even if that 'one we prepared later' never existed, NASA would have programmed enough time into their script for it to have been able to happen at least in theory. Hancock also says that the original text under 35A72 stated that it was 1.5km (1 mile) *across*. Subsequent information from other sources would state—correctly—that this sculpted mesa was actually one mile *in length*.

According to Hoagland, NASA numbered their Viking images in the following way: orbit-craft-frame. Therefore, image 35A72

meant thirty-fifth orbit, 'A' craft, seventy-second frame. Hoagland also stated that this frame in question was imaged at 6.00 pm local time with a 10° Sun angle. Soffen was known to be an engaging and sympathetic scientist with considerable credibility amongst the press and therefore they all accepted his statement as fact and the matter was forgotten. Gerry Soffen had not lied, because a few hours later this region of the planet would have been in total darkness and obviously it would all have "gone away". Dr. Soffen had only been somewhat economical with the truth.

It was to be three years before anybody outside NASA discovered that another image taken "a few hours later" *did actually exist*. So how many hours make "a few" for the historians at NASA? Numbered 70A13 this second image would have been taken some 35 orbits later *if* we take the numbering system at face value (no apologies!) and *if* it was taken by the *same* orbiter that took image 35A72.

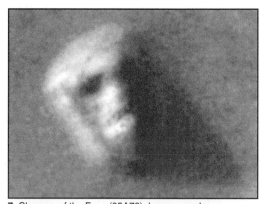

7. Close up of the Face (35A72), low sun angle.

NASA/CARLOTTO

Two facets

Carl Sagan made a fundamentally important statement concerning the Viking orbiter/landers in *Cosmos*. "When each of the two Viking orbiter-lander combinations was inserted into martian orbit, *it was unalterably committed to landing at a certain latitude on Mars.*" (our emphasis) The longitude could be selected by adjusting the speed of the orbit in relation to the rotation of the planet, and was therefore flexible.

This means that the decision as to which band of latitude would be imaged had to be decided *before the arrival of the probe into martian orbit.* NASA stated that they sent Viking 1 to the Chryse Planitia because this site fulfilled the paradigms of temperature, surface conditions, communications accessibility and that upon the successful arrival of Viking 2, this second probe would be able to live a little more dangerously—they would therefore send it up further up north at 44°N to Cydonia. Carl Sagan stated that Cydonia had been selected by NASA experts because "according to some theoretical arguments, there was a significant chance of [finding] small quantities of liquid water there". And also, "some scientists held that the chance of Viking finding life would be substantially improved in Cydonia".[11]

You bet they found life! Yet Carl Sagan repeated three times in the same chapter that the martian landing sites were selected for their dullness! After examining the martian images numbering 100,000 (allegedly) Sagan finally concluded, "that no evidence of *intelligence* appears." (emphasis added) More utter hokum.

As we know, the Viking 1 landing site was reviewed for five weeks and retained while the Cydonia site was abandoned(!) and Utopia Planitia allegedly chosen instead. As for responding to ultimate safety requirements for

---

Carl's marks

Basing his evaluation on data from the Nimbus satellite which had a resolution of a few 10ths of a km,

Carl Sagan estimated that:

"Convincing photographic evidence of intelligent life on Earth

requires a resolution of 10 metres/33 ft or better."

NASA and all who fear ET invasion can relax, for by these standards the Great Wall Of China, visible from Space is not evidence of intelligent life!

The opinion of Dr. Sagan is obviously not that of the authors.

0/12

---

these landers, neither too dusty nor too soft, not too high in altitude and not too windy, the final sites chosen were in fact very rocky and the landers had a trial finding a footing, one nearly tipped over as it set down.

David Baker's *Spaceflight and Rocketry: A Chronology* records that Viking 2 arrived in orbit on August 7 and the lander descended on September 3 at 47.97°N, 225.71°W, as does *Encyclopaedia Britannica* and the *National Geographic.* This same work by Baker also has Viking 1 landing rather off course at around 27°N, 47°E, instead of the 'official' 22.38°N, 47.49°W. This total confusion of data on the part of both NASA and highly respectable reference sources is what we have come to expect, but that does not make it in any way acceptable. Moreover, Baker states that the Viking 2 lander failed to transmit data *just as it was arriving on the surface of the planet and no record of its descent and arrival on the planet existed* (emphasis added). Naturally, (our sarcasm) this "minor systems failure" partially re-established itself once the lander was ensconced on Mars and was fully up and running by the next morning. What a surprise! What did they not want officially imaged on the way down? Could it be that Viking 2 was landing near the D&M pyramid (the Tor) and this, looming up, was not going to be a desirable feature. Pretty difficult to pretend Viking 2 was over the other side of the planet if everybody saw those flat, megalithic walls filling their view!

In case this data is confusing you as much as NASA might like it to do, in essence:

A) Each orbiter/lander combo was inserted into its latitudinal orbit around Mars. (This was unchangeable.)
B) Each lander surveyed its choice of landing sites. (This site selection could be altered by slowing down or speeding up the craft until it was at the desired longitude.)
C) Each lander was then commanded by radio to descend to the selected site.
D) Each lander communicated with its orbiter. The orbiters then communicated with Earth.

According to the selected NASA latitudes

for Vikings 1 and 2, either the outcome of this latitudinal restriction means that the Viking 2 orbiter took the pictures of Cydonia and the Face, or both orbiters were in that region.

Throughout this book we have uncovered (sadly) many instances of NASA's perfidy and so we do not hesitate to assert that there was another scenario for the Mars exploration than the official record. Following the Cydonia mapping, images received via Mariner 9 (and perhaps the Soviets' craft) we suggest that a decision was made to place an orbiter over the Cydonia region and place a lander near the pyramidal structures the agency had previously observed. The decision as to where to place the second Viking would depend upon the outcome of that first landing.

From the very start of the project, the first Viking had been destined for the Cydonia orbit which would mean scanning 41° north latitude.

Upon arrival at Mars, NASA was perhaps somewhat astonished to find something in their imaging that had not been apparent on the Mariner images: the Face. Those five weeks of deciding to find another landing site for Viking 2 represent the time it took to reconfigure a plan of action in order to investigate further. We suggest that Viking 1 was landed just beside the D&M Pyramid (the Tor) and that following the successful landing we consider that Viking 2 was *also* landed at Cydonia, but over to the east of the area near to an extremely large, flat-topped rock.

This intriguing site is a large mesa that NASA has studiously avoided mentioning since the beginning of the furore over Cydonia. If anything screams "artificially flattened" it is this rock platform. Where there might be room for manoeuvre regarding tricks of light and shadow concerning the Face, there are certainly no doubts as to the utter flatness of this large mesa to the south-east of the Face.[12]

Facing the facts

The magazine *Soviet Life* published an article on the martian structures in which it stated that

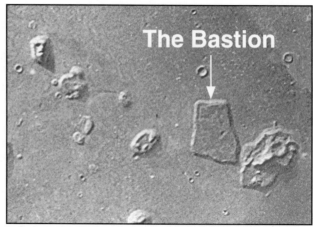

8. Cydonia, the Bastion. An apparently artificially-flattened rock, *more than two miles in length*. Compare its flatness with its natural neighbour to the east. NASA

the original images were transmitted to Earth from *Mariner 9* and *Viking 1*. Allegedly, there was also a top-level conference at the Kremlin between the Soviet Space Agency and religious leaders. From 1976 through to 1979 NASA showed *absolute* reluctance to commit to any sort of re-imaging of this region—on the grounds that there was not enough proof of an artificial structure or structures for it to be worth their while returning specifically to the Cydonia arena. Such unreasonable expectations closed the door to further investigation by NASA—at least officially.

Carl Sagan considered that scientists only abide military secrecy *by prior agreement*, and not 'ex post facto' (after the event). However, as NASA is a US Government agency—and many of its employees, its contractors and *their* employees are bound by enforced security—this "securing the defense of the United States" would not have been a problem.

The Face on the cutting room floor

It was not until 1979,[13] that Professor Vincent DiPietro and his colleague Gregory Molenaar were looking through the picture library of the US National Space Science Data Center when they unexpectedly came upon that second image 70A13 of the Cydonia Face—which they found had been mis-filed. They were *amazed* at what they saw—and we use their own word. And we too are amazed at the desperate attempts of NSSDC/NASA to 'mis-file' their priceless images from Mars. Image (9) was taken at a higher Sun angle of around 27°. With the Face clearly visible when viewed from *two different Sun angles*, we can be quite sure that this remarkable phenomenon is in no way due to any "trick of the light" (see also pictures 6 & 7).

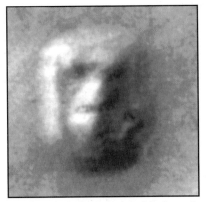

9. The Face (70A13, high Sun) part of the image found by Professor Vince DiPietro and Gregory Molenaar.

NASA/CARLOTTO

Subsequently in 1979-1980, DiPietro and Molenaar carried out their valuable research and enhancement on this data from Cydonia and further computer enhancement of the NASA images was performed by Dr. Mark Carlotto in the US. More recently in London, we have carried out additional rectification and enhancement of the material. Yet NASA still refused to be drawn as to the future plans for the Cydonia region, although they had to pay some kind of lip service to the furore that erupted after DiPietro and Molenaar discovered this second image.

In the mid 1990s NASA HQ issued a list of 'all' the images taken over the Cydonia plain in 1976 by Viking. In addition to the six pictures eventually located by DiPietro and Molenaar, this list included four new images, as well as ten pictures taken over the complex that included the Face. In all, eighteen images were taken of the region by the Viking I and 2 orbiters. The pictures with the best resolution of the Face are the two images we have been discussing namely 35A72 and 70A13.

Staying ahead?

NASA's image of what has come to be popularly known as the Face was catalogued at Goddard Space Archives as 'the head'. Yet another source of these pictures, the Jet Propulsion Laboratory, had no recollection of having such an image! When this image was requested from JPL in 1977 by Walter Hain, he was told by one Don Bane, that unless Hain was able to quote the exact archive number he would not be able to help him. "Those nicknames that you give the pictures (like 'Mars face') mean absolutely nothing to me..." wrote Don Bane, obeying the first of Wople's Ways.

Walter Hain comments that back in the seventies the numbers of the images were not systematically issued with the image, so there was not necessarily any way of requesting an image by numerical reference. However, by 1978 Don Bane managed to equate 'Mars face' with an image and sent Hain a print. JPL's co-ordinates were incorrect, especially for the actual latitude of the Face, which is rather surprising—but the significance of this 'mistake' will become very relevant, as we will soon find out!

Don Bane also stated that the incidence of light was at 20°—this is not in agreement with subsequent data which gives 10° Sun elevation for 35A72 and 27° Sun elevation for image 70A13. Bane subsequently corrected his information, advising Walter Hain that the Sun angle was in fact 10°. Oh dear! What a tangled web they wove. First they couldn't/wouldn't find the images, then they can't/won't remember what the Sun angle was. Given that this image was at that time allegedly *UNIQUE* amongst the NASA data, knowing the Wople's Way, we are no longer surprised by the 'amnesia' virus rampaging through the halls of NASA. However, if NASA was unable or unwilling to make the connection between the two words 'Head' and 'Face' in relation to the Cydonia complex on Mars, then should we be worrying about their intelligence quotient, or their integrity quotient?

Just before his death in February 1997, Carl Sagan, astronomer and defender of the NASA faith, actually said that Dr. Soffen had been ill advised in denying the existence of the Face, and in his 1996 book *The Demon-Haunted World,* Sagan expanded on this statement. Adopting the popular Humpty Dumpty attitude, Sagan himself still did not think that there was anything meaningful to this structure and considered that it was most unlikely—even most improbable—that it was an artificial construction. But he went on to say that the questioned structures of the Cydonia region were certainly "worth examining". He expressed the hope that the future Mars missions carried out by both the Russians and the Americans would make special efforts to investigate the Cydonia region. Unfortunately, it turns out that Dr. Sagan's statements suffer from misleading innuendoes. Sagan managed to acknowledge the careful and professional work of image processing specialists Carlotto, DiPietro and Molenaar, while at the same time ignoring these very same qualifications, when asserting that transmission error 'dots' on these images are deluding these very same researchers into thinking that they are seeing a symmetrical face.

Perhaps NASA and the 'masters of infinity' wish us all to believe that this whole matter of Mars has been an illusion, fostered by themselves, and foisted on us, in order to raise funding for Mars space research. It is an idea, certainly. The problem is that it is an idea that only works in isolation. When taken together with the evidence presented in this book—from 1908 through to 1998—we can see that the rules of the game have now changed. The methodology of the 'masters of nothing' is still apparent but now they are no longer fully in charge of the outcome. They can only attempt to bend their responses to fit the event, or in other words, "try to rearrange their molecules in all of their energy fields".[14]

Little wonder the 'problems' have been blamed on a 'galactic ghoul'.

Eagle's eyes

It is unsurprising that the agency will not commit publicly to an investigation of this region in detail. It cannot be sure of what it will find. Yet we can say that it is *totally aware* that the Cydonia area is full of artificial constructions—because military-trained remote viewers have taken a "closer look" at these structures. Bringing in remote viewers is an example of how seriously the findings in this region of Mars are being taken. Short of actually landing and investigating these structures, there is simply no other way of 'viewing' (externally or even internally) at close quarters artefacts that are simply out of reach to Earth visitors.

According to the American military (who do not care very much either *why it works,* or *how it works*, as long as they get results—which they do), remote viewing is described as the ability to translocate the *mind* anywhere in space and time and report back efficiently what is seen. The findings are reported in words and/or by drawings. Incidentally, this skill should not be confused with 'out of the body' experiences. The sessions are totally controllable by those running the experiments. Generally the remote viewer is given a trigger, such as a set of map co-ordinates and asked to go to that place, and report. The leader of the experiment does not 'lead' the viewer but simply notes and monitors the progress. Opinions as to actual methodology vary but remote viewing was and is taken very seriously by the American military and the intelligence community.

This investigation was carried out principally at Fort Meade in Texas and at SRI, organised by Hal Puthoff and his colleagues. It is interesting that in 1972 Uri Geller was also at SRI during that period—was he remote viewing as well as working with the military on laser and computer technology? Whatever the opinions on actual methodology, one thing on which most organisers are agreed was that Joe McMoneagle was the best remote viewer of the program. However, it would appear that he was presented with misleading location data.

Allegedly co-opted into the SRI program in 1978, McMoneagle declared in his 1993 biography *Mind Trek* that he was given the Mars images to remote view in 1984.[15] Remarkably, Joe McMoneagle has published co-ordinates for the images viewed that are incorrect, even ac-

Target Number Seven: 15° North Latitude, 198° East Longitude **Pyramid Structures** (*Figure 35*).

Figure 35. Pyramid Structures, Blowup of Frame 70A77.

10. Joe McMoneagle's remote viewing target # 7. This image is actually part of Cydonia's Altea City (see below), which has been rotated through 90° and given false map co-ordinates.

cording to NASA's own terms of photographic reference. For example, 70A13 is located by McMoneagle at 44°N. And when we remember that the Viking probes had to stay in the latitude into which they were inserted, then how can frame 70A77 possibly be at latitude 15°N?

QUESTION: Was McMoneagle misled by his superiors as to the actual location of the artefacts?

QUESTION: Has McMoneagle been required to disguise them for security purposes?

QUESTION: Or is he too obliged to assist in the artifice that these artefacts are scattered all over the planet?

Mr McMoneagle is certainly a remote viewer but he was also in the military and an employee of the US Government until his retirement. He recognised that "the events described are essentially true" and that although he had given evasive answers to some direct questions, his answers, nevertheless "held an *element* of truth".

Notwithstanding the locations given, we immediately recognised these sites from the perceptions and sketches that McMoneagle provided *before he was shown the actual photographs of these locations*.

When describing the image that McMoneagle received for the first photograph, he made no mention of the Face. It is our understanding that McMoneagle was perhaps viewing from an angle that did not give him an overview of the area, or that the comments relating to the Face were excised from the account in his book, or that the published image 35A72 in the book does not correspond to the photograph that was actually being used for the experiment. It is also notable that 70A77, allegedly taken at 15° above the equator appears to have been taken some 64 frames after the second image of the Face— which was of course 70A13. Then again, perhaps Dick Hoagland is only partially correct with regard to NASA's classification system, 'A' might simply mean 'orbiter'.

However, the military are not the only people able to deploy remote viewing techniques and we can assure Joe McMoneagle and our readers that despite the published co-ordinates, these sites *are all* in or near the Cydonia region.

The overall impression from this and other books by researchers in this arena, is that the seeds have been planted for a scenario that accommodates the NASA policy. Joe McMoneagle described the pyramidal structure he viewed as megalithic, okra coloured, (as okra is a green vegetable, did he mean ochre?) And then McMoneagle said that he had an impression of severe clouds, more like a dust storm (shades of Mariner—is this an indication that the image used was a Mariner 9 picture and that the Face was therefore not visible on it?). And then he states that he was looking at the after effect of a major geological trauma. We suspect that he was looking at partial damage to the Five-sided pyramid, the Tor—see next page and (18). However it could be that this damage was not caused by a planetary geological catastrophe, but by a local event which we, the authors have described elsewhere.[16]

As a final word on remote viewing, would it surprise you to learn that the aptly named Lambert Dolphin, a physicist at SRI, who worked with Hoagland on the Cydonia material was involved in remote viewing projects that concerned not only Mars but also the artefacts on the Giza Plateau?[17]

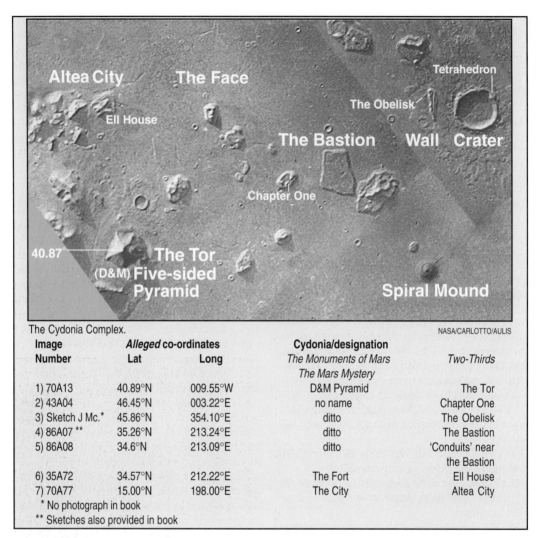

The Cydonia Complex.   NASA/CARLOTTO/AULIS

Image Number	Alleged co-ordinates		Cydonia/designation	Two-Thirds
	Lat	Long	The Monuments of Mars The Mars Mystery	
1) 70A13	40.89°N	009.55°W	D&M Pyramid	The Tor
2) 43A04	46.45°N	003.22°E	no name	Chapter One
3) Sketch J Mc.*	45.86°N	354.10°E	ditto	The Obelisk
4) 86A07 **	35.26°N	213.24°E	ditto	The Bastion
5) 86A08	34.6°N	213.09°E	ditto	'Conduits' near the Bastion
6) 35A72	34.57°N	212.22°E	The Fort	Ell House
7) 70A77	15.00°N	198.00°E	The City	Altea City

* No photograph in book
** Sketches also provided in book

Giza gazers

The establishment generally does not relish any connection between Mars and the Egyptian artefacts—censorship is exercised as and when necessary. On November 27 1994 *The Age of The Sphinx,* part of the well-respected *Time-Watch* Series, was first broadcast on British television. This TV documentary contained a section concerning possible links between the Sphinx and the Face on Mars.

In July 1995 this program was re-peated—*only this time the section of referring to these martian connections had been cut.*

For those who had seen both broadcasts, this was rather a surprise! We questioned the BBC and the *TimeWatch* producer told us that: "We were obliged to cut the length for programming purposes."[18] Scheduling is always done weeks in advance of transmission, and in the summer season British TV is overrun with repeats. There were no major news items that disrupted the schedules that day. It looks very much as if a judicious edit was executed and sounds as if someone had been shouting "Off with her head!"—but who was the judge, who were the jury and what was the crime? We also wonder why the BBC should go to the bother of high-

have a bearing in the future? Whatever the hidden motives of the powers behind the Beeb's throne, paradoxically, by eliminating this sequence, the detractors of the Mars/Giza theory very publicly drew attention to it. Does this sound at all familiar, somewhat like the business with UFOs? While on the one hand announcing that something does not exist the 'authorities' seemingly emphasise its importance by taking action against the non-existent factor.

Again, curioser and curioser.

The Lion lines

The original NASA images of the Face on Mars indicated that it was symmetrical. It was *assumed* by those that studied these images that the side of the Face in *shadow* was similar to the *sunlit* side. However, after examining computer enhanced images employing local contrast equalisation, one could observe detail in the shadow side, which has been brought up to the same standard as the sunlit side.

11. Local contrast equalisation. NASA/CARLOTTO
The Face on Mars was clearly intended as a beacon.

lighting the matter by repeating a doctored version so soon after the first transmission? Someone obviously perceived a need to redefine the record.

We noted that July 1995 was the broadcast month for the Roswell autopsy film. This production received massive pre-publicity both in the American and UK press and was screened at around the same time in both countries. Did this have a bearing on the matter? Or would it

As a result of this processing, we can compare the two faces of Cydonia and Egypt, because it is possible to demonstrate that the Face on Mars is in fact a *Sphinx*. In other words, it incorporates both man and lion in its

DARK MOON

design. For with the Face on Mars, we find the hominid representing consciousness, and the lion for courage, representing the heart. We can best evaluate this imagery by matching sides, that is—if we take the left side as you look at it, (the right side if you imagine you *are* it) match it and 'flip' it, we see that we have the image of a primate (12).

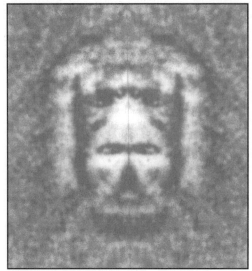

12. The Primate side matched.

When we take the right side of the Face as you look at it (the left side if you *are* it) match and 'flip' that—we have the image of a lion (13).

It is not the remit of this book to explain in great detail all the encodings of this Sphinx, the very specific reasons why the martian Sphinx is primate on the left and leonine on the right are all addressed in detail in *Two Thirds*. This chapter is concerned with drawing attention to the key points that link the planets of Mars and Earth. The best example that we have on Earth of a Sphinx is of course, the sculpture sited on the Giza Plateau, near Cairo, in Egypt.

We consider that our Great Sphinx was linked both in essence and in mathematical relationship to the Face on Mars and we maintain that these two Sphinx-like structures have a common ancestry. An intensive survey of our planet's mythology is also beyond the

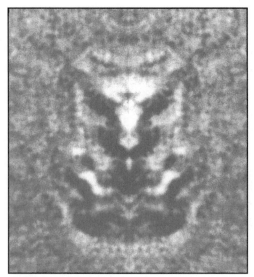

13. The Lion side matched.

scope of this particular book, but it is worth noting here, that Hindu mythology called Mars 'Nr-Simha'—the planet of the man-lion. As with the Hindu mythology (which is laden with references to UFOs and the 'becoming of things'), the martian Sphinx sculpture is, among other things, a commemoration of the architectural, artistic and encoded philosophical aspects of the beings who constructed the Cydonia complex on Mars. This statement also

14. This facial expression increases access to what is called the 'vomeronasal region'. Covered in sensor cells, and located above the palate, it permits the tiger to take in all the scents pertaining to her/his territory.

484

holds true for the Giza Sphinx and the arte-facts on the Giza plateau. The martian Face was sculpted on the top of a 1 mile/1.6 kms long mesa in order that it would be *visible from space* when viewed, remotely or other-wise. This would of course occur at the point when an observer, particularly mankind, had evolved sufficiently to be able to despatch a probe designed to orbit and photograph Mars.

In February 1992, Darryl Anka the psychic transcommunicator of 'Bashar' was asked specific questions about the Great Sphinx at Giza.[19] Whatever one's personal views on the means used to acquire it, in this case a deep-trance communication, the information re-ceived is apposite. When the questioner en-quired on our behalf about the feminine aspect of the Sphinx, Bashar replied:

16. Etching of side view of the female side of the Great Sphinx at a time when the Sphinx basin was filled with sand.

Many thousands of years ago on planet Earth, the feminine power and energy was more understood, female and male were more in balance, whereas now the energy of this planet is fundamentally based on a patriarchal (male) system.

The Sphinx is a very good primal exam-ple of the blending and balancing of the female and male energy in one particu-lar physiological symbol. Therein is the concept of feline grace as it connects to human consciousness, both represented by the way of feminine intuition and masculine power in receptivity.

Assertiveness is depicted in the leonine reclining position. By combining the animal body with human features, this statue is then used as an indication of the potential energy that can be re-leased. It is therefore a blending of the *'idea'* of the physiological prowess of animal power with the *'idea'* of spiritu-ality—or psychic instinctive ener-gies—which are usually ascribed to the female.

Thus sculpted, this symbol becomes a representation not only of the blending

15. Aerial view of the Great Sphinx (viewed from the left, the male side)　　　C DAVIES

485

17. The Great Sphinx female side.   C DAVIES

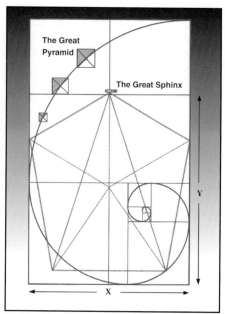

18. The Giza Plateau illustrating its underlying layout based on a transD spiral (X = 0.866% of Y) The five-sided outline is the groundplan of the Five-sided (D&M Pyramid, the Tor) on Mars (see also 20).

of female and male, but also of Heaven and Earth; in your contemporary times, the cat generally symbolises the bridge between your physical and non-dimensional physicality.

The Sphinx was created for several reasons:

A) As a remnant/reminder of the civilisation that *you* call Atlantis.
B) As a symbolic 'look-out' for the future.
C) As a symbol to guide the future back to its former level.
This is similar to the *'idea'* of the Sphinx on what you call Cydonia, Mars. *That* Sphinx was also created...to allow future humanity to be lured back to   itself.

Thus the 'Sphinx' has always been used to cast an eye into the future. As a psychic monument to allow humanity to find its former glory and level.

In that way, the Sphinx acts as a marker.
Both the Sphinx on Mars and the Sphinx on Earth were created for this same purpose and impart information which is encoded into its form, its structure and within the nearby regions of the location of the Sphinx.
In solving the 'riddle of the Sphinx' you can uncover and crack the codes of your former knowledge and *regain* your for-

mer understanding of your connection to nature and to the Universe.
The Crop Glyphs are the beginning of this decoding, expressed in another way.

Nine lives
We have already made passing reference to *The Only Planet of Choice.* This book is a collection of transcommunications selected from material accumulated over some twenty years of meetings with the Council of Nine. Among the many people, famous and private, who have had the privilege of speaking to Tom, the Council's spokesman, were Gene Rodenberry (who received much guidance for the early scripts of *Star Trek),* and the famous American researcher Dr. Andrija Puharich, who worked on PSI research projects such as those carried out by Puthoff at SRI. Both the authors of this book have also had the pleasure of speaking with Tom, who was transceived by the well-known deep trance medium Phyllis

486

Schlemmer. During one session Dr. Andrija Puharich who is called Andrew in the book) asked if it was true that there were secret chambers within the Great Pyramid—and that, "if entered by certain people, it will mark the end of a cycle for humanity"?

Tom had replied: "It is to a degree. The entrance is from the Sphinx."[20]

Tom's answers are generally not as literal as they first appear, or at least the first take is only one of many answers carefully encoded into his words. A further understanding of his answer is that endings are beginnings and vice versa, for we have been given to understand that the very first artefact sculpted on the Giza Plateau was not the Great Pyramid, but the Great Sphinx.[21] Many people are expecting to find a Hall of Records under the Sphinx, as predicted by the famous psychic, Edgar Cayce. And although scientific instruments have found spaces that suggest there are chambers within or under the Sphinx, to date the Egyptians will not let anyone *publicly* explore this possibility.[22] However, it is rather immature and literal thinking to imagine that these will be filled with *writings* pertaining to possible 'answers'.

We suggest that humankind is already in possession of the messages, the information. It is currently here in our architecture, the encoded landscaping, planetary relationships, Crop Glyphs, and yes, ET craft and UFO sightings. These 'artefacts' are all clues *that we have to work things out for ourselves*—albeit with a little help from our friends. And everywhere that we look, *the 'language' is the measurement and the 'writing' is the artefact itself.* Tom's reply to Dr. Andrija Puharich also relates to the *number of degrees* made by the Causeway in relation to the Great Sphinx's *right paw*. This turns out to be an angle of—19.47° (see 19).

Two key points:

- 19.47° is the latitude for the point of 3D energy upwelling of a planet (q.v.). The Cydonia Sphinx is sited at a point on Mars *one-third* of the way (one vertex of a tetrahedron) from Olympus Mons, the energy upwelling on Mars. And as we have stated, this volcano is located at a latitude namely 19.47°

19. The front paws of the Great Sphinx   C DAVIES *are not parallel.* The right paw deliberately rests at 19.47° to the causeway, which is visible at the top left hand corner of the picture.

which is the base latitude on the sphere of a circumscribed tetrahedron.

- 1947 is the year that the Roswell Incident occurred and the public start of the UFO events of modern times. How could 19.47°/1947 possibly be dismissed as any kind of coincidence?

A one way ticket too wide

Following the considerable controversy over the Viking data, the next effort from the space agencies was a very publicised program of probes for the 1990s—destination Mars.

In September 1992 NASA launched an imaging probe, the *Mars Observer,* which had the capability—beginning in December 1993—of re-imaging the Cydonia complex. NASA was potentially able to capture surface details down to three feet in size. There was strong evidence supporting the hypothesis of the intelligent construction of the Cydonia complex on Mars, a hypothesis that devolved from the careful and persistent study of the Viking orbiter images carried out by non-government (and therefore unbiased) researchers—who then presented their findings to NASA in Washington during 1992 with subsequent follow-ups.

What did NASA do in response? Or rather what did it *not* do?

NASA refused to make any effort whatsoever to re-image the area in which the Cydonia complex is located. The British Prime Minister, Tony Blair, when elected in 1997 immediately disassociated the Bank of England from government (thereby avoiding any accountability or responsibility for British base rate which would, over time, affect the pound sterling and foreign exchange rates). NASA too, has used similar manoeuvres when (prior to the Mars Observer probe launch) it 'gave away' the ownership and responsibility of the Mars images to Michael Malin, a staunch upholder of the anti-Cydonia Artefacts Camp. The agency did concede that if, by chance, any images of that area were captured, then they would be made available to the public *approximately six months* after their arrival on Earth.

Why a delay of such a period? Apparently that would be the time it would take for Malin to prepare the images for release in a scientific and adequate way. But these clever tactics did not matter in the end, for just as the NASA craft was entering into orbit around the red planet on August 21 1993 (the day that the

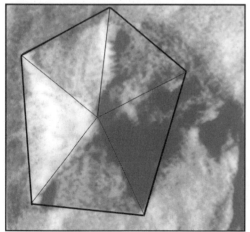

20. The Five-sided pyramid (the Tor) on the Cydonia complex, Mars.   NASA/CARLOTTO/TORUN

work *Two-Thirds* was first published) Mars Observer 'failed'. Graham Hancock notes the extreme lack of haste and endeavour on the part of NASA in its attempts to re-establish contact with its craft, and he is astonished by NASA's seeming lack of enthusiasm in this matter. We suggest that their lack of enthusiasm might be put down to the fact that they knew quite well that this craft had gone AWOL. Perhaps it was another example of interference by what they call the 'Great Galactic Ghoul' that has been plaguing NASA & Co. over the years.

It would seem that if NASA was not going to make the Mars images immediately available to the people of planet Earth, then NASA was not going to have the pictures either.

Facades

We started this chapter by discussing the Face on Mars. But there are other structures within the Cydonia region that are of interest including the highly significant five-sided D&M pyramid which we call the Tor. Whether they be the authors of voluminous tomes, writers of articles in the popular press, or specialist magazines, a number of researchers have expressed opinions as to the origin of the Cydonia structures. Opinions vary from conventional scientific explanations of natural forces such as wind, to an ancient martian civilisation that perished, through to colonisers from 'elsewhere' who then travelled onwards when the climate of Mars changed. Some have even asked if these artefacts were not created by *human* beings—which is giving NASA & Co. far more credit for their technological capabilities than they deserve! However, let us take these various theories one by one.

EROSION

When the Crop Glyphs of Southern England's fields (which, since 1989 have evolved from simple circles into patterns containing rectangles and other precise geometrical wonders and then fractal-like glyphs—rather beyond the capacity of any human hoaxer), what was known as the *Meaden hypothesis,* suggesting their natural occurrence due to plasma vortices was blown away! Similarly, the theory that natural erosion was responsible for the martian structures on Cydonia bites the dust, not only from the sheer limitations of the physics of erosion, but also by reason of the very intricate geometrical relationships inherent in the layout of the Cydonia region.

The overlaid picture (20) emphasises the straight lines of the five-sided pyramid (the Tor) located to the south-east of the Cydonia 'City'. (Also known as the D&M pyramid, after the discoverers Professor Vincent DiPietro and his colleague Gregory Molenaar.) Erol O Torun, a geomorphologist with the American Defense Mapping Agency, has stressed that an object with five *straight* sides cannot be formed, or at any rate cannot be *maintained* by the action of wind and weather. For the force that is sharpening one face will at the same time be causing erosion to any existing opposite straight sides or edges. Given the relative proximity of the further forms of which it is a part, this remark is equally valid for the nearby area known as the City. We should also remember Dr. Carl Sagan's statement: "Intelligent life on Earth first reveals itself through the geometrical regularity of its constructions".

CONSPIRACY CASTLE

While very few people subscribe to the conspiracy theory, it has nevertheless been bandied about in the popular UFO press that Mars is harbouring secret bases, thanks of course to NASA's travel club. We hope that by now the reader will have understood the sheer impossibility of such a theory. The idea that human beings are responsible for the creation of these pyramids on Mars is laughable—we are not even able to travel to the Moon and back safely, let alone construct a five-sided pyramid on a planet that currently lies far beyond our grasp.

CLEVER NATIVES

As for an indigenous population emerging on Mars, the requirements relating to the emergence of self-aware life that we have set out in "Essentials" and "THE Triangle" preclude this possibility. We apologise for the repetition but—without a moon of an appropriate size

and a companion planet of an equal size (in this case to the size of Mars) *no planet is capable of bringing forth self-aware life.*

EXTRA-TERRESTRIALS

That leaves the hypothesis of a colonising civilisation which was obliged to leave Mars when the climate changed. This theory *assumes* traumatic climate change rather than a more interesting alternative: the possibility that the climate became incapable of supporting life *following* the departure of a colonising civilisation that had been artificially maintaining the planet.

We claim that Mars could *never* naturally become a blue-green planet upon which self-aware beings could evolve—because it does not have any of the criteria required: no companion planet of the correct size and Mars is spinning naturally at too slow a rate to generate the essential magnetic field.

But we do claim however that with the correct technology, Mars *was* made to spin at the 'right rate' and thus became habitable for *colonising* self-aware beings. Further, that it was in the same Cydonian complex that the technology for speeding up the rotation of Mars was installed by those who temporarily colonised the red rock planet. This technological possibility would be valid for many planets that spin too slowly and human beings will probably end up learning how to perfect this technique also—for as a species it is already too late for us to turn back. Mankind has already embarked upon our cosmic voyage by attempting to explore our solar system. It is no

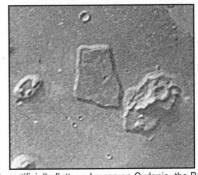

21. The artificially-flattened mesa on Cydonia, the Bastion.

good pretending that what is in space is not there, especially as some of us have already pretended that they are rather clever at travelling around and about 'out there'.

We further maintain that within this martian complex there are a number of structures including—in many ways even more obvious than the Face—*an artificially flattened mesa* that we mentioned earlier, which we call the Bastion.

This now flattened mesa to the south-east of the Face, (which would have entailed massive working of the hitherto natural feature, not unlike the adjoining mesa to the right (see 21) bears an interesting resemblance to the Egyptian hieroglyph or determinative for 'nose'. Derived from 'face' it is also a determinative in words connected to nose, to the sense of smell, and to enjoyment.

We consider that it is this mesa Joe McMoneagle remote viewed and sketched for the US Government's PSI program (labelled as number 4/NASA 86A07) although it was claimed to be located at 35.26°N 213.24°E.

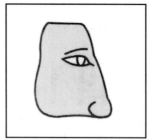

23. The Egyptian hieroglyph for nose.

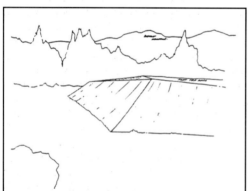

22. Copy of McMoneagle's sketch, side view of a flat mesa—with more rugged terrain behind—compare (21).

Picture (22) above is a copy of his sketch.

To the east of the Bastion is a mound with a very distinctive ascending spiral. This mound is estimated to be a mile in diameter and about 500ft/152m high.

To the north-east of the martian Sphinx there is a large crater together with what we claim is an artificial construction called the Wall, on the western side of the crater's ejecta blanket. This Wall is remarkably straight and some

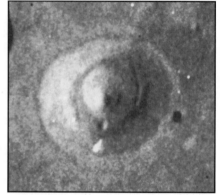

24. The Spiral mound on Mars. NASA/CARLOTTO

two miles long.

The Wall clearly *sits on top* of the ejecta blanket (the material resulting from the forming of the crater) which obviously means that the Wall *post*-dates this 'splash' of material. On the crater's rim above a gap there is a three-sided (tetrahedral) pyramid. One can also see two white marks on the floor of the crater. We believe that they are the location of the two base rings of levitating magnets that were asso-

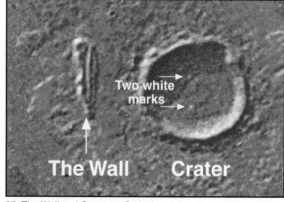

25. The Wall and Crater on Cydonia. NASA/CARLOTTO/AULIS

490

ciated with two enormous Spinning Disks built inside this crater.

Three steps to Heaven, the art of terraforming

Why would anyone want to site two Spinning Disks in a crater on Mars? Rapidly spinning disks lose mass and release gravitrons in the process—as we saw in "Essentials". Loss of mass equals loss of gravity. These rapidly Spinning Disks therefore would have infused the surface of the planet with gravitrons, thereby increasing its effective mass, facilitating a computer-controlled *increased spin rate of the planet*. This is part of the requirement for colonising a planet but such a concept flies 'in the face' (there we go again!) of current scientific thinking as to how to set about terraforming Mars.

Arthur C Clarke in *The Snows of Olympus* sets out the current thinking (his at least) on the way to adapt a planet like Mars to man's requirements. While it is possible to run a variety of computer simulations, and envisage robot self-replicating machines, what is the point, if an atmosphere is not retained by the planet? Unless we blinked when we read his book and missed them, notably absent from ACC's index—as items in their own right—are the words:

'atmosphere'
'rotation'
'radiation', as in 'damage from'.

Specifically, we cannot find any scientific reference as to how an appropriate atmosphere is going to be retained in his proposals. The red planet is currently rotating at 24 hours 37 minutes and 23 seconds, which is 41 minutes 19 seconds *slower* than our rate of 23 hours 56 minutes 4 seconds. However, we maintain that if you were to put two sets of computer-controlled Spinning Disks at the correct sites (in relation to the theoretical tetrahedron) you would be able to gradually infuse the planet with gravitrons, thereby increasing the effective mass of the planet's surface and bring it up to the necessary rotational speed. It is our contention that it is only acceptable to *increase* the

rotational speed of planets, so planets that either spin too rapidly (or that do not possess certain amounts of water), are not suitable for colonisation.

As the correct rotational speed is achieved, so does the magnetic field increase and facilitate the conveyance of the vital planetary energy all over the planetary surface, which is the *essential* requirement for self-aware beings to be able to live and work on a planet for any length of time.

While self-aware beings can certainly get used to a different gravitational field, they will not in our view, be able to survive *for any length of time* without a flow of hyperD energy around them. It is our belief that for a being that has *already evolved* to the composite state of self awareness—as demonstrated by the creative linear-thinking being, it could be possible to exist on a planet *without* a moon such as ours, provided that the planet has a sidereal day of 23 hours and 56 minutes. This we feel would have been the case on Mars, once its rotational speed was so adjusted.

Mars was also landscaped somewhat. Firstly to emphasise the metaphor inherent in the lateral hemispheric difference. Readers of *Two-Thirds* will appreciate the relevance of the fact that the demarcation between the northern and southern hemispheres on Mars is at an angle of around 37° to the horizontal. Secondly to emphasise both the metaphorical and practical messages inherent in the siting of the giant volcanoes that dominate its northern hemisphere. Olympus Mons not only points up the 19.47 tetrahedral constant but is also in a geometrical relationship with the other three volcanoes on Tharsis Ridge and these three relate to the philosophical concepts of both the Bastion, the Face on Mars, and the pyramids and Sphinx at Giza, Egypt. And thirdly, this landscaping contributes to an eccentric orbit for Mars that is influential in maintaining the Earth's revolution of 365.26 days.

Step one

As we have outlined, to adjust the axial rotation of a planet, Spinning Disk technology produces a continuous bombardment and infusion of gravitrons which increases the effective mass of the planet undergoing adjustment. This infusion of gravitrons results in the increased spin rate of the planet. It is only *then,* when the planet is spinning at the rate of 23 hours 56 minutes and 4 seconds that it becomes capable of retaining the gases needed to build its atmosphere. These can then be infused into the very thin natural atmosphere of the planet undergoing terraformation. Finally, the separation of oxygen molecules from the existing water on the planet joins this combined atmosphere.

We maintain also that a planet has to be given an atmosphere of sufficient density and depth that will enable the Sun to heat it to acceptable temperatures for the life that is desirous of living upon it. If the 'masters of infinity' do not study this fundamental, they will never be able to orchestrate the colonisation of a planet such as Mars. They should not colonise the Moon this way because the Moon is an essential component to the functioning of Earth and to tamper with the dynamics of the Moon in any way whatsoever, even by mining, could endanger life forms on Earth. For even the mass of each planet in a binary or three-planet system plays a part in the little-understood hyperD requirements that are part of the new physics.

Step two

The next step in this process of making Mars habitable, is the infusion of a breathable combined atmosphere. Nitrogen and other required liquefied gases have to be sprayed around the planet. When these liquefied gases hit the thin natural atmosphere they abruptly return to their natural gaseous states. In so doing, these gases create gigantic clouds of mist which eventually dissipate, as the atmosphere of the planet becomes denser and warmed by the energy emitted from the Sun.

Once the calculated amount of nitrogen and other gases have been infused into the new combined artificial and natural atmosphere of Mars, the next phase of the process to produce breathable air can begin. Oxygen is extracted from the northern ice sheet and allowed to mix

freely with the transitional combined atmosphere. The hydrogen released by the extraction process then floats up into the atmosphere and beyond, too light to be held by the gravity of that planet. When the projected amount of oxygen has mixed into the atmosphere the extraction ceases, and the new combined atmosphere of the planet is almost ready.

The air would be breathable but still too cool, especially at night, for anyone to settle on the planet. This planet's orbit is far from its Sun, so the heat absorbed by its thin natural atmosphere, almost totally composed of carbon dioxide, would only manage occasionally to raise the midday equatorial temperature above the freezing point of water. The infusion of a breathable atmosphere about 1,500 feet thick (extremely shallow when compared with a naturally breathable atmosphere like that of Earth) does not ensure much greater warming. On its own, the infused artificial atmosphere's ability to absorb and retain more heat from the Sun is still insufficient to raise atmospheric temperatures.

Step three

The presence of a natural atmosphere on Mars *plus* an added artificial atmosphere brings about the slow climb of atmospheric temperatures to an afternoon temperature of about +75°F/24°C at mid-latitudes. Incoming short-wave radiation from the Sun is able to pass directly through the combined atmospheres, but most of the incoming ultraviolet radiation is absorbed at the upper limits of the combined atmosphere, thereby protecting life below. The short-wave radiation which penetrates to the surface is absorbed by the surface and then, as long-wave infrared radiation, sends the heat out into the combined atmosphere.

Without the natural atmosphere of the planet, this infrared radiation would, for the most part, continue upward and beyond the artificial atmosphere which would remain too cool for comfort. However, the natural atmosphere of a planet such as Mars consists almost entirely of carbon dioxide, which is a gas that absorbs infrared radiation and therefore gives off heat. Some of that heat is directed towards space but

492

the rest is deflected back to the surface of the planet. So the combined atmosphere gradually warms to near ideal temperatures. Then additional carbon dioxide has to be carefully and precisely released into the combined atmosphere of the planet so that atmospheric temperatures rise to prescribed levels.

The process of warming the combined atmosphere of a planet with Mars' 'qualifications' is relatively easy and of short duration compared with many other planets. Mars' current natural atmosphere is almost perfect in its ability to provide the *temperature-raising component* of the combined atmosphere. Even though the temperature at mid-latitudes should be maintained at around +75°F the temperature near the polar ice caps will remain below the freezing point of water—even during periods when one or other of the ice caps point towards the Sun.

A planet prepared in such a way as was Mars does not, in our opinion, require solar mirrors reflecting the heat back onto the planet, as suggested by some scientists. Nor would it take 21,000 years to achieve, which is the interval set by the British Interplanetary Society for the safe inhabitation of Mars by self-aware beings in an appropriate atmosphere, as opposed to a situation of living within biospheres equipped with airlocks.

This principle of terraforming has been distilled from our detailed study of UK Crop Glyph findings, the encoded data therein being another gift from ET. We suggest that technological capabilities of the magnitude described have already been deployed on the red planet in order that the colonising beings could live for an extended period on Mars.

We hope that NASA, and those who find the discoveries of the Cydonia complex difficult to take, will come to understand the significance of mankind's special relationship with the red planet—for Mars is special. And it is special to human beings. Mars shows us the way forward, but we still have much more to learn about ourselves and the important relationships between our Earth monuments and Cydonia.

It is our understanding that if those who clearly did settle temporarily on Mars had not

achieved their aims, human beings would not be living on planet Earth today. Our reconstructed history of the colonisation of the red planet, the reasons for that, the technology involved and the outcome of that colonisation have been set out in detail in our earlier work.[23] It does not involve the catastrophic demise of civilisations due to the incoming 'big one'. We are a precious part of the Universe, probably the highest form of physical existence: a creative and linear thinking self-aware being, and far too special to be disposed of at the drop of a comet. And in our view this is yet another prime reason why Earth will not be the recipient of an incoming destructive 'big one' either.

26. The Great Sphinx has a circle of contrasting material on the crown of the head, that can only be seen from the air.   C DAVIES

CONCLUSION

The Moon was and always will be, our nearest and dearest. Mars is special because we have always been connected to the red planet, and without our consciously being aware of it Mars beckons, encouraging us to take another step towards our future and our past. What a pity that NASA has failed to do this in the spirit that was intended, in openness, in joy and with a sense of humour. The Universe is fun—except for those who live with fear and greed.

27. Silbury Hill, Wiltshire, Southern England.   AULIS

Ironically, considering the main thrust of this book, author and researcher Richard Cavendish points out that the construction of Silbury Hill would have consumed a proportion of the gross national product of the times "comparable to that expended by the United States on its *entire* Apollo program." Silbury Hill is *not* a burial mound. And in fact, officially, the entire purpose and massive effort of the Silbury and the adjacent Avebury complex remains a complete mystery. It has been said that if Stonehenge is thought of as a church, then by comparison Avebury is a cathedral. Avebury circle, measuring a quarter of a mile across, is the mightiest in size and grandeur of all stone circles on this planet. It consists principally of an outermost rampart with a deep inner ditch formed from the building of this rampart. The resulting internal platform of earth, criss-crossed by four tracks-become-roads, contains circles of standing stones: one circle delineating the outer edge of the entire Avebury platform, with the remains of two separate inner circles in the

Back to Earth—around the mounds

As an encoded site, Stonehenge has been discussed in the context of its modelling in stone of the Spinning Disk technology. It is not alone as a major archaeological centre, because located in the same English county of Wiltshire we also find Avebury Circle and Silbury Hill. Both these structures are of considerable significance, and relate to the Cydonia region of Mars.

Silbury Hill is the largest prehistoric mound in all Europe. It was constructed from nine million cubic feet of earth and chalk. It has been calculated that to move the amount of material required to build Silbury Hill would have taken 700 people (kited out with no more than antler horns and wicker baskets) ten years of labour! Or putting it another way, *every man, woman and child presently living in the British Isles* would each have needed to bring a bucketful of earth to build it.

28. Avebury Circle, comprising a ¼ mile wide earthen rampart and ditch   AULIS
surrounding the remains of three stone circles.

494

north-east and the south-east sectors. Today a village nestles comfortably within its circumference, which is most appropriate.

Clear reflection

Our initial insights and later research suggested that the Avebury rampart and ditch was in fact an analog of the Cydonia crater and that Silbury Hill represented the Spiral mound on Mars. So we carefully compared these two obviously similar sets of items and found these measurements to be *stunningly proportionate.* That is to say, when the Cydonia complex (30) is reduced by a ratio of 14:1 *it fits exactly* over Avebury/Silbury (29).

The centre of Silbury Hill is (proportionately) exactly the same distance from the centre of Avebury Circle as the centre of the Spiral Mound is from the centre of the crater on Cydonia. And the two pairs of structures are at exactly the same angle to each other. Each pair is a copy of the other. The combined overlay (31) illustrates the result of this exercise, which essentially superimposed the UK Ordnance Survey map of the Avebury area (29) onto the

NASA imaging of the Cydonia region of Mars, (30) with fourteen miles in Cydonia equalling one mile on the Avebury landscape.

The staggering nature of this successful superimposing exercise cannot be over-stressed. Even the most hardened sceptic must ask, how could it be the result of any kind of chance or coincidence that the two most spectacular archaeological structures in all Europe just happen to superimpose perfectly on two identical structures on Mars? It is simply beyond the bounds of chance that the respective proportionate dimensions of these two sets of structures (or formations) and the linear distances between them could be coincidental.

But there is much more!

We started evaluating the rest of the complex on Mars and looked to see if we could find anything at Avebury that would approximate the long straight Wall on the crater's ejecta blanket in Cydonia. As a first step, we drew a line projecting from the centre of the Spiral Mound on Mars to the centre of the Wall (as in 30). Similarly, we drew a line from the centre of Silbury Hill to the centre of Avebury

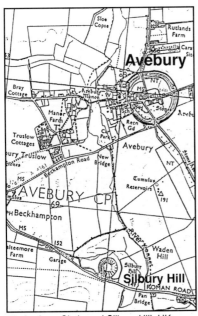

29. Avebury Circle and Silbury Hill, UK Ordnance Survey. © Crown Copyright

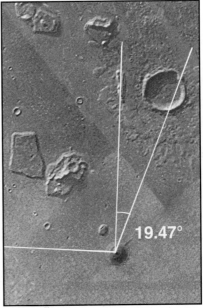

30. Cydonia Spiral mound, the Wall and crater on Mars. NASA

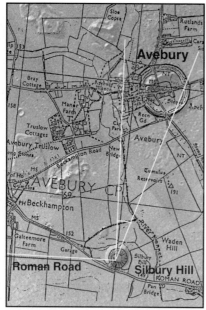

31. Avebury area map and Cydonia combined.
© Crown Copyright/NASA

Pyramid pairs

We had already noted a small mark on the Ordnance Survey map of Avebury outer rampart. This Avebury mark (a tumulus in ordnance terms) was just above a gap in the rampart, identical to the siting of the tetrahedral pyramid on the martian crater rim—also above a gap (32). When we examined this tumulus we found it to be tetrahedral in shape! So a tetrahedral pyramid on a crater ruin, above a gap in the rim on Mars, is matched by a tetrahedral pyramid *at precisely the same point on the Avebury Circle*—above a gap in the rim through which runs the lane that leads to the east.

But when we drew a line from the centre of Silbury Hill to this point on the Avebury rim we realised we had replicated the angle of 19.47° that we had found on the Cydonia complex! Put another way, the angle between the vertical Wall line and this new line was once again, 19.47°. How could the constant recurrence of this number be any kind of coincidence? We have once more another location full of genuine wonders for our contemplation.

Manor, to the west of Avebury Circle—and found that we had a virtual ninety degree angle at the junction of this line and an ancient east/west Roman road (as in 31). Additionally, a combination of the boundary of Avebury Manor and the River Kennet appears to outline the boundary of the Wall on the Avebury landscape.

33. Side view of the tetrahedral pyramid on the rim of AULIS Avebury Circle, Southern England.

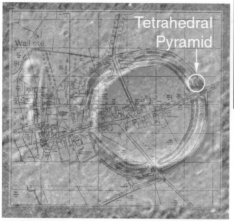

32. Cydonia Crater with superimposed Avebury map further demonstrating the stunning correspondences between Earth and Mars. © Crown Copyright/ NASA

Following these extraordinary findings, we examined the Avebury analog of the tetrahedral rim pyramid on Cydonia, in still more detail.

This Avebury pyramid has obviously eroded somewhat since the time of its construction (officially some 5,000 years BP but we think it is vastly older than that) and must have been an impressive structure originally. It is indeed tetrahedral in construction, with two long sides and one short side, so that in one direction it projects in an almost lozenge shape. *These very same features appear to be duplicated by the Cydonian rim pyramid.*

This tetrahedral pyramid on the Avebury rampart, north of a gap, mirrored by the tetrahedral pyramid on the Cydonia rim, north of a gap, surely sets the final seal of proof, on a case which was nevertheless already proven without it.

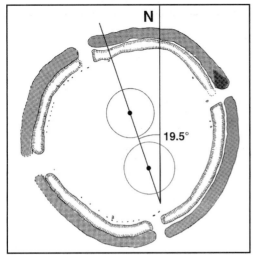

34. Avebury Circle and the two (reconstructed) Spinning Disk stone circle analogs.

Avebury asides

We have demonstrated that the martian crater is represented on Earth by Avebury Circle. But is there anything within the rampart and ditch, to represent the two Spinning Disks that we claim would have been positioned in the Cydonia crater? We find, amazingly enough, that two stone circles were indeed originally constructed inside Avebury Circle, with an offset from north of approximately nineteen and a half degrees.

Our claim is that these circles themselves could be analogs of the two Spinning Disks that we propose were once operating in the martian crater. As we have already pointed out, in the NASA photograph of Cydonia, one can see two white marks inside the crater (25). We consider that these original Avebury stone circles, in particular their *centre stones*, are analogs of the two *base rings of levitating magnets* associated with the two Spinning Disks located in the crater on Cydonia, Mars.

It already seems established beyond reasonable doubt that Mars was once inhabited by self-aware beings. The links with Avebury, Stonehenge and the Giza Plateau, demonstrate a very strong and very real physical and mental connection between Earth and Mars.

This second discovery reinforces the first. Or rather, taken together, the two sets of data form a totally unshakeable case.

In the popular and specialist press, there is much reporting that sides with NASA and cannot envisage the possibility of intelligent beings having created the structures on Mars—still less the fact that there are irrefutable correspondences with our home planet. But let us remember that these correspondences are not only of artificial structures on a distant planet that compare with artificial structures on our home planet. There are also artificial structures on our planet that correspond with natural volcanic and crater features on Mars. The three pyramids on the Giza plateau overlay exactly over the three volcanoes on Mars. (35)

Stunning co-incidents

We must stress again the sheer *impossibility of mere coincidence of:*

1) A mound plus crater rim on Mars—in the Cydonia region, and a mound plus earthen rampart on Earth—at Avebury.

2) The paired items having also the same relative size and being the same relative distance from each other.

3) The Cydonian crater rim, with gap, plus tetrahedral pyramid, and the Avebury earthen rampart, with gap, plus tetrahedral pyramid.

4) These Mars/Earth sites both displaying the above physical occurrences at *identical locations.*

And remarkably, both sets of structures on two different planets sharing an identical *geography*, an identical *geometry*, and an identical *topography*.

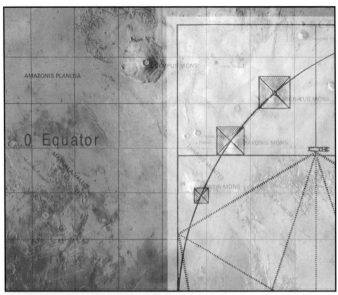

35. The three pyramids at Giza superimposed over the three volcanoes on Mars. Note the Great Sphinx is tangent to the martian equator.

Whistle-Blowing

We maintain that the Face, the beacon for the layout of the Cydonia complex, in many aspects is highlighting the encoded workings of the Universe and the new (to us) transD physics and technology. Scientists could commence work experimenting and investigating this decoded information *NOW,* if they were inclined to allow their perceptions to encompass the enormous ramifications of these findings.

By virtue of the fact that we have discovered them, such encoding on another planet infers that we are ready to decode this information at this time. To say, as one Mars researcher has stated, "We are not ready to understand this information", is to stick our heads back into the sand in an ostrich-like attempt to ignore the significant evolutionary stage mankind has reached.

However, observing anomalous structures on the surface of our neighbouring planet is one thing. *Understanding* the meaning of such a layout creates other demands on ourselves.

Does the fact that NASA has been not only publicly ignoring this artificially landscaped terrain on Mars, but has also apparently refused to make any effort to find out more about Cydonia mean that the masters and their servants are not ready for the ramifications of such a discovery? Or do they wish to keep their findings to themselves? And if so, why? The very fact that the general public have been denied a dialogue on this matter is indicative of the contempt that the masters, their servants and the military-industrial complex have for its own people who, as taxpayers, actually finance NASA's exploits.

Those who are entrusted with decision making concerning the exploration of space (together with those who issue the orders)—if they were worth their salt—would be exploring every indication of an intelligence extraneous to this planet in an open way. But that is not yet to be. Instead, the establishment ridicules any suggestions that contradict the web of terminological inexactitudes the agency has spun, and it is now attempting a passable imitation of 'the spider who sat down beside her' by

---

Called to order

The McDaniel report on the failure of Executive Congressional and Scientific responsibility in setting mission priorities for NASA's Exploration Program stated that:

"Any reasonable degree of doubt regarding the natural origin of any of the debated features [on Mars]
creates a profound and compelling ethical obligation for NASA to give extremely high priority to obtaining high resolution photographs of those landforms."

Stanley V McDaniel, Professor Emeritus & former Chairman of the Dept of Philosophy

at Sonoma State University, California

---

indoctrinating everyone with *fear of the un-known.*

Mankind went to Mars to look for life.

What could be more wonderful than finding there signs of *intelligent* life?

It may have become rather sobering to NASA that the Face on Mars grew to be one of the agency's most frequently requested pictures! And perhaps as a result of the continual, unrelenting pressure from enthusiasts and experts alike, these new images were released much more quickly when Cydonia was eventually re-imaged by the Mars Global Surveyor (MGS).

This re-imaging took place on April 5 1998. MGS acquired pictures of part of the Cydonia complex including the Face on Mars. But this re-imaging may have been done under protest as a result of all that lobbying over a number of years. As the original Viking pictures and the newly-released MGS images were acquired with the Sun in totally different positions, and as the new image was not taken directly overhead (as was Viking 70A13 for example), but more to one side, image processing expert Mark Carlotto found it necessary to map the new data on top of his previous Viking 3D image processing in order to provide a means by which meaningful comparisons could be made.

We must remember that this is, after all, a *face* that we are talking about. But alas, although the new image has greater definition, initially we were denied the opportunity of comparing like with like. As the Viking lighting was 'overhead' or at the top and to one side—which is the more normal or flattering way to light any face; and as the new MGS image was *not* taken with the light source overhead *but from underneath*—that is to say from 'below'—certainly very *un-flattering,* there is no way that the two images of the same subject were going to look the same. Verification would become difficult and the casual observer might be forgiven for concluding that the original images were a 'trick of the

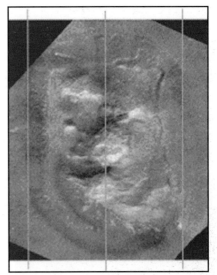

36. Mark Carlotto's rectified MGS 1998 image of the Face on Mars.   NASA/CARLOTTO

light' as claimed by NASA. Was the decision to re-image from a different viewpoint i.e. from one side and under totally different lighting conditions perhaps intentional? Were those responsible hoping to make life difficult for serious researchers? Did they perhaps hope for (and get) a grotesque-looking lump of rock this time? Remember this face could well have been on Mars for hundreds of thousands of years. And please remember the severe weather on the planet—the fact that winds sometimes sweep dust and sand over the surface at up to 300 miles per hour.

Consider how your great grandfather would your look in an obscure portrait with the sole source of light under his chin!

However, as a result of the excellent work by Mark Carlotto we can see that indeed it is still a face.[24] Compare (37 & 38) on the next page).

The Ministry of silly talk

We realised that there was something very wrong with the Apollo missions by studying the recorded TV material, the film and the still images. Have we not, once more, come full circle? Here we are again, discussing images from Mars, only this time NASA seems to be attempting to *withhold* the evidence rather than

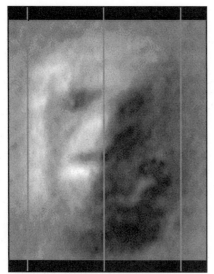

37. Viking (170A13) 1976 image of the Face on Mars.   NASA/CARLOTTO

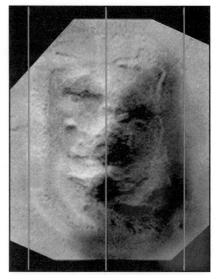

38. Mark Carlotto's rectified MGS 1998 image of the Face on Mars with lighting adjusted to match as near as possible the Sun position for 70A13 in 1976.   NASA/CARLOTTO/AULIS

creating it. The clues to the Apollo hoax lay in the *images*. It was the *filmmakers* that started it all, with illusion driving reality starting as early as 1927 in Europe and again in 1964 in America. The Apollywood photographer/filmmakers repeated the cycle in 1969. If anyone was going to unmask the hoax of Apollo then it would be the photographer/filmmakers. Has it started all over again with this martian saga?

NASA Administrator Dan Goldin suggested that in 35 years time we would have routine space travel, the technology would be there and human beings would be setting up colonies on the Moon, and on Mars. When asked during a 1994 interview with British journalist, Sheena McDonald, if such adventures would be available to all and sundry, he intoned his mantra, "I don't know what I don't know". It seems to be one of Goldin's stock replies and he has used it on several occasions. He added that *how* such an achievement would be accomplished was beyond his knowledge base, "he didn't know how that could be done!" So we won't all be taking vacations on the Moon then. What a surprise!

NASA is being faced with more than the Face on Mars (on which subject we could suggest a variation on the Goldin mantra: "I don't know what I don't want to know"). It is also faced with the problem of how to revert to being a private or underground military operation in terms of space exploration, while simultaneously maintaining enough public interest in selected activities in order to keep the cash flowing into its coffers.

This approach is yet another reason for all the meteorite scare stories. They enable the masters to mobilise public opinion behind NASA guarantees for the building of the Space Station, while at the same time ensuring that the launching of such technology does not necessitate the use of astronauts beyond the Van Allens. Secretly they can attempt to develop the technology they wish to use, not against a meteorite but against their idea of ET. If you are considering buying into the meteorite scare scenario then you should be aware that Spaceguard UK have already stated how stupid it would be to blow up a meteorite.[33] In so doing, not only do you increase the problem rather than eliminate it, you also contaminate the solar system with nuclear waste—for to use such a device is our only option at this time.

The Americans, good at telling everybody else what to do with their nuclear power, ignore such problems and continue to push for the Strangelovian approach to life—nuke it first, ask for its identification afterwards.

Times up

We started out with the intention of demonstrating that the Apollo photographic record was faked, that we could not have been to the Moon with the named Apollo astronauts. When depicting a real scene such as Columbus arriving at the new world, artists can paint only what they see. This also goes for photographers and all those who wish to register a major event for posterity. When the available materials or technology are found (through circumstances beyond one's control) to be inadequate or the actual results to be "unsuitable for publication", and when there is an absolute necessity to have proof that the event actually took place, there is a great temptation to provide a substitute.

In the Apollo scenario, we, the public were 'shown' that prospective Moon travel was a like a beautiful film, as many of us saw in *2001: A Space Odyssey*. Then we had the 'reel' thing—grainy, fuzzy TV pictures. And because our expectations were trained on smooth, sharp colour images, we understood that 'reality' is less attractive than 'fiction'. In that way, we all viewed the pictures of the astronauts on the Moon without really 'seeing' them, but we enjoyed the moonscape shots—some did rather resemble scenes from *2001*.

Our belief is that we were all led by the nose along the visual path that NASA wanted us to follow. But the agency has consistently refused to discuss the fact that the imagery relating to Apollo appears to be booby-trapped (thanks to the Whistle-Blowers) and displays technical problems that are contrary to the laws of physics as we know them. Nor do the lunar surface photographs correspond to the conditions under which they were said to have been taken.

Taking into account section 102 (b) of the declaration of the NASA policy and purpose, reproduced below, there is only one conclusion that can be drawn from such an attitude. For what reason, other than that they were bound by the regulations of the DODmen at the Department of Defense, would NASA refuse to discuss the matter of their faked Apollo material?

The Apollo missions with the named astronauts must have been activities peculiar to the research and development carried out "for the defense of the United States". In other words, a cover for the real Apollo surrogate missions which, by definition, must have been primarily associated with military operations and personnel *fully equipped with weapons*. Arms by definition experimental, due to the fact they were being taken into an environment never before experienced by human beings.

In its stubborn refusal to be accountable for

Declaration of NASA Policy and Purpose

Sec 102 (b). The Congress declares that the general welfare and security of the United States require that adequate provision be made for aeronautical and space activities.

The Congress further declares that such activities shall be the responsibility of, and shall be directed by, a civilian agency exercising control over aeronautical and space activities sponsored by the United States,

except that activities peculiar to or primarily associated with the development of weapons systems, military operations, or the defense of the United States (including the research and development necessary to make effective provision for the defense of the United States)

shall be the responsibility of, and shall be directed by,

the Department of Defense;

and that determination as to which such agency has responsibility for and direction of any such activity shall be made by the President in conformity with section 201(e). (emphasis added)

Countdown to zero

It was Fritz Lang who thought up the now famous '10, 9, 8' countdown to 'lift off' for his film *Frau im Mond*. "Another of my damned touches", he once said.[25] He used the phrase as a way of injecting some drama into the departure of his mock-up rocket to the Moon.

Throughout his life, Lang maintained that NASA had incorporated his invention into *their* space dramas.

Confirmation that those who know recognised this fact might be inferred by an event in 1968, when Fritz Lang was the guest of honour at a Space Science Seminar in Huntsville, Alabama.

Lang was considered to be "in a certain way, *the father of rocket science".*

---

its deeds and through one section of its own enabling legislation, NASA has finally blown a whistle—on its own activities.

Today, little by little, NASA is quietly burying the shortcomings of its 1960s rocketry and bringing out into the open what the agency has been practising privately since 1945, technical co-operation in space with the Soviets, the Russians—ace rocket builders—true masters of their art. However everybody is quietly going underground, for unless some profound changes occur within the mentality of the 'masters of infinity' (reduced through their own density to 'slaves of limitation') NASA & Co. have no intention whatsoever of letting Joe Public and his family wander around in our own back yard.

Not least because it is classified 'Top Secret'.

Let's go to Mars and find our inheritance

For the last four decades we have been consistently misled regarding the aims and motivations of NASA and for the last five decades we have been misled concerning our heritage.

It is time to drop the illusion.

We could travel onwards from this planet with courage, honesty and generosity of spirit; not with fear, lies and attitudes of contempt. Sadly, *all* those researchers who have asked for responses from NASA have found an agency where an atmosphere of cover-up continues to linger and it is, as we have seen from its behaviour over Cydonia, still business as usual. Can NASA prove itself to be both responsible and accountable for its actions?

Whichever way we turn we cannot escape the fact that:

Only NASA can say why its photographs are at odds with the fundamentals of photography and the way light behaves.

Only NASA can say what problems were actually encountered which incited the agency to fake their evidence for the Apollo missions.

Only NASA can say why for nearly 30 years, it chose to hide from us all the real story of Apollo.

Only NASA can say why it is continuing to do so, even after precise scientific evidence that demonstrates the woeful inadequacies of its accounts.

Only NASA say us why it is being persistently obstructive regarding the discussions over the case for artificial artefacts on Mars.

The Face is such a beacon and is so clearly a deliberately-positioned sculpture that NASA neither needs, nor wants to discuss the ramifications of Cydonia. Through their reluctance to acknowledge the problems and discoveries encountered during their attempts to go to the Moon, the masters have created an unsolvable puzzle for themselves and their space agencies. They cannot send astronauts to Mars safely and at the same time they cannot explain why! They are therefore *obliged* to dismiss the idea of artefacts on Mars, whatever their true thoughts on the matter. To date budgetary excuses and limited technology for the martian voyage can mask these inadequacies, but if they *do not* find the way to travel safely, either astronauts will be killed unnecessarily or these masters will oblige NASA to replay the scenario that we have exposed in this book.

Welch rabbit

When NASA's Brian Welch issued that challenge to us concerning the laser measurement from the Moon we already realised that the presence of a reflector on the lunar surface did not *automatically* mean that human beings have walked on the surface of the Moon. We even considered that the reflector could have been part of a soft landing probe.

As it happened we did not even have to speculate on this point.

In 1962 a ruby laser was used to shoot a series of pulses at the lunar surface—then *240,000* miles distant.

> The beams (sic) illuminated a spot *just under a mile and a quarter in diameter.* This laser beam was reflected back to Earth *with enough strength to be measured by ultrasensitive electronic equipment.* [26] (emphasis added)

But that was in the good old days! By 1969, when the 'Apollo 11' laser equipment was supposed to be working, the divergence of the beam on reaching the LR[3], the lunar surface had somehow become *"only a few miles wide".* [27] How extraordinary! In fact, taking into account the difference in Earth/Moon distance on those two dates the variation between the 1962 and '69 beam widths *should actually* have been in the region of only 277 feet! This detail aside, the answer to the question set by NASA's Brian Welch is quite simply:

> It is not necessary to have a laser retro-reflector *on* the Moon in order to receive a return laser signal *from* the Moon—as was demonstrated in 1962.

Would NASA now care to answer our questions?

Planet Earth's prospective space exploration will have to be handled differently in future. The attitudes of those who were too scared to

speak out, the courage of our Whistle-Blowers who have been, and are still outspoken, plus a general disinclination to have the future of this planet held in the hands of people like the 'masters of infinity' and their representatives, means that there has to be change. But we all have to play a part in bringing about the required changes.

The first step towards that process is by recognising that the majority of us are more naturally inclined to laughter, joy and life, rather than fear, war and death.

It is for these reasons that we have written this book. It is for these reasons there is an even stronger indication that ETs are with us, and not against us, that ETs are both intelligent and care passionately about our future, because ETs are related to us as we are to them.

But some of those who already know these things, sadly, do not want the rest of us to know.

With regard to those Apollo lunar landings, we leave the last word on this subject to Una Ronald, the Whistle-Blower who alerted us to the 'artefact' used to write *FAKE* across the 'Apollo 11' TV material transmitted in Western Australia:

> Our integrity is insulted by these set-ups and fakes. It is not right that an elite in this world should censor the truth of this matter. All the people who believed that the Moon landings were real *deserve* the truth and so do our children. We should all know, simply because as adult human beings, we should share in the discoveries that concern this planet.

Chapter Thirteen

Hurmaze

At the outset of this chapter can we, the authors, momentarily get down on our knees and beg any hardened sceptics in these matters to reconsider precisely what we find when we compare the structures found at Avebury/Silbury in Southern England with those at Cydonia on Mars. Remember here that our planet's set of structures just happen to be the largest man-made megaliths found anywhere in Europe. Briefly recapping:

We have in each case a large stone circle and a large mound. The two sets of structures are of *precisely* the same proportions (on a ratio of 14:1). The two items, mound and circle, on the two planets are *exactly* the same position relative to each other. Each of the craters on the two planets has a gap on its north-east rim at the same point; and *in each case above the gap* is placed a *tetrahedral pyramid*. The two gaps at the same point are remarkable. The two gaps plus tetrahedral pyramid are dumbfounding.

Alongside the crater on Mars is a wall. Alongside Avebury Circle is a manor boundary. When one draws a line from the centre of each mound to the centre of the wall/boundary respectively, and another from the centre of each mound to the centre of the tetrahedral rim pyramid respectively, the angle between the two lines is 19.47°. (And 19.47° just happens ofcourse to be the latitude of a circumscribed

tetrahedron and the point on many planets in our solar system where the most violent energy upwelling occurs.

How can this collection of *facts,* of *totally parallel facts* be any kind of coincidence? How can they?

We get up off our knees.

Amazing face

Arthur C Clarke has said that he considers the Face on Mars to be a natural phenomenon, but *hopes* that he is wrong and that Mars is certainly worthy of further study.[1]

Even without the visual and geometric evidence that links the volcanoes of Mars and Egypt's Giza plateau in Egypt on Earth, the entire Cydonia complex on Mars and its corresponding analogs with England's Avebury complex on Earth, there is yet another key to demonstrate that Cydonia is a massive lesson in philosophy, mathematics and transD physics. By extension therefore, the Face on Mars, (or the Hurmaze, *Two Thirds*) is by no means a natural phenomenon. Furthermore, human beings cannot possibly have constructed the lock into which a vital key can be inserted and turned.

The name of this special key is *topogly* and this key is further evidence that we are not alone in the Universe.

504

Literally, topogly means the art of 'sweet positioning' (from the Greek). Two or more sites are linked in a relationship that depends uniquely on mathematics involving the exact co-ordinates (the latitude and longitude) and specifics of the topographical details relating to each site.

The precise centre points between any given locations measured from the planet's prime meridian are applied to a universal constant, for example pi (3.14159 et seq.). There are literally many hundreds of such sites on Earth but these ancient sites are not necessarily limited to locations on a single planet. From the resulting topogly calculation one can appreciate a unique representation of any given structure (whether natural or artificial). The particular relationship between structures, monuments, or places (other than their relative 3D positions) is revealed *by each structures' topogly reference within the overall encoding.*

Carl Munck is an American encryptographer who has devoted many years of his life to re-cataloguing this encoded topogly and he has named this catalogue *The Code.*[2]

Munck does not get particularly excited by the idea that extra-terrestrials might have visited this planet. In fact, while he is an open minded and open hearted person, this line of thought has no place in his philosophy and is definitely *not* the driving force that motivates him to spend his days hunched over maps decoding details of our planet-wide topogly grid. He is however, aware that all our historic sites incorporate ancient encoded information, which can be broken using *The Code.* Munck does not care for the way that our most important mathematical systems are being "lost", "buried" or carefully disregarded by "the powers that be".

In topogly "number talks to number" as Carl Munck explains:

> The problem is, while most folks can do simple math, they are not comfortable with it. Mathematics (like our legal system) is seemingly a cold rigid realm of law, with no room for emotion and if we can avoid it we will. But if we really want to 'talk grid' we *cannot* avoid math and as grids involve maps,

---

Constant

A constant is any quantity or parameter, which remains the same, while the variables change.

Constants assume different values for different initial and boundary conditions but are constant for each particular set of conditions.

An absolute constant such as Pi is always the same.

---

we must also become familiar with them; because where this ancient grid system is concerned it involves both.

The ancient grid of sites was mathematically oriented both here on Earth and on the red planet and quite likely beyond that. Since we cannot have a grid without math, those who speak of it should become conversant with how it works. Only with understanding can we have understanding. In making [topogly] calculations, we need to remember that in the pyramid age, the *Prime Meridian* was at Giza in Egypt, 31 degrees 08 minutes 8 seconds east of the current meridian at Greenwich in England.

Further TechnoSpeak

A cryptographer is a person who encodes/manipulates data and information (such as architectural dimensions, landscaped earthwork details) in order to hide differing levels of knowledge within the structure itself.

This encrypted data is revealed to those in possession of the appropriate set of keys.

Many of the ancient sites on our planet are also positioned on geophysical energy lines, which the English have called ley lines (the word 'ley' means 'a clearing' in English). The Chinese base their system of Feng Shui upon these lines, which they also refer to as Dragon lines. These energy lines are also known as Drakon lines (from the Greek). However, when dealing with topogly it is important to bear in mind that while the site *might* be situated on such an energy line, the geographical location is in fact *irrelevant* to the interpretation of the topogly number.

505

So if number talks to number, what are the odds on such a system being more than just mystical mumbo jumbo, where the figures are made to fit the theory? In response to an enquirer as to whether the martian structures were artificial or accidental, Anatoly I Kandiew, a top American mathematician with patents in computing to his name, established a method for evaluating the accuracy of Munck's code After rigorous analysis he published his conclusion in the respected *Journal of the Louisiana Mounds Society:*

> The chances of properly positioning two structures, to conform with this topogly Grid Matrix Relationship [Carl Munck's Code] — would be approximately 1 in 100 *TRILLION*. Furthermore, these odds do *not* include the odds for *more* than two structures maintaining these relationships.

In the Appendix, together with Anatoly Kandiew's analysis, we have set out Carl Munck's calculations in full demonstrating that the Face on Mars was positioned by intelligence.

Carl Munck also says:

> Unfortunately, Western science—including NASA—insists that Cydonia's Face was *not* intelligently made by whoever it is that isn't 'out there' and of whom we're all supposed to be afraid. But, the mathematical language of these cartographers (wherever they were from) shows it for what it is:

- A valid communication system capable of transmitting meaningful data without resorting to slow, cumbersome writing.
- The features key its message.
- Acknowledge the 9th power at Giza and the Face on Mars will 'speak'.
- Deny it and learn nothing.
- It is all cartographically and mathematically verifiable.

The proof as always is in the detail—the numbers, the mathematics.

We are only at the beginnings of our understanding of transD physics and topogly, but so far the results of our research, together with the evidence presented in these chapters, underline the fact that a 'lost civilisation' of human beings, whether from the Antarctic, Atlantis, or elsewhere here on Earth, *cannot possibly* have constructed *and so precisely positioned* the Great Sphinx, the Great Pyramid, or Stonehenge. Nor indeed any of the other *megalithic* sites that were beyond the incredibly precise siting and construction capacities of the respective societies—not only at the alleged time of building but even today! These encoded structures were located relative to each other in the grid locations to at least *eight decimal points* of accuracy.

To argue, as Graham Hancock does in *Heaven's Mirror*, that this lost civilisation built such places according to the stars they saw in the sky is a step in the right direction, it gets us thinking and relating 'down here' to 'up there'.[3] But the significance of relationship between a particular constellation and a structure on Earth *entirely* depends upon the date

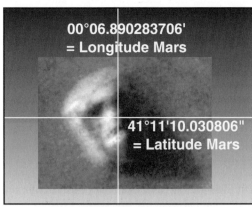

00°06.890283706'
= Longitude Mars

41°11'10.030806"
= Latitude Mars

1. The following details indicate that the Face on Mars was positioned by intelligence:

Pi x ⅓ rd Pi x ⅔ rds Pi = 6.890283706
00° 06.890283706′ = the precise longitude
of the Face on Mars.

The angles of a tetrahedron, 720° x 2 = 1440 x Pi =
4523.893421 thereby encoding
41° 11′ 10.03080581″ = the precise latitude
of the Face on Mars
Verified by 41 X 11 X 10.03080581 = 4523.893421.

selected as that of the site's construction. While agreeing with Hancock that there is an interesting alignment in the dates expressed via the architecture of these structures, we do not necessarily agree with all the conclusions drawn.

Topogly on the other hand is the number derived from one site talking to the number from any of the other ancient sites. Therefore this mathematical code is, so to speak, set in stone. It does not depend on the tastes or inclinations of current scientific thought but upon a mathematical calculation based on precise latitudinal and longitudinal co-ordinates which themselves are not susceptible to vast change. Further, in order for these megalithic sites to work out in a mathematical relationship it would have been necessary to have an overview of our entire planet, to understand at the very least that it was a sphere and to have already established an incredibly accurate system of determining latitude and longitude. Furthermore, for the code to be broken in the late 20th Century a complete prediction of future plate tectonic movement would have to have been undertaken! Clearly an impossible task for any indigenous culture living tens of thousands of years ago on Earth.

To suggest, as some have done, that this supposed advanced (but since disappeared human civilisation) sailed the globe and had even invented flight, is to ignore the fact that these constructors must have had the ability to travel not only on the high seas and the airwaves, but had also mastered manned flight into space! For there still has to be an explanation (difficult to accept or otherwise) for the fact that the *artificial* structures on Mars correspond totally with this mathematical code here on Earth.

Round faces

Which of course brings us back full circle to our first problem—to this day we do not have the technological means for elevating such megaliths, nor for travelling safely into deep space. It also puts ET firmly back into the picture. The contemplation of the secrets uncovered by topogly, might help us re-examine our understanding of "why these sites are where

they are", as that archaeologist enquired—for with this newly-discovered relationship between our monuments and our planets, we expand our horizons on all levels. We suggest that mankind is currently in possession of the messages, and the information. It is already here in our architecture, the encoded landscaping, topogly, planetary relationships, Crop Glyphs, and yes, ET craft or UFO sightings. These 'artefacts' are all clues *that we have to work out for ourselves*. Everywhere we look, whether it be to the structures of Cydonia and the images from Mars, or the megalithic structures of Earth and the images of the Apollo photographic record, the 'writing' is the artefact and the 'language' is the measure.

We consider that the topogly relationships are one of the irrefutable proofs that the construction and positioning of the artefacts on the Cydonia complex are the result of intelligence, and not just natural features of martian terrain or technical aberrations of the imaging processes. This certain fact is a prime reason why the Cydonia complex is such a thorn in the side to NASA & Co. To deny that these first findings on Mars are artificial constructions is also to deny the irrefutable evidence in the mathematics.

It is not the remit of this book to explain in great detail all the encodings of the Hurmaze—the Face on Mars. The very specific reasons why the martian Sphinx is primate on the left and leonine on the right are addressed in detail in our other works.[4] Here we will elaborate briefly regarding such encodings as they are also relevant to the Sphinx on Earth. Then again, these two structures are important components of two key complexes, Cydonia and Giza, constructed on two different but neighbouring planets in our solar system.

In structural terms we have two intentionally carved mesas. As we have already seen on Mars the Face is sculpted with a *vertical* split 'I'. Whilst on Earth the Sphinx's head displays a *horizontal* split '—' as we will see shortly. When combined, this results in '+' which, among other interpretations, could be taken to represent the two final stages of evolution to self-aware, modern man: Neanderthal and Cro-

2. The Primate side.

Magnon respectively. Moreover, the red planet is distinctly different in a roughly horizontal split of northern and southern hemispheres; our Moon's near and far side are definitely different—again a vertical split; and Earth is generally symbolised by a sphere within which we find a '+' and is of four roughly equal quarters (not dissimilar to the shape made by Avebury Circle which is also divided into four quarters.

Do these three planets encode the same message for us as do these two Sphinxes? Are these 'coincidences' a reflection of the contribution towards the evolution of our species by these planets? We think so. Both planets are tempting us to leave our nursery and explore. The Moon, as we have already said, has always been our nearest and dearest. Mars, due to a shared past, is encouraging us now to take another step towards our future.

Rosy cheeks

We now have yet another reason for the encoded arrival of the Roswell craft. It was the seeding of the *idea* that travel between planets was possible, indeed essential for the development and survival of an emerging species. It was also the seeding of the *idea* that we are ready for this adventurous exercise. Having been given every opportunity to share these realisations with the rest of the world, the administrators of our space program have always chosen poorly and done so with a singular lack of humour.

Learning about the Universe is fun—except for those living in denial who cannot tolerate the message left for us all on Cydonia which is well worth repeating: on the landscape of two different planets within the same solar system there are two sets of structures with the same concept. They are both a Sphinx adjacent to pyramidal structures of great significance. As no one born on Earth has yet developed the

capacity to visit Mars, it would be reasonable to conclude that any beings capable of visiting Mars from elsewhere were also capable of travelling to Earth.

Face to face

3. The Lion side matched.

The Sphinx on Mars and the Sphinx on Earth are beacons that cannot fail to attract attention—"Look at us carefully, contemplate!" they cry. "Perhaps there is more to us than meets the eye!"

Indeed there is.

From the research that we have carried out we propose that the head of the Great Sphinx in Egypt was carved in two phases: the first phase consisted of the head, the front paws and one-third of the body all of which were sculpted from the rock, and the second phase modified the initial sculpture into the head that we see today. Our research suggests that this head is 'divided' vertically in that its left profile (from the point of view of the Sphinx) is 'masculine' and its right profile 'feminine'. Not only does the masculine left side profile and the female right side profile grace it with a translucent beauty but additionally the head of the Sphinx at Giza comprises a summary of the two preceding evolutionary stages that led to modern man. This is encoded into the horizontal division which across the bridge of the nose—whereas the Face on Mars displays a *vertical* cut representing the quality of courage (the leonine), representing the heart, allied with the original material (the hominid) required for the genesis of human beings. The martian Sphinx is a sculptured statement of the past and future requirements for the evolution of self-aware life on Earth.

The Egyptian Sphinx on the other hand, represents the last two stages of the development of mankind—through a *horizontal* split the two final evolutionary stages are linked—the stages that resulted in the emergence of both creative and linear thinking in a self-aware being. It is our understanding that Neanderthal

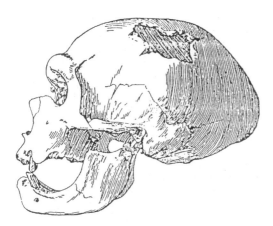

4. Neanderthal skull.

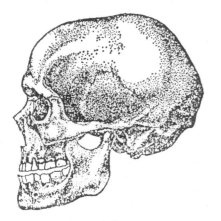

5. Cro-Magnon skull.

and Cro-Magnon were two separate stages of an assisted evolutionary program that resulted in ourselves—Homo Sapiens Sapiens.[5]

The missing link is only in our minds—thanks to the self-aware beings that *colonised* Mars in fact we are all relatives of ET.

Taking a line across the head of the Egyptian Sphinx we suggest that the top half (eyes, forehead, top half of the ears and from the bridge of the nose upwards) represents Cro-Magnon Man, while the lower half (lower half of ear, bridge of nose downwards to mouth and jaw) represents Neanderthal Man.

Illustrations (4) and (5) are of Neanderthal and Cro-Magnon respectively. Illustration (6) shows the result of combining the lower sec-

tion of the Neanderthal skull (unchanged) with the upper section of the Cro-Magnon skull (unchanged). Illustration (7) then shows the superimposition of this new combined skull on the profile of the Great Sphinx. We consider the fit to be excellent and that this design could have only been executed by those who *knew* that Neanderthal was a highly significant stage in our evolution as was Cro-Magnon man.

Neanderthal man was in full control of Europe and the Middle East around 35,000 BP. Then Cro-Magnon abruptly appeared in Europe at this time—from exactly where no one knows, although it seems his passage took him through the Middle East. In very short order Cro-Magnon now assumed control of Europe, driving the remnants of Neanderthal into the mountains and deep forests.

It is not the remit of the present book to go fully into all these matters. However, on Mount Carmel in Israel are found two sets of skulls—the Tabun and Skühl relics—dated around 35,000 BP. These skulls show a dramatic mixture of Neanderthal and Cro-Magnon characteristics—and are proof that the two species *did* interbreed. It is also the case that during the past 35,000 years Cro-Magnon as a species has disappeared (as orthodoxy reluctantly agrees). *We* are *not* Cro-Magnon. The disappearance of Cro-Magnon is best understood by the injection of a (relatively small)

Cro-Magnon

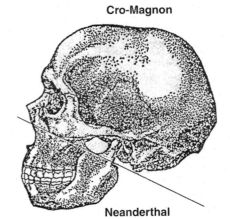

Neanderthal

6. The combined skulls.

509

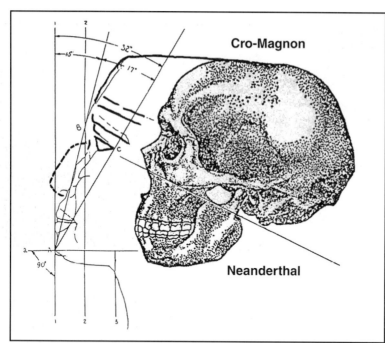

Cro-Magnon

Neanderthal

7. Combined skulls and profile of the Great Sphinx, complete with its large Neanderthal nose (dotted), based on the Sphinx profile drawn by Frank Domingo.

and the limitations of atmospheric protection at that time was eminently sensible). Stan Gooch also believes that Neanderthal was predominately left-handed, had a short big toe and the proud owner of a very large nose—that looked both Jewish and Amero-Indian. Some of these views—the large nose, for instance—are at last now beginning to be accepted by orthodoxy.[6]

Noses

We consider that some years after its second stage carving which altered the head, this great Neanderthal nose was deliberately damaged, thus leaving the basis of a 'Cro-Magnon' profile. This act resulted in a multi-level encoding among which were clues as to the development of self-aware beings.

proportion of Neanderthal into the Cro-Magnon gene pool.

Stan Gooch has described and defended this position at all cultural and psychological levels in some nine books notably in *Cities of Dreams, The Neanderthal Question,* and *Total Man.* He is also convinced that the Sphinx's head is a monument of very considerable antiquity which incorporates and enshrines this intermingling of Neanderthal and Cro-Magnon, and which produced this gifted hybrid which is ourselves. Neanderthal's head was considerably larger than that of Cro-Magnon. It is therefore clear that any Cro-Magnon woman fertilised by a Neanderthal male would almost certainly have died in childbirth, due to the large head of the offspring (a residual problem still with us to this day).

Gooch's views concerning the detailed anatomy of Neanderthal man are generally considered heretical by the academe of anthropology. His findings include the fact that Neanderthal was primarily nocturnal in habit, preferring the night-time for being awake and the day for sleeping (which given the strength of the Sun

8. Pharaonic headgear *copied from the head* of the Great Sphinx.

We have concluded that this already damaged nose of the Sphinx was then reconstructed at a *much* later date by the indigenous peoples of Egypt, who also added the beard (partly from the traditions infused into the Egyptian race and partly to disguise the original receding Neanderthal jaw line). In so doing they purposefully linked the Sphinx and its attendant artefacts on the Giza plateau to their form of King line, the Pharaoh.

Most people, including the Egyptian Museum authorities, assume that the Sphinx is masculine because the head covering resembles the Pharaonic headgear. As we saw in "Prints of Mars", the Great Sphinx is a physiological symbol of both the masculine and the feminine and in our view it was the *Pharaonic headgear that was copied from the ancient head-dress of the Great Sphinx.* (8)

It was this *second* nose, we suggest, that was used for target practice, by either the Mamelukes or Napoleon's soldiers—both groups have been accused of this misdemeanour. If Napoleon's troops are to blame, we are tempted to ask whether their vandalism was in part prompted by their perception of a passing re-

9. Napoleon Bonaparte at Giza July 21 1798.

semblance between the Sphinx's large, rather prominent nose and Napoleon's own proboscis?

Whatever the reason, the result has been to recreate a damaged nose for the Giza Sphinx, as was originally intended.

The damaged nose of our Great Sphinx could also be taken as another encoding: that the knowledge represented by the Egyptian Sphinx and its surrounding artefacts would be virtually imprisoned until the beings represented by this statue—Homo Sapiens Sapiens, us—have the courage and understanding to perceive that creative and linear thinking are of equal value.

A prisoner of circumstance?

In Ptolemaic Egypt prisoners held at the ancient port of Rhinocolura (modern day El Arish had their noses cut off.

Presumably as a symbol of their downgraded status and also ensuring that they could not leave the port area without being immediately spotted.

The name of the town leads to an association with the eastern practice of cutting off Rhino's horns from a the belief that they transmitted sexual potency (male dominance).

Both situations lead one to think of the damaged nose of the Sphinx and the implied metaphor.

We also seem to have named the exact centre of the Moon *Sinus Medii*—related to the nose again!

In Egypt, the practice of defacing or mutilating a statue's nose was symbolic of the intention to deny the person represented an afterlife—as was the erasing of the written name of the unfortunate individual.

This latter practice somewhat resembles the habit of authority even today, to change the name of a nuclear site in an attempt to forget its unfortunate past.

And as we have seen the US Government have pushed the ancient practise even further by altering entire locations and dates!

Our new horizon

We the authors do appreciate that for many—certainly initially—this book will seem to be a mixture of fact and fantasy (although for us the authors it is all equally factual, and forms one seamless unit). So faked photographs? Well yes. But a massive Spinning Disk driven by human consciousness generating gravity that will take us to the stars???

Our proposal to any baffled or bewildered readers is as follows.

Take on board the facts—the undeniable facts. Then, by all means, and by any means available, look for your own explanation of these facts. Should you disagree with the explanatory and exploratory path we ourselves have offered, where, for you, do the facts lead?

It is a *fact* that the still photographs of the lunar EVAs are studio fakes. We are quite sure our evidence for this claim would stand up in a court of law. So *why* then, in your opinion, did NASA and its counterparts undertake this massive deception? What explanation for this behaviour do *you* come up with?

It is a *fact* that the view through the two LM windows was filled with the colour blue rather than the inky-blackness that should have been visible at the time of the 'Apollo 13' 'accident' some 200,000 miles from Earth. What is *your* explanation for such an occurrence?

It is *a fact* that the physical parallels between the Cydonia structures on Mars and the Avebury/Silbury complex on Earth are absolutely beyond argument and beyond any coincidence. How do *you* explain the circumstance that each set of structures is a copy of the other?

It is a *fact* that the solar system is 4.6 billion years old. However as stated at the Fourth Lunar Science Conference, the Moon has upon it rocks which are, conservatively, 5.3 billion years old. Some dating methods put the age of these rocks at between 7 billion and 20 billion years. Why are no such ancient rocks found on *our* planet? What is *your* explanation for this amazing situation?

It is a *fact* that light is *drawn into* black holes. Clearly therefore, light is affected by gravity. Is it not then likely—or indeed certain—that the speed of light within our solar system differs from the speed of light between stars, and this again from the speed of light between galaxies? Should not light speed measuring instruments be launched into deep space on probes to travel beyond our solar system to test this situation?

In respect of the last two items above, we appreciate that the general reader is hardly in a position to pursue matters of this kind in any direct sense.

Our appeal there, then, and likewise in respect of other specialist topics raised throughout this book, is for university and high school students of the subjects in question to determinedly and persistently badger their lecturers and professors in search of answers. Students can be quite sure, incidentally, that their teachers will never raise these matters with them!

By means of such grass roots revolution—and perhaps only through grass roots revolution—will the breakthrough come for which we the authors fervently hope. And indeed, precisely in pursuit of which we have written this book.

Let us release our binds by acknowledging our connection to *all* that is and become the harmonious creative-linear thinking beings that we truly are. Then we shall be able to use trans-dimensional physics for the benefit of both our planet and space travel. And we shall succeed in opening the way to the stars—for the *future* of all mankind.

Of course the Moon is not really dark at all. Together with our Sun, it is truly the light of our lives.

Chapter Notes

Chapter Notes

"They're not going to the Moon, not in this book." Sheila Wolfe to Tom Wolfe during the writing of *The Right Stuff*. As it turned out she was more right than she knew.

Chapter One "Photocall"

1. See Eric Jones' *Apollo Journal*, Apollo 11 mission on the NASA website for more on this EVA. (also see Appendix)
2. Ralph René, *NASA Mooned America*, René, 1994.
3. *ibid.*
4. HJP Arnold, "First Man On The Moon: The Missing Picture*", Spaceflight* Volume 30, July 1988. Also by HJP Arnold, *Images from Space: The Camera in Orbit*, Phaidon Press Ltd, 1979.
5. See chart of Sun angles in box on page 63. It has been suggested that earthshine (the light reflected onto the lunar surface from Earth) would be a factor in these images. Given the angle of the Earth in relation to the Sun and the Moon—surely we should expect to see *two shadows* (obviously one much brighter than the other) for each object, not one—but this was not the case. Moreover, even in areas out of the sunlight there would be a feint shadow from any earthshine, but there was none. We therefore conclude that in the Apollo lunar surface photographs earthshine was not a factor.
6. *Colour Films*, Focal Press, 1966.
7. Focal Press, 1960.
8. A full report on this photographic analysis is to be found in the Appendix.
9. *idem.*
10. Ed. Michael Dempsey, Robin Kerrod (compiler), *The Concise Encyclopaedia of Science*, Purnell & Sons Ltd, 1974 reprinted 1980. This photograph was full page and measured approximately 11¾" x 8". Therefore the 'C' would have been impossible to miss had it been left in!
11. James Lovell's letter of June 24 1996 addressed to Bill Kaysing.
    In Act 1 of Oscar Wilde's *The Importance of being Earnest* Lady Bracknell actually said: "To lose one parent, Mr Worthington, may be regarded as a misfortune; to lose both looks like carelessness".
12. Interestingly, a significantly high percentage of the American black population and homosexuals were suspicious of these flights (as compared with other groups) which we take to be indicative of these groups' ability to be more 'in tune' and aware. In 1969 over 70% of the population worldwide doubted the authenticity of the Apollo missions, European newspapers openly questioning the matter. Although NASA had hoped that the result of a 1970 poll of 1,721 Americans from six cities across the nation—(that 30% figure) would reduce, over time, it has not done so. Today NASA admits that "many millions" of people still doubt the veracity of these missions. Despite the media circus surrounding the 25th anniversary of 'Apollo 11', and the movie *Apollo 13,* over 50% of the American population *still does not believe* that NASA went to the Moon.

Chapter Two "Northern Exposures"

1. Brian Harvey, *The New Russian Space Programme*, John Wiley & Sons, 1996.
2. *National Geographic,* January 1965.

3. *ibid.*
4. *ibid.,* September 1973.
5. Astronaut Joe Allen, article on orbital mechanics, 1996. NASA administrator Thomas Paine, defined deep space as starting after LEO, therefore below the VABs.
6. British TV documentary series, *The Reel Truth, 1995.*
7. A *Sunday Times* part-work, *The History of Cinema.*

Chapter Three "Radiant Daze"

1. Carsbie C Adams, *Space Flight*, McGraw-Hill, 1958.
2. John Davidson, *Radiation,* C W Daniels, 1986.
3. Paper by Rein Silberberg, Chen Tsao, James Adams Jr, US Naval Research Laboratory & John Letaw of Severn Communications Corp, "Radiation Hazards in Space", *Aerospace America,* October 1987.
4. Arthur C Clarke in his foreword, written in 1980 for Kenneth Gatland's *Space Technology,* Salamander, 1981.
5. J R Murphy, *Medical Considerations For Manned Interstellar Flight*, JBIS 1981 Volume 34; also sourced: Gregory, "Cosmic Ray Shielding For Manned Interstellar Arks And Mobile Habitats", JBIS, 1976 Volume 30; Tobia & Grigor'yev, "Ionizing Radiation in Foundations of Space Biology & Medicine", VII bk II, 1976; Report on Space Colonisation by the ASEE/NASA Ames Stanford University Engineering Design Summer Study Group, 1976.
6. *National Geographic,* 1955.
7. Also sourced: "Basic Environmental Problems Relating to Man and the Highest Regions of the Atmosphere as Seen by the Biologist"; "History of the Development of Radiation Protection Standards for Space Activities"—and other papers published by the National Council on Radiation Protection and Measurements (NCRP), USA (see also 31 below). Additionally: *Working in Orbit and Beyond* (Ed. David B Lorr, Victoria Garshnek, and Claude Cadoux, Volume 72 Science and Technology Series, American Astronautical Society, 1989.
8. William J Walter, *Space Age,* Random House, 1992.
9. W N Hess, *The Radiation Belt and Magnetosphere*, 1968;
   Francis S Johnson, Ed. *Satellite Environment Handbook*, revised edition, 1965;
   B M McCormac, *Earth's Particles and Fields*, 1968;
   Radiation Trapped in the Earth's Magnetic Field, 1966.
   J G Roederer, *Dynamics of Geomagnetically Trapped Radiation*, 1970.
10. BBC TV *University Challenge* Quizmaster Jeremy Paxman, September 1997.
11. Maurice Cotterell, *The Supergod,* Thorsons, 1997.
12. *ibid.*
13. Interview with Professor Clive Dyer at DERA Farnborough, England, June 1996.
14. Quote from H Friedman, *Sun & Earth*, Macmillan, 1985.
15. Walter *op. cit.*
16. Baker, *Spaceflight and Rocketry: A Chronology*, Facts On File, 1996; entry for March 20 1959.
17. Encyclopaedia Britannica, 1997.
18. Bill Wood interview, California, USA, October 1996.
19. *National Geographic*, October 1974.
20. Striepe/Nealy/Simonsen NASA Langley Research Center, "Radiation Exposure Predictions for short-duration stay Mars Mission", *Journal of Spacecraft & Rockets,* Volume 29 # 6, November-December 1992.
21. Rein Silberberg, Chen Tsao, James Adams Jr, US Naval Research Laboratory & John Letaw of Severn Communications Corp, "Radiation Hazards in Space", *Aerospace America,* October 1987.
22. *ibid.* Referenced papers by the above authors also include "Galactic Cosmic Radiation doses to Astronauts outside the Magnetosphere".
23. "High-Energy Radiation Environment During Manned Space Flights".
24. Bill Wood at Goldstone/JPL, California, December 1997.
25. *Aerospace America, op. cit.*
26. John H Mauldin MA PhD, *Prospects For Interstellar Travel,* Volume 80 Science and Technology Series, American Astronautical Society, 1992.

27. *ibid.*

28. Also of interest is "The Sun Unveiled", *National Geographic,* October 1974; and two films:
    1) *Beyond the Stars* (1989): Although the entire film is well worth watching, the opening scene is particularly relevant to this chapter. Colonel Andrews, one of two astronauts on a lunar EVA, gets caught by a burst of solar radiation. By the end of the film he will have died from its effects.
    2) *Plymouth* (1991): This film concerns the community of an entire town shipped to the Moon after a nuclear accident in the USA. Their subsequent dealings with SPEs/solar flares and the sociological aspects of lunar colonisation are also relevant to this chapter.

29. Interview with Professor Clive Dyer at DERA, Farnborough, England, June 1996.

30. Quoted by Ralph René, *op. cit.*

31. NCRP report # 98 (see also Chapter Nine pg 376). Other NCRP papers sourced for this chapter:
    "History of the Development of Radiation Protection Standards for Space Activities", Sinclair 1996;
    "Philosophy on Astronaut Protection: A Physician's Perspective", Holloway 1996;
    "The Space Radiation Environment", Robbins 1996; "Biology Relevant to Space Radiation", Fry 1996.

32. *Aerospace America,* October 1987, *op. cit.*

33. Bernard Lovell in response to authors' letter of July 1997.

34. Andrew Chaikin, *A Man On The Moon: The Voyages of the Apollo Astronauts,* Viking Penguin Group 1994 (hbk) & Penguin, 1995 (pbk).

35. *Saga* UFO special # 3 and Don Wilson, *Our Mysterious Spaceship Moon,* Sphere Books, 1976.

36. Andrew Chaikin, *op. cit.*

37. Eric Jones, *Apollo Journal* Apollo 17 transcript, NASA website, November 1997.

38. *National Geographic,* December 1969.

39. Ralph René, *NASA Mooned America,* René, 1994.

40. *National Geographic,* May 1961, January 1965, May 1969, December 1969.

41. David Shayler, *Apollo 11 Moon Landing,* Ian Allen Ltd, 1989.

42. Hawkes, Lean, Leigh, McKie, Pringle, Wilson, *The Worst Accident In The World: Chernobyl The End Of The Nuclear Dream,* Heinemann, 1986 and Pan Books, 1986.

43. *National Geographic,* May 1961, January 1965, May 1969, December 1969.

44. Shayler, *op. cit.*

45. Jim Irwin to Andrew Chaikin, *op. cit.*

46. In conversation with the authors, California, October 1996.

47. Glenn Lutz during a British TV documentary, 1996.

48. Ralph René, *op. cit.*

49. *ibid.*

50. NCRP, *op. cit.*

51. Rhodes, *The Making of the Atomic Bomb,* Penguin, 1988;
    National Geographic, "Farewell to Bikini", July 1946; "Operation Crossroads", April 1947;
    "Nevada Learns to Live with the Bomb", June 1953 and
    Ed. Ferris, *The World Treasury of Physics Astronomy & Mathematics,* Stanislaw M Ulam pg 705, Little, Brown & Co., 1991.

52. BBC TV documentary, *People's Century 1945-95,* October 1996; and this extract (reported by E Jane Dickson in the British TV magazine *Radio Times)*: "The impact of nuclear power has been enormous—in the sorrow, the pain and the discomfort and loss to many, many people. And I think the thing that I feel terribly bad about is that we have lost confidence in our government. We really daren't trust them anymore." Sheldon Johnson of St. George, Utah, USA.

53. Rhodes, *op. cit.* and also Ernest Volkman, *Espionage, The Greatest Spy Operations Of The Twentieth Century,* John Wiley & Sons, 1995.

54. Alperowitz, *The Decision To Use The Atomic Bomb,* HarperCollins, 1997.

55. David Baker, *Spaceflight and Rocketry: A Chronology,* Facts on File, New York, 1996: August 1 1946 and May 1947.

Chapter Four "Rocket Rackets"

1. Carsbie C Adams, *Space Flight,* McGraw-Hill, 1958.

2. Most had been repatriated to Germany by 1953.
3. We have adopted the grammatically correct spelling of 'Matériel', according to the *Harraps New Shorter French and English Dictionary*, Bordas and Harrap & Co. Paris. In the texts we have encountered the American writing of this word has not necessarily been identical in the use and placement of the accent.
4. Andrija Puharich, *Uri,* WH Allen, 1974.
5. *National Geographic,* January 1953 and August 1955; also *Spaceflight*, Volume 38, July 1996.
6. Information is consistent on this point throughout the major space histories.
7. T A Heppenheimer, *Countdown, A History of Space Flight,* John Wiley & Sons Inc., 1997.
8. Reg Turnill, *The Language of Space, Dictionary of Astronautics,* Cassel, 1970. Turnill was one of the BBC's Apollo period commentators.
9. Bill Kaysing & Randy Reid, *We Never Went to the Moon*, Eden Press, 1976. All the space historians deal with the Apollo 1 incident but Kaysing does go into greater depth than most.
10. *ibid.*
11. Kaysing, *op. cit.*
12. David Shayler, *Apollo 11 Moon Landing,* Ian Allen Ltd, 1989.
13. Kaysing, *op. cit.*
14. Piers Bizony, *Focus*, UK, March 1997.
15. Kaysing, *op. cit.*
16. Brian Harvey, *New Russian Space Programme,* John Wiley & Sons Inc., pg 25; and Adams, *op. cit.*
17. See Appendix for USSR/USA lunar 'timeshare' launch date schedules.
18. The Russians Suvorov/Sabelnikov offer a different set of dates for the N-1 tests compared with Baker, only agreeing with the date of the first test. The Russian version states: 2nd test July 1970; 3rd test July 1971; 4th test December 1972. These N-1 'launch failures' occurred around the time of Apollo launches. Was that July 1969 N-1 'test' recorded by Baker actually a successful launch?
19. Suvorov & Sabelnikov, *The First Manned Spaceflight, Russia's Quest for Space*, Nova Science Publishers Inc., 1997 (see also Appendix).
20. Harvey, *op. cit.*
21. David Baker, *A History Of Manned Spaceflight,* Crown Publishers Inc., 1982.
22. Bill Wood interview, October 1996.
23. Baker, *op. cit.*
24. Andrew Chaikin, *A Man On The Moon: The Voyages of the Apollo Astronauts,* Viking Penguin Group 1994 (hbk) & Penguin 1995 (pbk).
25. *ibid.*
26. Shayler, *op. cit.*
27. Baker, *op. cit.*
28. *National Geographic*, December 1969.
29. The LM/CSM combinations were numbered: 'Apollo 8' LM nil-CSM103; 'Apollo 10' LM4-CSM106; 'Apollo 11' LM 5-CSM107; 'Apollo 12' LM6-CSM108; 'Apollo 13' LM 7 (7 the good luck number)-CSM109; 'Apollo 14' LM8-CSM110; 'Apollo 15' LM10-CSM112; 'Apollo 16' LM11-CSM113; 'Apollo 17' LM12-CSM114. Note between the 'Apollo 14' & '15' allocations the serial numbers LM9-CSM111 are 'missing'.
30. George Pinter, born June 16 1916 in Budapest, completed his education at the Swiss Federal Institute of Technology in Zurich where he also pursued post-graduate studies in thermodynamics. Holder of four patents and author of nine technical papers Pinter emigrated to America in 1953 and worked for General Electric and Aerojet before joining Grumman in 1963, following extensive checks on his education and background. Having been given a high security clearance he worked on the cryogenic systems of the LM through to 1971, then on the Space Shuttle systems, the ELM satellite, the Infrared Telescope Facility for the Shuttle after which he was assigned by Grumman to Princeton Plasma Physics Lab undertaking specialist work for the DOE (US Dept of Energy). Pinter received a *Certificate of Excellence* from Grumman for his services during 'Apollo 13' and a NASA *Apollo Achievement Award* for his contribution to the first manned lunar landing. George Pinter was also a member of the American Rocket Society and The American Institute of Aeronautics and Astronautics. He was very highly regarded by his friends and colleagues.

31. Interviews with Bill Kaysing, December 1995, and Bill Wood in California, October 1996.
32. *ibid.*
33. Letter to authors dated July 7 1997, from Raymond V Arnaudo, Science and Environment Attaché of the American Embassy in London. In response to our letter of June 30 1997 he informed us that he had sent copies of our questions to James Zimmerman of NASA US Embassy Paris and J Adamas at NASA's International Affairs Office. At the time of publishing, there was no response from either of these gentlemen. (See also copy of American Embassy acknowledgement in Appendix.)
34. Bill Kaysing interview, 1995. It should be remembered that as the craft was about to touch down, in addition to the dust and a great deal of smoke, there would have also been *flame from the rocket engine* which would have illuminated the lunar surface. This illumination would have been clearly visible from the windows of the LM. Rather like landing in the dark with a giant flame-thrower lighting the way, such a situation might have assisted the operation or simply made matters worse by illuminating the smoke—rather like automobile headlights in fog!
35. In corroboration of our statement, see "Media Review, Cold War Not So Cold After All", *Exposure* magazine, Volume 2 # 5 1995-6. The quote was from the *National Geographic*. NGM also ran articles on Antarctica, in which the friendly links between the Soviet and American scientists were much in evidence, especially during the run up (1957/8) to the International Geophysical Year. This was a period when America was building facilities on Antarctica for the Soviets—a time of Cold War between these two countries elsewhere on the planet.
36. Bill Wood, interview, October 1996.
37. Bernard Lovell, *op. cit.*
38. Also in 1967 Bernard Lovell noted that there "seemed to be a near parallelism in the [space] developments in both countries [USA/USSR], aimed at placing a man on the Moon before 1970".

Chapter Five "masters of infinity"

1. Lyndon Baines Johnson extract from speech at the Senate Democratic Caucus, January 7 1958.
2. Bernard Lovell, *Astronomer by Chance,* Oxford University Press, 1992; and
3. Carsbie Adams, author of *Spaceflight,* Macgraw Hill 1958; both colleague and friend of Wernher von Braun in the USA. (also see Appendix)
4. Patrick McGilligan *Fritz Lang, The Nature Of The Beast*, Faber & Faber, 1997 and most leading space biographies.
5. Ernst Stuhlinger & Frederick I Ordway III, *Wernher von Braun: Crusader for Space,* Krieger Publishing Co., 1994.
6. Dr. Helen B Walters, author of *Wernher von Braun: Rocket Engineer,* Macmillian, 1964; writes of an MA whereas Heinz Gartzmann, in *Men and Rockets* (a translation from the German by the Science Book Club—no date given), states it was a BA.
7. Stuhlinger & Ordway, *op. cit.*
8. *ibid.,* and H Walters, *op. cit.*
9. *ibid.,* and H Walters, *op. cit.*
10. H Walters, *op. cit.*
11. James Harford, *Korolev,* John Wiley & Sons Inc., 1997.
12. Wernher von Braun, *Space Frontier,* European publisher Frederick Muller Ltd, 1968; (copyrighted WvB 1963-1968); there is no reference to this book in the American bibliographies consulted.
13. Aleksandr Solzhenitsyn, *The First Circle,* Collins and the Harvill Press, 1968; *The Gulag Archipelago,* Harper & Row, 1973.
14. The impression that Peenemünde was a stark rocket research facility with no comforts for its inmates is generally fostered by most historical accounts of this period. Later in America these same scientists would make use of another hearth room—this time looking rather like a 'ranch house' and suspend a distinctively-decorated sign upon which could be found, among other in-jokes, the words "Curio Shop".
15. Ernest Volkman, *Espionage*, John Wiley & Sons Inc., 1995.
16. Gartzmann, *op. cit.*; and Manvell & Fraenkel, *Hitler*, Grafton Books, 1996.
17. British TV documentary, *Nazi Gold,* June 1997.

18. Adam LeBor, *Hitler's Secret Bankers,* Pocket Books, 1997.
19. The consensus of those who came into contact with them, was that the SS in mufti were esteemed to be more 'dangerous' than those in uniform.
20. Heinz Gartzmann, *op. cit.* Patrick. McGilligan *Fritz Lang, The Nature Of The Beast*, Faber & Faber, 1997.
21. An opinion stated by his friend Carsbie Adams and quoted in Stuhlinger & Ordway's biographical memoir of WvB, *op. cit.*
22. Helen Walters, *op. cit.*
23. Stuhlinger & Ordway, *op. cit.* pg 40.
24. Ignorance is bliss? WvB had always denied specific knowledge of what really went on at the Mittelwerks. Stuhlinger & Ordway relate that WvB's visits to Mittelwerk "lasted only a few hours, sometimes one or two days". They also state that: "a special organisation to operate this new subterranean production facility was established, this is how Mittelwerk came into being". However, in *Albert Speer: His Battle With The Truth* (Alfred A Knopf, 1995), author Gita Sereeny writes that the Peenemünde scientific team with Colonel Walter Dornberger and Wernher von Braun were to be responsible for the technical side of the Mittelwerks facility. (Magnus von Braun was also at Mittelwerk at that time.) How could that responsibility be fulfilled efficiently with just "sporadic visits"? William J Walter author of *Space Age* (Random House, 1992), writes that WvB told his friend A C Clarke, "I did not know what was going on, but I suspected. And in my position I could have found out, but I didn't and I despise myself for it".
25. Helen B Walters, *op. cit.*
26. Stuhlinger & Ordway, Baker, Harford, Gartzmann *op. cit.*
27. Stuhlinger & Ordway, Baker, Harford, Gartzmann *op. cit.*
28. Stuhlinger & Ordway, Baker, Harford, Gartzmann *op. cit.*
29. Stuhlinger & Ordway, Baker, Harford, Gartzmann *op. cit.*
30. Stuhlinger & Ordway, Baker, Harford, Gartzmann *op. cit.*
31. Another 2,100 V-2 rockets were found in field storage at various sites. Baker, *Spaceflight and Rocketry, op. cit.*
32. Betty Maxwell, *A Mind Of My Own,* Sidgewick & Jackson, 1994.
33. Stuhlinger & Ordway, *op. cit.*
34. Russell Davies, *Foreign Body: The Secret Life Of Robert Maxwell,* Bloomsbury, 1995.
35. H Walters, *op. cit.*
36. Ernest Volkman, *Espionage,* John Wiley & Sons Inc., 1995.
37. The Guggenheim Aeronautical Labs at the California Institute of Technology. The Guggenheims were sponsors of Robert Goddard.
38. H Walters, *op. cit.*
39. Peter Harry Brown & Pat H Broeski, *Howard Hughes the Untold Story,* Little, Brown and Co., 1996. Also of interest, though not specifically mentioning this particular comment, was the US TV production *The Secret History of Howard Hughes,* Parts One and Two, 1998.
40. Baker, *Spaceflight and Rocketry, op. cit.*: 1945 September 8. Of the 280 members of the society by December 31 1945 six were appointed as honorary fellows: Wernher von Braun, Willie Ley; Guido von Pirquet; Eugene Sanger; A V Cleaver and O W Gail.
41. Arthur C Clarke, *Odyssey,* Gollancz, 1992. Also see *Astounding Days,* Gollancz, 1989, for an interesting account of his own life.
42. Adams, *op. cit.*
43. Gartzmann, *op. cit.*
44. Timothy Good, *Beyond Top Secret,* Sidgewick & Jackson, 1996.
45. Baker, Adams, *op. cit.*
46. Baker, Adams, *op. cit.*
47. Baker, Adams, *op. cit.*
48. In July 1958, this 'year' was extended to 18 months, thus January 1 1959 became the final day of this International Geophysical Year.
49. Adams, *op. cit.* and also for hitherto unrevealed background to the Soviet space program see Suvorov & Sabelnikov, *The First Manned Spaceflight,* Nova Science Inc., 1997.

50. Baker, *op. cit.*
51. Stuhlinger and Ordway, *op. cit.*
52. *ibid.*
53. Gartzmann, *op. cit.* The propellant mixture was liquid oxygen & alcohol plus 30% admixture of water. According to the *Daily Express Book of the Year* 1935, Jules Verne was the pen name of M Olchewitz.
54. *ibid.*
55. *ibid.*

Chapter Six "Truth or Consequences"

1. Phil Cousineau *UFOs, A Manual For The Millennium,* Harper Paperbacks, 1995.
2. Simon Welfare & John Fairley *Arthur C Clarke's Mysterious World,* Book Club Associates, 1984.
3. Cousineau *op.cit. Roswell UFO Crash Update*, Cpt Kevin Randle (Retd.) Global Communications, 1995. Books other than those listed include: *Out There,* Howard Blum, Simon & Schuster, 1990; *The Roswell Message,* Rene Coudris, translated from the German, Gateway Books; 1997; *The Day After Roswell,* Col. Philip Corso, Simon & Schuster Pocket Books, 1997.
4. *Secret History: The Roswell Incident,* documentary on British TV, 1995, and see Appendix for cast list of the Roswell military.
5. A 1991 statement made during a home video, re-broadcast in *The Roswell Incident, ibid.*
6. Robert Morning Sky, a native American, is much involved with UFO phenomena and author of *The Terra Papers,* a book concerning 'alien'/Earth contact.
7, 13, 14 & 22. All sources Timothy Good, UFO researcher, see list of books in Appendix.
8. Ed. Richard M Hall, The National Investigations Committee on Aerial Phenomena (NICAP), *The UFO Evidence,* Barnes & Noble Inc., 1964. This edition published by arrangement with the UFO Research Coalition, 1997.
9. *National Geographic,* November, 1987.
10. Randle *op. cit.*
11. *The Roswell Report: Fact vs. Fiction in the New Mexico Desert,* US Govt. Printing Office, 1995; and *The Roswell Report: Case Closed,* US Govt. Printing Office, 1997.
12. The *Sunday Times,* UK July 29 1995.
15. *Encounters* magazine, issue # 1.
16. Prior to this autopsy footage 'release', Ray Santilli was chiefly known for his negotiation to obtain the British rights to the *Tintin, Exploration on the Moon* material.
17. NICAP report *op.cit.* By 1998 the press were running stories on the stepping up of radio telescope search for intelligence 'out there'. The US Project Phoenix is scheduled to run for ten years by UK's Jodrell Bank & Puerto Rico. Seth Shostak expects to find signs of intelligence within 15 years, while Jodrell Bank's Ian Morrison states that ET will send a 'beacon' signal rather than a readable message. Wake up chaps, they already have done so! (then again, see 21).
18. Stanton T Friedman & Don Berliner *Crash at Corona: The Definitive Study Of The Roswell Incident.* Marlowe & Co., Second Edition, 1994.
19. David Kahn, *The Codebreakers,* Scribner, 1967, 1996.
20. Stanton Friedman *op.cit.*
21. *National Geographic,* 1955. In 1998 SRI physicist Peter Sturrock stated that his investigative panel found that UFOs were not a fantasy and then announced that: "they had found no violation of any natural laws and NO convincing evidence of extra-terrestrial intelligence". Which statement manages to keep Einstienian physics firmly on its pedestal and appear to be forward thinking on the subject of 'alien' contact while actually acknowledging one type of UFO and dismissing the flying saucer variety. Hopefully they will remember to request their colleagues at Jodrell Bank and Puerto Rico not to waste their time. Or does Project Phoenix mean: yet another round of disinformation?
23, & 25. British TV documentary, *The Day The Earth Was Hit,* November 1997; Simon Welfare & John Fairley *op cit.*; Jack Stoneley, *Tunguska: Cauldron of Hell,* W H Allen & Co. Ltd., 1977.
24. Crop Glyph analysis has been undertaken by The BLT team headed up by ex Michigan State University biophysicist, Professor W C Levengood, together with John Burke & Nancy Talbott; Analysis of Crop Glyph Samples, a paper in the US *Physiologia Plantarum,* 1994, and the UK

Farmer's Weekly, 1995. Soil analysis undertaken by Dr. DiPinto, Delaware Radionics Labs, Oxford; also by Marshall Dudley, Oak Ridge nuclear physicist with Michael Chorost, physicist, "Analysis of Soil and Crop", for Project Argus, The British Ministry of Agriculture's R&D dept—ADAS ran tests on Crop Glyph samples in 1995. After finding anomalies therein (notably but not exclusively in the soil's nitrogen/nitrate content) the ministry promptly closed down the entire department. This action thwarted further open discussion on the subject of Crop Glyphs.

As with UFOs, governments are clearly very concerned, but *publicly* they remain "not interested".

26. Benoit Peeters Herge *The Making Of Tintin Mission To The Moon,* Methuen, 1989.
27. Phil Patton *Travels in Dreamland, The Secret History Of Area 51,* Orion Paperbacks, 1997.

Chapter Seven "Distant Horizons"

1. Helen Walters, *Wernher von Braun Rocket Engineer,* pg 91 Macmillian, 1964.
2. Rhodes, *op. cit.*
3. Gartzmann, *The Men Behind The Space Rockets,* The Scientific Book Club, London (subject matter included up to 1955).
4. Adam LeBor, *Hitler's Secret Bankers, op. cit.*; and Tom Bower, *Blood Money: The Swiss, The Nazis and The Looted Billions,* Macmillan, 1997; British TV documentary *Nazi Gold, op. cit.*
5. Timothy Green, *The World of Gold Today,* Arrow Books, 1973.
6. Oleg Penkovsky, *World's Greatest Spies & Spymasters,* Octopus Books, 1984, reprinted 1985, 1997; and Volkman, *op. cit.*
7. Green, *op. cit.*
8. For example the Soviets were very short of computers, components and allied technology.
9. Stuhlinger and Ordway, *op. cit.*
10. Clive James, the *New York Review of Books,* 1979.
11. All of ACC's output both fictional and non-fictional is highly enlightening—especially interesting is *Profiles of the Future: an Inquiry into the Possible,* Gollancz, 1962, Pan Books, 1964.
12. *Encyclopaedia Britannica, and* Arthur C Clarke, *How the World was One.*
13. *National Geographic,* 1958.
14. The High Frequency Active Aural Altitude Atmospheric Program based in Alaska and due on line by the end of 1999.
    Dr. Nick Begich, *Angels Don't Play This Haarp, advances in Tesla Technology,* Earth Pulse Press, Anchorage, Alaska. (PO Box 201393 Anchorage, Alaska 99520, USA.)
15. Baker, *Spaceflight and Rocketry, op. cit.*
16. Col. Philip J Corso, (Retd.) with William J Birnes, *The Day After Roswell,* Pocket Books, 1997.
17. Carl Koppeschaar, *The Moon Handbook: A 21st Century Travel Guide,* Moon Publications, 1995; Arthur C Clarke, *3001: The Final Odyssey,* Voyager, 1997.
18. Stuhlinger & Ordway, *op. cit.*
19. Baker, *Spaceflight and Rocketry, op. cit.*: entry 1959, March 20.
20. From paperwork published in Corso's *The Day After Roswell, op. cit.*
21. T A Heppenheimer, *Countdown,* John Wiley & Sons Inc., 1997.
22. One example of this Soviet thoroughness was the Ergorov paper. This publication dealt with "Problems and Dynamics of Flight to the Moon" and included 48 months of research material from the Russian Mathematics Institute.
23. Arthur C Clarke, *How the World was One, op cit.*
24. Malcolm Brown from a paper entitled "The Evolution of the Moon" in which he writes: "No terrestrial rocks can be directly measured as having such great crystallisation ages [as lunar samples]".
25. Malcolm Brown, "The Evolution of the Moon".
26. *Collins Dictionary of Astronomy,* HarperCollins, 1994.
27. Adrian Berry, *The Next 500 Years, Life In the Coming Millennium,* Headline, 1995.
28. The *Art Bell* show is the most popular coast-to-coast American talk show of its kind. It often deals with controversial topics, this quote was from Part Two of a six-part show transmitted on May 15 1996. A transcript of the program was published on the web by G Varano. Not unlike the Internet, such radio shows can be an ideal platform for any ideas that are 'required' to come into the public

domain. The distance between the two landing sites is a close approximation. We used the diameter of the Moon multiplied by Pi = circumference of Moon in statute miles, divided by 360° equalling the number of miles per degree, multiplied by the distance between the 'Apollo 14' and 'Apollo 12' sites, taking into account both latitude and longitude. Viz.: 2160 x Pi (3.14159526) = 6,785.84 miles divided by 360° = 18.85 miles per degree x 5.55° (degrees longitude eastward of the 'Apollo 12' site) = 104. 6175 miles. Note that the 'Apollo 14' landing site is also the location designated for 'Apollo 13' and it lies approximately 325 miles west of Sinus Medii.

29. Landing site lat/long data from Carl Koppeschaar, *op. cit.*
30. Brown, *op. cit.*
31. Berry, *op. cit.*
32. *National   Geographic.*
33. Don Wilson, *Our Mysterious Spaceship Moon,* Sphere Books, 1976.
34. Dr. Harold Urey, *Chemistry*, February 1974.
35. Wilson, *op. cit.*
36. *Science News,* August 16 1969: pg 129; and January 10 1970: pg 34.
37. French magazine *Mystères* [Mysteries], *Article Science Frontières Lunikhod: une fois, deux fois? adjuge!* 1994.
38. Interview, California, 1995.
39. Eric Jones, *Apollo Journal,* NASA web site, 1997.
40. British TV documentary 1997.
41. Dave Scott, *National   Geographic,* September 1973.
42. Dating confirmed by Dr. Stephen Morebath of Oxford University, during *Earth Story* BBC TV, 1998. No human beings are on record as having been killed by a falling meteorite; however, a dog was killed by the arrival of the Nahkla meteorite in Egypt. How much of a coincidence is it that this 1969 meteorite arrived five months before the scheduled Moon landing, at a location only a few hours drive from Houston and near a town with a dog's name? The Chihuahua breed of small smooth-coated dog takes its name from this Mexican town. Adrian Room (*Dictionary of Proper Names*, Cassell, 1992) gives the meaning of Chihuahua as dry or sandy. Whereas the Peruvian/Englishman Michael Bentine tells us that 'Huaca' relates to the natural force lines of the Earth (drakon lines).
43. Richard Hoagland during a public lecture at Ohio State University, June 1994.
44. Chaikin, *A Man On The Moon, op. cit.*
45. Good, *Above Top Secret, op. cit.*
46. *Spaceflight: A Smithsonian Guide*, Macmillian, 1995, A Ligature Book.
47. Good, *op. cit.*
48. Buzz Aldrin & John Barnes, *Encounter with Tiber,* Hodder & Stoughton, 1996.
49. *Saga* magazine, UFO Special # 3 quoted by Don Wilson, *op. cit.*
50. Wilson, *op. cit.*
51. Chaikin, *op. cit.*
52. Good, *op. cit.*
53. Are these names somewhat laborious 'ultra secret coding' designed for us all to work out (after a lot of nudges from Farouk El-Baz) and then get fearful? Apart from some researcher's theories that these names refer to clarification of diction as in B for Bravo, how does that then fit with B for Barbara? Perhaps Barbara is Santa Barbara/Santa Claus/ET? (remember 'Apollo 8'?) And what if AnnaBell was intended to relate to Barbara Ann/The Beach Boys/beached Buoys/ET craft?
54. David Baker, *Spaceflight and Rocketry: A Chronology:* entry for 1982, June 27.
55. Baker *op. cit.* entry for 1962, March 14.
56. This information is inherent throughout the reading of any profile on the named astronauts from the Apollo program.
57. Baker *op. cit.*
58. Bill Kaysing in conversation with authors 1995. The incident was recorded by Absolute Video, Nashville TN, USA.
59. *Art Bell* show, May 15 1996 1am to 4am PDT. Ed Mitchell and Richard Hoagland were primarily airing the possibility of anomalies existing on moonscape photographs in Hoagland's possession.

60. Jim Schnabel, *Remote Viewers: The Secret History of America's Psychic Spies,* Dell Books, 1997.
61. *ibid.*
62. Uri Geller: *My Story,* Praeger/Robinson; *The Geller Effect* Jonathan Cape. *Uri* Puharich, Doubleday.
63. Dr. Puharich was one of the prime movers and shakers (together with Sir John Whitmore) during the early days of the communications from Tom, of the Council of Nine, transceived by Phyllis Schlemmer. Their story by Stuart Holroyd was published by W H Allen in 1977 under the title *Prelude to the Landing on Planet Earth,* and Puharich also attended many other sessions with Tom. Selected sessions from the period 1974 through to 1994 have been published under the title *The Only Planet of Choice: Essential Briefings From Deep Space,* compiled by Phyllis Schlemmer & Mary Bennett, Gateway Books, 1994, Second Edition.
64. James Randi, *The Supernatural A-Z,* Brockhamton Press, 1995.
65. Geller, *op. cit.*
66. Schnabel, *op. cit.*
67. Geller, *op. cit.*
68. Kaysing, *op. cit.*
69. Stan Gooch in conversation with the authors, 1995.
70. The *Frank Skinner* series, British TV mid 1990s, source Peter Oakley (researcher and lecturer on space); edited version repeated in *The Best of Frank Skinner,* 1996.
71. Ex-astronaut and golfer Alan Shepard with British golfer Peter Alliss, during a British TV golfing interview transmitted in the late 1990s on British TV.
72. Aldrin's biography, *Return To Earth,* 1973.
73. Kaysing, *op. cit.*
74. This statement was made during an interview in 1994 with a source who wishes to remain anonymous. The exact time period quoted by Aldrin was, "maybe a couple of weeks ago, maybe more".

Chapter Eight "Servants of Circumstance"

1. Col. Philip Corso (Retd.), *The Day after Roswell, op. cit.*
2. Patrick Moore, *Exploring the Earth and Moon,* Regency House, 1996.
3. Bernard Lovell, *Astronomer By Chance, op. cit.* This is only one of several books concerning Jodrell Bank and Bernard Lovell's life and work.
4. Arthur C Clarke, *How the World was One, op. cit.*
5. Lovell, *op. cit.*; and Heppenheimer, *op. cit.*
6. It was necessary to cross reference several of the autobiographies by Sir Bernard in order to complete the broader picture. For example, in the incident concerning Colonel L, *Astronomer by Chance* is relatively succinct. Colonel Walter Hingston was the Chief Information Officer of the DSIR—the Department of Scientific and Industrial Research. Lovell states there was a division within that department responsible for administering government funding for "fundamental research". The DSIR took the Royal Observatories under its wing in 1965 and was retitled the Science Research Council (SRC) in 1981, without fundamentally changing its modus operandi it was again retitled as SERC: the Science & Engineering Research Council.
7. David Baker's *Spaceflight and Rocketry: A Chronology* provides a comprehensive overview of space exploration mainly from the Western point of view and Brian Harvey's *The New Russian Space Programme* covers the Soviet/Russian space program, albeit Harvey has written an account rather than a formal chronology. Also relating to the Soviet history is the earlier work by Philip Clark. *The Soviet Manned Space Program: an Illustrated History of the Men, Missions and Spacecraft,* Salamander, 1988. These, together with Jos Heyman's *Spacecraft Tables 1957-1990,* Univelt Inc., 1991, offer relevant reading.
8. Heppenheimer, *op. cit.;* and Lovell, *op. cit.*
9. Lovell, *op. cit.* This information tends to suggest that (at least at that stage in the technological development of the space program) it required much more powerful equipment to *send* information to spacecraft at any great distance from Earth than it did to *receive* signals from space.
10. According to Eric Jones' *Apollo Journal,* of the three landing sites at Tranquility, landing site # 1 was nominated for 'Apollo 8', landing site # 2 for 'Apollo 10' and landing site # 3 for 'Apollo 11'.

Patrick Moore's *Moon Flight Atlas* of 1969 cites the 'Apollo 11' flight ignoring site # 1 but confirms site # 2 as being the intended landing place for 'Apollo 10'. Which is contrary to NASA's own map of the 'Apollo 11' landing site (see Appendix page 545).

11. Most of the WvB biographies mention this incident.
12. Nigel Hamilton, *JFK Reckless Youth*, Random House, 1992; Jamie Doran & Piers Bizony, *Starman: The Truth Behind The Legend Of Yuri Gagarin,* Bloomsbury, 1998.
13. Jock Bruce-Gardyne, "Was Gagarin Russia's answer to the Piltdown Man?" *The Daily Telegraph* London, 21 April 1986.
14. *ibid.*
15. Lovell, *op. cit.*
16. The trajectory of the Vostok 1 flight was an west-east orbit of 105×194 miles at an angle of $65°$ to the equator, averaging 17,400mph/28,000kph. In fact this flight did not complete a perfect circle of the Earth, coming down to the west of its starting point (rather than on the button or to the east). The craft was tracked by ground stations in the Soviet Union for just under 30 minutes and then by their tracking fleet. The coded, unscrambled telemetry was fed back to computers in Moscow.
17. HJP Arnold in conversation with the authors.
18. James Oberg, *Uncovering Soviet Disasters,* Random House, 1988: Chapter 10 "Dead Cosmonauts". We have found various spellings of the name Golyakovsky, and chosen that which is printed in this manuscript. Oberg spells the Doctor's name with an 'H' as in Golyakhovsky. However, we are all referring to the same person.
19. Harvey, *op. cit.*
20. Doran & Bizony, *op. cit.*; referred to as D&B in this "voluntary best servants" section.
21. Oberg, *op. cit.;* also "The Men Before Gagarin", *Enigma* magazine issue # 1, December 1996.
22. Doran & Bizony, *op. cit.*
23. *ibid.*
24. *ibid.*
25. *ibid.* In the event of a problem during the Vostok 1 flight, it would have been necessary to produce a body. If the Vostok had failed at take off there would have been an unrecognisable corpse in the wreckage. That being the case, officially the Soviets could have 'postponed' the flight.
If the Vostok had failed during its orbit, the Soviets could 'send it a suicide note'.
If the Vostok had failed during or after re-entry, then there would have been a body in the crash wreckage. However, in the event, we suggest that the *surrogate* cosmonaut, Nelyubov ejected over a an undisclosed, secret location.
When the Vostok had returned to Earth safely, Gagarin was parachuted down over a location some two miles away from the already-landed Vostok, thus giving everybody the time to perform these manoeuvres. So Nelyubov had fulfilled his overriding ambition to be 'first in space', at the expense of never being publicly acknowledged for his bravery. Gagarin and Titov were regarded as being too precious to be risked during these initial stages of the manned program in what was without doubt a potentially dangerous flight. Of course, Gagarin's profile was the perfect emissary for the Soviets, (as was the case with Armstrong for the Americans).
It is our view that the unnamed junior gantry helpers were Anikeyev or Filyatev, conscripted into this manoeuvre to replace Gagarin with Nelyubov. All three were 'sacked' [or pensioned off] from the cosmonaut team in 1963 by Kamamin on a very flimsy pretext. Did the 'spare man' of this triumvirate perform another such surrogate role later on for Titov? Consult James Oberg and Doran & Bizony for more on that incident.
26. *ibid.*
27. Doran & Bizony, *op. cit.*
28. Kaysing, *op. cit.*
29. Johnston Island is south-east of Hawaii at $17°10'N$ $169°8'W$.
30. It would be easy to misconstrue this diagram and assume that it is possible to leave Earth for space via the 'unaffected' hemisphere furthest from the Sun, as this illustration, while showing the position of the artificial radiation belt, only shows a partial 'slice through' of the radiation belts *that fully encircle the Earth.*
31. Baker, *Spaceflight and Rocketry: A Chronology*; entry July 8 1962.

32. John Davidson, *Radiation,* C W Daniel, 1986.
33. Professor Clive Dyer, DERA, Farnborough, England, interview June 1996.
34. Refer to Chapter Three "Radiant Daze" for more on the Van Allen radiation belts.
35. Moore, *op. cit.*
36. Ian Fleming in the *Sunday Times Magazine* 1962; reprinted *Esquire,* 1997; reprinted *Cover* magazine, 1998.
37. In the Film *Diamonds Are Forever*, note that Bond's hotel was called the *Whyte House* and the owner of said hotel was one Willard Whyte. This scene is prior to Bond's investigation into the Techtronics US Government Restricted Area 'moon' set sited north of Las Vegas. Some have proposed an analogy to reclusive millionaire Howard Hughes as the inspiration behind '*Willard Whyte*', we suggest that there might be another line: It is alleged that as a result of amateur astronomer George Adamski's UFO sightings during the 'flap' of 1947, the military asked him to document his sightings. By 1951 he was a well known UFO researcher.
Are there links between the UFO flap of 1947/Roswell/George Adamski/The Willard Hotel/The White House/ET/the Moon landings/Project Horizon/Mars and Cydonia/Arthur C Clarke's *3001* character 'Uncle George', possessor of old video tapes and science fiction magazines?
38. Luna 9 landed at 7°08′N 64°33′W on January 31 1966 and transmitted images together with radiation data back to Earth.
39. *The Sentinel* was written in 1948 by Arthur C Clarke and copyrighted by Avon Periodicals in 1951. See Chapter Twelve "Prints of Mars" for more on this story;
Arthur C Clarke, *Encounter in the Dawn*, Ziff Davies Publishing Company, 1953.
In Clarke's introduction to *2001: A Space Odyssey* (Legend pbk edition, Arrow Books Ltd, 1990), Clarke notes the "uncanny connection" with the 'Apollo 13' mission, noting the three points that we specifically have highlighted, i.e. the name of CSM, the background music and the line of script. He wrote most of *2001's* book/film script at the Hotel Chelsea, 222 West 23rd Street, New York.
40. Bob Pritchard in correspondence with the authors.
41. Authors' correspondence with Parkes Observatory, Australia, 1997 and the "Apollo Color TV camera", a paper by L L Niemyer, Jr presented at the Electro-Optical Systems Design Conference, New York, September 16 1969.
42. Goldstone's Bill Wood and authors' correspondence with Parkes Observatory, Australia, 1997.
43. This refers to the American Embassy correspondence mentioned in Chapter Four "Rocket Rackets".
44. Baker, *op. cit.*
45. Correspondence with Jerry Wiant, McDonald Observatory, 1997.
46. Geller, *op. cit.*
47. 'Apollo 11' and 'Apollo 12' were alleged to have placed laser ranging reflectors of 100 corner cubes each while the 'Apollo 15' crew were alleged to have placed a laser reflector comprising 300 corner cubes. We have noted the relative distance between Lunikhod 2 and 'Apollo 15'.
48. US Weather bureau reports in our possession for this part of Texas—July & August 1968, July & August 1969 and July & August 1970. The total rainfall for July 1969 was 7.04 inches for the area in question and *all of this had fallen by July 18*. At the time of the lunar landing, July 20/21: maximum temperatures for July 20 were 85°F (rising to 91°F on July 21 1969); and minimum temperatures were 66°F on July 20 (and 60°F on July 21 1969).
49. During July 1969 the Moon was in the first quarter at the time of 'Apollo 11'.
Full Moon occurred on July 29 and the last quarter on August 5 1969.
Lunar night was therefore installed *all* over the lunar surface facing Earth by August 13 1969.
50. Eric Jones states that it was the seismometer that had failed to adjust correctly, but in any event this would still appear to be a technically impossible situation.
51. Shayler, *op. cit.*
52. Paddington & Minnett, "Microwave Thermal Radiation From The Moon", *Australian Journal of Scientific Research*, March 1949; and also the Arthur C Clarke biography, *Astounding Days*, Gollancz, 1989.
53. We have found a reference to the 'Apollo 14' & '15' LR[3] laser reflectors in Kenneth Gatland's *Space Technology*, Salamader, 1981. However, the disparity in the data between these two works of Baker is unexplained!

54. *The Daily Telegraph,* London, December 18 1997.

Chapter Nine "Slaves of Limitation"

1. In a very long biographical note posted on the world wide web titled *Who is Eric Jones* we are informed (among other things) that he is an employee of the Los Alamos National Laboratory and that it was in 1988 that Eric realised that "nothing had been done" with the Apollo mission transcripts. Given that David Shayler used these tapes and transcripts therefrom extensively in his 1989 publication *Apollo 11 Moon Landing,* written certainly in 1988 if not before; and given that Andrew Chaikin (ex editor of *Sky and Telescope)* also availed himself of these tapes during the eight years (from 1985 through to December 1993) of research and writing *A Man On The Moon* by 1994, Mr Jones' statement would appear to be somewhat exaggerated.
It is particularly significant that he has bolted his commentary onto these Apollo transcripts thus creating a vehicle for steering 1990s readers in a particular direction. Eric Jones considers that the most relevant information about himself is his marriage to Di (why should that be relevant to the *Apollo Journals?)* and that he has long been a friend of 'Bill W'. As it was one Bill Wood of Goldstone who took pains to make sure that we were aware of Eric Jones' *Apollo Journal* we wonder? More especially do we wonder, when Eric Jones underlines the fact that his e-mail address is 'Honais' because it "sounds like" Jones in Spanish. He has adopted this pronunciation since his college days. More charades? If you pronounce the whole name *'Eric Jones'* with a Spanish rhythm and accent then this 'looks like' Ericojones, 'sounds like' Ericohonais which 'is like' the Spanish word for biological balls.
2. Oxford Shorter English Dictionary.
3. Jim Lovell with Jeffrey Kluger, *Apollo 13,* Pocket Books, 1995.
4. *Speedmaster: The Moon Watch* published by Omega SA, Biel, Switzerland, 1995.
5. Never mind the height, feel the width! The astronauts (in the *Apollo Journal)* are agreed that it is a tight fit but that it doesn't present that much of a problem!
From Jeffrey Kluger's *The Apollo Adventure*: "A simple overlooked fact of Lunar Module design . . . the door of the LM opened inward and to the right".
6. On a journey to the Moon surely the conditions in space are only near to zero weightlessness when at the neutral point? Any other location along the trajectory being (to a degree) under the influence of either to the Earth's gravity or the Moon's gravity. NASA would have it (Baker, *A History Of Manned Space Flight)* that: "Debris can become trapped by the summed gravitational force between the two massive bodies". All right for floating space junk maybe, but this quote actually refers to the question of an ejected booster from Apollo. As NASA also declares that the calculated neutral point or equigravisphere is the place at which the gravitational force of each body (Earth & Moon in this instance) has dwindled to near zero, and the space craft has reduced its momentum to about 8% of the initial velocity required for leaving Earth orbit—and as this works out to around 2,127mph—no craft can become 'trapped' because not only does it possess booster rockets but also it is at this exact moment that the Moon starts pulling on the object in question.
See Chapter Ten "Essentials" for more on this subject. By the way, the ejected booster in the above mentioned conversation was left behind over 1,000 miles earlier.
7. Numerous space histories cite this incident.
8. Private correspondence with Stephen Clementson. *If* the craft had suffered such an explosion and survived, **it would certainly have been blown way off course** (see also Appendix for further details).
9. Diana Brueton, *Many Moons,* Prentice Hall Press, 1991.
10. Jim Lovell, *op. cit.*
11. Documentation in possession of the authors.
12. Harvey, *op. cit.*
13. Having contacted Harold M Watson at the Historical Electronics Museum Inc., Maryland, USA in September 1997, we received a package of information assembled by Larkin Neimyer the Engineering Manager and Stan Lebar the Program Manager of the Apollo TV camera(s). They very kindly sent us the lunar TV Camera Operations Manual, The TV Camera Handbook, a paper concerning this equipment written by Niemyer and photographs of the TV cameras used on the program.

14. Stuhlinger & Ordway, *op. cit.*
15. In discussion with the authors in California, December 1997.
16. Bob Dylan, *Ballad of a Thin Man, c.*1965, M Wittmark & Sons: the original words were: ". . . But you don't know what it is..."
17. Victor Pelevin, *Omon Ra,* originally published in Russian by Text Publishers, Moscow, 1992; first published in English by Harbord Publishing Ltd, London; and subsequently published in paperback by Faber & Faber, 1996.
18. Goldstone's Bill Wood, communication with the authors, December 1997.

Chapter Ten "Essentials"

1. Eric Jones relates that Armstrong leaned *back* at an angle of 45° pulling against the 'rope' or lanyard of the LEC conveyor, steadying himself with one foot placed behind the other. With his PLSS acting as additional weighting it is hard to see why such a dangerous attitude should be adopted, even with the help of the LEC 'rope'.
2. Carsbie C Adams, *Spaceflight*, McGraw-Hill Book Company Inc., 1958.
3. Personal correspondence with Dr. Percy Seymour, Principal Lecturer in Astronomy at the University of Plymouth. Dr. Seymour teaches astronomy and astrophysics, and also researches both the terrestrial and biological consequences of cosmic magnetic fields. As well as being the Director of Plymouth's William Day Planetarium and Astronomy Tutor with the Open University, this former Senior Planetarium Lecturer at the Old Royal Observatory in Greenwich also gives public lectures and has still found time to write several books, among which are *Adventures with Astronomy* (1983); *Cosmic Magnetism* (Adam Hilger, 1986); *Astrology: The Evidence of Science* (Lennard Publishing, 1988); *The Scientific Basis of Astrology* (Fulsham, 1997).
4. M Vertregt (Fellow British Interplanetary Society), *Principals of Astronautics,* 1965; F M Branley (astronomer), *Exploration of the Moon,* 1966; M H Ahrendt, *The Mathematics of Space Exploration* 1965; J A Eisele, *Astrodynamics, Rockets, Satellites and Space Travel,* 1967; *Colliers Encyclopaedia,* 1961.
5. Correspondence and conversation with George Pinter on both the 0.167 gravity, pg 392, and the neutral point figure given in box on pg 393 (see Appendix for calculations).
6. The LEM inserted into this Saturn V absolutely did **NOT** go to the Moon. So why did WvB adopt this particular image as his signature souvenir photograph of Apollo? Was he trying to tell us all something highly significant? The LEM in his photograph was a model designed in 1963, the year that the Soviets advised Bernard Lovell that they could not beat the radiation in space. Visually, at least, the 1969 version was a distant relation of this 1963 model—*but this LEM was never built.*
7. William Brian II, *Moongate*, Future Science Research Publishing Co., 1982.
8. Wigner was curious as to what exactly was responsible for the collapse of the wave function, and postulated that consciousness was the cause. Please refer to any good book on quantum physics for more on this fascinating subject.
9. J P McEvoy & Oscar Zarate, *Quantum Theory For Beginners,* Icon Books, 1996.
10. *ibid.*; and Felix Pirani & Christine Roche, *The Universe For Beginners,* Icon Books, 1993.
11. *Two-Thirds,* Aulis Publishers, London, 1993: Part 1, Chapter Three.
12. *ibid.*; Part 1, Chapter Two; Part 1, Chapter Four; Part 4, Chapter Four.
13. See Appendix for the relevant mathematical formulae relating to these speeds of light.
14. Dr. Rupert Sheldrake, *Seven Experiments That Could Change The World*, Fourth Estate, London, 1994 (see Appendix for details).
15. *ibid.*; The academe of Science in refusing to re-evaluate Einsteinian physics, took the arbitrary decision in 1972 to fix the speed of light by definition. This effectively halted any further discussion and the preceding variations in light speed were conveniently dismissed as "intellectual phase locking". Interestingly enough, *this linking of the speed of light to the metre* occurred in the same year that the 'Apollo landings' were terminated. Equally interesting is the fact that just over three months after 'Apollo 11', NASA converted to the metric system (the *first and only* government agency in a land of imperial measurement, to do so at that time), this conversion included all its post-Apollo technical and scientific paperwork. Such steps, however 'logical', automatically

relegate all pre-metric systems to the dungeons of the past, from which it would appear they rarely emerge with any degree of accuracy.

16. William Brian II's *Moongate* (Future Science Research Publishing Co., 1982), was entirely based on the premise that the gravity on the Moon was *more than* ⅙th of Earth. We find some common ground with William Brian but only up to a point. However, we most certainly agree that there appears to have been a cover-up relating to the Apollo mission data.

17. Phyllis Schlemmer & Mary Bennett, *The Only Planet of Choice*, Gateway Books, 1994;
Part 1, Chapter Five–Tom in conversation with a guest, who was in fact David Percy.

18. John Holman, the photographer, in conversation with the authors.

19. *The Only Planet of Choice, op. cit.*: Part 1, Chapter Five pp 55-58; and Part 3, Chapter Twelve pg 158.

20. Arthur C Clarke during a lecture on Unispace, 1992.

21. Interesting conclusions followed research undertaken between the years 1994–1996 by Wessex Archaeology and English Heritage (the current guardians of Stonehenge) using radio carbon dating methods to evaluate the surrounding organic material. This research suggested that Stonehenge was not built over a time period of 1,000 years, but that most of the stones were erected within a period of about 300 years between 4598 and 4298 BP, which is five hundred years earlier than hitherto was believed to be the case (BBC TV News, March 1996). Three months later it was concluded that prior to these stones, circles of pine poles had existed at Stonehenge. The wood was dated to around 9,998 BP. (*The Daily Telegraph,* London, June 1996).

22. Required reading: *The Avebury Cycle* and *The Silbury Treasure,* both by Michael Dames, Thames & Hudson.

23. Report by Robert Matthews and Ian Sample, *The Sunday Telegraph,* September 1 1996, and on BBC TV News, September 1996.

24. British TV documentary in the Horizon series, BBC TV, Autumn 1996.

Chapter Eleven "THE Triangle"

1. Stan Gooch, *Cities of Dreams*, Century Hutchinson 1989; Aulis Books (pbk), 1995.

2. *Two-Thirds*, *op. cit.*: Part 3, Chapter Thirteen.

3. *ibid.*; Part 1, Chapter Two.

4. David Bryant, *Enigma* issue # 1 "The Great Ozone Scam" and *Enigma* issue # 3 "Global Warming, Threat or Conspiracy?" *Enigma* magazine, Newsstand Publications, 1997.

5. The Adrian Berry column, *Astronomy Now*, September 1996.

6. *Two-Thirds*, *op. cit.*: Part 1, Chapter Seven: and also "Lunar Mission: by stabilising Earth's Tilt, the Moon may have made life possible", *Time,* March 8 1993.

7. *ibid.*

8. *ibid.*; pg 88; and also Don Wilson, *Our Mysterious Spaceship Moon*, Sphere Books, 1976.

9. *National Geographic*, August 1970, June 1975, February 1993 and BBC TV Horizon *Farewell Fantastic Venus,* February 1995.

10. *Two-Thirds, op. cit.*: Part 2, Chapter Thirteen.

11. Chaikin, *A Man On The Moon, op. cit.*

12. *The Only Planet of Choice,*; *op. cit.* Part 2, Chapter Eight "Accelerating Earth's Evolution", Tom in conversation with Dr. Andrija Puharich.

13. Barbury Castle, north of Avebury, Wiltshire (British Ordnance Survey Map grid ref: SU152 768) was the site of the Tetrahedron Crop Glyph. Among other things this glyph demonstrates the principles of a combinatorial hierarchy and the four forces of nature. See *Two-Thirds, op. cit.* for a detailed analysis of this glyph.

14. See Appendix for further information relating to Crop Glyph material.

15. From the start, *The X Files* more than any other sci-fi series since *Star Trek* was heavily supported by books and magazines promoting the TV show and subsequent films.

16. Jos Heymann, *Spacecraft Tables 1957-1990,* Univelt Inc., 1991.

17. The Cold War served as a 'standard excuse' as to why the manned lunar missions were cancelled. In 1998 ACC said that: "We should not be discouraged because there has been no follow-on from the Apollo programme, and dreams of exploring Mars are now on hold".

18. Administrators of NASA are 'officially' appointed by the American President, but the fact that Dr. Goldin withstood the change of government from Republican to Democrat, might well indicate that the *actual* choice of NASA Administrator lies somewhere other than in the Oval Office.
19. Dr. Daniel Goldin, interview with journalist Sheena McDonald, British TV, 1997.
20. British TV documentary on the MIR accident, 1998.

Chapter Twelve "Prints of Mars"

1. Graham Hancock, Robert Bauval & John Grigsby, *The Mars Mystery, A Tale Of The End Of Two Worlds,* Michael Joseph, 1998.
2. *ibid.*
3. Harvey, *op. cit.*
4. *bid,* and Richard C Hoagland, *The Monuments Of Mars: A City On The Edge Of Forever,* North Atlantic Books, 1987.
5. Harvey, *op. cit.*
6. Hoagland, *op. cit.*
7. Carl Sagan, *Cosmos,* Random House, 1980.
   This book was based on Sagan's eponymous thirteen-part TV series.
8. *Two-Thirds, op. cit.*: Part 2, Chapter Ten.
9. Hoagland, *op. cit.* who also quotes Gerry Soffen on pg 476.
10. Hancock, *op. cit.*
11. Sagan, *op. cit.*
12. NASA Viking imaging of the Cydonia region clearly shows this large, flat rock. See *Two-Thirds* Part 2, Chapter Four.
13. Hoagland, *op. cit.*
14. *The Only Planet of Choice, op. cit.*: Part 6, Chapter Twenty One "The Next Millennium". Tom in conversation with Mary Bennett.
15. Joe McMoneagle, *Mind Trek, Exploring Consciousness, Time, and Space through Remote Viewing,* Hampton Roads, 1993, 1997.
16. *Two-Thirds, op. cit.*: Part 2, Chapter Eight.
17. Randolfo Rafael Pozos, *The Face On Mars,* Chicago Review Press, 1986.
18. Telephone conversation between Aulis Publishers and the *TimeWatch* producer, July 1995.
19. Bashar in a private communication with Caroline Davies, asking questions on behalf of the authors.
20. Tom of the Council of Nine in conversation with Dr. Andrija Puharich.
21. *Two-Thirds, op. cit.*: Part 3, Chapter One.
22. This refers to the general situation on the Giza plateau at the end of 1997. Please refer also to Colin Wilson's *From Atlantis to the Sphinx* (Virgin, 1996); Erich von Daniken's *The Eyes Of The Sphinx* (Berkley Books, 1996); Graham Hancock's *Fingerprints of the Gods* (Heinemann, 1995). Rudolf Gantenbrink's *Robot 'Upanaut' ('Opener of the Way')* was used to explore a shaft in the Queen's Chamber. Subsequent to this exploration Gantenbrink was unable to obtain further permission to explore this shaft.
23. *Two-Thirds, op. cit.*: especially concerning terraforming: Part 2, Chapter Three, and also Part 2, Chapter Four.
24. Mark J Carlotto, "Digital imagery analysis of unusual Martian surface features", *Applied Optics,* Volume 27, pp 1926-1933, 1988; "Evidence in support of the hypothesis that certain objects on Mars are artificial in origin", *Journal of Scientific Exploration,* Volume 11, # 2, pp 123-145, 1997; *The Martian Enigmas: A Closer Look,* North Atlantic Books, Second Edition, 1997.
25. McGilligan, *op. cit.*
26. *National Geographic,* December 1966; and referring to an Earth/Moon ruby laser ranging of 1962 when the Moon was 240,000 miles distant. The beams illuminated a spot less than two miles in diameter. Given that *even at that time* astronomers were able to measure the results reflected back to their instruments on Earth, with a further seven years of experience and doubtless improved technology, this makes the McDonald and Lick Observatories' results of the 1969 'Apollo 11' laser ranging even more astonishing!
27. *National Geographic,* December 1969.

Chapter Thirteen "Hurmaze"

1. Richard Hoagland during a public lecture at Ohio State University, June 1994.
2. Carl Munck publishes a newsletter on *The Code* at a rate of US $25 for six issues per annum. Post paid in the USA only. Europe and the Middle East add $10, The Far East Add $18. Available from *THE CODE* Carl P Munck, PO Box 418, Flemington, W VA 26347, USA.
    For previous issues of published material and videos, contact L L Productions, 700-112 Ave N E Suite 302, Bellevue, Washington, 98004 USA. E-mail: www.lauralee.com (see also Appendix).
3. Graham Hancock & Santha Faiia, *Heaven's Mirror*, *Quest for the Lost Civilisation,* Michael Joseph, 1998.
4. *Two-Thirds, op. cit.*; and also the video *The Face on Mars*: *The Avebury Connection* VHS 0797 distributed by Aulis Publishing available from SKS, 20 Paul Street, Frome, Somerset, BA11 1DX UK. Video also available from: Nexus, 55 Queens Road, East Grinstead, W Sussex, RH19 1BK UK.
5. *ibid.*; Part 2, Chapter Five, especially pg 149.
6. Stan Gooch, *The Neanderthal Question*, Wildwood House, 1977; and also *Cities Of Dreams,* Aulis Books, 1995.

The last word

In that 1948 short story by Arthur C Clarke, the original *Sentinel* was a crystal pyramid, roughly 12 feet tall, sitting on an artificially-flattened plateau above the Sea of Crises. It appeared to be protected by an invisible spherical force field. Arthur Clarke told Richard Hoagland that he had in mind a *tetrahedral* pyramid. Was ACC aware of the Barbury Castle Crop Glyph design (with its sphere around the tetrahedron) as early as 1947?

And just as the Moon was only a stepping stone on the way to Mars—was the Fra Mauro landing site a screen test for Cydonia?

Appendix

Appendix

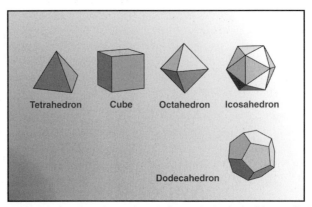

An infinite number of regular polygons, but only five regular 'perfect' solids—see Prologue.

Chapters One and Two
NASA DATA
Hasselblad 500 EL/70 Lunar Surface Camera
Some details are at variance with other sources

This electrically powered camera, carried on the LM, featured semiautomatic operation. It used a 60mm Biogon lens exclusively. The operating sequence was initiated by squeezing a trigger mounted on the camera handle. *A reseau grid was set in front of the image plane to provide photogrammetric information in the analysis of the photography.* The camera was bracket mounted on the front of the astronaut's suit. The settings and ranges for equipment on this camera were:

Lens focal length	60mm Biogon
Focus:	3ft to infinity
Aperture:	f/5.6 to f/22
Shutter speed:	1 sec to 1/500 sec
Field of view:	49.2° side, 66° diagonal

Films
The films used throughout the Apollo 11 mission were as follows:

SO-368 Film (CEX)
Description:	Ektachrome MS color reversal, ASA 64
Use:	Terrain and general photography

SO-168 (HCEX and CIN)
Description:	Ektachrome EF high speed color reversal, ASA 160 for surface and interior photography; no filter required
Use:	Surface and interior photography at low light levels

Accessories
Accessories for the Apollo 11 photographic equipment included the following:

A polarising filter was used on the lunar surface superwide-angle camera for the photo-geology experiment.

NASA DATA
Apollo 15 lunar photography—extract from Data Users Note December 1972

Lunar surface TV camera
Regarding the RCA television camera color was achieved by using a rotating disk driven by a synchronous 600 rpm motor. Lunar color scenes were scanned, field sequentially, and down-linked serially to the Manned Space Flight Network (MSFN). Video was received and recorded from lunar distances at any of the three Deep Space Stations: Goldstone (California), Madrid (Spain), and Honeysuckle [Creek] (Australia). Color conversion was required at the Manned Spacecraft Center (MSC) *in order to provide commercial standard signals for display monitors.*

NASA DATA
Apollo 17 lunar photography—extract from Data Users Note December 1974
Some details are at variance with other sources—see Chapter Two.

RCA TV camera
The scanning rate for the RCA TV camera was the commercial 525 scan lines/frame. Scan conversion for black and white monitors was not required.

All of the TV coverage was recorded on black and white 16mm kinescope roll film.

Chapter One
Apollo Photographic Analysis
David Groves PhD

Determination of the direction of illumination in the image of the Astronaut Descending Ladder

The best estimate of the horizontal direction of illumination using (Photograph D[38]) can be determined from the position of the highlight on the heel of the right hand boot. The calculation requires knowledge about the dimensions of the boot, the focal length of the camera lens and film format and the ability to identify the centre of the image. Other reasonable assumptions are made and stated at the point of application.

The plane of the sole of the boot is approximately parallel to the direction of view of the camera and approximately parallel to the horizontal axis of the image. In photograph D the distance (d1) in the plane of the sole between the furthest left point visible on the bottom of the sole and the point directly below the bottom corner of the Velcro fastener can be measured.

$$d1 = 5.00mm$$

Similarly, the distance between the bottom corner of the Velcro fastener and the furthest right point visible on the bottom of the sole (d2) can be measured.

$$d2 = 3.15mm$$

The ratio is $\quad \dfrac{d1}{d2} = 1.5873$

(I had no close up of this portion of the image, limiting the accuracy of the ratio determination. However, this turns out not to be critical due to the curvature of the sole at the point through which the highlight passes.)

Photographs and photocopies of a 'sample' boot were provided. The sample boot was a larger 'shoe size' than the one in photo D, the latter having fewer 'tread bars' on the sole. However, the 'actual size' photocopy of the sole (Photocopy F) of the sample can be used to determine the rotational orientation of the boot in the image, if it is assumed the width and length of the boots have the have the same ratio for both sizes.

The photocopy was used to determine the 'direction of view' required to give the same ratio of visible sole each side of the bottom corner of the Velcro fastener, measured in the plane of the sole. The required direction of view is shown on photocopy F. (The given direction of view drawn onto photocopy F yields a ratio of 1.5817 (i.e. 126.3mm/79.85mm), demonstrating a reasonable estimate of boot orientation).

Using photograph D, the distance (d3) in the plane of the sole between the furthest left visible point of the sole and the point on the sole directly below the highlight can be measured.

$$d3 = 2.15mm$$

Using photograph D, distance (d4) in the plane of the sole between the furthest right visible point of the sole and the point on the sole directly below the highlight can be measured.

$$d4 = 5.95mm$$

The ratio $\quad \dfrac{d3}{d4} = 0.3613445$

(The total distance (d5) across the visible sole of the right boot in photo D is 8.1mm).

In photocopy F, the distance (d6) across the visible sole in the plane of the sole (measured at 90° to the direction of view) is 206.4mm.

Therefore, the distance (d7) of the highlight in photocopy F from the inside of the boot is

$$d7 = \frac{d3}{d5} \cdot d6 = 54.7851mm$$

This point is marked on photocopy F on the line at 90° to the direction of view. A perpendicular is dropped to the edge of the sole to show the position of the 'highlight'.

At the point of intersection with the edge of the sole, a tangent has been carefully constructed. The normal to the tangent is measured to be at an angle of (ß1) 1.1 ° to the direction of view of the camera imaging the heel protector.

Now we can trace the ray's path, projected onto the horizontal plane parallel to both the horizontal edge of the image and the optical axis of the camera. The ray has travelled from the light source, been reflected in the heel (at a known position and angle reflection) and onto the camera lens.

To carry out the ray tracing accurately, we need to know details about the camera lens and the distance between the camera and the highlight on the boot.

The camera lens has a focal length of 60mm recording an image on square format 70mm film. Camera/lens data sheets tend not to have scientific accuracy and the 'angle of view' of a lens can be quoted ambiguously, either across the image or across a diagonal of the image.

The angle of view of a 60mm lens on a 70mm film camera was determined practically by measuring the angle of view across a 70mm film image recorded using a 120 Bronica camera fitted with a 75mm lens. The angle of view that a 60mm lens would exhibit on a 120 film/70mm camera was then calculated by virtue of the inverse linear relationship between width of object imaged and focal length of the lens.

A ruler, placed 897mm from the imaging plane, parallel to the horizontal edge of the image and passing through the centre of the image was recorded using the Bronica, as shown in Figure 1. The width of ruler imaged was 494mm.

The 'half angle' of view (ß2) is simply

$$ß2 = Tan^{-1} (247/897) = 15.39°$$

For a 60mm lens on a similar 70mm film camera the distance across the ruler imaged is inversely proportional to the focal length of the lens.
Therefore ß3, the 'half angle' of view of a 60mm lens on a 120film/70mm camera is

$$ß3 = Tan^{-1} \frac{247 * 75}{60 * 897} = 18.99°$$

Therefore the angle of view across the image (ß4) is

$$ß4 = 37.989°$$

The full width of the image (d8) is shown in photograph D, measured (close to the bottom, passing through the 'United States' emblem, parallel to the lower horizontal edge of the image) to be

$$d8 = 185.6mm$$

Assuming the lens on the 500 EL/70 camera has insignificant barrel or other non-linear distortions, the angle of view will vary linearly with distance across the image. For photograph D the change in angle of view (relative to the centre of the image) per unit distance from the centre of the image G is:

$$G = \frac{ß4}{d8} = \frac{37.987}{185.6} = 0.2046713° \; mm^{-1}$$

or, converting to radians

$$G = 0.00357219 \; radians \; mm^{-1}$$

From photograph A, given the (approximate) length of the boot, the distance from the bottom of the sole to the top of the 'heel protector' (d9) is approximately 68.4154mm.
(A direct measurement could be used for better accuracy. As well as being unsure if this dimension is the same in both the sample boot and the boot in the NASA transparency, the photograph of the sample boot has significant distortion from the use of a wide angle lens, contributing additional inaccuracy in the estimation of d9).

In photograph D, the top of the heel protector and the bottom of the sole are clearly visible. The horizontal part of the centre of the image reticle 'cross' is visible and the vertical line of the cross can be determined by geometric construction from other reticle crosses in the image.
As the variation in angle of view with distance along the image has been determined relative to the centre of the image (i.e. relative to the optical axis of the camera) the difference in angle of view between the top and bottom of the heel protector can be determined.
The distance between the centre of the image and the top of the heel protector in the direction parallel to the vertical edge of the image was measured to be 7.95mm and the distance between the centre of the image and the bottom of the heel protector in the direction parallel to the vertical edge of the image was measured to be 10.5mm.

Let the angle between the optical axis of the camera and the ray passing between the top of the heel bar and the camera lens projected onto the vertical plane (the plane which is parallel to both the vertical axis of the image and the optical axis of the camera) be ß5, determined as

$$ß5 = 7.95 . G$$

Similarly, the angle between the optical axis of the camera and the ray passing between the bottom of the heel bar and the camera lens projected onto the vertical plane be ß6, determined as

$$ß6 = 10.50 . G$$

If it is assumed in figure 2 the distance between the camera and heel protector(R) is much greater than the distance between the top and bottom of the heel protector (d9) and the difference in angle of view between the top and bottom of the heel protector (ß6-ß5) are related by

$$d9 = R . (ß6-ß5)$$

or

$$R = d9/G. (10.50 - 7.95)$$
(Where G is expressed in radians mm^{-1})

Therefore $\quad R = 7510.70mm$ (i.e. 7.5107 metres

This is the distance of the heel protector from the camera. The only 'questionable' measurement is the actual height of the heel protector. To cross check, the range calculation can be repeated using the extreme left and right edges of the sole visible in the image of the right hand boot. The sample boot, according to the direction of view determined on photocopy F, has a width in this orientation of 206.4 mm.
Therefore the range (of the mid point of the sole) by the method used above

$$R = 206.4/G. (21.3 - 12.85)$$
(Where G is expressed in radians mm^{-1})

$$R = 6837.8mm$$

The discrepancy in estimates is an indication of the difference between the dimensions of the sample boot and the boot in the transparency. As it is the major cause of uncertainty in the calculation the two estimates (one determined across the boot and one determined vertically through the boot) it will be used later in the estimation of the accuracy of the final result of the position of the source of illumination.
We now have enough information to trace the ray of light (in the horizontal plane, the plane parallel to the optical axis of the camera and parallel to the horizontal edge of the image) emanating from the light source, being reflected in the heel protector and entering the camera lens at a known orientation to the optical axis of the camera. Consider Figure 3, the projection of the ray path onto the defined plane.

As the distance in photograph D between the centre of the image and the highlight on the heel protector in the direction parallel to the horizontal edge of the image can be measured (15.35mm), the angle between the optical axis of the camera and the ray emanating from the illumination reflecting in the heel protector (ß7) can be determined as

$$ß7 = 15.35 . G$$
(Where G is expressed in $°mm^{-1}$)

$$ß7 = 3.1417 °$$

Now the beam from the source of illumination is reflected in the heel protector such that the angle of incidence is equal to the angle of reflection, measured relative to the 'normal' to the surface (i.e. the line perpendicular to the tangent of the surface of the heel protector at the point through which the 'highlight' passes).
From photocopy F we have determined that the 'normal' at the point of the 'highlight' on the heel protector is 1.1 ° to the direction of view of the beam passing between the heel protector and camera lens. Therefore, as shown in figure 4a, the beam emanating from the source of illumination has the same angle on the other side of the 'normal' to the tangent, a total angle (ß8) of 2.2 °.
Therefore, as shown in figure 4b, we have a triangle with two known angles and a known side length.

where

$$\frac{A}{\sin (a)} = \frac{B}{\sin (b)}$$

or

$$A = B . \sin (a)/\sin (b)$$

Therefore X, the distance of the light source to the right of the camera (assuming it is the same distance from the heel protector as the camera) is

$$X = B . \sin (a)/\sin (b)$$

or

$$X = 7510.7 * \sin (2.2)/\sin (90.942)$$

or

$$X = 288mm$$

Now the (worst) estimate of R was 6837.8mm which would result in an estimate of X of 262.20, an error of approximately 25.8mm

$$e1 = 25.8 \ mm$$

The angle of the 'normal' was measured to an accuracy of about 0.1° (assuming the boot photocopy fairly reflected the shape of the actual boot), therefore the 'error' in the position due to the angle (S = R.. ß) is

$$e2 = 7510.7 * 2.2 * \Pi/180 = 26.2mm$$

The total maximum error on the position of the light source is

$$e + e1 + e2 = \pm 52mm$$

Therefore, the light source is between 23.6cms and 34.0 cms to the right of the camera.

Photocopy F.

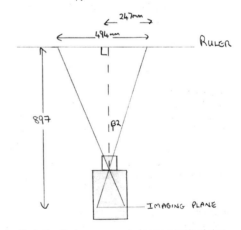

Fig 1. Practical measurement of camera angle of view.

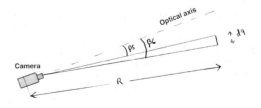

Fig 2. Rays from top and bottom of heel protector projected onto the 'vertical' plane as defined in the text.

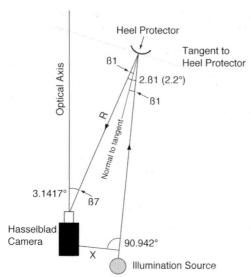

Fig 3. Ray path projected onto the 'horizontal' plane as defined in the text.

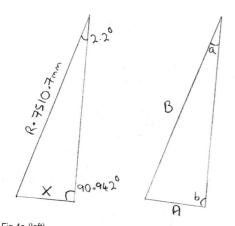

Fig 4a (left).
X, the distance to the right hand side of the camera, of the source of illumination, assuming the same approximate distance away from heel protector as the camera.
Fig b (right).
Relationship between angles and 'opposite' side length for all triangles.

Determination of the position of the camera in the image of the Astronaut Standing

Calculation of the Camera's Height from Photograph A[48]

The best estimate of the height of the camera can be deduced from photograph A, using the 'divergence' of the camera lens (defined by the focal length of the camera

lens and the 70mm film format), the angle of declination of the camera (defined by the position of the horizon relative to the centre reticle of the image) and the distance between the camera and the astronauts visor (defined by the 'divergence' of the camera lens and the actual width of the visor).

I am informed that the focal length of the camera lens used on the Hasselblad 500 EL/70 Lunar Surface Camera was a 60mm (Zeiss Biogon) lens.

1. Camera Height with 60mm Focal Length Lens Used to Record Photograph A[48]

1.1 Divergence of the 60mm focal length lens

To carry our 'ray tracing' to determine the position of the camera, we first require to know the 'angle of view' or 'divergence' of the camera lens. This can never be 'exact' as the divergence varies slightly with focus. As camera/lens data sheets tend not to have scientific accuracy and the 'angle of view' of the lens can be quoted ambiguously, (either across the image or along a diagonal of the image) the angle of view was determined practically.

An image of a ruler was recorded using a 120 Bronica camera fitted with a 75mm focal length lens. The ruler was positioned to pass through the centre of the image, its sides being parallel to the top and bottom edges of the image.

As shown in Figure 1, the imaged width of the ruler was 494mm and the orthogonal distance (i.e. along the optical axis of the camera) between the ruler and imaging plane was 897mm. The 'half angle' of view of the 75mm lens is simply

$$\text{ß1} = \text{Tan}^{-1} (247/897) = 15.39°$$

For a 60mm lens on a similar camera, the distance across the ruler imaged is inversely proportional to the focal length of the lens. Therefore ß2, the 'half angle' of view of a 60 mm lens on a 120 film/70mm camera is

$$\text{ß2 132} = \text{Tan}^{-1} ((247 * 75)/(60 * 897)) = 18.99°$$

Therefore, the angle of view (through the centre) of an image recorded using a 60mm lens on a 120 film /70mm camera, ß3 is

$$\text{ß3} = 37.987°$$

1.2 Angle of Declination of the Camera in Photograph A[48]

Assuming the lens on the 500 EL/70 camera has insignificant barrel or other non-linear distortions, the 'angle of view' will vary linearly from the centre of the image. For photograph A, if taken with a 60mm lens, the change in angle of view per unit distance (mm) (measured radially from the centre of the image) is

$$\text{G60} = \text{ß3/d1} = 37.987 / 186.7° \text{ mm}^{-1}$$

536

were dl is the distance measured on photograph A between the edges of the visor intersecting with camera axis 'y'.

$$G60 = 0.2034654° \text{ mm}^{-1}$$
$$G60 = 0.00355114 \text{ radians mm}^{-1}$$

Now, in photograph A, let us assume the line of the horizon is orthogonal to the 'true' vertical in the vicinity of the astronauts. Assuming that the terrain to the horizon is approximately flat and that the Moon is spherical, the angle of the horizon to the 'true vertical' can be determined from the radius of the moon and the (approximate) height of the cameras viewpoint.

Figure 2 shows the Moon of radius $Rm = 1740,000m$ (ref Philips Atlas of Stars and Planets). The angle of elevation of the horizon to the true vertical ßm at a height of $D2$ from the surface can be determined as

$$\sin(\text{ßm}) = Rm/(Rm + D2)$$
or $\quad \text{ßm} = \sin^{-1}(Rm/(Rm + D2))$

Therefore, in the range of height of viewpoint 2m to 10m, the angle of elevation of the horizon to the true vertical is 89.91 to 89.80°. Taking into account the various uncertainties in the shape of the Moon, flatness of the terrain etc., the horizon can be taken as defining the plane of the true horizontal in all images.

Using the horizon as a 'spirit level' the angle of declination of the optical axis of the camera can be determined. In photograph A, axes 'x' and 'y' have been drawn through the centre reticle of the image, the axes being parallel to the 'horizontal' and 'vertical' edges of the image. Note that the camera is rotated relative to the horizon

The angle of declination of the camera in the true vertical plane can be determined from the distance between the horizon and the centre of the image along the line passing orthogonally through the horizon, d3.

$$d3 = 76.6mm$$

Therefore, the angle of declination of the camera to the true horizontal in the plane of the true vertical is

$$\text{ß8} = d3 * G60$$
$$\text{ß8} = 76.6 * 0.2034654°$$
or $\quad \text{ß8} = 15.58544964°$
$$\text{ß8} = 0.27202 \text{ radians}$$

Therefore, in the true vertical plane, as shown in Figure 3, the angle of elevation ß9 of the optical axis to the true vertical is

$$\text{ß9} = 90 - \text{ß8}°$$
$$\text{ß9} = 90 - 15.58544964°$$
$$\text{ß9} = 74.41°$$
$$\text{ß9} = 1.2988 \text{ radians}$$

1.3 Distance of the Centre of the Camera's Imaging Plane Above the Moon's Surface

The distance between the centre of the imaging plane and the vertical plane which passes through the left and right hand edges of the visor can be determined from the divergence of the lens and actual width of the visor.
The width of the visor is 280mm. The distance between the edges of the visor d4 in photograph A[48] is

$$d4 = 20.5mm$$

Therefore, the scale of the photograph in the vertical plane passing through the left and right edges of the visor in the vicinity of the visor is

$$\text{scale A} = 20.5/280$$

In photograph A[48], the distance d5 between the edges of the visor intersecting with camera axis 'y' is

$$d5 = 19.7mm$$

Therefore the 'actual' distance between the edges of the visor intersecting with camera axis 'y' is

$$D5 = d5/\text{scale A}$$
$$D5 = 19.7 * 280/20.5 \text{ mm}$$
$$D5 = 269.073 \text{ mm}$$

Now, the difference in angle between the edges of the visor intersecting with camera axis 'y', as shown in Figure 4, is

$$\text{ß12} = \text{ß11} - \text{ß10}$$
or $\quad \text{ß12} = d5 * G60$
$$\text{ß12} = 4.0083°$$
or $\quad \text{ß12} = 0.0699 \text{ radians.}$

Now, from Figure 4, the ß12 and $D5$ can be used to determine $D6$, the distance between the imaging plane and the vertical plane passing through the edges of the visor, as

$$\sin(\text{ß12}/2) = D5/(2 * D6)$$
or $\quad D6 = D5/(2 * \sin(\text{ß12}/2))$
$$D6 = 269.073/(2 * \sin(0.0699575/2))$$
$$D6 = 3847.02mm$$

Therefore, as shown in Figure 5, the distance $D7$ in the true vertical between the centre of the imaging plane of the camera and the plane parallel to the true horizon passing through the point on the optical axis which intersects with the vertical plane passing through the edges of the visor is

$$D7 = D6/\text{Tan}(\text{ß9}) \text{ mm}$$
$$D7 = 3847.02/\tan(1.29877891517313) \text{ mm}$$
$$D7 = 1073.05 \text{ mm}$$

From photograph A[48], the distances D8 and D9 cannot be determined directly. However they can be estimated

537

from this data and photocopy B, assuming the astronaut in both images have a similar stance, are of similar height and the ground in the vicinity of astronaut and photographer in photograph A is flat. If these assumptions are valid, the data in Figures 4 and 5 can be used to draw the 'rays' and position of the camera onto the (extended) photocopy B. The scale of the photocopy can be determined as the distance between the top and the bottom of the visor is 260mm. The distance between the top and bottom of the visor in photocopy B is 29mm

$$scale\ 8 = 29.0/260$$

If the beam in the true horizontal (which intersects with the horizon) is used to 'overlay' the ray trace data, the optical axis intersects with the shins of the astronaut, perhaps a little higher than in photograph A due to departures from the stated assumption. If the optical axis of the camera is drawn on photocopy B so as to intersect with the 'correct' position on the astronaut's shins, a 'range of uncertainty' (e = 80.7mm from photocopy of known scale) in the height of the position of the camera above the surface can be determined.

From photocopy B of scale 'scale 8'

The height D11 of the centre of the imaging plane above the surface is

$$D11 = D7 + D8 + D9$$
$$D11 = 1073.05 + 453.60$$
$$D11 = 1526.65$$

Therefore the range at which the camera is above the surface is between D11 and D11 - e.

That is

THE CENTRE OF THE IMAGING PLANE OF THE CAMERA WAS BETWEEN 1446mm AND 1527mm ABOVE THE SURFACE OF THE MOON WHEN PHOTOGRAPH A WAS RECORDED.

Further, assuming perfectly flat terrain from horizon to horizon, the reflection of the opposite horizon and the centre of the imaging plane of the camera should appear in the same horizontal plane, consistent with (within reasonable variation) visor reflection in photograph A.

Finally, the above calculations provide an accurate estimate of the camera's height above the surface, provided all the assumptions stated are valid. The only assumption which could make a significant difference if not valid is the assumption that the terrain beneath and between the photographer and astronaut is flat. This assumption can be tested and a 'typical' value for the variation in height of the surface between the astronaut and photographer can be estimated using shadow on the surface of the outside edge of the astronauts left leg.

Consider photograph A. If the ground was flat, the shadow of the outside edge of the left leg should be

approximately straight. The curvature of the shadow on the ground is due to the surface not being perfectly flat. An approximate estimate of the range in height of the surface between the photographer and astronaut can be determined from the distance between the straight line pining the shadow of the left foot and hip and the actual shadow, measured along camera axis 'y'. This is (approximately, by observation) the maximum distance between line and actual shadow, representing the largest discernible 'hill' between astronaut and photographer.

Consider Figure 6. C is the position of the centre of the imaging plane of the camera, B is the position of the shadow if the surface was flat and A is the actual position of the shadow. ß13 is the angle of the line at the intersection with camera axis 'y'. From photograph A[48] d12 and d13 can be measured, the distance between the centre of the image and the straight lines intersection with the camera's y axis and the distance between the centre of the image and the actual shadow's intersection with the camera's y axis respectively.

$$d12 = 32.9mm$$
$$d13 = 25.5\ mm$$

Therefore
$$ß13 = d12 * G60$$
$$ß13 = 6.694°$$
$$ß13 = 0.116833\ radians$$

From figure 6
$$ß15 = 90 - (ß13 + ß8)$$
$$ß15 = 67.7206°$$
$$ß15 = 1.18195\ radians$$

As
$$\cos(ß15) = D11/Dl2$$
$$Dl2 = 4027.709mm$$

But
$$ß14 = d13 * G60$$
$$ß14 = 5.18836°$$

From figure 6
$$ß16 = 90 - (ß14 + ß8)$$
$$ß16 = 69.226°$$
$$ß16 = 1.208226\ radians$$

As
$$\cos(ß16) = D14/D12$$
$$D14 = D12 * \cos(ß16)$$
$$D14 = 1428.643mm$$

Therefore the 'displacement' of the shadow of the outside edge of the left leg on the ground from the straight line joining the shadow at of the foot to the shadow of the hip is due to a rise in the surface height D15.

$$D15 = D11 - D14$$
$$D15 = 99mm$$

This 'hill' is seen to fall and rise between the astronaut and photographer. Its maximum height is in the order of only 10cm, indicating that the surface's height beneath both astronaut and photographer is not significantly different.

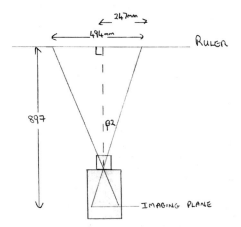

Fig 1. Practical measurement of camera angle of view.

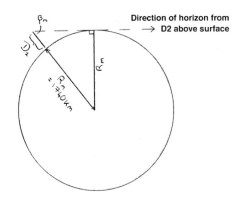

Fig 2. Angle of elevation of horizon to the 'true' vertical on the Moon.

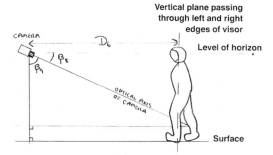

Fig 3. Angles of declination and elevation of the camera relative to the 'true' vertical.

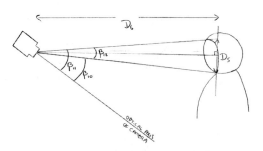

Fig 4. Distance between camera and vertical plane passing through edges of visor.

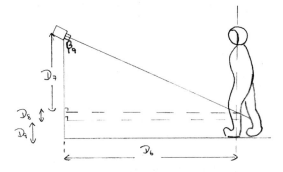

Fig 5. Height of the centre of camera's imaging plane above the surface when 'photograph A' was recorded.

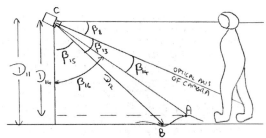

Fig 6. 'Typical' variation in surface height between astronaut and photographer.

539

Evaluation of Ionising Radiation (X-rays) on Ektachrome ISO 160 Professional 120 Colour Reversal Film—David Groves PhD

1) INTRODUCTION

I am informed that Ektachrome EF ASA (ISO) 160 high speed colour reversal film was used for lunar photography during the Apollo lunar surface EVAs.

2) AIMS

This investigation aimed to establish the effect of ionising radiation on 'correctly' exposed latent images on fresh Ektachrome 160T film.

3) METHODS

A Bronica ETRSi 120 roll film camera was used for the tests. Five rolls of Ektachrome 160T film were exposed at the 'correct' exposure of a JOBO Labortechnik colour test chart. The chart consisted of six colour patches (additive primary blue, green and red and subtractive complementary colours yellow magenta and cyan) and six neutral 'grey scale' patches from white to black with a density difference of one aperture difference (0.3D) between each.

For exposure the test chart was illuminated evenly using two 60 Watt tungsten lights, one placed each side of the camera. 'Correct' exposure (1/60th sec @ f5.6) was determined using a spotmeter on the mid grey tone to an accuracy better than 0.6 of a stop (0.18D).

The exposed films containing latent images of the test chart were then exposed (without any surrounding shielding) to 8 MeV x-rays using a linear accelerator. The film was then E6 processed in the normal manner. The results are given in the next section.

4) RESULTS

Film Strip 8

Film strip 8 contains 'correct' exposures (1/60th sec @ f5.6) of the test chart which were then exposed to 25 rem of ionising radiation (8 MeV x-rays). The film was processed in the normal (E6) manner. The images, although visible are seriously damaged rendering them unusable.

Film Strip 9

Film strip 9 contains 'correct' exposures (1/60th sec @ f5.6) of the test chart which were then exposed to 50 rem of ionising radiation (8 MeV x-rays). The film was processed in the normal (E6) manner. The images are barely visible, the x-rays having near obliterated the latent images.

Film Strip 10

Film strip 10 contains 'correct' exposures (1/60th sec @ f5.6) of the test chart which were then exposed to 100 rem of ionising radiation (8 MeV x-rays). The film was processed in the normal (E6) manner. The images are completely obliterated by the x-rays.

5) DISCUSSION

Ektachrome ISO 160 appears to be significantly sensitive to x-rays. Above 100 rem exposure to x-rays any latent image is completely obliterated. Between 50 rem and 25 rem exposure to x-rays the remaining image is visible but extremely faint. The estimated radiation dose required to degrade the image to the level produced by four hours exposure to the maximum temperature expected on the lunar surface (+82.2°C—see next test) is estimated from the above results to be in the order of only 5 rem.

6) CONCLUSION

Even a modest radiation dose to the film (5 rem and greater) would produce significant reduction of contrast and image density in the resulting Ektachrome ISO 160T transparencies.

Evaluation of High Temperature on Ektachrome ISO 160 Professional 120 Colour Reversal Film—Extract from report by David Groves PhD

1) INTRODUCTION

The following test was undertaken with fresh Ektachrome 160T film.

According to NASA's own data, the temperature range the Hasselblad 500 EL/700 camera was subjected to whilst on the lunar surface was +180°F (+82.2°C) to -180°F (-117.8°C).

This range of temperature is well outside Kodak's recommendation. The purpose of this investigation was to establish the behaviour of Ektachrome ISO 160 roll film when used at the high end of the temperature range.

2) AIMS

This investigation aimed to evaluate the photographic behaviour of the film at +82.2°C by recording images at the 'correct' exposure to test the effect on image density and colour hue.

3) METHODS

The same Bronica ETRSi 120 roll film camera as was used for the radiation tests was employed for the image density and colour hue tests. Again the JOBO Labortechnik colour test chart was illuminated evenly using two 60 Watt tungsten lights. 'Correct' exposure was determined as before (again 1/60th sec @ f5.6) using a spotmeter on the mid grey tone to an accuracy better than 0.6 of a stop (0.18D).

A test on the effect of persistent high temperature (+82.2°C) on the latent image recorded on Ektachrome 160T was then carried out. A time of 4 hours was chosen as a number of lunar EVAs lasted for this period. Film strip 7 contains 'correctly' exposed images recorded at room temperature as described above. After recording the latent images, the film was baked in an accurate temperature-controlled oven for four hours at +82.2°C.

4) RESULTS

When compared to the control strip the resulting transparencies in test strip 7 show significant 'lightening' apparent both on the test patches and on the unexposed areas of the film between and to the side of each exposed image.

5) CONCLUSION

Extended exposure to the higher end of NASA's anticipated temperature range on the lunar surface may be expected to significantly decrease the image density of the resulting Ektachrome ISO 160 transparencies.

Total number of hours Apollo astronauts spent on the lunar surface—according to the record			
Mission	Crew LM	Time spent on lunar surface	EVA duration
'Apollo 11'	Armstrong & Aldrin	21 hrs 36 mins	02 hrs 31 mins
'Apollo 12'	Bean & Conrad	31 hrs 31 mins	1st) 03 hrs 56 mins 2nd) 03 hrs 49 mins Total) 07 hrs 45 mins
'Apollo 14'	Shepard & Mitchell	33 hrs 30 mins	1st) 04 hrs 47 mins 2nd) 07 hrs 12 mins Total) 11 hrs 59 mins
'Apollo 15'	Irwin & Scott	66 hrs 54 mins	1st) 06 hrs 32 mins 2nd) 07 hrs 12 mins 3rd) 04 hrs 49 mins Total) 18 hrs 33 mins
'Apollo 16'	Duke & Young	71 hrs 02 mins	1st) 07 hrs 11 mins 2nd) 07 hrs 23 mins 3rd) 05 hrs 40 mins Total) 20 hrs 14 mins
'Apollo 17'	Cernan & Schmitt	74 hrs 59 mins	1st) 07 hrs 11 mins 2nd) 07 hrs 36 mins 3rd) 07 hrs 15 mins Total) 22 hrs 02 mins

Hasselblads flown on Apollo missions

(see Chapter Two)

'Apollo 8' 2 pcs 500 EL/70

'Apollo 10' 2 pcs 500 EL/70

'Apollo 11' 1 pcs HEDC 500 EL/70—or *Super-Wide**

*according to NASA data

2 pcs 500 EL/70 (in Command Module)

'Apollo 12' 2 pcs HEDC 500 EL/70

5 pcs 500 EL/70 (in Command Module)

'Apollo 13' 3 pcs HEDC 500 EL/70

1 pcs 500EL/70 (in Command Module)

'Apollo 14' 2 pcs HEDC 500 EL/70

2 pcs 500EL/70 (in Command Module)

'Apollo 15' 3 pcs HEDC 500 EL/70

1 pcs 500EL/70

'Apollo 16' 2 pcs HEDC 500 EL/70

1 pcs 500EL/70

'Apollo 17' 2 pcs HEDC 500 EL/70

1 pcs 500EL/70

This list does not include any other cameras such as the Data Acquisition Camera, stereo cameras or TV cameras etc.

Chapter Three
Radiation

"The difference between an active Sun and a calm Sun is enormous. For example, if this activity were in the spectrum of visible light—we would all be blind".
J F Mangin astronomer and laser specialist. Observatories de Nice, France.

Sputnik 3 is rarely mentioned but in the context of the Van Allen belts it is worth noting that Brian Harvey, author of *The New Russian Space programme* asserts that *this* was the Soviet probe that returned the Van Allen data! Sputnik 3 successfully gained orbit on May 15 1958 after a launch failure on April 27 1958—according to Harvey. Interestingly, American space chronologers Baker and Heyman both give February 3 1958 as the launch failure date for this radiation detecting probe. Had it been successful, the Sputnik 3 launch would parallel the US Explorer 1, which was also geared to detect radiation and bears out our claim that both space agencies were probably aware of these zones of radiation since November 1957.

A note on orbital data: 141 x 581 means that the nearest point of the orbit was 141 miles from Earth and the furthest was 581 miles from Earth. The inclination is the angle at which this orbit is inclined to the equator. The end date is the date at which the probe re-entered the atmosphere and burned up, this does not necessarily coincide with the end of data transmission which can have occurred months before. For example Sputnik 1 had power and therefore the ability to transmit data for 14 days and Explorer 3 stopped transmitting at least 12 days before re-entry.

Chapter Four
Rockets

We are used to seeing the familiar black and white squares on American rockets—an embellishment designed to aid visibility. However, it is little known that this aid was initially employed by the Nazis at Peenemünde on October 3 1942. The A-4/V-2 rocket (which would later attempt to inflict serious damage upon London and elsewhere) completed a triumphant trial on that October day and was emblazoned with these black and white squares.

Korolëv

On reading of von Braun's Apollo program exploits in the early 1960s Korolëv had remarked that they "should be friends".

Like von Braun, Sergei Korolëv was a charismatic team leader.

Unlike von Braun, Korolëv was not allowed to be a media star, his existence being kept secret by the Soviet government until his untimely death at the age of 59, in 1966.

Also, unlike von Braun, amongst his peers Korolëv was truly unequalled in his sphere of rocketry and space technology.

In 1966 Sergei Korolëv asked his Doctor how long his heart would last. The reply was "about twenty years"—to which Korolëv replied: "Ten years will be enough".

He would be dead within hours of his admission to hospital—of either heart failure or peritonitis, depending on which account you read recording his death.

Suvorov

In *The First Manned Spaceflight* Alexander Sabelnikov, (nephew of Vladimir Suvorov), has collated material from the diaries of his famous uncle and produced an important book which provides a remarkable insight into the Soviet Space program. Suvorov was probably the most important of the photographers and film makers assigned to the Soviet space agency, having already worked on other top secret assignments such as recording the research and technology of the Soviet nuclear program. It was Vladimir Suvorov who took those shots of Yuri Gagarin that (at the time) we all believed were 'live'. However, Suvorov had carefully avoided any mention in his diaries of either a Soviet manned Moon program or even a military space program. Given the very high levels of security clearance under which Suvorov worked, this fact is hardly surprising. But Sabelnikov has also interviewed

Embassy of the United States of America

24 Grosvenor Square
London W1A 1AE

July 7, 1997

Mr. David S. Percy

Dear Mr. Percy:

I have forwarded a copy of your letter to the NASA Representative in Paris, as well as NASA Headquarters in Washington, and asked that they reply directly. There is no one currently at the Embassy with the expertise to answer your specific questions.

Sincerely,

Raymond V. Arnaudo
Science & Environment Attache

cc: James Zimmerman
    NASA - Embassy Paris

    J. Adamas
    NASA, International Affairs Office

Despite this acknowledgement from the United States Embassy in London replies to our questions were never forthcoming from NASA.

various retired participants in the Soviet program in a post-Glasnost attempt to fill the gaps left in history by his uncle. It was not until 1990 and the publication of an article on the subject of the N-1 project in the Russian newspaper *Krasnaya Zvezda* that Sabelnikov considered that he had obtained the level of confirmation required concerning the seriousness of the Soviets' intent to achieve a Moon landing by the late 1960s.

We strongly recommend his book.

Rockets

Referring to the Challenger Space Shuttle disaster, executives from Morton Thiokol were adamant that it was too dangerous to risk the Challenger flight as the ambient temperatures were "outside of their experience".

That being so, surely the conditions in which the Apollo craft were expected to perform could also be described as "outside of their experience"? The CSM/LM engines and fuels were required to operate in ambient temperatures far more extreme than those experienced overnight by Challenger sitting on the launch pad.

Lunar 'timeshare' launch date schedules for the USSR/USA space agencies
(see text Chapter Four, page 162)

Space agency	Date	Mission	Space agency	Date	Mission
USSR	Jan 02 1959	Luna 1	USA	Jan 10 1968	Surveyor 7
USSR	Sep12 1959	Luna 2	USSR	Apr 07 1968	Luna 14
USSR	Oct 04 1959	Luna 3	USSR	Sept 14 1968	Zond 5
USA	Aug 23 1961	Ranger 1	USSR	Nov 10 1968	Zond 6
USA	Nov18 1961	Ranger 2	USA	Dec 21 1968	'Apollo 8'
USA	Jan 26 1962	Ranger 3	USA	May 18 1969	'Apollo 10'
USA	Apr 23 1962	Ranger 4	USSR	July 13 1969	Luna 15*
USA	Oct 18 1962	Ranger 5	USA	July 16 1969	'Apollo 11'*
USSR	Apr 02 1963	Luna 4	USSR	Aug 07 1969	Zond 7
USA	Jan 30 1964	Ranger 6	USA	Nov 14 1969	'Apollo 12'
USA	Jul 31 1964	Ranger 7	USA	Apr 11 1970	'Apollo 13'
USA	Feb 20 1965	Ranger 8	USSR	Sept 12 1970	Luna 16
USA	Mar 24 1965	Ranger 9	USSR	Oct20 19 70	Zond 8
USSR	May 09 1965	Luna 5	USSR	Nov 10 1970	Luna 17/ Lunikhod
USSR	June 08 1965	Luna 6	USA	Jan 31 1971	'Apollo 14'
USSR	July 18 1965	Zond 3	USA	July 26 1971	'Apollo 15'
USSR	Oct 04 1965	Luna 7	USSR	Sept 02 1971	Luna 18
USSR	Dec 031965	Luna 8	USSR	Sept 28 1971	Luna 19
USSR	Jan 31 1966	Luna 9	USSR	Feb 14 1972	Luna 20
USSR	Mar 31 1966	Luna 10	USA	Apr 16 1972	'Apollo 16'
USA	June 02 1966	Surveyor 1	USA	Dec 07 1972	'Apollo 17'
USSR	Aug 24 1966	Luna 11	USSR	Jan 08 1973	Luna 21/ Lunikhod 2
USA	Sept 20 1966	Surveyor 2	USSR	May 29 1974	Luna 22
USSR	Oct 22 1966	Luna 12	USSR	Oct 1974	Luna 23
USSR	Dec 21 1966	Luna 13	USSR	Aug 09 1976	Luna 24
USA	Apr 20 1967	Surveyor 3			
USA	July 14 1967	Surveyor 4			
USA	Sept 11 1967	Surveyor 4			
USA	Nov 10 1967	Surveyor 6			

* Matched missions.

Chapter Five

The main sources of reference for Chapter Four are listed in the Chapter Notes but here are some further comments and background.

An astronaut in a rocket leaves the Earth at X moment in time on X day for X period and XYZ events occur during the trip. Such facts should be indisputable and therefore all space histories should correspond on these points. Naturally, the *interpretation* of such events will be as individual as the writers themselves. Nevertheless it was astonishing to find numerous discrepancies between the various space histories on fundamental points. These discrepancies do not automatically imply inaccuracy on the part of the authors but they are certainly an indication of a problem—a problem that could stem from the distribution and/or in the content of the space program information that has been made available to the researchers of the Apollo records.

David Baker, the author of two seminal reference books, *A History of Manned Space Flight* and *Spaceflight and Rocketry: A Chronology,* is an acknowledged expert on the history of space and its attendant technology. His attention to detail is unparalleled. The material in his *Spaceflight and Rocketry* took him over thirty years to compile.

Heinz Gartzmann, author of *The Men and The Rockets* was assistant to Zborowski, the German rocket scientist and engineer at BMW's Rocket Technology Research, and Gartzmann worked for German Rocket Program throughout the Second World War. Encompassing the years from 1895 to 1956 his book is a translation from the German by the Science Book Club.

James Harford, author of *Korolev,* is the Executive Director Emeritus of the American Institute of Aeronautics and Astronautics and formerly Verville Fellow at the US National Air and Space Museum. This biography, published in 1997, was a key reference for this chapter (although we cross referenced with other published material and also used the fruit of our own 1997 meetings in Moscow).

Ernst Stuhlinger and Frederick I Ordway III have written an invaluable biographical memoir of von Braun. Stuhlinger was a veteran of Peenemünde and one of the 127 men shipped to the United States after WWII. The American-born Frederick I Ordway III worked with Wernher von Braun at ABMA and at NASA's Marshall Space Flight Center.

Dr. Helen B Walters, author of *Wernher von Braun, Rocket* intended this book to be read by the younger reader and was produced with the approval of von Braun—who penned the introduction.

The *Hutchinson Dictionary of Scientists was* published in 1994. In this book von Braun is named Wernher Magnus, instead of Wernher Frieherr. Magnus was actually the name of his father and his younger brother, the latter worked with WvB both in Germany and in the United States.

Willie Ley always said that he left Germany for the States in 1933 due to the fact that he detested fascism. He maintained lifelong close connections both professional and personal with Oberth, Fritz Lang and von Braun. Ley wrote several books on space exploration while in the US and ended his career in charge of the National Air and Space Museum.

Willie Ley's works include:
Bombs & Bombing, 1941;
Exploration to Mars (with Wernher von Braun), 1946;
Ranger to the Moon, 1965;
Watchers of the Skies, 1963;
Rockets, Missiles and Men in Space, 1963.

BIS

Although a clearing house of astronautical information, do not confuse the BIS with that other BIS (the Bank of International Settlement). Founded with just five members on October 13 1933, the British Interplanetary Society grew to a modest fifteen members within ten weeks of its birth. In the opinion of Heinz Gartzmann the BIS has been the single most influential society to bring about a state of "space consciousness" in the world population. Gartzmann cites others who have contributed towards the reputation of the society, men such as the 1948 and 1949 Chairman AV Cleaver, the rocket engineer, and Arthur Clarke, a leading English writer on astronautical subjects and chairman of the BIS no less than five times. Cleaver states that at the time of writing (the mid 1950s), its founder Philip Cleator was the only survivor of the original fifteen members.

Chapter Six
The Roswell cast

Major Jesse Marcel	Staff Intelligence Officer, Roswell Army Air Field.
Lt Col Joseph Briley	Operations Officer, Roswell AAF from mid July 1947.
Col William Blanchard	Commanding Officer, 509th Bomb Group, Roswell AAF.
Major Edwin Easley	Provost Marshall, 509th Bomb Group, Roswell AAF.
First Lt Walter Haut	PR Officer, 509th Bomb Group, Roswell AAF.
Colonel Thomas J Dubose	Chief of Staff, 8th Army, Fort Worth AAF.
Brig-Gen Roger Ramey	Commanding Officer, 8th Air Force, Fort Worth AAF.
Col Al Clarke	Base Commander, Fort Worth AAF.
Brig-Gen Arthur Exon	Brig-Gen, Wright AAF (now Wright Patterson AFB).

The VLA with its *nine* dishes per Y-shaped arm is sited on 'the Playa'·(as it is known locally) and is located northwest of Bat Cave, the most ancient agricultural site in North America, where 4,500 year old corn kernels were discovered. This 'Y' layout is similar to that of the Tetrahedron Crop Glyph which was activated in a 1991 wheat field at Barbury Castle, Southern England.

Had that particular tetrahedral design (featuring the top view of a tetrahedron) already been seen at that particular place in 1947?

Chapter Six *ET update*
In the late 1990s during a British TV program chaired by TV personality and presenter Michael Aspel and devoted entirely to the subject of UFOs, a representative of the American military declared that there had been no UFO (as in ET spacecraft) investigations going on—since 1969! This cut-off date conveniently encompasses 'Apollo 11'. However, given the contents of *Title 14,* July 16 1969 it would be surprising if many of the armed forces personnel desired to inform their superiors of a sighting, which therefore would make the foregoing statement correct—from a military point of view. Never mind that according to these same people, there were no such things as ET spacecraft to investigate in the first place!

Other books by UFO researcher Timothy Good:
Above Top Secret, 1987;
The UFO Report, 1991;
The UFO Report, 1992;
Alien Update, 1993;
Alien Base, 1998.

Chapter Eight
Lasers
In 1998, during a conversation with the astronomer and laser specialist, J F Mangin of the Nice Observatory, France, we were advised that the laser used in France at the time of Apollo "was not around any longer". Mangin was unable to tell us what had become of it, but thought that it had been dismantled. The personnel who were at the observatory at that time were no longer working there and he was unable to fulfil our request for either the time it was first used or for the exact Earth/Moon distance then recorded by this laser. We were led to believe that although this laser was installed at the time of Apollo with much celebration between America and France, the results had been less than glorious. Today a YAG (yttrium /aluminium/grenat) laser is in use, rather than the ruby lasers used during Apollo. The YAG laser is a continual pulse laser which emits in the infrared range and has an accuracy that far exceeds the ruby laser.

Laser ranging—
conflicting reports from the same source
In his *Apollo Journal* Eric Jones tells us that Bruce McCandless wanted to give the crew the news that the laser ranging had been successfully achieved by scientists at Lick Observatory—but that it was decided by the flight director they should not be distracted.

As stated by Jerry Wiant of McDonald Observatory, no readings were received from 'Apollo 11' at McDonald due to bad weather and as stated in *National Geographic* Lick Observatory was unable to get a ranging during July 1969 on account of the prevailing sunlight. Yet *despite* these facts, NASA tape transcripts demonstrate that Houston did tell Collins (in the CSM) that at about 29 after the astronauts had installed the LR[3], apparently Lick *had indeed* received a reading!

According to Eric Jones this laser ranging readout

"could refine the position of the landing site".
Here is the NASA transcript of that conversation:

112:34:29 McCandless: You might be interested in knowing, Mike, that we have gotten reflections back from the laser reflector array they deployed, and we may be able to get some information out of that a little later.

But according to *Time* July 25 1969, Lick Observatory were 50 miles off target.

What does all this say about the comms/navigation links between the CSM, the LM and Mission Control on Earth? From the above reported speech by Capcom Bruce McCandless, we must deduce that the tracking data and the LM guidance telemetry during 'Apollo 11' were virtually useless. Collins, orbiting the Moon in the CSM, was equally unable to 'see' the Eagle from the sunlight reflecting off its mylar covering. Even when Houston allegedly had the Lick Observatory laser reading they still did not know *even approximately* the area that the LM Eagle had landed in and were unable to locate the 'Apollo 11' landing site using that method. (Which is hardly surprising when we know that this laser reading did not officially happen at all.)

The fact of the matter is *nobody on Earth knew exactly where on the Moon these intrepid astronauts were,* and as it later turned out, neither were the EVA astronauts sure of their own position either!

Jones also states that 'Apollo 14' and '15' erected LR[3]'s. But the otherwise very detailed and timed-to-the-minute EVA reports for these two 'mission impossibles'(?) totally neglect to slot in this LR[3] activity—(to date!).

How surprising is that?

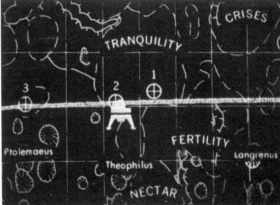
Three alternative landing sites for Apollo at Tranquility.   NASA MAP

Further comments on table 39, page 376
The Gemini dose readings were taken *below* the Van Allen belts and can only compare with the ASTP flight which took place within the same region.

The Skylab dose readings were taken just inside *the lower* Van Allen belt and the daily dose rate apparently reflects this difference.

Apollo missions, '8','10','11' through to '17' were said to have taken place principally *beyond* the Van Allen belts. Therefore they *cannot* be compared with either the Gemini, Skylab or Apollo 9 flights.

This matter being firmly established—the figures for the nine claimed lunar orbital flights (and six of those supposedly placed crew members on the even more exposed lunar surface) are actually *lower than the average daily dose rate of Skylab.*

How can that possibly be the case?

Are these figures only relating to the orbits made around *the Earth* by the CSM?

Furthermore, to make it all the more difficult for the lay person to equate rads, rems or sieverts, the doses in table (39) are expressed as:

1 mGy equalling 100 millirad.

1 mGy = 100millirad = 0.1 rad.

Taking readings from the above table as an example, 1.80 mGy = 0.18 rad purporting to represent the total mission dose for 'Apollo 11', we find this 0.18 rad figure corresponds with the data in Eric Jones' *Apollo Journal.* Jones also summarises the situation by stating in his commentary that neither Armstrong nor Aldrin's radiation readings changed since landing. (But omits to state whether this means since landing on the Moon or landing back on Earth.) He also informs us that the total uncorrected dosages received by the 'Apollo 11' crew were about 0.25 rad but again this is for three astronauts—yet conditions for two of them were completely different to that of the CSM pilot. He then states that the adjusted readings were evaluated as being 0.18 (the "post-mission corrected true reading") but that most of that was received on the trips through the VABs. Thus apparently implying that deep space is safe!

Below are the personal radiation dosimeter (PRD) readings (as published by NASA). They are in fact two different conversations, one from the CSM and the other from the LM but they appeared in the following format in the Jones journal:

112:48:27 Collins: I say again, I am manoeuvring to the P52 attitude, and do you want a crew status report?

112:48:34 McCandless: Roger. And go ahead with your crew status report.

112:48:40 Collins: Roger. No medication. Radiation 100 point 16.

112:59:39 Armstrong: Houston, Tranquility Base. The CDR's PRD reads 11014.

112:59:51 McCandless: Roger. 11014 for the CDR.

113:00:01 Aldrin: Roger. LMP reads 09018. Over.

113:00:06 McCandless: Roger. 09018.

Presumably Armstrong and Aldrin's readouts, like Collins actually read 110 *point* 14 and 090 *point* 18 respectively.

Chapter Eight *Communications*

Bill Wood, the USB Engineer at Goldstone stated:

"The signal coming from the LM was a much stronger than had been expected, so it ran into clipping. As the signal was inverted—that is white on black instead of black on white, and as the clipping was on the black side, the picture was coming down to Goldstone almost completely black, with very little white, there was no detail. When we saw the switch from Goldstone to Honeysuckle Creek there was a pronounced improvement in video quality."

Ed von Renouard was the TV technician at Honeysuckle Creek (HC) during the Apollo period and informed us that the B&W picture from 'Apollo 11' was 800 lines but at only *10 frames per second.* In order for it to be converted to the US (EIA) TV standard of 525 lines at *60 frames per second* it had to be displayed on a monitor and the 'scanned' off the monitor by a vidicon 525 line TV camera pointed at the screen. From this set-up the 10 frames per second were recorded onto a magnetic disc, and then replayed *five times* from the disc to make up the 60 frames per second.

But surely the US TV standard then, as now, requires 30 FRAMES per second and at two fields making up each full picture that would be 60 FIELDS per second. Something not quite right here?

Apparently this replaying delay is the explanation for the pictures we all saw at the time manifesting a ghostly appearance whenever the astronauts moved about.

- Bill Wood at JPL/Goldstone describes the Goldstone 210ft Mars link as the *backup* support to the tracking of the Apollo spacecraft (whilst in another paper he refers to it as the *primary* receiving station).
- Apparently it was considered unnecessary for this type of prime support for the crews of 'Apollo 8' and 'Apollo 10' (who seemingly flew before completion of the link installation)? Despite the fact that they were not landing (allegedly) on the lunar surface they were still using TV and voice transmissions and on 'Apollo 10' they were flying a LM just off the surface *for the first time.*
- Apparently HC were ready and able to cope with the "higher than expected" FM downlink deviation (which initially resulted in the high contrast inverted image at Goldstone.)
- Jodrell Bank could only pick up the Apollo craft once they were "near to the Moon". This turns out to be a distance of around 1,000 miles out from the lunar surface. Jodrell Bank used a 50ft radio telescope at a frequency of 2300Mhz with a ⅝th degree beam width.
- According to Goldstone's Bill Wood, the MSFN (Manned Space Flight Network) operating frequencies were:

for the CSM (transmitting voice data) 2287.5 Mhz;

" (TV) 2277.5 Mhz;

for the LM (ALL) 2282.5 Mhz.

- As these frequencies were *below* the Deep Space Tracking Network's (DSTN) normal range, namely 2290Mhz-2295Mhz—it was therefore necessary to retune the low noise amplifiers.

All these frequencies were *well below* the stated Jodrell Bank frequency.

Chapter Eight
Plaques and medals

According to Eric Jones, in Buzz Aldrin's 1989 book *Men From Earth* Aldrin detailed the items that he tossed onto the lunar soil in memory of those who had gone before. Eric Jones describes this event and lists the objects which were allegedly thrown onto the surface at the very end of the EVA (apparently almost as an afterthought) by Aldrin and nudged into place by Armstrong's moonboot.

On that list two items are rather more specifically described:

A *Soviet* medal commemorating the Soyuz cosmonaut Vladimir Komarov who died during re-entry on April 23 1967.

A *Soviet* medal honouring the Vostok cosmonaut Yuri Gagarin, who died in an aircraft accident on March 27 1968.

The inference has always been that this little 'in memoriam ceremony' was to be NASA's homage to all those from 'both sides' who had died in the 'space race'. Indeed other sources certainly describe a medallion, but omit to state its provenance.

QUESTION: If there was truly a race to the Moon in a Cold War situation, why did the Soviets not put their medals on their own probe Luna 15, which ostensibly left Earth before 'Apollo 11'? After all, the Soviet's Luna 15 was present on the Moon at the same time as 'Apollo 11' and it too contacted the lunar soil.

Or were these accounts actually the actions performed by an astronaut from the Luna 15/LM during that unforgettable month of July 1969?

Items taken to the Moon 1969. Note that the Soviet medals were not included in this official NASA presentation.   NASA

Chapter Nine *Radiation Data*
Apollo Journal

We are specifically informed by Eric Jones that the 'Apollo 14' crew received an average dose of 1.14 rad (as compared with the 0.18 rad for 'Apollo 11' "in part because their trajectory took them closer to the *centre of the belts* than any of the other crews".

Let us unstitch that remark:

The Van Allen belts are rather like sausage shapes wrapped around the Earth, there is no specific centre but these belts do vary in intensity according to altitude. As the Saturn V rockets were launched from a location near to the equator the Apollo craft passed through all of the various slices of intense radiation that are within this area. The only way of minimising *the length of time* spent in the belts (when on a Saturn V rocket) would have been to leave Earth from a launch site as near to the North or South Pole as possible, where the belts are at their thinnest.

However, if the intended trajectory for 'Apollo 14' required a longer time in the Van Allen belts, that is another matter. Equally, if the designated trajectory from Earth required transit through the Starfish Prime artificial radiation belt, that too is another matter.

Eric Jones is at pains to point out that the 'Apollo 14' doses were not indicative of "significant medical risks"—especially when compared to all the other risks that a trip to the Moon entailed. In relation to the figures published in the Gemini/Skylab/Apollo table (39) on page 376 he is no doubt correct.

'Apollo 13' oxygen tank inconsistencies
Observations by Stephen Clementson

Exposing a hoax becomes more difficult when the evidence burns-up in the Earth's atmosphere, so 'blowing-up' the service module was very convenient!

There would have been no story if the CSM had vaporised, so NASA must have cooked-up the entire scenario. The agency ensured that the 'explosion' would appear to take place at a non-return distance, providing a more nail-biting plot.

How, one might ask, can a pressurised oxygen tank explode, when in a vacuum, without completely destroying the CSM. Whilst under Earth's atmospheric pressure, the level of damage that can be inflicted by an exploding oxygen tank is considerable. The totally inexplicable thing about the 'Apollo 13' story is the fact that *it did not even result in a rocket fuel explosion*. There should have been an explosion of such a magnitude that the electrical system and the cryogenic oxygen supply would have completely failed. Filled with pressurised liquid oxygen, to a level which was undoubtedly greater than 50%, the *potential to cause havoc would have known no bounds*. Bits of metal, accelerated to supersonic speeds, would have *smashed through the structure as though it was made of putty*.

It was truly a media epic, the operation was deemed a total success, with the general public now aware of the difficulties of space-flight, and any suggestions that the previous missions might have been hoaxed were also dispelled.

The 'Apollo 13' Command Module showing damage following the explosion 'accident' on April 13 1970.

NASA

The table below lists the total time spent in space by the Apollo astronauts over their careers. An asterisk indicates that the mission time was in relative safety, i.e. below the radiation belts. Although these figures give the impression of much exposure to the hazards of space travel, in our view only the flights *below* the Van Allen belts are of interest. We maintain that the named Apollo astronauts would have been vulnerable to potentially lethal radiation in deep space beyond the Van Allen belts, if they were in the CSM and/or LM built to the published specifications.

Name	Year	Spaceflight	Mission duration
Anders	December 1968	Apollo 8	147hrs 0min 42sec
Aldrin B	November 1966	Gemini 12*	94hrs 31min 34sec
	July 1969	Apollo 11/LM	195hrs 18min 35sec
			289hrs 50min 9sec
Armstrong N	March 1965	Gemini 8*	10hrs 41min 26secs
	July 1969	Apollo 11/LM	195 hrs 18min 35sec
			206hrs 0min 1sec
Collins M	July 1966	Gemini 10*	70hrs 46min 39sec
	July 1969	Apollo 11/CM	195hrs18min 35sec
			266hrs 5min 14sec
Conrad P	August 1965	Gemini 5*	190hrs 55min 14sec
	September 1966	Gemini 11*	71hrs 17min 8sec
	November 1969	Apollo 12/LM	244hrs 36min 25sec
	May 1973	Skylab 1*	672hrs
	over a period of 8 years Conrad totals		**1,117hrs 49m 12sec**
Bean A	November 1969	Apollo 12/LM	244hrs 36min 25sec
	July 1973	Skylab 2*	1,416 hrs
	over a period of 4 years Bean totals		**1,660hrs 36min 25sec**
Borman	December 1965	Gemini 7*	330hrs 35min 0 sec
	December 1968	Apollo 8	147hrs 0min 42sec
	over a period of 2 years Borman totals		**477hrs 35 min 42 sec**
Gordon R	September 1966	Gemini 11	71hrs 17min 8sec
	November 1969	Apollo 12/CM	244hrs 36min 25sec
	over a period of three years Gordon totals		**315hrs 53min 33sec**
Haise F	April 1970	Apollo 13	142hrs 54min 41sec
	plus further missions with the Space Shuttle.		
Lovell J	December 1965	Gemini 7*	330hrs 35min 0sec
	November 1966	Gemini 12*	94h 31min 34sec
	December 1968	Apollo 8	147hrs 0min 42sec
	April 1970	Apollo 13	142hrs 54min 41sec
	over a period of 5 years Lovell totals		**713hrs 1min 57sec**
Swigert J	April 1970	Apollo 13	142hrs 54min 41sec
Mitchell E	January 1971	Apollo 14/LM	216hrs 01min
Roosa S	January 1971	Apollo 14/CM	216hrs 01min
Shepard A	May 1961	Mercury 3/ MR-3*	0hrs 15 min 22 sec
	January 19	Apollo 14/LM	216hrs 01min
	over a period of 10 years Shepard totals		**216hrs 16 min 22 sec**
Irwin J	July 1971	Apollo 15/LM	295hrs 11 min 53 sec
Scott D	March 1965	Gemini 8*	10hrs 41min 26sec
	March 1969	Apollo 9*	241hrs 0min 54sec
	July 1971	Apollo 15/LM	295hrs 11 min 53 sec
	over a period of 2 years Scott totals		**546hrs 54min 21sec**
Worden A	July 1971	Apollo 15/CM	295hrs 11 min 53 sec
Duke C	April 1972	Apollo 16/LM	265hrs 51min 05sec
Mattingley K	April 1972	Apollo 16/CM	265hrs 51min 05sec
	?	Shuttle STS-4 *	no data
		Shuttle STS 51-C*	no data
	in one year Mattingley accrued		**265hrs 51min 05sec** Contd.

549

Continued from previous page:

Name	Year	Spaceflight	Mission Duration
Young J	March 1965	Gemini 3*	4hrs 53min
	July 1966	Gemini 10*	70hrs 46min 39sec
	May 1969	Apollo 10	192hrs 2min 23sec
	April 1972	Apollo 16/LM	265hrs 51min 05sec
	1980	Shuttle STS-1*	no data
		Shuttle STS 9/spacelab 1*	no data
	to 1972 a period of 7 years Young totals		**533hrs 33min 7sec**
Cernan E	June 1965	Gemini 9*	72hrs 56min
	May 1969	Apollo 10	192hrs 2min 23sec
	December 19	Apollo 17/LM	301hrs 51min 59sec
	over a period of 7 years Cernan totals		**565hrs 54min 22sec**
Evans R	December 1972	Apollo 17/CM	301hrs 51min 59sec
Schmitt H	December 1972	Apollo 17/LM	301hrs 51min 59sec

NASA DATA

19.47° and the sites of energy upwellings on planets in the solar system
Latitudes of emergent energy phenomena

PLANET	FEATURE	LATITUDE	COMMENT
Venus	Alta Regio	19.5° N	Current volcanic region.
	Beta Regio	25.0° S	Current volcanic.
Earth	Hawaiian Caldera hot spot	19.4° N (now active at 19.6° N)	Largest shield volcano.
Moon	Tsiolkovsky	19.6° S	Unique, far side 'mare-like'
			lava extrusion.
Mars	Olympus Mons	19.3° N	Largest shield volcano (non active).
Jupiter	Great Red Spot	22.0° S	Vast atmospheric vorticular
	(The surface of Jupiter is hidden from sight)		upwelling'.

Voyager confirmed that this feature is a hurricane-like disturbance in Jupiter's atmosphere, surrounded by smaller vortices.

PLANET	FEATURE	LATITUDE	COMMENT
Saturn	North Equatorial Belt	20.0° N	Region of storms
	South Equatorial Belt	20.0° S	observable from Earth.
Uranus	Northern IR 1-2K	20.0° N	
	Southern IR 1-2K	20.0° S	
Neptune	Great Dark Spot	20.0° S	Similar to Jupiter's Great

Red Spot, the scale of this feature is immense—planet Earth is approximately the same size as Neptune's Great Dark Spot.

Some of **Jupiter's** moons have also provided data:

Io /Loki:2	19.0° N (Voyager 1&2 recorded volcanic plumes)
Maui: 6	19.0° N
Pele:1	19.0° S
Volund: 4	22.0° N

Source: NASA & US Geological Survey

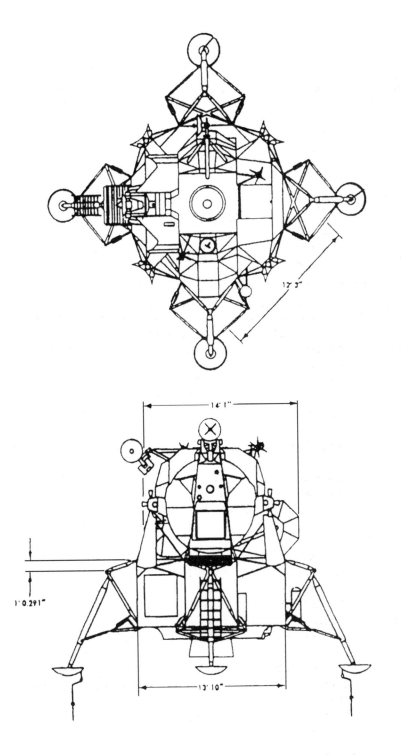

NASA

**Top view and side view of the LM with overall dimensions from the
LMA790-3-LM APOLLO OPERATIONS HANDBOOK SPACECRAFT.** (see Chapter Nine)

551

Chapter Ten
The Neutral Point
The precise difference between the CNP and the ENP at the time of the 'Apollo 11' trajectory was 18,759 miles.

The History of Rocketry and Space Travel was first published by Thomas Y Crowell, New York, USA in 1966 with reprints in both 1969 and in 1975.

WvB's co-author on *The History of Rocketry and Space Travel* was Frederick I Ordway III, who worked with WvB at ABMA and then at the Marshall Space Center and was a member of von Braun's team until 1964. Thereafter Ordway joined the faculty of Huntsville's University of Alabama and subsequently the Department of Energy in Washington. Ordway co-authored another four books with WvB and is co-biographer, along with Ernst Stuhlinger, of the posthumous biography *Wernher von Braun: Crusader For Space.* In this biography Ordway states that he was aware of WvB's work since 1947 and that he first met him in 1952 and retained "close personal and professional" ties with WvB throughout his life. Interestingly, Walters (the author of *Space Age*) lists the original Crowell publishing date as 1967 and also lists a reprint from New York publishers Harper and Row that appeared in 1985, after WvB's death. This reprint was titled: *Space Travel: A History—An Update of The History of Rocketry and Space Travel.*

Chapter Ten
The speed of light
Between the years of 1928-1945 the speed of light was found to be 3% slower than the accepted value of 186,282 miles per second. In fact it was only in 1947 that the speed of light returned to the values of 1927.

During that period many major historical events occurred—marker points in the history of our planet. The Wall Street crash and great depression in America. Ghandi's opposition to the British in India, Mao Tse Tung's long march in China. The Spanish Civil War, the rise of the Nazis, the Second World War and the development of the A-bomb. The period from 1945 through to the mid 1950s was one of transition and then regrouping after much horrific conflict. The activity of a significant proportion of the world's population, taken together with this fluctuation of the speed of light, is truly worthy of note—especially when considered from the viewpoint of quantum physics.

Further details of the three speeds of light
In illustration (20) on page 404, the circles along the axis of the two glyphs have been marked from right to left A, B, B1, C, D and E. All the above circles have been telescoped down the axis and superimposed over the largest circle E, in order to illustrate the way in which the three light speeds were encoded. The diameter of the circles and other measurements within these glyphs are in most instances the average, or the near average, of these two *almost identical* formations.

For example, the true average between the two circles marked C on the two glyph surveys, namely 18.6666' is a close approximation to the value of 18.6282' for circle C. 186,282.3959 is the speed of light in miles per second as defined by a team led by Kenneth M Evenson during tests in Boulder, Colorado during October 1972 deploying a chain of laser beams.

Circle **C** is 18.6282	x 2 =	37.2564
Circle **B** is 8.0944	x 2 =	16.1888
Circle **A** is 11.3100	x 2 =	22.6200

$$76.0652 \quad \text{(E)}$$

C x 2	=	37.2564 **(D)**
B x 1	=	08.0944
A x 1	=	11.3100

B namely 8.0944 x 7	=	**56.6608** (B1)
8.09441624 + 11.3100	=	**19.40441624** (A+B)

24/25ths or 96% (the maximum percentage of local light speed physically attainable—see text *Two-Thirds*) of **A + B x 10** namely **194,044.1624** is **186,282.3959 = C^1** *Solar System* light speed in miles per second, the speed of light in a vacuum anywhere within a solar system.

And 19.40441624 x 2 = 38.80883248
96% of 38.80883248 = 37.25647918 x 10 =
372,564.791 = C^1 x 2 _____
E = 76.06531166 :
18.62823959 = 4.08333333

408,333.333 is the interstellar factor (see *Two-Thirds* text references to interstellar light speed over 400,000 times faster than solar system light speed). **408,333.333 x C^1** namely **186,282.3539** = **7.60653116^{10}** the *Interstellar speed of light* C^2 **Bl** namely **56.6608 = 8.0944 x 7 7 is the factor applied to calculate the *Intergalactic speed of light* C^3** (see also text *Two-Thirds).*

Summary
C^1 Solar system light speed
= **186,282.3959 miles per second.**

C^2 Interstellar light speed (186,282.3959 x 408,333.333)
= **7.60653116^{10} miles per second.**

C^3 Intergalactic light speed (7.60653116^{10} x 7)
= **5.32457181^{11} miles per second.**

Analysis of the Fractal *Two-Thirds* Crop Glyph activated at Alton Barnes, England in 1997. (see Chapter Ten)
The small circles are ⅔rds the size of the larger circles and similarly the triangles decrease in size by ⅔rds.
Calculations by Martin Noakes.
Many Crop Glyphs form part of what we call the ancient Topogly Matrix (see text Chapter Thirteen).

Chapter Ten
Neutral Point calculations

The Earth/Moon distance at the time of 'Apollo 11'
(measuring centre-to-centre) was:

246,322.134 miles/396,654 kms.

Applying Newton's Law of Universal Gravitation

Y   =   distance from Moon's centre to the
        neutral point
T   =   centre to centre distance between the
        Earth and the Moon
R_e =   radius of the Earth = 3,960 miles
R_m =   radius of the Moon = 1,080 miles
X   =   distance from the Earth's centre to the
        neutral point
Y   =   distance from the Moon's centre to the
        neutral point
G_e =   Earth's surface gravity
G_m =   Moon's surface gravity
T   =   246,322 (miles)
Y   =   24,736 (miles)
X   =   221,586 (miles)

$$G_e \frac{R_e^2}{X^2} = G_m \frac{R_m^2}{Y^2}$$

$$\frac{G_m}{G_e} = \frac{R_e^2 Y^2}{R_m^2 X^2}$$

$$= \frac{(3,960)^2 (24,736)^2}{(1,080)^2 (221,586)^2}$$

Therefore, $G_m = 0.167\ G_e$

However, the distance from the Moon to the Neutral Point
in July 1969 was stated to be (see text):
43,495 miles from the Moon's centre.
The new calculation therefore would be:

$$\frac{(3,960)^2 (43,495)^2}{(1080)^2 (202,827)^2} = 0.61825$$

We know that the G_m of 0.61825 is incorrect for the true
gravity on the lunar surface—it is known to be or ⅙G_e or
0.167 G_e.

553

Chapter Twelve

Mars 'timeshare' launch date schedules for USSR/USA			
USSR	1960		2 launches
USSR	1962		3 launches
USSR	1964	November 3	1 launch
USA	1964	November 5	2 launches
USA	1964	November 28	1 launch
USA	1969	February 24	1 launch
USSR	1969	March 27	2 launches
USSR	1969	April 2	1 Launch
USA	1971	May 8	2 launches
USSR	1971	May 10	3 launches
USA	1971	May 30	1 launch
USSR	1973	July x 2 & August x 2	4 launches
USA	1976	August & September	2 launches
USSR	1983	failed on arrival around Phobos	
USA	1993	Mars Observer-failed	1 launch
RUSSIA	1996	November Mars 96	1 launch
		failed to leave Earth orbit	
USA	1996	November Mars Global Surveyor	
USA	1996	December Pathfinder	2 launches total

Pyramid construction findings

1) In 1979, Dr. Klemm, a qualified mineral expert, analysed 20 different rock samples from the Great Pyramid and concluded that each stone had come from a different region in Egypt. However, each sample contained a mixture of ingredients from the various regions. Furthermore on testing granite samples, instead of the uniform density that such material possesses naturally, he found too many air bubbles and that the density of the material was massed to the original base of the block.

2) The Director of the Institute for Applied Archaeological Science at Barty University, Miami, Florida, Professor Joseph Davidovits thinks that the arguments about scaffolding, ramps, sleds of tree trunks, ropes and pulleys are irrelevant. He suggests that the builders of these monuments used some material not unlike concrete.

Joseph Davidovits, in the *Revue des Questions Scientifiques 1986* stated that the Great Pyramid has also been subjected to electromagnetic readings. High frequency waves were shot through the rock, which scientists thought to be completely dry. The scientists expected to receive 'bounce-back' from the waves (which could help discover anomalies and/or additional passageways. They failed to get the result they were anticipating, in fact they found the opposite effect. The rock absorbed the HF waves 100%. The building blocks of the Great Pyramid contained more moisture than natural rock. Therefore, it is the conclusion of Professor Davidovits that these stone edifice are made of artificial stone. i.e. concrete. Professor Davidovits used ancient Egyptian recipes to mix cements and concretes. He found that the result was a quick drying well-balanced concrete, which made it more resistant to the environment in which it had to perform—more so than any concrete currently in use. One French and one American company have already started manufacturing concrete according to these old recipes.

Rotation/revolution				
ed = Earth days; ey = Earth years; rp = retrograde precession; rr = *retrograde* rotation east-west.				
Planet	Rotation	Revolution	Axis tilt	RP
Mercury	58 ed 15 hrs 36 mins	088.0 ed	002.00° approx.	no
Venus	243 ed/rr	224.7 ed	177.30°	no
Earth	23 hrs 56 mins	365.3 ed	023.45°	yes
Mars	24 hrs 37 mins	687.0 ed	025.19°	no
Jupiter	09 hrs 55 mins	11.86 ey	003.12°	no
Saturn	10 hrs 39 mins	29.46 ey	026.73°	no
Uranus	17 hrs 20 mins/rr	84.0 ey	097.86°	no
Neptune	16 hrs 6 mins	16.0 ey	029.56°	no
Pluto	06 ed 9 hrs 18 mins/rr	248.0 ey	122.46°	no

Chapter Thirteen
Topogly

In order to see how Topogly actually works, we will take the example of the Face on Mars and allow Carl Munck to guide us through its relationship to sites on both planets:

We *know* where this Face is—on planet Mars, staring at us from its nearest point of just over thirty five million miles at 41 degrees, 11 minutes and 10.0308 seconds north of the Martian Equator and at 00 degrees 06.890283706 minutes east of Cydonia's gigantic five-sided pyramid [the D&M, the Tor].

In math, we have certain well-established *constants*: such as the 360 degree system for reckoning such geometric shapes as circles and spheres.

The 'radian' (57.29577951) of these same spheres and circles.

Then we have Pi (3.14159255363).

We also have the fractions of these constants such as 1/3rd Pi; 2/3rds Pi. Together with their multiples such as double Pi (or Pi x 2 = 6.283185307); the double Radian; these are all *constants* and can be used with one another, for example:

1/3rd Pi x 2/3rds Pi x Pi = 6.890283706

Which is a number that should look familiar to you. Of course! It is the grid longitude of Cydonia's *Face*—which tells us that *intelligence* placed the Face on Mars. To argue against it is to mandate the idea that nature sculpts according to mathematical law.

Now, we do not know who it was that left us Cydonia's Face. What we do know, and can prove, is that intelligence *was* behind it.

How can we prove it?

By way of our own Great Pyramid over in Giza, Egypt: a four sided, four cornered, single apex monument which shows *everyone* a total of NINE features. Ever wondered why? There are *many* reasons, and among them is what we find when we raise the grid longitude of the Cydonia *Face* to the 9th power (for those whose math is rusty that simply means to multiply a number by *itself* nine times.)

Doing so for the *Face* we get:
6.890283706 = 35,005,310.83, which is of course, precisely the closest approach Mars makes to Earth—expressed in terms of our statute mile—*not* meters or any of the other degenerated astrological units of measure that have been forced on us over the ages. Anyway, now we know why the Face *had* to be centred on its meridian of 6.8902837 minutes longitude.

Next we have its latitude to contend with.

Why is it at 41 degrees 11 minutes 10.0308 seconds north of the Martian equator?

Why do we not find this Face anywhere else? Indeed what is it doing over there anyway?

Again, it doesn't really matter just yet, because demonstrating that this positioning is the product of intelligence is quite easy.

Pi x1/3rd Pi x 2/3rds Pi = 6.890283706
00° 06.890283706′ = the precise Longitude of the Face on Mars.

The angles of a tetrahedron, 720° x 2 = 1440 x Pi = 4523.893421 encoding 41° 11′ 10.03080581″
= the precise latitude of the Face on Mars verified by 41 X 11 X 10.03080581 = 4523.893421.

Most clear thinkers today realise that primary in the construction of nature—wherever we find it—is the *tetrahedron* (a three-cornered pyramid featuring a total of 720 degrees of surface angle and when two tetrahedra meet we have a *double tetrahedron* —1,440 degrees of reality! And again basic mathematical law involving constants.

Munck then asks:

What happens when we merge the double tetrahedron with Pi? 1440 x Pi = 4523.893421.

Of course, when any two *constants* merge, the outcome is always another constant. In this instance, it's quite enlightening, because the ancient *cryptographers* used it to 'hide' data from the wrong eyes. This answer encodes another three figures, which we find by:

4523.893421 divided by 41 then divided by 11 = 10. 03080581. 41°, which is the actual latitude of the Cydonia Face, namely

41° 11′ 10.03080581″.

Which, one again, demonstrates that the Face on Mars was placed by intelligence.

Extract from
Anatoly I Kandiew's calculations regarding the accuracy requirement for Topogly codification
Through the decoding of the various locations, a message comes out loud and clear:

R (real) =T (transcendental) *N (whole) *I (irrational)

That is, any real number R(real) (with finite representation), is the UNIQUE product of a transcendental number T(transcendental), a whole number N(whole) and an irrational I(irrational) within a prescribed accuracy.

Let us look at the 'magnitude' of our R number: Since R is a product of degrees, minutes and seconds with two digits for fractional seconds (with P = A * B * C), then to measure C within two digits after the decimal point would require absolute accuracy in equatorial degrees, minutes, seconds and fractional seconds.

The longitude (or latitude) of any site would require a measurement accuracy within 1 foot. Since, most measurement involves measure above the equator, that accuracy would have to be greater—let us say it could be performed to within 1/12th of a foot (one inch). Then, the minimum P could be: 0.01 and the maximum for P would be: 129,587.40 (360 * 60* 59.99).

That is, more than six places of resultant accuracy.

Since the most frequent transcendental number encountered in the Topogly Matrix is Pi, the square root of

(2, 3 and 5), all these numbers need to be known to 12 places of accuracy—Why?

Since their product would be affected by half as many digits, and we require a minimal six digit result, we would require 12 digits of accuracy for each and every one of them.

Finally, we notice that even if we could produce such pin-point accuracy for the transcendental and irrational numbers we still have N choices left, with which to make a mistake!

Even for a relatively small N of 100 or so, we would require a total of 14 digits of accuracy.

Anatoly I Kandiew concludes that:

"Thus the chances of properly positioning two structures, to conform with this [Topogly] Grid Matrix Relationship—would be approximately 1 in 100 TRILLION."

"Now do you think that the Topogly Matrix was an accident, or does the work arise from intelligence?"

These odds do not include the odds for more than two structures maintaining these relationships!"

It is important to bear in mind that many of the significant **Crop Glyphs** also are activated on sites that are part of this Topogly Matrix.

Bibliography

Carl Munck is author of the book on The Code: *Whispers from Time.* Published 1998 and obtainable from the author, the ordering details including postal rates are listed in the Chapter Notes.

Crop Glyphs

A selection of books which document the Crop Glyph phenomenon:

Delgado & Andrews, *Circular Evidence,* Bloomsbury, 1989.
Delgado & Andrews, *Crop Circles: The Latest Evidence*, Bloomsbury, 1990.
Ed: Ralph Noyes, *The Crop Circle Enigma,* Gateway Books, 1990.
Ed: Bartholomew, *Crop Circles, Harbingers of World Change,* Gateway Books, 1991.
J Michell, *Dowsing The Crop Circles,* Gothic Image, 1991.
F C Taylor, *Crop Circles Of 1991,* (photographs) Beckhampton Books, 1992.
Davies, *Ciphers In The Crops,* Gateway Books, 1992.
Delgado, *Conclusive Evidence,* Bloomsbury, 1992.
Martineau, *Crop Circle Geometry,* Wooden Books, 1992.
Collins, *The Circlemakers,* ABC Books, 1992.
Myers & Percy, *Two-Thirds,* Aulis Publishers, 1993.
Schlemmer & Bennett, *The Only Planet of Choice,* Gateway Books, 1994.
Martineau, *A Book of Coincidence,* (solar system/glyph Geometry), Wooden Books, 1995.
Ruby, *The Gift,* Blue Note Books, 1995.
Thomas, *Fields of Mystery,* (Sussex Crop Glyphs), SB Publications, 1996.
Thomas & Bura, *Quest for Contact,* SB Publications, 1997.
Thomas, *Vital Signs,* SB Publications, 1998—(includes a personal comment on each book, plus information on specialist journals, videos, web sites, and conferences.

Moonorama

This LM 7 badge is extraordinary in that it illustrates a LM actually having landed on the Moon beneath which is the descent engine's crater.

It is surrounded by mountains very like the sharp peaks of the **Frau im Mond** film set but totally unlike the soft rounded highlands of NASA's **Fra Mauro** location.

The hugely out of proportion Earth suggests that the LM was indeed not so very far away.

Lucky LM 7 was assigned to unlucky 'Apollo 13 '—the mission that *NEVER* landed on the Moon.

Index

All the world's a stage
And all the men and women merely players:
They have their exits and their entrances;
And one man in his time has many parts,
His acts being seven ages.

William Shakespeare, *As you Like It* Act II Scene VII

This Index is in seven sections:

1. Cast & Crew   558
2. Transport & Equipment   563
3. Actions & Reactions   564
4. Photography   565
5. Earth Locations   566
6. Moon Locations   567
7. Mars Locations   568

1. Cast & Crew

509th Airborne Division USAAF, 210

ABMA, Huntsville, 193, 196, 199, 257, 260, 291

Adams, Carsbie, 84, 91, 96, 101, 172, 197, 383, 390

Adamski, George, 314

ACC, see Clarke, 245, 291, 314, 345, 394, 456, 491

AEC, Atomic Energy Commission, 112, 124, 234, 251, 309

Aldrin, Buzz, astronaut, 11, 13, 16, 18–20, 25, 31–38, 39, 48, 53, 62, 63, 66, 70, 101-102, 106, 146, 147, 224, 242, 255, 278, 279, 284, 288-289, 311, 316, 326, 335, 336, 340–343, 349, 352, 356, 369, 377, 378, 407

Algranti, Joe, 150

Allen, Joe, astronaut, 54, 74, 155

American Congress, 162

American Consulate, 153-155

American Defense Mapping Agency, 489

American Government, 164, 182, 195, 197, 412, 425

Anders, Gunter, 121

Anderson, Gerry, 231

Angels, 47

Anka, Darryl, 485

Armstrong, Neil Alden, astronaut, 7, 11, 13, 16, 18–21, 23, 26, 32–37, 39-40, 46, 49, 53, 62, 63, 66, 70, 101, 105, 146, 149, 150, 152, 156, 224, 258, 277–279, 282–285, 289, 311, 316, 326-327, 331, 335, 340–342, 355, 359, 369-370, 377, 379, 407

Army Ballistic Missile Agency, ABMA, 121, 260

Arnold, HJP, 9-10, 15-16, 49, 50-51, 58, 60, 62-63, 67, 93, 102-103, 285, 426

Arnold, Kenneth, 205–209, 217

Artyukin, cosmonaut, 455

Aspect, 398

Azhaza, Dr. Vladimir, 278

Babakin Bureau, the, 468

Baker, David, 86, 89, 158, 174, 177–182, 193, 206, 259, 308, 326, 328, 393–395, 455, 470, 477

Bailey, Nick, 453

Bane, Don, 479

Bank of England, the, 488

Bank of International Settlement, BIS, 252,

Barnett, Grady L, 221

Baron, Thomas, 130-131, 163

Bartley Jr, William F, 132

Bauval, Robert, 483

Bay, Zoltän, 292

Bean, Al, 159, 165, 263, 348, 352

Becker Lt Col, 168

Bell Aerosystems, Buffalo, 150

Bell Aircraft Co., 168, 249

Bell, John, 397-398

Belyayev, Pavel, cosmonaut, 371

Berkner, Lloyd V, 234

Beria, Lavrenti, 169

Berry, Adrian, 264

Binder, Otto, 277-278, 283

Bizony, Piers, 132, 297

Black, Fred, 132

Blair Tony, 488

Blanchard, Col William, 212-213

Bondarenko, Valentin, 298–303, 305-306, 366

Bormanis, Andre, 387

Bormann, Frank, astronaut, 89

Brazel, William 'Mac', 210-215, 218, 220, 223, 227, 232

Brezhnev, Leonid, 172

Briley, Lt Col Joe, 220, 222

British Foreign Office, 293, 312-313

British Interplanetary Society, BIS, 144, 182, 193, 315

Bronk, Dr. Detlev, 240

Brown, Sgt Melville E, 225, 263, 266, 268, 283, 363

Brown, Sir Malcolm, 262, 265, 266-267

Bush, Dr. Vannevar, 234-235

Bykovsky, Valeri, 299, 314

Byrd, Eldon, 287

Capen, Charles, 233

Carlotto, Dr. Mark, 479, 499-500

Carter, Chris, 453

Cavendish, Richard, 494

CERN, Switzerland, 387-388, 397, 414

Cernan, Eugene, astronaut, 105, 146, 356

Chaffee, Roger, astronaut, 129-130, 149

Chaikin, Andrew, 19, 40, 89, 100, 102-103, 132, 141, 146, 156, 159, 266, 273, 284-285, 352, 391, 451-452

Chatelaine, Maurice, 277-278, 283

Chertok, Boris, 177

Chodas, 464

Churchill, Sir Winston, 175, 252

CIA, 212, 217, 234, 238, 242, 247, 252-253, 324, 346, 363, 413, 464

Clark, Col Al, 212

Clarke, Arthur Charles, 78, 113, 144, 183, 195, 200, 245, 255, 258, 266, 276, 283, 291, 313–316, 345, 456, 458, 460, 472, 491, 504

Clauser, 397, 398

Clifford, Dr. Brian, 282-283

Collier, Jim, 191, 194, 259, 328, 337, 375

Collins, Michael, astronaut, 74, 93, 96, 99, 106, 284, 407

Columbus, Christopher, 19, 457, 501

Conrad, Pete, astronaut, 14, 27, 104, 159, 258, 353

Cooper, Gordon, astronaut, 58, 338

Corso, Col Philip, 259

Cronkite, Walter, 128

Cunningham, Wally, astronaut, 51, 329

Darwin, Sir Charles, 263

de Moor, Robert, 251

Dennis, Glenn, 231

DERA, Farnborough, England, 79

Dietrich, Anthony, 182

DiPietro, Vincent, 478, 479, 480, 483, 479

Disney, Walt, 195

DOD, Dept of Defense, 126, 192, 217, 247, 256, 261, 283, 287, 501

DOD men, the, 247, 260-261, 452-453, 501

Dolphin, Lambert, 481

D&B, Doran Jamie & Bizony, 297-298, 300, 303, 305

Dornberger, Walter, 118, 167–169, 172–174, 176, 180, 183-184, 188, 198

Dryden, Hugh, 310

Duke, Charlie, astronaut, 103, 280, 281

Dubose, Brig-Gen Thomas, 215

Durant, Fred & Mrs, 195, 196

Dyer, Professor Clive, 79, 88, 93, 97, 114 , 310

Easley, Major Edwin D, 218

Eastman Kodak Company, Rochester, New York, 7, 9, 14, 30, 52, 224

Eastman, George, 56, 75

Edison, Thomas, 74, 75

Eisenhower, Dwight, 112, 195–197, 235, 246, 251, 256-257, 260, 292, 294, 307, 383

Einstein, Albert, 396–399, 403-404, 410

Ellington AFB, Lunar Geology Room, 354

Emerson, Ralph Waldo, 77

Engel Rolf, 168, 187, 188

English Heritage, 421-422

E T, 123, 201, 229, 232, 234, 236, 242-246, 275-277, 279-283, 373, 413, 452, 460-461, 464-467, 472-473, 477, 487, 493, 500, 503, 507, 509

Evans, John G, 291

Exon, Brig-Gen Arthur E, 218-219

Fairchild Industries, Maryland, 120, 394

FBI, the, 132, 224

Felz Charlie, 141

Fidelity Bank of Oklahoma, 132

Fleming, Ian, 313, 456

Foale, Michael, astronaut, 458

Forrestal, James V, 234-235

Foss, Dr. Ted H, 355

Fowler, Pauline, 223

French, Bevan, 267

Friedman, Stanton, 234–236

Friedmann, William, 235

Frolov, Yevgeni, 137

Future Projects Office, 259

Gagarin, Yuri, cosmonaut, 136, 139, 169, 296–299, 301-307, 310, 314, 317, 351, 366, 373, 383, 456

Gallai, Mark, 305

Gartzmann, Heinz, 176, 185–189, 194, 197-199

Gazenko, Oleg, 298

Geller, Uri, 120, 286-287, 324-325, 394, 480

General Electric Corporation, 178, 182

German Army Weapons Dept, GAWD, 118, 168, 188

German Rocket Society, 166

Ghoul, the Great Galactic, 96-97, 467, 488

Gilruth, Robert, 18, 157, 283, 339, 352, 353

Glenn, John, astronaut, 9, 109, 258

Glushko, Valentin, 170, 172, 174

Goddard, Robert, 122, 149, 179-180, 210, 316

Goebbels, Paul Joseph, 188, 190

Gold, Dr. Thomas, 327

Goldin, Dr. Daniel, 377-378, 457–459, 500

Golyakovsky, Dr., 298, 300

Gooch, Stan, 288, 510

Good, Timothy, 211, 213, 221, 278, 279, 281

Goodavage, Joseph, 280

Gordievsky, Oleg, 254

Gordon Bennett, James, 340

Gray, Gordon, 234

Grottrupp, Helmut, 191

Grigsby, 483

Grissom, Virgil 'Gus', astronaut, 129-130, 133, 149, 246, 258, 352

Groves, Dr. David, 32, 36-38, 41, 50, 66, 76

Groves, General, 179, 249

Grumman Aerospace, 142-143, 147–151, 153, 157, 184, 315, 337

Guggenheim Aeronautical Lab, GALCIT, 180

Hahn, Otto, 179

Hain, Walter, 479, 483

Hamberger, Hans, 200

Hancock, Graham, 467, 476, 483, 488, 506

Harford, James, 174, 178, 191

Harmon, Richard G, 132

Harvey, Brian, 298, 455-456, 468-470

Hasselblad, Victor, 9, 54, 56-57, 70

Haut, Walter, 218, 231

Hawking, Stephen, 385

Hayek, Nicholas, 340

Hendel, F J, 130

Heppenheimer, T A, 260, 292, 293

Herge, 243

Heulvemans, Dr. Bernard, 243

Heymann, Jos, 455

Hillary, Sir Edmund Percival, 19

Hillenkoetter, Roscoe, 212, 217, 234

Himmler, Heinrich, 172

Hitler, Adolf, 118, 165, 167–169, 171–176, 185, 188, 190, 198–200, 252

Hingston, Col Walter, DSIR, 294

Hoagland, Richard C, 283, 473, 475-476, 481, 483

Holman, John, 411

Homer, 347

Homo Sapiens Sapiens, 509, 511

Hubbard, Ron, 287

Hughes Aircraft Company, 47, 181, 226, 323

Hughes, Howard Robard, 47, 181, 182, 244, 321

Hughes, Richard, 424

Hunsaker, Dr. Jerome, 234

IAF, International Astronautical Federation, 193, 196

Ilyushin, Vladimir, 302, 303

Inman, Admiral B Robert, 413

International Astronomical Union, 178

International Latex Corporation, Delaware, 107

Irwin, Jim, 100, 108, 156

Isaev, Alexei, 177

Italian Admiralty, 200

Ivanovsky, Oleg, 304

Jacobs, Paul, 268

James, Clive, 255

Jet Propulsion Labs, JPL, 96, 180, 464, 467, 479

Jodrell Bank, (NRAL) Cheshire, England, 101, 291–295, 297, 317, 321, 358, 361, 364, 374

Johnson, Dave, 217

Johnson, Lyndon B, 132, 165, 201, 245, 257, 383

Johnston Space Center, Houston, 109

Jones, Eric, 104, 334–336, 340–343, 349, 369-370

Kammler, Hans, 175-176

Kandiew, Anatoly I, 506

Kaysing, Bill, 48, 100, 124, 126-127, 133, 135-136, 150, 162-163, 268, 273, 288-289, 357

Kazantsev, Dr. A, 278

Kennedy, J F, 52, 90, 132, 169, 201, 235, 253-254, 257, 310, 314, 383, 456

Kennedy, Joe, 166, 235

Kerr, Senator, 132

Kerrod, Robin, 42

KGB, 169, 192, 236, 254, 305

Killian, James, 257

King, Elibert, 274

Kluger, Jeffrey, 343-344

Koelle, Dr. Hermann, 260

Komarov, Vladimir, cosmonaut, 139, 306

Koroëv, Sergei Pavlovich, 136, 167, 169-172, 174, 192, 236-237, 261, 300, 302-306, 371

Kremlin, the, 478

Kruschev, Nikita, 136, 314

Kubrick, Stanley, 121, 276, 283, 315, 316

Lagergren, Gustav, 56

Land, Edwin, 256, 257, 334, 367, 368, 409

Lang, Fritz, 171, 183–191, 198-199, 362, 502

La Paz, Dr. Lincoln, 209

Lebar, Stan, 70, 72

Leed II, Col William D, 224

Lemania, 338

Lenin, Vladimir Illyich, 238, 252

Leonov, Alexei, 67, 169, 170, 366

Ley, Willie, 167, 183–186, 189, 195-196, 199, 362

Lick Observatory, California, 315, 326, 327

Lindbergh, Charles Augustus, 48, 221, 383

Lippman, Walter, 162, 163

Livermore Laboratories, California, 287, 324, 461

Locke, John, 461

Lost Tribe, the, 357

Lovell, Jim, astronaut, 48, 214, 221, 258, 281, 337-338, 344-345, 347–349

Lovell, Sir Bernard, 101, 139, 162, 167, 240, 291–295, 297, 307–312, 317-318

Lundberg, Jan, 56, 60, 66, 68, 353

Lutz, Glenn, 109

MacArthur, General, 112

MacCarthy, Senator, 180

Magnay, Keith, 384

Majestic 12, 234-235, 467

Malin, Michael, 488

Malina, Frank J, 180

Marcel, Jesse, Jr, 213-216

Marcel, Major Jesse, 212–217, 232

Marshall Space Flight Center, 120, 260

Marshall, George C, 112

Martin Marietta Aircraft Company, 132

Marx, Karl, 122

Masevich, Professor Alla, 102

'masters of infinity', 110, 165, 173, 193, 198, 201, 225,
229, 234, 236, 240, 243, 246, 250, 253, 256, 262,
274, 284, 291, 295, 304, 308, 311, 319, 334, 341,
351, 360, 363, 369, 373, 378, 386, 408, 411, 424,
452, 453, 457, 460, 466, 473, 481, 493, 499, 501,
503
Mauldin, John H, 98-99
Max Planck Institute, Germany, 286, 287
Maxwell, Dr. Elizabeth, 178, 179
Maxwell, Robert, 178-179, 193
McCandless, Bruce, astronaut/Capcom 'Apollo 11', 26
McCormack, Percival D, 99
McDaniel, Stanley V, 499
McDonald, David, 110
McGilligan, Patrick, 184-190
McKinnon, J A, 99
McMoneagle, Joe, 480-481, 490
McMullan, General, 223
Medaris, Gen John Bruce, 193-194, 196-197, 257, 259,
260, 290, 460
Menzel, Donald, 209, 234, 238
Merlin Productions, 225, 226
Metro Goldwyn Meyer, MGM, 196, 315, 316
Milroy, Dr. C M, 223
MIRE, 454
Massachusetts Institute of Technology, MIT, 257
Molenaar, Gregory, 478-479, 480, 483, 489
Molotov. Vyacheslav, 169
Mona Lisa, the, 201-202
Montague, Samuel, 240
Moore, Bill, 235
Moore, Dr. Patrick, 310
Morning Sky, Robert, 216
Morse, Ralph, 355
Mossad, 287
Munck, Carl, 505-506
Muybridge, Edwearde, 75, 352
Myers, David P, 483
Napoleon, 511
National Academy of Sciences, USSR, 246
National Space Institute, USA, 394
Neanderthal, 507–511
Nebel, Rudolf, 186–188
Niemyer, Larkin, 70, 358
Nelson, Alan A, 338
Newcomb, Simon, 383, 425
Newton, Sir Isaac, 387, 391–393, 396, 426, 430, 461
NICAP, 220, 230
Nixon, Richard, 258, 285, 295, 339, 344-345, 377, 383

Noetus, 287
North American Rockwell, 132
Noyes, Ralph, 310
Nuffield Foundation, 295
Nuffield, Lord, 295
Oberg, James, 298
Oberth, Hermann, 117, 121, 135, 164-168, 171, 173,
180, 184-189, 191, 198-200, 316, 362
Ogden, Dennis, 298, 303-304
O'Higgins, Dr. Paul, 226
Omega SA, Biel, Switzerland, 337-340, 353
Oppenheimer, Robert, 112, 249
Ordway, Frederick Ira III, 133, 172, 175-176, 181,
183, 199, 378
Paine, Thomas, 132, 345
Pal, George, 248
Palin, Michael, 59
Pelevin, Victor, 371-372
Penkovsky, Col Oleg, 253-254
Pentagon, the, 181, 195-197, 282-283, 460
Phillips, Major-Gen Samuel C, 130, 132
Piguet, Albert, 338
Pinter, George, 150-155, 157
Popovich, cosmonaut, 299, 455
Pozos, Randolph R, 483
President Kennedy, see Kennedy, J F, 132, 201, 254,
297, 310, 314, 456
Pritchard, Bob, 317-318, 358, 361
Puharich, Dr. Andrija, 286-287, 486-487
Purcell, Edward, 256-257
Puthoff, Hal, 287-288, 325, 385, 481, 487
Quantec Image Processing, 31-32
Quarlse, Donald, 197
Ramey, Major-Gen Roger, 212, 214-215, 217, 221
RAND Corporation, 193, 220, 287
Randle, Kevin, 218, 220
Reagan, Ronald, 282-283, 383, 456, 467
Rees, Eberhardt, 121, 378
René, Ralph, 11, 42, 98, 108-109, 163
Riedel, Klaus, 174, 187
Ritter, Dr., 187
Rocketdyne, 48, 124, 126-127, 150-151, 357
Rockettes, the, 119, 122, 134, 136, 181-182, 198-199,
259-260, 373
Rodenberry, Gene, 486
Rosbaud, Paul (Griffin), 171, 173, 179-180
Royal Academy of Sciences, 333
Ruppelt, Capt Edward, 209, 229
Rynin, Nikolai, 166

Santilli, Ray, 222–225

Shepard, Alan, astronaut, 258, 272-273, 288-289, 297, 328

Schaber, Dr. Gerald, 447

Schaefer, Hermann J, 103, 110

Scheikart, Fred, 177

Schlemmer, Phyllis, 287, 487

Schmitt, Harrison 'Jack', astronaut, 69, 103, 104, 146, 266-267, 356

Schmitt, Don, 218-219

Schnabel, Jim, 287

Scott, Dave, astronaut, 11, 54, 75, 108, 273-274

Sekania, 465

Sergeyev, see Korölev, 261, 298, 300, 302

Seymour, Dr. Percy, 59, 349, 391

Shackleton, Ernest, 241

Shandera, Jaimie, 234

Shaw, George Bernard, 75

Shapalov, Vladimir, 304

Shayler, David, 106, 321, 325, 327

Shell, Bob, 224

Shelus, Dr. Peter, 331

Schirra, Wally, astronaut, 9, 58, 62, 281, 338

Skinner, Frank, 288

SKY TV News, 59, 66, 68, 333

Slayton, Deke, astronaut, 328

Smithsonian Institute, the, 181, 207, 391, 426

Soffen, Gerry, 475-476

Souers, Sydney, 234

Soviet Academy of Sciences SAS, 238

Soviet Embassy, London, 137, 183, 196, 316

Spaatz, Carl, 112

Space Task Group, Langley, Virginia, 149, 308-309

Spaceworks Incorporated, Kansas, 340

Speer, Albert, 171, 173

SS, the, 171-176

Stafford, Thomas P, astronaut, 68, 259

Stalin, Josef, 136, 169, 172, 182, 192, 236, 238, 246-252

Stanford Research Insitute, SRI, California, 220, 286-287, 324, 325, 385, 480

Stehling, Kurt, 251-254

Stimson, Henry, 112

Stringer, Dr., 222

Strom, Professor Robert, 447

Strughold, Dr. Hubertus, 83, 84, 182, 192, 194

Stuhlinger, Ernst, 121, 134 , 172, 176, 181, 183, 195, 199, 378

Suvorov, Vladimir, 303-304, 454

Swann, Inigo, 287

Targ, Russell, 286-287, 324

TASS, 261

Temujin-Genghis, Khan, 27, 220

Tenzing, Norgay, 19

Tereskova, Valentina, cosmonaut, 314

Teske, Richard, 399

Thatcher, Margaret, 282, 297

Timoshenko, 169

Tissot, 338

Titov, cosmonaut, 299, 301–303, 305

Toftoy, Major-Gen H, 121

Torun, Erol O, 488-489

Trudeau, Gen Arthur G, 260

Truly, Richard, 457

Truman, Harry, 112, 192, 217, 288, 383

Tsar Nicholas II, 174, 237

Tsien, Dr. Hsue-Shen, 180

Tsiolkovsky, Konstantin, 134-135, 316

Una, Ronald, 319-320, 503

University of London, 222

Urey, Dr. Harold, 271

Van Allen, Dr. James, 83, 84, 86, 149, 310-311, 375

Vandenberg, Gen Hoyt, 234

Vasilieyev, Dr., 240

Verne, Jules, 199, 236, 324

VfR, Association for Space Travel, Germany, 166-168, 183-188

Volinov, cosmonaut, 455

Voluntary best servants, 299, 302

von Braun, Magnus, 176-178, 180

von Braun, Wernher Freiherr, 84, 117, 118, 120, 123, 127, 134, 165–178, 180–184, 187, 190–194, 196, 198–200, 249, 253, 255, 259-260, 287, 296, 298, 345, 348, 371, 377, 393-394, 408

von Harbou, Thea, 184, 185, 189, 190

von Hoefft, Dr. Franz, 166

von Karman, Theodore, 180

von Pirquet, Guido, 166

Walker, J A astronaut, 220, 315

Walter, William J, 84

Walters, Dr. Helen, 175-176, 183

Webb, James, 132, 149, 239, 250, 253, 310, 332, 343

Welch, Brian, 60, 65, 67, 69, 95, 323, 325, 334, 504

Westinghouse Defense and Space, Baltimore, 70–72, 323, 369

Wigner, 397

Wilde, Oscar, 48

Wheeler, John, 398

Whipple, Prof Fred, 178
Whipple, Babbie, 178
Wiant, Jerry, 324-330
Wise, David, 289
White, Ed, astronaut, 27, 129, 338
Whitehead, Professor, 437, 439, 451
Winkler, Johannes, 166
Wolpe, Howard, 465
Wood, Bill, 108, 127–129, 143, 156, 161,
Wood, Bill, Goldstone, 96, 335, 359-360, 369-370
Wright, Bishop, 382-383, 424
Wright, Orvill and Wilbur, 91, 382, 383
WvB, see von Braun, Wernher Freiherr
Yeager, Chuck, 345
Yeomans, 465
Zeiss, Germany, 56, 58, 61, 68
Zholotov, cosmonaut, 455-456

2. Transport & Equipment

Aggregate, 117
Air Force One, 343
airlock, collapsible, 343
Almaz 1, 454, 455
Ascent engine, LM, 144, 148, 152-155, 325-327, 342, 367
ATS 6, satellite, 395
Baikonur Cosmodrome, Khazakstan, 17, 199, 296, 300-301, 303-304, 306, 364, 366
Challenger, Space Shuttle, 26, 161, 186
Clementine, lunar probe, 51, 395, 441, 467
computers, desktop, 48
CSM Columbia 'Apollo 11', 70, 73, 283, 321, 364,
CSM, command module, 9-10, 15, 70-73, 101–104, 145, 281-282, 318, 322-323, 338, 344, 347-348, 359, 363-365, 375-377
CSM, Odyssey 'Apollo 13', 337, 344-346, 348
DC-X, 156
descent engine, LM, 146-147, 150, 152, 155, 159, 343
dish, radio, 231, 292, 294-295, 317–319, 322, 361-363, 376, 394
Early Bird, satellite, 321, 358
electronics, 88-89, 92-93, 182, 310, 408
Explorer probes USA, 83, 86, 96, 137, 256, 307, 309
flying craft, 209, 400, 401
flying saucer, 205, 207, 212, 214, 218, 220, 228-229, 231, 244, 277
Gemini missions, 27, 53, 58, 129, 140, 149, 258, 277, 314, 338, 354, 364, 458
gnomon, 68-69
hatch, LM, 29, 33, 35, 63, 103, 278, 340–343, 349, 366

Hubble Space Telescope in LEO, 50, 94
Intelsat, 319, 321
ladder, LM, 23, 31, 33-35, 39, 62, 64, 71, 173, 192, 242, 278, 343, 357, 359, 369
lasers, 322-324, 333, 367
laser reflector, LR^3, 325–330, 367, 373, 503
LEM, prototype lunar module, 141, 143, 354
LM Aquarius 'Apollo 13', 337, 343, 346, 349
LM Casper 'Apollo 16', 103, 141
LM Eagle 'Apollo 11', 146, 147, 150, 326, 349
Lusitania, 74
Luna 3, USSR, 17, 139
manned space station, 191, 195, 382, 440, 455-456, 457-458
Mariner probes, 446, 466–476
Mars 2 probe, 466, 468, 469, 473
Mars 3 probe, 139, 468-470
Mars Antenna Goldstone, (DSS-14), 319-321, 355, 368
Mars Global Surveyor, 499, 500
Mercury missions, 9, 258, 281, 294, 297, 299, 308, 314, 338, 339
MIR space station, 60, 88, 91, 94, 458
Omega Speedmaster Chronograph, 337-340
Pioneer 1, 294
PLSS, backpacks, 29, 32, 45, 107, 109, 123, 340, 366, 389
porch, LM, 34, 64, 340, 343
Proton USSR, 139-140
Ranger, USA crash landers, 17, 136, 159, 290, 295, 314
Rover, USA, 42–44, 46, 313, 328, 373
    Lunikhod rover, USSR, 296
Salyut 2, 454, 455
Salyut 3, 455
Salyut 5, 456
Saturn V, USA, 8, 101, 109, 120, 127–129, 133, 137, 139, 141, 145, 161, 363-364, 394, 457
Skylab, space laboratory in LEO, 93-94, 316, 376
Snoopy communications hat, 106-107
Soyuz, USSR, 139, 140, 351, 364–368, 371, 374, 376–378, 384, 455, 468, 470
spacesuit, 11, 29, 101, 106-107, 339, 341
    – gauntlets/pressurised gloves, 7, 10-11 16, 21, 61, 104-106, 339
    – helmet, 54, 60, 63, 103-104, 106, 342, 369, 371
    – moon boots/over-boots, 53, 104-105, 233, 313
    – underwear, 104, 107-108
    – visor, 11, 22, 26, 27, 36–38, 40, 41, 46, 54, 63, 66, 103-104, 266, 272, 342, 357, 360, 369

Spinning Disk, 388-389, 402, 413–417, 421–427, 439, 491, 494, 497, 512

Sputnik, USSR satellite, 84–86, 137, 139, 194, 197, 198, 243, 252, 255, 260, 292, 293, 296, 297, 305, 308, 312, 314, 374, 384, 456

STS, Space Shuttle, LEO, 9, 88, 91, 92, 103, 107, 155, 161, 196, 222, 259, 283, 316, 335, 346, 366, 383, 389, 429, 437, 457

Surveyor, USA soft landers, 17, 160, 188-189, 290, 295

Tank, the, 299, 300, 301, 342

tank, oxygen 'Apollo 13', 349
    Soviet isolation tank, 342

Telstar, satellite, 256

Tetra satellite, 358

Toyota, 28

tracking ships, 318

tunnel, LM, 336

UFO, 126, 206, 209-210, 212, 216–221, 225, 227–229, 231, 233, 236, 239, 241, 244-245, 246, 276, 278, 282, 283, 403, 414, 458, 487, 490, 507

umbrella antenna, 46

Viking probes, USA, 467, 476, 478, 479

Voskhod, USSR, 139, 140

Vostok, USSR, 139, 141, 299, 302, 305, 314

X-33, 458

Zond probe, USSR, 122, 139, 466

3. Actions & Reactions

American Civil War, 74

anthropomorphic dummies, 227-228, 301,

'Apollo 13', 98, 100, 151, 343-349, 355

Apollo lunar scientific experimental packages, ALSEP, 92

Apollo targets, 332-333

Apollo transcripts, 334-335

artefacts, 275, 276, 316

balloons, weather, 11, 212, 214-215, 219-220, 227, 233
    research, 18

barbecue mode, 92, 101

belts, radiation, see Van Allen belts

Berlin Wall, the, 121

BIG G, see also gravity, 387

biomedical results of Apollo, 102

blueprints, 118, 119

Brookings Report, the, 275

Cold War, the, 67, 121, 122, 132, 159, 201, 236, 255-256, 295, 306, 316

consciousness, 165, 276, 286

Crop Glyphs, 1, 196, 205, 240-241, 261, 271, 290, 296, 310, 364-365, 368, 372, 374, 385-386, 399, 4030404, 410-412, 415, 422-423, 429, 453, 460, 486, 488, 493, 507

cryogenic systems, LM, 150-151

crystals, 272

Cuban Crisis, the, 121

deterministic effects, 78-79, 80, 113, 309

dummies, USSR, 305-306

Earth mechanics, 79, 81-83, 90, 98, 110, 115, 139, 142, 162, 245-249, 258, 261, 282, 313, 323, 431-436, 436

ESP, 74, 286-287

ET dummies, 229

Feature Films:
    2001: A Space Odyssey, 276, 313-316, 344, 363
    Apollo 13, 343-346
    Diamonds are Forever, 312-313
    Frau im Mond, 184-185, 188–191
    Independence Day, 225
    Star Wars series, 312

FOA, circumvention of, 465-466

Foo Fighters, 205

fractals, 385,

future space travel, 386-387, 412-425

genetic encoding, 510

gravity, 84, 87, 89, 137, 200, 387-409, 423, 428, 434-435, 460-461, 463, 465, 491-492

HAARP, 247, 256

harmony, 70, 285

hypergolic fuels, LM, 137, 141, 145, 150-155

impact/invasion scenario, 452

International Geophysical Year, IGY, 91, 178, 196, 256, 293

isotopic dating system, 269

Jupiter, 'cometary' impact, 464

knowledge, prevarication, 482

laser, 282, 286, 287, 290, 294, 297, 322–326, 328, 329, 330, 333, 367, 399, 451

laser ranging, 103, 282-287, 290, 322-325, 335, 382, 480, 503

latitude & logitude, 391

light, see speed of

Luna 15 and Jodrell Bank, 361-365, 412

Mars mechanics, 461, 463

Mars policy, 377

Mars missions, 466-46

mascons, 408

Majestic 12, 234-236

Mercury missions, 281, 308, 294, 297

micrometeorites, 82, 90-91 103-104, 147-148

Monte Carlo Simulation, 447

Moon mechanics, 265-270, 427-430, 437-438,

Moon/HIP intelligent placement, 438-442, 445

NACA, established 1915, 246

NASA, Space Act, 246

NASA, budgets, 143, 251, 260, 377, 459

NASA, Ceramics Laboratory, 268

NASA, Goddard, image archives, 479

NASA, simulator facilities, 351-351-357

NASA, Apollo video facilities, 357-9

National Security Act, signed 1947, 192

nautical miles, 391

Neutral Point, CNP/ENP, 390-396, 406-408

Operation ALSOS, 179

Operation Argus, 307-308, 310

Operation Echo, 110-111

Operation Hydra, 173

Operation Magic, 327

Operation Overcast, 118-119, 177, 179, 181-182

Operation Paperclip, 119, 121, 168, 180, 181, 182, 199

Operation Peter Pan, 460-461

Operation Starfish Prime, 308

Panels, SAP, 257

Panels, TCP, 257

Pearl Harbour, 282

plate tectonics, 448-450

Pluto mechanics, 386, 416, 428, 432

precession, retrograde, 431

Project Able, 293, 295

Project Argus, 307-308, 310

Project Blossom, 123, 200

Project Horizon, 257, 259-260, 290-291, 294-295, 306, 331

Project Manhattan, 109-110, 113, 121, 196-197, 249, 251

Project Mogul, 219

Project Slug, 195

'project sterling', 349

physics, 52, 77, 81, 127, 168

quantum physics, 398

Quebec Agreement, 113

radar, 126, 129, 158, 230, 276, 290-296, 322

radar target, 214-214, 220

radiation, various, 77-114

remote viewing, 480-481, 490

Roswell Incident, the, 2, 210-226, 231-234, 244, 346

autopsy footage, 222-225

Roulette, Russian, Solar Flare, 79, 96, 100-101

Roulette, American, Solar Flare, 333, 378, 385

Russian Revolution, the, 134

Scientology, 286

Sentinel, the, see 2001: A Space Odyssey

Soffen and Viking PR, 476

solar flares, 78-79, 93-104

solar particle events, SPEs, 51, 79, 90-101

South Atlantic Anomaly, 88

Space Treaty, the, 258

space rescue drills, 306

speed of light, the, 390, 396-412

spiders webs, 428

spin, 14, 105

Star Wars, see SDI

statute miles, 392

stochastic effects, 78, 113

Strategic Defense Initiative, SDI, 192, 212, 247, 256, 282-283, 312

terraforming, planetary, 491-493

tests, Omega Speedmaster, 339

tests, Tank, 341

tests, 'vomit comet', 342, 355

tetrahedra, 453, 487, 497

Theory of Relativity, the, 397-399

Three Rs, the, 431

Tintin, Exploration of Moon, 242-243

Title 14, 282-283

Topogly, 507

transcommunication, 485-486

transD physics, 397-407, 409, 452, 498

trash (space junk), 180

on Moon, 343-349

Treaty of Versailles, the, 115

UPP, upwelling planetary position, 443-444, 487

USAAF dummies, 227-229, 231

Van Allen radiation belts, 79, 83-100, 103, 114

Venus mechanics, 295, 416, 432, 436-437, 445-448, 463

VLA, the, siting, 230-231

Yalta Agreement, the, 118, 119, 177-179

Zero gravity, see gravity

4. Photography

aperture, 10-11, 15, 60, 63, 294, 340, 341, 369

Ektachrome, 13, 20, 30, 60, 62, 64, 334

emulsion, 12, 21, 59, 334

exposures, 12–16, 20, 29-31, 52, 58, 62, 95, 368

film stock, 9, 12–15, 20, 21, 29, 30, 59, 60, 64, 75, 93, 102, 103, 148, 334

filters, 20, 21, 54, 61, 78, 257

Hasselblad, 500 EL/70, 21, 56, 58, 60-62, 69

Instamatic, 9, 12
Lunar Surface Camera, see Hasselblad
lenses, 10, 11, 17, 20, 30, 49, 50, 56, 58–63, 68, 72, 80,
    111, 266, 369
lubrication, (camera), 60
magazine, 10, 12–16, 21, 30, 39, 46, 53, 56, 58, 61-62,
    93, 104, 108, 156, 191, 194, 255, 259, 274, 342, 351,
    360, 369, 478
Mars image (Viking), 86A07, 482, 490
Mars image 35A72, 474–476, 479, 481, 482
Mars image 70A13, 476, 478, 479, 481, 482, 499, 500
Mars, mapping cycles (Mariner), 468-469, 470, 478
Nikon, 69
paint, 92, 114, 323
paint, aluminium, 59, 72,
polarising filters, 20, 56, 61-62, 257
Polaroid, 56, 257, 334, 367-368
reticle, 36, 49, 67-69
shutter speed, 15
SFX, special effects, 73, 76, 183-184, 194, 248, 303,
    312, 314, 344, 351
shutter speed, 60, 74, 369
TV Camera, lunar, 17, 18, 27, 40, 43–45, 70–72, 266,
    299, 339, 348, 352, 358, 369
viewfinder, 11, 20, 30, 40, 45, 49, 57, 61, 67
Viking images, 474–476
wire, Peter Pan, 354

5. Earth Locations
Albuquerque, New Mexico, 214, 226, 234
Almogordo, New Mexico, 181
Alton Barnes, England, 261, 385
Amesbury, England, 418-419
Antarctica, 73, 256, 258, 273
Antwerp, Belgium, 119
Argentina, 197
Arizona, 61, 315, 355-357, 358
Atlantic Ocean, 449, 468
Avebury Circle, England, 419, 494–497, 504, 508
Avebury, England, 419, 429, 494–497, 504, 508, 512
Avebury Manor, England, 497
Avebury pyramid, England, see tetrahedral pyramid
Baikal, Lake, 239
Baikonur Cosmodrome, see also Tyuratam, 135, 136
Barbury Castle, England, 399, 410, 453
Berlin, 84, 117, 118, 121, 166–169, 172, 184–188, 190,
    248, 297
Bleicherode, 175–177, 183, 192
Boise, Idaho, 205, 216
Borehamwood Film Studios, England, 315-317

Brooks AFB, Texas, 132
Budapest, Hungary, 248, 292
Canberra, Australia, 318, 322, 376
Cape Kennedy, Florida, 57, 115
Chernobyl, Russia, 93, 105, 106
Chihuahua State, Mexico, 274-275
Chilcomb Down, England, 364-365, 422, 424
Corona, New Mexico, 211, 213, 217, 220, 232–236
Cuxhaven, 183
DSTN, 319, 322, 358, 360, 362, 365
Ellington AFB, Texas, 149, 354
ecliptic, 361, 431, 435
Equinox, 433
Erebus, volcano, 241
Etna, Mt, volcanic, Sicily, 155
Felixdorf, nr Vienna, 171, 188
Feucht, Germany, 200
Flagstaff Observatory, 469
Fort Bliss, Texas, 120, 178, 181–183, 191, 193, 194
Fort Meade, 480
Fort Strong, Maryland, 181
Fylingdale, England, 295
Giza Plateau, Egypt, 481, 484, 486-487, 497
Glastonbury Abbey, 422-423
Gorodomyla Island, 192
Grand Canyon, the, 354
Greece, 429
Ground Zero, 111
Hawaii, 267, 308, 321, 330, 445
Hiroshima, 112, 113, 121, 240
Hollywood, 184, 191, 197, 248, 316, 340, 350
Honolulu, 308
Indian Ocean, 321, 371, 456
Johnston Island, 308
Kasputin Yar, Astrakan, 193
Kennedy Space Center, the 127, 355-356
Kolmya, Magadan, Siberia, 170
Kummersdorf, nr Berlin, Germany, 117, 118, 168, 169
Las Vegas, Nevada, 110, 126
Leningrad, 297
London, 75, 122, 153, 156, 175, 179, 183, 194, 201,
    222, 225, 252-253, 268, 297, 315, 320, 330, 479
Los Alamos, New Mexico, 184, 210, 424, 464
Los Angeles, California, 293-294, 335
Madrid, Spain, 319, 322, 376
Magdalena, New Mexico, 211, 220-221, 230-231
Medias, Romania, 184, 187
Mineral, Washington State, 206

Moscow, 85, 134, 137, 167, 169, 170, 172, 174, 178, 183, 187, 192, 193, 197, 237, 254, 278, 293, 296–298, 301-302, 304, 316, 361, 370, 371, 457
Nagasaki, 112, 121
National Space Science Data Center, USA, 478
Nahkla, Egypt, 275
New Orleans, Louisiana, 119, 180
Nightingale Road, London, 201
Norad, Colorado, 219
Nordhausen, Bavaria, 119, 173, 175, 177-178
Oberammergau, 176
Oberjoch, 176, 177, 179-180
Overton, Wiltshire, England, 402
Pacific Ocean, 308
Pad 34, Cape Kennedy, 129, 130, 132, 133, 162
Paris, 76, 175, 177, 179, 181, 194, 203, 253, 314
Parkes Observatory, Australia, 319-320, 322
Perth, Western Australia, 320
Plotsenzee, nr Berlin, 188
Ranch, the Foster, 211, 214, 217-218, 220, 226, 232-233
Randolph Air Force Base, Texas, 84, 111
Redstone Arsenal, Alabama, 120, 194
Reinickendorf, nr Berlin, 188, 190
Reno, Nevada, 151
Rio Grande, 355
River Kennet, 496
Roswell, New Mexico, 123, 210–229, 231–237, 240–244, 245, 282, 403, 412, 424-425, 444, 467, 483, 487, 508
San Agustin, New Mexico, 220, 231
Santa Susana California, 126
Sharaga, 170, 172, 174, 237
Silbury Hill, England, 419-420, 494-496
Socorro, New Mexico, 220
Solar system, the, 384-406, 415-416
South Pole, 59, 73, 443, 446
South Atlantic, 88, 307, 321
Sri Lanka, 78, 394, 456
San Francisco, California, 75
Star City, nr Moscow, 298, 301
Stonehenge, England, 417–425, 427, 494, 497, 506
Station, Apollo, Goldstone, 335, 359
Sweden, 9, 50, 55–58, 69, 175, 182, 198, 289, 338
Switzerland, 172, 194, 198, 200, 201, 251-252, 273-274, 337, 339, 374, 414
Sydney, Australia, 319-320
Tampere University, Finland, 423-424
tetrahedral pyramid, Avebury, England, 496-497, 504

The Doldrums, 460
The Ranch, Nevada test site, 126
The Great Sphinx, Egypt, 475, 484-487, 491, 493, 498
The Wolf's Lair, Rastenberg, Prussia, 173, 186
Trader Vic's, 315
Trinity, White Sands, New Mexico, 111-112
Truth or Consequences, New Mexico, 208, 220, 229, 233, 244, 274
Tunguska, Siberia, 237–241, 245, 271, 306, 464
Tyuratam, see also Baikonur Cosmodrome, 135
Vandenberg AFB, California, 115
Walker AFB, 217
White House, the, USA, 257, 267, 276, 283, 297, 310, 314
White Sands Proving Grounds, New Mexico, 120, 156, 192, 210, 220, 223, 228, 233-234
Wolgast, Baltic coast, Germany, 169, 171
Wimbledon Common, London, 74
Yakima, Oregon, 207
Yatesbury, England, 291

6. Moon Locations

albedo, 65-66, 281
Aristarchus, 269
breccia, 265, 266
caves, 245, 267
Clavius crater, 315
Cold Mooners, 262
craters, 40, 240, 266, 315, 357, 441, 442, 447-448, 504
crustal thickness, 328, 440, 441, 442
EVA, 'Apollo 11' moonwalk, 10, 12, 27, 35, 47, 54, 61, 62, 70, 99, 104, 107, 109, 142, 278, 279, 319, 325, 336, 338, 339, 340, 343, 350, 362, 370, 376
farside, 440, 441, 442
feldspar, 265, 272
Flag A&B scenario, 43, 44
Fra Mauro 'Apollo 13' & '14', 267, 328, 349
GIT, 263-264, 265, 442
Hadley Rille, 15, 11
highlands, 65, 266, 373, 447
HIP, 436, 438, 445, 452
Hot Mooners, 262
isotopes, 270, 442
landing sites, spacecraft, 35, 47, 264, 268, 295, 296, 324-325, 328
    'Apollo 13', 349-350, 361, 373
    Viking, 477
lava, 265, 267, 355, 369, 447-448
Lunikhod, 139, 236, 296, 324-325, 328, 329

lunar crust, 264

lunar temperatures, 59, 72, 76, 291, 353

maria, 65, 265, 268-269, 408, 440-441

mascons, 408

moonwalk, see EVA

nearside, 440-442

Ocean of Storms, 267, 269

olivine, 272

revolution, 386, 387, 423, 429, 431–435, 438, 440, 447, 463, 468, 491

rocks, lunar, 13, 22, 25, 28, 29, 54, 65-66, 159, 264–276, 281, 288, 311, 336, 354-355, 512
terrestrial, 436,

rotation, 319, 386, 387, 391, 402, 415, 428-429, 431–435, 440, 445–447, 463, 477, 489, 491

soil, 110, 157, 238, 241
lunar, 139, 158, 262–265, 267–272, 276, 296, 357, 361, 367, 418, 442,
Sun angle, 11, 13, 22, 25, 35, 63, 141, 476, 479

Taurus Littrow, 28

terminator, the, 63, 349-350, 369, 429, 430

Tsiolkovsky crater, 135, 350

Tycho crater, 315

7. Mars Locations

Altea City, 481-482

Arsia Mons, volcano, 208

Ascraeus Mons, volcano, 208, 470

Bastion, the, (flattened mesa) 478, 482, 489, 490-491

Chryse Planitia, 477

Cydonia, 201, 470–484, 486–490, 493–499, 504–508, 512

D&M pyramid, see also the Tor, 470, 477-478, 482, 486, 488-489

Elysium, 471, 473

Face on Mars, the martian Sphinx, Hurmaze, 470, 474-475, 482–484, 486, 488, 490-491, 499-500, 505-508

Hurmaze, see above

megalithic structures, 475, 477, 481

Olympus Mons, volcano, 207-208, 444, 463, 469, 472, 487, 491

Pavonis Mons, volcano, 208, 469

Sphinx, martian, see Face on Mars

tetrahedral pyramid, 471, 496-497, 504

Tharsis Montes, 469

Tor, the, 470, 477-478, 481-482, 486, 488-489

Utopia Planitia, 477

Wall, the, 472, 490, 495-496

About the authors

Born and brought up in Thaxted, England, Mary Bennett was educated both in East Anglia and at Dartington College of Arts. Bennett has spent much of her adult career researching, writing and translating many subjects related to protected knowledge. She edited *Two-Thirds* and *The Only Planet of Choice* (Gateway Books) a best seller that has been recognised as unique in its category by the trade and the public alike.

Unusually talented, Mary Bennett has developed the PSI abilities that have been with her since childhood, among which is the natural gift of remote viewing.

This skill has provided valuable additional insights and checks on the astonishing information unearthed during the research for this in-depth analysis of Apollo and other space-related subjects.

David Percy was born and educated in London. Percy is a member of the British Interplanetary Society, an Associate of the Royal Photographic Society and was nominated Film Cameraman of the Year by the British Industrial and Scientific Film Association. An award winning film and television producer, Percy is a well-established professional communicator in the world of commerce, working regularly with leading multi-national corporations.

David Percy is heard on radio regularly and frequently appears on the 'other side of the camera' on TV. He lectures widely, has written many articles and is co-author of the work *Two-Thirds*. In 1997 he produced the video *The Face on Mars: The Avebury Connection,* a continuation of his previous production on this subject *The Terrestrial Connection.*